CASES IN MARKETING MANAGEMENT

Cases in MARKETING MANAGEMENT

by

Ralph Westfall, Ph.D.

Professor of Marketing

School of Business

Northwestern University

and

Harper W. Boyd, Jr., Ph.D.

Professor of Marketing

Graduate School of Business

Stanford University

1961

RICHARD D. IRWIN, INC.

HOMEWOOD, ILLINOIS

First Printing, July, 1961
Second Printing, August, 1963
Third Printing, June, 1964
Fourth Printing, September, 1965
Fifth Printing, January, 1966
Sixth Printing, February, 1967
Seventh Printing, July, 1967
Eighth Printing, February, 1968
Ninth Printing, January, 1969

The Library of Congress Catalogue Card No. 61–14493

PRINTED IN THE UNITED STATES OF AMERICA

To

IRA D. ANDERSON

PREFACE

Over the past several years marketing has received increasing attention from businessmen and academicians alike. With the growth of an affluent society, it is inevitable that the role of marketing in the economy will grow in importance. The concept of the market-oriented firm has received so much attention that not only marketing people, but many outside the field are today aware that a firm's success depends on serving efficiently the needs of the consumer.

Strangely enough, the term *marketing management* is of recent origin. Only a decade ago most books dealing with the management of marketing activities were published under the heading of *sales management*. They reflected a preoccupation with the management of the sales force. Today this activity, while still very important, is only a part of the broader field of marketing management.

The scope of the marketing manager's job has grown steadily as has his authority. In addition to managing the sales force, he now also manages the advertising and marketing research activities. More and more marketing executives are assuming greater responsibility in product planning, setting marketing objectives, determining what markets to cultivate, pricing, determining the level and location of inventories, and production scheduling. The chief marketing executive not only supervises, but he co-ordinates all these various activities to produce the most efficient combination.

It is the purpose of this book to present a range of cases which reflect the problems facing the marketing manager. The title, *Cases in Marketing Management,* reflects the attempt by the authors to offer cases dealing with the day-to-day problem-solving activities facing the chief marketing executive, *regardless* of the size of his company or the industry in which it operates. The cases have been selected and organized to fit into the administrative process sequence; they cover the important administrative areas of setting objectives, planning, organization, operation, control, and reappraisal.

The cases were developed over a number of years and have all been tested in the classroom. They are analytical in substance and require the student to "take action." They represent typical problems, and many offer the student the opportunity to use quantitative tools of analysis as well as his knowledge and awareness of concepts from the behavioral sciences.

Students using this book will probably find outside readings of considerable value. The instructor may wish to assign all or part of an advanced textbook in marketing management and/or selected journal articles. Such readings will provide useful background knowledge and, in some cases, helpful analytical techniques. It is not the authors' intent that the text material appearing at the beginning of each major section will do more than orient the student to the subject areas in that part of the book.

The authors owe a substantial debt to many. Our greatest debt is to those firms which co-operated to make these cases a reality. Many top marketing executives gave generously of their time as did many of their subordinates. Each case represents an actual marketing problem from the real world. While it was sometimes necessary to use fictitious company names and to alter confidential data to protect the firms, every effort has been made to preserve the integrity of the situations.

We are indebted to Northwestern University's Institute for Management which helped to finance the gathering of cases presented in this book. We are also grateful to the Ford Foundation which provided Northwestern University's School of Business with a grant to study its curriculum and gather teaching materials. Dean Richard Donham and Associate Dean Ira Anderson have been the motivating forces behind our efforts. To Associate Dean Anderson, a colleague and friend of long standing, we owe much for his constant interest and encouragement.

Our associates have been helpful in providing case leads, testing cases in class, and evaluating them as they went through numerous revisions. We thank Steuart Henderson Britt, Richard Clewett, Vernon Fryburger, James R. Hawkinson, and Lynn Stockman for such help. To Merle Wittenberg, who worked with us for the better part of two years and who participated in the development of many of the cases, we owe a great deal. We also thank Eric S. Stein and F. B. Rabenstein for their work in collecting many cases. We deeply appreciate the highly skilled work of Edith N. Silver, Frances W. Shuford, and Marion B. Bernhardt in typing, editing, and assembling the manuscript.

RALPH WESTFALL
HARPER W. BOYD, JR.

Evanston, Illinois
January, 1961

TABLE OF CONTENTS

SECTION III—PLANNING TO ACHIEVE MARKETING OBJECTIVES

A. Product

B. Channels of Distribution

SECTION VII—REAPPRAISING THE MARKETING PROGRAM

INDEX OF CASES

Marketing Management and the Administrative Process

THE ADMINISTRATIVE process consists of setting objectives, planning the operations necessary to achieve the objectives, organizing to put the plan into action, putting the plan into action, and controlling the operations in such a way as to know whether or not the objectives are being achieved. The concept of this process provides a useful framework for analysis of the problems facing a marketing manager. It enables the administrator to perceive the total operation of the firm and the relationship of the marketing activities to this totality. It also furnishes him with an orderly sequence of steps by which to think through his job, and it provides a perspective from which he can make a more realistic diagnosis of the day-to-day problems that come across his desk, distinguishing between symptoms and basic problems.

The administrative process is simple to comprehend yet difficult to apply. It involves a way of administrative life and, as such, should permeate the everyday business life of all executives. It is essentially nonquantitative, although quantitative techniques are helpful in "solving" the problems that are involved in its implementation. The process provides a way of taking fragments of information and putting them into categories that, in the long run, will provide the executive with data that will facilitate decision making.

Setting Objectives

The broad objective of a firm is to make profits, but a company also has responsibilities to the stockholders, the community, and its employees. None of these, however, provides a specific rationale for the firm's existence. Some writers have suggested that management think of its basic objective in terms of the firm's specific products or services, but a more useful approach is to think of a firm's objective in terms of "the niche or part of the market that the company wishes to acquire by offering some product or service. In thinking about a company's objective, in

1

other words, we can go beyond the product or service itself to the kind of demand involved—for example, the demand for finely tailored men's clothes or specific types of food products."[1]

This line of thinking has become known as "the marketing concept" and is well summarized as follows: "Management must think of itself not as producing products but as providing customer-creating value satisfactions. It must push this idea (and everything it means and requires) into every nook and cranny of the organization. It has to do this continuously and with the kind of flair that excites and stimulates the people in it. Otherwise, the company will be merely a series of pigeonholed parts, with no consolidating sense of purpose or direction. In short, the organization must learn to think of itself not as producing goods or services but as buying customers, as doing the things that will make people want to do business with it."[2]

Most firms must confine their basic objective to some particular part or segment of the market. Rarely, if ever, can a firm, regardless of its size, satisfy the needs of all segments comprising the market for a given product. This is particularly true if one thinks in terms of product use as contrasted with specific products or services. Those firms producing for the mass market typically find that they cannot actually produce successfully for all market segments, e.g., they cannot satisfy both the segment demanding low-priced products and the segment demanding highest quality regardless of price. Despite this need to concentrate on a specific market segment, it is essential that management not think too narrowly about the firm's niche, since to do so will prevent management from being perceptive to slow trends that may ultimately erode substantially the need for its product. The case of the railroads and their narrow objective of moving goods and people only over steel rails is a classic example.

Before deciding what niche to aim for, a firm must, of course, know the demands of the various market segments, how competing firms are attempting to satisfy these demands, the resources of the present and potential firms comprising the industry, and its own resources. A realistic accounting of a firm's own resources is difficult, since it includes an appraisal of human resources. Some firms make the mistake of using the resources of the other firms in the industry as a standard for measuring the worth of their own resources. While such a criterion is useful, it is ultimately the needs of the market niche that the firm seeks to fill that determine the value of its resources.

Once the firm has determined a market niche that is consistent with its resources, it is then, and only then, ready to meet the problems of plan-

---

[1] Edward T. P. Watson, "Diagnosis of Management Problems," *Harvard Business Review*, January–February, 1958, p. 70.

[2] Theodore Levitt, "Marketing Myopia," *Harvard Business Review*, July–August, 1960, p. 56.

ning, organizing, and controlling its operations. The market niche becomes "the broad umbrella that governs the total business life."[3]

Planning

Management has the responsibility of developing a program or plan of action that is consistent with the needs of the market niche, the trends and conditions existing in the economic environment within which the firm operates, and the firm's resources. While a firm's total plan encompasses far more than merely the marketing aspects, the major strategies upon which the detailed plans are built are market oriented. It is not easy to categorize these strategies, but a useful (and generally accepted) classification includes four categories: the strategies of product and product line; channels of distribution; advertising, personal selling, and promotion; and pricing.

Each of these strategy categories is very broad; each can be divided and then subdivided into many parts. All are highly interdependent. The product strategy that a firm adopts is conditioned by and in turn influences the other strategies. Putting these various strategies together to obtain the optimum over-all "mix" is one of management's most difficult problems. At any one time, one activity may dominate the marketing "mix," causing other activities to be adjusted accordingly. At another time, this activity may be of minor importance. Research and development, for example, may be most important at one point, but later the development of competent channels of distribution may become the most essential need. The ability to adjust to changing conditions is necessary. "Strategy becomes embodied in company policy, and a policy can sometimes become a sacred cow, which succeeding managements hesitate to change either because of a feeling that it is difficult to argue with success or a belief that present trends are fads that will soon disappear."[4]

Once the various strategies have been determined, planning of a different type must be effected. Scheduling or programing must be carried out and provisions made for co-ordination. A marketing program is a continuous activity. It should specify *what* to do, *how* to do it, *when* to do it, and *who* is to do it. It is specific—establishing quantitative forecasts and quotas. It involves the construction of a budget, or a series of budgets, in which sales, margins, and expenses are specified in total and by operating units down to individual salesmen. The plan shows the role to be played by each activity within the marketing department and, where applicable, activities located in other areas of the firm. The construction of a plan will often bring into the open operational inconsistencies that have prevailed in the past; for example, the failure to co-ordinate sales and adver-

---

[3] Fred J. Borch, "The Marketing Philosophy as a Way of Business Life," American Management Association, Inc., Marketing Series No. 99, 1957, p. 4.

[4] Watson, *op. cit.*, p. 72.

tising or the goal of "signing up" certain large outlets without "upgrading" the sales force.

A marketing plan helps co-ordinate the activities of the marketing department. It fixes responsibility and alerts executives as to what to do and when to do it. It does not insure against failure. Plans must be carried out by people who do not always perform as expected. This may be failure on the part of the operating individuals or failure on the part of the planners to forecast accurately. Conditions in the market also change, so the plan must be considered a flexible instrument, to be changed as changing conditions require. Properly used, there is little doubt that operation according to a marketing plan increases the probability of achieving the marketing objectives.

Organizing

The previously discussed steps in the administrative process—setting the marketing objective and developing the marketing plan—predetermine, to a considerable extent, the organization system of the firm. "The dominant values in industry have shifted from those of the manufacturing executive to those of the marketing executive. It is the manufacturing executive or engineer who is concerned with the system, who models his organization after the machine, who gets excited about input, output, and feedback, who strives to eliminate human sentiments and values from the work and market place, who strives to develop the one and only system, and who places a premium on standardization. It is the marketing manager who looks out into the external world and views the changing, shifting needs of the market, the relativity of business objectives, the need for flexibility, the importance of constant adjustment, etc. These shifts in organization patterns would appear to represent a shift in occupational dominance and a re-integration of industry in terms of marketing values."[5]

Since the marketing department usually serves as the firm's line of communication with the market, it is essential that the firm's over-all organization provide for a communications system which permits—indeed, encourages—the flow of relevant information from the market as well as to the market and helps the information flow through the marketing department to the various other departments and to top management. One of the most difficult organizational problems is how to co-ordinate the marketing, engineering, and production departments. While the departmental organizational systems can be structured so that they are "plugged into" one another, it is not always possible to overcome the inevitable human weakness that people tend to hear and believe only those things that they

---

[5] David G. Moore, "Marketing Orientation and Emerging Patterns of Management and Organization," in Eugene J. Kelley and William Lazer (eds.), *Managerial Marketing: Perspectives and Viewpoints* (Homewood, Ill.: Richard D. Irwin, Inc., 1957), p. 248.

want to hear and believe. Typically, the marketing department wants many product variations and frequent, quick product changes. Engineering and production tend to favor standardized products and infrequent changes. While this conflict is not without its advantages (a better balance may result from countervailing power), the firm's organization must be such that head-on clashes are detected and differences reconciled quickly.

The organizational system within the marketing department must recognize and establish the proper relationships between line and staff personnel, the scope of each individual's job, the authority system, and the system for controlling the organization over time. Such concepts as centralization versus decentralization; profit centers; and geographic-, customer-, or product-centered organizational breakdowns are important.

There are many dimensions of the organizational system, for example, the organization shown on the chart, the organizational system through which communications flow, the system for exercising authority, the system for control, and others. They are interrelated and changes in any one will inevitably affect the others. The organizational system is one of the most sensitive areas with which management has to contend. Failure by management to adjust the organization to changes in the market or within the firm will quickly lead to organizational problems.

Putting the Plan into Action

No matter how complete the definition of objectives, the planning of marketing strategies, and the organizing activities, nothing happens if these are merely left on paper. The organization must put the plan into action.

The field sales force is one of the main centers of such action. Salesmen must be recruited, trained, supervised, and paid. Plans for these activities are developed in the planning step of the administrative process. Such plans will take into account sales-force needs in view of the objectives. If more salesmen are needed to accomplish the sales objective, the plan will call for this increase. It is in the action step, however, that recruiting activities are begun, actual individuals selected, training programs put on, salesmen sent into the field—inspired, encouraged, or pushed as the case may require.

Advertising programs must also be activated. The advertising personnel, often in conjunction with an advertising agency, develop the actual advertisements to be used, the media in which to place them, and the other promotional activities, such as point-of-purchase advertising materials and special promotions.

The marketing research department determines the projects on which it can work most profitably and then carries out the actual data collection and analysis. Physical distribution of the product must be accomplished.

Stocks are established and maintained at the necessary points, and orders are processed so that shipments arrive on time and intact.

Controlling

The control function consists of following up to determine that the actual operation is proceeding according to plan. No executive can anticipate the future with certainty, and thus there is the probability that events will occur that will necessitate changes in the plan, the organization, or even in the objectives. Management must keep informed on both long-range market trends and short-run changes in the strategies employed by competitors. In another sense, control deals with mistakes; it attempts to identify them, rectify them, and prevent them from recurring.

Standards are an essential part of the control operation, since performance cannot be appraised unless it is measured against some criteria. It is not always possible to measure the performance of parts of the marketing operation, for example, the advertising function. Wherever possible, however, standards must be established; quotas and budgets are common types. They may be broken down by individual salesmen, territories, and products.

Reports are an essential part of the control system. Common reports are those dealing with actual sales versus quotas, brand share within individual markets, consumer brand preferences, attitudes of channels toward the company and its personnel, and cost ratios such as sales expenses to sales. In many companies the marketing research department spends a large part of its time and budget obtaining control information.

Another type of control that is essential is accomplished by personal supervision. Reports will rarely indicate what people are thinking or what their attitudes are. There is no effective substitute for the chief marketing executive finding out how members of his department think or feel about a given situation through personal contact. Probably the most effective control over people is that which involves anticipating how they will react to a given situation. Once this is known with reasonable certainty, then management can adjust its decisions to utilize the typical reactions to best advantage.

Control leads to reappraisal. If it did not, control would apply solely to the present state of affairs and would not lead to any changes. Thus conceived, control would be a static process. Yet the market-oriented firm is flexible and dynamic, responding in a positive way to the changes in the market place. Reappraisal must be a continuous process whereby management assesses constantly the commitments of the firm's resources to a given set of strategies designed to exploit a given and definable market niche. The administrative process thus becomes an evolving circle in which objectives are changed, and this, in turn, produces a need for a change in the firm's marketing strategies, which in turn presents a need for a change in the organizational system, and so on.

UNION CARBIDE CONSUMER PRODUCTS COMPANY

PERMANENT-TYPE automobile antifreezes enjoyed rapid growth after World War II, but by 1958 the market had become increasingly competitive. The growth of "price" brands and the loss of effective fair-trade laws in an increasing number of states plus a trend toward consumer acceptance of off-brand glycol antifreeze as a substitute for the major antifreeze brands had seriously affected sales of the major brand producers of antifreezes. Additional problems arose from the growing reluctance of automotive wholesalers to stock antifreeze prior to the selling season. In preparing its promotional plan for the 1958–59 selling season, Union Carbide Consumer Products Company, manufacturer of Prestone antifreeze, was faced with the problem of how to deal with the current market situation.

The antifreeze market had originated in the early 1920's, when the spreading ownership of automobiles and the improvement of roads caused an increasing demand for a coolant that could be used satisfactorily in below freezing weather. Denatured alcohol was the antifreeze adopted, and later in the thirties methanol (essentially a synthetic wood alcohol) was used widely. Both these coolants boiled at relatively low temperatures, making frequent replacement necessary during a winter driving season. In 1927 Union Carbide Consumer Products Company, then the National Carbon Company, introduced Prestone, a glycol-base antifreeze, which had a much higher boiling point and hence would last all winter. Other brands of glycol-base antifreezes were gradually introduced, but these "all-winter" or "high-boiling-point" types gained acceptance slowly. Methanol-base products continued to dominate the market until World War II, after which glycol-base antifreezes moved ahead rapidly. By 1957 glycol-base products accounted for 82 per cent of the total antifreeze annual volume (Table 1).

TABLE 1

SHARE OF ANTIFREEZE MARKET HELD BY GLYCOL-BASE
PRODUCTS FOR SELECTED YEARS*

| Year | Share of Market | |
	Glycol-Base	Alcohol-Base
1927	0%	100%
1941	20	80
1955	72	28
1957	82	18

* Share of market is based on gallonage produced. In dollars, the glycol share would be larger.
Source: *Printers' Ink*, March 28, 1958.

Advantages of Glycol Antifreezes

Generally, when enough methanol or alcohol-base antifreeze is placed in a cooling system to protect it from freezing at a temperature as low as 20 degrees below zero, the solution will boil at 180 degrees or less at sea level. Prestone and other glycol products have a boiling point of about 223 degrees under similar conditions.

Many modern high-compression automobile engines operate with cooling systems under seven to thirteen pounds' pressure. Each pound of additional pressure tends to raise the boiling point of the coolant about three degrees. The purpose in operating modern automobile engines at higher temperatures is to obtain more efficient performance. Most thermostats now have start-to-open temperatures of 160 degrees or higher. This prevents the cooling solution from circulating through the radiator until that temperature is reached. The temperature of the coolant, however, may rise as much as 20 degrees after the engine is stopped and the pressure drops. If this happens, the margin of safety between the coolant temperature and the boiling point of methanol solutions vanishes, "after-boil" occurs, and the pressure of the steam in the engine water jacket can force the coolant solution out the overflow pipe. The higher boiling points of the glycol-base antifreezes make them less susceptible to this "after-boil" and hence more desirable. In addition, a very real danger of flash fire exists in using the methanol solution if the solution should be released from the cooling system and spill over a hot engine block. Some danger from the fumes of hot methanol also exists. These fumes are toxic and could be detrimental to the occupants of the automobile if a small leak developed in the heater of the car. These factors partially accounted for the tendency of glycol antifreezes to replace methanol products in consumer preference. An additional factor was the decline in price spread between glycol and methanol products. Glycol had steadily declined in price because of improved production methods, while methanol prices were increasing.

The management of Union Carbide estimated that in 1957 about 101 million gallons of antifreeze were sold at retail—about 85 million glycol-base and 16 million methanol-base. As Union Carbide had been the first to market a glycol-base antifreeze, it had orginally enjoyed the entire market. Competition had not entered until 1939, when Du Pont introduced Zerex. By 1957 there were over two hundred competitive brands of glycol-type antifreezes on the market. Union Carbide's sales had increased steadily over the years, but its share of the market had been dropping as more competitors sprang up. Nevertheless, Prestone antifreeze was the largest-selling brand in the industry.

Union Carbide also produced a methanol-base antifreeze called Trek, but did not promote it actively. It had been introduced in the antifreeze market in the early 1940's, when Du Pont, which until that time had marketed only Zerone, a methanol-base antifreeze, decided to market Zerex, a glycol-base product. Union Carbide's reason for introducing the Trek brand was to round out a complete line of antifreeze in order to compete with Du Pont. However, by 1957 sales of Trek were still only a fraction of Prestone antifreeze sales. The average retail price of Trek was about $1.60 per gallon, and the wholesale price to the service station was about $0.90 per gallon.

Prestone antifreeze was distributed through two channels. The greatest gallonage was sold through automotive-supply wholesalers, who acted as agents for Union Carbide. They sold both to smaller jobbers and direct to dealers, primarily service stations and garages. On sales direct to dealers, the wholesaler's commission was 20 per cent, but on sales to other jobbers it was considerably less.

The second channel of distribution for Prestone antifreeze was to national marketers, such as the large oil companies and automobile manufacturers. The number of these accounts was considerably smaller than the number of agent accounts, and the product was sold outright in this case. Regardless of the method of distribution, Union Carbide suggested that Prestone antifreeze be sold at retail for $3.25 per gallon. Where fair-trade laws existed, this price became the fair-trade price. Other leading national brands of glycol-base antifreeze, such as Zerex, Pyro, and Peak, also had suggested list prices of $3.25 per gallon at retail.

Company executives had looked forward to a constantly expanding market as the number of cars on the road increased. Although the number of cars was increasing, total sales of antifreeze were apparently fairly constant. The average 1957 model car required six quarts of antifreeze to protect it against freezing at temperatures as low as zero. In the three years 1955–58 the number of motor vehicles increased from 62 million to 67 million, but the sale of antifreeze dropped from 110 million gallons to 107 million. Leaders in the industry believed this paradox was partly the result of the use of the word "permanent" to describe glycol antifreezes. Some motorists had come to believe that these antifreezes could be used for several years or even indefinitely. Surveys had been made that indicated that about 40 per cent of all car owners used their antifreeze for two years or more.

Sales of antifreeze were also greatly affected by weather. Sales could vary as much as 10–15 per cent above or below normal, depending on whether the winter was very cold or exceptionally mild. Sales had to be estimated and production scheduled almost one year ahead of the next selling season. Overestimation could result in costly warehousing and inventory extended over a nine-month period. Underestimation or maldistribution of the product could result in sales lost to competition. Part of the sales drop from 1955 to 1958 was the result of some mild winters.

Another marketing problem centered about a trend toward more antifreeze sales to consumers through outlets not offering installation service, such as supermarkets, chain drugstores, and discount houses. During the 1957–58 season an estimated 25 to 30 per cent of antifreeze sales was made through these outlets. A few years previously, automobile service-type outlets (filling stations) accounted for 95 per cent of all anti-freeze sales. The over-the-counter, nonservice-type outlets' market pene-tration had been accomplished largely through lower retail prices, which ranged as low as $1.79 per gallon for some private brands, as compared to the suggested $3.25 per gallon for the nationally advertised brands.

Union Carbide's management believed that it could cope with price competition from private brands, but, with the loss of effective fair-trade laws in a great number of states, many nonservice outlets had begun us-ing Prestone and other national brands of antifreeze as loss leaders. Ad-vertised retail prices in some cases were lower than wholesale prices. This type of competition was fairly new to automobile service outlets, and, in areas where it was most severe, traditional distribution channels were hurt. Service outlets in these areas tended to delay stocking of antifreeze until the season actually started, which resulted in increased warehousing costs for the company. Some service outlets reacted by refusing to push nationally advertised brands.

It did not appear that the declining trend of antifreeze sales through service-type outlets would continue. Analysis indicated that service sta-tions would continue as the primary outlets for antifreeze. Among other classes of retailers, only the grocery store approached the service station in the number of local neighborhood locations. As compared to a grocery store's greater traffic, the service station was in a position to sell either over the counter or installed, to offer sounder advice to the "do-it-your-self" trade as to quantity required and installation procedures, and to service and test antifreeze protection for brands handled, and was normally open seven days a week for long hours, which was important if cold weather arrived suddenly. Also, newer model automobiles were becoming more complicated, and the average car owner had neither suffi-cient skill nor the proper tools to install his own antifreeze.

Union Carbide had conducted continuing research for product im-provement from the time Prestone antifreeze was first marketed. As a result, the company executives were convinced that Prestone was supe-rior to any other antifreeze on the market. The glycol base was essen-tially the same in all these products; the important quality differences were in the rust-inhibitor additives. A rust inhibitor of some type was essential in a glycol-base antifreeze because, with usage, the solution of antifreeze and water became acid and corrosive as a result of normal con-tamination with combustion exhausts. This contamination took place with any type of antifreeze. The mixing of glycol or methanol with water did not, in itself, increase the tendency toward corrosion. If rust inhibitors were not present in any type of engine coolant, chemical reactions oc-curred with exhaust gases, and rust was formed in the engine water jacket and the radiator, eventually clogging the cooling system. Although borax was widely used as a rust preventive in antifreezes, those using borax were far from being equal to Prestone, with its "two-phase" inhibitor, which had been developed in its laboratories.

Union Carbide's two-phase inhibitor contained both a chemical inhibitor and a polar-film or magnetic-film inhibitor. The chemical inhibitor prevented the breakdown of the glycol through protection of the coolant from acid contamination and through reduction of the corrosive action of water on iron and other metals. According to the company chemists, the magnetic-film inhibitor formed a thin, tough barrier between the coolant and the metal surfaces, where all corrosion began. Union Carbide executives believed this exclusive blend of inhibitors would prevent the breakdown of glycol for a much longer time than the widely used borax inhibitor, which was only a rust preventive. Their analysis of the better-known, nationally advertised brands of glycol antifreezes indicated that no other brand currently being marketed carried an inhibitor combination equal to that used in Prestone.

In spite of the fact that Union Carbide believed Prestone antifreeze was superior to all other antifreezes, the company did not advertise its product as a "permanent" antifreeze because executives believed the rust inhibitors in any antifreeze would eventually wear out with use. A statement from *The Engine Cooling System*, a manual developed by Union Carbide for garage and service-station men, summed up the company's thinking as follows:

How long antifreeze will last depends on many factors such as cooling system condition, the speed and mileage the car is driven, and the rate of contamination. For example, even minor exhaust gas leakage into the coolant can break down the rust inhibitors in any antifreeze. No two engines are exactly the same and tests show that rust preventive life may vary as much as 4,000 per cent between two similar cars, depending on type of driving, mechanical condition, and general maintenance. There is no simple, dependable way to determine rust inhibitor condition in used antifreeze. Even complicated laboratory tests cannot tell how much longer the rust and corrosion protection will last. Rust-scale build-up in the engine starts before there is any visible sign of rust in the coolant.

This manual had been distributed widely to service-station men and mechanics for over twenty-five years. Union Carbide also maintained a national field-service organization staffed by about thirty technicians, who were available for contact and consultation concerning any cooling system problem that might develop. The company felt that the goodwill developed over the years by this organization helped maintain prestige for Prestone antifreeze and enabled the firm to develop a valuable fund of information about cooling-system problems. This information was of value to both the research and the product-development departments.

The advertising budget for the fall of 1958 was expanded considerably

EXHIBIT 1

over previous years to a total of approximately $4.4 million. Three million dollars of this was to be allocated to network television ("Playhouse 90," "Perry Mason," "Cheyenne," "Sugarfoot," a "Sportacular" on the eve of the World Series, and "NBC News"). Another $800,000 was for radio spots on 544 stations covering 369 markets, and $600,000 was for newspaper ads in over five hundred papers, including four-color, full-page Sunday-supplement ads and a page in the *Saturday Evening Post*.[1] The

---

[1] *Advertising Age,* August 1, 1959, p. 164.

themes plugged in these ads would be the "double guarantee" plan, which would emphasize the importance of proper installation of antifreeze and the "Magnetic Film" protection of the radiator. (See Exhibit 1.) The advertising program was designed to further promote Prestone's reputation as a top-quality product.

The "double-guarantee" advertising theme was based on a marketing idea that a number of the national-brand manufacturers and large petroleum companies had decided to use. This idea was a guarantee to the consumer that the dealer installing the antifreeze would add any additional antifreeze needed "to restore protection lost from mechanical leakage, provided you have leaks repaired promptly." In the case of Prestone, the "double guarantee" referred to the dealer's guarantee and the guarantee that Union Carbide had given for many years, which stated: "Union Carbide Consumer Products Company, Division of Union Carbide Corporation, specifically guarantees that 'Prestone' Brand Antifreeze, if used according to printed instructions, in normal water cooling systems, will protect the cooling system of your car against freezing and clogging from rust formation for a full winter; also that it will not boil away, will not cause damage to car finish, or to the metal or rubber parts of the cooling system, and that it will not leak out of a cooling system tight enough to hold water."[2]

To gain dealer support for this plan, Union Carbide planned a sales program along the lines described in the brochure reproduced as Exhibit 2. Dealers were given free instruction booklets, customer guarantee "logs," dealer guarantee stickers, and tie-in posters. A price schedule, as shown in Table 2, was established.

TABLE 2

PRESTONE ANTIFREEZE PRICE SCHEDULE: 1958

| Size of Can | Cans per Case | Wholesale Price per Gallon | | Suggested Retail Price per Gallon |
		Unbroken Cases	Broken Cases	
1 gal............ 6		$2.17	$2.50	$3.25
1 qt.............24		2.27	2.60	3.40

On all orders for delivery prior to October 31, 1958, an allowance of 6½ cents per gallon was given to the dealer. It was estimated that this allowance would exceed the cost of any replacements of antifreeze made under the guarantee, particularly if the dealer did a proper job of "readying" his customers' cars before installing Prestone. It was emphasized, however, that dealers did not have to use the dealer-guarantee part of the plan; the dealer could write any guarantee plan he wanted to, includ-

---

[2] *The Engine Cooling System: a Manual for the Service Man* (Union Carbide Consumer Products Company, Division of Union Carbide Corporation).

EXHIBIT 2

Here's what the **PRESTONE** BRAND **ANTI-FREEZE**

DOUBLE GUARANTEE PROTECTION PLAN

can mean to you . . .

- **MORE NEW CUSTOMERS...MORE SATISFIED REGULAR CUSTOMERS** — Because you offer both the "Prestone" Anti-Freeze PRODUCT GUARANTEE and your own PERSONAL GUARANTEE *in writing!*

- **MORE EARLY SALES** — By convincing customers you need plenty of time for proper servicing when offering *your* guarantee, you'll be able to get them in early!

- **MORE PARTS AND SERVICE SALES** — You'll sell more radiator chemicals, thermostats, hoses, fan belts, etc. if you offer complete cooling system service backed by your personal protection plan guarantee.

- **MORE NEW FILLS** ...You'll benefit your customers by discouraging re-use of last season's anti-freeze — all car manufacturers and leading automotive authorities recommend fresh anti-freeze each fall.

DEALERS WHO ARE PREPARED TO DO PROPER SERVICING CAN DO A PROFITABLE ANTI-FREEZE BUSINESS EARLY — BY OFFERING THEIR CUSTOMERS THE "PRESTONE" ANTI-FREEZE "DOUBLE GUARANTEE PROTECTION" PLAN

HERE'S HOW THE PLAN WORKS—

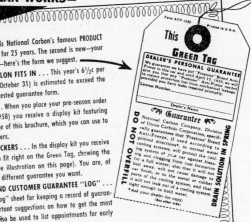

1. **TWO GUARANTEES** . . . The first is National Carbon's famous PRODUCT GUARANTEE which has been in effect for 25 years. The second is new—your own DEALER'S PERSONAL GUARANTEE—here's the form we suggest.

2. **HERE'S HOW THE 6½¢ PER GALLON FITS IN** . . . This year's 6½¢ per gallon allowance (on deliveries by October 31) is estimated to exceed the cost of replacements under the suggested guarantee form.

3. **FREE DISPLAY TIE-IN POSTER** . . . When you place your pre-season order (for delivery before October 31, 1958) you receive a display kit featuring the poster, shown on the front page of this brochure, which you can use to announce the plan to your customers.

4. **FREE DEALER'S GUARANTEE STICKERS** . . . In the display kit you receive sheets of special stickers, made to fit right on the Green Tag, showing the suggested form of guarantee. (See illustration on this page.) You are, of course, free to write any other or different guarantee you want.

5. **FREE INSTRUCTION FOLDER AND CUSTOMER GUARANTEE "LOG"** . . . The display kit also contains a "log" sheet for keeping a record of guarantees you give and includes important suggestions on how to get the most out of the plan. The sheet can also be used to list appointments for early installations.

SOME IMPORTANT POINTS—

It is optional whether or not you wish to take advantage of the dealer's guarantee part of the plan.

The maker's product guarantee remains in effect whether or not you take advantage of the dealer's guarantee part of the plan.

The dealer's guarantee is your personal guarantee and can be written in any terms you wish. You decide what guarantee to give and what cars to cover.

FREE*

BIG 1958 DISPLAY KIT HELPS YOU PUT YOUR DOUBLE GUARANTEE PROTECTION PLAN TO WORK...
Selling more Anti-Freeze and Service!

New version of famous "FLAPPER" Motion Display Sign
that proved an overwhelming favorite last year! . . .

This section goes on outside of glass...FLAPS IN SLIGHTEST BREEZE to attract plenty of attention!

This section goes on inside of glass . . . tells customers at once you offer the great 1958 "Prestone" Anti-Freeze Double Guaranteed Protection Plan.

PRESTONE BRAND ANTI-FREEZE *with Exclusive* MAGNETIC FILM...Prevents Rust

Large banner measures 50" x 10". Really catches the eye at a distance!

Two 17" x 8" streamers

DEALER'S PERSONAL GUARANTEE
We guarantee we have put "Prestone" Brand Anti-Freeze in this car and until April 15, 1959, we will give you free any "Prestone" Anti-Freeze needed to restore protection lost from mechanical leakage, provided you have leaks repaired promptly.

License Number_____

_____
Dealer's Name

_____
Dealer's Name

These stickers showing the suggested form of personal guarantee are supplied in quantity. They are made to fit the "Prestone" anti-freeze Green Tag to identify the cars on which your personal guarantee applies.

Dealer's special "log" to keep track of his guarantees. Contains many helpful hints on how to get the most out of the Plan.

8-page "Prestone" Anti-Freeze Protection Chart ...includes data on all late-model vehicles. SPECIAL NEW FEATURE THIS YEAR . . . Chart of all drain locations for every late-model passenger car.

* With Pre-Season Order for requirements of "Prestone" Anti-Freeze. Order must be placed early for delivery before October 1, 1958.

ing no guarantee at all. Union Carbide's guarantee would remain in effect regardless of the dealer's action in this respect, and orders for delivery prior to October 31 would receive the 6½ cents per gallon allowance regardless of whether or not the dealer used the guarantee plan.

1. *Was the Prestone marketing program for 1958–59 sound?*
2. *Are there any other marketing strategies that Union Carbide could use effectively in addition to, or in the place of, the promotion plan established?*

2

ELGIN NATIONAL WATCH COMPANY

THE NINETY-THIRD annual report of the Elgin National Watch Company for the fiscal year ending March 1, 1958, showed an operating loss for the year of $2,442,000. Sales had dropped from $42 million in the previous year to $31 million. Net operating profit for the previous year had been $671,000. These results were naturally disturbing to the management. It was not difficult, however, to identify the major causes of the poor showing. Discount houses had been cutting long-established retail prices and had disrupted conventional distribution channels. At the same time, low-priced imported watches had been cutting into sales of the more expensive watches, further upsetting the market. Therefore, the Elgin management began an evaluation of its product and distribution policies.

Elgin had been one of the best-known American watch manufacturers ever since its founding in 1864. For years it had enjoyed the prestige of building the finest watch in America. A long-established tradition of fine watch craftsmanship was a matter of pride on the part of all personnel in the company. The Elgin reputation was still strong in 1957. In that year the company surveyed the market. Among questions asked was "What is your brand preference for the next watch you purchase?" The five leading brands mentioned were as follows: Elgin, 30.9 per cent; Bulova, 29.4 per cent; Hamilton, 21.9 per cent; Longines, 14.9 per cent; and Timex, 2.9 per cent.

Elgin had diversified in recent years into electronics, micronics (production of highly precise and miniature devices for guided missiles and aircraft), and a quality line of abrasive products for the metalworking field. The watch division, however, still accounted for considerably more than half the company's sales volume. In 1958 the newer divisions were not yet operating profitably, but, for the most part, the operating loss in the preceding fiscal year was attributable to the watch division.

In addition to the operating loss sustained in the 1958 fiscal year, special "write-offs" of $4,500,000 were made against earned surplus. Most of these special charges applied to the watch division. They included a write-down of fixed assets that resulted from plant relocations and consolidations and a more realistic valuation of the finished-product inventory, which included many models of watches that were not selling well.

Elgin's unfavorable results were accounted for partially by the recession of 1957–58, but the general unrest and confusion that had existed in the watch market for a number of years was a major factor. Following World War II, imports of Swiss watch movements had increased at the expense of domestic movements. Bulova Watch Company produced its own cases, but Swiss movements were used in about 50 per cent of its finished watches. Gruen and Longines used Swiss movements exclusively in their cases. Many "off-brand" Swiss watches were sold in the lower-price field. On February 28, 1958, the Office of Defense Mobilization ruled that the American watch industry was not essential to national defense. This decision precluded the possibility that higher tariffs might be imposed to restrict imports in the foreseeable future.

Price-cutting was another disruptive influence that was closely related to the influx of low-cost watches. After World War II discount houses became important factors in retailing. The wide established margins on watches, typically 50 per cent of selling price, and the well-known brand names made them popular promotion items for the discounters. The emphasis that these discounters put on price in their promotion of watches encouraged aggressive selling by manufacturers of low-priced watches. Some manufacturers began advertising fictitiously high prices so that retailers could offer consumers what appeared to be larger discounts. Indicated retail prices as high as three times the retailer's cost were common.

These practices were at their peak in 1957. In addition to its financial loss that year, Elgin suffered a major loss in its share of the market. Elgin estimated the total number of wrist watches sold by the industry in 1957 to be 12.2 million, well above the 9.2 million sold in 1956. Elgin's share of the market, however, dropped, as did the share held by most of the major jeweled-watch manufacturers. The major pin-lever watch manufacturers gained in market share.[1] The disruptive market factors described above were major causes of Elgin's loss in market share, but the management did not think that they were the sole cause. Elgin had not kept completely abreast of such changing trends as the increased demand for round watches; sweep second hands; and shockproof, waterproof, and self-winding watches. As a result, Elgin followed its competitors in introducing these changes.

The market for watches had also been changing by price lines (Table 1).

---

[1] A pin-lever watch is constructed without the use of jewels as bearings. This is the typical construction in watches retailing for less than $15.00.

TABLE 1

Share of Wrist Watch Movement Unit Sales by Price: Selected Years
(Thousands)

	1950		1952		1954		1956		1958	
	No.	Per Cent	No.	Per Cent	No.	Per Cent	No.	Per Cent	No.	Per Cent
Jeweled watches*										
Under $30......	2,000	20.0	2,686	24.6	2,597	29.8	3,293	37.0	3,000	40.0
$30 and over....	7,992	80.0	8,233	75.4	6,118	70.2	5,607	63.0	4,500	60.0
Total jeweled	9,992	100.0	10,919	100.0	8,715	100.0	8,900	100.0	7,500	100.0
Pin-lever watches†.	4,800	....	6,300	....	5,900	....	7,700	....	8,000‡	....
Total all watches..	14,792		17,219		14,615		16,600		15,500	

* Total jeweled-watch-market data from U.S. Tariff Commission; price breaks, estimated from Elgin studies, indicate retail value of complete watch, not merely movement.
† U.S. Tariff Commission.
‡ Estimated.

In 1950, jeweled watches selling for less than $30 accounted for only 20 per cent of jeweled-watch sales, but by 1958 this was 40 per cent. Watches selling below $30 were generally considered low priced, but this market consisted of two separate segments—jeweled watches, retailing between $15 and $30, and pin-lever watches, which usually sold for less than $15. Pin-lever watches did not use jewels for bearings. The total volume of low-priced watches was large in dollars as well as units. At manufacturers' selling prices, the "$15 to $30" market totaled $23.5 million in 1957 and the "under $15" market totaled $12 million.

Elgin had always emphasized high-priced watches, and the top price bracket, $75 and up, had lost significantly in market share in 1957, as shown in Table 2.

Prior to 1958 Elgin had not produced a watch that could be retailed below $33.75 with the customary trade margin of 50 per cent. Company policy had been positive and explicit in refusing to produce a watch under the Elgin name to retail in the lower price brackets. The management had felt that selling a low-priced watch with Elgin's name would degrade the tradition of quality and craftsmanship built up by the company over many years. Some executives cited the Packard automobile as an example of what would happen if a lower-priced watch were marketed. They said the Packard name at one time stood for the top in automobile quality. When that firm put out a medium-priced car, its reputation suffered; it lost its top-quality market and failed to gain a medium-price market. These officials believed that, if Elgin should try to compete in the lower-priced market, the results might be similar to Packard's.

As the low-priced-watch market expanded, however, Elgin officials

TABLE 2

DISTRIBUTION OF WRIST-WATCH SALES BY RETAIL PRICE: 1956 AND 1957*

	1956		1957	
Price	Units	Per Cent	Units	Per Cent
$75 and up................1,514,000		16.5	1,380,000	11.3
$50 to $74.99..............1,889,000		20.6	3,000,000	24.6
$30 to $49.99..............2,015,000		22.0	2,666,000	21.8
$15 to $29.99.............1,805,000		19.6	1,728,000	14.1
Under $15................1,965,000		21.3	3,460,000	28.2
	9,188,000	100.0	12,234,000	100.0

* Data compiled by Elgin National Watch Company. Data are for watches, not merely movements, as shown in Table 1. The large difference in the totals in Tables 1 and 2 is primarily the result of differences in estimating pin-lever watch sales. During this period, Timex was just getting started and a major portion of its production went into "pipeline filling" of new channels of distribution. The practice in repairing pin-lever watches still under guarantee was to replace the movement entirely instead of repairing it. Elgin estimated that this would account for approximately 25 per cent of the pin-lever movements in Table 1. Also, many pin-lever movements went into timing devices other than wrist watches. The Elgin estimate probably understated purchases of pin-lever watches because it did not include individuals under fifteen years old, who bought an estimated one-half to one million pin-lever watches.

were under greater and greater pressure to enter that field. Rather than compromise the Elgin reputation, they brought out in 1952 a lower-priced watch under the name Wadsworth, which sold primarily at $19.95 and $29.95. Executives believed that with adequate promotion this watch would capture its fair share of the lower-price market. Sales were disappointing despite the fact that low-priced watch sales generally continued to grow. Executives believed the Wadsworth was adequately promoted, but it never obtained more than 3 per cent of the "under $30" market in any year. In 1956 Elgin estimated the Wadsworth accounted for about 2.3 per cent of the "under $30" market, but this dropped to 1.9 per cent in 1957.

In a general appraisal of the watch market, Elgin executives concluded that there was an increasing acceptance of inexpensive "fashion" watches, such as the Swiss timepiece in the $20 and $30 bracket, and of the cheaper pin-lever watches, primarily American brands such as Timex. Appreciation for fine watches as jewelry was declining, particularly among the younger generation. No longer was a watch bought or presented as a gift with the idea that it would be used for a lifetime. The market for expensive watches was faced with increasing competition from other goods and services such as hi-fi sets, outboard motors, sporting equipment, cameras, vacation trips, and other items that the expanding American "middle class" was enjoying in its leisure time.

Elgin officials interpreted the development to mean that the expensive watch was no longer the symbol of social standing that it had been a generation before. Consumer surveys indicated that the largest number of watches retailing for less than $30 were purchased for teen-agers as gifts. The tendency was to give less expensive watches, which would be functional for some years but which neither the givers nor the recipients expected to last a lifetime. Style changes emphasizing the latest in design and fashion were also encouraging the tendency to pay less for a watch and to buy more often.

Watch ownership was high in all age groups, so that a large share of the market would be in the form of replacement sales. An Elgin survey showed, however, that there was a significant number of men in the teen-age and 30–39 age brackets who did not own a wrist watch or even any watch (Table 3).

TABLE 3
PERCENTAGE OWNERSHIP OF WATCHES BY AGE AND SEX: 1957

	14–19		20–24		25–29		30–39		40–49		Over 50	
	Men	Women	Men	Women	Men	Women	Men	Women	Men	Women	Men	Women
Use wrist watch	56	68	87	70	81	80	75	75	69	86	54	69
Own, don't use wrist watch	4	1	2	4	1	2	1	2	1	1	5	2
Don't own wrist watch	40	31	11	26	18	18	24	23	14	13	16	26
Use pocket or lapel watch	0	0	0	0	0	0	0	0	15	0	26	3
Percentage of men or women in group	11.7	11.0	8.6	8.6	9.5	9.3	20.1	20.1	18.3	18.1	31.8	32.9

Elgin had distributed its watches directly to jewelers and high-class department stores for many years. Surveys indicated that 90 per cent of all Elgin watches had been purchased at jewelry stores. Elgin's management had always felt a great loyalty for the established, legitimate local jeweler who had distributed the product so successfully. Such loyalty had become almost a tradition, and the management hesitated to break away from such a distribution policy in spite of the dynamic changes that were taking place in the watch market. The low-priced watches, however, were being sold through different channels than had been customary for expensive watches (Tables 4 and 5).

TABLE 4
DISTRIBUTION OF SALES OF WRIST WATCHES BY PLACE OF PURCHASE: SELECTED YEARS

Place of Purchase	1954*	1956†	1957†
Jewelry store	67%	61%	56%
Department store	5	7	5
Discount house	4	6	11
Mail order	3	5	7
Drug store	3	7	9
All other	18	14	12
	100%	100%	100%

* A. C. Nielsen Consumer Survey.
† Crossley–S. D. Consumer Survey.

TABLE 5

DISTRIBUTION OF SALES OF DIFFERENT-PRICED WRIST WATCHES BY PLACE OF
PURCHASE: 1956 AND 1957

Watch Price	Jewelry Stores	De-partment Stores	Dis-count Houses	Drug Stores	Mail Order	All Others	Total
$75 and up.........84%	84%	6%	3%	1%	0	6%	100%
$50 to $74.99........76	76	2	6	2	6	8	100
$30 to $49.99........75	75	3	10	1	4	7	100
$15 to $29.99........50	50	12	15	4	6	13	100
Under $15..........16	16	10	7	30	10	27	100

The jewelry stores still dominated the retail sale of watches above the $30 price bracket. This was Elgin's strong field, but even here its share of this market had dropped.

In 1958 Elgin's management again considered the question of whether to enter the low-priced market. To aid in arriving at a decision, a mail and personal interview survey was conducted among Elgin's dealers. Nine hundred and seventeen dealers answered the question, "Would an Elgin watch retailing at about $25 help your sales?" The results are shown in the accompanying tabulation.

	Personal Interviews	Mail Survey
Yes................................76.5%	76.5%	66.1%
No.................................23.5%	23.5%	30.9%
Number answering..................... 47	47	870

Additional comments were solicited, and the principal reasons for and against the introduction of a watch in the $25 range that were given are shown in Table 6.

In June, 1958, the marketing department presented a plan for increasing Elgin's total watch sales, with special emphasis on the "under $30" market. The first step in the suggested plan was to eliminate the production and marketing of the Wadsworth watch in spite of the fact that considerable investment had been put into advertising this watch over the preceding five years.

The next recommendation was that Elgin's prestige line, the 21-jewel "Lord" and "Lady" Elgins, which retailed from $71.50 to $175, be continued as the top Elgin line but that the starting retail price be reduced to $59.50. This price reduction would, it was believed, enable Elgin to compete in the $50 to $65 market, where it might presently be losing many sales. It was recommended that this quality line continue to be distributed directly to retail jewelry dealers. Dealers were to be franchised, however, and tightly policed by the company. Franchises would be granted

TABLE 6

REASONS GIVEN BY DEALERS FOR AND AGAINST LOW-PRICED ELGIN WATCH

	No. of Mentions
Reasons for:	
Would get business from Swiss (private brands)...................	169
People want this price watch. This *is* where market is..............	127
Need a good-name watch at lower price..........................	81
We need an inexpensive watch for teen-agers.....................	55
It would outsell Wadsworth....................................	15
Elgin name alone would sell it.................................	8
Reasons against:	
It would hurt Elgin name......................................	71
It would interfere with Wadsworth sales.........................	40
You couldn't give the mark-up..................................	22
There is no demand for this type of watch.......................	20
It would hurt our higher-priced watch sales......................	12
Other reasons...	55

to a limited number of perhaps 7,000 dealers out of the 17,000 on Elgin's dealer list. Franchises could be withdrawn at Elgin's option from dealers whose activities did not enhance the prestige name of the "Lord" and "Lady" Elgin line.

The third recommendation was that a medium-priced line of Elgin watches of the 19-jewel variety be introduced to sell at from $34.95 to $69.50, or perhaps higher in models with solid-gold cases or diamond ornamentation. This line of watches would be distributed to all jewelry stores as well as to many other types of retail outlets. The Elgin sales force would sell the line direct to large mass distributors such as department stores, catalogue houses, low-margin retailers, certain house-to-house operations, and trading-stamp redemption stores.

The fourth recommendation was that a 17-jewel, lower-medium-priced Elgin watch, retailing from $19.95 to $29.95, be produced or, if necessary, assembled with imported movements in company designed cases. This lower-priced line would be offered to all outlets to which Elgin sold direct, including jewelry stores, department stores, and the large mass distributors, to be used for the medium-priced line. In addition, distribution would be sought through wholesale distributors who sold to good "merchandising" drugstores, gift stores, specialty stores, and through premium channels. Distinctive names were planned for this low-priced line; the men's wrist watch would be called the "Sportsman" and the ladies' the "Starlite." The word "Elgin" would appear in the title along with the model name. This would distinguish this lower-priced line from the medium-priced line, which would use only the word "Elgin," and the top line, which would always be identified as the "Lord" or "Lady" Elgin. Packaging on all three lines was to be distinctively different, so that there would be little confusion on the part of the consumer as to which quality of Elgin watch he was buying.

It was believed that this program could hold the loyalty of the jewelry retailer, who, although he might be competing with the discount house on the medium-priced line or the drugstore on the low-priced line, could point out to his customer that only he, the jeweler, could supply the finest in the Elgin line—the "Lord" and "Lady" Elgins.

The marketing department made no recommendation that Elgin attempt to enter the "under $15" market, where the great volume of the nonjeweled or pin-lever watches was sold. It was believed that the lowest-priced Elgin line would automatically take some sales from this low-priced market, in that some customers might be induced to upgrade their purchases on the strength of the fact that for a few dollars more they could purchase a jeweled-lever, quality Elgin watch.

The "Lord" and "Lady" Elgin lines would continue to be marked with a suggested retail price that would provide the retailer with the conventional 50 per cent margin. The medium-priced line would carry a suggested retail price that would give the retailer a margin of 50 to 60 per cent, depending on the specific model. In the low-priced line, suggested retail prices would provide margins of 40–45 per cent, somewhat less than the common industry margin of 50 per cent.

Elgin's sales force numbered about fifty men, who sold direct to about 17,000 active accounts. Each salesman had between 300 and 400 accounts. Salesmen called on the typical accounts four times a year; they called more frequently on the larger accounts, some as often as once a month. Where a small account was inconveniently located, a salesman might not call more than once a year.

If the new marketing plan were to be adopted, salesmen would continue to sell direct to retail jewelers and the mass distributors. The same salesmen would handle any drug or other wholesalers in his territory. The new plan would expand the number of Elgin accounts an estimated 15–20 per cent, or about 3,000 accounts. It was estimated, however, that this would expand the number of retail outlets from 17,000 to about 40,-000. Initially some special sales personnel would probably have to be added to open up new accounts, especially the drug and tobacco jobbers. After these were started, regular salesmen would take over. The number of salesmen would be increased as necessary and as experience showed the desirable number of calls and time per call that the new accounts would require.

Long-term promotion plans called for most advertising to support the entire Elgin line with such broad terms as "Elgin watches from $19.95." It was planned, however, to spend part of each year's budget on each line separately, featuring new models and new model features. If the low-priced "Sportsman" and "Starlite" models were added to the line, a major share, perhaps 75 per cent, of that year's budget would be spent in introducing them. In general, however, the "Lord" and "Lady" Elgin lines would receive the largest percentage of specific model advertising. As a general policy, new models and other innovations would be introduced in the "Lord" and "Lady" Elgin lines first. The franchised dealers who handled these lines would also get special display materials.

Should Elgin adopt the new product line and distribution plan?

3

NATIONAL THREAD COMPANY

NATIONAL THREAD COMPANY was a small selling organization for all types of industrial threads, and it also acted as a manufacturer's agent for a line of industrial zippers. In 1953, its first year of operation, the company's sales were less than $50,000, but they increased steadily thereafter to $250,000 in 1958. Mr. Silver, the company president, believed that, if the firm were to continue to grow and prosper, it would have to organize its sales operations according to some plan. He was uncertain as to what kind of sales program was best in an industry as changeable and competitive as the thread industry.

The thread industry was composed of two large companies, American Thread Company and Coats and Clark, which together accounted for 70 per cent of the thread business. About six firms accounted for another 15 per cent of the business, and seventy-five to one hundred firms of about the same size as National Thread accounted for the remaining 15 per cent. Coats and Clark was the only firm that produced thread for sale to household consumers. A number of thread manufacturers concentrated their sales with the dress, coat, and suit industry exclusively; others sold to other industries. Mr. Silver decided not to sell to the garment industry because of the intense price competition there. In total, he sold to about fifty different industries, the more important of which were work clothing, mattresses, furniture, gloves, canvas goods, shoes, and automotive.

About 85 per cent of all thread is cotton, 10 per cent is synthetic (nylon, dacron), and 5 per cent other material, such as silk and glass. Cotton thread is finished in three basic ways: soft finish, glazed, and mercerized. The latter gives a silky, shiny appearance to the thread. There are some 17,000 shades of colors, but a range of 200–250 colors account for most sales. Thread runs from 2 to 10 ply, i.e., the number of strands twisted together. National made each of the three basic types of cotton thread and all standard plys in about 200 colors.

Thread-buyers were usually not aware of the quality difference in threads. Thread purchases were generally made on the basis of requests by sewing-machine operators. These operators in most companies were on a piece-rate method of production. Once accustomed to a certain brand of thread, they would not accept another brand even of higher quality. Experiments had shown that any change resulted in lower production rates and operator animosity.

A plant in the South produced all National's thread. Mr. Silver had found the arrangement satisfactory because he did not need to tie up his limited capital in production facilities, did not have to be concerned with idle plant facilities, and was able to purchase thread at costs that were substantially competitive.

National handled a top-quality thread that required the best grade of cotton. Only about the top one-half of 1 per cent of all cotton could be used to produce this quality of thread. The cotton was bought through a broker in a southern exchange in quantities sufficient to fill anticipated requirements 90–120 days in advance. This meant that National owned a stock of 30,000–45,000 pounds of cotton at most times. Top-grade cotton cost twice as much per pound as the next best grade. The high-quality thread was superior to others in that it did not break so easily and so was more efficient in high-speed industrial sewing machines. National attempted to sell this thread at prices that were competitive with most threads of lesser quality. It made an average gross margin of 10–12 per cent; its break-even point was at a volume of about $125,000. The typical thread order was for about 100 units (pounds) and was valued at $100 to $400. Most customers reordered four or five times a year.

In addition to its thread business, National was a manufacturer's agent in its area for a small zipper manufacturer. It did the actual selling, but the zipper manufacturer performed all the other marketing functions and services. National's commission rate was 5 per cent, but the earned commission frequently was less. While the company could cut the manufacturer's price to complete a sale, part of the price cut came out of its commission when this was done. Many small thread manufacturers had similar arrangements to sell zippers. Mr. Silver believed the zipper was a good addition to the thread line because:

1. The line often complemented thread sales, especially in the work-clothing industry.
2. Any profits made on zippers added to the company's total profits. Zippers could be sold with little additional sales effort and caused no additional expenses. Zippers were occasionally the basis of entree into a new account when thread could not be sold. After zippers were sold, thread orders were obtained.

The zipper industry was dominated by Talon, which accounted for about 40 per cent of the total zipper business; one medium-sized firm, Connar, which did about 20 per cent of the volume; and some fifteen other manufacturers, who shared the remaining 40 per cent of the zipper market. Talon and Connar had their own sales forces calling on accounts. Talon had a separate sales force for its industrial division and another for its retail division, while Connar's sales force sold to industrial users only. The remaining fifteen manufacturers generally employed such a sales representative as National Thread to handle their lines. National was expected to sell a minimum of $50,000 a year in zippers to continue as the representative in its area. A typical zipper order was for 10,000–15,000 units or $300–$500. Most customers reordered twelve to twenty-four times per year.

National sold in a seven-state area that included Illinois, Michigan, Ohio, Indiana, Iowa, Minnesota, and Wisconsin. A large share of National's sales were for custom threads, those manufactured to order. The period between order and delivery was from three to six weeks, which was considered good in the industry. Ability to deliver quickly was important, and National had a good reputation in this respect.

Mr. Silver and his partner did all the selling. Each of them took responsibility for one-half of the seven-state market and attempted to call on all manufacturers that would use thread or zippers in that territory, except garment manufacturers. In each city they located prospects by checking the classified directory for firms in the industries that were likely to use thread. Initially, they tried to call on the owner of a plant. After an order was obtained, however, later contacts were usually with purchasing agents or factory supervisors. Some reorders were obtained by telephone or mail, but about 85 per cent of all sales were made on personal calls.

Price was an important factor in purchases of thread, but there was relatively little price bargaining. National based its sales effort on quality. The industry leaders commonly gave 2 per cent cash discounts, free delivery for orders of 200 pounds or more, and quantity discounts that ranged up to 5 per cent. National had the same terms.

In 1958 the firm had about 250 accounts, of which approximately 20 per cent bought both thread and zippers and 10 per cent bought zippers only. Manufacturers accounted for 90 per cent of the business, with distributors and government contracts accounting for the remaining 10 per cent. Each partner spent about 70 per cent of his time selling. On the average, they called on each account once every four to six weeks, but this varied from once a week to once a year, depending on the size and needs of the account. In 1958 they picked up thirty new accounts and lost about fifteen accounts. The average sales were as follows: accounts buying (1) thread only, $150; (2) zippers only, $200; and (3) both thread and zippers, $350.

The big thread manufacturers advertised in a large number of trade journals—usually in one or more of the trade journals serving each of the main thread-using industries. Coats and Clark also advertised in national consumer magazines; and the big firms participated in all the large trade shows of the thread-consuming industries—probably twenty-five or more per year. National had never participated in these shows because the minimum cost was $1,000 to $2,000 per show. Most of the small thread manufacturers, including National, limited their advertising to some direct mail pieces of an institutional nature.

National's profit and loss statements for 1957 and 1958 are shown in Exhibit 1.

EXHIBIT 1

OPERATING STATEMENTS FOR NATIONAL THREAD COMPANY: 1957 AND 1958

	1957	1958
Sale of threads	$125,000*	$150,000*
Gross margin	22,500	30,000
Marketing expenses	16,000	19,000
Sales salaries	(10,250)	(15,000)
Advertising (direct mail pieces)	(250)	(500)
Traveling expenses and gifts	(5,500)	(3,500)
Administrative expenses	9,000	10,000
Net profit or loss on thread	2,500 (loss)	1,000 (profit)
Zipper sales†	100,000	100,000
Zipper commissions	3,250	3,750

* All figures rounded.
† Mr. Silver believed that all expenses should be charged to the thread operation because the expense of keeping the records required to separate thread expenses from zipper expenses would far exceed its value, especially since zipper sales were relatively small.

Mr. Silver believed that, if National were to continue to grow, it would be necessary to organize better sales programs, but he did not know how to proceed. Presumably a sales forecast for the coming year was a first step, but he believed that he could not make a forecast accurate enough to be of any value because of the following factors.

1. Demand within most of the thread-consuming industries varied widely from one year to the next and even from one month to the next. Table 1 shows the monthly variations in sales experienced by National over the past four years.

TABLE 1

MONTHLY SALES NATIONAL THREAD COMPANY: 1955–58

Month	1955	1956	1957	1958
January	$ 16,900	$ 16,200	$ 17,900	$ 21,300
February	14,100	15,400	16,900	17,200
March	21,300	15,400	18,600	15,000
April	19,000	18,200	19,900	21,900
May	16,300	15,200	20,500	19,000
June	15,500	14,300	15,800	20,000
July	17,000	17,400	13,200	18,500
August	17,100	19,500	24,000	22,800
September	18,400	15,200	18,400	25,300
October	16,500	25,400	22,700	30,000
November	18,000	18,500	18,300	21,000
December	17,500	17,300	19,200	18,000
Total	$207,600	$208,000	$225,000	$250,000

2. There was no consistency in sales by industry. In any given industry, each manufacturer had different requirements. National's sales to each industry varied widely from year to year, although Mr. Silver did not have a breakdown of sales by industry. National did not know how many potential customers there were in its territory. The *1954 Census* showed the number of manufacturers in National's main consuming industries to be as given in Table 2.
3. Manufacturers were constantly changing processes, e.g., from sewing to heat sealing. This could not be predicted.
4. No industry statistics could be trusted enough to be used because the smaller thread producers all believed that the giants dominated the trade association, and hence they (the small producers) were reluctant to give information to the association.

TABLE 2

NUMBER OF MANUFACTURING FIRMS BY INDUSTRY IN
NATIONAL THREAD COMPANY'S MARKET AREA*

Industry	Illinois	Michigan	Ohio	Indiana	Iowa	Minnesota	Wisconsin	Total
Work Clothing.....	10	22	23	34	0	14	14	117
Mattresses.......	0	0	41	0	13	14	19	87
Furniture.........	86	72	75	42	120	21	26	442
Gloves...........	10	14	0	14	0	0	17	55
Canvas goods.....	77	50	64	32	19	14	29	285
Shoes............	100	9	28	7	0	12	61	217
Automotive†......	126	282	139	136	25	30	34	772
Total......	409	449	370	265	177	105	200	1975

* *Census of Manufacturers: 1954.*
† Includes auto part producers who do not use thread.

5. Manufacturers buying thread and zippers ordered only as needed to produce for current orders. Traditionally, thread and zippers were available when needed. Mr. Silver believed that it was useless to promote long-range purchase orders, regardless of inducements made, because manufacturers traditionally did not carry any thread or zipper inventory. One of the major factors that caused Mr. Silver to stay out of the garment industry was that purchases were made in very small quantities and buyers often wanted to return any part of the order that was not used.
6. There was no way to forecast unusually large orders that might be placed by large manufacturers or by the federal or state governments. One or two such windfall orders could completely distort production, sales, and advertising plans.

Mr. Silver believed in the value of advertising but was not sure whether the company should advertise or not; if it did advertise, he did not know how much to spend for advertising or what media to use. He was especially concerned with the advertising problem because it was his general belief that a small company such as National could not justify spending funds for participation in trade shows because sales obtained at such events were generally very small. Since he dealt with some fifty industries, each having one or several trade journals, he did not see how he could possibly advertise to reach all his potential market. He was not convinced that direct mail was productive, but he had been doing some because all the other small thread firms did.

Mr. Silver was also uncertain as to whether he should hire one or more full-time salesmen. If he did try to get an additional man or two, he was not sure where he could get qualified individuals. The following factors influenced his thinking on this matter.

1. Generally, it took a salesman considerable time, perhaps more than a year, to acquire a workable knowledge of the thread line. A salesman needed to know such things as what thread to use for each of the many different purposes, when substitutions could be made without loss of quality in the final product, and how to aid manufacturers in maintaining sewing quality while cutting costs.
2. Mr. Silver estimated that it would cost approximately $5,000 to train such a man.
3. Selling thread was a discouraging business because it took a long time to get prospects to switch to a new line. The type of customer and the product itself held little glamour for most salesmen.
4. Mr. Silver estimated that there were less than 50 salesmen in the thread industry. Most of these men worked for the large companies and would have little interest in working for such a firm as National.
5. Mr. Silver wanted to hire a college graduate but wondered whether he could realistically expect to attract such a man.

What sales program should Mr. Silver develop?

4

HEATHLEY COMPANY

THE HEATHLEY COMPANY was one of two leading producers of standard household food mixers.[1] In addition to standard mixers, which accounted for approximately 80 per cent of Heathley's dollar sales volume, the company also manufactured and sold electric heating pads, electric corn poppers, and hot plates. In 1959 total sales were near $7 million. The small-appliance industry, however, was changing rapidly with the introduction of new products. Heathley had fallen behind the industry in this respect but in 1960 was trying to develop a marketing plan for introducing new items.

The small-appliance industry consisted of over thirty firms that manufactured small electrical housewares, such as coffee makers, toasters, blankets, hot plates, frying pans, fans, irons, roasters, and mixers, all of which typically sold for less than $50. Small-appliance sales had doubled since 1949 and in 1959 amounted to over $1 billion. Most of this increase, however, was the result of the introduction of new products (see

---

[1] A standard food mixer consists of an encased motor, feeder blades, a bowl, and an upright stand.

Table 1). Despite this recent market growth, a large potential still appeared to exist. Sales of small appliances were seasonal; for example, an estimated 40 per cent of all mixers sold in 1959 were sold in November and December. General Electric and Sunbeam, both full-line sellers, were acknowledged leaders in the industry; however, many small limited-line firms were considered outstanding in one or two products. The market was highly competitive, with sellers constantly vying with one another on such matters as price, advertising, and product differentiation.

TABLE 1

PERCENTAGE OF TOTAL ELECTRICAL HOUSEWARE SALES
ACCOUNTED FOR BY NEW ITEMS AND STAPLE ITEMS: 1950–56*

Year	New Items	Staple Items
1950	11.82	88.18
1951	14.25	85.75
1952	22.45	77.55
1953	30.69	69.31
1954	35.17	64.83
1955	37.52	62.48
1956	38.37	61.60

* Source: *Electrical Merchandising*, January, 1957. Data not available for years 1957–59, but information indicated that new items were accounting for a still larger portion of total sales.

The Heathley line of products, which was sold under the brand name of "Perfect," was considered to be of high quality and had an excellent reputation both in the trade and at the consumer level. The line received strong competition from a variety of sellers who also produced quality lines. Retail list prices on the Perfect line were competitive with comparable models of most other producers.

The Heathley Company employed eleven salesmen and also used eleven manufacturers' agents to sell its line. These salesmen and agents sold to more than six hundred distributors, who, in turn, sold to typical appliance outlets, such as appliance stores, department stores, hardware stores, and drugstores. The density of distribution and sales varied considerably from market to market. The company deployed its salesmen mainly in the East and the Midwest. Most company salesmen and agents were paid a 5 per cent commission on sales. They were expected to pay all their own expenses, including travel and entertainment. The company's sales territories ranged in size from one metropolitan area (New York) to the entire Pacific Coast (California, Washington, and Oregon). Usually a territory covered more than one state and included several major metropolitan areas. Other firms in the small-appliance field typically had a more intensive coverage of their markets; in fact, some of them, such as General Electric and Westinghouse, had their own company-owned distributorships. These firms, however, also sold to independent distributors.

Salesmen of the large companies handled a relatively smaller number of accounts (from 10 to 20 distributors), which permitted them to make more frequent calls on the distributors and also to spend more time with key retailers. For example, Sunbeam was thought to have about 1,200 distributors and 150 salesmen, of which 75 were classed as junior salesmen and merchandising men.

To support its personal selling program, Heathley budgeted about $300,000 annually for national advertising. In 1959 the bulk of this advertising was placed in such consumer magazines as the *Saturday Evening Post, Life, Better Homes and Gardens,* and *Brides' Magazine.* Also, the company frequently used newspapers to combat local competitive pressures or to take advantage of a special situation. In addition to the $300,-000 budget, Heathley set aside about $40,000 in 1959 for dealer co-operative advertising. This plan provided the dealer with advertising funds amounting to 2 per cent of his annual purchases of Heathley products. Actually, the company paid 50 per cent of the cost of any ad of its appliances up to the 2 per cent figure. In 1959 General Electric was estimated to have spent between $3 and $5 million on national advertising and a similar amount for local-market promotions. Sunbeam was thought to be spending over $5 million for both types of advertising combined. Most firms in the small-appliance field conducted aggressive in-market promotions, with emphasis on special "deals." The trade usually advertised one product at a time; rarely was the entire line featured.

Industry sales of standard mixers had declined substantially since 1950, while sales of portable mixers had been increasing (see Table 2).[2] The

TABLE 2

INDUSTRY SALES OF PORTABLE MIXERS: 1950–56*
(In Thousands)

Year	Units Sold	Year	Units Sold
1950	145	1955	1,625
1951	125	1956	2,645
1952	455	1957	2,400
1953	615	1958	1,995
1954	1,274	1959	2,250

* Source: *Electrical Merchandising,* June, 1960.

introduction of a portable mixer in the fall of 1958 represented the company's first attempt to expand its line of mixers. Heathley's portable mixer was not visually differentiated from competitive models and was made only in white and yellow, although most competitors offered four colors. The new product was of the standard Heathley high quality. In introduc-

---

[2] A portable mixer performed the same functions as a standard one. It consisted primarily of an enclosed motor and beaters. It was truly portable and, for example, could be used to "beat" products on the stove.

ing the new portable mixer, Heathley did not allocate any additional advertising funds or offer any introductory deals. It expected the new product to be carried by the general reputation of the Perfect line, especially that of the standard mixer. Sales in 1959, the portable mixer's first full year, amounted to only about $400,000, a disappointing figure to the firm's executives.

Heathley planned to introduce a new frying pan at the housewares show in July, 1960. This electric skillet was to be offered in two sizes, 10 inch and 12 inch, and would be priced competitively. While this product had no unusual or distinctive features, the Heathley executives believed that it was of excellent quality. Industry sales of electrical frying pans had increased rapidly following the product's introduction by Sunbeam in 1955.

In January, 1960, the Heathley management decided to employ the services of a management consulting firm to determine what kind of marketing program was needed to improve the firm's competitive position. One of the first things the consultants attempted to do was to evaluate the performance of each sales territory in sales of the standard mixer. This was done by measuring the trend of Heathley's share of industry sales in each territory over the last four years. The National Electrical Manufacturers Association (NEMA) collected data on industry sales. These were summarized by Heathley sales territories, and Heathley's share in each territory was computed. The results are shown in Table 3.

TABLE 3

HEATHLEY'S SHARE OF MARKET FOR STANDARD MIXERS: 1956–59

	Index of Heathley Sales				Index of Industry Sales*				Heathley Share of Market			
	1956	1957	1958	1959	1956	1957	1958	1959	1956	1957	1958	1959
New York..................100	116	119	116		100	99	100	108	36%	42%	43%	39%
Chicago–Milwaukee...........100	80	84	85		100	102	100	108	32	26	28	26
Philadelphia–Washington......100	99	74	77		100	92	76	82	39	42	38	36
Los Angeles–San Diego........100	88	87	95		100	88	106	115	40	41	33	34
Boston–New England..........100	111	103	103		100	91	83	90	29	34	35	32
Cleveland....................100	75	110	95		100	76	101	109	36	35	39	31
Cincinnati–Indianapolis.......100	82	85	66		100	84	87	95	28	27	27	19
San Francisco.................100	101	94	131		100	119	124	134	47	40	36	47
Minneapolis–St. Paul..........100	82	93	98		100	81	86	92	38	38	41	40
Buffalo......................100	92	84	85		100	97	87	95	31	29	29	27
Newark......................100	101	133	192		100	80	95	103	27	34	37	50
St. Louis.....................100	114	88	88		100	110	91	98	19	20	19	18
Pittsburgh....................100	69	82	83		100	72	80	86	36	35	38	36
Dallas–Houston...............100	103	119	114		100	91	98	105	19	22	24	21
Portland.....................100	55	83	73		100	72	103	111	39	29	31	25
Miami–Atlanta...............100	124	105	176		100	115	112	120	38	39	35	53
Seattle......................100	107	100	97		100	106	104	112	41	41	39	36
Denver......................100	70	109	112		100	80	116	125	27	23	25	24
New Orleans.................100	124	110	98		100	102	105	114	23	26	22	18
Detroit......................100	79	73	68		100	78	74	80	40	41	40	34
Total Sales..............100	94	97	99		100	92	95	103	32	33	33	31

* NEMA data cannot be published; the index numbers shown here indicate the direction and size of the sales changes.

Between the first and the last of the four years, seven of the twenty districts showed an increase in market share, and thirteen showed a decrease. As shown in the table, however, the share of market figures shifted from year to year in an irregular manner.

The consultants also found that Heathley had many small accounts among its distributors (see Table 4). Over 45 per cent of the distributors accounted for less than 10 per cent of Heathley's dollar sales in 1959.

TABLE 4

DISTRIBUTION OF SALES BY DISTRIBUTORS: 1959

Sales Volume	No. of Distributors	Per Cent of Total Distributors	Sales	Per Cent of Total Sales
Under $2000................131		21.8	$ 130,400	1.9
$2000–$4999................150		24.9	497,600	7.3
$5000–$9999................147		24.5	1,039,000	15.0
$10,000–$19,999.............. 87		14.4	1,187,000	17.2
$20,000–$29,999.............. 27		4.5	646,000	9.4
$30,000–$39,999.............. 23		3.8	779,000	11.3
$40,000 and over............. 37		6.1	2,611,000	37.9
Total.................602		100.0	$6,890,000	100.0

At the other extreme, 10 per cent of the distributors accounted for 50 per cent of sales.

In a survey among distributors and retailers, the consultants found that Heathley's distribution at wholesale was incomplete and that very few wholesalers stocked the complete line. The Heathley line was a secondary product with most distributors and was considered a poor third to Sunbeam and General Electric.

The consultants pointed out that the influx of new items in the small-appliance industry; variations in established products, such as the addition of various colors; and the declining demand for some old standbys, such as deep-fat fryers, standard mixers, and roasters had forced wholesalers and retailers alike to effect closer control over their inventories. This had been done by weeding out slow-moving items and by reducing the number of lines. In this sorting-out process, limited-line manufacturers such as Heathley had suffered.

The consultants believed the introduction of Heathley's portable mixer had been handled poorly and had caused a loss of prestige among both distributors and dealers. Many distributors had complained about poor delivery on the new mixers and about the lack of promotion to introduce the new item. They also complained about the lack of an introductory "deal," i.e., special discounts or free merchandise.

After completing their study, the consultants made the following recommendations:

1. New products should be introduced in order of their ease and worth of introduction. Since Heathley was coming into the market "late," they believed it was imperative that the firm turn this disadvantage into an opportunity by marketing a product that was visually better than any other on the market.

2. No new item should be introduced until the previous new item had gained both trade and consumer acceptance.

3. Efforts should be made to identify dealers essential to Heathley's success. These would not necessarily be those firms already selling the Heathley line. A priority list of these essential retailers should be constructed for each sales territory and a definite plan developed to get these firms not only to stock Heathley products but also to sell them aggressively. Such a plan should spell out details on the improvements made in the product line, the new products still to be added, the national advertising program, the local co-operative advertising plan, the special offers or deals, and the plan for working with key retailers. As part of this plan, the consultants urged that Heathley reduce the geographical size of its sales territories and the number of its distributors in each. Increased sales from the addition of new products were expected to offset the reduced potential in each area.

4. Every effort should be made to use the present sales force as efficiently as possible by adding agents, thereby freeing salesmen. These salesmen should control and work with the agents helping them to do a better job. The sales force and the agents need to be strengthened by the addition of new merchandising ideas and plans to stimulate distributor and dealer sales effort. Sales help should be available to help distributors and dealers handle difficult local situations. The two individuals in the home-office merchandising division should be augmented.

5. Heathley was heavily outgunned in advertising by its competitors. While this was expected in an industry dominated by General Electric and Sunbeam, it was not realistic to assume that the Heathley Company could market new products successfully without the addition of substantial sums to its advertising budget. National advertising should be tied in with local advertising and merchandising. In this regard every effort should be made to get distributors and dealers to do as much local advertising as possible. In the long run Heathley must be prepared and must commit itself to spend large sums for advertising, not merely on national advertising alone but on all advertising. The co-operative budget for the coming year should be increased substantially and point-of-purchase display materials developed.

Since the consultants were not requested to make any organization and personnel recommendations, the report contained nothing about the organization that was needed to implement the various suggestions made in the report. In a verbal presentation made to the Heathley president, the consultants did recommend that the marketing department be strengthened substantially. They felt it desirable to have at least five different divisions within the marketing department as follows:

A. Advertising and merchandising.
B. Consumer sales force.
C. Commercial sales, including export.
D. Marketing research.
E. Sales training and selection.

In commenting on the consultants' report, the president of the Heathley Company said, "I think they covered just about all our defects, but what I don't find is a workable plan. We are trying and have been trying for the past several years to do the very things that they indicate we must do. We know, for example, that we should be spending more money for advertising, but the question is: Where do we get this additional money? Certainly we can't borrow it from a bank, and our profits are so small that they do not permit us to make an investment in the kind of advertising budget that the consultants are talking about. We've known for years that we don't have the kind of retail distribution that we should have. But here again, what can we do about it?

"We have a small sales force, and of course we'd like to have a larger one; in fact, we must have a larger one if we are to increase sales and profit. But again, I'm not sure that the consultants really understand that problem. Certainly it doesn't make sense to me that we collapse our sales territories and put more agents in charge, because for the most part we don't really have control over these men. I'm convinced that we should go in the other direction and that, if anything, we should take money from our advertising funds and hire more salesmen and fire some of our agents. I think this is far more important than either hiring agents or increasing our advertising budget. After all, we do have a name with the consumer and, if we don't advertise as much as we have been doing for the next year or two, I don't think we'll lose too much ground. I'm convinced that the answer lies in the introduction of new products. Even if these new products are not as successful as we would like, they do help us utilize plant capacity and enable us to use our present distribution system more effectively. We do get some profit from the number of new units we sell. Take for example the hand mixer which we introduced last year and on which we only had $400,000 in sales. If it hadn't been for that product I don't think we would have had any profits."

What sales plan should Heathley adopt?

SECTION II

Establishing the Firm's Marketing Objectives

THE CONCEPT of market niche and use of product is of greater value to the firm in setting its objectives than is an evaluation of the kind or types of products or services it produces. Given this concept, there still exists the problem of determining which niche(s) the firm shall attempt to exploit. To decide this question, the firm must develop a procedure for segmenting the total market and determining the relative importance of the individual segments, in both the present and the future. The needs or characteristics of each segment must be evaluated in relation to the firm's resources and in relation to the competing resources that are attempting, or may attempt, to exploit the given segment.

An example may help clarify the foregoing. Assume that a given firm produces timepieces. Its objective may be thought of as satisfying man's need to measure time. This total need can be segmented in a wide variety of ways, of which the following is only a beginning:

I. Need to measure time by consumers by place
  A. Within home
    1. Kitchen
    2. Bedroom
    3. Playroom
    4. Other rooms
  B. Outside of home
    1. Car
    2. At place of business
    3. At other places where physical surroundings are less controlled by consumer
II. Need to use time measurement mechanism as an activation device
  A. Activation of noise
    1. For awakening individuals
    2. For alerting or warning individuals or masses (alarms, oven timers)
  B. Activation of mechanical devices
    1. Timers for industry (control of automatic processes, vault doors)
    2. Timers for the home (start radio, turn on oven, turn on furnace)

From a product point of view, such a classification would suggest that the firm *could* produce a line of clocks, watches, and timers. Within the clock line, the firm could produce items powered mechanically or electrically; it could produce kitchen clocks, playroom clocks, decorator clocks for various rooms, alarm clocks, and travel clocks. It could produce expensive or inexpensive clocks. The watch and timer markets could be segmented in similar fashion. Each segment must be analyzed as to its "needs." For example, the travel clock segment has such needs as:

1. Dependability in a time-measurement device because of the importance of catching transportation and keeping appointments.
2. Rugged construction, since the unit will be placed in luggage that will likely be handled roughly.
3. Smallness and compactness, since luggage space is usually limited.
4. Simplicity of operation. Since travel clocks are used infrequently, they should not pose a memory problem as to how to start, adjust, and set and turn off the alarm.
5. Reasonably attractive. Many people who are traveling are in a festive mood and the unit may be viewed by others.
6. Reasonable price. Since a travel clock is not used constantly and since it is frequently purchased as a gift, it does not warrant as high a price as some other timepieces.

The firm then assesses its resources relative to the stated needs, keeping in mind the resources of other firms in the industry which may compete for the travel-clock business.

Many firms attempt to sell several market segments simultaneously. Where the various segments have similar needs and where they are comprised of approximately the same individuals, this may pose no major problems. But where the needs of segments differ substantially, the firm must be careful to consider how these differences will impinge upon the firm's resources. If the needs of two or more segments are in conflict, it may be difficult or impossible for the firm to sell successfully to each segment. An example of this situation is found frequently in the needs of the high-price-market segment versus the needs of the low-price segment. Few firms sell successfully to both.

The system to use to segment the total market depends upon many things. Wherever possible, the system used should be related to available market information, thereby facilitating measurement of the market segments. The system should provide as much information about the needs and characteristics of the segments as possible. But primarily the system of segmentation must attempt to separate all market segments with needs that differ from those of other segments. The consumer market is frequently segmented by occupation, age, income, city size, position in life cycle, geographical location, sex, and race. The industrial market may be segmented by such factors as industry, size, quality of product, market served, and geographical location.

Quantitative Objectives

To make a sound decision as to the market segment(s) that it will attempt to exploit, the firm's management must estimate the amount of a given good or service that a segment will consume during some stated time period. Once a segment has been selected, estimates or forecasts of the firm's sales to the segment are necessary as a guide for planning the marketing program.

Forecasts of demand by a particular market segment are sometimes made by estimating sales to individual customers and adding these figures to get totals. More often, total purchases of the market segment are estimated through a series of forecasts beginning with a forecast of over-all business conditions. Next, the firm forecasts the market segment's demand for the product in light of these anticipated business conditions, and then forecasts the firm's share of this industry total.

Once a forecast of the firm's sales has been completed, the total is broken down by geographical territories. Two different breakdowns are often made—one that is a forecast of actual sales by territory and one that indicates the distribution of sales in proportion to sales potential, that is, what sales would be if the same share of potential were obtained in each territory. The latter breakdown is needed as a guide for allocating sales resources among the territories. Ideally, a firm will allocate sales resources (men and dollars) among different geographical areas so that the marginal return per unit of resource is the same in each area. This means that territories with more potential will normally get more resources.

The sales forecast can be distributed among territories by using a standard market potential index as a guide or by developing a special index for the purpose. Such indexes may be single factors, such as industry sales or personal incomes. Other indexes are made up of a number of factors, which are weighted and then combined to form an index.

The sales-potential estimates for each territory serve as a standard against which to compare past sales. Where share of potential has lagged behind the average, special investigations are made to determine why. Sales costs per unit of sales and per unit of potential are computed and compared. From these analyses, the plan for allocation of sales resources can be developed.

Once the firm has determined what its sales activities will be in the various territories, it is in a position to set quotas, that is, the amount it actually expects to sell in each area. Quotas are performance standards against which actual results can be compared. They are used to measure efficiency and thus are control devices as well as objectives.

The foregoing abbreviated discussion on setting qualitative and quantitative marketing objectives is an oversimplification of the subject. The cases in this section were selected to show the variety of approaches used by a number of widely different firms in attempting to determine objectives. Each case affords an opportunity for analysis of the procedures used and an opportunity for creative thinking in developing better methods.

A. Qualitative Objectives

5

UNITED AIR LINES

In 1959 United Air Lines was confronted with the problem of whether to ask the Civil Aeronautics Board for permission to institute a new promotional type of airline fare that would be known as an "economy" fare. Such a fare would be lower than the coach fare, which was the cheapest fare currently offered by domestic scheduled airlines, but would be higher than the fare on nonscheduled airlines.

Different classes of service had been introduced into the air-transport industry from time to time. As a result, by 1958 the consumer had a confusing variety of services from which to choose. When jet service was introduced early in 1959, there were as many as seven different types of fares available between major cities. Table 1 shows the different types of services and the corresponding fares between New York and Los Angeles.

TABLE 1

FARE STRUCTURE FOR NEW YORK TO LOS ANGELES
FLIGHT—2,474 MILES

	Fare	
Class of Service	One Way	Round Trip
First-class jet*........................	$176.25	$352.50
First class...........................	166.25	332.50
Coach jet*...........................	115.50	231.00
Custom coach.......................	107.00	214.00
Regular coach.......................	104.00	208.00
Air-coach excursion†.................	No one way	168.40
Supplemental air carrier‡.............	88.00	160.00

* Proposed by American Airlines.
† Available only on DC-6 planes. Flights must begin on Monday, Tuesday, Wednesday, or Thursday, and round trips must be completed within thirty days.
‡ Commonly known as nonscheduled airlines.

Air coach service had been introduced after World War II. In the late 1940's the airlines' equipment began to catch up with the demand for air transportation, and there appeared to be a possibility of excess capacity. Coach service was introduced at that time and apparently was responsible for the tremendous increase in passenger traffic that followed thereafter.

Between 1950 and 1957 total air travel grew from 7,955 million passenger-miles to 25,250 million, or 217 per cent, while air-coach travel grew from 1,057 million passenger-miles to 9,510 million, or 800 per cent. During this same period, air transportation's share of all common-carrier traffic increased from 14.2 per cent to 40.1 per cent (see Table 2). By 1958, air

TABLE 2

UNITED STATES INTERCITY PASSENGER MILES TRAVELED
AND AIRLINE SERVICE AVAILABLE AND USED:
SELECTED YEARS
(Millions)

	1938	1946	1950	1954	1957	1958
Pullman and air travel						
Rail Pullman (first class)....	7,354	19,801	9,338	6,850	5,349	4,249
Air—first class............	457	5,910	6,898	11,375	15,740	15,180
Air coach................	...	...	1,057	5,321	9,510	10,076
Total air.................	457	5,910	7,955	16,696	25,250	25,256
Pullman and air combined...	7,811	25,711	17,293	23,546	30,599	29,505
Per cent airline of com-						
bined total..............	5.85	22.99	46.00	70.91	82.52	85.60
Other common carriers						
Rail coach................	10,240	39,119	17,473	17,710	16,365	14,300
Intercity motor bus.........	8,800	26,293	21,254	16,934	16,023	14,588
Total....................	19,040	65,412	38,727	34,644	32,388	28,888
Total common carrier........	26,851	91,123	56,020	58,190	62,987	58,393
Per cent airline of common						
carrier...................	1.70	6.49	14.20	28.69	40.09	43.3
Private intercity automobile....	226,279	253,570	402,843	548,763	655,400	650,000
Total common carrier and auto						
carrier...................	253,130	344,693	458,863	606,953	718,387	708,393
Per cent airline of total inter-						
city travel................	.18	1.71	1.73	2.75	3.51	3.6
Passenger-miles per capita.....	1,950	2,461	3,045	3,765	4,218	NA
Available airline seat-miles						
flown....................	908.4	7,490.4	12,385.6	25,646.5	39,838.2	53,069.6
Airline revenue passenger-miles						
flown....................	457.3	5,903.1	7,766.0	16,246.3	24,499.5	31,481.9
Airline passenger-load						
factor (%)................	50.35	78.81	62.70	63.35	61.50	59.32
Airline revenue plane-						
miles flown.................	65.4	304.5	327.1	497.2	711.1	972.1

Source: *Air Transport Facts and Figures*, 20th ed., 1959.

fares were competitive with rail fares and only slightly more than bus fares (see Table 3).

Since the price of a given class of air transportation was subject to approval by the Civil Aeronautics Board (C.A.B.), the type and the quality of service were often the most important competitive tools available to the individual airlines. If a particular type of service were introduced by one of the major airlines (with the approval of the C.A.B.) and was successful, other major lines soon offered similar service. Some domestic airlines offered two different services on a single flight, and most airlines

TABLE 3

COMPARISON OF BUS, RAIL, AND AIR FARES: 1958

	First Class*		Coach*		
	Rail	Air	Rail	Air	Bus†
Chicago–New York.............$ 74.35		$ 47.95	$37.33	$ 34.10	$27.35
Detroit–Boston................. 51.21		42.30	31.03	32.35	25.40
New York–Los Angeles......... 163.50		166.25	92.91	104.00	88.75
Philadelphia–Atlanta........... 47.83		48.10	24.92	30.35	24.00

* Source: *Air Transport Facts and Figures*, 20th ed., 1959.
† Source: Greyhound Corp.

anticipated that there would be two classes of service on jets. By re-arranging seats so that more were accommodated in the same amount of space in some parts of the plane and by building partitions between the different sections, different classes of service were offered on the same plane. United Air Lines did not combine two types of service on any of its domestic flights because the management believed that its flights were more desirable to the first-class passenger if there were no other fare classes on board. Likewise it scheduled its custom-coach flights separately. Custom coach differed primarily from coach in that meals were served aboard the former at a slight extra cost, while no meals were provided on coach flights. The custom-coach meals were not as fancy as the first-class meals. The other principal distinguishing features between custom-coach and coach were that newer equipment was used for custom-coach flights, seats were reserved, and two stewardesses were provided. Supplemental carriers did not operate daily schedules, since they were limited to ten days of operations per month, seating arrangements were more crowded than the coach flights, no meals were served, and older equipment was generally used. The major airlines did not offer this service.

The entire airline industry was suffering from a profit-margin squeeze. Profit margins had fallen from 5.1 per cent of net revenues in 1952 to 2 per cent in 1957, and the rate of return on investment for the same period had dropped from 10.9 per cent to 5.1 per cent (Exhibit 1).

This situation was of particular concern to the larger airlines because it was estimated that the scheduled airline companies had 474 new aircraft on order for delivery in the period 1959–61. Out of this total, 230 were jet craft, 167 turbo-props, 70 piston-type, and 7 helicopters. The total value of this equipment was approximately $2.5 billion.

The airlines attributed their margin squeeze primarily to the refusal of the C.A.B. to grant adequate fare increases to cover increased operating costs. The Air Transport Association, the trade association of the scheduled airlines, pointed out that between 1938 and 1958 the average revenue per airline passenger-mile had gone down from 5.32 cents to 5.25 cents while the over-all cost of living had increased 98 per cent during the

EXHIBIT 1

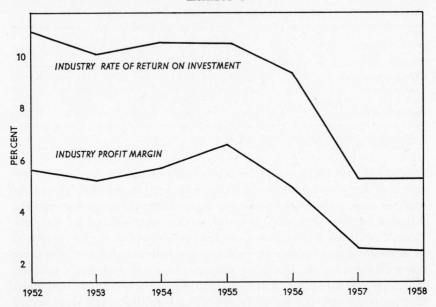

same period and even the cost of bus tickets had gone up 35 per cent.

Since 1956 virtually every trunk-line operator in the airline industry had filed requests with the C.A.B. for fare increases ranging from 12 per cent to 20 per cent. In unison the major companies had pointed to their precarious profit position, particularly in view of the tremendous additional capital that would be needed to equip them for the "jet age." Their case before the C.A.B. was based primarily on the fact that, with such low returns, bank financing was difficult to obtain and additional equity capital was almost unavailable.

In February, 1958, temporary relief was granted by the C.A.B. in approving proposals for what would amount to a 6.6 per cent average interim fare increase. Increases allowed were based upon a 4 per cent over-all increase plus an additional charge of one dollar on each ticket. It was estimated by the C.A.B. that the increase would result in additional operating revenues to the airlines of $85 million in 1958. The Air Transport Association pointed out that such an increase would boost 1958 industry profits only to about 2.6 per cent of net revenue as compared to the 2.0 per cent realized in 1957.

The C.A.B. announced that it would continue comprehensive investigation of the industry's rate structure but also warned that, in the event of further deterioration of airline earnings, it would make a "searching review" of scheduling practices. It was implied that excessive scheduling on the part of most airlines was responsible for the lower earnings in recent years. The C.A.B. could point to the passenger-load factor

(Table 3), which had been declining since 1946 despite a substantial increase in the passenger-miles flown.

United Air Lines filed a request in September, 1958, for some changes in its domestic-fare structure, including cancellation of round-trip discounts applicable to first-class transportation; cancellation of stopover privileges, available without additional charge on first-class trips; and reduction of the family-plan discount from 50 per cent to 33 ⅓ per cent.[1] All these requests, in effect, raised fares. The C.A.B., in granting approval to United and several other lines to make such rate changes, stated that it was incumbent on the airlines to develop and submit to the Board new types of fares designed to promote additional traffic. In a minority report, C.A.B. member G. Joseph Minetti indicated that he would approve tariffs proposing elimination of first-class-fare discounts only if they were accompanied by proposals to reduce coach fares or to inagurate an economy service with high-density, low-fare features.

United officials observed that, as more jet equipment was put into use, an excess of piston-type planes would probably become available. The airlines had had little trouble in the past disposing of older equipment as new planes became available, partially because passenger equipment had been in short supply since World War II. Demand for older equipment had been forthcoming from both the smaller, scheduled, feeder airlines and nonscheduled operators and the foreign airlines. Resales of used aircraft had been relatively profitable for the major trunk lines in the ten years previous to and including 1958. But the jets were making the DC-7's technically obsolete, since both were primarily long-range airplanes. The DC-7 had higher operating costs than the DC-6 but had had a speed advantage. The jets wiped out the speed advantage and cost less to operate.

United had purchased most of its fleet of over 50 DC-7's in 1954 and 1955 and had added a few in early 1958. These had all been purchased new at a cost of approximately $2 million each. The C.A.B. permitted DC-7's to be depreciated over a seven-year period, but the actual life of the plane was considerably longer, at least ten years, since after a series of overhaul operations it was virtually a new airplane. A study by the Transportation Center at Northwestern University indicated that the price of a used DC-7 would drop to between $160,000 and $240,000, approximately salvage value, as the number of jets increased. United officials thought that this estimate was too low but that the value would be as low as $300,000 by 1960. American Airlines, which was one of the first

---

[1] Family-plan fares (not shown in Table 1) were special fares offered to the families of first-class passengers on certain days of the week when business was slow. If a businessman had a first-class ticket, his wife and children could each travel with him for one-half the regular fare. The service received was the same as that offered on the regular first-class fare.

to receive jet equipment in 1958, was reported by a trade publication to have received $22,875,000 for 25 DC-7's traded in for jets. The Used Aircraft Exchange, which listed most used commercial planes for sale, had not shown a DC-7 sold to another user since early 1958. United planned to trade in ten DC-7's for new jet equipment and to convert another six to cargo planes. The remaining part of the fleet could be considered for use in an economy service.

United Air Lines made a study of transcontinental fares as compared to trans-Atlantic fares. Since trans-Atlantic fares were considerably higher per mile than transcontinental fares, an index number was developed. First-class fares in each case were set at 100, and index numbers

TABLE 4

INDEX NUMBERS SHOWING RELATIVE SIZE OF VARIOUS AIRLINE FARES*

	Trans-continental One Way	Trans-Atlantic One Way	Trans-continental Round Trip	Trans-Atlantic Round Trip
Deluxe..........................	..	111.5	..	111.5
Jet first class...................	106.0	..	106.0	..
1st class......................	100.0	100.0	100.0	100.0
Tourist........................	..	72.4	..	72.4
Jet coach......................	70.4	..	70.4	..
Custom coach..................	64.4	..	64.4	..
Coach.........................	62.6	..	62.6	..
Economy......................	..	57.9	..	57.9
Nonschedule...................	52.9	..	..	48.1
Excursion......................	..	..	50.6	..

* The index numbers in each column are relative to each other but cannot be compared to the numbers in other columns. Actually, the lowest trans-Atlantic fare is higher on a per passenger-mile basis than the highest trans-continental fare.

of the other fares were computed on these bases. The results are shown in Table 4.

Typical seating capacity on a DC-7 coach flight was 86. Executives estimated that this could be expanded to 100 for the proposed economy service.

An analysis of the experience of all air carriers during the quarter ending December 31, 1957, gave operating data for DC-7 aircraft as shown in Exhibit 2.

From its own experience, United estimated that direct costs made up about 60 per cent of the total costs that the airline had to cover. The other 40 per cent included passenger service, ground service, sales and advertising, and general administration costs.

In considering applying for permission to introduce an economy fare, United was interested in the experience of trans-Atlantic airlines with a similar service. Economy fares had been instituted in the summer of 1958 by trans-Atlantic airlines. Trans-Atlantic air travel was increasing rapidly,

EXHIBIT 2

OPERATING STATISTICS FOR ALL DC-7 AIRCRAFT*
QUARTER ENDING DECEMBER 31, 1957

Revenue miles flown		36,324,974
Direct costs:		
Flying costs		
Flight crew	$ 7,049,672	
Fuel and oil	13,581,992	
Other	3,321,923	$23,953,587
Maintenance		13,714,872
Depreciation		13,892,652
Other		1,022,701
Total direct costs		$52,583,810

* Gotch and Crawford, *Air Carrier Analyses* (Washington, 1958).

and the introduction of economy fares appeared to further the growth. Third-quarter trans-Atlantic figures for 1957 and 1958 are shown in Table 5. Tourist class on trans-Atlantic flights was analogous with coach travel on domestic lines.

United executives were interested in the effect that economy fares had had on tourist fares in trans-Atlantic service. In a period of one year economy fares had practically crowded out the tourist class. One international airline, SAS (Scandinavian), had already eliminated tourist class on the simple argument that very few wanted to pay an extra $113 round trip for an extra five inches of space. It was anticipated that as the jets shortened the trans-Atlantic flight to six and one-half hours, the premium on luxury would recede even further. A prominent trans-Atlantic airline official stated that first class would soon become an airborne version of the genteel, but anachronistic, railroad parlor car.

In observing the first year's results of the economy fare on trans-Atlantic flights, United Air Lines was interested in what was known as the "battle of the sandwiches." Trans-Atlantic fare schedules were regulated by a voluntary organization of all carriers, International Airlines Transport Association (I.A.T.A.). With fares fixed, a great battle developed among the competing airlines over the food to be served to pas-

TABLE 5

TRANS-ATLANTIC REVENUE PASSENGERS: THIRD QUARTER, 1957 AND 1958

	1957			1958			
	1st Class	Tourist	Total	1st Class	Tourist	Economy	Total
Eastbound	29,700	109,400	139,100	34,180	28,425	126,344	188,949
Westbound	37,400	161,400	198,800	43,443	41,028	193,473	277,944
	67,100	270,800	337,900	77,623	69,453	319,817	466,893

Source: 1957 data: "Summer Traffic Continues To Gain," *Aviation Week*, October, 1957, p. 38; 1958 data: "Trans-Atlantic Air Travel Reaches New Peak," *American Aviation*, December 1, 1958, p. 53.

TABLE 6

UNITED AIR LINES' PASSENGER PLANE FLEET: 1959*

Type of Plane	No. Owned	Average Cost (Millions)	Passenger Capacity
Mainliners			
DC-8............40 (on order)		$5.0	111–151
B-720............11 (on order)		3.7	100–125
DC-7............40		1.911	58
DC-6B..........36		1.173	58
DC-6............14		0.799	50
Convair..........52		0.6	44
Coaches			
DC-7............15		1.964	86
DC-6B..........5		1.280	75–78
DC-6............28		0.864	72

* Moody's Transportation Manual: 1959.

sengers traveling on the economy fare. It had been agreed that a sandwich would be the maximum amount of food served. Pan American charged, however, that some of the European lines were serving whole meals of such items as paté, fish, and even fruit on a slice of bread and calling it a sandwich. I.A.T.A. was called upon to hand down an official definition of a sandwich, which was as follows: "Each sandwich to be a separate unit, the whole meal not to give the appearance of a cold plate. A substantial and visible part of each unit to consist of bread, rolls, or similar breadlike materials. . . . Each unit to be simple, that is, not complicated. . . . This calls for a minimum of garnishing. Each unit to be inexpensive. This calls for an avoidance of materials normally regarded

TABLE 7

SELECTED OPERATING DATA UNITED AIR LINES: 1954 AND 1958*

Item	1954	1958
Revenue miles flown (000,000)........	98.3	135.5
Available seat-miles (000,000).........	4,986.1	8,034.3
Revenue passenger-miles		
Total (000,000)..................	3,305.6	5,163.5
Coach (000,000).................	967.4	2,206.4
Revenue passengers (000).............	4,769	6,839
Revenue per passenger-mile............	5.31¢	5.45¢
Average miles per passenger...........	694	715
Passenger-load factor.................	66.4%	64.5%
Plane utilization per day.............	8 hr. 30 min.	8 hr. 33 min.
Revenue (000)		
First-class passengers} $175,566		$281,533
Coach passengers }		
Total.......................$200,719		$319,961
Operating gross margin (000)........$ 21,887		$ 33,698

* Moody's Transportation Manual: 1959.

as expensive or luxurious, such as smoked salmon, oysters, caviar, lobster, game, etc." This controversy emphasized to United Air Lines' executives the extent to which items other than price affected competition in the industry.

United was a major factor in the air-transportation industry, in both coach and first-class flights. In 1958 its air-coach flights serviced thirty-three cities and accounted for 43 per cent of all passenger-miles flown by the company. This was a 19 per cent increase in the share of its business attributed to coach flights as compared to 1957. Tables 6 and 7 present selected information on United's operation.

Should United Air Lines institute the new economy fare?

6

KROEHLER MANUFACTURING COMPANY

FOR SOME time Kroehler Manufacturing Company, the largest United States furniture manufacturer, along with the furniture industry in general, had been concerned about the fact that furniture sales had failed to keep pace with the increase in disposable income of the American people. A brochure prepared and published by the Home Furnishings Council of America in the fall of 1958 outlined the following statistics:

In nine years—1948 through 1956—the money Americans had to spend after taxes and living costs (food, clothing and housing) rose from $97 billion to $169 billion. This was an increase of 73 per cent. In the same period the percentage of this money spent on furniture slid downward, from 2.7 per cent to 2.5 per cent. The failure of furniture sales to keep pace with growing buying power has lost the industry an estimated $2,100,000,000 since 1948.

Federal Reserve Board figures show that in 1956, the last year for which figures are available, 83 per cent of all American families bought no furniture at all. The amount spent for furniture was appallingly low—$62. This compares with $115 for tobacco and $190 for liquor.[1]

Kroehler Manufacturing Company had annual sales of more than $90,-000,000 in 1957. This total compared to yearly sales of about $50,000,000 for Bassett Furniture Industries, the second largest company in the industry. The balance of the industry was made up of about fifty medium and many small-size manufacturers, none of which approached Kroehler or Bassett in gross sales. Total sales for the furniture industry were about $2.5 billion. Kroehler accounted for about 8 per cent of the living-room-furniture market in the United States and 25 per cent in Canada.

---

[1] *What's the Future of the Furniture Industry* (Chicago: Furnishings Council of America, 1958).

Kroehler had been in business for about sixty-five years and had grown from a small plant in Naperville, Illinois, to an organization with fourteen plants in the United States and three in Canada. It had advertised extensively and had carried on national advertising on a large scale since about 1913. In 1957 its advertising and promotion budget was about $2,000,000.

Kroehler had always aimed its appeal at the average American family. Its designing was developed with the middle-class consumer in mind; the "high style" or extreme types of construction were avoided. As a general rule, "period" furniture, such as "French Provincial" styles, were not a part of its line. Style trends were, however, highly important to Kroehler's design department, and, while the furniture produced had to be sturdy, useful, and comfortable, it was the definite intent of the company to stay out of the "low end" or "borax" field. Seventy-five per cent of sales were in the popular-priced Kroehler brand. A chair and sofa set in this brand sold at wholesale somewhere between $117 and $250. Kroehler's Valentine Seaver brand of higher-styled furniture accounted for 9 per cent of sales. A sofa and chair set of this brand ran from about $200 to well over $300 at wholesale. The rest of the sales were in the Case-Goods Division, which produced bedroom and dining-room furniture that was sold under the Kroehler name.

Kroehler marketed most of its furniture directly to 12,000 dealers located in every state; about 12 per cent of sales went to mail-order houses. Dealers varied from Marshall Field, J. L. Hudson, and Gimbel's to small one-man stores. Contact with dealers was maintained principally through two hundred salesmen, each responsible for all dealers in a specific geographical area. Dealers were developed on a selective basis so that the distribution in a particular area could be to the greatest advantage of the company. Salesmen were responsible for "educating" their dealers and for getting them to use the company display and "in-store" promotional materials. The salesman would recommend that a change be made when he felt that the franchised dealer in an area was not doing the type of job that was needed.

Kroehler salesmen were highly paid. An average salesman grossed about $18,000 per year, out of which he paid all his own expenses, which, on an average, ranged from $4,000 to $5,000 per year. Salesmen were paid entirely on a commission basis. Commission rates varied from 3 to 7 per cent on Kroehler upholstered furniture, depending on the customer's volume and trade-discount bracket. On the Valentine Seaver line the rate was 6 per cent and for Case Goods 5 per cent.

Of the $2 million spent by Kroehler on advertising and promotion in 1957, about two-thirds was spent on national advertising, principally in such magazines as *Life*, the *Saturday Evening Post*, the *Ladies' Home Journal*, *Better Homes and Gardens*, the *American Home*, the *Farm Journal*, and *Living for Young Homemakers*. Spring and fall campaigns were usually followed with national ads of similar or identical types concentrated in all these media in a three-month period. The remaining one-third of the advertising and promotion budget was used to provide dealer helps, such as direct-mail pieces, pennant sheets and window banners, radio-transcription records, dimensional cutout letter signs and emblems to identify the dealer as the "Franchised Kroehler" dealer, special photos for TV use, ad mats, spot announcements for radio and TV use, and a host of other point-of-purchase items, all of which were distributed to the dealers by the salesmen.

Kroehler had no co-operative advertising program, but the advertising department estimated that in 1957 dealers used more than one million column-inches of company-prepared mats without any change from the original layout other than insertion of the dealer's name. These mats were designed to tie in with the national advertising and featured the Kroehler brand name prominently. It was estimated by Kroehler that the one million column-inches of advertising done by dealers was the equivalent of another million dollars of Kroehler advertising.

The failure of the consumer to spend even so large a percentage of his disposable income on furniture in 1956 as he did in 1948 was disturbing to Kroehler. After discussing the situation with its advertising agency, the company decided to conduct a study of what women think about furniture, what motivates them to buy, and, even more important, what psychological factors keep them from buying. Social Research, Inc., a well-known organization in the motivation research field, was chosen to do the job. The results of the study, which came to be known in the advertising field as "The Kroehler Report," presented a comprehensive picture of the furniture market, what women looked for in furniture, the attitudes that influenced their buying, and a summary that made some definite observations based upon the research conducted. Some of the highlights of the findings of this research project are presented below.

The research agency separated the population into five socioeconomic classes and analyzed their furniture-buying habits. Table 1 shows the makeup of these classes.

TABLE 1

DISTRIBUTION OF SOCIOECONOMIC CLASSES AS PER CENT OF POPU-
LATION AND PER CENT OF SPENDABLE CONSUMER INCOME

Socioeconomic Class	Per Cent of Population	Per Cent of Spendable Consumer Income
Upper and lower upper	1.5	5
Upper middle	8.5	15
Lower middle	25–30	25–30
Upper working	40–45	40–45
Lower working	20	5–10

Source: *The Kroehler Report.*

Occupations represented in the upper, lower upper, and upper middle classes were professional people (lawyers, doctors, some college professors, etc.), managerial and executive people (typical salaried employees receiving more than $10,000 per year), and the owners of prosperous businesses. Both men and women in this class were typically college educated. People in the lower middle class were white-collar workers, small businessmen, and the top layer of the blue-collar workers (railroad conductors, highly paid foremen, small contractors, etc.).

The upper working class primarily included blue-collar and service personnel, as well as some of the more impoverished white-collar workers. In considering buying attitudes and habits, the report disregarded the lower working class, which received less than one-tenth of the disposable income.

In analyzing the buying habits of the three economic classes, it was found that income level was not necessarily the determining factor in a family's attitude toward furniture. For example, "a young lawyer or perhaps a college professor earning $8,000 a year is inclined to spend a relatively larger share on housing (in a "select" neighborhood), furnishings, and cultural amusements; these people are upper middle class. A 35-year-old shoe salesman or lithographer earning the same amount probably spends his earnings on good housing also, without as much care about a glamorous neighborhood. This kind of man and his family would be classified as lower middle class. On the other hand, a cross-country truck driver, with annual wages of $8,000 is usually classified as upper working class; his money usually goes in larger measure for food, sports, and 'quick pleasures.' "

The upper middle class, according to the research report, based its judgment in buying furniture on whether it would serve "as an adequate testament of my 'taste,' my financial status, and my social position." The upper middle class was the principal market for "antiques," "authentic" period furniture, high-priced contemporary, and the ultra-sophisticated, designer-styled modern lines.

The research found that people in the upper middle class had a strong tendency to buy expensive furniture, assuming that by doing so they were obtaining durability of construction. This class was important in the furniture market beyond its share of actual purchases because its members served as the nation's taste leaders, and if a style or trend "caught on" with this class, it was then handed down after a few years to the mass market.

More than any other class, the lower-middle-class women were found to be furniture conscious. "They are more dependent on furniture to establish their social reputations." This class of women followed furniture trends more avidly than did upper-middle-class women and were less likely to take "quality construction" for granted. Such a characteristic increased their apprehension over the sturdiness and durability of the furniture they considered.

The upper working class looked for comfort, sturdiness, and "up-to-date" appearance in its furniture. The main consideration, in addition to price, was "Can it take a beating and be comfortable for a long time to come?" In addition to this prerequisite, this class preferred "modern" furniture, not in the sense of the aesthetically modern style, but in the sense of "the latest thing on the market." This class was represented by the bargain hunter or "price-conscious" buyer.

The research report stressed the confusion and uncertainty felt by the average woman in buying furniture. Lack of confidence in her own taste and confusion created by the numerous styles and style names, such as Contemporary, Danish Modern, Early American, Swedish Modern, French Provincial, etc., all tended to make the average woman approach the buying of new furniture with a great deal of apprehension. Related to the apprehension of the buyer was a distrust of the average retail-furniture salesman. The report indicated that they (the buyers) would like to rely on the salesman to guide them and in effect be an "authoritative counselor in furniture selection" but lacked enough confidence in the salesman's good taste to allow themselves to be guided by his recommendations.

In summary, the Kroehler Report drew numerous conclusions and made recommendations, the more important of which were as follows:

1. Furniture buying in many cases is approached with a feeling of uneasiness.
2. The traditional American conception of "the home" as a symbol of "family relationships" should be stressed in promotion of furniture.
3. Furniture merchandising should stress an association of furniture in use with people.
4. Pleasure and respect should be stressed in connection with furniture images.
5. Promotions should provide direction, definition, and reassurance relating to many diverse elements, such as taste, style, price, quality, and integration into the home.
6. The retail salesman could benefit by knowing the human elements making up his market as well as by having a better knowledge of his product.
7. Presently owned furniture should not be ridiculed because often an insult to her present furniture may be considered by the customer as an insult to herself.
8. Furniture should be displayed in a surrounding or setting similar to its end use and not in a massed display.

On the basis of the research report, Kroehler made a number of changes in its marketing strategy. One change was in the design of its furniture. Kroehler had always catered to the middle and upper working classes. Furniture for this market was designed in "Commercial Heavy Modern," a massive type of design which would withstand heavy wear

EXHIBIT 1

<small>Typical Kroehler Ad before Research Study</small>

over a long period. Colors tended to be dark and intense in order to be "practical." After studying the research report, Kroehler executives decided that they should emphasize "higher" style—less heavy, more simple construction and lighter fabrics. They did not believe this meant that durable construction should be sacrificed. In general, their popular line should be smart and contemporary in design, sturdy in construction, and modest in price.

Kroehler advertising was also changed. Exhibit 1 shows a typical ad

EXHIBIT 2

TYPICAL KROEHLER AD AFTER RESEARCH STUDY

Be confident with **KROEHLER**

Presenting the **SMARTSET '59 GROUP...**

Be confident of quality and comfort! When you choose Kroehler furniture, you buy for the years ahead. Lasting satisfaction is assured by the vital "Hidden Qualities" you get only with Kroehler furniture! It is scientifically tested for truly comfortable living. Feel the comforting difference! See what solid comfort really means!

Be confident of styling and value! Designed to be admired, Kroehler furniture will stay in style with the passing years. Designed, too, to be "friendly" with your present furniture. From *every* point of view, you get more for your money when you look for the brand name of Kroehler, world's largest furniture manufacturer.

Sectional sofa in bouclé textured fabric. Choice of either end or curved corner section, $95 each . . . with Air-foam cushions, $110 each. Armless center section, $59.50 . . . with Airfoam cushions, $69.50. Pillow-back lounge chair in textured Nylon frieze, with Airfoam seat and back cushions, $119.50. Round cocktail table, $39.50. End table, $29.50. Dining table, $74.50. Side chairs, $17.50 each. Buffet, $99.50. Open hutch china cabinet, $149.50. Prices slightly higher in some areas. Convenient terms offered by most Kroehler dealers. Dining and bedroom furniture and living room tables shown in Saddle Walnut Finish. Also available in Pongee Walnut Finish. *See your Kroehler dealer now!*

KROEHLER MFG. CO., General Offices: Naperville, Illinois. In Canada: Stratford, Ontario

before the research. No people were used in the ad and, while the furniture was bulky, it was presented with the theme: "There's a feeling of luxury in the new fleetness of line." As a result of the research, ads were changed to the type shown as Exhibit 2. The furniture was still sturdy appearing. The accessories and colors were keyed to this styling. More people were used in the ads. "Be confident with Kroehler" appeared in every ad. Prices and construction details were given in the copy.

A "Performance-Tested" tag was developed that would be placed on each piece of furniture. This indicated that the fabric had been tested and approved for cleanability, wear resistance, seam strength, tear and breaking resistance, resistance to fading, anti-fuzzing, and wrinkle resistance.

Kroehler also took steps to develop a new program of dealer aids. Instead of banners and streamers for the stores, the program was to emphasize dealer education so that he would know more about furniture and would inspire consumer confidence.

Were the changes in the Kroehler marketing program sound?

7

MOTOROLA, INC.

ALMOST from the industry's beginning, Motorola, Inc., was one of the leading manufacturers of television sets. The company's sales, however, were concentrated in the lower-priced lines. In an effort to gain a larger share of the higher-priced console television sets, Motorola entered into an unusual arrangement with the Drexel Furniture Company by which the latter would have the responsibility for designing the cabinets for the more expensive Motorola television sets.

Motorola originally specialized in car radios, from which it got its name. By 1930 and thereafter it was the leader in that field and was known for producing high-quality, reliable car radios. In 1949 the management decided to enter the television field and to compete primarily on a price basis. Most competitors at that time was selling sets with seven-inch screens for about $300. By cutting production costs wherever possible, Motorola was able to bring out a set for $179. This set was successful, and Motorola soon became the fourth largest television manufacturer in the country.

By 1954 the management decided that medium- and high-priced sets accounted for a significant share of the industry's volume and would account for an increasing share in the future. For this reason it decided to produce a line of television sets in all price brackets. Accordingly, the following lines were established:

Leader line—{ Table models, $179–$199
{ Console models, $229–$249

Main Deluxe line—{ Table models, $199–$219
{ Console models, $259–$279

Accent furniture line—Console models, $300–$450

These prices were for the 21-inch screen sets, which had become standard for the industry. The price range in each line was the result of different woods and finishes of the cabinets. The television set was the same in all models of a line. The higher-priced Main Deluxe and Accent lines, however, had better television sets as well as better cabinets.

Total industry sales of television sets declined after 1954, as did the share of sales in the "over $300" price class, as shown in Table 1. Estimates for 1959, however, indicated a rise in total sales and an increase in the share of the market accounted for by sets retailing at over $300.

TABLE 1

TELEVISION INDUSTRY SALES FOR SELECTED YEARS

Year	Total Sets Sold (Millions)	Percentage of Sets Sold by Retail Price		
		$100–$199	$200–$300	Over $300
1954	7.3	27	41	32
1957	6.5	N.A.*	N.A.	N.A.
1958	5.25	41	39	20
1959 (est.)	5.5	35	39	26

* Not available.

By 1956 it was clear that the Motorola medium- and high-priced lines were not successful. In the 1954–6 period, Motorola made approximately 70 per cent of its dollar sales in the Leader line, which produced a low profit margin for both Motorola and its dealers. About 28 per cent of sales were in the Deluxe line, and only 2 per cent in the Accent Furniture line. Executives thought the higher-priced lines could compete in appearance and performance with other brands on the market. Consumer and dealer surveys showed, however, that consumers did not associate the Motorola name with higher-priced television sets and that the Accent Furniture line did not fit into typical living and lounging room furni-

TABLE 2

PERCENTAGE OF CONSUMERS WHO WOULD LIKE TO
HAVE EXPENSIVE MOTOROLA TELEVISION SET
IN HOME: 1956

Income Group	Per Cent
Upper	35
Upper middle	50
Lower middle	47
Lower	47

ture settings. In one survey consumers were asked whether they would like to have the most expensive Motorola set in their homes. The results are shown in Table 2.

To overcome this consumer attitude, Motorola set out to improve the design of its high-priced line. Television manufacturers usually bought cabinets from cabinetmakers, but late in 1956 Motorola's director of styling called on a number of furniture manufacturers seeking their help in producing television cabinets that would compete in the high-price market. It soon became obvious that the well-known furniture manufacturers were not interested because previous experience of furniture companies in making television cabinets had shown that (1) there was no identification of the furniture maker with the cabinet; (2) styling was determined by the television manufacturer; and (3) construction of cabinets as they were needed caused considerable fluctuation in production. Furniture makers were generally not accustomed to these ups and downs, since their industry had rather stable production throughout each year.

TABLE 3

SHARE OF TELEVISION INDUSTRY SALES HELD BY
MAJOR PRODUCERS: 1957

Company	Per Cent of Industry
RCA	16.0
Zenith	13.5
Philco	11.0
GE-Hotpoint	10.0
Admiral	9.5
Motorola	8.0
Silvertone (Sears Roebuck)	6.0
Sylvania	5.0
Westinghouse	4.0
Emerson	3.5
Magnavox	3.5
Remainder of industry	10.0
Total	100.0

The Drexel Furniture Company had made heavy use of advertising tie-ins with companies manufacturing related products, for example, Firestone with its Velon upholstery yarn and B. F. Goodrich with its foam rubber. Also, Drexel had been urged by a number of sources to produce custom-made high-fidelity phonographs, but it lacked experience in electronics. In 1957 the executive vice-president of Motorola arranged to meet with the vice-president and treasurer of the Drexel Furniture Company to discuss the possibility of joining in a co-operative venture. The two executives agreed at this meeting that it would be to their mutual advantage to join forces. Drexel knew how to make furniture and was one of the best known and most respected names in the furniture business. It was the largest producer of furniture in the upper-middle-class line. Motorola knew electronics. Also, Motorola television sets would move into quality furniture outlets that had never handled TV or Motorola TV before. Similarly, Drexel furniture styling would be shown in TV outlets and would have entree into thousands of homes already furnished in one of its four lines, whose owners wanted electronic components to match. An agreement between the two was developed which had the following provisions:

1. Drexel would design the cabinets for the Accent Furniture line.
2. The Drexel name would be featured in all advertisements and merchandise tags involving television sets with Drexel cabinets.
3. Motorola would give Drexel firm orders for cabinets for twelve weeks at a time so that Drexel would not have excessive production-schedule changes. Motorola would buy all cabinets called for in each twelve-week agreement. If demand ran ahead of production, Drexel would increase production if feasible.

Motorola and Drexel agreed on three general cabinet stylings that would be used for high-priced television sets and for matching stereophonic phonographs—the Provincial, Modern, and Conventional designs. The Drexel-designed line would retail from $500 to $540 for the television and $470 to $520 for the phonographs. The companion speaker to go with the phonograph retailed for $80.

EXHIBIT 1

Only from

MOTOROLA

Stereo High Fidelity

in custom-crafted

cabinets by Drexel

CABINETS AS BEAUTIFUL AS THE PERFORMANCE

Sound to satisfy
the sensitive ear

French Provincial Fouraine

Motorola adds new charm to the most elegant room settings with Stereo Hi-Fi (and matching TV) in superb, mastercrafted cabinets designed by Drexel®. Rich, handrubbed finishes. Controls tastefully concealed behind doors.

Combined with this exclusive individuality in styling are the components needed to reproduce the finest stereo high fidelity sound possible.

More to enjoy

® MOTOROLA

World's Largest Exclusive Electronics Manufacturer

Motorola® Stereo Hi-Fi
and TV also
available in these fine
furniture stylings

Contemporary *Declaration*

Traditional *Travis Court*

No test marketing was tried. A small number of the new designs were produced in the latter part of 1958. Plans for early 1959 called for increased production and the addition of a fourth style.

In 1957 sales of television sets had been split among the major manufacturers as shown in Table 3. RCA, Zenith, and Dumont dominated the high-priced television market.

It was estimated that about 45 million homes had television sets and that about 10 per cent of these had more than one set. Portable sets (17-inch) accounted for about 30 per cent of total sales at a typical retail price of $179. The 21-inch cabinet model was the most popular, accounting for about 60 per cent of the market at a typical price of $225. Replacement sales were increasing and by 1958 accounted for 48 per cent of all sales, original purchases accounted for 30 per cent, and additional sets accounted for 22 per cent.

Motorola sold its television sets exclusively through about 100 distributors, who sold to about 25,000 retailers. The distributor's margin varied from 12 per cent on the less expensive sets to 17 per cent on the higher-priced sets. Drexel sold its furniture directly to approximately 2,500 selected retailers.

The Motorola-Drexel agreement called for Drexel to sell the Motorola Accent line, which had Drexel cabinets, to its retailers. Actual distribution would be handled through Motorola distributors. Each company planned to promote the Motorola-Drexel line as part of its regular advertising. Drexel typically advertised in furniture trade magazines and consumer magazines, such as *House Beautiful* and *Better Homes and Gardens*. Motorola planned to advertise Motorola TV sets in Drexel cabinets (Exhibit 1), while Drexel would advertise Drexel cabinets with Motorola television sets. Neither Motorola nor Drexel planned any special emphasis on advertising the new line in the first year.

One marketing problem developed immediately. Motorola distributors were reluctant to handle the new high-priced line because of past difficulties. This hurt distribution to both the Motorola and the Drexel retailers. To help overcome this problem, the executive vice-president sent a letter to all Drexel dealers and a bulletin to Motorola distributors with a copy of the Drexel letter attached. A copy of the bulletin with attached letter is shown as Exhibit 2.

EXHIBIT 2

Bulletin to All Motorola Distributors

I wish you would pay special attention to the attached letter which is going to all Drexel dealers today. The reason for this letter is to:

1. Enlist the support of Drexel dealers in our Motorola-Drexel program.
2. Allay any suspicions that this is a short-range activity. Let me assure you that we plan to continue with Drexel cabinets for many, many years and we firmly expect that the power of this program will increase as we go along.
3. Indicate to you my concern over the apparent lack of attention on the part of many of our distributors to follow through at their local levels to promote this program.

In regard to Point 3, let me state that Motorola without question has scored a tremendous scoop on all competition by making this tie-in with Drexel. We know for a fact that several competitors are frantically looking for similar tie-ins with other manufacturers, but the beauty of it is that Motorola has the best. Some manufacturers have even contacted Drexel with promises of far greater volumes than we're giving them to try and woo Drexel away from Motorola.

On the one hand, Drexel is a fine, ethical, highly reputable manufacturer and we know that they would do nothing that would in any way work against Motorola's best interests. On the other hand, we must be realistic and recognize that the only way we can continue to win this loyalty is through active support and aggressive promotion of the merchandise.

Some of our people attended the High Point furniture show this week and came back with distressing stories that some Drexel dealers have tried for weeks to contact our distributors but have been unsuccessful in reaching them or in getting salesmen to call on them. In my estimation this is entirely inexcusable.

As you will note in the attached letter, I'm telling the Drexel dealers that if they cannot get an answer from our distributors then they should write to me directly. This program must succeed. Its benefits to you and to Motorola far exceed the volume potentials. Nevertheless, there is tremendous volume available in this category of merchandise, and I don't have to tell you that here is where the greater profits lie.

May I ask that you give this Drexel program your own personal attention. This is the only way that we'll get the job done.

Sincerely,

(*signed*)   ED TAYLOR
Executive Vice-President

Letter to All Drexel Dealers

As you know, Motorola joined forces with the Drexel Furniture Company this year in offering television and phonograph-stero units in authentic Drexel furniture designs, namely, Touraine, Travis Court, and Declaration. The success that has greeted this program far exceeds our fondest expectations. In fact, the demand for these new models is so great that we have been in a constant back-order condition despite several increases in production schedules.

Proof that here is something that the public has long desired can be found in editorial columns of the country's leading magazines and newspapers. Further proof is evidenced by you and other Drexel dealers who wholeheartedly endorse the program.

At the High Point Furniture Show just concluded, hundreds and hundreds of dealers expressed themselves to Motorola and Drexel representatives that, "At last someone has brought good styling and good taste to television-phonograph cabinetry."

Motorola entered into negotiations with Drexel on the basis that this was no short-term program. It was agreed by both companies that this activity would continue and grow over the years. In fact, we are so delighted with the consumer reaction to our new Drexel series that we are expanding it to include a Profile television model early in January.

As you know, Motorola sells through wholesale distributors only. All of these distributors have been alerted to the importance of this Drexel program and the necessity for selective dealer appointments. On the other hand, we learned at the High Point show that some qualified Drexel dealers were having difficulty contacting our distributors and having distributors' salesmen call on them. If this is your experience, I wish you would write to me direct and I'll make sure that your inquiry is answered promptly.

We firmly believe that the Motorola-Drexel relationship is as good for you as it is for us, and we very earnestly solicit your support.

Sincerely,

(*signed*)   E. R. TAYLOR
Executive Vice-President

Was the agreement between Drexel and Motorola sound from Motorola's viewpoint?

8

EASY LAUNDRY APPLIANCES DIVISION

EASY Laundry Applicances Division of the Murray Corporation was one of the oldest and best-known names in the laundry appliance field. It had been a family-owned company for eighty years until 1948, when it merged with the Syracuse Corporation. In 1955 the merged organization was bought by the Murray Corporation of America but was continued as a separate operation known as the Easy Laundry Appliances Division. The Easy Spindrier—a semi-automatic washing machine that got its name from the fact that instead of a wringer it had a spinner tub to damp-dry clothes—was developed in the early 1920's. The Spindrier was one of the fastest selling machines on the market in the 1920's and 1930's. In the late 1930's the first fully automatic washer appeared on the market but did not become a major factor in the industry because further developments were curtailed by World War II. Soon after the war, however, the automatic washer captured a dominant portion in the laundry appliance market. Easy did not add an automatic washer to its line until 1954.

This delay was costly, for, while Easy maintained its share of conventional washer sales, its share of total washer sales declined severely as automatic washers captured a larger and larger proportion of the industry. By 1957 automatic washers accounted for more than 70 per cent of the total washer units sold. Exhibit 1 shows Easy sales and share of

EXHIBIT 1

EASY'S SHARE OF CONVENTIONAL WASHING MACHINE SALES AND TOTAL
INDUSTRY SALES*
(Units Sold)

Year	Easy	Industry Conventional Sales* (Thousands)	Easy Share of Conventional Sales	Industry Total Sales* (Thousands)	Easy Share of Industry Total
1946	164,197	1,691	9.7%	2,047	5.2%
1947	291,581	2,695	10.8	3,165	9.2
1948	370,544	3,421	10.8	4,387	8.4
1949	256,535	2,119	12.1	3,476	7.4
1950	328,296	2,666	12.3	4,387	7.5
1951	227,926	1,795	12.7	3,476	7.6
1952	192,775	1,591	12.1	3,267	6.0
1953	144,181	1,461	9.0	3,500	4.1
1954	156,952†	1,137	10.6	3,610	4.3
1955	186,586†	1,154	10.8	4,391	4.2
1956	179,221†	1,117	9.8	4,713	3.8

* Industry data taken from trade association compilation and considered accurate.
† Including automatic washer sales but not sales of combination washer-dryers.

market from 1946 to 1956. The automatic dryer had also become a major part of the laundry appliance market by this time, and Easy had lagged behind the industry in developing this item. Easy's first automatic washer and first dryer were introduced in 1954. By this time competing brands were well established in the market.

In 1953 the Bendix Appliance Division of Avco introduced the first combination washer-dryer in which the entire washing and drying process took place automatically within one machine. Whirlpool, Westinghouse, and General Electric brought out competitive models in the following three years. Easy marketed its combination washer-dryer, the Combomatic, in 1956. Sales were disappointing; the new machine was not accepted quickly by either consumers or the trade. In 1958 Easy undertook a research project designed to measure the long-term potential for the new washer-dryer and to furnish data that would help sell the product. A summary of the results is shown as an appendix to this case.

After studying the research results, the Easy management was convinced that, by concentrating on the Combomatic, Easy could regain its market position. This optimism was heightened by the industry trade-association forecast of sales of combination units over the next four years. Exhibit 2 shows this forecast along with sales from previous years.

EXHIBIT 2

ESTIMATED COMBINATION WASHER-DRYER SALES: 1953–62
(Units)

1953	48,000*	1958	164,218†
1954	52,000*	1959	375,000‡
1955	58,000*	1960	538,000‡
1956	102,406†	1961	613,000‡
1957	175,841†	1962	700,000‡

* Estimated; records of sales had not been kept prior to 1956.
† Actual sales.
‡ Trade association forecast.

The executives of Easy recognized a number of problems that they faced in gaining a strong position in the combination washer-dryer market. The major appliance market was dominated by seven or eight large companies that manufactured a full line of appliances, including, in addition to laundry equipment, refrigerators, freezers, water heaters, dishwashers, garbage disposal units, air conditioners, ranges, television sets, and sometimes a line of smaller electrical appliances. These companies were able to offer full lines to builders to install in new houses. The builder had to deal with only one source, could install matched items, and could often get a price advantage because of the large total order. Full-line manufacturers could also maintain closer ties with dealers by furnishing the entire line he would handle. There were some additional advantages in brand advertising; the full-line firm could promote one name over many items.

A change in retailing also affected Easy's future. There was a trend toward large discount houses that handled all the major brands. These dealers were major factors in the large metropolitan markets, such as Chicago, where 40 per cent of the appliance sales were made by Sears, Roebuck and Company; a local chain, Wieboldt Stores, Inc.; and three discount houses, Polk Brothers, Hudson-Ross, and Bruno's. The discount houses liked brands for which there was a strong demand. Since they bought in large quantities, they were able to bargain effectively for low prices.

Easy's management believed that there was still room for two or three independents in the laundry appliance field. The large full-line manufacturers' market strength did not extend through all their lines, and only a few of them were especially strong in the laundry appliance market. The executives of Easy thought that a smaller company was more able to adjust quickly to market changes than were the large companies. In 1957 there were three independent washing machine companies in the national market: Easy, Speed Queen, and Maytag. In addition, there were several smaller companies that competed on a regional basis, for example, Blackstone on the East Coast and Duchess in the Middle West.

The Easy sales organization was headed by a vice-president and general manager, who had under him a general sales manager and a national field sales manager. Under the national field sales manager were four divisions, each of which had from two to four regional offices. The service representatives and three or four special representatives who did market tests or special promotion work were directly under the national sales manager. Service was handled primarily through distributors except in the large metropolitan areas, where separate service organizations were appointed by the company. The organization is shown in Exhibit 3.

Easy sold to retailers both direct and through distributors. In general, if no distributor met the company standards in a certain area, the company would sell direct to retailers through company controlled distributing offices; if a good distributor was available, the company preferred to use him. Approximately one-fourth of the company's sales were direct to retailers, and the remaining three-fourths were through distributors. Easy had 78 distributors in the United States and 6,000 active retailers plus 2,500 dealers who were considered moderately active. Franchise agreements between Easy and dealers were essentially a gentleman's agreement. Historically, appliance dealers had been free to pick and choose the products they would handle, and the number of exclusive franchises in the industry was negligible. For this reason, there were few controls over dealer sales practices. The company worked with dealers, however, in planning local promotional activities to stimulate sales, and most advertising was done on a local basis.

With the Combomatic, Easy management thought it could regain a favorable position in the laundry appliance market. It was, in fact, looked on as the company's main hope for continued success. Up to 1958 the industry generally had not been successful in selling the combination washer. The Easy executives believed greater promotional efforts were needed. The public had to be sold on combination washers before Easy could sell its brand. Easy executives believed that this was a problem they could not tackle alone. Promotion by the larger appliance manufacturers, who had more money for promotional activities, would be necessary before these units would be generally accepted. The management believed that, if the entire industry pushed combination washer-dryers, Easy's sales would rise with industry sales. In fact, in 1958 the

EXHIBIT 3

EASY SALES ORGANIZATION

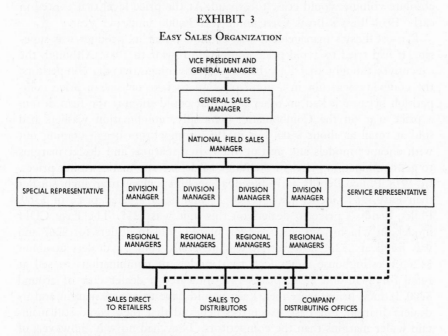

management thought that Easy had a competitive advantage that would enable the firm to benefit more than most of its competitors from an expansion in general demand.

In the development of the Combomatic, several patentable innovations had been developed that the company felt would give them an advantage. One of these innovations was in the construction of the machine itself. The Combomatic was smaller and cost less to produce than competitive machines because of these patentable innovations. The Combomatic was only 27 inches wide and as such was the smallest combination washer-dryer yet developed that could handle a standard wash load. The resultant lower cost gave Easy the opportunity to offer its dealers a wider margin at competitive prices and thus more price flexibility in meeting price cuts. Another innovation was in the washing method, which used less water and washed clothes cleaner, in the management's estimation, than any other combination on the market at the time. The company believed the Combomatic was the only true one-unit combination washer-dryer that had component parts designed specifically for this type of machine. Most competitors' machines were composed of washer and dryer components combined in one cabinet.

Easy's goal was a 15 per cent share of market in the initial years of growth of the combination washer-dryer. The management anticipated that as combination sales grew and more of the industry became active in the market, Easy's share would decrease, but not to the extent that its absolute volume would cease to expand. At the price level that existed in early 1958, Easy's break-even point was 30,000 units per year.

Because Easy's management was confident that its product was superior, it had tried to avoid price competition prior to 1958. Although the executives thought that Easy had a cost advantage over its competitors, the company was not in a good position to take on severe price competition because it had no other lines that could support the firm during a price war on the Combomatic. Generally, combination washers had sold at retail at about $500, but in 1957 competitors began coming out with cheaper models and cutting their own margins and dealer margins to get combination prices in the range of deluxe automatic washer prices. In 1958 Philco-Bendix introduced a machine one-quarter inch smaller than Easy, 26¾ inches wide versus 27 inches, at a retail price of $369. Philco-Bendix's price to dealers on this unit was $255. The Easy CDH model, on which main emphasis was placed, sold to dealers for $267 and was listed at $529; however, it was generally sold by dealers at about $420. Westinghouse announced two models of combinations to sell at retail for $330 and $350, prices that indicated a dealer cost of around $200. If such prices were met, Easy would have to cut its margin and its dealers' margin, but Easy executives believed that they could still maintain wider margins than the competitors. They had no way, however, of knowing competitors' exact costs.

Easy's management decided that the firm would benefit from a rapid growth of the combination washer industry before major competitors caught up with Easy's advantage. Therefore, they took the data developed in the 1958 survey and prepared a special presentation and made it available to individual washer manufacturers, appliance manufacturers', dealers' associations, and consumer groups. The purpose was to encourage more rapid expansion of the combination washer industry. The information given was essentially that shown in the appendix to this case, with the exception of the data pertaining to the brand competition situation.

To be sure to capitalize on any expanding market, Easy decided to make every effort to keep it name synonymous with quality. On two occasions when improvements were made in the Combomatic, the firm offered one-for-one trades to people who had the previous, inferior models. In this way the company hoped to keep the product's reputation high among consumers and to get the newest models before the public.

In the future, Easy planned to change models only when it had significant innovations to offer, rather than every year as a planned obsolescence program. It was felt that this would also keep costs down in comparison with those manufacturers who changed models annually.

APPENDIX A

Methodology and Findings of Survey of the Washer-Dryer Market

Methods and Samples

1. *Nonowners of combination washer-dryers.* A sample of 850 was selected from three national panels of 1,000 families each. All families selected were homeowners with incomes over $4,500. There were 712 responses to the questionnaire mailed to 850 families, but only the first 603 were tabulated because of the need for early results. Of these 603 families, 584 did not own combination washer-dryers and constitute the bulk of the tabulations. Nineteen families owned combination washer-dryers.

2. *Laundry appliance retailers.* A total of 47 personal interviews were conducted with retailers in 11 markets. Of these, 29 were Easy dealers and 18 were not Easy dealers. Neither the dealers interviewed nor the interviewers were informed of the client involved.

3. *Independent service agencies.* A questionnaire was mailed to 26 independent service agencies that serviced washing machines. No evidence of Easy participation was given in the questionnaire, and the mailing was made under a research firm's name.

4. *Combomatic owners.* There were 279 telephone interviews conducted in 25 metropolitan areas with owners of Combomatics, model CDH. The sample was selected from warranty cards returned to Easy. The interviews were all conducted with the housewife. The median age of the Combomatic owned in this sample was 3.2 months.

Findings: The principal findings of the survey are summarized in the fourteen tables that follow.

TABLE 1

Percentage of Respondents Who Expressed Intention of Buying These Appliances

Period within Which Will Buy	Wringer Washer	Combination Washer-Dryer	Automatic Washer	Automatic Dryer
Within 6 months	1	Less than 0.5	1	1
Within 6–12 months	1	1	3	3
Within 2–3 years	3	3	12	10
Do not plan to buy within 3 years	33	32	40	36
Don't know	1	1	1	1
No answer	61	63	43	49
No. of respondents	(603)	(603)	(603)	(603)

TABLE 2

AVAILABILITY OF 220-VOLT WIRING IN HOMES OF NONOWNERS
OF A COMBINATION WASHER-DRYER

Have 220-volt wiring.......................	83%
Do not have 220-volt wiring.................	15
Don't know.............................	Less than 0.5
No answer..............................	2
No. of respondents........................	(584)

TABLE 3

KNOWLEDGE OF COMBINATION WASHER-DRYER
AMONG NONOWNERS

Have heard of units.............................	95%
Have not heard of units..........................	5
No. of respondents..............................	(584)

TABLE 4

INTEREST AMONG NONOWNERS IN OWNING
A COMBINATION WASHER-DRYER

Not interested.................................	60%
Interested.....................................	36
Don't know....................................	3
No answer.....................................	1
No. of respondents.............................	(584)

TABLE 5

ADVANTAGES AND DISADVANTAGES OF OWNING A COMBINATION WASHER-DRYER IN
OPINIONS OF NONOWNERS

Main Advantages		Main Disadvantages	
Less handling of clothes........	19%	Too slow.....................	33%
Time-saver....................	18	More repairs needed...........	14
Convenience...................	8	Can't wash and dry at same time...	14
Less space....................	6	Both units out if one needs repair..	11
Less cost.....................	6	Repairs more expensive.........	8
Save some steps................	5	Cost more to operate...........	7
No advantage..................	8	None.........................	11

TABLE 6

OPINIONS OF NONOWNERS AS TO WORK IN USING COMBINATION WASHER-DRYER
COMPARED TO SEPARATE UNITS

Combination Requires Less Work	58%	Combination Requires More Work	37%
Less handling of clothes........	44%	Takes too long.................	20%
Laundry ready for ironing.......	5	Would require more sorting of	
Only one unit to clean..........	5	clothes......................	4
Save steps....................	4	Present washer satisfactory......	4
		Other........................	9

No opinion 5%

TABLE 7

Nonowners' Opinions of Cost of Combination Washer-Dryer Compared to Separate Units

Cost more..17%
Cost less..59
Cost same...18
Don't know... 6

TABLE 8

Nonowners' Opinions of Service Problems with Combination Washer-Dryer Compared to Separate Units

More service problems................................71%
Less service problems................................23
Don't know... 2
No answer.. 4

TABLE 9

Brands of Laundry Appliances Sold by Easy Dealers and Other Dealers

	Easy Dealers			Other Dealers			Total Sample		
Brand	Washer	Dryer	Combination	Washer	Dryer	Combination	Washer	Dryer	Combination
Easy..............	86%	79%	100%	..	..	..	53%	49%	62%
Frigidaire..........	48	41	..	44%	44%	..	47	43	..
G.E..............	55	55	38	33	33	22%	47	47	32
Whirlpool.........	62	62	62	50	50	33	57	57	51
Maytag............	38	41	..	28	22	..	34	34	..
Philco-Bendix.......	41	45	38	17	11	28	32	32	34
Norge.............	55	52	..	39	39	..	49	47	..
Westinghouse......	38	38	24	28	22	17	32	32	21
Hamilton..........	28	31	..	6	6	..	19	21	..
Speed Queen.......	17	17	..	11	6	..	15	13	..
Hotpoint...........	31	31	17	11	11	11	23	23	15
Kelvinator.........	7	7	..	28	27	..	15	15	..
A.B.C.............	3	3	..	11	6	..	6	4	..
O'Keefe............	..	..	..	..	..	11	..	..	4
Other.............	10	10	..	17	17	..	13	13	..
None..............	..	..	..	..	6	11	..	2	4

TABLE 10

OPINIONS OF DEALERS ON BRAND OF COMBINATION WASHER-DRYER WITH
FEATURE EASIEST TO SELL AND WITH LEAST SERVICE PROBLEMS

Brand	Easy Dealers Brand with:		Other Dealers Brand with:		Total Sample Brand with:	
	Best Selling Feature	Least Service Problems	Best Selling Feature	Least Service Problems	Best Selling Feature	Least Service Problems
Philco-Bendix..	17%	17%	28%	27%	21%	21%
Easy..........	45	36	..	..	28	21
G.E..........	7	3	11	11	9	6
Hotpoint......	..	3	..	6	..	4
Sears Kenmore.	..	..	6	6	2	2
Whirlpool.....	21	24	28	22	23	24
Westinghouse	3	7	11	11	6	9
Refused.......	7	10	17	17	11	13

TABLE 11

OPINIONS OF DEALERS ON SERVICE PROBLEMS OF COMBINATION WASHER-DRYER
COMPARED TO SEPARATE UNITS

	Easy Dealers	Other Dealers	Total Sample
Combination has fewer service problems.............	28%	39%	32%
Combination has about the same service problems.....	28	6	19
Combination has more service problems..............	44	44	45
No answer...	..	11	4

TABLE 12

DEALER OPINIONS ON APPLIANCE WITH GREATEST AND SECOND GREATEST
EXPECTED SALES INCREASE DURING 1958

Appliance	Easy Dealers	Other Dealers	Total Sample
Air-conditioning units			
First............................	59%	33%	49%
Second...........................	7	38	19
Automatic dishwasher			
First............................	7	11	9
Second...........................	21	6	15
Combination washer-dryer			
First............................	14	22	17
Second...........................	41	11	30
Color television			
First............................	17	33	23
Second...........................	14	28	19
No answer			
First............................	3	...	2
Second...........................	17	17	17
Total			
First............................	100%	100%	100%
Second...........................	100%	100%	100%

TABLE 13

RATING OF COMBOMATIC WITH PREVIOUSLY OWNED
LAUNDRY APPLIANCE BY COMBOMATIC OWNERS

	Percentage of Owners		*Percentage of Owners*
Washing clothes clean		Drying of clothes	
Excellent	50	Excellent	56
Good	38	Good	25
Fair	8	Fair	11
Poor	3	Poor	6
No opinion	1	No opinion	2
Time saving		Ease of operation	
Saved lots of time	73	Very easy	96
Saved little time	9	Somewhat difficult	2
Did not save much time	13	No opinion	2
No opinion	5		
Over-all satisfaction with unit		Over-all convenience of unit	
Extremely well satisfied	40	Very convenient	87
Very well satisfied	31	Just convenient	9
Just satisfied	15	Not very convenient	1
Not very satisfied	13	No opinion	2
No opinion	1		

TABLE 14

OWNERS WHO WOULD RECOMMEND COMBOMATIC TO FRIENDS

	Per Cent
Would recommend	72
Would not recommend	22
Don't know	6

1. *Appraise Easy's promotion program for the Combomatic.*

2. *Should Easy concentrate on the Combomatic as its best hope for improving its market position?*

9

SHAEFNER COMPANY

THE Schaefner Company produced a line of products that it sold direct to the electronics industry.[1] Its line included resistors, capacitors, transistors, diodes, power transformers, switches, fuses, condensers, tuners, and I-F transformers. Sales had increased several fold since 1946 and were

---

[1] The electronics industry was composed of firms producing products in which electronic tubes, transistors, and similar items were used.

over $10 million in 1959. Competitors included such large, well-known firms as American Radio Corporation, Conn Electronics, and National Products Company, as well as many smaller, more specialized firms that typically produced only a limited line of products. Despite a favorable sales growth, which exceeded that of most firms in the industry, the Shaefner Company management was trying to find ways by which they could make further gains. To help guide their efforts, the vice-president in charge of marketing requested that an "image" study be undertaken to determine how customers actually viewed the company.

Items in the company's line sold for prices ranging from a few cents to over $1,000. Items were usually ordered in thousands of units; the average-size order was in excess of $1,000. Because of the technical nature of the products, a number of different individuals within an electronics company typically had some influence on the selection of the specific firm from which a given product would be purchased. This meant that any study of the Shaefner image would involve interviews with a variety of electronics executives. Gilbreth and Associates, a firm with wide experience in research among corporation executives, was retained to do the study.

The vice-president of marketing stated that the primary purpose of the study would be to determine the attitudes of electronics company executives toward the Shaefner Company along the following lines:

1. The level of awareness of Shaefner and its products.
2. The strong and weak attributes of the Shaefner image.
3. The strong and weak attributes of the images of Shaefner's major competitors.

Research was conducted in two phases. The first consisted of 20 interviews in four selected cities to test the questionnaire and to obtain an estimate of the field costs. As a result of this test, the questionnaire was reduced in length and was simplified. A total of 107 interviews in twenty-six cities across the country was then completed. The original sample included 135 individuals, but 28 persons refused to co-operate or had been transferred to positions that were not deemed pertinent for the purpose of the study. Neither the interviewers nor the respondents were aware that Shaefner Company was the sponsor of the study.

The sample was selected from a list of individuals prepared by Shaefner. The list included electronics industry executives ranging from upper-middle management to top management. The former included such persons as those doing the actual purchasing or engineering work, while the latter were individuals holding such administrative positions as executive vice-president and general manager. The 107 interviews were accomplished among 76 companies.

Interviews were opened by asking respondents to indicate how much they knew about their firms' suppliers—mostly with reference to what companies produced what products. This information measured the level of the respondent's awareness of individual suppliers and also provided a point of reference for evaluating the rating scales and questions that asked for descriptions of suppliers.

Images were sought for four major suppliers of electronic components, American Radio, Conn Electronics, National Products, and Shaefner. The specific factors for which measurements were obtained included such things as dependability, company engineering skills, flexibility, product quality, research activity, promptness of delivery, extent of product line, management's contact with customers, location of warehouses, promptness in settling complaints, and the company as a source of information. A summary of the results is shown below.

Utility Executives' Awareness of "Who Produces What Products"

Respondents were asked what electronic supply companies made the following items:

1. Resistors	6. Electronic switches
2. Capacitors	7. Fuses
3. Transistors	8. Television tuners
4. Diodes	9. I-F transformers
5. Power transformers	10. Condensers

Many respondents thought that Shaefner produced all the products in the list, but several products were not associated with Shaefner by a significant number of executives. Only 28 per cent mentioned Shaefner as a producer of diodes, 48 per cent as a producer of condensers, and 51 per cent as a producer of tuners.

Relative Awareness

It was thought important to evaluate the relative awareness of each respondent as to what companies manufactured each of the products in the ten product-line categories. Each company was ranked by product line according to the number of respondents who mentioned it as a manufacturer of that line. Schaefner was mentioned by more respondents, and therefore ranked first, for two product lines. It ranked second for two product lines, third for four product lines, and fourth for two product lines. Table 1 summarizes the results relative to Shaefner.

No one company was mentioned by all respondents as a supplier for each product category. American Radio, however, was recalled more times than any other company for seven product lines. This was true for resistors, capacitors, transistors, diodes, switches, condensers, and I-F transformers. On two of the three remaining product lines, Shaefner was mentioned more times than any other company, and a smaller company was recalled more times as a producer of power transformers.

Unaided Recall Descriptions

For the second part of the interview, respondents were asked to give a description of each of the four selected electronics supply companies.

This question gave the respondent full opportunity to say anything that came to mind about each particular company.

More than one-third of all respondents discussed Shaefner in terms of company growth, diversification, and product-line expansion. These same features were mentioned by about 19 per cent of the respondents for National Products, whereas none of the respondents mentioned growth or expansion for Conn Electronics or American Radio. Nearly one-fourth of the executives associated Shaefner with prompt delivery of equipment and over-all good service, but about 20 per cent described Shaefner as a company that did not supply all products used in the electronics industry. Conn Electronics and American Radio were described as companies that did supply all such products. About 14 per cent of the respondents spoke of Shaefner as a major supplier for electronics supplies.

TABLE 1

Awareness of Shaefner as a Producer of Each of Ten
Product Lines Based on Unaided Recalls

Product Lines	Shaefner's Rank
Fuses	First
Television tuners	First
Capacitors	Second
Power transformers	Second
Transistors	Third
Electronic switches	Third
I-F transformers	Third
Condensers	Third
Resistors	Fourth
Diodes	Fourth

Most associations and descriptions for Shaefner were related more closely with National Products than with Conn Electronics or American Radio.

In general, Shaefner was described by electronics industry executives as a company that:

1. Did not have as complete a line of products as some other companies.
2. Showed aggressiveness in developing new equipment.
3. Gave very prompt delivery.
4. Had demonstrated relatively large growth.
5. Carried more products that were frequently ordered.
6. Always had parts available.

The electronics executives spoke mostly of Conn Electronics as the "other of the two leading companies." Conn Electronics was continually associated with American Radio but almost always with the qualification that it was not as large. There were no indications that Conn Electronics' personality was distinguished from American Radio.

There were practically no negative descriptions given for Shaefner and

National Products. American Radio was recognized as the leader in the electronics manufacturing industry but was also subject to more criticism than the others. Some respondents said that American Radio was more interested in showing a profit than in satisfying the customer. It was also indicated that there was relatively less confidence in American Radio representatives than in those of the other three companies.

Conn Electronics was seen as a company that:

1. Was number two in the electronic manufacturing industry.
2. Spent millions of dollars on basic research and development.
3. Manufactured a complete line of equipment.
4. Had the most competent engineers.
5. Made daily contact with customers.

National Products brought up comments similar to those mentioned for Shaefner, but to a lesser degree. About 19 per cent discussed National Products with regard to company growth, expansion, and diversification. The executives offered comments to indicate that National Products was doing the right thing in buying smaller companies and expanding its product lines. Although it was said to be a moderate-size company, it was seen as advancing with the times.

Executives' Suggestions for Improving Supply Companies

Several suggestions were offered by the electronics executives to improve the general operations of the various supply companies. They particularly emphasized that the supply companies should lower prices on equipment, or at least hold them where they were. All companies were seen as needing to set up a system for informing buyers of the status of their orders. This was needed to permit buyers to make any necessary adjustments in their schedules.

A few respondents said that Shaefner should expand and improve its products. More pointed suggestions of this type, however, were directed toward the other companies. For example, several respondents mentioned that Conn Electronics could do a better job on capacitors and fuses; American Radio should arrange closer co-ordination of manufacturing with sales and service so as to make for more prompt delivery service; and American Radio should return to salesmen the authority to commit their various departments to specific prices and delivery dates. Suggestions made for National Products included providing more and better warehouse facilities and more salesmen and improving its line of transistors.

Image Characteristics of Shaefner

In the last part of the interview, the electronics executives were asked to rate the four supply companies on thirty-three different and specific attributes. These attributes were given in the form of statements or phrases. The executives were asked to check in the appropriate space whether the particular statement applied, probably applied, probably did not apply, or did not apply to the company being rated.

There were several specific areas in which Shaefner received higher ratings than those given to National Products, Conn Electronics, or American Radio. These were over-all company flexibility, readily sensing the needs of customers, manufacturing products with the highest reliability, settling complaints the fastest, willingness to respond to special requests by customers, and delivery of equipment when promised. It also obtained a relatively high rating for good location of its sales offices.

Shaefner was rated behind American Radio and Conn Electronics but above National Products on over-all research and development activity. Electronics executives thought it unlikely that Shaefner spent more than 5 cents out of every dollar on research. They felt that American Radio and Conn Electronics did spend more than 5 cents out of every sales dollar for research, but not more than 10 cents. American Radio and Conn Electronics were thought to keep the industry better informed on research and results than did Shaefner.

Relative to American Radio and Conn Electronics, Shaefner's top management was viewed as having little contact with electronics companies. Shaefner salesmen were rated as having less product knowledge than American Radio or Conn Electronics salesmen. The salesman's message was rated over-all equally worthwhile to that of American Radio but slightly below that of Conn Electronics. Shaefner representatives, however, were said to do much more than "just look for orders." The two giant firms did not rate so well in this respect.

Although Shaefner was rated relatively high for most service functions, including its willingness to respond to special requests by customers, it was thought to be a company that copied from competitors more than did the other three supply companies.

Shaefner executives were pleased with some of the findings but disturbed about others. In commenting on the study, the vice-president of marketing said, "I know as a fact that we have scored more 'firsts' in new products over the past several years than any of our competitors. And they were all significant firsts. Perhaps we did follow the big firms when we were just another small company, but no longer. We've got a wonderful laboratory and are spending more than 5 cents out of every sales dollar for research and development. We have to have good research people to turn out so many new products.

"Our image as less than a full-line producer hurts. While we don't produce all items, we have the third most complete line in the industry. And we've spent a lot of money on our advertising these past few years to point up the breadth and depth of our lines."

In discussing the report with the president, the vice-president of marketing stated that, until the image of the company was revised substantially, the company's sales would increase only slowly. He was not sure what action he should initiate to change the image.

What action, if any, should the vice-president of marketing take?

10

GOLDBLATT'S DEPARTMENT STORE

LATE IN 1954 the management of Goldblatt's Department Store was approached by a group of businessmen with the proposition that the store establish a large branch outlet in a planned shopping center on the outskirts of the city of Racine, Wisconsin. The proposed center would include one large department store and a variety of smaller specialty and shopping goods stores. It would have a large parking space available for roads in southwestern Racine.

At the time that Goldblatt's was approached by the Racine group, the company consisted of a chain of fourteen department stores located in the city of Chicago and its trading area. It had grown to this position from a single store with a frontage of 15 feet in 1914. The basic policy of the company had been that of seeking rapid turnover through low markup. By 1945 the company had purchased or acquired a total of twelve units located within fifty miles of Chicago. Each store purchased was renamed "Goldblatt's" and made to conform to the general merchandising policies of the company. The company also maintained two warehouses in Chicago, one for furniture and appliances and one for soft goods.

After World War II the management found itself with stores that were largely thirty years of age and a market that was moving rapidly from the city to the suburbs. In 1947 Goldblatt's departed from its policy of acquiring existing stores and built a new unit, without parking facilities, in a neighborhood shopping center. In 1951 another neighborhood store, this time with parking facilities, was built. By 1953 another suburban store was built. To speed and to aid in further expansion, a new position was established, assistant to the president, to acquire real estate leases for the building of stores in new shopping centers. By the time of the Racine offer, Goldblatt's was building another branch west of Chicago and was considering two others in Rockford and Hillside, Illinois. Top management's policy was to open new units just as soon as desirable shopping center locations were available. Management had established the following criteria as a basis for judging each proposed location:

1. The store must be designed to do from $3 to $5 million in annual sales volume.
2. The store must be located in a one-stop shopping center only.
3. The store must not be located in a major metropolitan center, but rather in secondary areas, such as found with most suburban shopping centers.
4. The store must be in an area with population and consumer income growth potential, not in an area past its peak.
5. The store must not be located more than two hundred miles from the central Chicago store.
6. Each store unit property must be leased and not bought.
7. There must be a minimum trading area of 100,000 persons.

The city of Racine was located seventy miles directly north of Chicago and fronted on Lake Michigan. The population of the city proper was estimated at about 80,000 in 1953, and the retail trading area held approximately 125,000 people. Seven miles south of the proposed shopping center location was Kenosha, Wisconsin, with a population of 55,000. Racine was primarily an industrial town, composed of skilled laborers who worked in the plants of such companies as Johnson Wax, Massey Harris, J. I. Case, and Hamilton Beach. Racine had grown, partially from annexing adjacent areas, from 67,000 in 1940 to 71,000 in 1950. No new industry or expansion of present firms, however, was anticipated in the near future.

In attempting to determine whether to accept the proposal to establish a branch in the city, the management of Goldblatt's hired a marketing research specialist to study the potential of the location. His report, completed in February, 1954, contained information from which the following has been extracted.

The Elmwood Shopping Center was to be located in the extreme southwest section of Racine on a triangular-shaped parcel of land bounded by three highways, Route 11 on the north, Taylor Avenue on the southeast, and Lathrop Avenue on the West (Exhibit 1). The site was to become a terminal point for two intercity bus runs. In 1949 the state of Wisconsin recorded an average of 2,750 vehicles per day passing the site on Route 11, and 2,200 on Taylor Avenue. Route 11 was a major artery leading into Racine from the western areas, including Sturtevant, Union Grove, and Burlington. Lathrop Avenue was lightly traveled but was being improved by road work. All traffic had increased since 1949. Lake Shore Drive (Route 32), located about 1¼ miles east of the proposed center, carried the largest number of cars traveling from Kenosha to Racine.

Access to the site was extremely difficult from northern areas of Racine because of the limited number of bridges over the Root River. The routes that were available for shoppers were all poor as a result of congestion, the narrowness of the streets, and the distances involved.

The effective potential trading area for the proposed site was judged

EXHIBIT 1

SHOPPING CENTERS IN RACINE

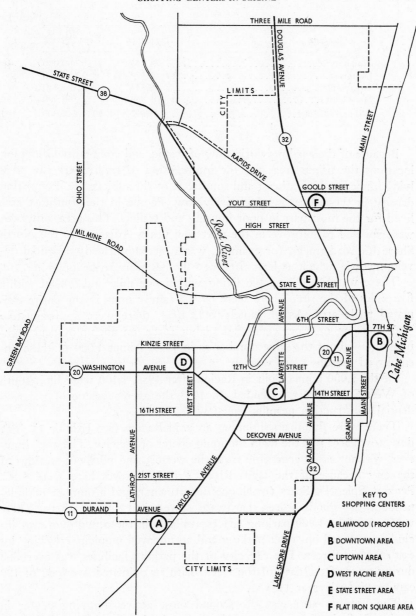

KEY TO
SHOPPING CENTERS

A ELMWOOD (PROPOSED)

B DOWNTOWN AREA

C UPTOWN AREA

D WEST RACINE AREA

E STATE STREET AREA

F FLAT IRON SQUARE AREA

to be delimited by a series of concentric part-circles drawn around the site with radii five miles in all areas east of the site (except where they intersect the lake), five miles also to the north-northwest, ten miles to the south-southwest, and twenty-five miles to the west-northwest and west-southwest (Exhibit 2). The population and income within this zone were as shown in the accompanying tabulation.

Quadrant	Population	Gross Income
Northeast	74,341	$118,660,000
Southeast	3,199	2,628,000
Northwest	50,433	80,597,000
Southwest	105,924	152,340,000
Total	233,897	$354,225,000

Because of the road network, flow of traffic, and competitive shopping locations the prime areas for the interception of trade were the areas lying immediately southeast and southwest of the subject site. Population density in these areas was relatively low. People in the southeast area lived for the most part in poor housing and trailers. This area, however, was expected to improve in the next few years. Adjacent to the North Shore Railroad tracks, for example, was a medium-priced residential development in which at least fifty new homes were to be built in 1954.

There were 11,397 people living within one mile and 90,380 within five miles of the site. There were 69,607 family units in the entire estimated trade area. As of January 11, 1954, there were approximately 3,000 persons, or 6 per cent of the labor force, on unemployment compensation—about the same number as in 1949. About 1,000 of these unemployed persons were women.

Of the 2,000 homes built in Racine after 1950, 1,100 were built south of West Sixth Street, extended. In 1953 the average value of the residential construction permits issued was $10,795.

There were five main shopping areas in Racine (see Exhibit 1). The downtown area was the main shopping center of the city. The area, however, was not easily accessible from the western and northern sections of the city because of the Root River. Principal stores here were J. C. Penney, Spiegel's, Sears (catalogue department), and a number of independent dry-goods stores, hardware stores, and supermarkets. There were a total of 1,800 parking spaces available in the downtown area including metered on-street parking and an unpaved municipal parking lot east of Main Street. The capacity of the parking facilities was exceeded during most of the days of the week, with an estimated overload of 180 cars on Saturdays at 11 A.M.

The uptown area was the second most active shopping center in Racine. It had numerous convenience goods shops and several limited-line stores carrying clothing for women and children. Parking facilities were overloaded for sixteen hours during the week, with some additional 50–60 spaces needed over the existing 347 to accommodate the shopping peak on Saturdays.

EXHIBIT 2

POTENTIAL TRADING AREA FOR PROPOSED ELMWOOD SHOPPING CENTER

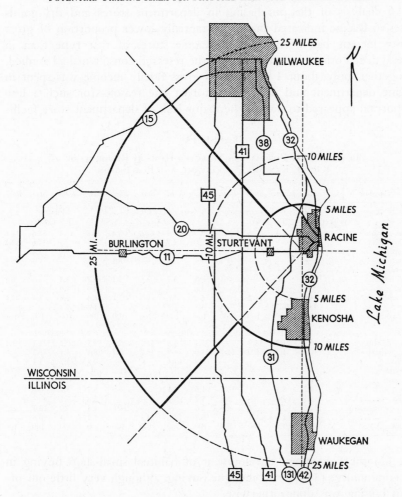

West Racine was a shopping center located directly west of the up-town area. It had a total of 324 parking spaces, with slight overloads on Thursdays, Fridays, and Saturdays. An estimated 50 additional spaces were needed. Stores in the area included convenience goods shops, several clothing stores, and a furniture outlet.

The State Street area served the northern section of Racine. Stores in this area were of poor quality and offered limited supplies of merchandise. Convenience goods stores predominated, and there were a number of eating and drinking places. Parking never exceeded 62 per cent of the total 151 spaces available.

Flat Iron Square also served the northern part of Racine. This shopping area had 175 parking spaces. Stores were mostly of the convenience goods type. Parking facilities were overloaded on Fridays and Saturdays to the extent of about 25 cars.

An analysis of the purchasing in department stores and dry-goods stores in Racine indicated that a substantially lower proportion of gross family income had been spent in Racine stores of that type than in several dozen other communities that the research consultant had studied. Altogether, only about 4 per cent of gross family income was spent in Racine department and dry-goods stores. The reasons for such a low proportion appeared to be (1) the major lack of department store facili-

TABLE 1A

PLACE OF LAST PURCHASE OF SELECTED ITEMS BY RESIDENTS OF
RACINE, KENOSHA, STURTEVANT, AND BURLINGTON

Place of Purchase	Rac.	Ken.	Stur.	Burl.	Rac.	Ken.	Stur.	Burl.	Rac.	Ken.	Stur.	Burl.
	MEN'S WORK CLOTHING (Per Cent)				MEN'S CLOTHING (Per Cent)				DRESSES (Per Cent)			
Racine (downtown)	36.4	2.4	65.6	6.3	44.9	2.4	62.0	9.4	55.8	13.4	58.6	12.6
Racine (other)	8.0	3.9	17.2	3.1	32.0	4.7	31.0	6.3	21.0	—	34.6	12.5
Kenosha	—	64.6	—	—	1.2	76.4	—	—	1.6	74.0	3.4	—
Burlington	—	—	—	78.1	—	—	—	78.1	—	—	—	65.5
Sturtevant	—	—	—	—	—	—	—	—	—	—	—	—
Milwaukee	2.0	1.6	—	3.1	6.1	4.7	—	3.1	8.7	5.5	—	6.3
Chicago	—	0.8	—	—	3.6	5.5	—	—	4.9	3.9	—	—
Other and unknown	4.9	—	17.2	9.4	6.9	1.6	7.0	3.1	6.4	2.4	3.4	3.1
Never	48.7	26.7	—	—	5.3	4.7	—	—	1.6	0.8	—	—
Total	100	100	100	100	100	100	100	100	100	100	100	100
	SHOES				CHILDREN'S WEAR				FURNITURE			
Racine (downtown)	46.8	1.2	56.9	—	35.1	4.8	51.7	6.3	55.5	10.2	24.3	3.1
Racine (other)	30.4	1.2	38.0	14.1	21.0	—	13.8	6.3	28.4	3.1	55.2	—
Kenosha	—	83.0	—	—	0.8	64.4	—	—	0.8	74.2	3.4	—
Burlington	—	—	—	67.2	—	—	—	71.8	—	—	—	90.6
Sturtevant	—	—	—	—	—	—	—	—	—	—	—	—
Milwaukee	4.2	6.3	—	12.5	1.6	2.4	—	—	6.5	3.1	—	—
Chicago	3.5	2.4	—	1.5	1.2	0.8	—	—	2.8	3.1	—	—
Other and unknown	11.5	3.4	3.4	4.7	3.6	—	—	15.6	4.8	3.9	10.3	6.3
Never	3.6	2.4	1.7	—	36.7	27.6	34.5	—	1.2	2.4	6.8	—
Total	100	100	100	100	100	100	100	100	100	100	100	100

ties; (2) the consequent development of habitual small-shop buying in the community; (3) heavy catalogue buying, although very little out-of-town buying was done otherwise.

Since a Goldblatt store would offer a considerable addition to the city's department store facilities, the consultant estimated that it would increase department store buying to 6 per cent of gross income.

Tables 1A and 1B contain the results of a shopping survey made during January 1954. In all, 435 interviews were taken in the cities of Racine, Kenosha, Burlington, and Sturtevant. The survey research group believed that the sample might have been biased somewhat toward the middle-income ranges, with fewer than the proper proportion of low-income and high-income families. They also believed the sample to be somewhat biased toward the residents of new homes. An area sampling technique was employed, and the areas selected were mostly "critical" areas. More of these were in outlying sections than were in the central city.

The survey also showed that 80–90 per cent of the residents of all the cities covered owned cars and generally traveled by car to shop in downtown Racine. On the average, 40 per cent of the shoppers found that they had to park three blocks or more away from the downtown store where they made their major purchases. The survey also showed that 87.7 per cent of the residents of Racine shopped, on the average, once a month or oftener in downtown Racine. The proportions of residents in Kenosha, Sturtevant, and Burlington who shopped in downtown Racine once a

TABLE 1B

PLACE OF LAST PURCHASE OF SELECTED ITEMS BY RESIDENTS OF
RACINE, KENOSHA, STURTEVANT, AND BURLINGTON

	Appliances			
Place of Purchase	Rac.	Ken.	Stur.	Burl.
Racine (downtown)	55.4	2.4	20.6	—
Racine (other)	23.8	2.4	65.8	—
Kenosha	0.4	92.8	—	—
Burlington	—	—	—	87.5
Sturtevant	—	—	3.4	—
Milwaukee	4.5	0.8	3.4	6.3
Chicago	4.0	1.6	—	3.1
Other and unknown	5.2	2.4	6.8	3.1
Never	6.7	—	—	—
Total	100	100	100	100

month or more were 12.6 per cent, 89.7 per cent and 12.5 per cent, respectively. Thirty-four per cent of the residents of both Kenosha and Burlington never shopped in downtown Racine.

Should Goldblatt's establish a branch in the planned shopping center?

11

DAVIS SUPER DRUGS

IN THE fall of 1955 Davis Super Drugs, an independent retail drugstore located in Holton, Illinois, was considering changing from conventional clerk service to a self-service operation. At that time self-service in the drug field was relatively new, having been stimulated by the success of the supermarkets, which were handling more and more drug products—

as a result, it was believed, of the supermarkets' use of self-service displays.

Many druggists were becoming alarmed at the loss of business that they felt should logically be theirs. According to a survey made in 1953 by the *American Druggist*, there were about 636 self-service drugstores in the United States and about 7,000 others that were on a partial self-service basis. The 636 self-service stores represented only about 1 per cent of the nation's drugstores.

A self-service drugstore, as defined by the *American Druggist*, was one in which practically all merchandise, except products sold in the prescription department and at the fountain, was sold on a self-service basis. Others defined a self-service drugstore as one having (1) a wrapping counter (or checkout stand) near the front of the store, (2) some open-wall shelving, and (3) self-service islands. If these three factors were present, the store was considered self-service even though some departments, such as cameras, high-priced cosmetics, fountain, and prescriptions, were of the service type. Mr. Davis, owner and operator of Davis Super Drugs, thought of self-service along the latter lines except that he thought "some open-wall shelving" should be "all open-wall shelving" for those products other than presceiption items, photographic equipment, watches, clocks, and other higher-priced items, which were by their nature less adaptable to complete self-service.

At the time Mr. Davis was considering changing from service to self-service, there were nine drugstores, including Davis Super Drugs, in Holton, a city of 18,000 population. Eight of the stores were independently owned, and one was a unit in the Ford Hopkins chain. None of the nine was a self-service operation.

Competition was extremely keen in the retail drug business in Holton, as indicated by the fact that there were nine drugstores serving a city population of 18,000 plus a trading area with a radius of only about ten miles. *Standard Rate and Data Service* showed the following information on Holton: estimated population January 1, 1955, 17,700; total retail sales, 1954, $29,223,000; and retail drugstores sales, 1954, $1,137,000.

All the independent stores had been established in the community for many years, except the Davis store, which was established in 1935. In 1946 Davis had remodeled his store completely, purchasing all new fixtures. These were not completely depreciated and were still functional and modern in appearance. At the time of remodeling he had doubled his square footage by taking over a store building next door. His store layout, as a clerk-service operation, was probably superior to that of any of his independent competitors.

Exhibit 1 shows the general location of drugstores in Holton and Table 1 gives Davis' estimate of the floor space and sales volume of his competitors.

The total floor space available in Davis Super Drugs was 2,600 square

EXHIBIT 1

LOCATION OF DRUGSTORES IN BUSINESS SECTION OF HOLTON

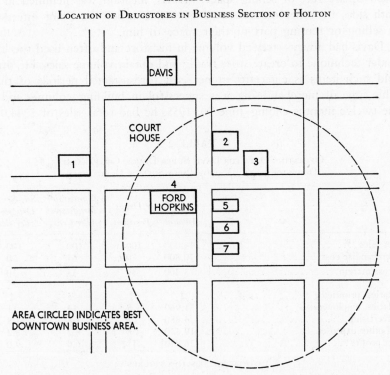

AREA CIRCLED INDICATES BEST
DOWNTOWN BUSINESS AREA.

feet. *Chain Store Age* reported on self-service drugstores as follows: "A
self-service store must have a selling area of at least 5,500 square feet in
order to do an effective selling job, according to most operators. A few
chains insist that 7,000 square feet is ideal, and a minority place the figure
from 8,000 to 10,000 square feet. Chains with successful small self-service
stores say they would not open a new store having less than 4,500 or

TABLE 1

ESTIMATED FLOOR SPACE AND SALES OF HOLTON DRUGSTORES

Drugstore	Approximate Sq. Ft. in Store	Davis' Estimate of 1954 Sales
Davis	2,600	240,000 (actual sales)
1	1,000	60,000
2	1,000	60,000
3	1,400	110,000
4 Ford Hopkins	3,000	300,000
5	800	110,000
6	1,500	175,000
7	1,500	60,000
8 (neighborhood store, outlying location, not on map)	1,200	50,000
Total	14,000	$1,165,000

5,000 square feet of selling space." Davis' location was hemmed in on both sides by other business establishments, which were not interested in selling or renting part of their space to him.

Davis had always stressed volume in his store and often used the loss-leader technique to create store traffic and obtain volume sales. He often sold such items as cigarettes at net cost for sustained periods of time. This type of merchandising was successful in building volume, and in the twelve months ending June 30, 1955, he had total sales of $244,000.

TABLE 2

OPERATING DATA FOR DAVIS SUPER DRUGS, COMPARABLE
DRUGSTORES, AND VARIOUS SELF-SERVICE DRUGSTORES

	Davis Super Drugs		Comparable Drugstores* (Per Cent)	Self-Service Drugstores† (Per Cent)
	Amount	Per Cent		
Net sales..........................	244,000	100	100	100
Merchandise cost.....................	170,800	70	65	70
Gross margin........................	73,200	30	35	30
Salaries, proprietor..................	‡	‡	5	‡
Salaries, employees..................	21,960	9	14	11
Advertising.........................	4,880	2	1.8	1.8
All other expenses...................	19,520	8	8.2	8.2
Net profit..........................	26,840‡	11‡	6.0	9.0
OTHER COMPARATIVE FIGURES				
Average merchandise investment at cost...	$47,000		$40,000	$49,000
Stock turnover (times per year)..........	3.4		5.0	6.3
Per cent of prescription sales to total sales...	5.0%		24.2%	15.0%

* *Lilly Digest for 1953.* Data are from stores with "over $200,000" in sales, located in cities between 5,000 and 20,000 in population. No information on number of self-service stores included, if any.
† Lynn H. Stiles, "The Development and Operation of Self-Service Drugstores." Average percentages from 65 independent drugstores operating on self-service.
‡ No breakdown for proprietor's salary. In these cases proprietor's salary is included in net-profit figure.

A wide line of merchandise contributed to the total volume. Among the items sold were toiletries, cosmetics, vitamins and all types of ethical packaged drugs, baby goods, photo supplies, cameras, watches and clocks, toys, boxed candies, carry-out ice cream, tobaccos, liquors, magazines, newspapers, greeting cards, and such sundry items as light bulbs and shoe polish. He had no soda fountain.

Table 2 shows a comparison between the Davis Super Drug operating figures for its fiscal year 1955 and the percentage figures reported by the *Lilly Digest* for a selected group of drugstores in the "over $200,000" sales class reporting to the Ely Lilly Company. All the stores were located in cities having a population between 5,000 and 20,000. The table also shows pertinent average percentages taken from operating statements of sixty-five independent drugstores that had already converted to self-service. These figures were gathered by a graduate student at the University of Illinois.[1]

As indicated in Table 2, Davis Super Drugs' prescription business amounted to only 5 per cent of total sales compared to 24.2 per cent figure from the Lilly survey and a 15 per cent figure from Stiles's survey. Davis believed that there were two important reasons for his small percentage of this type of business. The first was the fact that his extremely large volume generated by the loss-leader tactics made his prescription volume small as a percentage of total sales, since prescription business did not lend itself to this type of promotion. The second reason, Davis believed, related to his newness in the community. It was difficult for him to break into the prescription business because local doctors directed their patients to the older stores as a result of years of association with the owners.

In reading condensations of Mr. Stiles's thesis published in *American Druggist*, Davis was particularly interested in the reasons given by eighty-nine drugstore owners or managers interviewed as to why they switched service stores to self-service (Table 3).

TABLE 3

REASONS FOR CONVERTING SERVICE DRUGSTORES TO SELF-SERVICE

Reason	Independent Stores*	Chain Stores*
Self-service is the trend	42.6%	4.8%
It's what the patrons want	39.7	28.6
To cut salary ratio	35.3	47.6
To boost total volume	29.4	28.6
To boost average sale	11.8	14.3

* Percentages total more than 100 per cent because some operators gave more than one reason.

Also of interest to Davis were the figures concerning the average sale of the eighty-nine stores whose managers were interviewed by Mr. Stiles (see accompanying tabulation). The average sale of these stores increased by more than two-thirds when they converted to self-service. The average sale for Davis Super Drugs in 1955 was $1.16.

Davis was inclined to believe that self-service was the coming thing and that, if the chains were as convinced as they seemed to be that self-service was the answer, he as an independent who stressed volume should seriously consider making the change. He was aware of the criticisms leveled at self-service operations by the older, conservative, independent druggists, both in his community and nation-wide. In his opinion, the

---

[1] Lynn H. Stiles, "Development and Operation of Self-Service Drugstores" (thesis submitted for Master's Degree, University of Illinois).

	Independent Stores	Chain Stores
Average sale as clerk-service store.............$0.458		$0.625
Average sale as self-service store............... 0.766		1.19
Per cent increase........................... 67.4%		89.6%

most important criticism was that which concerned the professional nature of the drugstore. Many druggists felt that customer confidence in the pharmacist was not inspired by the more cold, commercial atmosphere of the self-service store, where some of the personal contact between pharmacist and customer was lost. Davis believed this criticism was not as important when applied to his operation as it might be in the case of some of his competitors in Holton who prided themselves on the highly professional nature of their stores, particularly in respect to their prescription services. Davis doubted very much whether any of his seven independent competitors were seriously considering a change-over to self-service. He was unable to learn whether the Ford Hopkins store was considering such a move.

Davis estimated that the cost of fixtures necessary to change his store to self-service would be about $10,000. He was interested in the costs given in Mr. Stiles's thesis (Table 4).

TABLE 4

AVERAGE COST OF FIXTURES FOR EQUIPPING SELF-SERVICE DRUGSTORES

	Independent Stores	Chain Stores
Excluding fountain...........................$ 7,650		$23,500
Including fountain........................... 14,437		35,250

One of the most important reasons given by chain drugstores for the change from clerk service to self-service was the hope and intent to cut salary ratios. Davis' existing salary ratio of 9 per cent was considerably lower than the 14 per cent average shown in the Lilly survey and the 11 per cent average in the Stiles' survey (see Table 1). Davis was somewhat doubtful whether he could bring his figure below 9 per cent by changing to self-service. He believed that he would have to have at least two check-out counters, which would have to be manned at all times. There would have to be some clerks on the floor to help customers who could not find the merchandise they wanted. In addition, the actual physical stocking of merchandise would probably require more personnel than it had in the clerk-service store because of the necessity of keeping all merchandise marked and of replenishing all stocks immediately.

If he changed to self-service, Davis did not intend to add any more types or varieties of items than he already carried, but he hoped that better exposure of the products to customers would increase volume and thus increase his stock turnover rate. Self-service grocery stores had turnstile-type entrances and exits. Davis was undecided whether these would hurt the general atmosphere of a drugstore but believed that they would help control pilfering.

Should Davis Super Drugs convert to a self-service operation?

12

AMERICAN INSTITUTE OF LAUNDERING

THE AMERICAN INSTITUTE OF LAUNDERING was a trade association organized to provide the laundering industry with a wide range of services. These services included the preparation and dissemination of informations regarding plant operations, distribution and sales, the conduct of a laundering school, maintenance of a textile-testing laboratory, and the operation of a full-scale model laundry. Over the past twenty years, the physical volume of laundry processed in power laundries had remained level, while population, disposable income, and gross national product in the United States had increased steadily. Overcapacity existed in the industry and future expectations in new textiles and home-laundering equipment indicated radical changes in laundry services. With this prospect, the American Institute of Laudering (AIL) engaged the Armour Research Foundation (ARF) to develop a long-range research program to meet the present and future needs of the laundry industry.

The ARF study team found that, although the number of power laundries (i.e., laundries using commercial laundering equipment) had not changed significantly since 1935, there had been a 50 per cent increase in neighborhood laundries between 1935 and 1957. These neighborhood laundries were typically small establishments using family-type washers. Total dollar receipts of power laundries had doubled since 1939, but so had the consumer price index covering all consumer purchases. Estimated physical volume had apparently shown no growth and probably was declining, since the consumer laundry price index had been increasing more rapidly than the total consumer price index.

A survey of the laundry industry indicated that there had been little or no change in the operations of power laundries in the past fifteen years. Laundries picked up dirty clothes and returned clean clothes to consumers through delivery routes or dealt with customers over the counter. Most laundries, regardless of size, did not have over two over-the-counter outlets. On the other hand, the number of delivery routes increased with the volume of business. The majority of laundries served a market area of twenty miles or less around their plants, and 80–100 per cent of their business was concentrated in the area within ten miles of their plants.

There was relatively little active sales promotion by laundries. The survey indicated that more than half the power laundries spent less than 2 per cent of sales for advertising and sales promotion. Newspaper ads, bundle inserts, and radio ads were most commonly used. Only 14 per cent of the laundries had attempted to attract business from such institutions as motels, hotels, and hospitals.

There did not appear to be any one factor that related to profitability, but laundries specializing in family-bundle work had a slightly higher profit level than others. There was some indication that laundries that did more over-the-counter business and less pickup and delivery business tended to have a higher profit level. The survey showed that profits of 4 per cent of sales before taxes were average, regardless of the size of the laundry. Overcapacity in excess of 10 per cent existed.

The laundry industry leaders placed a great deal of emphasis upon the need for better quality of work and the development of revolutionary equipment to accomplish this. Some suppliers to the laundry industry were conducting research into new equipment, but most indicated that sales to the industry were not large enough to justify large-scale research programs.

Home washers and neighborhood laundries were the main competitors of the power laundries, with home washers being by far the most important. An estimated 88 per cent of all wired homes contained electric clothes washing machines in 1957. This was near the saturation point, and most washer producers aimed their sales efforts at the replacement market. Another survey indicated that a large number of washer owners still used outside laundry service on occasion, when the weather was unfavorable or they did not feel up to the general trouble of hanging clothes to dry. Only 13 per cent of all wired homes contained either an electric or a gas clothes dryer. It appeared reasonable to expect that the volume of power and neighborhood laundries would be adversely affected by increased dryer sales.

New scientific developments indicated that home washing, drying, and ironing might become even more effortless by 1980. Advances in supersonic washing and forced-air drying could cut washing and drying time to a matter of minutes. Other advances indicated the possibility of easy ironing through the use of electrostatics.

The trend toward more informal and leisure clothing was expected to continue, including more and more of the "wash-and-wear" fabrics. This would have adverse affects on the laundry industry. Disposable clothing, which could be priced so low that it would be disposed of after a couple of wearings, was also nearing commercial reality. Coveralls and painting smocks made of disposable materials were already on the market.

These factors made the future outlook for the laundry industry such that the ARF team recommended that no long-range research projects be embarked upon by the Institute. Any long-range research might be completely inapplicable before it was completed. Research in marketing and production appeared preferable to research on the development of new equipment. The former would be less expensive and could be done quicker.

Five major areas of possible research were developed by the ARF team: marketing research, production and cost-control research, technological research, communications research, and management-development research. In each of these major areas, specific research projects were considered and analyzed as to cost of the research, probability of technical success, cost of development, probability of commercial success, and research and development time. From these estimates an over-all "measure of commercial effectiveness" was determined. This procedure is explained in Exhibit 1. The first three areas of possible research listed above were considered to be the most promising. The fourteen research projects considered most practical are shown in Exhibits 2 and 3.

The American Institute of Laundering could not support a large research program under current conditions. Membership dues amounted to $400,000 for the 1956–57 fiscal year. No idle funds were on hand. The best method for raising funds appeared to be by requesting voluntary subscriptions from members. Other methods included more extensive use of trade shows, increasing the Institute's laundry operations, raising membership dues, and short-term borrowing. There were also possibilities of getting support from allied industry associations and from government agencies and/or foundations.

EXHIBIT 1

METHOD OF ESTIMATING PROBABILITY OF TECHNICAL SUCCESS, PROBABILITY OF COMMERCIAL
SUCCESS, AND COMMERCIAL EFFECTIVENESS

Probability of Technical Success

This factor measures the chance that no unforeseen scientific or technical impasse will be encountered. A high probability of success does not necessarily indicate that the research will result in favorable findings; it simply implies that an answer will be obtained. In this study the probability of technical success is rated in terms of the following ratios: 0.9, 0.7, 0.5, 0.3, and 0.1. A ratio of 0.9 may be interpreted as indicating an excellent chance of success, 0.7 as a good chance, 0.5 as a fair chance, 0.3 as a poor chance, and 0.1 as a very poor chance.

Probability of Commercial Success

This measure considers primarily the degree and extent to which the industry will accept and implement the research recommendations. Tacit con-

EXHIBIT 1—*Continued*

sideration is given to the probable effect of the implemented recommendations upon the laundering market. As in the case of the probability of technical success, the degree of commercial success is measured by the ratios 0.9, 0.7, 0.5, 0.3, and 0.1.

Measure of Commercial Effectiveness

This is predicated on several assumptions:

1. The power laundry industry is comprised of 6,500 establishments; the American Institute of Laundering membership includes approximately 3,000 power laundries.
2. Total industry sales are somewhat over $1 billion and total sales of AIL members are about $800 million.
3. Operating costs and profits of the industry are distributed as shown in the accompanying tabulation.[1]

	Annual Cost (Millions)	Per Cent of Total
Productive labor	$265	33
Productive supplies	80	10
Power	40	5
Buildings	16	2
Machinery	40	5
Indirect overhead	55	7
Distribution	128	16
Sales	48	6
Administration	96	12
Profits (before taxes)	32	4

4. An increase in sales volume would not materially alter the distribution of costs.
5. All the research recommendations possess the same useful life, and therefore annual or one-year savings provide a valid base for comparison. (Not necessarily true but no means exist for estimating the economic life of research findings.)
6. All the research programs are financed and adopted by 100 per cent of the AIL membership where applicable.

Sample Calculation

Effect of research: 5 per cent increase in the sales of AIL members and a 5 per cent reduction in distribution costs. A 5 per cent increase in sales is equivalent to an increased dollar volume of $4,000,000; at a profit margin of 4 per cent this results in a $160,000 increase in profits. A 5 per cent decrease in distribution costs results in a $6,400,000 addition to profits.

$$\text{Measure of commercial effectiveness} = \frac{\text{Annual addition to profits resulting from research}}{\text{Cost of research and development}} = \frac{6,560,000}{190,000} = 34.5.$$

---

[1] Based on AIL Special Report No. 227, "Operating Cost Percentages, 1955."

EXHIBIT 2

EVALUATION OF FOURTEEN PROPOSED RESEARCH PROJECTS

1. *Market Definition*
   Research cost:
   Field survey, $35,000.
   Probability of technical success:
   Excellent (0.9)—many similar studies have been previously con-
   ducted.
   Cost of development:
   A redirection of advertising effort would probably be required to im-
   plement the research findings. The preparation of illustrative copy
   ($10,000) and dissemination of recommendations to AIL members
   (3,000 members × $5/member) would result in a total cost of about
   $25,000.
   Probability of commercial success:
   Fair (0.5)—advertising is in a sense an intuitive art. A general reluc-
   tance on the part of individual AIL members to forego personal ad-
   vertising preferences may be expected.
   Research and development time:
   Two years—one year for research and one year for development.
   Measure of commercial effectiveness:
   26.7—arising from increase in sales of AIL members of about 5 per
   cent.
2. *Diversification: New-Markets Study*
   Research cost:
   Literature and field survey, $15,000.
   Probability of technical success:
   Excellent (0.9)—similar studies are continuously being conducted suc-
   cessfully.
   Cost of development:
   Distribution of findings to the industry in terms of specific case studies
   and recommendations, $25,000.
   Probability of commercial success:
   Good (0.7)—the national trend toward greater leisure indicates that
   markets for new services exist—they remain only to be uncovered and
   exploited.
   Research and development time:
   Two years—one year for research and one year for development.
   Measure of commercial effectiveness:
   40.0—arising from 5 per cent increase in sales of AIL members.
3. *Media Research*
   Research cost:
   Consumer field survey, $20,000.
   Probability of technical success:
   Excellent (0.9)—this is a common type of advertising study.
   Cost of development:
   Primary costs lie in the dissemination of the research findings to AIL
   membership for utilization—$15,000
   Probability of commercial success:
   Good (0.7)—a relatively minor effort would be required on the part
   of the individual laundry owner to redistribute present advertising
   expenditures in such a manner as to reach a larger potential market.

EXHIBIT 2—*Continued*

The simplicity of the effort greatly enhances its widespread acceptability.

Measure of commercial effectiveness:
4.6—resulting from 0.5 per cent increase in sales volume of AIL members.

4. *Appeal Research*

Research cost:
Limited consumer motivation survey, $25,000.

Probability of technical success:
Excellent (0.9)—a good deal of progress in this kind of research has been achieved in recent years.

Cost of development:
The development of several sample advertising approaches would be required. Total cost for distribution to AIL membership would approximate $45,000.

Probability of commercial success:
Fair (0.5)—appeal research is relatively new and as such its comprehension and acceptance may prove difficult for a number of laundry owners.

Research and development time:
Three years—one and one-half years each for research and for development.

Measure of commercial effectiveness:
45.9—arising from estimated 10 per cent increase in AIL membership sales volume.

5. *Packaging Research*

Research cost:
Laboratory study and field survey, $20,000.

Probability of technical success:
Good (0.7)—many packaging research studies have previously been completed successfully.

Cost of development:
Dissemination of research findings to AIL membership, $20,000.

Probability of commercial success:
Good (0.7)—adoption of the recommendations would probably entail little or no additional expense. The prospect of increasing sales in this manner would have widespread acceptance.

Research and development time:
One year for research and development.

Measure of commercial effectiveness:
Nil—in the large majority of cases laundry packages come only to the attention of individuals already using laundry services. It is unlikely that the present consumer would increase his laundry use merely as a result of a packaging change.

6. *Study of Route versus Over-the-Counter Costs*

Research cost:
Field study and records analysis, $20,000.

Probability of technical success:
Excellent (0.9)—this is a relatively straightforward study.

Cost of development:
Dissemination of research findings to AIL membership, $20,000.

Probability of commercial success:

EXHIBIT 2—*Continued*

Good (0.7)—the research findings are based upon historical case data and are easily understood and applied.

Measure of commercial effectiveness:

64.0—arising from anticipated 2 per cent reduction in average distribution costs.

7. *Operations Research Over-the-Counter Location Study*

Research cost:

Field survey and mathematical analysis, $30,000.

Probability of technical success:

Good (0.7)—a good number of similar studies have previously been successfully completed.

Cost of development:

Mathematical analysis of individual laundryman's distribution system ($10 per AIL member × 3,000 members) plus cost of distributing the research findings ($10,000), $40,000

Probability of commercial success:

Fair (0.5)—while it is unlikely that the research findings would result in the relocation of present outlets, they do present a workable guide for the planning of new outlets.

Research and development time:

Two years—one year for research and one year for development.

Measure of commercial effectiveness:

9.1—arising from anticipated 2 per cent increase in sales of AIL members.

8. *Equipment Catalogue Evaluation*

Research cost:

Compilation of equipment catalogue and a number of field surveys, $35,000.

Probability of technical success:

Excellent (0.9)—this is a relatively straightforward type of study.

Cost of development:

Distribution of equipment catalogue to AIL membership, $30,000.

Probability of commercial success:

Good (0.7)—the use and acceptance of equipment catalogues is quite common throughout the industry.

Research and development time:

Two years—one year for research and one year for development.

Measure of commercial effectiveness:

20.4—arising from anticipated 0.05 per cent reduction in direct labor costs.

9. *Equipment Evaluation Study*

Research cost:

Field survey, $20,000.

Probability of technical success:

Good (0.7)—some difficulty may be encountered in obtaining completely reliable field information, since there would be need, in many cases, to rely on the memory of laundry owners.

Cost of development:

Presentation of research findings and solicitation of funds and support to construct expensive testing laboratory facilities, $100,000.

Probability of commercial success:

Fair (0.7)—testing facilities are quite commonly employed in many

EXHIBIT 2—*Continued*

industries, but the high cost of development may prove restrictive to the laundry industry.

Measure of commercial effectiveness:

22.1—arising from anticipated 1 per cent decrease in direct labor costs.

10. *Renting versus Purchasing Equipment Study*

Research cost:

Field survey, $20,000.

Probability of technical success:

Good (0.7)—numerous similar analyses have been successfully concluded.

Cost of development:

Dissemination of study findings to AIL membership, $6,000.

Probability of commercial success:

Good (0.7)—leasing of equipment usually allows for the conduct and expansion of business with minimum capital requirements. The resulting relative flexibility in plant capacity would probably prove attractive to laundry owners.

Research and development time:

One year for research and development.

Measure of commercial effectiveness:

15.4—arising from probable 1 per cent reduction in capital costs (depreciation) for AIL members.

11. *Industrial Engineering Team Evaluation*

Research cost:

Field study, $40,000.

Probability of technical success:

Good (0.7)—similar studies are common, but some difficulty may be encountered in relating specific profit improvements to the recommendations of the industrial engineers.

Cost of development:

Dissemination of research findings to AIL membership and solicitations of industrial engineering firms to undertake a full-scale improvement program, $10,000.

Probability of commercial success:

Good (0.7)—industrial-engineering concepts are common in the industry and bear a relatively high degree of acceptance.

Research and development time:

Two years—one and one-half years for research and one-half year for development.

Measure of commercial effectiveness:

103.0—based upon anticipated 2 per cent reduction in AIL members' direct labor costs.

12. *Re-evaluation of AIL Publication Policy*

Research cost:

Field study, $30,000.

Probability of technical success:

Fair (0.5)—the need to consider an exceedingly large number of possible combinations of volume and detail of published material presents an extremely difficult problem of experimental design. Relating field-operating improvements to changes in AIL publication policy presents another difficult problem.

Cost of development:

EXHIBIT 2—*Continued*

Nil—a simple redistribution of current effort and expense is all that would be required.

Probability of commercial success:

Good (0.7)—presentation of information in an effective and efficient means usually meets with widespread acceptance; some objection might arise on the basis of somewhat restricted coverage.

Research and development time:

Two years' research time—little or no development time would be required.

Measure of commercial effectiveness:

17.6—arising from anticipated 0.2 per cent decrease in direct labor costs of AIL members.

13. *Information Exchange Research*

Research cost:

Field research, $10,000.

Probability of technical success:

Fair (0.5)—difficulty may be encountered in measuring the absolute effectiveness of each form of information exchanged and tested.

Cost of development:

Dissemination of research findings and organization costs of initiating a long-range information exchange program, $15,000.

Probability of commercial success:

Fair (0.5)—difficulty may be encountered in obtaining the full scale and enthusiastic support of industry necessary to the success of the program.

Research and development time:

Two years—one and one-half years for research and one-half year for development.

Measure of commercial effectiveness:

10.3—arising from anticipated 0.1 per cent reduction in average direct labor costs.

14. *Evaluation of Traveling Information Team*

Research cost:

Field trial, $20,000.

Probability of technical success:

Fair (0.5)—the accurate correlation of operational improvements with the information provided by the information team may be difficult to obtain. In many instances the laundry owner's memory would be the only source of such information.

Cost of development:

Dissemination of the research findings to AIL membership and the solicitation of funds to select, train, and maintain a number of information teams in the field, $40,000.

Probability of commercial success:

Good (0.7)—there is a strong natural tendency to accept and place relatively high value upon the direct recommendations of an expert as opposed to "wading through" printed matter.

Research and development time:

Three years—two years for research and one year for development.

Measure of commercial effectiveness:

22.1—arising from expected 0.5 per cent reduction in average direct labor costs.

EXHIBIT 3

SUMMARY EVALUATION OF PROPOSED RESEARCH PROJECTS

Research and Development Projects	Cost of Research (Dollars)	Probability of Technical Success	Cost of Development	Probability of Commercial Success	Research and Development Time (Yrs.)	Effect of Research*	Measure of Commercial Effectiveness
1. Industrial engineering team	40,000	.7	$ 10,000	.7	2	−2% productive labor/yr.	103.0
2. Study of route vs. over-the-counter costs	20,000	.9	20,000	.7	1	−2% productive labor/yr.	64.0
3. Appeal research	25,000	.9	45,000	.5	3	+10% sales/yr.	45.9
4. Diversification and new market study	15,000	.9	25,000	.7	2	+5% sales/yr.	40.0
5. Market definition	35,000	.9	25,000	.5	2	+5% sales/yr.	26.7
6. Equip. evaluation study	20,000	.7	100,000	.7	4	−1% productive labor/yr.	22.1
7. Information team	20,000	.5	40,000	.7	3	−0.5% productive labor/yr.	22.1
8. Equipment catalogue evaluation	35,000	.9	30,000	.7	2	−0.05% productive labor/yr.	20.4
9. Re-evaluation of AIL publication policy	30,000	.5	nil	.7	2	−0.2% productive labor/yr.	17.6
10. Renting vs. purchasing equipment study	20,000	.7	6,000	.7	1	−1% depreciation/yr.	15.4
11. Information exchange research	10,000	.5	15,000	.5	2	−0.1% productive labor/yr.	10.3
12. O.R. over-the-counter location study	30,000	.7	40,000	.5	2	+2% sales/yr.	9.1
13. Media research	20,000	.9	15,000	.7	1	+0.5% sales/yr.	4.6
14. Packaging research	20,000	.7	20,000	.7	1	nil	0.0

* + = increase, − = decrease.

What research, if any, should the American Institute of Laundering undertake?

B. Quantitative Objectives

13

INTERNATIONAL HARVESTER FARM EQUIPMENT DEPARTMENT (A)

THE farm equipment sales department of International Harvester had the problem of establishing reasonable sales potentials for industrial wheeled tractors for each of its fifty-seven sales districts. This problem had confronted the company for several years and was becoming more important each year because of the expanding number of industrial tractor sales as a percentage of the total domestic tractors sold, as shown in Table 1. By the latter part of 1958 the need for a solution to the problem was imperative because, under the present system, International had little control over sale to this segment of the market.

TABLE 1

DOMESTIC FARM AND NONFARM TRACTOR SHIPMENTS: 1955–57

Year	Total*	For Farm Use	For Nonfarm Use	Percentage Nonfarm
1955	286,000	263,000	23,000	6.9
1956	191,000	170,000	21,000	11.0
1957	204,000	179,000	25,000	12.6

* Except contractors' "off highway," garden, and crawler-type tractors.
Source: Department of Commerce, *Facts for Industry, 1955, 1956,* and *1957.*

Statistics on tractors sold for nonfarm use were available for only the years 1955 and after. Prior to 1955 the Department of Commerce and various groups reporting statistics lumped all domestic shipment figures of tractors for nonfarm use with shipments for farm use.

As the sale of industrial tractors became more important, Harvester's farm equipment sales department felt that it was imperative that some method be devised to determine potentials for tractors sold for nonfarm use for each sales district. The company had for many years established sales potentials for farm tractor sales. The procedure for doing this had changed over a period of time; the current one was quite simple. The

EXHIBIT 1

```
┌────────────────────────────────────────────────────────────────────────┐
│  COMMERCIAL SALE OF AN INTERNATIONAL TRACTOR        MR. DEALER—          │
│                                                     FILL IN AND MAIL TO YOUR DISTRICT │
│        MODEL_____ SERIAL NO._____  OFFICE IMMEDIATELY ON DELIVERY │
│  NAME OF PURCHASER_____     OF TRACTOR.          │
│                                                                          │
│  TOWN_____ COUNTY_____ STATE_____               │
│                                                                          │
│  A.  TYPE OF BUSINESS OR ESTABLISHMENT WHERE TRACTOR WILL BE USED  _____ │
│                                                                          │
│  B.  NUMBER OF TRACTORS OWNED BEFORE BUYING NEW IH TRACTOR                │
│                                            ☐ NONE OWNED                   │
│                                                                          │
│        IH TRACTORS (NUMBER_____)        OTHER TRACTORS (NUMBER_____) │
│                                                                          │
│  C.  STATUS OF NEW IH TRACTOR  (CHECK ONE ONLY)                           │
│        ☐ FIRST PURCHASE OF A TRACTOR                                      │
│        ☐ REPLACES ANOTHER TRACTOR (MAKE REPLACED_____ . AGE IN YEARS____) │
│        ☐ AN ADDITION TO OTHER TRACTORS ALREADY OWNED.                     │
│                                                                          │
│  D.  SPECIFIC JOBS OR KIND OF WORK FOR WHICH NEW TRACTOR WILL BE USED     │
│        _____                 │
│        _____                 │
│        _____                 │
│                                                                          │
│  E.  SPECIAL-DUTY EQUIPMENT SOLD WITH TRACTOR   (CHECK ONE OR MORE)       │
│                                    ☐ NONE SOLD                            │
│        ☐ BACK HOE                   ☐ PLATFORM CARRIER                    │
│        ☐ BLADE—CENTER               ☐ POST-HOLE DIGGER                    │
│        ☐ BLADE—FRONT                ☐ RAKE                                │
│        ☐ BLADE—REAR                 ☐ ROLLER                              │
│        ☐ CEMENT MIXER               ☐ SAW                                 │
│        ☐ CRANE                      ☐ SCRAPER OR SCOOP                     │
│        ☐ FORK LIFT                  ☐ SNOW PLOW                           │
│        ☐ HALF-TRACKS                ☐ SWEEPER OR BROOM                     │
│        ☐ LOADER                     ☐ TRAILER OR WAGON                     │
│        ☐ MOWER—CUTTER BAR           ☐ TRENCHER                            │
│        ☐ MOWER—HAMMER KNIFE         ☐ WINCH                               │
│        ☐ MOWER—REEL                 ☐ _____                         │
│        ☐ MOWER—ROTARY               ☐ _____                         │
│                                                                          │
│  DEALER_____    ADDRESS_____          │
│  DISTRICT OFFICE_____   DATE_____                   │
└────────────────────────────────────────────────────────────────────────┘
```

Census of Agriculture gave the farm tractor population for each county. Past experience had shown that the average life of a farm tractor was fourteen years. On this basis it was concluded that one-fourteenth of this tractor population would be replaced each year. Since replacement sales accounted for almost the entire market for farm tractors, this figure was used as the county potential. From these potentials, sales quotas or sales goals for the various districts were determined. Such quotas were important to management, particularly in judging sales performance. They would become more important because, starting in 1959, salesmen's compensation would be determined on the basis of their ability to meet or exceed their quotas.

The fact that some counties had a much greater potential for tractor sales, now that industrial sales were becoming more widespread, was obvious. The only method that the company had for setting a county quota or sales goal for total tractor sales in 1958 was to determine the approximate potential for tractors used for agricultural purposes as described above, to estimate International Harvester's share of the market, and to add to this figure a "best guess" of the tractors that would be sold for industrial purposes. The "best guess" was usually made on the basis of the proportion sold the previous year for industrial purposes. It was the responsibility of the district manager to break his quota down by zones, which usually consisted of a number of counties. Under these circumstances, the farm equipment sales department manager did not know whether a district that sold fifty tractors per year for industrial use was doing as well as a district that sold only twenty-five.

As early as November, 1955, the sales department had instructed its fifty-seven district offices to obtain a detailed dealer report on the sale of each tractor for other than farm use. A copy of this form is included as Exhibit 1. Dealers continued to report the sales of tractors for industrial use for the years 1956 and 1957, but the sales department found that there was difficulty and confusion on the part of dealers as to which of their tractor sales were for industrial use as opposed to those for farm use. To clarify the classifications, a letter defining industrial and farm use was sent to all district managers on May 7, 1958. A copy is shown as Exhibit 2.

EXHIBIT 2
Farm Equipment Sales Department

All F. E. and Combination Districts

May 7, 1958

District Manager
Asst. District Manager

CLASSIFICATION OF TRACTOR SALES—
FARM OR COMMERCIAL

In order to fully participate in the large and growing market for tractors sold for use in commercial job applications, it is necessary, of course, to keep fully informed on the current sales and distribution pattern of these units. For this reason, you are reporting separately those units of your weekly tractor deliveries which are for commercial use.

We recognize that it is sometimes difficult to correctly classify a retail tractor sale as either commercial or farm. Therefore, we believe it will be helpful to set forth the following standards and criteria to assist you in determining the classification in which a sale belongs:

  I. A tractor sale should be classified as "farm" if it is to be *used primarily* for: (1) the growing, harvesting, farm storage, and preparation for market

EXHIBIT 2—*Continued*

or use of any crop, including orchard and specialized crops; (2) the production of all poultry, livestock, and related products; (3) the general maintenance and care of the farmstead. This classification should apply whether the work is done for the owner of the tractor or as custom work for other farm operators.

II. A tractor sale should be classified as "commercial" if it is to be *used primarily* by: (1) any industry other than agriculture; (2) private homes and estates; (3) public and private schools and social institutions (except where used on a farm in connection with the institution); (4) recreational clubs and similar groups; (5) political divisions, subdivisions, and governing boards; (6) dealers or others for rental to commercial users.

III. A further criterion that should be useful is the type of equipment that will be used with the tractor. The "Special Duty Equipment" has been developed largely for commercial applications; however, some of the machines can be used for agricultural purposes. Again, the final basis of judgment should be the *principal use* for which the tractor and machines were purchased.

It is our expectation that the above criteria will materially assist in maintaining a uniform basis for reporting commercial sales at all districts. *District Management will have the final obligation* of correctly reporting farm and commercial sales, and we ask your full co-operation in carrying out this responsibility.

(signed) B. H. Bagby

The sales department had analyzed the report forms for the period from November 1, 1955 to June 30, 1956. In that eight-month period, 3,847 tractors were sold that were reported by dealers as being purchased for industrial purposes. In the same period International Harvester sold 36,841 tractors for farm use. The reliability of the figures was not considered to be 100 per cent because of the difficulties mentioned above. No further studies of these reports of tractors sold for industrial use had been made by 1958.

In studying the results of the eight-month period in 1955 and 1956, the market research department noted that the 3,847 tractors sold for industrial use by International Harvester represented only 18.3 per cent of total sales of tractors for nonfarm use in 1956. Harvester's eight months' sales of tractors for farm use represented 21.5 per cent of industry tractor sales for farm use in the entire 1956 calendar year. Harvester's total sales of tractors for industrial use for the eight months were divided among various types of tractors, as shown in Table 2.

In the spring of 1958 the market research department initiated a further analysis of industrial tractor sales. This second survey was for a six-month period beginning May 1, 1958 and ending October 31, 1958. Some of the results for the two most important models sold for industrial use, the International Cub and the Series 300, are shown in Table 3. Contractors, political subdivisions, and service and maintenance users appeared to be the biggest market for tractors for industrial use. Contractors of all types, including general, building, and excavating, used tractors for bulk-material handling, excavating, and grading. Political subdivisions and institutions, such as states, counties, townships, parks, schools, and hospitals, used tractors in grading, excavating, landscaping, and mowing. Service and maintenance users, such as dealer rentals, florists, estates and private homes, cemeteries, motels, and resorts used tractors for grading, mowing, landscaping, hauling, excavating, and loading.

International tractors were distributed principally through some 1,500 farm equipment dealers, who handled only farm equipment, and about 3,400 combination dealers, who handled both farm equipment and the International line of motor trucks. In addition, there were about seventy-

TABLE 2

TYPES OF TRACTORS SOLD FOR INDUSTRIAL USE
IN EIGHT-MONTH PERIOD, 1955–56

Type of Tractor	No. Sold for Industrial Use	Average Price F.O.B. Shipping Point*
International Cub (includes both Lo-Boy and Farmall Cub)	539	$1,250
100 Series (Farmall 100 and Super A)	217	2,000
300 Series (includes International 300 Utility and Farmall 300)	3032	2,400
400 Series	54	2,800
600 Series	5	4,600
Total	3,847	

* Prices are for tractor only and do not include any attachments.

five company-owned, farm equipment stores that sold tractors. Each district manager was responsible for all sales in his district, which usually consisted of six zones. Each zone had an average of twelve dealers. Zones were usually composed of a number of counties. Each dealer had a county or a specific part of a county assigned to him in which he was responsible for all International Harvester sales. If a franchised dealer could not be established to cover a specific area and if such an area appeared to have a reasonable potential, then the district manager might recommend that a company-owned, farm equipment store be established. Generally, it was felt that an independent dealer was the most desirable type of outlet, and, where company-owned stores were in existence, it was the policy to sell them to a qualified local man whenever an opportunity for such a sale arose.

The study of industrial tractor sales indicated that sales of tractors for industrial use were to individuals or organizations that were entirely different from the normal farmer, whose needs and wants were familiar to the franchised farm equipment dealer. The problem of whether a different channel of distribution was needed arose, but it was decided that, before this problem could be properly solved, a method of determining sales potentials for industrial tractors had to be devised.

One method of setting potentials that the research department considered was to use actual sales of tractors for industrial use as an indication of the potential. If a given district sold 10 per cent of the industrial tractors sold by Harvester in 1958, that district could be given a quota of 10 per cent of the firm's forecasted 1959 industrial tractor sales. The company was not satisfied with this method. It realized that a better way of establishing potentials for industrial tractors should be devised so that quotas could be developed from a reasonable potential instead of from the previous year's sales figures.

In studying the figures from the survey, the research department noted that sales of industrial tractors were related to the size of the population, particularly in the metropolitan areas, within each district. The rate of growth of an area also seemed to be associated with sales for industrial purposes. Logic and experience also suggested that industrial sales were related to the type of industrial activity in the district; the extractive industries, such as mining, logging, and oil well drilling; the density of estate-type homes, which could use a small industrial tractor for mowing and maintenance purposes; and the trend of municipalities and other political subdivisions to substitute machines for hand labor in such

TABLE 3

SELECTED STATISTICS FROM MARKET RESEARCH DEPARTMENT ANALYSIS OF
INDUSTRIAL TRACTOR SALES FIGURES: May 1,–October 31,1958

Chief Occupation or Business of Purchaser of I 300 or I.H. Cub Tractor	I 300	Cub
Contractors	54%	17%
Political subdivisions and institutions	14	13
Services and maintenance	9	52
Retail dealers and suppliers	8	5
Industrial and commercial applications	7	10
Logging	5	1
Oil fields	2	1
Mining operations	1	1
Number of tractors owned before buying an I 300 or I.H. Cub tractor		
Owned none	35	62
Owned one	35	28
Owned two	16	2
Owned three or more	14	8
Makes of tractors owned before buying an I 300 or I.H. Cub tractor		
Owned none	35	62
Owned I.H. tractors only	20	21
Owned both I.H. and competitive makes	9	4
Owned competitive makes only	36	13
Status of new I 300 or I.H. Cub tractor		
First tractor purchase	35	62
Addition to tractors already owned	29	19
Replaces another tractor	36	19

TABLE 4

Comparison of States by Rank According to Sales of Tractors for
Industrial Use, Population, and Rate of Growth of Households

	No. of International Tractors Sold for Industrial Use 5/1/58–10/31/58	Rank by Industrial Tractor Sales 5/1/58–10/31/58	Population Rank 1/1/58	Rank by Percentage Increase in Households 1/1/55–12/31/57
U.S. total	5,009	..	..	..
New England				
Maine	13	42	36	44
New Hampshire	21	37	45	33
Vermont	13	43	47	48
Massachusetts	77	26	9	39
Rhode Island	10	47	40	43
Connecticut	88	23	26	19
Middle Atlantic				
New York	268	6	1	3
New Jersey	91	22	8	9
Pennsylvania	283	5	3	8
East North Central				
Ohio	363	2	6	2
Indiana	204	9	10	12
Illinois	388	1	4	7
Michigan	206	8	7	4
Wisconsin	153	10	15	11
West North Central				
Minnesota	84	24	18	14
Iowa	145	11	24	26
Missouri	238	7	12	20
North Dakota	29	35	43	37
South Dakota	41	32	41	38
Nebraska	38	33	34	32
Kansas	116	17	39	31
South Atlantic				
Delaware	20	39	46	29
Maryland	80	25	22	10
Dist. of Columbia	13	44	39	45
Virginia	97	21	14	15
West Virginia	72	27	30	42
North Carolina	105	19	11	17
South Carolina	60	20	25	25
Georgia	122	14	16	22
Florida	60	31	13	6
East South Central				
Kentucky	233	3	21	34
Tennessee	145	12	17	24
Alabama	124	13	19	35
Mississippi	69	29	28	47
West South Central				
Arkansas	71	28	32	49
Louisiana	110	18	20	23
Oklahoma	118	16	27	46
Texas	303	4	5	5

TABLE 4—*Continued*

	No. of International Tractors Sold for Industrial Use 5/1/58–10/31/58	Rank by Industrial Tractor Sales 5/1/58–10/31/58	Population Rank 1/1/58	Rank by Percentage Increase in Households 1/1/55–12/31/57
Mountain				
Montana..................	32	34	42	36
Idaho.....................	17	40	44	41
Wyoming.................	14	41	48	40
Colorado..................	21	38	33	16
New Mexico..............	11	45	37	28
Arizona..................	11	46	35	18
Utah.....................	8	48	38	27
Nevada..................	7	49	49	30
Pacific				
Washington..............	68	30	23	13
Oregon...................	29	36	31	21
California................	120	15	2	1

activities as street sweeping, snow removal, and trench digging. The best method of incorporating all these factors into a statistical procedure that would "pinpoint" the actual potential in each area was not clear.

In the fall of 1958 no solution had yet been found to the problem of setting district potentials for industrial tractors. The research department ranked all states according to industrial tractor sales during the six-month period from May 1 to October 31, 1958, and compared this with rankings based on population and rate of growth of households. Table 4 shows the results. Some correlation existed among these three measures, although in some cases the relationship was far removed. It was noted that in most of the exceptions there was some valid explanation. For instance, Kentucky ranked third in the forty-eight states in industrial tractor sales for the period, but its population rank was twenty-first, and its household increase rank was thirty-fourth. This extreme deviation was caused by the fact that the state of Kentucky had placed a large order for industrial tractors for use in its highway department in the period analyzed. Despite these weaknesses, the research department believed that some statistical relationship of this type offered the best possibilities for measuring potential industrial tractor sales.

1. *How should International Harvester proceed in developing a measure of the potential for sales of tractors for industrial use?*
2. *Would such a measure be worth the expense of developing and maintaining it?*

14

CHERRY-BURRELL CORPORATION

EARLY in 1959 the management of the Cherry-Burrell Corporation was considering whether to expand the firm's program for measuring market potential. In 1951 the advertising manager had devised a method of estimating market potential that had been used by the firm ever since for estimating potential in one industry. The advertising manager's own opinion of the measurement method was summed up in the final sentence of a memorandum he sent to the sales manager: "Let me say only that I hold no particular brief for this particular system as being the one and only system which will produce results. I do, however, say that it has produced usable results for us and I have yet to find a better." The question faced by the management in 1959 was whether to expand the technique to the firm's entire product line, to bring more current data into the measurement, or to leave the measuring of potential as it was.

The Cherry-Burrell Corporation, located in Cedar Rapids, Iowa, manufactured and sold throughout the United States equipment for the dairy, food, beverage, brewing, and chemical industries. Their products included filling and washing machines for glass and metal containers, pasteurizing and cooling equipment, freezers, steam generators, and storage tanks. The company also acted as a jobber in selling the supplies used in connection with its equipment; these supplies included disinfectants, measuring cups, milk racks, cans, bottles, bottle caps, and pails. Sales were about equally divided between equipment and supplies. Net sales in 1957 were $35 million; in the ten-year period since 1948 they had increased nearly $7 million. The company had approximately 1,500 employees.

The advertising manager originally set up his system for estimating market potential in 1951. He used data from the dairy industry only but believed the procedure was equally applicable to the other industries that were served by Cherry-Burrell. For a number of reasons, including the movement of the firm's offices from Chicago, the procedure had not been applied to the other industries, nor had the data been revised for the dairy industry.

As the advertising manager pointed out, the potential measurement system was quite simple to use after it was established, but to set it up required a great deal of detailed knowledge of the processes used in the plants of the company's customers. In the dairy industry, for example, there were five basic types of products—fluid milk; evaporated, condensed, and powdered milk; butter and cheese; and ice cream. The amount of equipment needed to process any of these types of products depended on the capacity of the plant. Milk capacity was specified in quarts per day, butter and cheese in pounds per year, and ice cream in gallons per year.

In preparing the estimates of market potential, the advertising manager first established classes according to the capacity of plants producing each of the five basic types of product. These classes were set, on the basis of his knowledge of the industry, to give about five groupings. Each included a significant number of actual plants. These classes are shown in Exhibit 1.

EXHIBIT 1
PLANT TYPE AND SIZE CATEGORIES

Fluid milk—capacity in quarts per day
  0–999
  1,000–4,999
  5,000–24,999
  25,000–49,999
  50,000 and over
Evaporated, condensed, and powdered milk—capacity in pounds of raw milk
    per year
  No size breakdown
Butter—capacity in pounds per year
  0–99,999
  100,000–399,999
  400,000–799,999
  800,000–1,499,999
  1,500,000 and over
Cheese—capacity in pounds per year
  0–149,999
  150,000–449,999
  450,000–749,999
  750,000–1,499,999
  1,500,000 and over
Ice Cream—capacity in gallons per year
  0–49,999
  50,000–199,999
  200,000–499,999
  500,000–999,999
  1,000,000 and over

Working with other Cherry-Burrell executives, the advertising manager then developed an itemized list of equipment that would be used by each type and size of plant. He determined the current cost of each piece of equipment from the firm's price list and estimated its useful life from data published by the Bureau of Internal Revenue for determining depreciation for tax purposes. The Bureau's life estimates were revised downward 10 per cent and rounded to the nearest smaller whole year, because the company had found the Bureau's life estimates to be too long in most cases.

The cost of each piece of equipment was divided by its useful life to get an "annual charge." By adding the annual charge figures for each plant, an estimate of annual purchases was obtained. This was, in effect, the total investment that a plant should make each year for new equipment to maintain itself.

In order to apply the annual charge computation to a specific plant, the figure was divided by the daily capacity of the average (median) plant in the class to arrive at a per quart or per pound figure. This average annual charge per quart or per pound could then be multiplied by a given plant's daily capacity to obtain an estimate of the amount that the given plant would spend annually for equipment. By adding up the estimates

TABLE 1

TOTAL EQUIPMENT COST AND "ANNUAL CHARGE" FOR FLUID MILK PLANTS
WITH CAPACITY OF 5,000–24,999 QUARTS PER DAY

Item—No., Type, and Size	Cost	Useful Life (Yrs.)	"Annual Charge"
2 Steam generators—50 H.P.	$ 7,288	16	$ 456
2 Hi-Flex conveyors—case and can—100' ea.	6,340	12	528
1 Can washer—3 cpm	1,744	10	174
1½ Bottle washer—TJ—½	1,039	12	87
CS—8W—½	2,507	12	209
K—12W—½	4,158	12	347
1 Case washer—141	1,053	10	105
1 Weigh can—750 lb. Higrade	1,357	10	136
1 Receiving vat—1500 lb. Higrade	1,060	13	82
1 Bottle conveyor—50 ft.	1,909	12	159
1½ Bottle filler—K-16	10,095	10	1,010
1 Tri-Flo cooler—18 inch—24T	252	10	25
3 Storage tanks—2,000 gal.	11,100	14	793
1 Sweet water cooler—5-S-10	1,535	15	102
3 Pasteurizers—CC 300	6,285	16	393
2 Pumps—Flexflo—VA	446	14	32
2 Pumps—Meterflo—PV-2M-2A	2,500	14	179
1 Shortime pasteurizer—8,000 lb.	8,685	12	724
1 Plate cooler—10,000 lb.	2,130	12	178
1 Homogenizer—6,000 lb.	4,963	13	382
2 Cheese vats—500 gal.	2,528	18	140
1 Culture cabinet	60	16	4
1 Separator—No. 272-A	4,600	13	354
1 Clarifier—No. 266-C	3,725	12	310
1 Tester—TD-12	265	14	19
1 Surge vat—300 gal.	1,035	14	74
Total	$88,659	13.3	$7,002
Per quart handled daily*	$4.43		$0.35

Where entire output is packaged in paper, the washers, fillers, and bottle conveyors are omitted and the following factors apply:

Total—original cost	$68,951		
Total—annual charge			$5,190
Per quart daily	3.45		0.26

* Based on average of 20,000 quarts per day.

for individual plants, management could estimate the potential annual industry purchases in a territory by type of plant (fluid milk, ice cream, or butter, etc.) or by individual pieces of equipment in any area of the country or for the United States as a whole.

TABLE 2

"Annual Charges" for Dairy Product Plants of Various Sizes
per Daily Unit of Product*

| | Machinery | | Supplies§ | |
Plant—Type and Size	All Glass†	No Glass‡	Including Container	Excluding Container
Fluid milk—quarts per day				
0–999	$0.65	$0.43	$4.23	$0.34
1,000–4,999	0.48	0.37		
5,000–24,999	0.35	0.26		
25,000–49,999	0.28	0.20		
50,000 and over	0.23	0.15		
Ice cream—gallons per year				
0–49,999	N.A.	0.024	0.049	0.0018
50,000–199,999	N.A.	0.015		
200,000–499,999	N.A.	0.011		
500,000–999,999	N.A.	0.008		
1,000,000 and over	N.A.	0.008		
Butter—pounds per year				
0–99,999	N.A.	0.009	0.0172	0.0035
100,000–399,999	N.A.	0.003		
400,000–799,999	N.A.	0.003		
800,000–1,499,999	N.A.	0.002		
1,500,000 and over	N.A.	0.002		
Cheese—pounds per year				
0–149,999	N.A.	0.0048	0.015	0.0074
150,000–449,999	N.A.	0.0023		
450,000–749,999	N.A.	0.0019		
750,000–1,499,999	N.A.	0.0023		
1,500,000 and over	N.A.	0.0021		
Evaporated, condensed, powdered milk and misc. products	N.A.	0.00018		0.0006

* All factors are in dollars per year, in terms of the units stated. Thus, $0.34 multiplied by daily volume in quarts of a fluid-milk plant gives annual expenditure of that plant for all processing supplies, excluding containers.
† All milk packaged in glass containers.
‡ All milk packaged in paper containers.
§ Supply prices are the same per unit for all volumes.

Tables 1 and 2 illustrate this estimating method as it was applied to the dairy industry. Table 1 shows the itemized list of equipment that a fluid-milk plant with a daily capacity of 5,000 to 24,999 quarts would have, and the cost, useful life, and annual charge for each piece. The total cost and total annual charge figures were then stated on a per quart basis for a daily capacity of 20,000 quarts. From similar data for other plant sizes and for other products, the advertising manager developed a summary that is shown as Table 2. In addition to the annual charges for equipment, Table 2 also shows estimated expenditures for supplies, including and excluding containers. From this table it was possible to compute expenditures per year for equipment and supplies of dairy plants of any type

EXHIBIT 2

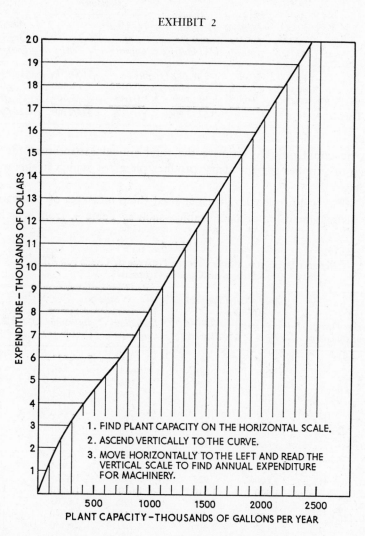

1. FIND PLANT CAPACITY ON THE HORIZONTAL SCALE.
2. ASCEND VERTICALLY TO THE CURVE.
3. MOVE HORIZONTALLY TO THE LEFT AND READ THE VERTICAL SCALE TO FIND ANNUAL EXPENDITURE FOR MACHINERY.

and size. For example, assume a plant has a daily capacity of 40,000 quarts of milk and an annual capacity of 200,000 pounds of butter and 1,500,000 gallons of ice cream. The plant packages milk in bottles. The estimated annual potential sales of Cherry-Burrell to this plant would be as shown in Table 3.

To make quick estimates of the possible potential, the advertising manager developed charts such as the one shown as Exhibit 2. From these

TABLE 3

ANNUAL MARKET POTENTIAL OF A DAIRY COMPANY WITH PRODUCT CAPACITIES AS SHOWN

| Product | Capacity | "Annual Charge" for Machinery | Annual Expenditure for Machinery | Annual Expenditure for Supplies Including Containers | | Total Annual Potential |
				Per Unit of Capacity	Total	
Milk.........	40,000	$0.28	$11,200	$4.23	$169,200	$180,400
Butter.......	200,000	0.003	600	0.0172	3,440	4,040
Ice cream.....	1,500,000	0.008	12,000	0.049	73,500	85,500
Total...	...	...	$23,800	...	$246,140	$269,940

charts he could quickly estimate the total annual expenditure for machinery or supplies for any dairy product plant for which he knew the capacity.

The Cherry-Burrell sales manager used these measures of potential to guide his salesmen. He prepared tables, such as Table 4, from which his

TABLE 4

MARKET POTENTIAL AND SUGGESTED NUMBER OF CALLS FOR MILK
PLANTS OF VARIOUS CAPACITIES

| Average Daily Output (Quarts) | Annual Market Potential Machinery | | Supplies | | Suggested Calls per Year |
	No Paper*	All Paper†	Excluding Containers	Including Containers	
100.............$	65	$ 43	$ 34	$ 423	3
200.............	130	86	68	846	3
300.............	195	129	102	1,269	3
400.............	260	172	136	1,692	3
500.............	325	215	170	2,115	3
750.............	488	323	255	3,173	4
1,000............	480	370	340	4,230	4
1,250............	600	463	425	5,288	6
1,500............	720	555	510	6,345	6
2,000............	960	740	680	8,460	9
2,500............	1,200	925	850	10,575	9
3,000............	1,440	1,110	1,020	12,690	12
3,500............	1,680	1,295	1,190	14,805	15
4,000............	1,920	1,480	1,360	16,920	15
5,000............	1,750	1,300	1,700	21,150	18
7,500............	2,625	1,950	2,550	31,725	24
10,000............	3,500	2,600	3,400	42,300	30
12,500............	4,375	3,250	4,250	52,875	36
15,000............	5,250	3,900	5,100	63,450	52
20,000............	7,000	5,200	6,800	84,600	52
25,000............	7,000	5,000	8,500	105,750	52
30,000............	8,400	6,000	10,200	126,900	52
40,000............	11,200	8,000	13,600	169,200	52
50,000............	11,500	10,000	17,000	211,500	52

* All milk packaged in glass containers.
† All milk packaged in paper containers.

salesmen could determine the "proper" number of calls to make each year on any given customer or prospect.

The advertising manager was well aware of the fact that the cost data from which the market potentials were computed were out of date. In discussing this point in his memorandum on the subject he said:

Actually, that is not too much of a drawback, since most of the time we are after relative figures and comparisons rather than absolute answers in any one individual case. For instance, what we mainly want to know is how is Salesman A doing relative to Salesman B, or how is Branch A doing compared to the company average. In such cases, of course, it does not make too much difference whether your yardstick is 32 inches or 40 inches long, provided it is the same length for everybody. Before you raise your eyebrows too far, let me say that I am well aware of the drawbacks here and well aware of the opportunity for serious overstatement or understatement of the company position relative to the industry as a whole.

As an aid to determining what action should be taken with respect to the market potential estimates, the advertising manager estimated the number of man hours that would be involved in updating the data for the dairy industry and in making original computations for other industries. He concluded that three man-months of clerical time would be needed in each case. He was unable to estimate the executive time that would be involved but knew from the previous experience that the estimating of equipment needed to operate plants of various sizes would take at least several executive weeks.

1. *Should Cherry-Burrell update its market potential measurements for the dairy industry? Should it compute potentials for other industries using similar methods?*

2. *What other methods of estimating potential could Cherry-Burrell use?*

3. *For what purposes, besides those described in the case, could Cherry-Burrell use the market potential data?*

15

WESSEL STARCH COMPANY

IN 1957 the Wessel Starch Company purchased the assets of the Gleason Corporation, which was in bankruptcy following the death of its founder and owner. The Wessel Company produced a line of consumer and industrial dry starches that was distributed nationally. Sales were made through the company's own sales force to wholesalers, large chains, and large industrial users. Wholesalers, in turn, sold to both industrial users and retail outlets, primarily food stores. For several years the company had been searching actively for an opportunity to purchase a small liquid-starch company, since the management was convinced that the best way to enter this part of the starch business was to purchase a small manufacturer already operating successfully. When the opportunity arose to purchase for $300,000 the assets of a small regional firm, the Gleason Corporation, the Wessel Company executives took immediate action. Shortly after the acquisition, the company was faced with the need to decide on the consumer marketing areas in which to concentrate initial sales effort. Because of the widespread consumer acceptance of the trade name Wessel, it was decided to drop the Gleason name and to market the new item under the Wessel brand.

The company planned to use the same consumer channels that it had used with its dry-starch products, that is, company salesmen to wholesalers and major chains. It was recognized that the production capacity of the Gleason plant was limited; however, management did not wish to undertake an expansion program until it knew more about the consumer acceptance of this new item in the line. Executives also recognized that, instead of one central plant, a number of small plants scattered throughout the country would be needed in the long run. Water was a substantial part of the contents of a bottle of liquid starch; therefore important transportation cost savings could be effected through this locational strategy.

Consumer market potential data for liquid starch were an urgent need. While the company planned to commence marketing its liquid starch in the area surrounding the Gleason plant, executives thought it necessary to commence immediate planning as to where and in what priority other plants would be located. The company's marketing research director was assigned the task of determining potentials for various market areas.

In the course of investigating sources of potential data, the research director considered the services provided by the A. C. Nielson Company and the Market Research Corporation of America. These research organizations collected data on consumer purchases of liquid starch by major marketing areas. To obtain such information, the company would have to subscribe to one of the services on an annual basis at a cost of $20,000–$30,000. Because of the expense, the research director reluctantly turned elsewhere for the needed data and finally evolved a plan whereby he would use the data contained in various newspaper studies. These studies, many of which were done on an annual basis, provided data on "per cent of families using" each brand of a wide variety of products. In the studies, a newspaper typically mailed questionnaires to a sample of consumers selected from the market area that the newspaper covered. These questionnaries asked for the brand purchased most recently for each of the products in which the paper was interested. Starch was usually included. Consumers who completed the questionnaires usually were rewarded with a gift, often a basket of groceries.

After locating thirty-two such studies, the research director grouped them by regions and prepared several tables, which he forwarded to the sales manager. Extracts of these are shown in Tables 1 and 2. The full

TABLE 1

PERCENTAGE OF FAMILIES USING LIQUID STARCH AND USING SPECIFIC
BRANDS FOR SELECTED YEARS IN SELECTED MARKETS

Metropolitan Market	Per Cent of Families Using Product	Per Cent of Families Using						
		Sta-Flo	Zippy	Linit	Dazzle	Perma-Starch	Sun Light	Bright Sail
Portland, Me.								
1957..............50.4		12.5	34.0	20.9	5.5	4.8	5.3	2.1
1956..............49.3		10.6	33.2	15.6	7.3	3.9	6.0	4.6
1955..............47.0		8.9	40.3	13.0	6.1	2.4	6.7	4.9
1954..............41.1		6.0	38.9	16.0	7.4	1.9	10.0	5.2
1953..............35.2		3.5	43.9	10.5	8.4	2.2	5.4	4.3
Washington, D.C.								
1958..............52.0		14.0	17.5	12.8	..	7.4	..	3.8
1957..............55.7		11.8	23.1	10.8	..	8.4	..	2.3
1956..............54.4		10.5	30.1	14.9	..	9.2	..	3.3
1955..............51.0		8.9	29.1	14.6	..	9.4	..	2.2
1954..............47.6		..	38.9	13.7	..	7.5	..	2.1
1953..............44.5		2.1	36.1	15.7	..	8.5	..	1.7
Chicago, Ill.								
1958..............40.5		45.9	..	20.3	..	6.0	..	4.4
1957..............37.5		52.5	..	6.8	..	5.6	..	4.3
1956..............36.9		53.3	..	5.3	..	4.9	..	4.9
Phoenix, Ariz.								
1958..............32.6		59.6	..	..	..	8.5	..	..
1957..............31.2		68.2	..	..	..	7.3	..	..
1956..............29.2		64.9	..	..	..	10.3	..	..
1955..............24.5		62.0	..	..	..	6.4	..	..
1954..............21.4		53.1	..	..	..	8.0	..	..
Los Angeles County								
1958..............44.8		12.4	6.5	..	..	7.4	..	..
1957..............48.8		12.8	5.1	..	..	7.2	..	..
1956..............50.8		9.1	6.6	..	..	5.5	..	..

tables showed data for ten regions that corresponded fairly closely with census regions. The thirty-two studies available were all for the metropolitan areas in which the newspapers were located.

One table provided a detailed analysis of the per cent usage of all liquid-starch brands found in the thirty-two markets.[1] The table was arranged by region and included figures from 1953 to 1958 where they were available. The percentage of families using each brand was reported for the major brands, Sta-Flo, Zippy, Linit, Dazzle, Vano, Gloss-Tex, Perma-Starch, Dura-Plastic, White Magic, Quick Elastic, Sun Light, Prim, Plasta, Bright Sail, and Sunny Day. Some of these brands had only limited

---

[1] The thirty-two areas covered by reports were Portland, Me.; Newark, N.J.; Newcastle County, Del.; Washington, D.C.; Birmingham, Ala.; Ft. Smith, Ark.; Miami, Fla.; Chicago, Ill.; Akron, Toledo, Youngstown, and Columbus, Ohio; Indianapolis, Ind.; Milwaukee, Wis.; Duluth and St. Paul, Minn.; Omaha, Nebr.; Wichita, Kan.; Phoenix, Ariz.; Salt Lake City, Utah; Denver, Colo.; Portland, Ore.; Seattle, Wash.; Modesto, San Jose, Sacramento, Fresno, Long Beach, and Los Angeles County, Calif.; and Dallas and Houston, Texas.

TABLE 2

Calculation of Percentage of Users of Various Brands of Starch: 1953 and 1958

Regions and Metropolitan Areas	1958						1953					
	Linit Rank	Linit Usage	Pop. 1,000's	Weight	Weighted Usage	Regional Usage	Linit Rank	Linit Usage	Pop. 1,000's	Weight	Weight Usage	Regional Usage
New England............						20.9						10.5
Portland, Me............2		20.9	173	1.0	21		2	10.5	168	1.0	11	
Atlantic............						14.9						15.7
Newark, N.J............1		31.9	466	1.4	45		..	...	....	..	..	
New Castle Co., Del............2		23.5	334	1.0	24		..	...	....	..	..	
Washington, D.C............3		12.8	1914	5.7	73		2	15.7	1594	1.0	16	

Regions and Metropolitan Areas	1958						1953					
	Sta-Flo Rank	Sta-Flo Usage	Pop. 1,000's	Weight	Weighted Usage	Regional Usage	Sta-Flo Rank	Sta-Flo Usage	Pop. 1,000's	Weight	Weight Usage	Regional Usage
New England............						12.5						3.5
Portland, Me............3		12.5	173	1.0	13		4	3.5	168	1.0	4	
Atlantic............						12.5						2.1
Newark, N.J............4		6.8	81	1.0	7		..	...	....	..	..	
New Castle Co., Del............4		5.2	334	4.1	21		..	...	....	..	..	
Washington, D.C............2		14.0	1914	23.6	330		5	2.1	1594	1.0	2	

distribution among the thirty-two markets covered. A large number of other liquid-starch brands were reported in these newspaper studies; data were presented on a total of sixty brands. Table 1 above includes data on the seven major brands.

Table 2 shows the percentage of liquid-starch users in each area who used Sta-Flo and Linit for 1953 and 1958. These two brands were chosen because they were reported most frequently in the newspaper analyses. Table 2 is divided into six columns for both 1953 and 1958. These columns contain the following:

Column 1—The rank in that market of each of the brands.
Column 2—The percentage of liquid starch consumers using each of the brands.
Column 3—The population, in thousands, of the metropolitan area involved.
Column 4—The relative weight of each metropolitan area. These weights were based on the difference in population. For example, in the Atlantic region, Washington, D.C., was given a weight of 5.7 and New Castle County, Delaware, a weight of 1.0 because the population of the Washington metropolitan area was 5.7 times that of New Castle County.
Column 5—Weighted usage was obtained by multiplying the particular starch-usage percentage in each metropolitan area by the weight of that area.
Column 6—Regional usage was calculated by dividing the sum of the weight usages of the metropolitan areas within a region by the sum of their weights. This gave the percentage of liquid-starch users in the region who used each brand.

1. *For what purpose or purposes could the data in Tables 1 & 2 be used?*

2. *In view of the purposes determined in answer to the foregoing question, did the research director obtain the best data?*

16

BORDO, INC.

IN 1956, Blackwell Manufacturing Company, a leading manufacturer of laundry appliances, acquired control of Bordo, Inc., a manufacturer of refrigerators and freezers. Bordo had been one of the fast-growing independents in the major appliance industry and held a 15 per cent share of the freezer market and a 7.2 per cent share of the refrigerator market. Blackwell management believed that Bordo's share of the refrigerator market could be increased to 15 per cent in the next five years through proper planning.

Blackwell's marketing research department prepared annually a ten-year forecast of industry factory shipments of laundry appliances and in

1956 added refrigerators and freezers to their forecast. This forecast was based primarily on the number of wired homes in the United States, since most of these appliances required electricity. The data on wired homes were obtained from utility companies and government agencies. Long-term industry sales figures were available from the National Electrical Manufacturers Association (NEMA). With the aid of these figures and various market surveys, Blackwell's research department estimated the number of homes with each major appliance. The ratio of each of these estimates to the number of wired homes indicated the degree of market saturation for the different appliances.

From data on the expected housing starts, estimates were developed for the number of wired homes in the future. The degree of market saturation for each appliance was projected ten years in advance, based upon information on future economic conditions as predicted by government and private agencies. The degree of saturation applied to the number of wired homes for any year gave an estimate of the number of any given appliance that would be in existence in that year. The difference between this figure and the current figure was an estimate of the net growth (new or nonreplacement sales) of the market between the present date and the given year.

To estimate replacement sales, data were developed on the scrappage rate for appliances. Data from warranty cards[1] were pooled by the industry through NEMA. These data indicated the percentage of purchases that were nonreplacement and the percentage that were replacement. The United States Department of Agriculture also developed data on the scrappage of appliances. From these data, estimated life spans were developed for appliances, and the number of replacements needed annually was forecast. By adding these figures to the estimated nonreplacement sales, total industry sales year by year were predicted.

Consideration also had to be given to known or expected innovations. The combination washer-dryer was an example of this. Blackwell executives believed it would eventually have a serious effect on both washing machine and dryer sales. New factors involving preservation and storing of foods would affect refrigerator sales. Trends in frozen foods affected style and design of refrigerators. Trends in clothes, the development of new fibers, and other factors were carefully watched to determine possible effects on laundry appliances. When one of these factors appeared to be significant, an adjustment was made in the forecast according to the impact the new factor was expected to have. Three successive annual forecasts, for the periods 1957–66, 1958–67, and 1959–68, are shown in Tables 1, 2, and 3.

Planning for the next year started about midsummer. At this time the

---

[1] A warranty card attached to each appliance sold was to be returned to the manufacturer by the purchaser to confirm his purchase and warranty.

TABLE 1

1956 Ten-Year Forecast of Industry Factory Shipments for Selected Products
(Thousands)

Year	Freezers	Refrigerators	Automatic Washers	Dryers	Combination Washer-Dryers
1957.............	1,000	3,800	3,400	1,363	186
1958.............	1,035	3,900	3,500	1,477	243
1959.............	1,040	4,100	3,500	1,591	319
1960.............	1,040	4,300	3,540	1,728	425
1961.............	1,040	4,400	3,590	1,883	527
1962.............	1,050	4,700	3,724	2,045	662
1963.............	1,070	4,900	3,800	2,200	731
1964.............	1,110	5,100	3,800	2,300	797
1965.............	1,170	5,300	3,800	2,300	951
1966.............	1,250	5,500	3,800	2,400	1,281
Ten-Year Totals:					
1956–65..........10,555		44,200	35,904	18,087	4,974
1957–66..........10,850		46,000	36,454	19,287	6,122

management committee of the Bordo Division would meet to establish its
goal for the coming year in terms of share of market. These figures were
applied to the industry sales forecast to get a company sales forecast.
Bordo's share of the refrigerator market in 1956 had been 7.2 per cent,
up 2.2 per cent over 1955. Plans for 1957 had been based on the company's establishing itself more firmly in its new niche and not trying for
an increased share of the market. Sales were forecast accordingly. But in
1957 the country experienced a recession, and appliance sales dropped
considerably. Refrigerator sales fell 9.5 per cent, and Bordo's market
share dropped to 5.8 per cent. Thus, Bordo's actual sales were less than

TABLE 2

1957 Ten-year Forecast of Industry Factory Shipments for Selected Products
(Thousands)

Year	Freezers	Refrigerators	Automatic Washers	Dryers	Combination Washer-Dryers
1958.............	950	3,500	3,200	1,150	260
1959.............	1,000	3,700	3,450	1,300	400
1960.............	1,020	3,900	3,650	1,400	550
1961.............	1,040	4,100	3,750	1,500	700
1962.............	1,050	4,300	3,800	1,600	900
1963.............	1,070	4,500	3,950	1,675	1,100
1964.............	1,080	4,700	4,000	1,750	1,300
1965.............	1,090	4,900	4,050	1,825	1,500
1966.............	1,100	5,000	4,075	1,875	1,700
1967.............	1,110	5,100	4,100	1,925	1,900
Ten-Year Totals:					
1957–66..........10,280		41,920	36,725	14,975	8,575
1958–67..........10,510		43,700	38,025	16,000	10,310

75 per cent of its forecast sales. The forecast for 1958 was revised in light of the new developments but showed an expected increase over 1957. Again the management committee decided on an objective of maintaining Bordo's existing market position. Industry sales fell another 7 per cent in 1958, so that, even though Bordo maintained its share of the market, its sales were below the figure that had been forecast.

In midsummer of 1958 the management committee met to determine its goals for 1959. The industry forecast for 1959 had been revised to

TABLE 3

1958 TEN-YEAR FORECAST OF INDUSTRY FACTORY SHIPMENTS FOR SELECTED PRODUCTS
(Thousands)

Year	Freezers	Refrigerators	Automatic Washers	Dryers	Combination Washer-Dryers
1959	950	3,075	2,800	850	200
1960	1,000	3,500	3,100	1,000	260
1961	1,020	3,700	3,400	1,000	370
1962	1,040	3,900	3,750	1,200	480
1963	1,060	4,000	4,050	1,275	600
1964	1,080	4,100	4,280	1,325	720
1965	1,090	4,300	4,520	1,375	830
1966	1,100	4,500	4,675	1,400	1,000
1967	1,110	4,700	4,800	1,425	1,200
1968	1,120	4,850	4,900	1,450	1,600
Ten-Year Totals:					
1958–67	10,350	38,575	37,975	11,725	5,800
1959–68	10,570	40,625	40,275	12,400	7,260

show a decrease of 1.3 per cent in refrigerator sales for 1959 as compared to actual sales in 1958. The committee was under pressure from Blackwell's management to increase Bordo's market share. The company's distributor organization was capable of handling an increased load, production had been running at a reduced rate for the past two years and could be increased without any major problems, and dealers were eager to increase sales. The committee decided to try for an increase of 1 per cent in market share, which meant that Bordo would have to sell almost 30,000 more refrigerators in 1959 than in 1958, while the total industry sales were declining.

This decision was followed by four months of detailed planning. The 1959 forecast was broken down into shipments by months and by models. Refrigerator sales followed a seasonal pattern, the peak months being March, June, July, and August. Production was scheduled more evenly, which required detailed planning of the flow of products from production to inventory to distributor.

The sales department planned its distributor and dealer activities and promotions for the coming year. Inventory capacities had to be surveyed.

The advertising and promotion plan for the year had to be determined and budgeted. The national advertising budget had been cut in 1958 to $500,000 from $700,000 in 1957. Another $600,000 had been budgeted in both 1957 and 1958 for co-operative advertising with dealers. The national advertising budget for 1959 was set at $700,000, and the co-operative budget was increased to $700,000.

1. *Should the Bordo management approve plans based on the 1959 forecast?*
2. *Was the ten-year forecast of sales a useful tool for Bordo's management?*

17

CONTROLS COMPANY OF AMERICA

SHORTLY after the formation of Controls Company of America in 1956, executives of the company realized the need for forecasting future sales. Forecasts were available for sales of the major appliance industry for which Controls Company was a large supplier, but these gave only a rough idea of what the company could expect in future sales. Management believed that for marketing, production, and financial planning, they needed a more accurate forecast of expected sales. For this purpose, a method of forecasting based on salesmen's estimates of their own future sales was developed.

Controls Company of America was a major manufacturer of control components for electric appliances. Its line included timers and solenoids[1] for automatic washers, dryers, and dishwashers; controls for heating and air-conditioning equipment; fractional horsepower electric motors; and an extensive line of switches for numerous applications. The company was formed in 1956 by the merger of Soreng Products Corporation, which had been a manufacturer of electric control devices for home appliances, and A-P Controls Corporation, which had been a manufacturer of controls for the heating, air-conditioning, and refrigeration industries. Further acquisitions expanded the company's line. Sales in 1956 were $31.6 million and increased to $51.5 million in 1959.

The company organized its domestic operations into four autonomous divisions and two motor subsidiary companies: (1) the appliance and automotive division, (2) heating and air-conditioning division, (3) the control switch division, (4) the semiconductor division, and two separate subsidiary companies producing two different types of electric motor lines. Each unit was headed by a general manager who was responsible for all operations of the unit and for making a profit on those operations.

---

[1] A solenoid is a device that opens or closes valves or switches upon electrical command.

Each unit had its own sales force, which consisted primarily of technically trained sales engineers. The salesmen generally were paid a salary plus expenses.

Sales forecasts started with the salesmen. Annually, the salesmen submitted estimates of their sales for the coming year in total number of units by general classes, i.e., so many timers, so many solenoids, etc. This information was based on the salesman's knowledge of his customers and what estimates he secured from the customers. The unit's sales staff compiled the salesmen's forecasts and reviewed the totals in light of new products being introduced, general business trends, and economic fore-

EXHIBIT 1

CONTROLS COMPANY OF AMERICA, APPLIANCE AND
AUTOMOTIVE DIVISION, SALES FORECAST FOR 1959—
SUBJECT TO QUARTERLY REVISION*
(Thousands)

Month	Sales Forecast	Actual Sales
January	$ 1,629	$ 1,618
February	1,688	1,610
March	1,565	1,731
April	1,565	1,565
May	1,451	1,371
June	1,258	1,522
July	1,350	1,258
August	1,450	1,561
September	1,740	1,850
October	1,688	1,638
November	1,780	1,578
December	1,650	1,178
Total	$18,814	$18,480

* Data disguised to prevent disclosure; ratios remain unchanged.

casts. After the forecast was reviewed and any revisions made, it was forwarded to the corporate staff, where the various unit forecasts were combined into a consolidated company forecast. The forecast for the appliance and automotive division for 1959 is shown in Exhibit 1, along with actual sales per month. This annual forecast was subject to quarterly revisions, or more often if unusual circumstances arose.

This division's sales forecast for 1959 represented almost a 50 per cent increase over 1958 sales. On the basis of this, the company rented additional plant space and set up production facilities to meet the increased demand. The sales and engineering staffs were increased to handle the increased business. The advertising budget, which was used exclusively in trade publications, was increased almost proportionately to the increased forecast in sales.

A separate operating forecast was made by each division quarterly; this was used for production scheduling and inventory planning. Each quarter the salesmen submitted forecasts for the next six months, based, as the annual forecast was, on information from customers and the salesmen's own estimates. The quarterly estimates were more detailed than the annual forecasts, being broken down by actual device number, i.e., so many No. 15 timers, so many No. 16 timers, etc., and by customers. In addition to his estimates, the salesman was required to report the source of his information—purchasing agent, production manager, or customer orders.

The quarterly forecast served not only as a check on the annual forecast but also as a check on the salesmen's activities. From many of its customers the appliance and automotive division received "blanket" orders for the year. These served only as an indicator that the customer would do business with Controls Company for that year. They were not firm orders, as no quantity was shown, and they were subject to change or cancellation. Releases were issued against these blanket orders for monthly requirements. The releases were firm orders.

The quarterly estimates for any one particular month (Exhibit 1) showed considerable variation. In actual practice, the salesmen submitted revisions of their quarterly estimates each month. These changes reflected schedule changes by customers and changes in the appliance market. One salesman's monthly forecasts for one timer are shown in Exhibit 2. Normally, the company received final releases a month in

EXHIBIT 2

SALES FORECAST FOR NO. 15 TIMER FOR A SPECIFIC ACCOUNT
(Units)

Sales Forecast for Month of:	Month of Forecast								Actual Sales
	January	February	March	April	May	June	July	August	
June............	5,500	4,750	5,000	...	4,500	...	...	...	4,220
August..........	6,500	1,750	9,500	...	15,500	11,000	2,500	...	3,970

advance. These were still subject to revision but usually held firm. Production changes could be made on one week's notice.

A salesman's forecast for any one month was checked against the orders and/or releases the company had on the books. If the books did not show orders up to the salesman's expectations, he was called upon to explain where the additional business was coming from or why it did not materialize. Also, at the end of each month a check sheet was developed for each salesman, showing the forecast of sales versus actual sales by account and by device. Again, the salesman was called upon to explain any variations, either high or low, that existed. This not only provided a constant check on the salesman's activities and his relationships with his accounts, but also served as a check on any tendencies a salesman had to be overly optimistic or pessimistic. This check sheet was introduced in 1960 as a further refinement of the over-all forecasting method.

The appliance and automotive division had eight salesmen. They were each assigned a territory and were responsible for all accounts in that territory. Salesmen were paid a straight salary plus expenses. A quota was assigned to each territory based on past business plus what increases were expected as a result of general business conditions.

The forecast for 1959 was very accurate, even with the fact of the long steel strike in the second half of the year. The forecast for 1960 did not appear to be so accurate. Although a 9 per cent increase had been forecast, it appeared after the first six months that, unless things changed radically during the year, this increase would not be realized. The 1960 increased sales expected by the manufacturers of laundry appliances did not materialize; therefore, the components or controls purchased by these manufacturers from Control Company lagged behind original anticipation.

1. *What changes, if any, should Controls Company make in its forecasting procedure?*

2. *Were the forecasts accurate enough to be of value as a planning tool?*

18

CLAYTON METAL PRODUCTS COMPANY

CLAYTON METAL PRODUCTS, a supplier of fabricated metal parts for power mower, outboard motor, and power tool manufacturers, had been looking for products that it could market to consumers. In 1958 a manufacturer of small gasoline engines came to the company with an idea for an air-cooled outboard motor for boats. Clayton spent a year in further research and development of the motor; by that time the management believed that it had a reliable motor, one which eliminated many of the problems of the conventional water-cooled outboard motors. Before committing the company to a major investment in production facilities for the new motor, Clayton decided to investigate the outboard motor market more thoroughly to determine the potential sales volume.

The Clayton motor was comparable in performance to a conventional 5-horsepower outboard motor. It used regular gasoline rather than the oil and gas mixture used in the water-cooled outboards; this gave a cleaner, smokeless operation and cost less. Because it was not water-cooled, the motor needed fewer parts—particularly since the water pump and intake and outlet for the water were eliminated. Internal corrosion problems were also reduced. The estimated retail selling price for the 5-horsepower Clayton motor was $180, approximately $60 less than comparable models of water-cooled outboards. The Clayton motor weighed about 10 per cent more than water-cooled motors of the same size because the greater heat required a heavier block and more veins for dispersing the heat into the air.

Sales of outboard boats and motors had increased rapidly since World War II. An estimated 5.8 million outboard motors were in use in 1959. Sales had exceeded 500,000 units in each of the past five years. Sales of motors with less than 7 horsepower had declined steadily in recent years (see Table 1). In 1959 the average horsepower of all motors sold was 23.7, and the average price paid by consumers for an outboard motor was

TABLE 1

Selected Data on Outboard Motor Sales: 1939 and 1949–59

| Year | No. of Motors Sold (000) | Per Cent of Motors Sold, by Horsepower | | | Average Horsepower of Motors Sold |
		0.0–6.9	7.0–14.9	15.0 and up	
1939	120	..	..	..	..
1949	329	67	28	5	6.4
1950	367	61	30	9	6.9
1951	284	47	37	16	8.9
1952	337	52	33	15	8.4
1953	463	46	33	21	9.0
1954	479	42	34	24	10.3
1955	515	31	32	37	12.9
1956	642	27	35	38	14.2
1957	550	22	27	51	16.3
1958	504	17	25	58	20.7
1959	540	17	21	62	23.7

Source: Outboard Boating Club of America.

in the neighborhood of $475. The average price per unit of horsepower was about $22.50 and was declining steadily, primarily because the price per horsepower was less as the number of horsepower increased. The Outboard Boating Club of America forecast that annual motor sales would reach 1,256,000 units by 1970.

Statistics from the Outboard Boating Club of America reflected the growth in popularity of cruising and water skiing (see Table 2). Water skiing required an outboard motor of at least 35 horsepower. Although fishing remained the major reason for buying an outboard motor, it had been declining steadily in importance. Small-horsepower motors were generally used for fishing and hunting.

The Outboard Motor Manufacturing Association supplied data that indicated that in the past four or five years 50 to 60 per cent of outboard motor buyers were buying their second, third, or fourth motors. The figures did not show whether such purchases were of additional motors or for replacement, but it was suspected that most were larger-horsepower motors bought to replace smaller motors.

TABLE 2

REASONS GIVEN BY PURCHASERS FOR BUYING OUTBOARD MOTORS AND BOATS

Reason	Outboard Motors				Outboard Boats			
	1955	1956	1957	1958	1955	1956	1957	1958
Fishing	65.6	62.1	48.5	45.0	54.5	47.3	48.2	47.5
Cruising	18.6	20.4	28.0	28.8	27.1	29.7	28.0	27.5
Water skiing	7.1	8.3	14.4	17.7	8.8	14.2	14.4	17.0
Hunting	7.3	7.5	7.4	6.7	7.2	6.7	6.7	6.5
Racing	1.0	1.3	1.2	1.2	1.4	1.5	1.2	0.8
Commercial	0.4	0.3	0.3	0.4	0.4	0.3	0.3	0.4
Rental	0.1	0.1	0.2	0.2	0.6	0.3	0.2	0.3

Source: Outboard Boating Club of America.

The outboard motor market was dominated by several large companies, among them Johnson, Evinrude, and Gale, all divisions of Outboard Marine Corporation, and Mercury, Hiawatha, Scott, and Sea King. The public apparently had been educated to the use of water-cooled engines by these companies, each of which maintained extensive advertising programs. The advertising budgets of each of the two or three largest firms exceeded $2 million annually. At least one air-cooled outboard motor had been produced in the United States since World War II, but it had made no headway and was no longer being marketed.

Manufacturers sold most of their motors direct to retail dealers, which were quite varied in type. The most important dealers were outlets that specialized in marine supplies and equipment. Some of these—about 4,000, according to one trade estimate—were marinas, that is, they were located near the water and operated boat ramps and docking and fueling facilities. Other marine dealers, probably at least as many, were located in regular shopping centers. The mail-order houses were major retailers of motors. Over-all trade estimates placed the number of retail outlets

TABLE 3

TYPES OF RETAILERS SELLING OUTBOARD MOTORS

Type of Retailer	Number*
Marine	6,400
Sporting goods	3,800
Hardware and general merchandise	4,200
Department store	400
Mail order	†
Automotive parts	1,600
Auto service station	1,400
All other	2,200
Total	20,000

* Based on estimate of 20,000 as total number of outboard motor dealers.
† Less than 50.

somewhere between 15,000 and 25,000. Most of the dealers were franchised to one manufacturer on an annual basis. A few, primarily the smaller ones, handled more than one brand. Tables 3 and 4 show break-

TABLE 4

NUMBER OF RETAILERS SELLING OUTBOARD
MOTORS, BY SIZE

Number of Motors Sold Annually	Number of Retailers*
1–9	8,960
10–24	4,920
25–49	3,000
50–99	2,000
100–199	800
200–299	200
300–499	80
500 and over	40
Total	20,000

* Based on estimate of 20,000 as total number of outboard motor dealers.

downs of dealers as Clayton estimated them from data furnished by the boating trade association. The figures are based on an assumed total of 20,000 motor retailers in the entire country.

1. *What annual sales for each of the next ten years should Clayton forecast for its outboard motor?*

2. *What sales program would be necessary to achieve such sales?*

19

SERVEL OFFICE SUPPLY COMPANY

THE SERVEL OFFICE COMPANY manufactured a wide line of office cements, pastes, artists' supplies, stamp pads, ink, ink eradicators, crayons, tempera paints, marking pencils, and ink solvents. The sales growth experienced by the company from 1953 through 1958 is shown in Table 1. In December, 1958, the president received the final income statement for the company's fiscal year ending November 30, 1958. He was extremely disappointed in the net income figure of $23,595. Exhibit 1 shows the 1958 statement and others for recent years. The president immediately began an analysis of the company's plans for 1959.

Servel, which had originally specialized in the ink business, was an old and well-established company. With the decline in the sale of conventional writing ink as the result of the popularity of the ball-point pen, it

TABLE 1

ANNUAL SALES SERVEL OFFICE SUPPLY
COMPANY: SELECTED YEARS

Year	Sales
1953.....................	$1,504,881
1956.....................	2,120,111
1957.....................	2,065,149
1958.....................	2,359,337

had expanded into other lines of expendable office supplies. The policy of adding new products was successful, and the fastest-growing items in Servel's line at the end of 1958 were tempera opaque water-color paints, rubber cement, stamp pads and stamp-pad inks.

The Servel sales force consisted of twenty salesmen, five manufacturers' representatives, and a promotion man. Sales were made directly to large retail stationers and to wholesale office supply companies. Many customers were both wholesalers and retailers. Institutional and industrial customers were not typically sold direct; they generally bought from retail stationers. One salesman handled sales to all the major chains regardless of the location of the chain buying office. The balance of the sales force worked in specifically defined territories. The entire continental United States was covered by the sales force, with some salesmen having territories as large as five or six states. The same salesman who handled the chain-store business was also responsible for export sales, which were a growing factor accounting for about 6 per cent of the company's sales in 1958.

One manufacturer's representative covered the state of Washington, another Oregon, and a third northern California. These were supervised by the salesman in that territory. Another representative covered Colorado,

EXHIBIT 1

SERVEL OFFICE SUPPLY COMPANY ABBREVIATED INCOME STATEMENTS:
FOUR SELECTED YEARS

	1958		1957		1956		1953	
Net Sales	$2,359,337	100%	$2,065,149	100%	$2,120,111	100%	$1,504,881	100%
Cost of Sales	1,403,805	59.5	1,250,918	60.6	1,289,891	60.8	914,852	60.8
Gross Margin	$ 955,532	40.5	$ 814,231	39.4	$ 830,220	39.2	$ 590,029	39.2
Commercial Expenses								
Shipping and Delivery	$ 224,137	9.5	$ 166,093	8.0	$ 165,690	7.8	$ 104,999	6.9
Selling Expense	408,165	17.3	355,420	17.3	326,657	15.4	243,846	16.2
Administrative	198,184	8.4	178,099	8.6	184,031	8.7	133,206	8.9
Advertising and Promotion	101,451	4.3	70,880	3.3	69,914	3.3	77,553	5.2
Total Expenses	$ 931,937	39.5	$ 770,492	37.2	$ 746,292	35.2	$ 559,604	37.2
Net Operating Income	$ 23,595	1.0	$ 43,739	2.2	$ 83,928	4.0	$ 30,425	2.0

New Mexico, and Arizona, but he was dropped at the close of 1958 because his volume was too small to be worth while. The fifth manufacturer's representative covered almost all the rest of the United States. Salesmen from these representatives competed with Servel's own salesmen, who were often perturbed when the representatives got orders from their customers. The management felt, however, that this competition was good because it forced Servel's salesmen to be more aggressive and because it was one way to raise the firm's sales volume quickly.

The president believed that the recent policy followed by the company in selling more aggressively in all territories had resulted in sales growth over the past five years but that, in turn, it had been responsible for higher selling costs, thus reducing net income to a smaller percentage of sales. Salesmen had been placed in new territories where there was no established volume. The firm had to support these men until they developed the market to a profitable level. The president considered this "an investment in market development." Such investments could not be capitalized, however, and had to be carried as expenses, thus making a poor showing on the operating statement. He had the controller prepare a study of the sales potential for the company's products by areas. This study (Table 2) substantiated his belief that more effort had to be expended to develop areas in which Servel's present sales were relatively low, even if this meant a reduction in current profits.

Servel sales had always been relatively low in New York City, for example. This city had previously been part of two larger territories, but in 1957 two men, Clark and Woodbury, were assigned to New York City alone. One of these men, Woodbury, was to concentrate on industrial accounts to be sold directly—a new procedure for Servel. Strand and Stevenson were also new salesmen in 1958 who were given new territories in which to build up Servel's volume.

In checking selling costs in established territories with costs in some of the new areas, the president found that selling costs ran as high as 24 per cent of net sales in the latter. In the more established territories covered by experienced salesmen, the costs of selling averaged approximately 13 per cent (see Table 3). The company did not have a uniform sales compensation plan, as shown in Table 3, but believed that the ideal plan for controlling sales costs would be straight commission and hoped that ultimately all salesmen could be compensated on a straight commission basis.

In spite of the president's belief that the high cost of selling in the underdeveloped territories was justified on a long-term basis, he decided that in planning for 1959 a reappraisal of this policy should be made. He believed that in view of the fact that the net operating profit was small, the 1959 budget must be highly accurate. The precision of such a budget would naturally be dependent upon a correct estimate of sales for the coming year. With this situation in mind, the company had started to work on the 1959 budget in the fall of 1958.

TABLE 2

OFFICE SUPPLY POTENTIAL AND SERVEL 1958 SALES

Salesman	Territory	Share of U.S. Potential	Servel Sales 1958	Share of Servel Sales
Payne.......	New England and part of New York	5.4%	$ 130,943	7.1%
Clark.......	Part of New York City	4.1	45,641	2.5
Woodbury...	Part of New York City	4.1	63,793	3.4
Dillion......	Parts of New York, Pennsylvania, West Virginia, and Maryland	6.4	52,681	2.8
Strand.......	Delaware, New Jersey, and parts of Pennsylvania and New York	6.7	70,344	3.8
Adams.......	Virginia, District of Columbia, Tennessee, Kentucky, and parts of West Virginia, Maryland, and Indiana	6.5	125,915	6.8
Pospisil......	North Carolina, South Carolina, Georgia, and Florida	6.9	125,840	6.8
Berwick.....	Ohio	5.7	80,631	4.4
Stevenson....	Alabama, Mississippi, Louisiana, and Arkansas	4.7	50,037	2.7
Thomas.....	Southern Michigan and part of Indiana	4.3	64,655	3.5
MacRae.....	North Dakota, South Dakota, and parts of Minnesota, Wisconsin, and Michigan	3.7	104,547	5.6
Herbert......	Parts of Minnesota, Wisconsin, and part of Chicago	4.4	81,751	4.4
Finan........	Northern Illinois and northwest Indiana	4.7	167,043	9.1
Ragsdale.....	Part of Chicago	4.0	251,761	13.6
Henderson...	Missouri and Iowa	4.8	110,079	5.9
Lewis.......	Kansas, Nebraska, Oklahoma, Wyoming, Colorado, and New Mexico	4.8	69,937	3.7
Miller.......	Texas	5.6	97,604	5.3
Hinit........	Washington, Oregon, Northern California, Montana, Idaho, and northern Nevada	7.4	74,852	4.0
Dashiell.....	Southern Nevada, Arizona, and southern California	5.8	84,948	4.6
Total territroies.........................		100.0%	$1,853,002	100.0%
Strother.....	Chain stores and export......................		420,550	
Naismith.....	Promotion man.............................		3,964	
5 Manufacturers' representatives..........................			78,126	
House sales*...			3,695	
Total sales...................................			$2,359,337	

* Sales made by major officers of the company.

Sales forecasts were prepared in three independent procedures. First, each salesman was instructed to submit a realistic estimate of his 1959 sales, broken down by fifteen major product groups. This estimate was to reflect current trends in the salesman's territory. It was hoped that the newer territories would show encouraging expectations.

The second sales projection was made on a product basis—a separate estimate for each of the 150 items handled by the company. The presi-

TABLE 3

SERVEL SALES AND SELLING EXPENSES BY TERRITORY: 1958

Salesman	Sales	Salary and/or Commission	Expenses*	Total Selling Costs as Per Cent of Sales	Method of Compensation
Payne	$ 130,943	$ 13,094	$ 3,000	12.3	$250 monthly expense allowance plus 10% of net sales
Clark	45,641	8,645	1,000	21.1	Reimbursed expenses and salary
Woodbury	63,793	15,000	1,500	24.3	Car, reimbursed expenses and salary
Dillion	52,681	6,720†	2,400	17.3	$200 monthly expense allowance plus 12% of net sales†
Strand	70,344	8,400	5,500	18.3	Car, reimbursed expenses and salary
Adams	125,915	12,592	3,000	12.4	$250 monthly expense allowance plus 10% of net sales
Pospisil	125,840	12,584	3,000	12.4	$250 monthly expense allowance plus 10% of net sales
Berwick	80,631	8,063	2,400	13.0	$200 monthly expense allowance plus 10% of net sales
Stevenson	50,037	6,000	5,000	22.0	Car, reimbursed expenses and salary
Thomas	64,655	9,600	5,000	22.6	Car, reimbursed expenses and salary
MacRae	104,547	10,454	2,400	12.3	$200 monthly expense allowance plus 10% of net sales
Herbert	81,751	8,200	4,100	15.0	Reimbursed expenses and salary
Finan	167,043	12,000	2,800	8.8	Car, reimbursed expenses and salary
Ragsdale	251,761	15,500	3,200	7.4	Car, reimbursed expenses and salary
Henderson	110,079	11,008	3,000	12.7	Car, reimbursed expenses and salary
Lewis	69,937	8,392	3,000	16.3	$250 monthly expense allowance plus 12% of net sales
Miller	97,604	8,088	5,000	13.4	Car, reimbursed expenses and salary
Hinit	74,852	9,600	5,600	20.3	Car, reimbursed expenses and salary
Dashiell	84,948	11,000	4,300	18.0	Car, reimbursed expenses and salary
Strother	420,550	28,000	5,800	8.0	Reimbursed expenses and salary
Naismith	3,964	10,000§	4,300†	360.7§	Car, reimbursed expenses and salary
5 mfr's reps.	78,126	8,472‖	.....	10.8	See footnote ‡
House sales	3,695	‖	18,000‖	487.0‖	
Totals	$2,359,337	$241,412#	$90,600#	14.1	

* Rounded to nearest $100 because final expense reports were not in.
† Commission rate was 13 per cent part of year.
‡ Three representatives were paid commissions of 10 per cent; one got 15 per cent; and one had a sliding scale of 5 per cent on the first $5,000, 7½ per cent on the next $5,000, and 10 per cent on all sales over $10,000.
§ Naismith was the company promotion man. While his salary and expenses were properly chargeable to selling expenses in the broadest sense, they could not be compared directly with his own sales, since he spent only a small part of his time in face-to-face selling.
‖ House sales were made by company officers, whose salaries and expenses were not directly chargeable as selling expense. Travel expenses of $18,000 were not all properly allocated to selling.
The difference between total selling expenses shown here and the total in the operating statement is made up of the sales manager's salary and expenses and office sales expenses.

dent, controller, and sales manager worked on this forecast. A product-record card showing production by months for each item for the past three years was analyzed. A projection was then made for each month of the entire coming year. In making this projection the historical record was first considered and then modified by knowledge of industry conditions with respect to the specific item. Long-term trends in demand and competitive conditions were considered. For example, heavy sales promotions in the previous year, or price cutting that resulted in the dumping of unusually large supplies on the market, were factors which would affect sales in the following year. Upon completion of this analysis, all product forecasts were converted from units to sales dollars.

The third sales projection was made at a round-table discussion among the president, sales manager, controller, and several of the older, more experienced salesmen who represented widely separated geographical areas. At this conference, 1959 sales were forecast for each of the fifteen product groups: (1) writing ink, (2) stamp pads, (3) stamping ink, (4) paste, (5) gums and thinners, (6) cements, (7) tempera paints, (8) solvent, (9) ink eradicator, (10) artists' supplies, (11) indelible inks, (12) shipping supplies, (13) laundry-marking pens, (14) crayons and pens, and (15) specials. All Servel products were classified in one of these categories. Each group was considered as a unit, and dollar volume was estimated for the coming year from data on past sales, current trends, economic conditions, and any other information possessed by the salesmen. The estimated dollar sales of each group were then added to give a total company sales estimate.

The three independently achieved sales forecasts for each of the fifteen product groups were then considered and a "best" forecast selected. The three forecasts for writing ink, for example, were $240,000, $245,000, and $250,000. Since sales of writing ink had been declining, the conservative lower estimate was taken. On the other hand, the forecasts for tempera paints were $290,000, $300,000, and $327,000. Since this was a growing product line with Servel, the highest estimate was chosen. The total of the product group forecasts was $2,500,000. Since this represented an increase over 1958, but still seemed to be readily attainable, it was set as the company's sales forecast for 1959. This total was then broken down by salesmen on the basis of their forecasts and past performances (see Exhibit 2).

Next the controller was instructed to prepare the expense budget for the year based upon this level of sales. The most important selling expenses—those involving salesmen's salaries and/or commissions and traveling expenses—were projected, based upon the tentative sales volume expected from each salesman (see Exhibit 2). All other items of expense were also estimated and a forecast income and expense statement prepared (Exhibit 3).

The president directed that this statement be prepared based upon three different sales levels. In addition to a statement based on the pro-

EXHIBIT 2

FORECAST OF SALES AND SELLING COSTS BY SALESMAN: 1959

Salesman	Forecast Sales	Forecast Selling Costs	
		Salary and/or Commission	Expenses
Payne......................	$ 130,000	$ 13,000	$ 3,000
Clark......................	75,000	11,000	2,500
Woodbury..................	70,000	16,000	2,500
Dillion.....................	*	*	*
Strand.....................	74,000	8,000	5,500
Adams.....................	135,000	13,000	3,000
Pospisil....................	135,000	13,500	3,000
Berwick†...................	130,000	9,000	2,400
Stevenson..................	65,000	6,000	4,200
Thomas....................	80,000	9,600	4,000
MacRae....................	108,000	10,800	2,400
Herbert....................	80,000	8,700	4,000
Finan......................	182,500	13,000	3,000
Ragsdale...................	263,000	16,500	3,800
Henderson..................	125,000	12,500	3,000
Lewis‡.....................	90,000	9,900	2,400
Miller.....................	90,000	9,000	5,000
Hinit......................	85,000	10,000	5,600
Dashiell....................	95,000	11,500	4,000
Strother...................	450,000	36,000	6,600
Naismith...................	§	10,000	4,500
4 mfr's reps‖...............	75,000	7,500	.....
House sales**..............	5,000	†	12,000
Total................	$2,542,500	$255,000	$86,400
Less cash discounts...........	42,500		
Net Sales.............	$2,500,000		

* Dillion resigned. His territory was divided between Clark and Berwick.
† Berwick's compensation plan was changed, when he got part of Dillion's old territory, to a monthly expense allowance of $200 and a $9,000 salary.
‡ Compensation rate changed to $200 monthly expense allowance and 11 per cent commission on net sales.
§ It was planned that Naismith would devote all his time to promotion in 1959.
‖ One manufacturer's representative who had covered Colorado, New Mexico, and Arizona was dropped at the end of 1958.
** House sales would be made by company officers whose salaries could not be charged directly to sales.

jected sales of $2,500,000, he asked for a projected statement showing the results that would accrue if sales continued at the 1958 level of about $2,359,000, and for a third projection showing the results if sales should exceed the estimate of $2,500,000 by $100,000.

In order to make projected income statements for three levels of sales, the controller made extensive studies of which expenses would be variable and which would remain fixed. Exhibit 3 shows the resulting changes in net income based upon the three projected levels of sales. The president considered these budgets adequate to reappraise the problem of whether to continue to develop some territories at a high sales cost in order to continue increasing the company's sales volume.

Another use for the budgets developed early in 1959, when the president and the sales manager had to decide whether or not to take part in a

EXHIBIT 3

PROJECTED OPERATING STATEMENTS FOR 1959 AT THREE SALES LEVELS

Net sales...........	$2,359,000	100.0%		$2,500,000	100.0%	$2,600,000	100.0%
Cost of sales........	1,389,000	58.9		1,473,300	58.9	1,531,400	58.9
Gross margin.	970,000	41.1		1,026,700	41.1	1,068,600	41.1
Shipping and delivery—variable...	188,700	8.0		199,800	8.0	208,000	8.0
Shipping and delivery—fixed......	39,600	1.7		39,600	1.6	39,600	1.5
Total shipping and delivery	228,300	9.7		239,400	9.6	247,600	9.5
Selling expense—variable*.........	99,100	4.2		104,700	4.2	109,200	4.2
Selling expense—fixed............	316,300	13.4		316,300	12.7	316,300	12.2
Total selling expense....	415,400	17.6		421,000	16.9	425,500	16.4
Administrative expense..........	209,000	8.9		209,000	8.4	209,000	8.0
Advertising and promotion........	96,000	4.1		96,000	3.8	96,000	3.7
Total expenses	948,700	40.2		965,400	38.7	978,100	37.6
Projected net profit..	21,300	0.9		61,300	2.4	90,500	3.5

* Variable selling expenses included commissions only.
† Fixed selling expenses included salesmen's salaries, the salaries of five sales clerical people, sales meeting expenses, and miscellaneous other selling expenses.

$38,000 promotional program that had been presented to the company. This program had not been included in the 1959 budget. In general, the program involved a special dealer promotion on paste and the awarding of many prizes, including a number of English bicycles to leading salesmen and dealers. The president believed that this program had a great deal of merit. He planned to present it at a sales meeting early in 1959 in order to get the reaction of the entire sales force. The reaction he received would have some bearing on his final decision as to whether the expenditure of $38,000 for additional promotion would produce enough added sales to justify itself and whether it would be wise to take such a step at this time, when selling expenses were running well above the desired level because of heavy expenses in new territories.

Appraise the Servel sales budget as a planning and control device.

20

AUSTIN COMPANY

BERGEN EQUIPMENT COMPANY, a manufacturer of heavy cranes, materials-handling equipment, and earth-moving equipment, developed a special paste solder for use in its own plants to seal joints in air, fuel, and hydraulic lines. Over a period of several years a significant external demand developed, a separate company was formed, and by 1959 it was apparent that major decisions would have to be made on the general sales program.

The new solder had a definite advantage in that it could be applied before a joint was assembled. If heat were applied to the joint after assembly, the solder would make a permanent bond, completely sealing the joint. At the time Bergen developed the solder (1942), the company was manufacturing equipment for the Navy and presented the product to the Navy Department for approval. The Navy liked the item and saw other applications for it. Within a short time, Bergen had received several large orders for its solder. To fill these, it purchased a plant in Austin, Minnesota, and set up a separate division, the Austin Company, to handle production and distribution. In subsequent years Austin started producing a fairly complete line of solid and liquid solders so as not to be dependent on one product. By 1959 the new solder accounted for about 40 per cent of all sales. By this time, competitors had developed products comparable to the new solder.

During World War II there was no sales problem—demand exceeded supply and distribution was a matter of allocation according to priority. This situation prevailed to some extent throughout the Korean War. From 1946 on, however, the Austin management began work on a sales and distribution organization, looking forward to the time when the market would be competitive again. But the management of Bergen Equipment, the parent company, considered Austin a "war baby" only and refused to allocate any funds for the development or expansion of this division. As a result, little was accomplished.

This attitude changed in 1956, after Austin showed a good profit in several "normal" post-Korean years. On the basis of this record the management of Austin was able to convince the parent company that the solder business had a bright future. In 1957 Austin was given permission to go ahead and began to plan for the more competitive years to come.

At that time Austin had 135 distributors in seventeen sales districts in the United States and also had outlets through the parent company in Europe, South America, and Canada. The districts were the same as those maintained by the parent company. A salesman was maintained in each district to work with the distributors and to solicit business directly from large users. These salesmen were specialists who furnished technical advice both to direct customers and to customers of distributors. They worked out of the Bergen district offices, but sold only Austin products.

From industry publications the sales staff developed data on the total market for solder. These data were compared with their own sales figures, and it was found that Austin's pattern of solder sales by end use varied considerably from the industry (Table 1). The company's market share was higher among manufacturing users than among nonmanufac-

TABLE 1

TOTAL INDUSTRY AND AUSTIN SALES OF SOLDER BY END USE: 1956
(Millions of Pounds)

End Use	Total Industry Sales	Austin Sales	Austin Per Cent of Market
Manufacturing Industry	*354*	*31.9*	*9.0*
Electrical equipment and machinery	42	7.2	17.2
Fabricated metal products	58	8.4	14.6
Machinery (except electrical)	96	7.6	8.0
Primary metals	11	0.7	6.3
Transportation equipment	103	6.3	6.1
All other	44	1.7	3.9
Nonmanufacturing Industry	*157*	*10.6*	*6.8*
Construction	39	3.7	9.5
Utilities	22	0.6	6.6
Metal working shops	49	1.2	2.4
Transportation	25	0.3	1.1
All other	22	4.8	21.8
Total Market	511	42.5	8.3

turing users. Among manufacturers, Austin's sales were highest in the electrical equipment, machinery, and fabricated metal products segments. In the nonmanufacturing markets the company was strong in the construction and "all other" segments.

Total industry sales were broken down geographically and compared with Austin's geographic sales pattern (Table 2). Again it was found

TABLE 2

AUSTIN AND INDUSTRY SALES BY AUSTIN SALES DISTRICTS: 1956
(Millions of Pounds)

	Total Industry Sales	Austin Sales	Austin Per Cent of Market
Detroit	87	6.2	7
Pittsburgh	74	5.9	5
Chicago	64	2.5	4
Boston	41	2.7	7
Los Angeles	36	2.7	7.5
New York	35	0.8	2
Philadelphia	26	5.0	19
Kansas City	25	1.8*	7.5
Milwaukee	20	3.5*	17
St. Louis	18	2.0	11
Minneapolis	17.5	3.0	17
Seattle	17	1.3	8
San Francisco	14	2.9	21
Denver	11	0.7	6.5
Norfolk	10	1.9*	19
Dallas	7	0.8*	11
Washington, D.C.	7	0.5	8
Total†	509.5	44.2	8.3

* Includes shipments to warehouse stocks.
† Totals do not agree with those in Table 1 because of different sources and the inclusion of shipments to warehouse stocks.

that Austin's geographic sales pattern differed substantially from that of the industry. Three of the seventeen Austin sales districts accounted for nearly half the total solder industry market. Part of the variation was the result of shipping to warehouse stocks. Austin maintained a warehouse in each of four districts—Norfolk, Kansas City, Milwaukee, and Dallas—to serve areas where distributors were not readily available. Shipments to these warehouses were recorded as sales. The penetration of individual sales districts had been determined primarily by allocation to customers up to 1952. The sales pattern still reflected much of this practice.

TABLE 3

AUSTIN SHIPMENTS DIRECT AND TO DISTRIBUTORS BY SIZE OF ACCOUNT: 1956

	Accounts		Shipments	
	No.	Per Cent	Millions of lbs.	Per Cent
DIRECT SALES				
Under 1,000 lbs.	302	44	0.056	0.3
1,000–1,999	129	19	0.374	2
5,000–9,999	44	6	0.374	2
10,000–19,999	48	7	0.561	3
20,000–49,999	68	10	2.151	11.5
50,000–99,999	42	6	2.618	14
Over 100,000	47	7	12.529	67
SALES TO DISTRIBUTORS				
Under 20,000 lbs.	122	52	0.714	3
20,000–49,999	42	18	1.666	7
50,000–99,999	22	9	1.904	8
100,000–249,999	24	10	4.403	18.5
250,000–499,999	17	7	7.616	32
Over 500,000	8	3.4	7.378	31

Industry data showed that 54 per cent of all sales were made through distributors, while 46 per cent were made direct to end users. Austin's pattern was almost the same, 56 per cent through distributors and 44 per cent direct. Austin's policy was to attempt to sell direct to end users who purchased 50,000 pounds or more annually, even though in many cases this volume was bought from several suppliers. The percentage sold through distributors was exaggerated in those districts where shipments of solder were made to warehouse stocks, because these shipments were recorded as sales to distributors, although much of the warehouse sales were made direct to small users in the area. Actually, the warehouses were essentially sales branches. Sales analysis showed further that 81 per cent of the total tonnage of solder sold direct by Austin in 1956 went to eighty-nine accounts buying 50,000 pounds or more. These eighty-nine accounts represented only 13 per cent of the total direct accounts. The same pattern existed in sales to distributors where 82 per cent of the company's shipments went to 21 per cent of the distributors, all of whom purchased 100,000 pounds or more annually. Solder prices averaged about 10 cents a pound, so that a distributor handling less than 100,000 pounds accounted for less than $10,000 in sales. Table 3 shows the direct and distributor sales patterns.

Data on the sales of solder to different types and sizes of firms were obtained from trade publications and from Austin's own sales records. From these data, estimates were made of the potential sales of solder to

TABLE 4

NUMBER OF DIRECT SALES PROSPECTS AND POTENTIALS FOR DIRECT SALES
AND DISTRIBUTOR SALES BY SALES DISTRICT
(Millions of pounds)

Sales District	Number of Direct Sales Prospects	Direct Sales			Distributor Sales		
		Est. Poten-tial	Austin	Austin Per Cent of Potential	Est. Poten-tial	Austin	Austin Per Cent of Potential
New York	127	16.3	0.4	2.4	18.8	0.4	2.1
Boston	195	18.9	1.1	5.8	21.8	1.6	7.3
Los Angeles	211	16.8	2.2	13.1	19.5	0.5	2.6
Detroit	271	40.5	2.3	5.7	46.9	3.9	8.3
Pittsburgh	297	34.1	2.6	7.6	39.4	1.3	3.3
Chicago	150	29.6	1.2	4.1	34.4	1.4	4.1
Minneapolis	86	8.1	1.9	23.5	9.4	1.1	11.7
Dallas	25	3.2	0.2	6.2	3.8	0.6	15.8
San Francisco	36	6.3	2.4	38.1	7.4	0.5	6.8
Seattle	19	7.9	0.1	12.7	9.2	1.2	13.0
St. Louis	33	8.5	1.6	18.8	9.9	0.5	5.1
Philadelphia	85	12.1	1.6	13.2	13.9	3.5	25.2
Milwaukee	28	9.4	0.4	4.2	10.9	3.1	28.4
Washington, D.C.	9	3.2	0.3	9.4	3.7	0.2	5.4
Norfolk	12	4.6	0.2	4.3	5.3	1.7	32.1
Denver	25	5.0	0.3	6.0	5.8	0.4	6.9
Kansas City	33	11.5	...	...	13.3	1.8	13.5
Total U.S.	1,665	236.0	18.8	8.0	273.4	23.7	8.7

different types of firms according to their sales volumes. With these estimates and with data on the distribution of manufacturers in the United States from the Census of Manufacturers, the sales staff established sales potentials by district for both direct and distributor sales. All firms with an annual potential of 50,000 pounds or more were classified in the direct-sales group. The others were put in the distributor-sales group. The total was adjusted to make the total potential approximately equal the industry's total sales volume. Table 4 shows the breakdown of potential by sales district and the number of prospects for direct sales in each district.

A survey was made among solder users to determine future trends, but the results brought a different problem to the attention of the company. Although Austin accounted for 8.3 per cent of the total sales of solder, the survey showed that only 1.9 per cent of the users expressed a preference for Austin products when asked which brand of solder they preferred. Jansen solder had outstanding preference, with four to six times the percentage preferring it as preferred the next highest ranking brand. Jansen was the leading brand in the field and probably accounted for one-third of the industry's sales. Table 5 shows the relative preference ratings for all major brands of solder. There were no technical reasons expressed for preferring a particular brand, although each respondent was asked the reasons for his preference. Most respondents gave noncommittal replies, such as "We've always dealt with them" or "We just like them better."

TABLE 5

BRAND OF SOLDER PREFERRED BY USERS

Jansen	32.3%	Austin	1.9%
A & T	5.1	A. A. Metal	1.6
Harley	4.6	Bondex	1.3
Mueller	4.5	Fastet	0.8
Hobert	3.8	All Others	4.0
Permafix	3.5	No Preference	10.0
Metal Products	2.3	Don't Know	22.2
Solderall	2.2		
Total			100.0%

An executive committee was appointed to evaluate the information given above and recommend specific steps to be taken, as follows: (1) build Austin product preference, (2) set sales goals and quotas for direct and dealer sales, and (3) realign sales districts. In addition, the committee was to study the future trends of the solder market.

To build Austin product preference, the committee made the following recommendations: (1) distribute the facts of the market situation to the Austin sales organization; (2) give strong support to the sales organization through advertising and publicity; and (3) make a survey of present users to serve as a guide to future product improvement.

Another recommendation was that the company establish a goal in terms of the total tonnage of solder Austin should sell in 1958. Austin's market share was 8.3 per cent in 1956; 10 per cent was recommended as a reasonable and practical goal. The goal would be distributed among the sales districts in proportion to potential; e.g., if Detroit had 17 per cent of the industry potential, it would have 17 per cent of the Austin sales goal. The breakdown based on industry sales of 509.4 million pounds is shown in Table 6.

If there were any reason why a sales district should not have a goal relative to its potential, it would be given special consideration. The goal for each district should be divided into two parts, a goal for direct sales and a goal for distributor sales (Table 7). This division was based on the national sales pattern of 54 per cent through distributors and 46 per cent direct. Both these markets were to be developed equally. In many out-lying territories large accounts were being sold by distributors. It was recommended that a policy be established for direct solicitation of all prospective customers whose total solder purchases exceeded 50,000 pounds and that smaller accounts be left exclusively to distributors.

Many of the districts would be unable to attain their goals immediately, so each year quotas would be set that would permit them to move

TABLE 6

	Sales (Millions of Pounds)	Per Cent
Austin total goal	50.9	100
Detroit	8.7	17
Pittsburgh	7.3	15
Chicago	6.4	13

at a reasonable rate toward their goals. Some districts were already over the 10 per cent goal and would require quotas higher than their goals. An analysis of each individual district would be necessary in setting the quota to determine the district potential, the areas within the district that needed further development, and manpower requirements. The Chicago sales district was analyzed as an example (Table 8).

It was recommended that each area be further analyzed by class of user so that the company could tell more precisely the industries from

TABLE 7

	Sales (Millions of Pounds)		
	District Total	Direct	Distributors
Total company	50.9	23.4	27.5
Detroit	8.7	4.0	4.7
Pittsburgh	7.3	3.4	3.9
Chicago	6.4	3.0	3.4

which additional business should come. The company could provide each district with a detailed list of accounts that should be solicited. The committee further recommended that in the future a refinement of the market analysis be worked out on the basis of type of solder used. It also recommended that the company consider methods of realigning sales districts so that all would be approximately equal. The committee believed that it was desirable to divide the sales districts so that each would have a sales goal of between 2 and 3 million pounds annually.

The conclusion was reached that in the long term the demand for solder would remain fairly constant, with possibly a slight downward

TABLE 8

EXAMPLE OF BREAKDOWN OF SALES GOALS IN CHICAGO DISTRICT
(Millions of Pounds)

	Industry Total	Direct Sales			Distributor Sales		
		Industry	Austin Goal	Austin 1956 Shipments	Industry	Austin Goal	Austin 1956 Shipments
Total district	63.9	29.3	2.93	1.2	34.6	3.46	1.36
Chicago	41.9	19.2	1.90	1.1	22.7	2.27	0.83
Gary	7.2	3.3	0.30	0.1	3.9	0.39	0.41
Hammond	3.3	1.5	0.15	..	1.8	0.18	...
Waukegan	3.2	1.5	0.15	..	1.7	0.17	...
Rockford	2.7	1.2	0.12	..	1.5	0.15	0.01
Aurora	2.0	0.9	0.01	..	1.1	0.11	...
Peoria	1.4	0.7	0.07	..	0.7	0.07	0.05
Springfield	0.8	0.4	0.04	..	0.4	0.04	0.01
Elgin	0.7	0.3	0.03	..	0.4	0.04	0.04
Other areas	0.7	0.3	0.03	..	0.4	0.04	0.01

trend. New materials, such as plastic pipe, and new methods, such as printed circuits in the electrical industry, would have a noticeable effect on the solder market, but little change was expected in the next ten years. The demand for solder was closely tied to the demand for durable goods, which was expected to have a long-term upward trend. This trend would offset any loss resulting from new innovations during the next ten years.

1. *Are the committee's recommendations sound?*
2. *Are the sales goals and quotas valid and useful?*

21

WISCONSIN DOOR COMPANY

THE WISCONSIN DOOR COMPANY manufactured a line of aluminum combination screen and storm doors and windows. The primary market area for its product was limited to the Middle West and the Northeast; local competitive conditions, freight costs, and climatic factors made it uneconomical for the company to sell the line in the western or southern regions of the country. During the first four years of its existence, the company's sales grew rapidly, but in the fifth year there was a drop. The management became concerned and retained a consultant to analyze its marketing program.

The character and design of Wisconsin Door's products restricted the end-use market primarily to single- or two-family residential housing units; there was virtually no market for the line in either commercial or industrial building construction. Retail prices ranged from $31.50 for standard doors to $74.50 for sliding-door types and from $28.00 to $56.00 for windows. Even though its product was of excellent quality and enjoyed a distinct price advantage over competing makes, Wisconsin Door faced vigorous competition from several larger firms and occupied a relatively minor position in the industry. Nevertheless, there were many smaller firms in the industry. The company employed no direct salesmen of its own. In the past most selling activities had been handled by the president of the company, but his selling activities had been sharply curtailed as administrative demands took more of his time. The company was handicapped by a limited working capital position and a rather narrow profit margin, which prevented it from undertaking any sizable expenditures for sales or promotional efforts. While the company had sev-

TABLE 1

Wisconsin Door Company Annual Sales

Year Ending June 30	Sales Volume
1956	$100,700
1957	302,400
1958	577,600
1959	775,500
1960	730,000

eral "house" accounts, which it serviced and sold direct from the plant, it relied almost entirely on manufacturers' agents, building materials jobbers and wholesalers, and a few large retail dealers to distribute the line throughout its market territory. Retailer margins averaged about 50 per cent, and wholesale margins about 20 per cent.

Sales of the company had shown a consistent growth between 1955, when the business was started, and 1959, as shown in Table 1. Sales for 1960, however, declined to $730,000, and the company became concerned about its future.

At this point, the management decided to engage the services of a marketing consultant to examine the company's sales and marketing program and recommend a course of action. The consultant found the following situations in the company that he thought needed correction:

1. It had no established sales or marketing objectives.
2. It had little or no knowledge of the market potential of its territory upon which to base sound sales objectives.
3. Sales coverage of the market area was spotty and lacked co-ordination.
4. There was overlapping and duplication of distributive facilities and responsibilities. Some territories were covered by three types of distributors. None of the territories were clearly defined.
5. Almost 30 per cent of the company's business was concentrated with manufacturers of prefabricated homes, some of whom were diminishing in importance and were becoming poor credit risks.

6. Over 50 per cent of the company's total sales were concentrated in seven major accounts, two of which could not be counted on for much future business.

Based on his study and analysis of the situation, the consultant felt that two major factors were primarily responsible for Wisconsin Door's marketing problem: (*a*) an apparent lack of long-range sales and market planning and (*b*) a lack of full-time responsibility for sales and marketing management. The following recommendations are extracted from the consultant's report:

I. Establish annual sales objectives covering at least a five-year period.

Without established goals, no company can give proper direction or emphasis as to where it is going and how it plans to get there. Sales in 1960 were $730,000, slightly under the previous year, but in view of the past growth trend and an apparently increasing demand for this type of unit, the objectives as shown in the accompanying tabulation are suggested.

Fiscal Year	Sales Objective
1961	$1,000,000
1962	1,250,000
1963	1,500,000
1964	1,750,000
1965	2,000,000

These goals may not be attainable and should not be regarded as necessarily rigid objectives, but they do provide targets for which to aim.

II. Realign sales and distribution territories in relation to sales objectives and market potentials.

It is recommended that the company establish at least sixteen clearly defined sales territories in the northeast and middle-west regions of the United States, as shown in Exhibit 1. The suggested territorial alignment insures that all the company's principal market areas and major building centers are covered by some form of distributor representation. Table 2 shows the estimated industry market potential for each territory in the fiscal year 1961 (see Appendix A for method of computing potentials) and the share assigned to each territory. Some problems in distributor relationships may be created by re-aligning territories, but it is felt that it will aid the long-term development of the company.

III. Once territories are fixed, grant each distributor an exclusive territorial franchise.

Distributors should be given full responsibility for developing and servicing both old and new accounts in their territories. To achieve this, they must have company support against territorial encroachment by others, including the

TABLE 2

ESTIMATES OF TOTAL MARKET AND COMPANY SALES POTENTIALS,
BY SUGGESTED SALES AND DISTRIBUTION TERRITORIES

Territory	Estimated Industry Market Potential		Estimated Wisconsin Door Potential*
1.............................	$ 3,300,000	6.2%	$ 62,000
2.............................	9,756,000	18.3	183,000
3.............................	3,376,000	6.3	63,000
4.............................	3,148,000	5.9	59,000
5.............................	848,000	1.6	16,000
6.............................	1,236,000	2.3	23,000
7.............................	1,140,000	2.2	22,000
8.............................	3,396,000	6.4	64,000
9.............................	3,572,000	6.7	67,000
10.............................	6,244,000	11.7	117,000
11.............................	8,492,000	16.0	160,000
12.............................	2,192,000	4.1	41,000
13.............................	2,312,000	4.3	43,000
14.............................	968,000	1.8	18,000
15.............................	1,964,000	3.7	37,000
16.............................	1,324,000	2.5	25,000
	$53,268,000	100.0%	$1,000,000

* Wisconsin Door territory potentials computed by applying percentage of total market potential in an area to the firm's estimated total sales of $1,000,000.
Source: Appendix A.

company itself. For this reason, it is recommended that the company eliminate, insofar as possible, "house" accounts and turn these over to distributors. If a direct sale is made in a distributor's territory, it might be advisable to consider paying the distributor a token commission on this business.

IV. Select as territorial representatives those organizations best equipped, in terms of manpower and facilities, to sell and service a given territory effectively.

It is more important to get a distributor who can do the best sales job in a territory than to aim for a specific type of distributor. In some territories, a manufacturer's agent may be the best outlet; in others, a building materials wholesaler or even a dealer. In any case, the company should attempt to line up distributors who have a good following in their territory and who can perform the functions of stocking and delivery.

At this stage no attempt should be made to build up a direct sales organization. None of the suggested territories has a potential now that is sufficient to support direct salesmen.

V. Employ a full-time sales and marketing manager as soon as possible.

The absence of personnel to assume responsibility for over-all sales and marketing administration represents a major organizational weakness. A full-time sales manager should be hired to assume this responsibility. The man hired should have experience in sales management and should probably be between 35 and 50 years of age. His experience should include some connection with the building materials or hardware industry. A man of the caliber needed will probably require an income between $20,000 and $25,000. The base salary should range between $15,000 and $18,000 a year, with an incentive bonus scale added as follows: one-half of 1 per cent of all sales up to $750,000, 1 per cent of sales from $750,000 to $1,500,000, and 2 per cent of sales over $1,500,000. The company would also pay all business expenses. It may be wise to consider a profit-sharing arrangement in lieu of the bonus.

VI. Plan and develop a continuous, effective advertising program.

Occasional mailings of descriptive material to distributors and dealers and a few infrequent ads in leading building materials trade papers are insufficient to do an effective promotional job. Distributors and dealers need support from an effectively planned and continuous advertising program, even if it is of relatively modest proportions.

The company should also give consideration to providing distributors and dealers with more effective sales aids. Literature now being used seems to be little more than a price list. A true sales promotion piece should be more

EXHIBIT 1

RECOMMENDED SALES TERRITORIES

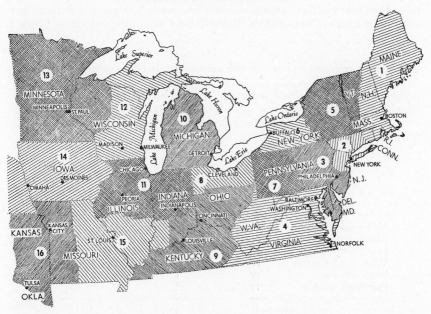

descriptive of the products and their features. Another possible merchandising aid would be the placing of a demonstrator model with each distributor and dealer. The company should also endeavor to promote brief sales demonstrations and training programs with distributors and dealers.

VII. Step up exhibiting activity.

Even though the company does not sell nationally, it should consider exhibiting at the National Association of Home Builders and other national trade shows. This would supplement the company's exhibits at regional jobber and dealer shows, and would add some prestige value and support to the entire promotion program.

APPENDIX A

METHOD USED IN DEVELOPING ESTIMATES OF MARKET POTENTIAL FOR ALUMINUM COMBINATION DOORS AND WINDOWS

Step 1

An estimate was first developed of the residential building activity in each of the 99 metropolitan trading areas in the northeast and midwest regions of the United States. A similar estimate was developed for the nonmetropolitan areas. This information was available from statistics on building permits issued. Because building permit activity fluctuated widely from year to year, a seven-year average for each area was computed as a base for subsequent projections.

Step 2

The data developed in Step 1 included both single- and multiple-type dwelling units. Since Wisconsin Door's products were primarily for single or double residential units, it was necessary to eliminate multiple-type structures housing more than two families. This adjustment was made by applying regional percentage estimates of one- and two-family structures to the estimates of Step 1.

Step 3

The next step was to estimate the number of dwelling units that would use screen and storm doors and windows. These data were available from a dealer panel study of sales for new construction made by *Building Supply News*. Although these data represented dealer figures only, they might reasonably be expected to follow those of the industry in general. The estimates for this were as follows:

Region	Estimated Per Cent of New One- and Two-Family Structures Using Screen and Storm Doors and Windows
New England	85
Middle Atlantic	70
East North Central	80
West North Central	80
South Atlantic	60
East South Central	70

Step 4

The next step was to estimate the number of dwelling units derived from Step 3 that would use aluminum combination storm and screen doors and windows. Data were available from the Bureau of Labor Statistics on the number of combination units installed in one- and two-family dwelling units in the first quarters of 1954–55–56 as a percentage of dwelling units using screen and storm doors and windows. These data showed a trend toward increased use of aluminum units. Projection of this trend indicates the following usages in market areas under study:

Region	Estimated Dwelling Units Using Aluminum Combination Doors as Per Cent of Total Dwelling Units Using Storm and Screen Doors and Windows
New England	50
Middle Atlantic	45
East North Central	45
West North Central	50
South Atlantic	40
East South Central	35

Step 5

From the data in Step 4 it was possible to develop a total market potential in dollar volume for each territory. By applying the percentages in Step 3 to get the total dwelling units using storm and screen doors and windows, then the percentage in Step 4 to get the number using aluminum combination doors, and multiplying by two (the average number of doors per unit), an estimate of the total units of aluminum combination doors used was derived. Multiplying this by the average manufacturer's price ($23.50) gave the territory door potential for all manufacturers. The trade estimates that four combination windows are sold for each door. Therefore, the total number of door units was multiplied by 4 and then multiplied by the average manufacturer's price for windows ($16.00) to get the territory window potential.

Step 6

A survey of dealers showed that, on the average, they sold an amount of aluminum combination doors and windows for replacement on existing dwelling units equal to what they sold for new construction. On this basis, the total potential of a territory was doubled.

The entire procedure for estimating market potential is illustrated for the St. Louis metropolitan area in Exhibit 2.

EXHIBIT 2

ESTIMATE OF TOTAL MARKET POTENTIAL FOR ALUMINUM COMBINATION DOORS AND WINDOWS: ST. LOUIS METROPOLITAN AREA

Step 1

New dwelling units authorized by local building permits issued:

1953	7,842
1954	10,234
1955	11,483
1956	9,947
1957	6,929
1958	10,547
1959	12,504
Total	69,486
7-yr. average	9,947

Step 2

Estimate of one- and two-family dwelling units: (9,927 × regional per cent of 89), 8,835.

Step 3

Estimate of one- and two-family dwelling units using storm and screen doors and windows: (8,835 × regional per cent of 80 for West North Central region), 7,068.

Step 4

Estimate of number of dwelling units using aluminum combination doors and windows: (7,068 × regional per cent of 50), 3,534.

Step 5

Estimated manufacturers' sales potential for aluminum combination doors and windows for new dwelling units: (3,534 × 2 × $23.50), $166,098; (3,534 × 2 × 4 × $16.00), $452,352; total, $618,450.

Step 6

Estimated manufacturers' sales potentials for replacement sales (equal to sales for new construction), $618,450.

Total potential of area (sum of steps 5 and 6), $1,236,900.

Should the Wisconsin Door Company adopt the consultant's report?

Planning to Achieve Marketing Objectives

AFTER the firm's market niche has been determined, its needs specified, and its resources appraised realistically, the next step is to plan the overall strategies that will, over the foreseeable future, maximize profits. This calls for an understanding of how the market will respond to inputs, which are largely comprised of the uniqueness of the product and the assortment in the product line; the activities of the company's channels of distribution; the extent of the firm's advertising and the imagination reflected in it; the size, judgment, and aggressiveness of the sales force; and the price or prices set. These major strategies are broad areas within which many precise decisions must be effected. In most companies one or a few of these areas are determined to be most important and are emphasized, but in every case they must all be considered—both separately and in their interrelationships.

Relatively little has been written on the problems of planning in the marketing field. In part, this paucity of information is a reflection of the fact that only recently have many firms changed from a sales organization to a full-fledged marketing operation. Extensive planning also usually depends to a great extent on the existence of a marketing research unit to gather facts from which alternative courses of action can be identified and analyzed. The growth of marketing research has come largely since the end of World War II.

One reason for a lack of formal planning in marketing is that this job is typically conceived to be the prerogative of the senior marketing line executive. In many cases this individual does not possess either the skills or the temperament to be a good planner. Planning calls for skills from many disciplines, not the least of which comes from the quantitative area. Temperamentally, the chief marketing executive is action oriented and is not an individual who "meditates" over a variety of alternatives. Even if he were so constituted, he would hardly have the uninterrupted time necessary to set down a detailed plan in writing.

Marketing planning has been done largely by staff personnel, usually those assigned to the marketing research unit. Really effective planning can be done only by a team comprised of both line and staff personnel. Not only must the chief marketing executive be behind the program, but the desire for planning must be evident throughout the firm. The marketing department is so intimately tied to the other functional areas that it cannot plan its own activities without co-ordinating with the plans of other major departments. The marketing manager must be a member of the company's over-all planning group.

Planning takes place at several administrative levels, and these individual plans must be co-ordinated both vertically and horizontally; that is, each unit must co-ordinate with other units at the same administrative level as well as with units above and below. Thus, there are a series of plans that become more and more specific at lower administrative levels. This book, however, will deal with planning primarily at the top marketing level, where major strategy decisions are made.

A plan is nothing more than a specification of the way(s) by which the firm intends to attain its objectives during some time period. In showing how the objectives will be reached, the plan specifies who will do what and when. Subordinate sections of the marketing organization develop their specific plans after they have received the broad plan for the firm. In the following paragraphs, each of the major strategy areas is considered briefly.

Product and Product Line

The company's product and product line are a reflection of how management has sized up the needs of the market segment(s) to which the company proposes to sell. Hopefully, the product will embody features that will enable it to satisfy these needs better than other available products at approximately the same price. Product(s) are typically in a state of constant change or evolution, since most firms seek to capture an increasing share of the market. Even staid products, which offer little opportunity for "improvement," are frequently given a new face through either a new package or a style change. The annual model change is another aspect of planned obsolescence, frequently a part of product strategy.

As a market segment grows, it offers increased opportunity for specialized service to subsegments in it. At some point, a given firm may decide to adapt a product to the needs of one of these subsegments, which then becomes a new market segment. Changes in production techniques may also make it practical to offer specialized products to smaller market segments. "There appear to be many reasons why formal recognition of market segmentation as a strategy is beginning to emerge. One of the most important of these is decrease in the size of the minimum efficient producing or manufacturing unit required in some product areas."[1]

In designing the product, it is necessary to have the needs of a specific market segment in mind. "All too frequently management (1) selects a group of functional features which 'are rated highly by consumers' when tested individually; (2) combines these with a style which is not too expensive to produce and is thought to be preferred by the largest number of consumers; (3) sells the product under a brand that has an image which has been built up over a period of years—partly without conscious guidance and partly according to what an advertising agency thought the image should be. And yet, when these three elements—each of them strong—are combined in the strategy, the result, as often as not, is a product with rather low overall consumer preference. The problem is this: the group of consumers that liked the features may be different from the group that liked the style, and the group that liked the image may have been different from either of the first two groups!"[2]

Product line strategy usually focuses on one or more of the following efforts of the firm:

1. To increase sales and reduce selling costs relative to sales, firms may expand the number of models, styles, and colors in which they offer their basic products. This effort may also lead to the addition of new products that it is believed can be sold to the same customers by the same sales force.
2. To make it possible for customers to buy more of their needs from one source and thus reduce the probability of competitors gaining a "foot in the door," companies may add more products to their lines.
3. To reduce dependence on one product or one market, companies may add unrelated products to their existing lines.
4. The general urge "to grow" may cause companies to add either related or unrelated items to their existing lines.

Product line expansion is not always the way to greater profits. Many companies have added new models or new products only to find that increased expenses more than offset any increase in sales achieved. Reducing the product line is, therefore, a strategy that is available to many firms. "The shibboleth of the 'full product line' is, in my experience, a major cause of American inability to compete. Typically, our manufacturing businesses offer a thousand 'lines.' Of these, 20 or 30 account for four-fifths of all sales and for all profits. . . . To be competitive, I have learned, companies have to concentrate on three or four products . . . that account for the overwhelming bulk of sales."[3]

[1] Wendell R. Smith, "Product Differentiation and Market Segmentation as Alternative Market Strategies," *Journal of Marketing*, July, 1956, p. 6.

[2] John B. Stewart, "Functional Features in Product Strategy," *Harvard Business Review*, March–April, 1959, p. 77.

[3] Peter F. Drucker, "This Competitive World," *Harvard Business Review*, March–April, 1961, p. 135.

Packaging, branding, warranty, and service are all important parts of product strategy and are essentially parts of the product itself.

Packaging of consumer goods has undergone drastic changes over the past few years for a variety of reasons, such as the development of new packaging materials and containers, the growth of new products, the increased emphasis on self-service, and the increased purchasing power that enables consumers to buy convenience. Packaging is a difficult undertaking, since there are many dimensions to the problem—production, transportation, retail display, and home use. All must be considered in order to produce a successful package. For consumer items, one of the most important functions of the package is to *sell* the product. A good package attracts attention, reflects the quality of the product, is cheap to produce, is light in weight, protects the product, is easy to stack in the retail store, and is easy to open, to handle, and to store in the home.

Branding is essential for product promotion. As an identification, a brand name assures the consumer of a level of product quality and may, in itself, influence the consumer's image of the product. In some cases, the brand may have a social value quite separate from the product itself.

Brand policy involves decisions as to whether to brand a product at all, what specific brand name to use, whether to produce for private brands, whether to use a family brand, and whether to use different brand names for different grades of the same product.

Warranties and guarantees are sometimes part of a firm's offer to sell and may pertain to characteristics of the product itself or to its functioning. Warranties are often more promotional devices than part of the product. A firm's service policy is tied closely to its warranty policy. Service policies frequently pertain to repair and maintenance service, but they may also involve prepurchase analysis of prospects' problems, installation, and training of operators.

Pricing Strategy

Pricing strategy is intimately associated with product strategy. The decision to produce a given product with specific characteristics to meet the use needs of a market carries with it an assumption as to price, if only that, in the long run, price will cover cost. Producers of standard commodities, such as many farm products, have little pricing independence. They must sell at the market price. Producers of differentiated products, however, may have planned pricing policies.

A firm must face up to a variety of pricing problems, including the price level for its products, the adjustment of prices to meet competitive pressures, the adjustment of prices during periods of rising or falling costs, price relationships among products within the line, and the discount structure, including quantity discounts, terms of payment, and margins for the various middlemen in the distribution channels.

Situations that involve price policy problems can be classified into three general groups, based on whether the product has: "(1) lasting distinctiveness; (2) perishable distinctiveness; (3) little distinctiveness and a few competitive sellers. The first two situations occur where the individual seller's product is differentiated enough to have some of the characteristics of pure monopoly demand."[4]

In situation 1—lasting distinctiveness—short-run costs must be compared against demand estimates to aid in determining what price will produce the greatest immediate profit. This price may be modified, depending upon how the firm estimates its effect on entry of competitors, on future sales, and on substitution of other products. In situation 2— perishable distinctiveness—a company must forecast the speed at which the product will move through the cycle of degeneration. Pricing in the pioneering stage will differ from pricing in the mature stages, since in the latter the company's product will possess few points of difference and the company will be forced to price it in accordance with competition. In the early stages a company may "skim" the market or may attempt to "penetrate" the market through a low price policy. In the third situation —pricing standard items—cost pricing will play a vital role.[5]

Channels of Distribution Strategy

In working back from the nature of the market and the product, it is usually possible to narrow down the strategy to be employed in selecting, selling, training, and controlling the channels of distribution.

The selection of channels to use is difficult because of the great number of alternatives, the conflicts between certain types, the fact that great variation exists among outlets of the same type, the large number of outlets, the variation in costs of servicing both similar types of outlets and different types, and the probability that the interests of the middlemen are different from those of the manufacturer. Typically, the manufacturer's product is but one of many that the channel either carries or may carry. This leads to differences of opinion on such matters as inventories, servicing, prime display space, price, discounts, and amount and frequency of local advertising.

In working with his channels, a seller has a number of alternatives. Frequent activities include advice to middlemen on better business practices and help with construction of displays, point-of-sale display materials, advertising ideas and materials, money for advertising purposes, and training of salesmen. Individual manufacturers may do all or none of these.

Advertising Strategy

All the major strategies are interdependent, but advertising is particularly influenced by decisions in other areas. It is impossible to determine a firm's advertising strategy without reference to the firm's product,

---

[4] Joel Dean, *Managerial Economics* (New York: Prentice-Hall, Inc., 1951), p. 402.
[5] *Ibid.*, pp. 410–56.

channels, and price strategies. Advertising and personal selling are, to some extent, interchangeable.

The complexity of the communication process, the importance of creativity, the large sums of money involved, and the difficulty of evaluating advertising results, all serve to make advertising a difficult problem. Advertising decisions center on how much money to spend, selection of and working with an advertising agency, determination of basic themes, selection of media, and creating the actual advertisements. Perhaps the most basic question is one that is frequently left unanswered—What is the precise purpose of the advertising? Most of the decisions in these areas depend heavily on judgment as opposed to scientific analysis.

Personal Selling Strategy

Personal selling and advertising have much in common in that they represent alternative ways of building sales volume and therefore need to be co-ordinated. They are communication vehicles and should reinforce each other. The advertising copy frequently paves the way for the salesman, thereby making his job easier. The salesmen may "merchandise" the advertising to the trade so as to point out the fact that the company is building and maintaining a consumer demand for the product.

The firm's personal selling strategy should be developed from a knowledge of the needs of the market and of the kinds of contacts that must be made to communicate to the market the way in which the company's product meets these needs. If middlemen can furnish this communication, the number and types of salesmen needed will be different than they would be if the sales force must communicate directly with the final customer. The character of this communication problem will also determine the relative roles given personal selling and advertising. Selling strategy may also be influenced by product service decisions, since salesmen may also serve to advise on installation, operation, and maintenance.

Once personal selling strategy is determined, the firm can start detailed planning on the frequency of calls, firms and individuals to be called on, work to be done on each call, length of time required to make a call, and size of sales territories.

A. Product

22

PARKER PRINTING COMPANY

PARKER PRINTING COMPANY, a leading publisher of guides to restaurants, hotels, motels, and resorts, faced the problem of changing its standard guidebook from a directory-type book to an illustrated book. Parker's trade sales of guidebooks were down 25 per cent in 1957 from 1956 and the decline appeared to be continuing in 1958. The management believed that this drop was a direct result of competition from an illustrated guidebook introduced by Sockett Guide Books, Inc., in 1956.

Parker Printing was one of the first printing shops started in Wisconsin. Initially it printed circulars and handbills and did some contract printing for small local newspapers in nearby towns. As Wisconsin developed into a resort area, Parker began printing circulars and guides for individual resort owners and resort associations to send as direct-mail pieces to prospective vacationers. In the early 1900's, when automobiles first became popular, Parker published a guidebook for Wisconsin vacationers that listed resorts, inns, and automobile gas and repair stations and gave directions on how to find them. This book was sold widely in Milwaukee and Chicago, but had little distribution outside these cities. In 1925 Parker published the first nation-wide *Traveler's Guide,* a book that listed restaurants, hotels, resorts, and scenic spots over the entire United States. At this time Parker began to broaden its publishing operations to include such things as business-data books and consumer-guide books. The company continued, however, to do a great deal of printing for resort associations and individual resorts and in this way secured much of the data included in its *Traveler's Guide.*

The Parker sales organization was divided into two parts, trade sales and commercial sales. Trade sales was responsible for all sales through retail outlets, which included sales of the *Traveler's Guide* and various consumer guides and business-data books. The commercial division was responsible for all sales to associations and businesses. Many such organizations bought these books to give away as promotion material.

In 1948 Parker Printing decided to make a greater effort to expand the *Traveler's Guide* among commercial users, such as insurance companies, banks, and manufacturers. The commercial division was given the responsibility for opening this market. A new position was created, national sales manager, to handle these sales, and one of the company's top salesmen was given this responsibility.

The results of this move were very successful, but not without problems. By 1957 the commercial sales of the *Traveler's Guide* had reached 1,302,000 units, as compared to trade sales of 288,000 units. The trade division complained that its sales were hurt by the commercial sales. Banks or other companies that used the *Guide* as a promotional item gave it away or sold it at half-price. This hurt retail sales in the area and also angered the retail outlets. The entrance of a competitor, Sockett Guide Books, into the retail market had further complicated things for the trade division. The commercial division still had no direct competition from other guidebooks.

The Parker management believed that the loss of business in the trade division was primarily the result of competition from the Sockett book. Parker had about three hundred independent magazine and paper-bound book wholesalers who sold nation-wide to bookstores, stationery stores, drugstores, and miscellaneous other retailers. An investigation of the sales of a representative group of these wholesalers indicated that just as many retailers were now handling the *Traveler's Guide* as in previous years but that re-orders were less frequent.

The Sockett guide sold for $2.35—30 cents more than Parker's guide, which sold for $2.05—but it seemed clear that the Sockett book was gaining in popularity. Four of Parker's largest trade outlets were critical of the *Traveler's Guide* as compared with the competitor's book. They gave the following reasons for their preference of the Sockett book:

1. Better general appearance because of the use of color and a better format.
2. More attractive and complete descriptions because illustrations, particularly colored illustrations, were used.
3. Better index.
4. Arranged by area rather than by class of business. Sockett showed all establishments in a city, whereas Parker had all hotels in one list, all restaurants in another, etc.
5. Competitive guidebook fully returnable if not sold. Parker's was not. Paper-bound book, magazine, and newspaper wholesalers generally operated on a full-return policy, but Parker had resisted this.

Parker's management committee met in the summer of 1958 to review the declining sales situation in the trade division and to investigate the possible alternatives open to the company concerning this problem. It was generally thought that, if the trade division were going to retain its market position with the *Traveler's Guide*, a book comparable to the competitive book would have to be published, which meant a colored, illustrated book. As far as the commercial division was concerned, there was no competition from other guidebooks, but there was competition with other products used for business gifts or as promotional pieces, and price was a major factor. The national sales manager thought that any increase in price would hurt commercial sales business. The price of the *Traveler's Guide* to commercial users had been raised 5 cents in 1957 to

77 cents per book. At that time, some customers objected to the price increase and threatened to stop using the book if there were any further price increases.

The trade division was not worried about price, since the main competitor, Sockett, was very successful at a higher price. The present *Traveler's Guide* was sold to wholesalers at $1.05 and resold to retailers at $1.20. No data were available on what effect a full-return privilege allowance would have on these prices, but it was estimated to be small because few returns were anticipated.

The committee established three alternatives: to continue with the present book, to publish an illustrated book, or to publish both types. The latter idea was dropped quickly because it was believed that printing costs would be prohibitive. The cost of material and printing of the present book, based on an annual printing of 1,000,000 copies was 42 cents per unit. There was little change in the unit cost at larger volumes. Unit cost of an illustrated book was estimated at 48 cents per unit on the same basis. There was an annual cost on the present book of about $13,000 to revise the data; it was estimated that this would remain the same for the illustrated book. The initial cost of creating an illustrated book was estimated at $130,000. There would be a small annual cost in keeping the illustrations up to date.

Which action should Parker take?

23

FOSTER STEEL DRUM COMPANY

THE FOSTER STEEL DRUM COMPANY manufactured 55-gallon steel drums, which it sold to the oil, paint, chemical, and food industries. The price of steel drums had risen steadily in the last ten years and another increase in steel prices was expected in June, 1957. Competitors were known to be testing fiber drums of similar size. Where they were on the market, 55-gallon fiber drums were selling at less than one-half the price of new steel drums. In February, 1957, the Foster management undertook a study of users' attitudes toward fiber drums and of comparative costs of such drums versus steel drums to determine whether Foster should begin manufacturing fiber drums.

Foster Steel Drum Company had been supplying steel drums for almost thirty years. It had ten salesmen, who called on over 650 active customers. Annual sales averaged about $5,000,000. The company had built a good reputation for quality and service and had maintained its share of market against larger competitors. In addition to 55-gallon drums, the company also manufactured 110-pound tins for shortening and lard. The shortening and lard industry accounted for a major share of Foster's volume in both sizes, and it was in this industry that the fiber drums seemed to have a potential market.

The costs of entering the fiber-drum business were estimated on the basis of facilities capable of producing two hundred drums per hour. An investment of $30,000 would be required in new equipment, $20,000 of which would be for a convolute winding machine for making drum bodies. Such a machine could produce up to twelve hundred 55-gallon drum bodies an hour. Machines under this size were believed to be economically impractical. An additional $50,000 would be required for expansion of the present plant and warehousing facilities. Present equipment could be modified at small cost to produce steel caps for the tops and bottoms of the drums.

At current liner-board and steel prices, the cost of materials for a complete 55-gallon fiber drum was estimated at $1.60. Manufacturing costs, including manufacture of steel caps and the winding and slitting of drum bodies, were estimated at 80 cents per drum. Warehousing and shipping costs would be approximately 5 cents per drum. Selling and administration costs had averaged 18 per cent of sales on steel drums, and executives believed that this was the best estimate for fiber drums.

Fifty-five-gallon steel drums generally cost shortening producers $7.00 new, but they were reusable. From companies that reconditioned used drums, it was learned that these companies purchased the used drums from bakeries at prices ranging from $2.50 to $3.00. After reconditioning, the drums were resold to shortening manufacturers at prices ranging from $4.50 to $4.75 per drum. Estimates as to the life of a steel drum varied from three to seven trips. Talks with shortening manufacturers and large bakeries indicated that there were no differences in the performance of a new drum and of a reconditioned drum. Some bakeries did not know whether they were receiving new or reconditioned drums. Only one large baker among the five interviewed insisted on receiving all shortening in new drums.

Information obtained from shortening manufacturers indicated that over 70 per cent of all shipments to the baking industry were in 55-gallon drums, 10 per cent in 110-pound tins and 10–20 per cent in 50-pound plastic-wrapped cubes. Some of the largest bakeries received shortening in tank-car lots.

Shortening manufacturers who had tried fiber drums reported two primary faults with them. First, the drums were not entirely leak-proof; grease gradually penetrated the paper and came through the sides. Second, the fiber drums' strength was limited, which limited the height to which they could be stacked in warehouses and created some dangers in handling. Despite these objections, only one of the eight shortening manufacturers expressed no interest in fiber drums. The others were testing or had tested fiber drums as a potential means of cutting packaging costs.

The bakeries interviewed expressed objections to the strength of fiber drums, as did the shortening manufacturers. In addition, bakers stated that a grease-soaked fiber drum would have no salvage value and that they would have to pay a scavenger to haul them away. The bakers also believed that it was more difficult to get the shortening out of the fiber drums. It was a general practice to heat the shortening in steel drums by applying a flame to the side so that the shortening could be poured and there would be no waste. This could not be done with fiber drums, with the result that some shortening would be left on the sides. All but one of the five bakers interviewed indicated an interest in fiber drums if there were a net saving in cost. The one exception bought most of its requirements in tank-car quantities.

The fiber drums for shortening currently on the market were selling for $3.10 each, but they were still primarily in the testing stage. One company was experimenting with polyethelene linings to stop the leakage problem and to keep the drums in a reusable condition. A tight-fitting but easily opened cap was another problem, but one company had apparently solved this with a new design.

Shortening manufacturers thought that there was a tendency among bakeries to turn away from the 55-gallon drum. Large users were going to tank trucks and tank cars, and smaller users were trying 50-pound cubes wrapped in cellophane or polyethelene. The cube had certain handling advantages, in that it could be dipped into the hot fat and melted, and the wrapping could then be pulled out. This left relatively no disposal problem. More institutional buyers were using 50-pound cubes. These manufacturers believed that the demand for 55-gallon drums would increase gradually with the increased demand for shortening over the next ten years, but in the long run the demand for drums would turn down.

Estimating the total market for 55-gallon drums for shortening was complicated by the fact that no statistics were available on the number of reconditioned drums used. Several of the large manufacturers of shortening and lard were known to use 10,000 drums a week each. The *Census of Business* indicated that in 1954 the baking industry used 764,000,000 pounds of shortening. Since there were 400 pounds of shortening in a drum, this was the equivalent of 1,910,000 drums of shortening. If 70 per cent of this were shipped in drums, 1,337,000 drum-trips would be needed to handle shipments to the baking industry. If each drum made five trips, this would required 267,200 new drums. Industry sources indicated that total production of fats and oils in the United States was over 10 billion pounds. About 3 billion pounds was inedible oils, which were purchased by manufacturers of soap, feed, and similar products—mostly in carload lots. Of the 7 billion pounds of edible oils, the largest part went to manufacturers who converted the basic product into branded shortenings for the consumer market. They bought in carload lots. The prepared mix manufacturers were another major market, but they also tended to buy in carload lots. This information indicated that the total market for drums for shortening was somewhat larger than merely the number required to supply the baking industry. How much larger was not clear. It was discovered that a competitive steel-drum manufacturer believed that shortening manufacturers shipped 3 million drums a year and that the average drum in this use made only three trips. This meant a total market of 1 million new drums a year for shortening.

Should the Foster Steel Drum Company enter the fiber-drum business?

24

GEORGIA BOND PAPER COMPANY

WHEN THE Georgia Bond Paper Company purchased a small Louisiana competitor in 1958 to acquire additional timber reserves, it also obtained a small paper mill as part of the acquisition. To utilize the 12-ton daily capacity of this mill, Georgia Bond management considered producing printing matrices, usually called "mats" by the industry. Before any final decision was made, it was decided to investigate the market more thoroughly, particularly to determine the reasons for the extremely strong position of the Mattrex Company, which held a virtual monopoly on the sales of such items.

Georgia Bond was an old and well-known company in the quality paper market. The company's primary customers were stationery and card manufacturers and printers who specialized in quality printing. Georgia Bond was the third largest in this field, with sales in 1957 of over $6.25 million. Its capacity before the acquisition of the new mill was 100 tons of high-grade paper per day.

To learn more about the market for mats, Georgia Bond interviewed a number of large mat buyers. These interviews indicated that Mattrex, for all practical purposes, held a complete monopoly on the market. The large users, however, indicated a willingness to receive a new supplier, provided that delivery, price, quality, and service matched that of Mattrex. In a few instances, buyers indicated an interest in a new source only if some price advantage were offered.

Some of the buyers indicated a willingness to split their business evenly between Mattrex and a new source, while other stated that they would not give more than 10 or 15 per cent of their business to a new supplier. Several buyers reported that Southern Paper had solicited mat business from them on several occasions but that they had refused because they doubted that Southern Paper would remain in the market permanently.

The primary reason for Mattrex' domination of the market appeared to be the quality of its product. Mattrex had developed the "dry mat," which had become the standard of the printing industry. Prior to this development, printing with mats had been done by pressing wet papier maché mats onto type held in a frame. The papier maché was then baked hard and dry and lead printing plates were molded from the impressions in the mats. With the wet mat process, there was little control over shrinkage and the paper fibers tended to limit the detail that could be reproduced. Mattrex' dry mats had controlled moisture content so that shrinkage could be controlled. Mattrex also had developed a special coating for the mats that permitted a perfect reproduction without any distortion from the fibers in the paper. These processes were a closely held secret; however, two Georgia Bond engineers had worked out similar or comparable processes that, in tests, accomplished the same results.

Mattrex' only competition was from the Southern Paper Company, which occasionally produced mats in emergency situations but was otherwise inactive in the market, and from imported mats, which were normally of low price and quality and were an insignificant factor in the market. Two other companies, Chicago Paper and Concord Pulp and Paper, had entered the mat market for a short period in 1954 and 1956, respectively, but were unsuccessful. Other paper manufacturers were known to have investigated the mat market. Some of these decided not to enter the market because of the opportunity costs involved. Papier maché, the type of paper involved in mats, required slow running of the paper mills. Unless profit percentages were higher than on other paper or there was excess capacity, this would make production of mats less profitable than the production of other papers.

Mattrex was well liked and respected by users of printing mats for its fairness, pricing, product, and service, and by its potential competitors for its engineering ability and marketing talent. Few buyers of printing mats were aware of Mattrex' monopolistic position in the market, and Mattrex did little to attract attention to the situation. Prices apparently were held relatively steady and profits allowed to fluctuate with material costs. Trade sources believed that Mattrex made a substantial profit on mats, but no actual figures were available.

The market was made up of about 1,800 purchasers, most of whom were small. There were seven buyers who represented about 11 per cent of the market. The largest mat users were stereotypers, who prepared mats for printers and publishers and large newspapers that had their own stereotyping departments. Table 1 shows the total estimated market and the seven largest buyers of mats.

The "all other" segment of the market was composed of smaller stereotypers and smaller newspapers, including most of the dailies, and publishers who maintained their own stereotyping departments.

Mattrex produced mats in two sizes only, 20″ × 24″ and 24″ × 26″, but the latter size was of minor importance. The 20″ × 24″ size was the standard size. Mattrex mats varied by moisture content and surface finish. These were controlled, however, and furnished only according to several standard specifications. No custom mats were made. The mats were sold in bundles of twenty and in cartons of ten bundles each. Mattrex selling prices varied slightly, according to specification and quantity, but sold at around 25 cents per mat.

Georgia Bond estimated Mattrex' mill capacity at 120 tons of paper per day. The total United States market was estimated at 150,000 mats

TABLE 1

TOTAL ESTIMATED MARKET AND SEVEN LARGEST BUYERS OF MATS: 1957

	No. of Mats	Per Cent of Market
Total Estimated Market.....................	39,000,000	100.0
American Stereotyping, Inc.................	1,210,000	3.2
Shorelane Stereotyping....................	780,000	2.0
Western Stereotypers.....................	663,000	1.7
Other stereotypers........................	1,500,000	3.8
Newspaper A..............................	507,000	1.3
Newspaper B..............................	468,000	1.2
Newspaper C..............................	429,000	1.1
Newspaper D..............................	351,000	0.9
Next 11 newspapers......................	3,500,000	9.0
Next 50 newspapers......................	7,350,000	18.8
All other newspapers.....................	5,642,000	14.5
All other...............................	16,600,000	42.6

20″ × 24″ or the equivalent per day. Assuming that Mattrex sold all the mats consumed in the country and that the Mattrex mill operated five days a week, the production of mats would take about 24 per cent of the firm's capacity. Most of the remainder of Mattrex' production capacity went into boxboard for several folding-box companies with which Mattrex had long-term contracts. At an average price of 25 cents per mat, Mattrex' total mat sales for 1954 were estimated at $9,750,000.

The long-term trend for printing-mat usage was thought to be slightly up. The number of newspapers and magazines was declining slowly, but total circulation was up. Many firms were experimenting on the use of synthetics in making mats, but none had been entirely successful. The tremendous investment in equipment that used mats made it unlikely that any innovation would suddenly eliminate the demand for mats.

Mattrex sold mats direct to users through a sales force of twenty-two men. These men also sold the company's other products, mainly boxboard. Georgia Bond was unable to determine what part of their time was spent selling mats. The Georgia Bond sales force consisted of six men who called on the large quality printers and approximately sixty manufacturers' agents. The salesmen worked with the manufacturers' agents in their territories and also handled their direct accounts.

To operate the new mill at a profit, assuming mats were sold at 25 cents each, the Georgia Bond management calculated that it would have to produce at more than the 66 per cent of capacity, five days a week, which was considered the breakeven point for that type of mill. One ton was the equivalent of approximately 5,000 mats. Thus annual mill capacity, at 12 tons per day, 5 days per week, 52 weeks per year, was about 15,600,000 mats. At 80 per cent of capacity, pretax profits would be about 8 per cent of sales, and at 95 per cent they would be about 17.5 per cent. Production problems seemed to pose no difficulties.

Should the Georgia Bond Paper Company produce and sell printing mats?

25

POLY PRODUCTS COMPANY

POLY PRODUCTS COMPANY manufactured and fabricated polyethylene, a plastic commonly used for a wide variety of consumer products. In 1958 the firm was looking for new plastic products to add to its retail line. One of the product areas under consideration was plastic kitchenware, such as dishpans, mixing bowls, covered pitchers, and refrigerator bowls. New plastic compounds developed in Europe had made the manufacture of this type of plastic item less expensive than it had previously been. As a result, kitchen containers made from polyethylene could be sold at a lower price than could either glass or metal containers. The company investigated the market for plastic kitchenware but was still not certain whether to proceed with the proposed new products.

Two men from a large plastics company had started Poly Products in 1947, with the objective of making a heavy polyethylene tube capable of replacing the standard metallic toothpaste tube. The tubes were engineered successfully, and mass manufacturing was initiated. The bulk of the company's sales, however, came from a few large accounts, primarily manufacturers of glue and antiseptic salves; the Poly tube was not accepted by toothpaste producers. Other polyethylene products were developed, such as a line of containers for frozen food and ice cream and heavy polyethylene bags. All sales were made direct through a sales force of seven men. Sales grew rapidly to $10 million in 1956 and $13 million in 1957.

The concentration of sales with a few large customers worried the company's management, since they felt that they had little control over their market. They thought that they would have greater balance in risk

TABLE 1

INDUSTRY SALES OF PLASTIC KITCHENWARE: 1952–57

1952..........$2,200,000	1955........$10,340,000
1953.......... 2,916,000	1956......... 12,760,000
1954.......... 5,500,000	1957......... 14,850,000

if they could produce a product line which could be sold to the consumer market. Accordingly, a consumer product program was started in 1956. A covered frozen-food container for use by housewives in freezing food or for refrigerator storage was introduced in that year. The company considered the product to be only a mild success, largely because it had to compete with cheaper paper containers made for these purposes. In 1957 Poly Products introduced an inexpensive waterproof plastic glove designed for household use. Both the gloves and the food container were marketed through food stores and variety stores. Food stores were reached through approximately thirty food brokers, who were handled by two regional managers. The same regional managers sold direct to the large variety chains.

Sales of these two products did not reach the anticipated level, so Poly Products hired Rabin & Associates, a marketing research firm, to collect some data on the market. Rabin estimated that sales of plastic kitchenware had increased more than six times since 1952 (Table 1). There was no reason to think a rapid rate of growth would not continue, at least for several years. One estimate was that total sales would be about $22 million in 1962. Conversations with other members of the industry indicated that many thought this figure to be conservative.

In his report, Rabin divided the market by retail outlets and industrial users. Over three-fourths of the industry's total production went to consumers through normal retail channels. Another 11 per cent went to consumers under private brands; this included sales to companies for resale

TABLE 2

INDUSTRY SALES BY MANUFACTURERS OF PLASTIC KITCHENWARE: 1957

Sales to			
Household users through retailers.....................$11,550,000			77.6%
Food stores.........................$5,198,000		34.9%	
Variety stores....................... 2,310,000		15.5	
Department stores.................... 1,732,000		11.6	
Hardware stores..................... 1,155,000		7.8	
All other........................... 1,155,000		7.8	
Private label users................................. 1,650,000			11.2
All other users: industry, institutions, and governments...................................... 1,650,000			11.2
Total industry sales.................................$14,850,000			100%

under their own name and sales to companies who used the product as a premium or promotional item. For example, one large soap company packaged 25 pounds of soap in a covered plastic pail for a special promotion. Table 2 shows this information.

Competition, according to Rabin's report, would primarily be from two large companies that dominated the market, Hilo Corporation and Plastics, Inc., each of which had about 40 per cent of the market. Plastics, Inc., had very strong distribution through food and department stores but was somewhat weaker in the other channels. On the other hand, Hilo Corporation was strong in variety and hardware stores. Both these firms were striving to broaden their market coverage in those areas where they were weak. Hilo Corporation particularly seemed to be increasing its market share by gaining better distribution through food and department stores. No one company, however, seemed to be really entrenched in any sales channel. The total industry volume was divided among five manufacturers and some imports, as shown in Table 3.

TABLE 3

SALES OF PLASTIC KITCHENWARE BY MANUFACTURERS: 1957

Hilo Corporation	$6,050,000	40.7%
Plastics, Inc.	6,050,000	40.7
Curd Enterprises	1,650,000	11.1
Imperial Mfg. Co.	550,000	3.7
Myers Bros., Inc.	220,000	1.5
Imports	330,000	2.3

To determine the attitude of retailers and wholesalers toward a new brand of plastic kitchenware, Rabin and Associates made detailed interviews with people in those fields. It was found that there was no enthusiasm in the trade for a new entry into this market. Chain-store managers in particular stated that they would not stock a new brand unless a demand was created by the manufacturer. In the private label, industrial, and institutional markets, more desire for another supplier was found. A consumer survey revealed that there was no appreciable brand loyalty or even brand awareness.

TABLE 4

EXPENDITURES FOR CONSUMER ADVERTISING FOR SELECTED COMPANIES

Year	Hilo Corp.	Plastics, Inc.	Curd Enterprises
1954	$221,176	$ 91,560	$41,289
1955	232,092	149,424	. . . . .
1956	119,953	202,116	66,186
1957*	102,790	140,324	15,216

* First six months only; does not include expenditures for newspaper advertising.

The top three manufacturers of plastic kitchenware allocated approximately 4 per cent of sales for consumer advertising. Table 4 shows total dollars spent for consumer advertising over the past four years by these companies.

Information was not available on the sales organization of Plastics, Inc., but there was some information on Hilo Corporation and Curd Enterprises. Hilo had three sales divisions reporting to a vice-president of sales. One division consisted of one man who handled sales to food brokers throughout the United States. The specialty sales division had eight regional managers under a general sales manager and was responsible for all sales except those to food brokers, large industrial accounts, and private label accounts. The Philadelphia region had six salesmen. The industrial sales division consisted of two men who were responsible for sales to private label accounts, large industrial companies, and government agencies. Curd Enterprises was known to have ten salesmen, who sold to 125 food brokers. Although no details were available about the Plastics, Inc., sales organization, it was known that from time to time they employed missionary men, who sold to retail grocers, booking the orders through the grocer's wholesaler.

Rack jobbers were a rapidly growing factor in the sale of specialty nonfood items through food and drugstores. Women's hosiery, for example, was sold in food stores largely through rack jobbers. These jobbers did not actually sell to retailers; instead they arranged to use a given space in the stores where they displayed their products. The rack jobbers took full responsibility for maintenance of the display, removal of damaged items, and replacement of items sold. When the retailer sold one of these items, he kept an agreed-upon percentage and paid the rest to the rack jobber.

Typically, rack jobbers obtained discounts of 50 or 50 and 10 per cent from the list price; 25–30 per cent of the selling price was kept by retailers. Food brokers usually received commissions of about 5 per cent, but this varied widely according to the services performed. General line grocery wholesalers usually obtained margins of 10–15 per cent on non-food items.

At this point Poly Products made a preliminary study of the production processes and costs involved. It was found that production was not a problem; the company was familiar with the processes and materials involved. It was estimated that an investment of $300,000 would be necessary in new equipment and facilities to produce a complete line of plastic kitchenware. Administration and other miscellaneous fixed costs were estimated at $77,000 per year. Estimates of material and labor costs were prepared on several of the most popular items. One of these was the 2-quart covered pitcher, which sold to jobbers and chains, at current competitive prices, for $16.20 F.O.B. factory per case of 24 and sold at retail for $1.40 each. Poly Products estimated that its material and labor costs per case would be $10.80. This relationship appeared to be the same for other items.

Should Poly Products add the plastic kitchenware to its line?

26

THE LIGGETT ADHESIVE CORPORATION

ON JANUARY 21, 1959, Mr. Edward West, senior vice-president of the Liggett Adhesive Corporation, was approached by the president of the Turner Research Co., Mr. John Turner, with a proposition that Liggett enter into an agreement with Turner to manufacture and market an adhesive known as Zipdry. This adhesive, a product of Turner Research, was developed as a sealant for shipping cartons and corrugated boxes. Because of its extremely short drying time, Zipdry had been found particularly adapted for use on rapid, automatic sealing machines. In addition, the product was highly moisture and water resistant, making it useful for cold storage and packaging moist products, such as fresh produce.

The Liggett Adhesive Corporation was a large Chicago manufacturer of a variety of adhesives for different industrial purposes. The company's volume of approximately $175 million was sold primarily in the Midwest and Southwest. The Paper Products Division of Liggett directed its activities toward the paper and pulp industries. Its chief product was an adhesive that was mixed with pulp in order to provide a binder for the paper fibers. This product was sold direct by the division's own small sales force. The division also produced and sold a limited volume of water resistant carton sealants of a lesser quality than Zipdry. Because of established marketing procedures, however, this group of products was not pushed aggressively and was handled practically as a side line.

Approximately a month after Mr. Turner's visit, Mr. West received a letter spelling out in detail the nature of the proposed venture. The letter read as follows:

February 12, 1959

Mr. Edward G. West
Senior Vice-President
Liggett Adhesive Company
4112 W. Grand Avenue
Chicago 10, Ill.

Dear Mr. West:
Pursuant to our conversation of January 21, 1959, concerning Turner Research Corporation's product, Zipdry, the following are my specific thoughts concerning the proposed relationship of Turner and Liggett in regard to exploiting this adhesive.

The Plant

We are at present leasing a 12,000 sq. ft. plant for $200 per month in Zanesville, Ohio. Additional equipment required for this plant is three 4,000-gallon storage tanks plus two pumps. This will bring the plant capacity to 300 drums of adhesive per month.

The Finished Product

Zipdry is a water resistant adhesive. Our costs and selling prices are as follows:

```
Sales price (F.O.B. Zanesville) ..........$137.50 per drum
Costs:
    Raw material ...............$39.04
    Nonreturn 54-gallon drum ......4.75
    Cash discount (usually taken) ...1.38
    Jobbing commission (30%) ....41.25
                                        86.42
    Gross profit to overhead ...............$ 51.08
```

The attached profit and loss sheet (Exhibit 1) shows the results for Turner Research Corporation for 1958 in some detail. Since the early part of the year was devoted to experimentation, production costs are greatly overrated. Some costs were also incurred on other projects that have been discontinued. It is contemplated that Turner's present sales price structure will be continued.

Market Potential

There are (according to 1953 figures from *Pulp and Paper*) over 15,000,000 gallons of water resistant adhesives and over 30,000,000 gallons of general adhesives sold per year. Zipdry is unique in that it can be used in applications where non-water-resistant adhesives are now used, but for purposes of this letter we will consider only the market for water-resistant adhesives. The following list of states, with their shares of the total United States market, is based on the number of box manufacturing plant employees, which is not precisely accurate but gives a general view of the markets.

1. Ohio 11.64%		7. Indiana 5.25%
2. Michigan 11.50		8. New Jersey 4.77
3. Pennsylvania 10.97		9. Connecticut 4.33
4. New York 10.33		10. Massachusetts 4.24
5. Illinois 9.23		11. Wisconsin 3.18
6. California 6.48		

In my opinion, the natural and long-range disposition of the foregoing markets would be as follows:

Chicago, Ill., plant, supplying the markets of:	*Zanesville, O., plant, supplying the markets of:*
Illinois 9.23%	Ohio 11.64%
Michigan 11.50	Pennsylvania 10.97
Indiana 5.25	
Wisconsin 3.18	
29.16%	

EXHIBIT 1

TURNER RESEARCH CORPORATION PROFIT AND LOSS STATEMENT:
JANUARY 1–DECEMBER 31, 1958

Sales			$23,341.14
Cost of sales:			
Factory payroll	$ 4,900.00		
Social Security tax	110.25		
Payroll insurance	40.60		
Containers	733.94		
Raw material	11,404.19		
Supplies	30.78		
Repairs and maintenance	331.77		
Insurance	50.87		
Rent	2,150.00		
Utilities	549.08		
Royalties	1,600.00		
Taxes and licenses	224.38		
Depreciation	1,434.72		
Miscellaneous expense	38.66		
Laundry expense	108.50		
		$23,707.74	
Less—Mfg. cost to samples	348.16		
Variation in inventory	889.16		
		$ 1,237.32	
			22,470.42
Gross Profit			$ 870.72
Selling and administrative expenses:			
Executive payroll	$ 8,750.00		
Selling compensation	7,325.00		
Social Security tax expense	173.25		
Payroll insurance	125.15		
Jobbing commissions	4,320.15		
Freight and express	1,653.08		
Telephone and telegraph	716.27		
Insurance	122.66		
Sales warehousing	177.74		
Sales expense accounts	5,048.38		
Samples	595.96		
Other advertising	100.94		
Office supplies	68.52		
Postage	22.45		
Taxes and licenses	258.79		
Discounts allowed	228.63		
Professional services	6,080.00		
Interest	3,030.00		
Depreciation	64.56		
Unemployment tax	193.13		
Miscellaneous expense	45.35		
		$39,100.01	
Loss for period			($38,229.29)

New York City plant, supplying the markets of:

New York 10.33%
New Jersey 4.77
Connecticut 4.33
Massachusetts 4.24
                     ——————
                     23.67%

Los Angeles plant, supplying the market of:

California 6.48%

At the present time Zipdry is being sold in only two market areas, Cleveland and Los Angeles. The following is a list of accounts which either are now testing Zipdry or are customers or have been customers, as indicated:

Cleveland

Horner Packing Co.
Inland Canneries
Ohio Produce Co.
Kraft
Cleveland Mfg. Co.
General Box Co.

Los Angeles

Sunkist
Valley Produce Co.
Citrus Growers Assn.
San Fernando Co-op
Export Packing, Inc.
15 other smaller packers and
    manufacturers

In addition to the foregoing accounts, we are selling on a house account basis West Virginia Tobacco Company, Wheeling, W.Va., and American Canneries, Inc., Fort Wayne, Ind. Also we have had as customers many fine firms, such as Wellington Packing Co., Harrison, N.J.; Johnson Co., Cleveland, O.; Cooper & Co., Philadelphia, Pa.; and National Manufacturers Co., Newark, N.J., which we have lost as a result of product instability. ·

Proposed Sales Organization

The plan of attack which I propose is simply this:

1. All customers presently using your own box sealants to be switched to Zipdry. I think it reasonable to assume that 75 per cent of the accounts could be switched, using only the present Liggett personnel assisted by our Mr. Miller. This would give you a fairly immediate sales volume of eighteen drums per month.

2. Carefully evaluate the large volume users in the Illinois market with a view to determining which accounts your present personnel in Chicago think they could sell with some specialized assistance. These accounts should be set up on a "house account" basis. Depending on the number of these accounts, sufficient manpower should be hired and trained by Mr. Miller to work with present Liggett salesmen. There should be one man for each fifteen or twenty accounts.

3. The finest manufacturers' representative available in Illinois should be induced to handle Zipdry to cover the remainder of the accounts in that state. Trained Liggett specialists should be assigned to assist him. Since we pay a relatively high commission (30 per cent), a plan should be introduced to have the manufacturers' representative hire one or more specialists to push the sale of Zipdry. These men would be trained by Liggett. Their salary and expenses would be paid by Liggett until such time as the manufacturers' representative had reached a previously agreed upon sales volume, then he would assume the specialists' overhead.

Joint-Venture Agreement

It is my suggestion that Liggett and Turner enter into a joint-venture agreement providing for the following:

1. Capital Contributions:

a) Turner would contribute all its manufacturing equipment, its leasehold on the plant, and the formula. In addition, Turner would sell its inventories and receivables to the joint venture for an amount in cash equal to the book value as of May 31, approximately $7,500.

b) Liggett would contribute initially $7,500 in cash to the joint venture to permit purchase of Turner's receivables and inventory. In addition, Liggett would contribute sufficient cash to purchase equipment previously mentioned for the Zanesville plant and $3,000 per month plus such additional funds as would defray travel expenses and the purchase of raw materials and containers as may be required. Additional cash may be required to bring base inventories up to an optimum amount. As soon as the monthly profits have reached sufficient levels, there would no longer be need for Liggett to make monthly contributions, since the operating expenses would be paid out of profits.

2. Division of Net Profits:

The net profits of the joint venture would be shared equally by Liggett and Turner, provided that Turner would be indemnified against any losses incurred in the venture. Liggett would be entitled to recoup such loss incurred by reason of such indemnity out of Turner's share of future profits.

In the determination of net profits, all sales of Zipdry would be credited to the net profit account of the joint venture, as would be all costs of operations, including monthly operating costs of Turner. The venture's overhead costs, including sales organization expense of Liggett incurred for the joint venture and a fair charge for over-all supervision and accounting, would be charged to this account. No distribution of profits would be made until the venture was in a position to operate with its own funds, and thereafter distributions of profits would never reduce the available cash below a minimum required for normal operations. Turner would receive a $2,350 a month management fee (included with the $3,000 operating requirement) to compensate it for the cost and expense of furnishing the services of its personnel.

3. Option by Liggett to Purchase All Turner's Outstanding Stock:

Turner would cause its shareholders to give an option to Liggett to purchase all Turner stock at a price of $702,000, the option to be exercisable at any time during the term of the joint venture. In the event that sales of the joint venture reached 750 barrels per month, Liggett would be obligated to purchase such stock.

If this letter sets forth your understanding of the points discussed in our conference of January 21, 1959, I suggest that the next step would be for your legal department to prepare the first draft of the joint venture agreement.

Sincerely,

(*s*) J. Turner
John Turner

This proposal was turned over to Mr. J. C. Williams of Liggett's market research division for analysis. He was asked to develop data to (1) evaluate the market potential for Zipdry, (2) determine the more important considerations involved in expanding the sales of Zipdry, and

(3) determine attitudes of previous Zipdry customers to a re-introduction of the product.

After a period of several weeks, during which time Mr. Williams reviewed company records and trade publications and conducted a number of personal interviews with purchasers of box adhesives, the following data were accumulated:

The Market

During 1957 Liggett sold approximately 21,000 gallons of water resistant box sealant. Of this total approximately 500 gallons was of the rapidly drying type that could be used upon fast machines. The remainder was of a low-price type used for slower and hand-fed machines. The total

TOTAL MARKET FOR BOX SEALANTS	
U.S. consumption of all types of box sealants	60–80 million gals.*
U.S. consumption of water resistant sealants	18–28 " " *
U.S. consumption of high-priced, water resistant, fast-drying sealants.	4.3–6.7 " " *
Consumption of high-priced, water resistant, fast-drying sealants in Liggett's market area	1.7–2.7 " " *
Number of plants using box machines in U.S.	21,518†
Number of plants using box machines in Liggett's market area	8,845†
Number of employees in plants using box machines	6,139,123†
Number of employees in plants using box machines in Liggett's market area	3,186,102†

* Data for 1957.
† Data for 1953.

market for box sealants was as shown in the accompanying tabulation.

The market for water resistant adhesives for box manufacture is growing substantially. This growth is coming from both a greater use of boxes in the economy and an increasing market share of the total sealant market. Water resistant adhesives accounted for approximately 27 per cent of all sealants sold in 1953. This is reported to have increased to 35 per cent in 1957. The trend toward greater use of water resistant adhesives is being caused by their generally cheaper price and ability to form a faster and better bond.

Buying Habits and Motives

Most adhesives for sealing machines are purchased in 55-gallon drums, some in 5-gallon cans. Very large users, such as Campbell's Soup, buy in truck-load lots of 60 drums, while small users order a drum at a time as the need arises.

Almost every user said that "next-day" delivery was available, but most users order two to three days in advance.

A 1953 study indicated that 74 per cent of adhesive purchasers bought through local distributors, 26 per cent purchased direct from the factory,

23 per cent bought from a manufacturers' agent, and 18 per cent from a manufacturer's salesman. (The figures add to more than 100 per cent because of multiple sources of supply.)

Most users have more than one supplier of adhesives, the number running up to five or six with larger users. Only one company interviewed had changed any of its suppliers in the last twelve months, and this was because a comparable product was obtained at a cheaper price. Other users interviewed had long-standing relationships with their present suppliers.

Acceptance of a new product by a user generally requires a number of tests, which sometimes take from three to six months. The testing of a new product may slow down or even stop a packing line. For this reason, products must have promise of great advantages before many plants will test them.

In small plants strong personal relationships often exist between suppliers' salesmen and shop personnel. This tends to make them resist new products.

Although purchasing agents have been deluged with adhesive salesmen, most are looking for new products that can cut costs and otherwise improve output. It appears that a product bearing a major brand name would stand a much better chance of being accepted for test than would an unknown independent brand.

The factors that purchasing agents reported to be most important in selecting an adhesive were, in order of importance, as follows: (1) quality of the bond made by the adhesive, (2) freedom from spoilage, (3) ease of cleaning the machine, (4) allowable speed and feed rates, (5) customer service, (6) freedom from harmful ingredients.

Competition

The box sealant market is characterized by a large number of suppliers. These include both large and small firms. The ease with which an individual can enter the field has caused the market to become overcrowded since World War II. Purchasing agents stated that they have as many as six box sealant salesmen a week calling on them, each claiming that his product will lower costs, increase production, etc.

Some suppliers have become firmly established in the market by specializing in offering a full line of sealants and related products and by applying heavy sales and promotional effort to the larger users. The smaller and less well-known suppliers often depend upon extravagant claims for their products in order to have them tested by a prospective customer.

All suppliers offer technical service to their customers both on an "on-call" emergency basis and on a periodic visit basis. The technical ability of many of the smaller companies' representatives was questioned by some of the purchasing agents, emphasizing the need for qualified box machine technicians to sell and service this type of product. Suppliers also offered to furnish specially compounded sealants for different kinds of box problems.

Product Quality

A sample of the adhesives for box sealing in the Chicago area revealed the information shown in the accompanying tabulation.

Tests conducted by the technicians on the Liggett staff revealed that under high-speed conditions Zipdry showed definite advantages over

		Coverage*		
Supplier	Product	Recommended	Actual	Price per Gal.
IN CHICAGO AREA				
Miller Glue Co.	T-140†	5,000	2,500	N.A.
Chicago Adhesives	Sealall	1,250	N.A.	N.A.
	#30†	3,750	3,750	$1.02
Cleveland Corp.	Cimglue†	N.A.	N.A.	$1.90–$2.00
Highwood Chemical	Trim†	2,500	3,750	$2.50
Animal Products	#1502	N.A.	2,500	$ .50
Standard Adhesives	Superla	N.A.	2,500	$ .50
Sun Company	N.A.	N.A.	1,800	$ .45
Johnson Products	Loseal†	N.A.	9,000	$3.50
Western Glue	#8LA†	N.A.	1,800	$1.55
IN EASTERN PLANTS THAT WERE FORMERLY TURNER ACCOUNTS				
Penn Products	Mikro Seal†	N.A.	1,800	$1.46
Animal Products	#1421†	N.A.	2,500	$ .55
Elm Chemical	N.A.	N.A.	5,000	$2.50
Miller Glue	T-200	N.A.	N.A.	$1.90

* Number of linear feet of coverage by a six-inch-wide double strip.
† Fast-drying, water resistant sealant.

Liggett's existing quality product. These advantages became evident, however, only under high-speed conditions, indicating that the product would find its best market among those plants producing a large volume of boxes.

Companies interviewed which had used Zipdry reported as follows:

Wellington Packing Co., Harrison, N.J.: Wellington used Zipdry from August of 1956 through the spring of 1958 with good results, and the central purchasing department had recommended it for all plants. They stopped buying Zipdry because of the tactics of the Turner sales representative, now no longer with the company, who apparently worked through plant personnel rather than the purchasing department. They would consider using Zipdry again if evidence could be presented that the spoilage problem had been completely solved.

Johnson Co., Cleveland, O.: The purchasing department records showed no reference to Zipdry, and the purchasing personnel had no recollection of ever having used Zipdry. They would not be interested in any product the price of which was not comparable to that of their present supplier, $0.55 per gallon.

Cooper & Co., Philadelphia and Harrisburg, Pa.: Personnel at the Philadelphia plant had no recollection of using Zipdry. The purchasing agent at Harrisburg remembered placing a small order for Zipdry in 1956, but had not reordered. They found nothing outstanding about the product.

National Manufactures Co., Newark, N.J.: They are still using some Zipdry left on hand but do not plan to reorder. They have found what they consider to be a comparable adhesive at a lower price.

Wilson Mfg. Co., Pittsburgh, Pa.: The Wilson Manufacturing Company's tests of Zipdry rated the product 84.7 per cent on their quality scale. They claimed that there were other products available that rated 116 per cent to 117 per cent on this scale and that sold for less than $2.50 per gallon. Penn Products' "Mikro-Seal" rated 90 per cent and sold for $1.46 per gallon.

Two tests run in Chicago brought diverse results as to Zipdry's quality. Fearn Products found that Zipdry did a superior sealing job and got roughly eight times the coverage as compared to the adhesive they were using.

Harper Company, on the other hand, had a serious problem with spoilage in a short time. Harper is a smaller company and their sealing machine operates only intermittently.

Should Liggett Adhesive Corporation accept the proposal of the Turner Research Company?

27

HOUSEHOLD LAUNDRY PRODUCTS COMPANY

THE HOUSEHOLD LAUNDRY PRODUCTS COMPANY produced and sold nationally a line of laundry aids, including dry and liquid laundry starch, bluing, laundry rinse, and bleach. Sales were made through twenty-three company salesmen to wholesalers who sold primarily to food stores. A separate sales force of eight men sold direct to corporate and voluntary-co-operative chain headquarters. Company brands were leaders in their respective product categories, and sales exceeded $36 million.

Because of the importance of transportation costs for each of its products, Household had established plants in ten markets. Each of these produced all the liquid bottled products. They were located in the following cities: San Francisco, Calif.; Portland, Ore.; Houston, Tex.;

Kansas City, Kan.; Minneapolis, Minn.; Chicago, Ill.; Memphis, Tenn.; Richmond, Va.; Cleveland, Ohio; Boston, Mass.

Household ammonia was a logical addition to the Household Laundry Products line. The problems of packing were similar to those for existing products in the line, many of the uses to which it was put were related to uses of present Household products, and channels of distribution were the same. In 1958 the Household vice-president in charge of marketing hired a consulting firm to study the market for household ammonia. A summary of the consultant's report follows:

Household consumption of ammonia is estimated at approximately $13 million per year. This reflects a slight upward trend in total sales. On a per capita basis, however, household consumption shows little change. In 1951 consumption per one thousand population was estimated at 366 quarts. In 1956 the estimate was 368 quarts. The estimated volume purchased in grocery stores appears to fluctuate between 234 and 247 quarts per one thousand population per year.

There are perhaps as many as two hundred brands of household ammonia in the market. Almost all of these brands are produced locally and sold at best regionally. Only two large so-called "national" brands are known. These are Little Bo-Peep, produced by the John Puhl Products Company of Chicago, which is a subsidiary of Spencer Chemical; and Parsons, which is produced by the Parsons Ammonia Company of New York City. Both these brands appear to have good consumer acceptance, although, as might be expected, their strength varies considerably from market to market.

The national chains and the larger voluntary groups secure their private-label ammonia from a number of regional producers. Other retailers secure their supply from one or more wholesalers or by direct dealing with bottlers. Some bottlers are known to use brokers in addition to wholesalers. It appears necessary for many small sellers to supplement the activities of brokers and wholesalers via bottler salesmen who work primarily at the retail level. Linco distributors, for example, report four regional sales managers and thirty-five salesmen so employed.

At the present time household ammonia is reported to be selling at retail at prices ranging from 12 cents to 25 cents a quart with retail margins of between 15 and 30 per cent. One trade source indicates that, on the average, the retail margin for household ammonia is 25.2 per cent versus an average of 28.4 per cent for all household supplies. Wholesalers' margins generally are about 9 per cent on net sales. Commissions to brokers vary between 5 and 7½ per cent, depending on the territory covered and the distribution of the product. Transportation costs are an important part of the final selling price. Freight costs averaged 23–27 cents per case of twelve quarts of ammonia (approximate weight, 45 lbs.).

There is some indication that ammonia is now being used for a wider range of household chores than it formerly was. It does not have, however, the acceptance of other special purpose cleaners. A check of a number of recent newspaper market surveys on brand usage in such cities as Sacramento, Milwaukee, Denver, and Cincinnati reveals a very consistent pattern. When asked what products were used for cleaning walls and woodwork, 40–50 per cent of the housewives named Spic and Span; another 20–25 per cent named Soilax. In contrast, only 1–2 per cent named ammonia (without specifying a brand). In two newspaper studies, which asked questions concerning window and glass cleaners (where ammonia was for many years predominant), 40–50 per cent of those using such products named Windex, 20–25 per cent named Glass Wax. Only about 4 per cent named ammonia.

Ammonia is a grease-cutting agent with both bleaching and water-softening properties. It can be used for almost all household cleaning chores from laundry to washing walls. Pure ammonia does not create any suds and needs no rinsing. Spic and Span and Soilax are detergents advertised as needing no rinsing. They do not cover the variety of uses that ammonia does. For cleaning windows, Windex and Glass Wax reportedly leave a "dirt resistant" film on the glass, whereas ammonia "just cleans." If it were possible to develop an ammonia with some spectacular qualities not found in present brands, a new entry into the field would be assured of success. There is a question, however, as to whether women would accept a new brand with qualities just like those found in the brands that they can buy now.

Factors involved in manufacturing a new household ammonia brand. Liquid household ammonia is a simple mixture of pure industrial ammonia and water. The amount of ammonia varies between 5 and 9 per cent. In addition, many household ammonias contain a small amount of detergent or other additives to give a milky, sudsy appearance. Ammonia, as a chemical, has been known for hundreds of years. It is a combination of nitrogen (one part) and hydrogen (three parts). Until World War II, most ammonia was produced as a by-product of coking operation. Because ammonia is a prime source of nitrogen, which in turn has many uses, including fertilizer and explosives, World War II led to the construction of a large number of plants producing synthetic ammonia. Many of these were financed by the federal government and, following the close of World War II, were disposed of to private interests. Producers of petroleum and natural gas also found it possible, and profitable, to produce industrial ammonia. Currently the nation's productive capacity exceeds demand by a considerable amount. Between 1953 and 1956 ammonia capacity nearly doubled. In late 1957 ammonia production was about 75 per cent of capacity.

The foregoing led to a market situation that finds industrial ammonia available from more than fifty producers, with plants located throughout the country. To a firm contemplating the production of household ammonia, this means that a reliable source of industrial ammonia would be available wherever and whenever needed. Further, the overcapacity and keen competition places considerable pressure on prices. High freight costs have brought about the production and distribution of household ammonia on a local and regional scale by many small producers. The distribution of the ammonia industry has made this possible.

Most bottlers of household ammonia use aqua ammonia. This is a solution of 24.9 per cent ammonia and distilled water, which is then prepared by the ammonia producer. This solution is available readily by tank car or by drums. To make money, the raw materials should be purchased in tank-car quantities—provided the plant has railroad facilities adjacent.

It is estimated that Parsons and Bo-Peep together account for between 50 and 60 per cent of the total volume of household ammonia. It is estimated that Parsons has net sales of about $3 million, with a gross margin of slightly in excess of $1 million. Advertising expenditures for these two brands were not available, but trade sources estimate that together they probably expend about $100,000.

Parsons has plants in Waco, Tex.; Portland, Ore.; Jacksonville, Fla.; Homewood, Ill.; Los Angeles, Calif.; and Passaic, N.J. Bo-Peep appears to operate on two bases—they own some plants and lease others. The company owns plants in Rensselaer, N.Y.; Trenton, N.J.; Brattleboro, Vt.; Lynbrook, Conn.; Wheeling, W.Va.; Gulfport, Miss.; and has ammonia plants in Chicago and Monticello, Ill.; Alliance and Cincinnati, Ohio; and Salem, Va. The company leases plants in East Greenbush, N.Y.; Rothschild, Wis.; and Meyerstown, Pa. It also leases an ammonia plant in Houston, Tex.

In terms of packaging, almost all ammonias are bottled in glass. The exception to this appears to be the Sunlight Chemical Corporation of Phillipsdale, R.I., who now packages household ammonia in a 22-ounce tinless can. American Can Company, which came up with this new container, says this is the first use of metal cans for household ammonia. Sunlight Company executives indicate that these cost more than glass containers, but they point out that the metal cans are not vulnerable to breakage. These cans have screw-top plastic caps and aluminum nozzles. Canco says they are similar to cans used for liquid detergents. One company has reported marketing its product in a dry form to the consumer. The presumption is that the consumer then literally makes his own household ammonia. Not much is known about this operation, but certainly it does not appear to represent a major innovation and sales to date could not have been substantial, else the trade would have picked up the item.

What action should the marketing vice-president take with respect to household ammonia?

28

CONSOLIDATED PACKING COMPANY

CONSOLIDATED PACKING COMPANY had been one of the "big five" in the food canning business for nearly eighty years. Its product line included a wide variety of canned fruits, vegetables, and fruit juices; frozen foods; and baby foods. In 1958 its sales of $266 million made it the third largest firm in the industry. Despite this apparent success, management was becoming increasingly concerned over the growth of private brands in the food field and believed the firm would have to take some new action to meet this threat.

Several factors pointed to the growing problem for Consolidated. Data compiled from several market research sources showed that private brands of canned foods had almost quadrupled their share of the market in the last eighteen years (Table 1).

Total canned food sales amounted to about $4 billion at retail prices. Consolidated's sales increased between 1952 and 1957, but not relative to total consumption of canned and frozen foods, as shown in Table 2.

Retail chains were growing steadily in size and in share of the food market. According to the U.S. Census Bureau, the chains' share of food-store sales grew from 30 to 43 per cent between 1929 and 1954.[1] A na-

---

[1] Four or more stores under single ownership constituted a chain.

TABLE 1

SHARE OF CANNED FOODS MARKET HELD BY NATIONAL AND PRIVATE
BRANDS IN SELECTED YEARS

Year	Private Brands	"Big Five" National Brands*	Other National Brands	Total
1940	4%	38%	58%	100%
1950	7	35	58	100
1958	15	30	55	100

*The "Big Five" and their 1958 sales: (1) California Packing Corporation (Del Monte), $350 million; (2) Libby, McNeill & Libby, $300 million; (3) Consolidated Packing Company, $266 million; (4) Stokeley's, $150 million; and (5) Green Giant, $100 million.

tional organization of retail grocers reported that concentration in the grocery business was growing and that, by 1960, 75–80 per cent of all grocery business would be accounted for by 20–25 per cent of the retail grocery firms.

The large chains were increasingly prone to adopt private brands. The Great Atlantic & Pacific Tea Company began in the 1920's to sell a few items, especially margarine, under its own private label. In the 1930's the Kroger chain began to feature its own private labels. By the 1940's the Jewel and National Tea food chains were actively selling canned goods

TABLE 2

CONSOLIDATED'S SALES, U.S. POPULATION AND PER CAPITA
CONSUMPTION OF CANNED AND FROZEN FOODS: 1952–57

Year	U.S. Population (Millions)	Per Capita Consumption (Lbs.) Canned Fruits and Vegetables	Frozen Fruits and Vegetables	Wholesale Food Price Index	Consolidated Net Sales
1952	157	63	11.9	104.9	$202
1953	159	64.6	12.5	104.5	206
1954	162	63	13.3	104.5	211
1955	165	65.1	15.5	105.5	242
1956	168	65.8	16	107.9	260
1957	171	66.3	16.5	103.9	241

under their own private labels. Consolidated executives estimated that the sales of canned foods of four of the largest chains were distributed between private and national brands as shown in Table 3. Retailer co-operatives, such as the IGA, were also increasing their emphasis on private brands.

There was some evidence that consumer interest in brands was declining. A trade survey found that the typical consumer shopping in a supermarket reported that she was interested primarily in the price of each item rather than in such factors as quality or the firm that canned the food.

TABLE 3

DISTRIBUTION OF CANNED FOOD SALES OF SELECTED CHAINS
BETWEEN PRIVATE AND NATIONAL BRANDS: 1958

Chain	Private Brands	National Brands
A & P.	90%	10%
Kroger.	50	50
National Tea.	15	85
Safeway.	35	65

Consolidated's line was sold through the firm's own sales force which was organized as shown in the accompanying chart.

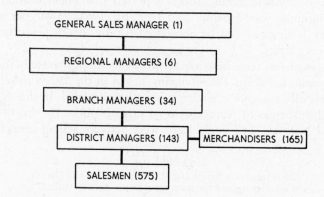

The branch managers were responsible for the sales and profits of their branches. The district managers had direct responsibility for sales to chains and jobbers in their areas and also supervised the work of the salesmen and merchandisers in their districts. The salesmen sold to the large retailers, other than those handled by the district managers, and helped the stores with merchandising ideas. The merchandisers worked with individual stores, both units of chains and stores sold by jobbers, helping them stack their shelves, build displays, and organize promotions.

As Consolidated considered the problem of maintaining and expanding the company's sales in the future, they noted the following possible alternative lines of action:

1. Consolidated could do away with all sales promotion and advertising allowances. It was the general practice in the industry to grant retailers such promotion allowances as free goods and/or 10 cents off on each case for special one-time promotions, and advertising allowances of 10 cents a case purchased. The allowances were generally believed to be much larger than what the retailer actually spent on promotion. Elimination of these allowances would permit the company to reduce its prices to a level more competitive with private-brand merchandise, which typically sold at 10–20 per cent less than the national brands. The industry pattern for allowances, however, had been established for many years, which raised the question of what would happen to Consoli-

dated's competitive position if it were the first, and possibly the only, firm not to grant such allowances.

2. A second alternative was to cut the price of each can one-half cent. The management estimated a cut of this size, but no larger, could possibly be made if expenses remained at their existing levels. Some executives believed that such a price cut would be so small as to be of no value in competition with private brands.

3. Consolidated could let its business under its own brand decline and concentrate on building a private brand business. Much of the current selling expense, which ran about 30 per cent of sales, could be eliminated, and significant price reductions could be made.

4. Another alternative was to raise prices and spend the larger margin on more advertising and selling. The soap-detergent and cereal manufacturers operated more in this manner. They used many promotion devices, such as contests and premiums, to obtain brand loyalty. Those industries spent 4–7 per cent of sales on promotion, while 1–2 per cent was more typical for the food-canning industry.

5. Consolidated could go into the retail grocery business by merging with an existing chain. This proposal did not have much appeal to the management, and there was some question as to whether it could be done legally.

6. Consolidated could cut its product line in order to promote a few items more heavily. Hunt, a medium-sized canner, began to cut its thirty-some-odd lines in 1947. By 1958 it had only three products: fruit cocktail, tomato products, and peaches. Within these lines, Hunt reduced the variety offered. For example, in peaches Hunt packed only one grade (choice) in one type of syrup (thick). This simplification was apparently very successful for Hunt. Its sales increased from $15 million in 1947 to $120 million in 1958. By that time it had the top brand in tomato sauce and tomato paste and was second in peaches and catsup. In addition to cutting down on the number of lines, Hunt also began a diversification program by buying out nonrelated companies, such as a manufacturer of matches.

7. Consolidated could change distribution policies and shift from its own sales force to food brokers. Del Monte used food brokers in some areas and its own salesmen in others; Stokeley's used food brokers exclusively. Brokers would sell to wholesalers for a commission, probably 3–4 per cent. There was a question, however, as to whether most brokers could handle a line as large as Consolidated's.

What action should Consolidated take in view of the threat of private brands?

29

ABBOT LABORATORIES (A)

IN THE middle 1950's the executives of Abbott Laboratories had become increasingly concerned about Abbott's corporate image. One of the factors that they thought contributed to a less-than-desired image was the company's packaging. Although many of the packages used by Abbott were unique in design (Exhibits 1 and 2), there was no strong

EXHIBIT 1

SOME OF ABBOTT'S ETHICAL DRUG LINE PACKAGES

EXHIBIT 2

SOME ADDITIONAL PACKAGES IN ABBOTT'S ETHICAL DRUG LINE

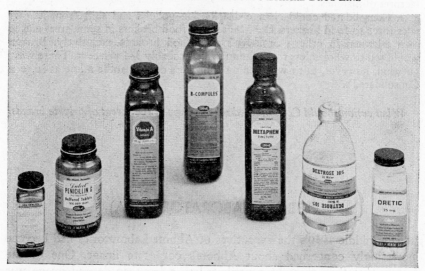

line of corporate identity, and some executives thought the packages
looked old-fashioned. The ethical drug line packages were characterized
by a blue color, often referred to as "institutional blue." Blue was a color
that was also used frequently by other drug manufacturers (Exhibit 3).

Only a relatively minor portion of Abbott's products were sold over
the counter; the majority were ethical drugs. Its advertising was directed
primarily to doctors, druggists, and hospitals, through trade journals and

EXHIBIT 3

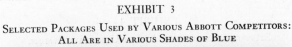

SELECTED PACKAGES USED BY VARIOUS ABBOTT COMPETITORS:
ALL ARE IN VARIOUS SHADES OF BLUE

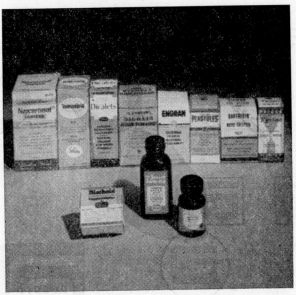

by direct mail. The company had done no consumer advertising prior to
1955, when it launched its promotion campaign for Sucaryl, a new noncaloric sweetener.

Abbott Laboratories was one of the leading manufacturers of ethical
drug products, but management thought that the corporation's image was
not as modern and progressive as the firm actually was. A major aspect of
this problem was the company's packaging. Not only was a clear corporate identity missing, but the management believed that the packages
were somewhat old-fashioned in appearance. In 1958 George Nelson &
Company, a firm of industrial designers, was engaged to redesign the
package line and, in the process, to develop a corporate symbol that
could be used on all packages and in other places where it was important
to identify Abbott—for example, on stationery, displays, and company
buildings and in advertising.

The industrial designers first attempted to find a symbol that would

reflect the desired modern, progressive image of Abbott Laboratories—
one that could be used throughout the company. Competitors' designs
were studied. The use of geometrical shapes, letters, and special geometric
shapes of letters was investigated. Symbols representative of the medical
or drug field or connected with phases of Abbott's work were considered.
Finally, from a fiftieth-anniversary medal designed for Abbott Laboratories, the designers developed the idea of the serpentine A. The steps
through which the concept evolved are illustrated in Exhibit 4. The

EXHIBIT 4

STEPS IN EVOLUTION OF ABBOTT CORPORATE SYMBOL

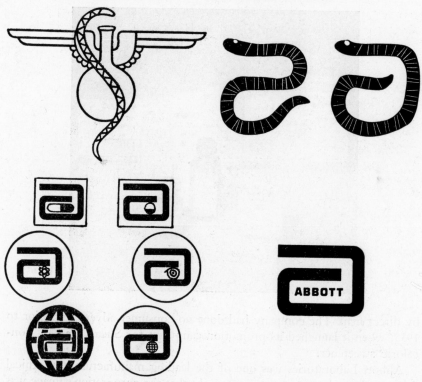

medal used a design adopted from the widely known medical symbol.
From this, the serpentine A in various geometric abstractions evolved.
This was modified and used with different supplementary design ideas
until the final solution, the abstract serpentine A with the name Abbott,
was selected.

With the basic corporate symbol determined, the designers turned to
the problem of adapting the design to Abbott's packaging. They believed
that the entire package line needed new, up-to-date design, with more
and better use of colors. Abbott's management agreed to the wider use of
colors but rejected any idea of color-coding its packages by products.

They believed that doctors, druggists, and hospitals objected to such coding. Doctors held that, in the use and administration of drugs, labels should always be read. Color-coding might lead to a dependence on the code, which would be dangerous. Some of the first designs submitted to management are shown in Exhibit 5 and are shown compared to competitors' packages in Exhibit 6. Colored portions of the packages were in such colors as red, pink, orange, blue, green, gray, and black.

EXHIBIT 5

SOME PROPOSED PACKAGE DESIGNS SUBMITTED TO ABBOTT'S MANAGEMENT; COLORED PORTIONS ACTUALLY WERE IN A WIDE VARIETY OF COLORS, SUCH AS RED, ORANGE, GREEN, BLUE, AND GRAY

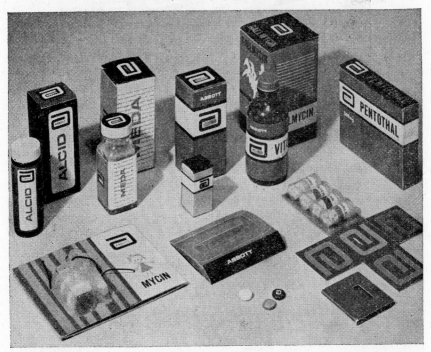

The use of solid colors or even of as much color as shown on the packages in Exhibit 5 proved to be unsatisfactory. A drug package had to carry a large amount of information about the drug, much of which was dictated by the federal Food and Drug Administration. The use of too much color on a package either did not leave room for the information or made it difficult to read if printed over certain colors. Still, the designers believed the company should make more extensive use of color. The final design selected is shown in Exhibits 7 and 8. The package was essentially black and white with a bar of color or two sides at the top and the corporate symbol at the bottom.

When the new design was introduced to the company, some veteran

EXHIBIT 6

PROPOSED ABBOTT PACKAGES, SHOWN WITH COMPETITORS' PACKAGES

EXHIBIT 7

NEW PACKAGE DESIGNS SELECTED BY ABBOTT

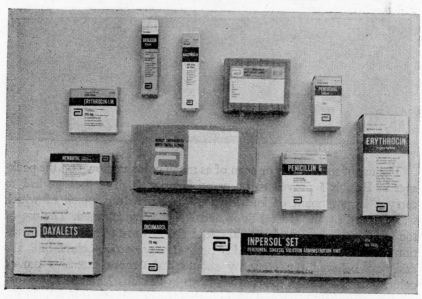

EXHIBIT 8

NEW PACKAGE DESIGNS SELECTED BY ABBOTT

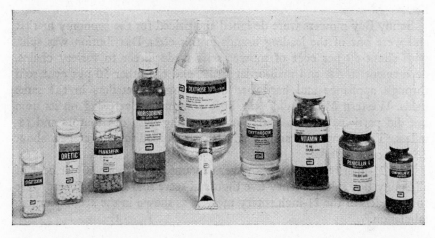

employees raised strong objections to changing the packages. The Abbott blue, which had been abandoned completely in the new design, was well known by customers after years of usage. These people asserted that the change would lose the value of this recognition and acceptance. Some field salesmen also complained that the variety of colors would make their job of checking stocks in hospitals and on druggists' shelves more difficult. With the existing packages, they could walk into a drugstore and immediately spot Abbott's products on the shelves, but with the new design they would have to search for them.

Were the new packaging policy and design sound developments?

30

WESTERN MOWER COMPANY

THE TREMENDOUS growth of the power mower industry following the Korean War attracted into the field many new companies, one of which was Western Mower Company. The intense competition that resulted from this influx of new firms led to reductions in prices and margins. Many of the smaller companies were forced out of business. Western Mower had experienced its share of difficulties but, by trimming expenses wherever possible, had remained profitable. As one aspect of this economy program, Western Mower redesigned the package on its power mowers. A year later it was reviewing this decision.

Western Mower's line included both reel and rotary power mowers; hand mowers; powered garden tools; and hand garden tools. Seventy-five per cent of the company's $10 million sales, however, were accounted for by power mowers, which were sold under the brand name Sunny Boy.

Sunny Boy mowers were designed and priced for the economy market and were one of the leading brands in this class. Distribution was split, with about 50 per cent of mower sales made direct to variety chains, department stores, and mail-order firms, and the other 50 per cent sold through appliance and hardware distributors to retailers in the same fields. Western Mower did very little consumer advertising on its own but did participate in co-operative advertising with distributors and retailers. The company's annual advertising expenditures averaged about 2.5 per cent of sales.

The 21-inch rotary power mower accounted for about 60 per cent of all Sunny Boy sales. Seventy-five thousand were sold in 1960. There were four models of the 21-inch rotary mower, as shown in the accompanying tabulation.

Model	Equipment	Suggested Retail Price
Economy.........	2-cycle engine	$ 74.50
Deluxe Economy..	2-cycle engine, leaf mulcher, handle controls	91.50
Deluxe...........	4-cycle engine, leaf mulcher	99.50
Special Deluxe....	4-cycle engine, leaf mulcher, handle controls, special trim and finish	109.50

Comparable models of "high-quality" mowers were priced in the range $89.95–$140.00. There was a considerable amount of price cutting in power mowers, however, so that actual retail prices on all brands were often lower than the list prices quoted by the manufacturers.

The same package was used for all models of the 21-inch rotary. It was composed of 200-pounds-test corrugated fiberboard 27″ × 26″ × 18″ and had three pieces of inner packing specially designed to hold the mower and parts in the box securely. The handle was removed from the mower and placed in the package separately. The mower was positioned in the box so that there was one-half-inch clearance on all sides and at the bottom and one-inch clearance at the top. This clearance was necessary to protect the mower from direct impact during shipment, which could crack the cast-aluminum deck. The packages for other mower models were all designed along the same lines. Most retailers set up one or a few mowers as models but sold most mowers in the package, as it was quite simple for the customer to attach the handle after taking the mower from the box.

All mower packages had been redesigned for the 1960 models in an effort to cut costs. The clearance of the mower inside the box was reduced one-quarter inch on four sides and at the bottom. This reduced the size of the box and inner packing, which resulted in a 12-cent reduction in the price of each box. The package for the 21-inch rotary cost the company 65 cents each in 1960. Similar reductions were achieved in packages for other models.

The reduction in clearances in the package resulted in increased damage from handling and shipment. The number of damaged mowers reported had previously averaged around 1 per cent of all shipments, but in 1960 it jumped up to 1.5 per cent. About 45 per cent of all damage claims were attributable directly to freight carriers. In these cases the dealer was able to recover the cost of the mower from the carrier. The other 55 per cent of damage claims were either disputed by the carrier or directly attributable to in-plant or warehouse mishandling or to distributor or dealer negligence. In the latter case distributors and dealers often made claims on Western Mower for damage that was the result of their own negligence or mistakes in handling or assembling the mower. This had always been a sore point with Western Mower executives because they felt that they should not pay such claims. Since it was hard to prove the source of damage and since the company did not want to lose the goodwill of customers, Western Mower actually paid most of such claims.

About 50 per cent of the damage claims were the result of cracking of the cast aluminum deck. The average cost of replacing a cracked deck was around $12, including shipping charges, plus $5 for labor for dismantling the mower to replace the deck. Other damage claims were for bent handles, broken wheels, or damaged motor parts. The average cost to the company of the claims, other than for cracked decks and excluding those paid by freight carriers, was estimated to be $20. This included the cost of the part replaced, labor charges and shipping, and administrative costs.

In addition to the cost of damage claims, the sales department was concerned about the reactions of their customers to increased damage. Complaints had increased in about the same proportion as had claims. While it could not be measured in dollars, the sales manager believed that there was a definite cost in goodwill that should be charged against the new package.

As a result of the 1960 record, the sales manager recommended to the packaging committee that Western Mower either return to the old package for 1961 or turn to a new package design that had increased clearance and possibly to higher-strength materials. In addition, he asked the committee to investigate the idea of developing a specially designed package for the 21-inch rotary line that would serve as a display in the dealer's store as well as a shipping carton. He cited the success of several of the top mower companies in the past year which had supplied displays to dealers at cost. He did not think that Western Mower had strong enough relationships with its dealers to be able to sell them displays, but he thought that, if each package could serve as a display, the dealer would be likely to use it.

This packaging problem was submitted to several of the company's package suppliers. Estimates were received on new designs and on the former design. Because of increases in paper costs, to increase clearances to the former size and to increase the strength of the inserts that held the mower in place would result in an increase of about 14 cents per package.

To produce a combination shipping carton and display unit for the 21-inch rotary presented more complicated problems. First, it involved better and more elaborate printing than the standard two-color design printed on four sides of the box, which had been used for a number of years. Several designs were submitted by packaging suppliers, some using the inner packing or special inserts to form a display, using the box as a platform, and others involving specially designed or printed boxes that could be formed into a display by folding or cutting them in a specified way. Cost estimates ranged from $1.23 to $1.75 per package for these design-type packages.

What type of package should Western Mower adopt for the 1961 season?

31

B. Channels of Distribution

INTERNATIONAL HARVESTER FARM-EQUIPMENT DIVISION (B)

SALES OF wheel tractors for commercial or industrial purposes by the farm equipment division of International Harvester were becoming an increasingly important portion of total tractor sales by 1959. Early in that year the division management reappraised the distribution channels for industrial tractors in the light of their increasing importance.

Table 1 shows the sales of tractors for farm and nonfarm use during a four-year period.

International Harvester had kept a careful record of the tractors that had been sold for industrial use for the six-month period from May 1, 1958, to October 31, 1958, and found that the total was over 6,000 tractors. Sales were reported in 1,528 of the 3,067 counties in the United States, or an average of approximately 3.9 tractors sold for industrial

TABLE 1

TOTAL DOMESTIC FARM AND NONFARM TRACTOR SHIPMENTS: 1955–58

Year	Total*	For Farm Use	For Nonfarm	Percentage Nonfarm Use
1955.........286,000		263,000	23,000	6.9
1956.........191,000		170,000	21,000	11.0
1957.........204,000		179,000	25,000	12.6
1958.........216,000		180,000	28,000	12.9

* Except contractors' "off-highway," garden, and crawler-type tractors.
Source: Department of Commerce, *Facts for Industry, 1955, 1956,* and *1957.*

use in each county where sales were made. During an average fiscal year Harvester sold about 70,000 tractors of all types.

International Harvester tractors, both for farm use and for industrial use, were being sold through the following number and types of outlets in the spring of 1959: McCormick farm equipment dealers, 4,445; selected-equipment dealers, 239; and company-owned McCormick stores, 98—a total of 4,782.

Of the total 4,445 farm-equipment dealers, about 3,000 handled both International Harvester trucks and farm equipment, while the balance handled only farm equipment. Not all dealers handled only International Harvester products, since some had other franchises for such products as appliances or automobiles. In some cases competing lines of farm equipment or trucks were handled.

International Harvester operated three distinct divisions—a farm equipment division, a construction equipment division, and a truck division. Sales by product lines in 1958 showed motor trucks, services, and parts to account for 47 per cent of total company sales of over $1,098,000,000; farm equipment, service parts and service sales, 36 per cent; and construction equipment, 12 per cent. Steel, pig iron, fiber and twine, and miscellaneous products made up the balance.

The motor truck division distributed its trucks through some 4,000 full-line motor truck dealers, of which 1,000 handled motor trucks only, while 3,000 were combination dealers, already mentioned as handling both the company's farm equipment and motor trucks. There were also about 900 dealers distributing motor trucks; these were known as "community contract" dealers. These dealers often handled only a selected portion of the full line of trucks and could be classified as either small country-town dealers, who had no reason to handle large over-the-road trucks, or as outlying dealers in metropolitan areas who were suitable outlets, not for large trucks but for light trucks for such users as truck gardeners, small ranchers, or others needing light delivery equipment. In addition, the company operated 174 motor-truck branches, which sold trucks at retail. These branches, usually located in large cities, were very important, accounting for about 40–45 per cent of all truck sales.

The company's farm equipment division was organized into six regions that covered the entire country. Each region had from ten to twelve districts, and each district was organized into about six zones. Zones were usually composed of about twelve dealers and consisted of geographical areas based upon one or more counties. The amount of territory covered was based primarily upon the potential in the counties assigned. In rich agricultural areas a zone might consist of only two counties. Basically the company's farm equipment dealers were located so that they were convenient to rural markets.

The six-month study of industrial tractor sales in 1958 indicated that the sales of tractors for commercial uses were to individuals or organizations that were entirely different from the normal farmer customer, whose needs and wants were quite familiar to the old-line, franchised farm equipment dealer.

In studying the reports from districts that showed the types of customers buying tractors for industrial use, it was found that contractors, political subdivisions, industrial and commercial firms, service and maintenance organizations, and retail dealers and suppliers were the principal customers for industrial tractors. Other data obtained from this analysis of industrial tractor sales are shown in Table 2.

TABLE 2

SELECTED STATISTICS FROM ANALYSIS OF INDUSTRIAL TRACTOR SALES

	I-300	Cub
Chief occupation or business of purchaser of I-300 or I.H. Cub tractor		
Contractors	54%	17%
Political subdivisions and institutions	14	13
Services and maintenance	9	52
Retail dealers and suppliers	8	5
Industrial and commercial applications	7	10
Logging	5	1
Oil fields	2	1
Mining operations	1	1
Number of tractors owned before buying an I-300 or I.H. Cub tractor		
Owned none	35	62
Owned one	35	28
Owned two	16	2
Owned three or more	14	8
Makes of tractors owned before buying an I-300 or I.H. Cub tractor		
Owned none	35	62
Owned I.H. tractors only	20	21
Owned both I.H. and competitive makes	9	4
Owned competitive makes only	36	13
Status of new I-300 or I.H. Cub tractor		
First tractor purchase	35	62
Addition to tractors already owned	29	19
Replaces another tractor	36	19

The company felt that the distribution and service facilities of its 4,500 farm equipment dealers furnished the most comprehensive coverage of rural areas of all companies in its field. Some of these dealers plus the company-owned McCormick stores, which were usually located only in the areas where the company felt that adequate coverage could not otherwise be obtained, covered larger towns, such as county seats, as well as the rural areas. Service facilities at most dealerships and at the company-owned stores were usually excellent. Since the tractors sold for commercial use were similar to those sold for farm use, no new service problems on these units were experienced. The basic difference between a tractor sold for farm use and one sold for industrial or commercial use was in the type of attachments. Typically a tractor for commercial use consisted of what was known as a 300 Series or 400 Series model equipped with a loader and back hoe combination. Units so equipped could dig trenches, move piles of earth, and load the earth that had been dug or moved. In the case of Cubs or the smaller 100 Series, the equipment that converted the tractor to an industrial unit could be a scraper for light grading jobs or snow removal, various types of mowers, post-hole diggers, street sweepers, or other special purpose attachments, in addition to the smaller loaders and back hoes.

Typical selling prices for industrial tractors ran as shown in the accompanying tabulation.

Type of Tractor	Price of Tractor	Typical Attachments	Total Price with Attachments
International Cub	$1,250	$ 100*	$1,350
100 Series	2,000	400†	2,400
300 Series	2,500	3500‡	6,000
400 Series	3,000	4800†	7,800

* Equipment included was rotary mower.
† Equipment included was loader.
‡ Equipment included was back hoe and loader.

The contractor, the estate owner, and the political subdivision buyers were not typically customers of the average International Harvester farm equipment dealer. Recognizing this situation, as well as the fact that many buyers of the commercial tractors were located in either metropolitan areas or fast-growing suburban areas, the company experimented with what it called "selected equipment dealers" as possible retail outlets. They were typically dealers who took on the sale of a segment of the Harvester line in addition to another type of business. They included landscape gardeners, equipment-rental dealers, garden and lawn supply stores, building material dealers, and even gasoline service station operators. Turnover was frequent among these dealers, and they did not appear to cover the potential market adequately. There were 239 such dealers in 1959. Although the survey of tractors sold for commercial use in the six-month period ending October 31, 1958, did not show sales by type of outlet, management estimated that 95 per cent of all tractors purchased for industrial use were sold by International Harvester farm equipment dealers and company-owned stores and less than 5 per cent by selected equipment dealers.

The Harvester truck division sold trucks of all sizes, but was especially successful with trucks weighing over 15,000 lbs. These trucks were distributed in metropolitan areas through 174 motor truck branches. Trucks were sold to a wide variety of customers, from a small farmer using a half-ton pickup truck to large trucking companies and fleet buyers, such as the Bell Telephone Company. In many ways these motor truck customers, particularly in metropolitan areas, appeared to be more typical users of tractors for industrial uses than the farmer market covered by the McCormick farm equipment dealers. Therefore, the tractor division decided to experiment with the sale of tractors through motor truck branches. The Los Angeles area was selected for this experiment, and late in 1958 an attempt was made to sell tractors in the Culver City branch, one of the seven motor truck branches in Los Angeles. A combination sales manager and salesman, who was independent of the motor truck branch manager, was set up to sell only industrial tractors. The extensive truck service facilities were to be shared by the industrial tractor department. By late spring of 1959 the experiment was considered a modest success from the standpoint of sales but unsatisfactory in maintenance and service. Trucks were given priority over tractors by service personnel.

As a result of this experience, it was decided to set up a separate, company-owned facility, similar to a company-owned McCormick farm-equipment store, to sell only tractors and equipment for industrial use. This experimental outlet was placed in the North Hollywood section of Los Angeles—an excellent, growing area. No operating results or conclusions had been reached concerning this test operation.

International Harvester's third most important product line was construction equipment, which consisted of such items as diesel crawler tractors and road scrapers. These products ranged in price from about $6,500 for a small crawler tractor to about $65,000 for a combination unit of a large tractor and scraper. These were sold by construction equipment distributors in about 180 locations in the United States. These distributors sold directly to construction contractors, such as road builders, heavy-construction companies that built dams and tunnels, and political subdivisions. All the principal cities in the United States were covered by the 180 distributors. Since the number of potential customers was relatively few for construction equipment as compared to farm equipment, the distributors needed correspondingly smaller sales forces. These distributors had been offered the opportunity to handle the

Harvester industrial tractors, but they had expressed very little interest and had made practically no sales of such equipment.

International Harvester's competition in the industrial tractor market included most of the major farm equipment makers, such as Allis Chalmers, J. I. Case, John Deere & Co., Ford, Oliver, Massey Ferguson, and Minneapolis Moline. Most of these companies entered into special contracts with allied equipment manufacturers to make the attachments that were necessary to make an industrial tractor functional. The equipment was then marketed along with the tractor by the tractor firm's regular dealers. Harvester had a similar arrangement with Pippin, Wagner, and Danuser, and the attachments were marketed under trade names identifying both parties, such as "International Pippin." Typical dealer margins on equipment and attachments were about 25 per cent, which was the same as the normal margin on tractors.

While competitors had generally marketed their industrial or commercial tractors through their regular farm equipment dealers, there was one exception. In 1959 Massey Ferguson set up an industrial equipment division for the expressed purpose of distributing its industrial tractor, which was called the "Work Bull." Although the Massey Ferguson promotional and advertising material implied that the tractor and attachments were developed specifically for the industrial market, they were essentially the same as those made by other manufacturers.

What channel of distribution should International Harvester use for its industrial tractors?

32

KITCHENS OF SARA LEE

THE KITCHENS of Sara Lee began local distribution of a very high quality of cheese cake in Chicago in 1951. Previously this quality of cake had been available only in specialty bakeries. The Sara Lee product was produced and packaged to sell to food chains, delicatessens, and other retail food outlets. The cake was offered in two sizes and was priced to sell to consumers at 79 cents for the large size and 59 cents for the small. A coffee cake of similar high quality was soon added to the line, and several other products later. Sales were concentrated within a three-hundred-mile radius of Chicago (overnight trucking distance) and within two years climbed to $3 million. When the firm found that it could freeze the items successfully, the management began to consider the possibilities of national distribution, despite the fact that such a product had never been handled on a national basis before.

In addition to developing the cakes, Sara Lee developed a new package, which helped in merchandising the product. The cakes were baked in foil pans, in which they were later sold. The pans were sealed with laminated pictorial covers. The cover for the all-butter pecan coffee cake was partially clear, so that the customer could see the contents inside. The package was so constructed that the customer could open it, remove part of the cake, close it, and still keep the cake fresh for several days.

Sara Lee found the distribution pattern used by packaged bread bakers to be applicable to its needs. The company's sales organization was designed to fit this method of distribution and prior to 1953 was set up as shown in Table 1. The Chicago driver-salesmen picked up the cakes at

TABLE 1

SARA LEE SALES ORGANIZATION PRIOR TO 1953

```
                        ┌─────────────────┐
                        │    PRESIDENT    │
                        └─────────────────┘
                                 │
                     ┌────────────────────────┐
                     │ GENERAL SALES MANAGER  │
                     └────────────────────────┘
                                 │
          ┌──────────────────────┴──────────────────────────┐
┌──────────────────────────┐          ┌──────────────────────────────────────┐
│ CITY OF CHICAGO SALES     │          │ DISTRIBUTION DIVISION SALES MANAGER  │
│ MANAGER                   │          │                                      │
└──────────────────────────┘          └──────────────────────────────────────┘
          │                                        │
┌──────────────────────────┐          ┌──────────────────────────────────────┐
│ ASSISTANT SALES MANAGER   │          │        SALES SUPERVISORS (4)         │
└──────────────────────────┘          └──────────────────────────────────────┘
          │                                        │
┌──────────────────────────┐          ┌──────────────────────────────────────┐
│   SALES SUPERVISORS (5)   │          │       FRANCHISED DISTRIBUTORS        │
└──────────────────────────┘          └──────────────────────────────────────┘
          │                                        │
┌──────────────────────────┐          ┌──────────────────────────────────────┐
│  DRIVER-SALESMEN (35)     │          │          DRIVER-SALESMEN             │
└──────────────────────────┘          └──────────────────────────────────────┘
```

the bakery and distributed them to the retail outlets in that city. The distributor sales division distributed the cakes throughout an area within a three-hundred-mile radius of Chicago, which included such cities as Detroit, Cleveland, St. Louis, and Indianapolis. Commercial carriers delivered the cakes to central terminal docks in these areas during the night or very early in the morning. The distributors' driver-salesmen picked up the cakes in the morning and delivered them to retailers.

The duties of both the Chicago and the distributor's driver-salesmen were to:

1. Call on every retailer on their routes every day or every other day, depending on the size of the account. In an average day each driver-salesman made about 60 calls.

2. Check to see how many cakes the retailer had on hand, rotate the stock to cause the older cakes to move first, and make certain the proper code was followed so that no stale cakes were ever sold.[1]

3. Advise retailers on the use of point-of-sale display material and on advertising promotions that were or would be taking place.

Driver-salesmen averaged about $1,000 sales per week. They were completely unionized and were paid a salary plus a commission based on weekly sales. The average driver-salesman earned about $7,000 annually. There were five driver-salesman supervisors in Chicago, who were paid a slightly larger salary for the added responsibility of supervising the drivers.

In those areas where a franchised distributor purchased the exclusive rights to distribute for Sara Lee, his driver-salesmen performed the same duties as the Sara Lee driver-salesmen. These distributors were required to comply with all Sara Lee policies and were supervised by one of the Sara Lee area supervisors.

In 1953 a food distributor in the South suggested that Sara Lee ship its cakes to the distributor for sale in that region. Sara Lee's executives declined because they believed that the distance was too great and that the cakes would spoil. The distributor then suggested that Sara Lee ship the cakes frozen. The Sara Lee management explored the possibility and found that, because of their high butter-fat content, the cakes could be frozen without impairing their quality. As a result, a regular shipment of frozen cakes was started to the southern distributor, who sold them to the frozen-food departments of retail food outlets. This business gradually expanded to include several other distributors.

As a result of the experience with these food distributors, Sara Lee executives began to think of distributing their products nationally. Frozen foods were growing rapidly in public acceptance; between 1940 and 1956 frozen-food production increased from 675 million pounds to 9,007 million pounds.[2] At the end of 1956 there were over nine million home freezer units in operation, and the number had been growing about one million each year.[3] Refrigerated warehouse capacity had grown from 86.6 million cubic feet in 1939 to 376.5 million cubic feet in 1955.[4] All these facts were strong evidence that the market for frozen foods was growing.

---

[1] To insure highest quality to the consumer, the quality-control laboratory determined the maximum shelf life for each type of cake. All cakes were marked with a special code that indicated the final date they could be offered for sale. In all cases this final date was set so that total shelf life would be several days less than the maximum determined by the laboratory. Cakes that had not sold by the final date were picked up by the driver-salesmen and returned to the bakery. They were then sold at half-price or less in a special retail outlet operated by the company. The percentage of cakes actually picked up was very small.

[2] National Frozen Food Distributors Association.

[3] *Ibid.*

[4] Gross space, 0° F., or below. Source: U.S. Department of Agriculture.

Since frozen foods had to be kept below freezing temperatures, public storage refrigerated warehouses had been growing at retail distribution points. Distributors, of which there were 610 according to the 1954 Census, were a key factor in the sale of frozen foods. They carried stocks of a wide line of frozen foods and delivered them in refrigerated trucks to the retailers' cold-storage cabinets. They also performed the other services common to food wholesalers. Many distributors serviced chain as well as independent stores and institutional outlets, but chains were developing more of their own refrigerated distribution facilities. The typical distributor's margin was about 18 per cent. Most distributors had sales between $500,000 and $5 million and facilities that were valued at about two-thirds of annual sales.

Refrigerated cabinet space in retail stores was the biggest factor limiting growth of frozen-food sales. A typical frozen-food cabinet in a retail store cost the retailer around $1,000. When he installed such a cabinet, it took space he would otherwise have used for other products. Thus the retailer did not add more cabinet space unless the potential increase in sales would justify the added cost. This meant that there were many more frozen-food products clamoring for space in retail frozen-food cabinets than could possibly be accommodated.

Sara Lee executives proposed that, if the frozen-cake line were sold nationally, it should be sold through frozen-food brokers and distributors. Brokers handled a number of noncompetitive frozen-food items, such as vegetables, Italian foods, sea foods, and meats. Some of them handled nonfrozen items as well. The brokers would sell to grocery chains and to frozen-food distributors. In addition to their actual selling activities, the brokers were expected to check on the credit of buyers, to arrange shipments, and to merchandise the selling at the retail level by such things as improving store displays and helping retailers tie in with Sara Lee promotions. Sara Lee proposed to pay the brokers a 5 per cent commission. The distributors would stock the cakes, or would draw on stocks maintained in public warehouses by Sara Lee, and would call on independent retailers on an average of twice a week. Very small accounts would be called on less often—perhaps once in two weeks. Retailers that purchased 400 dozen cakes at a time would receive direct shipments from the Sara Lee Chicago bakery. On direct shipments of this type, brokers would receive their normal margin; distributors would receive a reduced margin, lower according to the reduction of storage costs; and the retailer would receive a quantity discount.

Purchases by retailers of the frozen cakes were expected to vary widely. The typical small retail store would sell about a dozen cakes a week. Some small retailers might sell as few as three on a week end, and some large ones would sell 200–300 over a week end. Sara Lee planned to maintain the same price nationally—except west of Denver, where freight rates would require increases. By doing this, the company hoped to maintain the same retail price level as in Chicago—except on the West Coast, where retail prices would be about 10 cents higher per cake. Retailers could sell at any price they wished, though, and some retailers that offered special services, such as being open twenty-four hours a day, would undoubtedly charge higher prices. Retailers would pay distributors different prices for the cakes, depending on the quantity purchased. This would cause retail margins to fluctuate between 18 and 22 per cent if the established retail prices were maintained.

To supervise the frozen-cake operation, it was proposed to establish a third division in the firm, under the control of a frozen-foods sales manager, to be known as the "frozen-food division." The sales manager would have a small staff of regional sales managers to supervise the brokers.

Additional costs would be incurred by Sara Lee in producing and distributing a line of frozen cakes. First, there was the cost of freezing the cakes, then the cost of shipping them by refrigerated trucks. The 79-cent cakes weighed 19 ounces net, and the 59-cent cakes 11 ounces. The individual cake containers added a slight amount to this. For shipment over long distances the cakes would be packed twenty-four to a corrugated box, with four rows of six, each separated by corrugated dividers. Established truck-load rates for this service from Chicago were as follows: to New York City, $2.44 per cwt., 18,000 lbs. minimum; to Los Angeles, $5.21 per cwt., 20,000 lbs. minimum; to New Orleans, $2.54 per cwt., 20,000 lbs. minimum.

Warehousing charges for frozen cakes varied considerably in different parts of the country but averaged about as shown in the accompanying tabulation.

	Lots of:	
Warehouse Charge for:	Less than 2,000 lbs.	2,000 lbs. or More
Handling (in and out per cwt.)	$0.43	$0.33
Storage (per month per cwt.)	0.43	0.33
Special charge for type of product............	0.07	0.07

All large trucking firms handled frozen foods only by the truck load. Less-than-truck load rates were $4.50 per hundredweight to New York and $9.50 per hundredweight to Los Angeles. In all cases the minimum charge was for 100 pounds.

Sara Lee's advertising expenditures varied from market to market, depending on the management's judgment of what needed to be done and what was feasible in each case. For the company as a whole, however, advertising expenditures varied between 5 and 7 per cent of sales from year to year. This was higher than the ratio for the food industry generally. In most markets the advertising budget was distributed among the different media as follows: newspapers, 40 per cent; spot TV, 40 per cent; radio and other media, 20 per cent.

If no good TV spots were available at "reasonable" prices, a greater amount of the budget was put into radio. The Sara Lee executives realized that relatively high advertising budgets would be necessary to break into new markets, and they were prepared to increase their expenditure substantially if it appeared that this would establish the line in a given market.

Sara Lee could "go national" in at least two other ways. New bakeries could be constructed in major markets, each to serve an area of about a three-hundred-mile radius, as had been done in Chicago. In this case no frozen line would be necessary; each area would have the fresh line. It was anticipated that production cost could be held at the same level as in Chicago, but management hesitated to enter into this type of development because of the quality control problem that decentralization would bring. Sara Lee's success, they believed, was based on the uniform high quality of its products. The only way this could be guaranteed was to keep production centralized where it could be rigidly supervised.

Another alternative was to introduce the frozen line and handle the sales through a nation-wide company sales force.

What method of distribution should Sara Lee use to reach the national market?

33

DOLL HOUSE PRODUCTS, INC.

DOLL HOUSE PRODUCTS, INC., had manufactured a complete line of doll houses and accessories for the toy trade for many years. These items normally retailed from $3.00 to $7.00, and some were of the hobby-kit type. The products had a reputation for good quality and novelty in design. Prices were high compared to toys generally, but were highly competitive compared to other toys of comparable quality.

These doll houses and accessories were sold to standard retail toy outlets through toy jobbers and manufacturers' agents specializing in toys. When a new line of plastic toy dishes, pots, pans, and other household utensils was developed to sell at 15, 29, and 49 cents, the management decided to try some new retail outlets in addition to its established ones. Food and drug outlets looked like logical places to garner impulse sales, but the items were no sooner started there than Doll House's management received complaints from the regular channels.

The company occupied a strong, but not a dominant, position in the toy industry. Sales, which averaged between $1 million and $1.25 million annually, were handled by a select group of toy jobbers and manufacturers' agents that called on wholesale and retail toy outlets. Doll House had no salesmen of its own. The president was also the sales manager. Most of the president's sales contacts were with the jobbers and manufacturers' agents, but he usually attended the annual toy show in New York to be with the company exhibit there. In addition, he generally made a quarterly visit to the firm's permanent showroom in the New York City toy mart.

Besides these exhibits, the company carried on a modest but consistent advertising program in leading toy trade journals. This was supplemented by colorful, descriptive brochures and price lists for the use of the agents and jobbers and by a certain amount of direct-mail promotion to toy buyers of important retail accounts.

The company planned to package the new line of inexpensive plastic toy dishes, pails, and other doll-house equipment in transparent plastic coverings and to sell them as impulse merchandise in the usual toy stores and variety chains. Management also believed that a substantial market for these items existed in food and drugstores. The manufacturers' agents and toy jobbers that handled Doll House products did not cover food and drug outlets adequately in the management's opinion. In order to expand sales volume among these new retailers, therefore, the firm decided to use food and drug brokers as an added channel of distribution. When the toy jobbers and agents began to complain that the new channel encroached upon the accounts and territories that they served, Doll House executives decided they should make a complete appraisal of the policy.

Their first step was to get a thorough picture of toy distribution methods and trends. The *1954 Census of Wholesaling* gave a rough picture of the industry under the category "Toys, Games, and Athletic Goods." Neither food brokers nor wholesalers appeared under this category as distributors (Table 1). Specialty and general-line drug wholesalers together accounted for only 1 per cent of sales of this product category, and drug brokers were not shown at all. Wholesalers of amusement and sporting goods, which included toy wholesalers, accounted for the largest share of wholesale sales volume of the class "Toys, Games, and Athletic Goods." These data gave some indication of distribution but were limited in value because the information was not broken down for toys alone or by price ranges. Furthermore, these data showed total toy sales of only $723 million, whereas informed trade sources estimated sales in the range of $1.5–$2 billion at wholesale prices. The census data were six years old, which further limited their value.

A survey, "A Distribution Guide for Toy Manufacturers," done by the Toy Wholesalers Association of America, gave further information

TABLE 1

WHOLESALE SALES OF TOYS, GAMES, AND ATHLETIC GOODS: U.S., 1954

Type of Merchant Wholesaler	Amount of Sales (Millions of Dollars)	Per Cent of U.S. Total	Per Cent of All Lines Sold*
Amusement and sporting goods..................	$488.0	67.5	61.9
Hardware.......................................	119.1	16.5	6.4
Miscellaneous products.........................	42.8	5.9	1.8
Automotive equipment, tires, and tubes...........	21.8	3.0	0.8
Home furnishings...............................	9.9	1.4	0.8
Tobacco.......................................	6.3	0.9	0.2
Books, magazines, and newspapers...............	5.7	0.8	1.0
Specialty-line drug and toiletries.................	4.2	0.6	0.5
Specialty-line dry goods........................	3.8	0.5	0.2
Coarse paper and products......................	3.6	0.5	0.3
General-line drug..............................	3.2	0.4	0.3
Printing and fine paper.........................	2.8	0.4	0.2
Jewelry.......................................	2.7	0.4	0.4
Furniture......................................	2.3	0.3	0.4
Clothing and footwear..........................	2.3	0.3	0.1
Confectionery.................................	1.3	0.2	0.4
Stationery and office supplies....................	1.2	0.2	0.4
Transportation equipment.......................	1.0	0.1	0.3
Professional equipment and supplies..............	1.0	0.1	0.1
Paint and varnish..............................	0.4	..	0.2
Total.....................................	$723.4	100.0	

* Figures in this column represent the per cent of dollar sales of toys, games, and athletic goods to the total dollar sales of all commodity lines that are sold by each type of wholesaler. For example, while amusement & sporting goods wholesalers sold 67.5 per cent of all U.S. wholesale sales of toys, games, and athletic goods, this particular line of merchandise accounted for only 61.9 per cent of all commodity-line sales handled by these wholesalers.
Source: *1954 U.S. Census of Wholesaling.*

on the outlets covered by toy wholesalers. The results of this survey indicated that the toy wholesalers covered both drugstores and super-markets in varying degrees and that such coverage represented a fairly substantial part of their sales activity. Pertinent findings from this survey are shown in Tables 2, 3, and 4.

TABLE 2

NUMBER OF ACCOUNTS SERVICED BY 240 TOY WHOLESALERS

Number of Retail Accounts Serviced	Toy Wholesalers Servicing This Number of Accounts	
	Number	Per Cent of Total
100 or less...........................	8	3.3
101–300.............................	68	28.3
301–500.............................	67	27.9
501–1,000...........................	45	18.8
1,001–2,000..........................	35	14.6
2,001–5,000..........................	12	5.0
Over 5,000...........................	5	2.1
Total.............................	240	100.0

Source: Toy Wholesalers' Association of America.

TABLE 3

TYPES OF RETAIL ACCOUNTS SERVICED BY 221 TOY WHOLESALERS

	Toy Wholesalers Servicing Each Type of Account	
Type of Retail Account Serviced	Number	Per Cent of Total Respondents
Variety stores......................	192	86.9
Toy stores............................	185	83.7
Drugstores...........................	170	76.8
Department stores.....................	151	68.3
Supermarkets.........................	93	42.0
Stationery stores......................	82	37.1
Newsstands...........................	43	19.4
Hardware stores......................	9	4.1
Other types..........................	22	10.0

Source: Toy Wholesalers' Association of America.

TABLE 4

DISTRIBUTION OF RETAIL ACCOUNTS SERVICED BY TOY WHOLESALERS

	Number of Wholesalers for Which Each Type of Account Makes Up the Percentage Shown of All Accounts			
Type of Retail Account Serviced	Less than 10 Per Cent	10–25 Per Cent	26–50 Per Cent	51–75 Per Cent
Toy stores......................	40	61	40	20
Drugstores.....................	39	72	33	12
Variety stores..................	29	89	38	11
Department stores...............	56	69	15	2
Supermarkets...................	40	34	10	3
Newsstands.....................	35	7	..	..
Stationery stores................	39	34	3	3
Hardware stores.................	1	2	2	1
Other types....................	3	8	4	4

	76–99 Per Cent	100 Per Cent	No Per Cent Given	Total Accounts Serviced
Toy stores......................	14	3	7	185
Drugstores.....................	7	3	4	170
Variety stores..................	16	2	7	192
Department stores...............	1	1	7	151
Supermarkets...................	2	3	1	93
Newsstands.....................	..	..	1	43
Stationery stores................	..	..	3	82
Hardware stores.................	3	..	..	9
Other types....................	3	..	..	22

Source: Toy Wholesalers' Association of America.

Toys and Novelties Magazine, the principal trade magazine, had published "Marketing Toys" in 1957. This pointed out a basic change in toy buying habits that had occurred since 1938. Seventy-eight per cent of retail toy sales were made in November and December in 1938, but by

1957 this had dropped to 60 per cent, with the other 40 per cent spread over the preceding ten months. The number of exclusive toy shops doing an all-year business had increased to more than three thousand in recent years and was still increasing. Among the more important newcomers to the toy selling field, the brochure listed (along with the exclusive toy shops) supermarkets and hardware-housewares stores. The brochure commented that toys in supermarkets could be regarded as price promotional devices that were more important as traffic lures than as conveniences for shoppers. This brochure estimated that toy jobbers handled about 45 per cent of the total toy volume and were growing in importance. It stated that the jobber was necessary to reach the many small dealers handling toys. The "rack jobber" was also becoming an important link in the chain of distribution.

A survey by the Toy Manufacturers of the U.S.A. gave information concerning the toy-buying habits of the American public, and the data were separated by various toy price ranges. The survey showed that about 52 per cent of total toy sales were made through department and variety stores. Toy, drug, auto supply, hardware, and children's stores accounted for another 25 per cent of the retail volume. Supermarkets, discount houses, and mail-order firms each accounted for about 2 per cent of the volume. The woman in the family was the largest purchaser of toys. Women accounted for 67 per cent of all toy purchases made during the Christmas season. About two-thirds of all toys were purchased with some advance knowledge of what was wanted.

The survey indicated that the principal retail outlets for toys selling for $1.00 or less were variety and department stores (Table 5). Although toys in this price category represented 37 per cent of the unit volume of

TABLE 5

DISTRIBUTION OF PURCHASES OF LOW-COST TOYS BY TYPE OF OUTLET

	Percentage of Toys in Various Price Ranges by Type of Outlet in Which Sold		
Type of Retail Outlet	25 Cents or Less	26–50 Cents	51 Cents–$1.00
Variety	58%	53%	35%
Department store (independent and chain)	13	19	32
Toy store	7	5	6
Supermarket	6	3	1
Drugstore	7	8	6
Auto supply	1	1	4
Childrens' store	1	1	2
Discount house	*	*	1
Hardware store	1	2	3
Mail order	*	1	1
Other and not reported	6	7	9
	100%	100%	100%

* Less than 1 per cent.
Source: Toy Manufacturers of the U.S.A., Inc.

all toys, they accounted for only 6 per cent of the dollar volume. Toys in this price range were most frequently bought for children six years old and under. Socioeconomic characteristics of families affected distribution of toys in the under-$1.00 price range. About three-fifths of all toys in this price range were bought by people living in communities with less than 25,000 population, and nearly 50 per cent of this market was located in the northeast and southern regions of the country. From 73 to 78 per cent of all toys in the under-$1.00 price range were purchased by families with annual incomes ranging from $2,000 to $7,000 (Table 6).

TABLE 6

DISTRIBUTION OF LOW-PRICED TOY PURCHASES
BY GEOGRAPHIC AREA, CITY SIZE, AND INCOME

	Percentage of Toys in Various Price Ranges Bought by Families in Categories Shown		
	25 Cents or less	26–50 Cents	51 Cents–$1.00
Geographic area			
Northeast	28%	24%	25%
East North Central	17	18	20
West North Central	16	16	14
South	24	23	21
Southwest	6	8	7
West	9	11	13
Total	100%	100%	100%
City size (population)			
Under 2,500	42%	41%	44%
2,500–24,999	17	20	16
25,000–99,999	13	14	14
100,000–499,999	12	13	14
500,000 and over	16	12	12
Total	100%	100%	100%
Family income			
Under $2,000	8%	12%	9%
2,000–3,999	33	32	31
4,000–6,999	45	41	45
7,000 and over	10	9	9
Not reported	4	6	6
Total	100%	100%	100%

Source: Toy Manufacturers of the U.S.A., Inc.

Date from the American Rack Merchandisers Institute indicated that rack merchandisers had become a key factor in the distribution of non-food items through food stores. Rack merchandisers offered nonfood items to larger food stores on a service and guaranteed sales basis, leaving store managers free to concentrate on food sales. The rack merchandisers maintained inventories in the stores, and the stores paid only for the items sold. An estimated 81 per cent of the nation's supermarkets utilized the services of rack merchandisers to some extent. Retail volume done by rack merchandisers in nonfood items had increased from $17.5 million in 1949 to $400 million in 1958.

A study done by *Progressive Grocer Magazine* stated that toys ranked fifth among nonfood items in sales importance in the modern supermarket (see Table 7). Toys received from 10 to 12 square feet of floor

TABLE 7

RELATIVE IMPORTANCE OF SELECTED NONFOOD ITEMS IN
SUPERMARKETS

Nonfood Lines Sold in Supermarkets	Per Cent of Total Store Sales
Health and beauty aids	2.30
Housewares	0.92
Magazines	0.58
Soft goods	0.53
Toys	0.35
Records	0.30
Stationery	0.23

space in those stores handling them. Usually, more than ninety different toy items were handled, most selling for less than $1.00. The study showed that 67 per cent of the stores covered purchased toys through rack merchandisers, 17 per cent through wholesale grocers, 10 per cent direct from manufacturers, and 6 per cent were unspecified.

Data from the Super Market Institute confirmed the importance of rack merchandisers. A report by the Institute stated that eighteen out of twenty-one nonfood lines sold in supermarkets were supplied by rack merchandisers. This report listed the following points:

1. The percentage of all supermarkets handling nonfood items increased from 31 per cent in 1953 to 66 per cent in 1958.
2. In 80 per cent of the supermarkets the rack jobber was the major source of supply for toys, in 13 per cent it was the wholesaler, and in 7 per cent the manufacturer (direct sales).
3. Supermarkets in the southwestern and western regions of the country were less inclined to use rack jobbers as a source of toys than were those in other parts of the country.
4. Food chains with sales volume over $50 million annually were more likely to buy toys direct from the manufacturer than were those having lesser volume.

What action should Doll House Products, Inc., take with respect to its channel of distribution?

34

YOMANS PAINT COMPANY

YOMANS had been a well-known manufacturer of masonry paints for industry for many years. Sales had grown rapidly from $3 million in 1948 to $5 million in 1954, and gross profits had consistently averaged 30 per cent of sales. Sales in 1955 and 1956, however, showed little gain, and management believed that the company had reached a plateau as far as industrial sales were concerned and that further growth would come only gradually unless new markets were opened. In 1957 the decision was made to enter the retail market with Yomans' products. For the first time in the company's history, a marketing division was established. The first assignment was to develop an over-all market program for entering the retail market. The goal of this program was to double sales volume in the next five years by achieving national retail distribution.

Over its fifty-year history, Yomans Paint Company had built a reputation for producing only one high-quality paint. Its paint was accepted by industry as far superior to any other type for sealing and waterproofing concrete or brick surfaces. Although other companies manufactured paints for masonry, they were not competitive with Yomans in the industrial market. At present there was only one other smaller company that manufactured a paint that was considered competitive. It was known that several of the large paint manufacturers were attempting to develop a paint of competitive quality and would soon be entering the market. Yomans had limited itself to masonry paints and was a minor factor in the total paint market, having less than one-half of 1 per cent share of the market.

The company had 28 sales districts covering the United States, each under a factory representative. All the representatives, except one in a sparsely populated western district, were exclusive representatives for Yomans, handling only the Yomans line. They had full control over their districts, and all contacts with distributors were made through the factory representatives. All maintained offices in their district, and many had sales staffs. The factory representatives paid all their own expenses, including those of their sales staffs, and a portion of the advertising done in their district. The company paid the representative a commission on net sales in his district. The commission varied between districts, depending on the representatives' participation in sales activities and advertising, but was generally around 10 per cent.

The factory representatives established distributors as they were needed in their districts. However, the company did not allow them to discontinue a distributor without home office approval. In addition to handling all contacts with distributors, the factory representatives called directly on large accounts and aided distributors with other accounts upon request. In all cases, orders were always placed through the distributor in the area.

Yomans had about one hundred industrial distributors, mainly mill supply houses and industrial paint distributors. In addition to industrial accounts, their market included large painting contractors. Yomans paint was a special purpose product and was not a main line with these distributors. Most of the distributors handled three or four general lines of paint in addition to special purpose lines. Industrial users paid $7.00 a gallon for Yomans paint less a quantity discount up to 25 per cent. Distributors received a basic 50 per cent discount plus a quantity discount, which permitted the total discount to amount to as much as 55 per cent.

The plan developed by the marketing division called for gaining entry to the top twenty major retail market areas in 1957 and to the top 70 areas by 1959 and for putting Yomans' paints on the shelves of two-thirds of the retailers in these areas within two years after entry. A line of ten colors for consumer uses, packaged in retail sizes (gallons, quarts, pints, and half-pints), was developed for the consumer market.

No changes were planned in the sales organization, and the factory representatives would be given the responsibility for establishing retail distributors. Investigation showed that this was the sales organization used by most paint manufacturers. A few sold direct through company-owned stores or direct to large industrial users, but most sales were made through factory representatives and distributors.

The selection of retail distributors, however, was not left solely to the factory representatives. The new marketing division planned to make a survey of each market area to determine: (1) the potential of the area, (2) retailers' attitudes and expectations concerning Yomans paints, (3) which distributor or distributors were considered the best by retailers in the area, and (4) the number of distributors that would be required to gain full coverage of the area. This survey was to be done by the company's advertising agency with the aid of the factory representative and his staff in that district.

Full coverage of an area was considered to be two-thirds of the eligible retailers. The company eliminated about 30 per cent of those retailers who handled paint, because they were considered undesirable outlets either for reasons of type of operation, such as variety stores and drugstores that handled paint, or because they were poor credit risks. On this basis the total number of eligible retailers was arrived at as shown in Exhibit 1. The total potential of the United States was estimated to be six-tenths of 1 per cent of the total paint market, which was estimated to be $1.2 billion.

From the results of the survey, the company would select the distributors to be approached to handle Yomans' products. These selections would be given to the factory representatives for their consideration and approval, and they would approach the distributors. If an industrial distributor handling the Yomans line in an area also had a retail division, he would be given equal consideration with other distributors. If he rated high in the survey, he would be given the first opportunity to take on the retail line. If he did not rate high, he would be informed that he could not be considered as a retail distributor before any action was taken in his area with other distributors. The results of the survey were to be

EXHIBIT 1

NUMBER OF ELIGIBLE RETAIL OUTLETS FOR YOMANS PAINT IN THE
TOP 20 MARKETS AND EACH MARKET'S SHARE OF THE NATIONAL
PAINT MARKET: ELIGIBLE RETAIL DEALERS FOR NEXT 50
MARKETS AND FOR THE TOTAL UNITED STATES

Top 20 Markets	No. of Retailers	Share of U.S. Paint Market
1. New York	4,801	10.07
2. Chicago	2,161	4.56
3. Los Angeles	1,682	4.00
4. Philadelphia	1,500	3.07
5. Detroit	1,368	2.68
6. Boston	1,253	2.13
7. Cleveland	1,007	1.41
8. Pittsburgh	828	1.75
9. Minneapolis	770	0.89
10. San Francisco	761	1.85
11. St. Louis	696	1.28
12. Seattle	648	1.01
13. Dallas	591	1.00
14. Milwaukee	559	0.96
15. Buffalo	536	0.94
16. Baltimore	500	1.00
17. Portland	472	0.59
18. Cincinnati	466	0.83
19. Houston	525	0.85
20. Washington, D.C.	462	1.03
Total	21,656	
Next 50 markets	38,000	
Total United States	80,000	

put into a report that could be used by the factory representative as a sales tool in selling the desired distributor. This report would contain a summary of the reasons why a particular distributor was selected, the attitude of retailers toward Yomans paint, and the estimated potential for the area.

It had not been company policy to grant exclusive distributorships to its industrial distributors. Their territories were not limited, but the company required that they service what they sell. This policy would apply to retail distributors also. The company would reserve the right to establish distributors in an area as needed to gain coverage of at least two-thirds of the eligible retailers.

A steel display rack was developed that held approximately fourteen gallons of paint in various sized cans ranging from the half-pint to the gallon. This was to be distributed to retailers and also to constitute the minimum amount of Yomans' paint a dealer should stock. The cost to the retailer for the rack and paint was $70 and had a retail value of $130. The average retailer usually had one main line of paint and two or three supplementary lines. In addition to these were lines of special purpose paints, brushes, wallpaper, art supplies, and miscellaneous supplies for home decorating. The average retail paint store carried between 2,000 and 3,000 different items.

The retail price for Yomans paint was set the same as the industrial price, $7 per gallon. Retailers would receive a discount of 35 per cent. The retail distributors would receive a basic discount of 50 per cent plus quantity discounts, which permitted the total discount to amount to as much as 55 per cent. In net, this meant a smaller margin for the company because of the increased cost of advertising expenditures in supporting a market, particularly in its initial phase. Broken down by size of can, retail prices were $2.89 per quart, $1.69 per pint, and $0.98 per half-pint.

A consumer advertising program was planned that included display racks, point-of-sale advertising, and newspaper, radio, and television advertising. The money allocated for advertising in each area was to be based on the potential volume of the area in gallons of paint. A system was set up to credit 10 cents for advertising for each gallon of paint sold. At the end of the year the credits would be balanced against the expenditures. The company did not expect to achieve a balance in the first year, but, if the second year did not balance, a new evaluation of the distributor or distributors in the area would be made before further action was taken. It was company policy not to do co-operative advertising, and, with few exceptions, all advertising was determined and placed by the company through its agency. This policy did not extend to the factory representatives who occasionally participated with distributors in advertising programs.

Appraise Yomans' program for entering the retail paint market.

35

JESSUP SURGICAL DRESSINGS COMPANY

THE Jessup Surgical Dressings Company manufactured a line of surgical dressings (bandages and adhesive tape) for use in hospitals. Besides selling in the United States, the firm sold its products in several foreign countries, in each case through local distributors. In 1956 George Traver was made vice-president of a newly created international division, which assumed responsibility for all foreign business. In reviewing Jessup's foreign operations over the next few years, Traver became convinced that the distributor in Colombia was ineffective. No better distributor was available, however, so if Jessup dropped the existing distributor the company would have to handle distribution in Colombia itself.

Jessup was considered by the trade to be a small, specialty hospital supply firm. Its sales totaled $24 million. In the United States all Jessup's products were sold through Signet Surgicals, Inc., a large hospital supply wholesaler. This wholesaler sold a complete line of hospital supplies throughout the country, including some items that competed with the Jessup line. Except for the large, full-line manufacturers who distributed their goods through their own sales forces, most of Jessup's competitors also sold through distributors.

From the beginning of its foreign operation in the late 1930's, Jessup sold its line in other countries through one leading distributor in each country. These distributors handled the entire marketing program. Shortly after World War II, Jessup built a number of plants in foreign countries to produce the goods sold in those countries. The marketing of these goods, however, was left to the existing distributors. Plants were built in South Africa, Belgium, and Colombia.

Colombia had a population of thirteen million people, primarily concentrated in the western half of the country. Even in the western part the population was scattered, and in the eastern half the population was very sparse indeed. The income per capita was low, even by South American standards. The Andes Mountains cut the country into halves from north to south. Swamps, forests, and rivers added to the difficulty of the terrain. Roads were poor, and car and truck travel was limited. Railroads existed in only a few areas. Planes were the most frequent mode of transportation for long distances.

In studying the firm's situation in Colombia, Traver found the country had 365 hospitals with 33,700 beds, about 130 clinics with 4,000 beds, and several thousand drugstores. He believed that the hospitals made up about 80 per cent of the market for Jessup's products, with drugstores accounting for the remaining business. As a general rule of thumb, 40 units of both bandages and adhesive tape were considered the annual potential per hospital bed in the United States. Traver estimated that half of that figure, or 20 units of each product, would be the potential sales per hospital or clinic bed in Colombia. Therefore he estimated the potential for each of the two Jessup products to be about 750,000 units in the hospitals and clinics. In addition, there was an estimated potential of 187,500 units sold through drugstores. The products sold through drugstores were ultimately sold to doctors and small clinics rather than to consumers, since Jessup did not package its products for consumers. Jessup prices averaged about 70 cents per unit, so the total dollar potential for Jessup products was about $1,312,500.

Jessup's principal competition in Colombia came from two very large, complete line hospital supply manufacturers. One was Simon, Inc., a Colombian firm, which had about 80 per cent of the country's surgical dressings business. Hartman and Son, one of the large hospital supply producers in the United States, was the other competitor. Hartman tended to specialize in consumer products and so was not as serious a competitor as was Simon. Both firms, however, had plants and their own distribution systems in Colombia.

Jessup's distributor in Colombia sold approximately $100,000 of Jessup products in 1958. On the basis of the potential available, Traver believed that Jessup should have a volume of at least $500,000. The distributor had complete marketing responsibility for the Jessup line. He had a sales force of twelve men, who called on hospitals, clinics, and drugstores. In addition to the Jessup products, he handled a complete line of other hospital supply items, but none that competed directly with Jessup. Traver had no information on the advertising done by the distributor, if any, and knew only vaguely of the general selling policies. One of the important services furnished by the distributor was credit. Almost all sales were made on credit, and payments were very slow—six months not being uncommon. No interest was charged for these slow payments because it was customary not to make such charges.

The distributor's margin varied by product but averaged about 35 per cent. During 1958 the distributor pressed Jessup for a wider margin; this was one of the factors that made Traver consider dropping him.

Traver believed the primary market for Jessup's line was among the four million people living in or around the largest cities, which had populations varying from 50,000 to over 1,000,000 (Table 1).

TABLE 1

POPULATION OF THIRTEEN LARGEST COLOMBIAN
CITIES: 1956

Cities	Population (000)
Barranquilla	392
Bogotá	1,180
Bucaramanga	174
Buenaventura	50
Cali	504
Cartagena	162
Cucuta	126
Ibaqué	128
Manizales	156
Medellín	546
Pasto	106
Popayán	56
Tunja	47
Total	3,627

If Jessup were to undertake to sell direct, he would concentrate on hospitals and only on those hospitals with more than 25 beds. Many smaller clinics did not stock dressings but simply bought from local drugstores as needed. For this reason the drugstores handled the dressings packaged for hopitals. The salesman would call on smaller hospitals and clinics and drugstores only when they were close to larger hospitals and when he could make such a call with little additional expense.

Each hospital bought its own supplies and equipment, often on a bid basis. The purchasing agents handled the entire transaction, and price was an important factor in deciding which item to buy. Most of the larger hospitals were part of the government's socialized medical program. They tended to buy about a six-month supply at a time, while the smaller hospitals bought supplies only as needed.

Traver believed Colombia could be divided into six sales territories, each territory containing one or more major cities, which would be the basic market (Exhibit 1). These were: Territory 1, Cali, Popayán, and

EXHIBIT 1

PROPOSED JESSUP SALES TERRITORIES IN COLUMBIA

Pasto; Territory 2, Manizales and Ibaqué; Territory 3, Bogotá; Territory 4, Cucuta, Bucaramanga, and Tunja; Territory 5, Medellín; and Territory 6, Barranquilla and Cartagena. Raw materials were shipped from the United States to Buenaventura, a port located on the southwest coast, and hauled by truck or train to Cali, the location of the plant and central headquarters for Jessup's Colombian operation. Traver proposed to warehouse some of the finished products in Bogotá, from which he would supply the southern half of the country, and in Barranquilla to supply the northern half of the country. If an order was large enough to make a truck load, then it would be shipped directly from Cali. Such shipments would be slow. It was estimated that the trip from Cali to Barranquilla would take a truck approximately ten days.

To handle direct sales with this type of arrangement, Traver estimated that he would need the following personnel: one general manager in charge of both marketing and production; two sales supervisors, one for the northern region and one for the southern; seven to ten salesmen; two warehousemen; and an office staff in Cali for billing, credit, and collection.

On the basis of local price levels, each salesman would be paid a $2,000 annual salary and would have expenses of about $2,000. The sales supervisors would be paid $3,000 each, and the general manager $8,500. All other personnel together would cost about $8,000. Salesmen, using public transportation, should average six calls per day and should produce sales of $50,000 each per year. Promotion would be limited to participation in trade shows and direct-mail pieces.

Should Jessup undertake direct sale in Colombia?

36

INTERNATIONAL HARVESTER MOTOR TRUCK DIVISION (A)

INTERNATIONAL HARVESTER's share of total truck sales in the Los Angeles metropolitan area was low in 1952 and dropped even further in the following years. The western regional manager faced the problem of reversing this situation, as a proper share of the truck sales in this area was extremely important because of the size of the Los Angeles market and its rapid rate of growth.

A study of new truck registrations by gross vehicle weight (G.V.W.) for the four most important metropolitan markets in the United States for the years 1952 and 1953 and for the first ten months of 1954 (Table 1) presented the picture clearly.

International's share of the new truck registrations in the Los Angeles metropolitan market, which included all of Los Angeles County, had declined from 8.7 per cent of the industry total in 1952 to 5.6 per cent for the first ten months of 1954. International Harvester was concerned not only because of this drop but because, when compared to the three other major metropolitan markets, the company's industry share in Los

TABLE 1

NEW TRUCK REGISTRATIONS BY YEARS IN FOUR MAJOR MARKETS

| | 1952 | | | 1953 | | | 1954* | | |
| | In-dustry | International | | In-dustry | International | | In-dustry | International | |
Market		No.	Per Cent		No.	Per Cent		No.	Per Cent
Los Angeles....	17,825	1,542	8.7	23,540	1,768	7.5	19,513	1,085	5.6
Chicago.........	13,343	1,528	11.5	15,801	2,145	13.6	11,618	1,690	14.5
Philadelphia.....	6,924	719	10.4	8,213	838	10.2	6,233	660	10.6
New York......	17,236	2,179	12.6	20,549	3,037	14.8	14,587	1,897	13.0

*Figures for 1954 cover the first ten months only.

Angeles was extremely poor. In Chicago, International had 14.5 per cent of the industry's sales; in Philadelphia it had 10.6 per cent; and in New York 13.0 per cent. Los Angeles was by far the largest truck market in the country. In 1954 there were 208,834 trucks registered in Los Angeles County, as compared to only 119,335 in the five boroughs of New York City, the county with the second largest number of trucks.

The motor truck division of International Harvester Company manufactured and sold a wide variety of motor trucks and service parts, which were marketed under the trade name "International." Its product line ranged from small pickups and utility vehicles to heavy-duty models for all purposes.

Sales of motor trucks, parts, and service were a very important segment of the company's total sales, amounting to approximately $300,-000,000 in 1954—about 30 per cent of International's total sales. Harvester ranked third in the industry in total new truck registrations, but was first in the heavy-duty classification, which included trucks with gross vehicle weight of over 16,000 pounds (Table 2). Trucks weighing about 5,000 pounds tended to sell at a retail price around $2,500; trucks weighing 26,000 pounds retailed for about $7,500; while very large trucks might weigh close to 40 tons and sell for almost $25,000. Retail markups on the trucks averaged about 25 per cent. Almost all the large trucks were concentrated in fleets.

In 1954 industry truck production in the United States was 1,038,056 units, with a wholesale value of $1,588,046,000. Prior to 1954 approximately 850,000 new motor trucks were registered annually in the United States by the entire industry, and International trucks represented 11.5 per cent of that number. International had a goal of 15 per cent of the annual new truck registrations.

The 15 per cent market share goal was ambitious because, as shown in Table 2, the majority of new trucks sold were light trucks. In this field International was at a competitive disadvantage with the "big three" automobile companies. In light trucks many parts were interchangeable with parts used in passenger cars. Any of these interchangeable parts could be

TABLE 2

1954 New Truck Registrations by Makes and Gross Vehicle Weights

Make of Truck	Under 5,000 lbs.	5,001–10,000 lbs.	10,001–14,000 lbs.	14,001–16,000 lbs.	16,001–19,500 lbs.	19,501–26,000 lbs.	Over 26,000 lbs.	Total in U.S.
Chevrolet	161,382	56,206	12,635	62,856	……	……	……	293,079
Ford	141,837	45,298	14,103	46,916	8,941	7,800	2,902	267,799
International	30,007	12,603	2,497	14,131	10,565	7,197	7,322	84,222
GMC	24,626	11,821	2,728	12,479	6,035	4,682	4,273	66,644
Dodge	26,081	15,161	1,708	11,406	4,884	974	444	60,658
White	……	……	……	……	834	4,737	5,810	11,381
Studebaker	5,936	1,946	1,155	1,156	……	……	……	10,193
Willys Truck	3,099	6,826	……	……	……	……	……	9,925
Willys Jeep	7,598	……	……	……	……	……	……	7,598
All others	520	1,899	606	975	1,117	3,701	8,784	17,602
Total	401,088	151,760	35,432	149,919	32,376	29,091	29,435	829,101

Source: Automotive Industries, 37th Annual Statistical Issue: 1955.

produced at less expense by Chevrolet, Dodge, or Ford because of the great volume of passenger cars each had. International's management also believed that the company should continue to stress its heavier trucks. In this field Harvester already enjoyed a competitive advantage of customer acceptance. In addition, the volume was small enough that no other producer in the field could have the type of cost advantage that existed in the light truck field.

International trucks retailed through two types of outlets: franchised dealers and company-owned and -operated branches. There were about 5,250 dealers in the United States. Two-thirds of them were combination truck and farm equipment dealers and were located in small towns and rural areas. Most of the motor truck and parts business in the large cities was done through company branches, of which there were 165. This was particularly true for the large trucks; the dealers were more effective in selling the light trucks. In the average year, 40–45 per cent of all motor truck sales was handled by those branches.

International's activity in the retail field, as represented by its branches, was based on the following judgments founded on long experience:

1. International's branches, especially those at a considerable distance from its supervising district sales office, were invaluable as wholesale distribution points convenient to service neighboring dealers.
2. International must compete with other truck manufacturers who operate factory branches in many of the large markets.
3. Many large truck users preferred centralized dealings direct with the manufacturer for all their operations instead of multiple local arrangements wherever their trucks were located.
4. The technical knowledge and training of International's personnel was a definite advantage in servicing the varied needs of its large customers in metropolitan areas.
5. Branches provided an excellent training ground for employees and a ready source of trained and experienced individuals for advancement in the company.
6. The capital investment required for facilities, inventories, and other working capital in a large market was usually beyond the average dealer's financial limits.

Motor truck registration data for Los Angeles County were broken down by fleet size groups and number of owners and compared with similar data for the three other major markets. The results are shown in Table 3. Significant in the comparison was the large number of owners of four or fewer trucks in the Los Angeles market; Los Angeles had 25 per cent more owners in that category than New York and 300 per cent more than Philadelphia. The Los Angeles market contained a large number of small-farm owners and others with several acres for truck gardening, who combined to form a large potential for light-duty trucks. Often these individuals had employment in the city and used their trucks for transportation to and from work as well as for hauling produce.

TABLE 3

TRUCK OWNERS BY FLEET SIZE IN FOUR MAJOR MARKETS: 1954

Fleet Size	Los Angeles	Chicago	Philadelphia	New York
1–4.	98,387	45,312	25,061	77,374
5–11.	2,778	2,058	857	2,763
12–24.	654	578	227	721
25–49.	268	260	97	252
50 and over.	182	171	91	213
Total. 102,269		48,379	26,333	81,323

The scope of the Los Angeles market was revealed by other comparisons (Table 4). It was larger in area and number of motor truck owners than any of the others, and its area and number of owners were

TABLE 4

SELECTED STATISTICS ON FOUR MAJOR MARKETS

	Los Angeles	Chicago	New York	Philadelphia
Square mile area.	1,357	892	459	366
Number of truck owners.	102,269	48,379	81,323	26,333
Number of International dealers.	18	7	4	2
Number of International branches.	3	5	7	3
Number of branch salesmen.	38	36	35	21

four times as large as those of the Philadelphia market, but it had only the same number of branches.

All trucks registered within Los Angeles County were plotted on scatter maps according to the addresses where the trucks were principally garaged, as determined from branch sales and prospect records and salesmen's knowledge of accounts. Each truck registration was plotted on a clear acetate sheet, which was superimposed on a detailed street map of the area. One dot represented one truck. When completed, the scatter map reflected market concentrations. Exhibit 1 shows a rough approximation of this map.[1] The areas of greatest truck concentration are outlined on the map; the remainder of the trucks were distributed fairly evenly over the rest of the area.

A study of the overlay map disclosed heavy market concentrations in several industrial and commercial areas of Los Angeles proper, but generally the truck population was widespread. Prior experience indicated that a branch outlet, because of traffic congestion, could not expect to attract parts and service customers from beyond a five-mile radius in a metropolitan area.

Competitive makes of trucks were distributed principally through dealers whose main effort was devoted to passenger car sales and service.

---

[1] The small size of the map here does not permit showing the individual truck locations as was done on the original map.

EXHIBIT 1

MAJOR PORTION OF LOS ANGELES METROPOLITAN AREA, SHOWING CONCENTRATION OF
TRUCK LOCATIONS: 1954

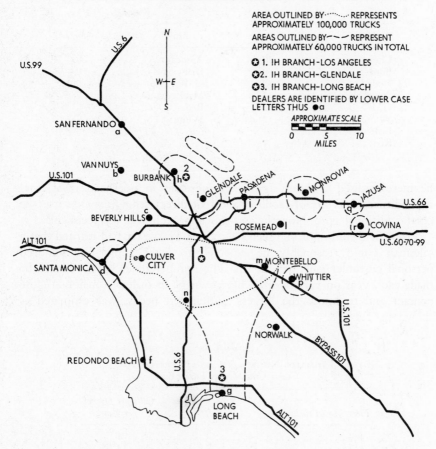

The large number of these dealers covered the market extensively and made competition severe. Few factory-owned branches of competitors served the market. Table 5 shows the number of competitive dealers and branches in late 1954.

International had three branches and eighteen dealers in the Los Angeles area. During the first ten months of 1954, branches accounted for 72 per cent of the 1,085 International trucks sold in that market. The company had experienced difficulties in franchising and holding good dealers in the area because of the strong competition from combination car and truck dealers with a sales volume advantage and because of the high capital investment required for land, facilities, tools, and inventories. The logical prospects for the International franchise were the automobile dealers who did not sell any line of trucks. In discussing contracts with these firms, International cited the fact that the motor truck line could

TABLE 5

COMPETITIVE OUTLETS IN LOS ANGELES: 1954

Dealers		Branches	
Make	Number	Make	Number
Chevrolet	70	Autocar	1
Ford	60	Diamond-T	1
Dodge	38	GMC	1
Studebaker	33	Mack	1
GMC	12	Reo	1
White	2	White	1
Federal	1		
Reo	1		
Total	217	Total	6

be merchandised without significant increases in overhead costs, tool expenditures, and size of facilities and that direct selling expense was the chief additional cost. Nonetheless, this approach was unsuccessful.

From field studies of salesmen's activities, Harvester had learned that a salesman could reasonably be expected to make about one hundred personal customer calls per month. The number of calls that should be made each year on various sized fleet owners, in order to maintain close contact and to know the buyers' anticipated needs, was estimated as shown in Table 6.

TABLE 6

ESTIMATED NUMBER OF CALLS NECESSARY FOR
CLOSE CONTACT BY FLEET SIZE

Fleet Size (Trucks)	Calls per Owner per Year
1–4	1
5–11	12
12–24	12
25–49	18
50 and over	24

The history of the three branches in Los Angeles indicated that a branch needed between 12,000 and 15,000 square feet of enclosed area for its operation. Rental costs averaged about $1.00 per square foot per year. Twelve to sixteen equipped service stalls were required per branch. Parts inventory averaged approximately 6 per cent of total sales and 30–50 per cent of parts sales, increasing with the size of the branch. Service revenue averaged $5.00 per hour of direct labor. Parts and service together accounted for 25 to 40 per cent of total sales, being higher in the smaller branches. Gross margins generally were between 12 and 15 per cent of total sales.

On the basis of the experience described above, the regional manager concluded that establishment of additional branches would entail a large capital investment on the part of the company. He also realized that it might be a number of years before a break-even point could be reached and that losses could be considerable for several years.

1. *Should International Harvester establish any additional branches in the Los Angeles area?*
2. *If yes, how many?*
3. *If no, are there alternative actions that the firm should take?*

37

VAN NORDEN AND COMPANY

FOR MANY years Van Norden and Company had distributed its wide line of plumbing equipment and supplies through a system of company-owned branches. Late in 1960 the management was considering a proposal to decentralize the manufacturing operation into four autonomous operating divisions and at the same time to shift its distribution from branches to independent wholesalers.

Van Norden's manufacturing operations, which were primarily concentrated in Pennsylvania, produced all types of plumbing equipment and fixtures, heating and air-conditioning equipment, and hot-water heaters. In addition to the products it manufactured, Van Norden branches also carried lines of allied products of other manufacturers. These allied lines accounted for approximately one-third of the firm's total sales of $430 million. For several products, Van Norden was the largest jobber in the United States.

Service to customers, often without much consideration of cost, was an early objective of the company and was the key factor in the development of the branch system. In addition, however, the lack of adequate channels of distribution in the early days of the 105-year-old company contributed to the impetus which caused the firm to develop its own distribution system. By 1918 the company had 70 branches and by 1930 almost 300. By 1960 the number had been reduced to 190 through consolidations and dropping of unprofitable branches.

Manufacturing and marketing had been clearly separated throughout Van Norden's history. The branch system was responsible for marketing all Van Norden products. The branches handled all sales to independent wholesalers and direct sales to users, except for a few large accounts which insisted on dealing directly with the main office. The sales organization was headed by a vice-president of sales (Exhibit 1). Under him were the director of advertising, the director of marketing services, and the director of sales. The director of sales was responsible for all

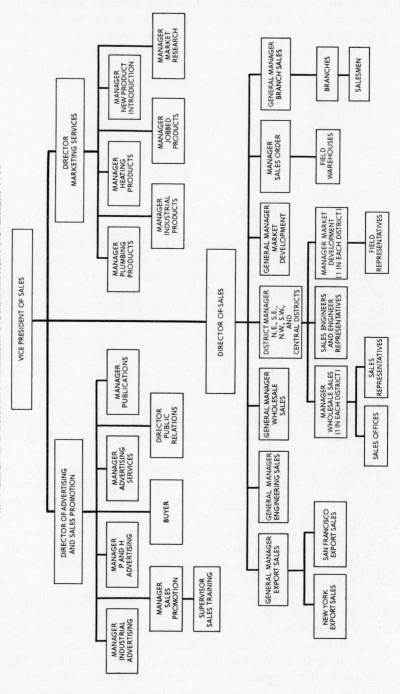

EXHIBIT 1

VAN NORDEN AND COMPANY MARKETING ORGANIZATION: NOVEMBER: 1960

personal sales functions. Reporting to him were the general manager of export sales, who was responsible for all sales outside the United States except Canada; the general manager of engineering sales, who was responsible for all sales of more complex equipment, such as valves for use in atomic energy developments; the general manager of wholesale sales, who was responsible for all sales to independent wholesalers; the general manager of market development, who was responsible for promotion work with architects and general contractors; the general manager of branches, who had charge of all branch operations; and the general manager of sales orders, who was responsible for internal sales problems, such as processing orders and controlling warehouse stocks.

There were five district managers under the director of sales. Each had under him a manager of wholesale sales and a manager of market development. Also reporting directly to the district managers were the sales engineers and engineering representatives. There were fifty-six wholesaler salesmen, who called on independent wholesalers in those areas where Van Norden did not have a branch. The branch salesmen sold to independent wholesalers in their territories.

The market development and sales engineering staffs had a total of one hundred and twenty-six field representatives. The market development representatives called on architects, general contractors, and other people who could influence the specifications for new construction to get them to specify Van Norden products. The sales engineers worked on more technical applications of products, such as applications in chemical companies or installations involved with radioactive materials. The market development and sales engineering personnel did not make actual sales. All sales, with very few exceptions, were made through local branches or independent wholesalers.

Each branch had a branch manager in charge and, depending on its size, possibly an office manager and a warehouse manager. The branches were responsible for all sales to users and independent wholesalers in their areas. In addition to Van Norden products, the branches also handled allied products of other brands. In general, these allied lines were not considered profitable, but did tend to fill in low points that resulted from the seasonal nature of the plumbing business. The branches carried the full Van Norden line. With respect to the allied lines, however, they could choose the products and brands they wished to handle so long as they selected from a list of suppliers approved by the main office purchasing department.

The branches received no credit for sales to wholesalers, which, on the average, accounted for about 15 per cent of branch sales. Valves and fittings were the main items sold to wholesalers. The branches sold to wholesalers at the same price at which they were billed by the parent company, yet had to bear the selling, paperwork, warehousing, and credit costs involved. Branch salesmen were compensated by salary plus commission. They received commission on sales to both users and wholesalers. Salaries averaged around $6,000, and commissions varied from $100 to $2,000 annually. Salesmen's expenses were paid by the company. This situation made it difficult for many branches to show a profit. In addition, good independent wholesalers were hard to get because of the direct competition they encountered from the branches. Branches priced their products competitively with local wholesalers. Both branches and wholesalers worked on a margin of 30 per cent on list prices. Another problem concerning wholesalers was that those handling Van Norden products did not maintain adequate stocks. If there was a branch nearby, they depended on the branch's stock to carry them. In fact, there were a number of wholesalers who featured the Van Norden name to add to their own reputation but actually carried little or no stock of Van Norden products. If a customer insisted on a Van Norden item, they ordered it from the branch, but otherwise they substituted inferior, high-profit brands.

With these problems in mind, Van Norden executives proposed to establish the Van Norden Supply Company as a separate division that would include all branches and would be responsible for making a profit on its own. The proposal also called for the dropping of weak branches and a switch in general emphasis to distribution through wholesalers. Three other autonomous divisions were also proposed, each complete

EXHIBIT 2

VAN NORDEN AND COMPANY PROPOSED ORGANIZATION CHART: NOVEMBER, 1960

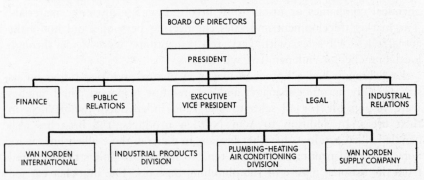

with its own manufacturing and marketing departments and responsible for making a profit from its operations (Exhibit 2). If the proposal were accepted, the firm would have four independent divisions as follows:

1. The industrial products division, which would encompass all products sold industrially. This would include such items as valves, fabricated piping, and boilers.
2. The plumbing, heating, and air-conditioning division.
3. Van Norden International, which would encompass all foreign operations and distribution.
4. Van Norden Supply Company, which would consist of approximately 70 branches. (Preliminary plans suggested that 120 existing branches be dropped in one way or another.)

The industrial products division and the plumbing, heating, and air-conditioning division would sell to the Van Norden Supply Company exactly as they would sell to independent wholesalers—same prices, same terms, same discounts, same treatment in every way. Each branch within the Supply Company would be responsible for all phases of its business, including making a profit.

The proposed change in the branch system called for the disposal of 120 branches; some of these might be converted into independent wholesalers, but others would be closed. In areas where branches were closed, new independent wholesalers would be acquired. A method of evaluation was offered for determining which branches would be kept and which would be dropped. The criteria proposed for determining the value of a branch to Van Norden were: (1) a branch should earn a 10 per cent return on investment, including facilities and inventory; (2) average monthly sales per salesman should be over $25,000; (3) average monthly sales per office employee should be over $18,000; and (4) average monthly sales per warehouseman should be over $18,000.

An analysis of several branches was made using the proposed plan of analysis. Exhibits 3, 4, and 5 show the results. Each analysis was to be made monthly and would show the individual figures for net sales, gross profit, shipping and handling expense, selling expense, administra-

EXHIBIT 3

ANALYSIS OF ABLE BRANCH OPERATIONS: 1960

	August	September	October	Total	3 Mos. (Per Cent)	10 Mos. (Per Cent)
Net sales.............	$116,638	$131,955	$120,420	$369,013		
Per cent of sales made out of stock.........	61	57	65		...	48
Gross profit on sales....$	24,970	$ 28,386	$ 24,913	$ 78,269	21.2	16.4
Shipping and handling expense.............	3,463	3,803	4,147	11,413	3.1	3.0
Selling expense........	3,936	3,973	4,764	12,673	3.4	3.3
Administration expense	6,106	5,381	6,081	17,568	4.8	4.1
Net income*..........	6,860	10,406	6,169	23,435	6.4	3.1
Investment account.....	339,499	345,333	322,924	335,918	(Average)	
Per cent return on investment*.........	24.2	36.2	22.9		27.9	18.4

No. salesmen.......................... 6	Av. sales/mo./salesman......$20,500
No. office employees (excluding manager)... 7	Av. sales/mo./office employee. 17,572
No. wholesale employees................. 4	Av. stock shipments/mo./
No. truck drivers....................... 3	wholesale employee........ 18,760
Total...........................20	

Av. number invoices per month.........1,428
Av. dollars per invoice................ 86

	November	December	January
Managers' sales forecast......................	$110,600	$107,800	$112,700

* Before state and federal taxes.

EXHIBIT 4

ANALYSIS OF BAKER BRANCH OPERATIONS: 1960

	August	September	October	Total	3 Mos. (Per Cent)	10 Mos. (Per Cent)
Net sales..............	$104,014	$129,956	$111,778	$345,748		
Per cent of sales made out of stock........	56*	56*	68		..	57
Gross profit on sales....	$ 15,806	$ 17,118	$ 17,355	$ 50,279	14.5	13.8
Shipping and handling expense............	3,571	2,540	5,061	11,172	3.2	2.7
Selling expense.........	4,662	2,711	4,266	11,639	3.4	3.3
Administration expense .	3,177	4,463	4,626	12,266	3.5	2.6
Net income†	2,534	4,820	1,985	9,339	2.7	3.3
Inventment account.....	609,544	533,621	456,281	533,149	(Average)	
Per cent return on investment†	5.0	10.8	5.2		7.0	11.7

No. salesmen...................... 3	Av. sales/mo./salesman..........$38,416
No. office employees (excl. manager)... 5	Av. sales/mo./office employee.... 23,050
No. wholesale employees............. 3	Av. stock shipment/mo./wholesale
No. truck drivers.................. 1	employee.................... 23,003
Total........................12	

Av. number of invoices per month............ 840
Av. dollars per invoice.....................$137

	November	December	January
Managers' sales forecast................$120,000	$120,000	$124,000	$120,000

* 9 Months' average.
† Before state and federal taxes.

tive expense, net income, and investment for each of the last three months. The average percentage for each of the income, profit, and expense items would be shown for the last three months and for the year to date, and the brach manager's sales forecast for the following three months would be included. The proposed branch analysis procedure would be used to weed out branches for the initial reorganization but would also be continued on a regular basis to help management spot trouble early and to determine the need to drop other branches as the occasion might develop.

Generally speaking, those branches that were low in return on investment tended to be low in the other categories of analysis, but not always. The investment account varied by branch according to the facilities of the branch and its age. A new branch might have a heavy investment charged to it, while an older branch might have written off most of the cost of its facilities. Gross profit also varied from area to area, depending on local competitive situations.

Exhibit 3 shows a branch that was earning a high return on investment but that did not meet the criteria for sales per salesman or per office em-

EXHIBIT 5

ANALYSIS OF CHARLIE BRANCH OPERATIONS: 1960

	August	September	October	Total	3 Mos. (Per Cent)	10 Mos. (Per Cent)
Net Sales............	$222,182	$106,153	$246,067	$574,402		
Per cent of sales made out of stock.........	33	61	40		..	42
Gross profit on sales....	$ 13,838	$ 10,163	$ 20,856	$ 44,857	7.8	8.7
Shipping and handling expense.............	4,848	2,760	3,147	10,755	1.9	3.0
Selling expense.........	3,251	5,889	8,741	17,881	3.1	3.7
Administration expense.	2,854	5,653	8,378	16,885	2.9	3.4
Net income*..........	673	(7,778)	(5,926)	(13,031)	(2.3)	(3.6)
Investment account.....	439,037	547,571	541,005	509,204	(Average)	
Per cent return on investment*..............	1.8	..	..	..	..	..

No. salesmen....................... 9	Av. sales/mo./salesman.........$21,274	
No. office employees (excl. manager)...10	Av. sales/mo./office employee.... 19,147	
No. wholesale employees............. 2	Av. stock shipments/mo./whole-	
No. truck drivers....................	sale employee................ 39,595	
Total.......................21		

Av. number of invoices per month............ 945
Av. dollars per invoice....................$203

	November	December	January
Managers' sales forecast................$425,000		$470,000	$400,000

* Before state and federal taxes.

ployee. Exhibit 4 shows a branch that had a ten-month average return on investment of 11.7 per cent but that had fallen below this in the last quarter. This branch met the criteria of sales per salesman and per office employee adequately. The branch in Exhibit 5 made a profit in only one of the three months shown and ran at a loss during the last ten months. Its sales per salesman did not meet the criteria established.

If the proposed plan were accepted, the branches in Exhibits 3 and 4 might be retained, but the branch in Exhibit 5 undoubtedly would be dropped or converted to an independent wholesaler.

The four new divisions were each to be headed by a vice-president and each was to have its own marketing department. The marketing departments of the plumbing, heating, and air-conditioning division and the industrial products division would be responsible for all sales of their divisions, both to independent wholesalers and to Van Norden Supply Company branches. Parts of the old organization would remain intact in one or more of the new divisions; for example, the market development section would come under the marketing department of the plumbing, heating, and air-conditioning division.

Exhibit 6 shows the proposed organization of the new plumbing, heat-

EXHIBIT 6

PROPOSED ORGANIZATION CHART FOR THE MARKETING DEPARTMENT OF THE PLUMBING,
HEATING, AND AIR-CONDITIONING DIVISION OF VAN NORDEN AND COMPANY

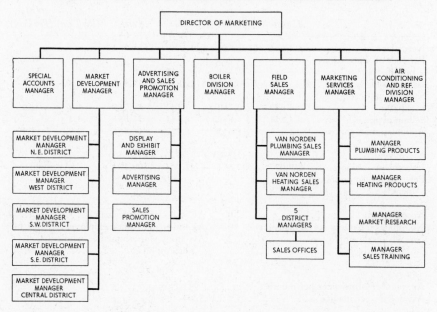

ing, and air-conditioning division. A director of marketing would be in
charge of all marketing activities. Under the director of marketing would
be the market development manager, advertising and sales promotion
manager, marketing services manager, special accounts manager, air-conditioning and refrigeration division manager, boiler division manager,
and the field sales manager. All direct sales activities would be under the
field sales manager. He would have five district managers for Van Norden

EXHIBIT 7

PROPOSED ORGANIZATION CHART FOR THE MARKETING DEPARTMENT OF THE INDUSTRIAL
PRODUCTS DIVISION OF VAN NORDEN AND COMPANY: NOVEMBER, 1960

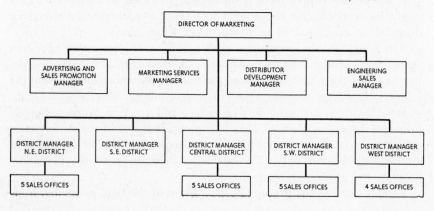

products reporting to him. The sales staffs under the district managers would sell to independent wholesalers and to branches of Van Norden Supply Company.

A director of marketing was also proposed for the industrial products division. Under him would be the advertising and sales promotion manager, marketing service manager, distributor development manager, and engineering sales manager (Exhibit 7). Five district managers would report directly to the director of marketing. They would be responsible for all sales to independent wholesalers and to the branches of Van Norden Supply. In addition, engineering sales would remain as it was in the old organization, handling special application problems.

The organization of the Van Norden Supply Company would consist of the director and the branch managers who reported directly to him.

Should the proposed reorganization plan be adopted?

38

BELL & HOWELL COMPANY

RELATIONS between dealers and manufacturers in the camera industry had been the source of increasing problems for several years. Rapid technological change and competition from imports and among domestic manufacturers were the primary factors creating this situation. Frequent price reductions and model changes had had serious effects on dealers' inventories. Camera specialty dealers were becoming alarmed at the volume of cameras and camera equipment being sold by other outlets. Complaints from dealers of defective merchandise and problems in handling defective merchandise had increased as the volume of cameras being sold increased.

To a company like Bell & Howell, which held a prestige position in the industry and was well known for the high quality of its products, the 3,491 camera specialty dealers in the United States were the most important retail outlets for its cameras. Not only was it important that these dealers display Bell & Howell products; it was also important that they have the knowledge necessary to sell and service quality cameras and equipment. Quality and feature differences in cameras were not always evident to laymen. External appearance could be deceiving. Since Bell & Howell's cameras were generally higher priced than most of its competitors, the company had to rely on the camera dealers to point out and demonstrate their products' features.

Bell & Howell had pioneered in the development of home movie equipment. It was the leading manufacturer of movie cameras and projectors, both for amateurs and commercial photographers. The company's continuing progress had been made possible by constant improvement of its line. Examples of the improvements that kept Bell & Howell in front of the industry were the electric eye camera introduced to the market in 1958, which automatically adjusted the lens of the camera to the light conditions, and the self-threading 8-mm. projector, which was marketed in 1959. The company also marketed a line of still cameras, high-fidelity equipment, and microfilm and graphic-arts film. In 1959 Bell & Howell merged with Consolidated Electrodynamics Corporation, which was known for its development of new techniques and electronic tools for science and industry. Bell & Howell sales in 1959 were in excess of $61 million, 4 per cent over 1958. The combined sales of Bell & Howell and Consolidated Electrodynamics were over $105 million.

The camera industry was made up of a variety of firms, some of which sold a full line of cameras in all price ranges, while others specialized in high-quality still cameras or movie cameras, or both. Most of the companies that made better-quality cameras sold direct to dealers. Some companies, primarily among the imports, limited distribution by granting exclusive franchises. Few domestic manufacturers granted exclusive franchises.

Besides being handled by independent camera dealers, photographic equipment was sold by a variety of other outlets, such as department stores, sporting goods stores, discount houses, jewelry stores, and drugstores. It was estimated that over one-half of all sales of photographic equipment and supplies, mainly film, was sold through drugstores. Eastman Kodak claimed to have 50,000 dealers, but this included film outlets. Such a firm as Bell & Howell might have as many as 10,000 of these retail outlets selling its products.

The typical independent camera dealer was small, with probably one to three employees, but his investment in inventory was sizable. He normally handled several lines of cameras and equipment plus a complete line of film and other photographic supplies. The camera specialty dealer also usually sold used equipment, which he had taken in trade on new purchases. He made his own deals on trade-ins. The average sale for the independent camera dealer was around $50.

The camera industry considered the dealer to be on his own. Once a dealer had purchased an item for resale, he assumed the risk of selling the item before new product features made the model obsolete. All manufacturers put their greatest sales effort into the annual industry trade show held each March. In recent years new product introductions at the show had taken place in ever increasing numbers. The resulting intense model competition often led to a chaotic price situation.

In August, 1959, Bell & Howell issued a "Declaration of Interdependence." (Exhibit 1.) This "Declaration" covered the major problems that existed in dealer relations and pledged Bell & Howell to take specific action in these areas to improve the dealer's position. It was to run for a trial period of eight months, from September 1, 1959, to May 1, 1960, and, if it proved mutually advantageous, was to be continued after this period.

EXHIBIT 1

THE DECLARATION OF INTERDEPENDENCE

ARTICLE I: Price Protection

> *Problem:* Sudden and substantial price reductions. Dealers have suffered severe inventory losses as an aftermath to March photographic conventions in recent years. Profits and inventory value dropped from one moment to the next as dealers went from one manufacturer's booth to another.

A price protection program, to be meaningful, must extend *beyond* the March photographic convention.

Any Bell and Howell product purchased by a franchised dealer from September 1, 1959, to May 1, 1960, will be fully protected against reduction by Bell and Howell of dealer net price of this product that may take place during this period, provided that this merchandise is in the dealer's stock at the time of the price reduction and remains in the product line. (Model change protection in Article II.) The full amount of any such reduction will be credited to the dealer's account.

ARTICLE II: Model Changes

> *Problem:* Abrupt announcement of discontinued models and frequent model changes. Dealers were unanimous in wanting improved product. However, they also wanted adequate protection against the effects of these changes on existing inventories.
>
> A specific criticism of Bell and Howell, for example, concerns our introduction of our new Sunometer cameras this spring. While the new meters were an improvement, dealers felt that the formal announcement of new models and sudden discontinuance of the older models created unnecessary inventory obsolescence.

Thus, in addition to price protection of current models, dealers must be protected against the effects of sudden model change. Bell and Howell will adopt a three-point policy to protect the dealer against changed or discontinued models: (1) Models will normally be continued in the line indefinitely, with no change in price or features until manufacturer and dealer inventories are exhausted; (2) when minor improvements in function or appearance are required, such changes will be incorporated in existing models and no formal trade or consumer announcements will be made; (3) if, as a last resort, it becomes necessary for Bell and Howell to discontinue a model, we will give ninety days' advance notice to franchised dealers. Any quantity of the discontinued model that remains in Bell and Howell's inventory at the end of ninety days will be offered to *all* franchised dealers at a reduced price for thirty days more.

ARTICLE III: Defective Merchandise

> *Problem:* Dealers report a disturbing increase in the amount of defective product received from manufacturers. We firmly believe that no responsible manufacturer would knowingly ship defective products. It is obvious, however, that action by manufacturers is called for.

EXHIBIT 1—*Continued*

It is the manufacturer's clear responsibility to provide its dealers and con-sumers with a quality product that functions according to satisfactory specifications.

To meet this responsibility, Bell and Howell pledges to enact a three-point program: (1) We will redouble quality control efforts. (2) We will also initiate immediate packaging changes to minimize damage during shipment, such as the new "egg-crate" packaging of projectors. (3) In the event that a franchised dealer receives defective Bell and Howell merchandise in spite of all quality-assurance measures, *we will assume all transportation costs*, to and from the dealer, and will strive to return replacement product to the dealer within 72 hours after its receipt by our warehouses or factory.

ARTICLE IV: Co-operative Advertising

> *Problem:* Profitless price promotion. Many dealers agreed that current trends toward price cutting and loss leader promotions are self-defeating. They are self-defeating from the standpoint of both the retailer himself and the industry as a whole, preventing the camera retailer from capitalizing on the services and products he alone offers.

We recognize that dealer advertising will best suit the long-term interest of Bell and Howell and its dealers if it emphasizes the product features and enhances the *quality reputation* of Bell and Howell products rather than emphasizing profitless prices.

The Bell and Howell retail co-operative advertising plan provides for factory participation with retailers who hold to this standard of retail advertising. No co-operative allowances will be paid for any retail advertising at retail prices other than those suggested in the Bell and Howell price catalogue.

ARTICLE V: Promotional Service for Retailer

> *Problem:* The need for action by the manufacturer to create a more favorable selling climate and to provide specialized promotional help was underscored by many dealers.

Bell and Howell will introduce a sales training plan for franchised dealers through its representatives. This plan will cover not only product knowledge but also retail selling techniques, which will benefit general store operations as well. In addition (with the help of the most expert advice available), Bell and Howell is preparing a "Dealer Merchandising Guide," designed to assist the camera retailer in developing profitable advertising and merchandising programs.

ARTICLE VI: Franchise Agreements

> *Problem:* Most dealers recognize that, as the industry grows, distribution problems grow with it. This has been the history of all growth businesses. The important thing is that manufacturers establish and enforce standards of doing business that permit retailers to prosper and that prevent predatory retailers from destroying the very foundations of profitable business.

Bell and Howell selective and comprehensive franchises will be strictly enforced. Dealers holding franchises will be expected to fulfill all terms and conditions as stipulated. If a dealer's franchise is terminated for any reason whatsoever, the provisions of the Declaration of *Inter*dependence will thereupon become null and void, and all ensuing benefits will be immediately cancelled.

EXHIBIT 1—*Continued*

CONCLUSION:

The Declaration of Interdependence will be given a fair test during the eight-month period from September 1, 1959, to May 1, 1960, a full six weeks after the March photographic show. What we do in the future depends upon whether this program is effective in overcoming principal dealer problems. We hope to demonstrate through our actions and policies the actual existence of a *spirit* of interdependence between Bell and Howell and its valued retail dealers.

(*signed*) CHARLES H. PERCY
President
Bell and Howell Company

In setting up the "Declaration of Interdependence," the management of Bell & Howell attempted to isolate the major problems affecting dealer relations. The six major problems were:

1. The dealer needed protection against sudden reductions in suggested list prices by the manufacturer.
2. The dealer needed protection against abrupt or unannounced model changes.
3. The amount of defective or damaged merchandise being received by dealers had to be reduced.
4. The dealer needed advertising help which would maintain price levels and stress quality.
5. The dealer needed help from the manufacturer in such marketing areas as sales training and merchandising.
6. The company needed to police and enforce its franchise agreements.

The need for price protection stemmed from the fact that both competition and new developments had put pressures on manufacturers to reduce suggested retail prices on many lines. These reductions were often made without sufficient warning to retailers. When Bell & Howell introduced its electric eye camera, all standard cameras in the same price range as the electric eye camera became obsolete. This depressed the price level of this group of cameras. Bell & Howell reduced the price of its three-lens turret camera from a suggested list of $169 to $139. This was done in January, 1960, while the "Declaration of Interdependence" was in effect. The company gave its dealers credit on all three-lens turret cameras purchased after September 1, 1959. The credit was an amount sufficient to maintain the normal retail markup. Management estimated that this cost the company an amount equal to the profit it would normally make on $5 million in sales.

In order to keep ahead of competitors, new camera models were constantly being introduced. In the spring of 1959 Bell & Howell introduced a new and improved version of its Sunometer camera. This camera had a built-in light meter that was calibrated to coincide with aperture settings so that the setting could be read directly from the meter. The new model sold at the same price as the old. This introduction caught dealers with sizable inventories of the old model. These had to be sold at reduced prices, and the dealers had to bear the losses.

The increase in complaints of defective merchandise were due primarily to the increase in the total number of units shipped. The percentage of defectives had not increased appreciably. Shipments of 8-mm. movie cameras had increased from 443,000 units in 1954 to 1,095,000 in 1958. Management believed that most of the increase in complaints was due to damage incurred in shipment. Shipping and handling methods had become rougher in order to achieve more speed and efficiency. Packages being used in 1958 and early 1959 were primarily folding cartons with corrugated inner packing to protect the camera. For shipment, these packages were packed in corrugated shipping containers.

In the fall of 1959 Bell & Howell developed a molded plastic package for its cameras. It consisted of two blocks of foam-type plastic molded to completely enclose the camera. These and the camera fitted into a base that would hold the camera upright for display purposes on the dealers' shelves. A plastic cover fitted over the entire package. Tests, including a football player kicking a field goal with the package, complete with camera, showed that this package provided much better protection than previous packages. If a dealer should receive any defective merchandise, Bell & Howell agreed to pay all transportation costs involved in return and replacement. In the past, the dealer had borne the cost of returning defective merchandise.

Management felt that Bell & Howell should offer more help to dealers in the operation of their stores. In 1959 the company published a *Camera Specialty Dealer's Guide to Marketing*. It covered five basic areas: (1) store atmosphere (ideas on displays and in-store promotions); (2) manpower (building sales staff and use of incentives for salesmen); (3) selling (credit selling, rentals, and ideas on tie-in selling); (4) promotion planning (themes); and (5) advertising (why, where, and what, how to use different media, and a guide to the graphic arts). The book was offered to dealers at a price of $30, which included three special promotion kits.

Bell & Howell sold direct to camera dealers through its own sales force. The salesmen were paid a straight salary plus bonus and expenses. There were two types of franchised dealers. Those on a comprehensive franchise handled Bell & Howell's full line, which included 16-mm., 8-mm., and slide equipment. Dealers with a selective franchise handled only 8-mm. and slide equipment. The franchises did not grant exclusive territories. Bell & Howell reserved the right to withdraw the franchise of a dealer if he did not conform to the company's standards as an ethical camera dealer.

Was the Bell & Howell plan for improving dealer relations sound?

39

TOWN AND COUNTRY HOMES

TOWN AND COUNTRY HOMES, a small prefabricated home manufacturer located in Hewitt, Nebraska, was faced with the problem of obtaining and holding satisfactory and reputable dealers to market its line of factory-built homes. Dealer turnover had been a serious problem for the company for a number of years. For the five years prior to 1958 a 10 per cent turnover in dealers had been about the average, and in the fall of 1958 it appeared that for the full year the 10 per cent figure would be reached and perhaps exceeded.

Since World War II prefabricated home construction had gained steadily as a percentage of the total single-family homes constructed in the United States, as shown in Table 1.

TABLE 1

PREFABRICATED HOUSES AS PERCENTAGE OF ALL NEW HOUSES
CONSTRUCTED IN THE UNITED STATES: 1946–57

Year	Prefabricated House Shipments	Single-Family Housing Starts	Per Cent Prefabricated Homes
1946	37,200	590,000	6.31
1947	37,400	742,000	5.04
1948	30,000	766,600	3.91
1949	35,000	794,300	4.41
1950	55,000	1,154,100	4.78
1951	50,000	900,100	5.56
1952	57,000	952,500	5.98
1953	55,000	937,800	5.89
1954	77,000	1,000,000	7.70
1955	93,000	1,189,000	7.88
1956	94,790	990,000	10.00
1957	93,546	872,700	11.00

Source: Home Manufacturers Association.

It was estimated by the Home Manufacturers Association, the recognized trade association and spokesman for prefabricated builders, that the total national production of factory-built homes for the year ending December 31, 1958, would exceed 105,000 units, which would top by more than 12 per cent the 93,546 units manufactured in 1957.

The factory-built or "prefab" home-building industry was composed of about one hundred companies turning out from as few as 50 units annually to as many as 20,000 units in the case of the National Homes Corporation, which was by far the largest in the field. United States Steel

Homes, American Houses, and Scholtz Homes were other large producers, but none of them approached the volume achieved by National Homes. It was estimated that at least half the companies in the industry turned out fewer than 200 units per year and had a total sales volume of less than $1,500,000.

Factory-built homes were generally defined as homes which were constructed in sections at the manufacturer's plant, shipped directly to the buyer's property, and assembled in a matter of days. The purchase price normally included the expense of erecting the house but not the cost of digging a basement or the cost of the lot on which the house was built. The cost of transportation to the buyer's site was high. This tended to limit the area in which a firm could operate and was one of the reasons for the large number of small companies in the industry. It was difficult for a company to compete effectively if shipments had to be made from a plant that was located more than five hundred miles from the buyer's lot.

Town and Country was one of the smaller producers in the industry; in 1957 it sold 203 units. Its homes emphasized quality and individuality

TABLE 2

PRICE RANGES FOR PREFABRICATED HOMES FOR
THREE SELECTED YEARS*

Price Ranges	Number	Per Cent
1953		
Under $8,000	Unknown	25
$8,000–$12,000	Unknown	60
1955†		
$6,000–$8,000	25,000	25
$8,000–$12,000	50,000	50
$12,000–$16,000	20,000	20
Over $16,000	5,000	5
1956‡		
Under $7,000	2,746	5.2
$7,000–$10,000	20,295	38.4
$10,000–$15,000	22,851	43.2
$15,000–$20,000	5,434	10.3
$20,000–$30,000	1,342	2.5
Over $30,000	187	0.4

* Prices are for houses erected, equipped, and painted, but do not include the lot.
† Estimates based on data representing 100,000 prefabricated homes.
‡ Estimates based on production data from 58 companies.
Source: Home Manufacturers Association.

of design. This meant that they tended to sell in the upper price levels for prefab houses. Trade association data indicated that most prefabs sold in the price range of $8,000–$12,000, as shown in Table 2.

Town and Country believed that these figures were not entirely correct and, in addition, believed that there was a considerable shift to lower-priced homes in 1958. In that year they thought perhaps 50 per cent of the prefab homes sold were priced below $7,500. Town and Country, however, did not sell many homes in this price class.

A large volume was necessary to compete effectively in the lower price ranges and Town and Country did not aspire to become one of the giants in the industry. The firm had originally been a contracting organization. It started prefab production in 1941 but did not emphasize home production until after World War II. Previous to and during the war, it concentrated principally on farm buildings, for which there was a large market. From 1950 to 1958, total output ranged up to 250 homes a year and in only one year dropped under 200 units. Mr. Henry, the president, did not wish to have the company grow much larger. Stable sales enabled employment of the same staff throughout the year. No employee had ever been laid off because of insufficient orders during the ten-year period from 1948 to 1958. The company felt a responsibility to its workers and to the community for maintaining constant employment. Company officials believed that an attempt to expand would necessitate bringing in outside labor, which might affect the status quo of the little community of Hewitt. They also believed that expansion would bring seasonal fluctuations, which the company had been able to avoid by careful scheduling as long as output remained relatively small.

Town and Country was located in the heart of a farming area and sold primarily to rural people and to those in small towns. As a result, most of the firm's units had been sold individually. The management had never tried to break into the "project" market, that is, the market for entire housing developments. This market was the volume market, however, and had to be developed by a home manufacturer seeking to build a large volume. Mr. Henry believed that volume could be expanded by promoting "projects." He hesitated to enter this market, however, because he knew of several companies that had expanded only to see their profits disappear in supporting large fixed expenses, which continued between projects.

Town and Country distributed its homes exclusively through dealers. About 110 dealers were located in a five-state area, which included Nebraska, Kansas, Missouri, Iowa, and South Dakota. The company had a rigid policy of no exclusive territories. It sought dealers in all localities in its marketing area. Since much of the market was among farmers, some dealers covered areas up to twenty-five miles in radius. All dealers were free to sell homes wherever they could find a prospect. The president and other company officials thought that assigning exclusive territories to dealers would destroy aggressive selling and limit the initiative that an active dealer could exercise. In 1957 ten dealers sold over 50 per cent of the homes shipped by Town and Country; the largest dealer sold twenty-six. Table 3 shows the dealers who displayed reasonable activity in selling homes in 1957 and the number of years each had been associ-

TABLE 3

Leading Town and Country Dealers with Units
Sold and Number of Years with Company: 1957

Dealer	No. Homes Sold	No. Years with Company
A	26	7
B	16	12
C	13	7
D	12	17
E	11	11
F	10	7
G	10	12
H	10	18
I	8	7
J	8	7

ated with the company as a dealer. There were twenty-six franchised dealers who did not sell a single unit in 1957.

As a general rule, dealers handled the homes as an extra line in addition to farm equipment, insurance, real estate, or contracting. A number of dealers were retired farmers who had many contacts in their own locality and who took on the selling of the homes as a part-time job. Mr. Henry estimated that about 75 per cent of the company's dealers were in either the insurance or the real estate business, while about 15 per cent were builder-contractors. It had always been difficult to determine who might become a satisfactory dealer. In one locality a junk dealer had tried to obtain a dealership. The company refused because his junk business was not in any way connected with the selling of factory-built homes. After several years of persistent inquiry by this individual, the management decided that no real harm could come from giving him a dealership. Much to the company's surprise, he became one of the most successful dealers.

Before a dealer was given a franchise, the management had to be convinced that he was of good character and standing in his community and had a satisfactory financial standing. Every effort was made to get a new dealer to erect a model home in his community, so that prospective customers could actually see one of the homes as it would appear when completed. This was not, however, an absolute requirement. The dealer was expected to finance such a model home himself.

Dealers paid the list price less 20 per cent when a house was delivered to a construction site. From then on the job was entirely theirs. They made arrangements for construction and equipping the home. This meant a dealer had to have financial resources of about $10,000 to finance a unit. This therefore became the minimum requirement for becoming a dealer. Mr. Henry estimated that 75 of the company's 110 dealers had erected a model house at one time or another during their relationship with Town and Country. Each dealer who erected a model house expected to sell it and to erect another, newer model. Every dealer franchise included a 30-day cancellation clause at the option of the company.

Town and Country's pricing policy was different from the generally accepted industry policy. Its retail prices included all prefabricated panels and materials necessary to complete the structure from the foundation up and were quoted F.O.B. the factory in Hewitt. Quoted retail prices did not include foundations—the owner was expected to contract with a local builder to erect the necessary foundations, as well as the chimney, porches, wiring, heating, plumbing, screens, storm sash, cabinets, and painting. Town and Country did not erect its prefabricated houses. This was usually done by a local contractor, whose services were obtained by the dealer or the owner. If neither the dealer nor the buyer could arrange for construction, the company would send a factory crew to erect the shell of the house. In such cases the purchaser was billed for this additional service.

List prices ranged from $3,055 to $10,645. The final cost of the total home, including the lot, erection costs, and equipment that had to be installed by subcontractors, could easily double the list price for a particular model. Mr. Henry estimated that the total value of an average house, in place, equipped, painted, and ready for the owner to move in, would be about $12,500. This average house would probably list at about $6,000.

In 1957 Town and Country spent about $35,000 or 3.5 per cent of sales on advertising. The principal mediums used were farm journals, such as the *Nebraska Farmer, Wallace's Farmer, House and Home,* and such construction industry publications as the *American Builder* and the *Practical Builder.* All company dealers were urged to use newspaper and other local advertising media. The company offered to pay half the cost of all such advertising.

In addition to the advertising mentioned above, Town and Country had participated for several years in the state fair in each of the states in which it marketed. At these fairs the company erected a model home and obtained the co-operation of a local merchant or merchants, who furnished the house completely with plumbing, heating, kitchen equipment, automatic utilities, furniture, floor coverings, and draperies. The co-operating merchants promoted their furnishings, as well as the home, by advertising the items in the model home. Town and Country benefited from this promotion. At the Nebraska State Fair in 1958, 18,000 people visited its newest model home, which featured a four-level arrangement.

All inquiries received by the company as the result of advertising or from visitors to the company's model homes at the state fairs were forwarded to the dealers in the localities from which the inquiries came. Dealers were expected to follow up all such leads. Six to seven thousand leads each year were forwarded to local dealers.

Company advertising emphasized the fact that Town and Country's homes stressed individuality and flexibility. Advertising pointed out that the homes were far removed from the common public conception of a prefab house, namely, something akin to a uniform "row" house. For instance, a wide choice of room arrangements was available because of a roof truss developed by Town and Country which eliminated the necessity for partitions to support the roof at any point. Dealers in the five-state territory were urged to bring their prospects directly to the company plant to consult with designers and draftsmen so that the customer could be shown how his individualized requirements and desires could be worked into his home through the customized designing offered by the company. The company's design department was supervised by a well-known architect, assisted by competent engineers. Company officials believed that this special service was one of their greatest competitive advantages. Through this service they could combat the most often heard criticism of a factory house: that mass production homes could not suit the individuality of the American public. Company records led the officers to believe that Town and Country was accomplishing this aim, in that two out of every three homes shipped from the factory were variations from the standard models.

Dealers sought leads wherever they could be found and followed up the leads that were sent to them by the home office. After making a contact, a dealer would appraise the interested party to determine whether he appeared to have either adequate financial resources or borrowing power to be able to purchase a home. If the prospect was genuinely interested and seemed to have the necessary financial backing, the dealer continued his efforts to sell the home.

As Town and Country had no subsidiary finance company, all prospects had to make their own arrangements for financing. One of the dealer's important functions was to help prospects arrange for the proper financing through a local lending agency. The homes were all eligible for F.H.A. and V.A. insured loans, and the dealers had to know the requirements of these agencies. In some communities there was a considerable problem in getting lending agencies to make loans on "prefab" houses.

If a prospect looked particularly likely, the dealer was urged by the company to bring the customer to the main office at Hewitt, where the customer could see the houses being constructed. There the prospect could confer with one of the company's designers on modifications of basic models to suit the prospect's own taste and needs. If any unusually difficult financial problems were involved, home office specialists could help work out a solution. Any proposed solutions, however, had to be carried out in the prospective customer's community with his local lending agency. It was an ironclad company policy that all financing had to be worked out before shipment unless the dealer himself was prepared to pay for the house and collect from the customer at a later date. Town and Country had no objection to any financing arrangement so long as the cost of the home, less the dealer's discount, was paid on delivery of the house to the building site.

The dealer's discount allowed was 20 per cent of the list price of the home, F.O.B. Hewitt. Mr. Henry believed that this discount was higher than that given by most prefab companies that marketed their homes through dealers. The average discount allowed dealers by other firms was about 10 per cent, but these dealers did not have to erect and display model homes utilizing their own capital. Many competing home manufacturers also handled the customer's financing problems, relieving their dealers of most of the work involved in this service. Many manufacturers in the prefab industry marketed their homes direct to consumers through their own salesmen. A survey made for the Home Manufacturers Association found that commission rates paid such salesmen averaged about 5 per cent. Table 4 shows more of the details of this survey.

Town and Country conducted no organized program of dealer training when a new dealer was signed. An annual meeting of all dealers was

TABLE 4

COMMISSION RATES PAID PERSONNEL CLASSIFIED AS SALESMEN IN
"PREFAB" HOUSING INDUSTRY

	Companies with Net Sales of			
	$1,500,000 and Over		Under $1,500,000	
Type of Compensation Plan	No. Com- panies	Commission Rates* (Per Cent)	No. Com- panies	Commission Rates (Per Cent)
Straight commission.........2		5(N)(x), 2½–5(G)(f)	1	5(G)(x)
Commission with drawing ac- count (no guarantee).......3		3½(G)(x), 5(G)(p), 3½–5(N)(p)	3	3(N)(f), 3(N)(p), 5(G)(x)
Commission and bonus.......–		— —	1	4(N)(p)
Commission with guaranteed drawing account..........1		5(GF)(p)	3	4(N)(f), 5(N)(p)
Salary and expenses deducted from total commission......1		2–4(G)(f)	4	4(N)(p),5(N)(f), 4(N)(x),4–5(N)(f)
Salary plus commission on sales above a quota.............1		1(G)(f)	–	— —
Salary, commission, and bonus.–		— —	1	½–2(N)(f)
Salary plus commission on all sales.................4		1(GF)(f), ¼–5(N)(p), ½–3(N)(f),	–	— —

* The capital letters in parentheses following the commission rates indicate the basis on which commission is computed: (G) gross sales, (GF) gross sales less freight or trucking, (N) net sales. The lower-case letters indicate the policy as to expense reimbursements: (f) full reimbursement, (p) partial reimbursement, (x) no reimbursement.
Source: Home Manufacturers Association survey of salesmen's compensation, September, 1958.

held at the company's expense, at which time the usual pep talks to stimulate sales were presented, particularly in connection with the introduction of new models. During the year a continuous flow of bulletins was sent to all dealers to keep them abreast of the latest developments. Additional contacts with dealers were maintained by the firm's two territory men, who, between them, attempted to see each dealer at least once a month. At the time of each call all leads that had been sent the dealer from the home office were checked, and the territory men often called on prospects with the dealer. At these monthly visits dealers were urged to ask the company representatives for help with any sales problems that might have developed either with prospects or with the home office. Mr. Henry, the president and sales manager, and other company officers often made trips specifically for the purpose of maintaining contacts with the dealers.

The local dealer adjusted any complaints by purchasers. This was a responsibility of the dealer, whether he had just sold the "shell" of the house as it came from the factory or had performed the functions of a contractor in erecting and equipping the finished house.

Mr. Henry thought that the 20 per cent discount adequately compensated Town and Country dealers. In spite of this higher-than-normal discount, the company was continuing to have trouble in obtaining reputable dealers with capital to finance a model home or to build homes for sale before customers actually bought them. The management was also concerned about the number of inactive dealers on their roster and often took steps to terminate dealerships in which no activity had taken place within a year's time. Such terminations, along with the voluntary withdrawal of other dealers, made up an annual 10 per cent dealer turnover. No data were available on the experience of other firms in the industry that had used dealers.

1. What should Town and Country do to reduce the dealer turnover?

2. Appraise the firm's complete marketing program.

C. Price

40

CONTAINER CORPORATION OF AMERICA

INCREASED competition and its resultant pressures on salesmen and profits led the Container Corporation of America, the largest manufacturer of corrugated and solid fiber shipping containers in the United States, to reappraise its market objectives. Part of the pressure on profits, in the opinion of management, was the result of salesmen's taking any orders they could get without regard to plant operating efficiency or profit. It was proposed that this tendency be controlled by changing the pricing procedure to make all types of orders approximately equal in profitability, even though this might result in lost sales. Since prices were established from cost estimates for each job, a program was outlined to revise the estimating system so that it would more accurately reflect the marketing objectives of the company.

The Container Corporation was a completely integrated company, with sales exceeding $250 million. Its own forests and wastepaper processing plants supplied its fifteen paper mills with raw materials. The paper mills supplied paperboard to the company's twenty-five shipping container factories and twenty folding carton and fiber can factories. Each of the forty-five container and carton plants operated independently and was responsible for meeting competition in its area and for making a profit. Paperboard was sold by the mills to the plants at market prices.

The shipping container market extended to all manufacturers who needed to package their products. Potential order sizes ranged from orders of one hundred or less units from a small manufacturer of specialized products to orders for 5 or more carloads at a time from large canners and brewers. Variations in types of materials ordered ranged from display materials, which required complicated manufacturing procedures, to plain regular "slotted containers," the industry term for ordinary boxes, which were run routinely at the rate of 10,000 per hour.

Container's shipping container factories were primarily designed for large-volume operation. For example, the Chicago plant had two corrugators for producing corrugated paperboard with a capacity in excess of 2.5 million square feet of corrugated board per day, which represented thirteen to fifteen carloads of finished boxes per day. The company did not manufacture any stock items or maintain an inventory of finished material. Everything was made to order.

The manufacture of an ordinary box, one for canned foods or beer, normally involved three operations. First, the order went to the corrugator, where the corrugated sheets were made, cut to size, and scored[1] to make the flaps of the box. The sheets then went to a printer-slotter machine, where they were printed, scored to form the sides, and slotted to separate the flaps of the boxes. In the final operation, the ends of the sheets were folded and joined either by taping, stitching (stapling), or gluing to form the finished box. The finished boxes were tied in bundles or palletized and moved almost immediately into trucks or freight cars

---

[1] "Score" is the industry term for creases put in the corrugated board so that it will fold at the proper points.

for shipment. Orders were timed to be finished at the scheduled time for shipment, since the volume of materials produced each day made storage impractical.

To get maximum production out of a box plant such as Container's Chicago plant, it was necessary to have a major proportion of large orders. This reduced the down time of machines for changing "setups" for each new order. But the large-volume business was generally low-profit business because of competition. Therefore, to maximize profits, it was necessary to have a mixture of large-volume orders and small or more specialized but more profitable orders.

Management believed that the cost-estimating methods led to prices that did not indicate the real profitability of an order. The estimating methods were thought to overstate profits on small-volume business and understate profits on large-volume business. This had led to a situation in which the plants were getting too many small orders to operate efficiently, because these orders looked more profitable than they were. Furthermore, some large-volume business was being lost because it did not look profitable when actually it was. A study of sales records revealed less than 10 per cent of the company's customers accounted for 90 per cent of the volume.

Further thought on this problem led management to the conclusion that a box factory was not primarily selling paper, but was selling the skills and process of converting paper into boxes. It was on these conversion costs that profits should be based. Under the existing system, sales and administrative expenses and profits were estimated as percentages of full cost, including materials. Also, under the existing estimating system, costs of certain groups of similar operations were averaged. It was thought that a new method should be found that would be based on the specific cost of each operation. This would make it possible to determine much more accurately the profitability of an individual order.

Exhibit 1 shows the prices arrived at from costs estimated by the existing average cost method and by the proposed specific cost system, with overhead and profits based on conversion costs. Four examples are shown. The first illustrates the case of an ordinary box, for which material costs were large in proportion to factory conversion costs, and the fourth example illustrates the case of a more complicated item, for which factory costs greatly exceeded material costs. The second and third examples are in between. Factory conversion costs consisted of two parts, the setup cost, or cost of preparing the machines for a particular operation, and the base cost, which was the cost of the machine time and labor used to run 1,000 units. All material and factory costs were for 1,000 units.

The profit percentage, 10.9 per cent of total conversion cost, including materials for the average cost method and 24 per cent of total conversion costs for the specific cost method, was calculated to bring a return of 20 per cent on invested capital after taxes. Factory costs that were

EXHIBIT 1

Two Methods of Cost Estimating for Four Hypothetical Jobs

	Example							
	1		2		3		4	
	Setup	Base	Setup	Base	Setup	Base	Setup	Base
Average Cost Method with Profit Calculated on Full Cost								
Material..............		$ 70		$ 60		$ 40		$ 30
Factory conversion costs..............$10	$10	20	$10	30	$10	50	$10	60
Total factory conversion costs, including materials................$10	$10	$ 90	$10	$ 90	$10	$ 90	$10	$ 90
Sales and administration costs, 10 per cent of total factory conversion costs..........	1	9	1	9	1	9	1	9
Total conversion-cost, including materials......$11	$11	$ 99	$11	$ 99	$11	$ 99	$11	$ 99
Profit, 10.9 per cent of full cost...........	1.20	10.80	1.20	10.80	1.20	10.80	1.20	10.80
Price................$12.20	$12.20	$109.80	$12.20	$109.80	$12.20	$109.80	$12.20	$109.80
SPECIFIC COST METHOD WITH PROFIT CALCULATED ON TOTAL CONVERSION COSTS								
Factory conversion costs..............$10	$10	$ 20	$10	$ 30	$10	$ 50	$10	$ 60
Sales and administration costs, 25 per cent of factory conversion costs..............	2.50	5	2.50	7.50	2.50	12.50	2.50	14
Total conversion costs........$12.50	$12.50	$ 25	$12.50	$ 37.50	$12.50	$ 62.50	$12.50	$ 74
Profit, 24 per cent of total conversion costs.....	3	6	3	9	3	15	3	18
Materials.............		70		60		40		30
Price................$15.50	$15.50	$101.00	$15.50	$106.50	$15.50	$117.50	$15.50	$122.00

included in factory conversion costs were allocated to units on the basis of an assumed minimum volume. The sales and administration cost percentage and the profit percentage were also based on this assumed minimum volume. In the case of the Chicago plant the assumed minimum volume was 63 million square feet of corrugated board per month.

Base and setup costs were not ordinarily quoted to customers. Prices were quoted for a specific quantity or quantities and were always quoted on a per thousand basis. These prices were arrived at by dividing the setup cost by the quantity in thousands and adding the base cost. For example, given a setup cost of $10 and a base cost of $100, the price quoted for 1,000 units would be $110 per thousand; for 500 units, $120 per thousand; and for 5,000 units, $102 per thousand.

Exhibit 2 shows the prices that would be quoted for orders of different quantities when the prices were determined by both the old and the new methods. Prices are shown for the same four hypothetical products shown in Examples 1, 2, 3, and 4 of Exhibit 1. The specific cost method resulted in generally higher prices, especially for small quantities. Where factory conversion costs were less than material costs, as in Examples 1 and 2, however, the specific cost method of computing prices resulted in lower prices than the average cost method. For products in which the conversion costs exceeded material costs, prices were consistently higher under the specific cost method than under the average cost method. Since

EXHIBIT 2

PRICES CALCULATED FROM EXHIBIT 1

		Price per Thousand	
Quantity	Example	Average Cost	Specific Cost
100.....................	1	$231.80	$256.00
	2	"	261.50
	3	"	272.50
	4	"	277.50
500.....................	1	134.20	132.00
	2	"	137.50
	3	"	148.50
	4	"	153.00
1,000..................	1	122.00	116.50
	2	"	122.00
	3	"	133.00
	4	"	137.50
10,000.................	1	111.02	102.55
	2	"	108.05
	3	"	119.05
	4	"	123.05

most of the company's business, particularly the large-volume business, resulted from items similar to Examples 1 and 2, the specific cost system would improve Container's competitive position.

The responsibility for establishing the actual prices quoted to customers rested with the sales managers at a step beyond the cost-estimating process described above. The estimated price was the price needed to give the standard profit. The price actually quoted to a customer might vary up or down from the level, depending on information the sales manager had on market conditions and competition for the specific account involved. There were no "standard prices" in the industry. It was not unusual for two companies buying boxes identical in size and material from the same box manufacturer to pay different prices. Some box companies tried using a "price list" that would permit the customer to calculate what the price would be on a given box by using the number of square feet of corrugated board in the box, multiplying this by a price per square foot, and then adding special charges for printing or other special features. In all cases, these "price lists" had been short lived.

Examples of two typical pricing situations are shown in Exhibit 3. In both situations the estimating department figured estimated prices based on the minimum return desired by management. The sales manager established the market prices, i.e., competitive prices, on the basis of his knowledge of the market and information from salesmen as to competitors and the prices they usually quoted these accounts. In the first situation the market price was lower than the estimated prices. It offered no profit under the average cost method of estimating costs, but it showed a

EXHIBIT 3

Two Typical Pricing Situations

	Average Cost Method	Specific Cost Method
PRICE PER THOUSAND FOR 20,000 ORDINARY BOXES SIMILAR TO EXAMPLE 1, EXHIBIT 1		
Estimated price................	$110.41	$101.78
Full cost......................	99.55	95.63
Market price..................	99.55	99.55
Profit........................	..	3.92
Per cent profit		
On total conversion cost.......	N.A.	12.4%
On full cost.................	0	3.9%
PRICE PER THOUSAND FOR 500 COMPLICATED BOXES SIMILAR TO EXAMPLE 4, EXHIBIT 1		
Estimated price................	$134.20	$153.00
Full cost......................	121.00	129.00
Market price..................	146.20	146.20
Profit........................	25.20	17.20
Per cent profit		
On total conversion cost.......	N.A.	17.4%
On full cost.................	20.8%	13.3%

profit of 12.4 per cent on conversion costs if the specific cost estimating method was used. In the second situation, which represents a small order that required more conversion, the market price was above the average cost price and below the specific cost price, but showed a profit in both cases. The average cost method showed more profit on market price than did the specific cost method.

With this information at hand, the sales manager could decide how badly he wanted these particular orders. Container's policy was to develop long-standing accounts that were profitable. Once a profitable price level was established in these accounts, it was generally maintained to the best of the company's ability. Constant attention was necessary, however, because of possible price cutting by competitors.

Constant attrition of accounts because of product changes, moves, and losses to competitors required the regular addition of new accounts if the company was to maintain its position. Container's main emphasis in acquiring a new account was on quality and design rather than on price. Price competition was avoided whenever possible, but it was sometimes necessary, particularly in large accounts using relatively standard types of boxes. Generally, when a company designed a new package for an account, it got the first order before the other box companies quoted on the item. Competitors could be expected to bid on later orders.

Salesmen were given some latitude for bargaining with an account. If the price the sales manager quoted was high, the salesmen could, if the customer was willing to bargain, meet the competitive price to get the order. Experienced salesmen were even given the authority to go below competitors' prices for some accounts.

Management did not expect that a change to the specific cost method of estimating prices would result in radical price changes and immediate improvement in profits. The estimating system approximated prices; actual prices were established by the sales manager in light of market conditions. Since the latter would not change, no great changes could be made in Container's prices. Management believed, however, that the new pricing system would cause sales managers to re-evaluate the importance of various accounts and hence to make some price adjustments.

1. *Would the new pricing system lead to higher profits for Container Corporation?*

2. *What other actions, if any, could have been taken in lieu of or in addition to the new pricing system to accomplish the same objectives?*

41

THE CAPEX COMPANY

THE CAPEX COMPANY of Evanston, Illinois, had specialized in manufacturing point-of-sale displays made of corrugated paperboard for local manufacturers and retailers. The company also built wooden exhibits for many of its customers to use at trade shows and conventions. As the result of several requests by customers for a less expensive exhibit booth, Capex had built some exhibits using corrugated paperboard. These experiments had proved successful, and Mr. Pease, president of Capex, decided to produce a line of prefabricated corrugated exhibit booths. In planning the marketing program for this addition to the Capex line, Mr. Pease was particularly concerned with how to price the product.

Capex had specialized in corrugated, self-supporting displays on which the art work was reproduced by the silk-screen process. This type of display had been particularly popular with manufacturers of "large ticket" items, such as television sets, ranges, air-conditioning units, water heaters, and other items that necessitated large display areas. These manuturers usually bought such displays in quantities of 500–1,000. In quantities of this size, Capex displays offered sizable savings over the cumbersome wood and cardboard units. Several of their larger accounts asked Capex to build enlarged displays for use at trade shows. After a number of such requests, Mr. Pease became convinced that there must be an extensive market for some type of sturdy, colorful, but economical trade display units. He designed a prefabricated unit, built in a manner similar to the store displays, to fill this demand.

The prefab exhibit units were built of Rigicor, a corrugated paperboard developed especially for display building. It had the thickness of wallboard, was lightweight, but had considerable strength. Capex used a spray finish with custom colors, which gave an appearance believed equal to that of the highest-priced wooden displays. The prefabricated exhibit consisted of a number of panels that could be locked together with fiber plugs. This interlocking arrangement, coupled with the rigidity of the Rigicor material, made a sturdy unit that could meet almost all trade-show needs. A "prefab" exhibit could do exactly the same jobs as a wooden display in presenting the exhibitor's product and selling story. Special lighting, motion picture projection, or other devices to make the exhibit attractive and effective could be used with the prefab units as easily as with the standard booths.

One of the important advantages of the Capex exhibit was in the ease of assembling and disassembling. The average ten-foot prefab display could be set up by two men in less than an hour. It took two men from four to six hours to set up a comparable wooden display. Most exhibit halls and hotels insisted that displays, either prefab or wooden, be assembled by union carpenters. The normal hourly rate charged per setup man was $13.50.

Tests indicated that the life expectancy of the prefabs was between eight and twelve showings. Wooden displays could be used about twice as long. Refurbishing was usually necessary for both types of displays after two or three shows, and often exhibitors wanted minor changes made between showings. Capex' current dollar volume from exhibits was divided among sales of new exhibits, 60 per cent; refurbishing and redesign, 30 per cent; and storage and handling, 10 per cent.

The prefab exhibit had further advantages for manufacturers who participated in many trade shows. A prefab display weighed approximately one-tenth as much as a wooden display of equal size. This would result in considerable savings in shipping charges.

For help in estimating the size of the potential exhibit booth market, Mr. Pease obtained data from the Chicago Convention Bureau on the size and trend of trade show activity in Chicago, probably the nation's leading trade show city. Although it did not have similar data on other cities, the Bureau believed that the trend in Chicago was typical of that in other large cities. Table 1 summarizes the Bureau data.

TABLE 1

CONVENTION AND TRADE SHOW ACTIVITY IN CHICAGO IN
SELECTED YEARS

Year	Number	Total Attendance	Total Money Spent (Millions)*
1932	694	460,000	$ 23
1946	882	522,000	52
1952	1,028	1,000,000	159
1955	1,127	1,300,000	210
1957	1,231	1,150,000	190

* It was estimated by the Chicago Convention Bureau that approximately 20 per cent of the total money spent represented the cost of exhibits, exhibit space, and personnel involved. Exhibit space typically cost $3–$4 per square foot.

Mr. Pease believed that the trade show was growing in importance as a marketing device. More and more manufacturers were entering trade shows to sell their products direct to dealers. Trade shows were losing the party atmosphere that they had had in the thirties and forties and were becoming serious business. Mr. Pease estimated that 50 per cent of Capex' customers ten years before were exhibiting at their first trade show. Furthermore, the use of displays by church organizations, educational institutions, and charity organizations at conferences and meetings was increasing.

Mr. Pease reasoned that two segments of the potential market for exhibit displays would be the most likely customers for the Capex units. They were (1) the small manufacturers and organizations that did not want to spend more than $500 for an exhibit (wooden exhibits generally ran from $800 up) and (2) the large manufacturers who participated in many national and local shows. Large manufacturers were often put under strong local pressure to participate in small local shows. The large number of these shows and their relatively small potential value caused these manufacturers to seek inexpensive ways of meeting this demand. For example, a large national food company, which was a Capex client, participated in fifteen national shows and about two hundred local shows in 1957.

Capex developed sixteen standardized display models. Because of the advantages of the product, especially its low shipping cost, and the fact that no other firm produced a similar item, Mr. Pease thought that he could distribute it successfully on a national basis. Wooden exhibits were generally constructed under contract by a firm located in the city where the show took place and at which the exhibit was first used.

Capex was a small firm, its sales volume approaching $1 million. In addition to Mr. Pease, the executive staff was composed of the vice-president, factory superintendent, treasurer, and sales supervisor. In planning the distribution of the new product, Mr. Pease considered the following:

1. Capex had virtually no reputation outside the general Chicago area.
2. Capex had no existing channel of distribution that could be used to sell the new line outside the Chicago area.
3. In view of the uncertain potential and Capex' limited resources, it would probably be unwise to establish a distribution system that would cause Capex to incur any fixed costs.
4. The sales volume that a salesman could obtain in most cities would probably not be high enough to support him if he carried only the Capex line.

In view of these considerations, Mr. Pease planned to use his own sales force in Chicago only. He proposed to employ four salesmen to sell there under the supervision of a sales supervisor who would also do some selling. In all other major cities and industrial areas, Capex would seek to establish brokers. This meant the number of brokers would total approximately twenty-five. The desirable brokers were those who handled related lines of other firms, such as advertising and display materials, sales aids, decals, and neon and electric signs. To set up these brokers and to supervise their activities, Capex considered employing three traveling sales supervisors.

The brokers would sell to their own contacts and to leads furnished by the Capex home office. They would receive a commission of 10–25 per cent, depending on the type of order and the method by which it was obtained. The commission was based on the quoted price of the display. If the broker received a lead from Capex and merely acted as an order taker, the minimum commission rate would be paid. If the broker developed a lead himself, sold a large order, or sold certain specially designed units, the commission rate increased. Each broker was given a catalogue showing all models and prices.

Mr. Pease believed that mail promotion methods could be a large source of business. Capex obtained a list of all convention and trade shows from the Exhibitors' Advisory Council in New York. This showed the trade shows planned in all major cities throughout the country. In addition, a number of private firms published the names and schedules of firms who would have exhibits at these shows. Capex planned to mail a card to each name on these lists informing them of the Capex product line. If an interested response was received, Capex would furnish the potential client a complete portfolio showing the models and styles that were available. If a broker were near one of these prospects, Capex would notify him and allow him to try to close the sale. If no broker were close, Capex would attempt to close a sale through the mail. Trade magazine advertising would be used as an introduction for salesmen and to develop leads. It was expected that many sales would be closed entirely by mail.

Mr. Pease had a difficult problem in pricing the new prefab exhibit units. Wooden displays typically cost exhibitors about $100 per lineal foot for original construction. Comparable prefab units would cost between $40 and $50 per lineal foot to manufacturer, including factory and administrative overhead. Mr. Pease believed that he could sell such units at prices between $60 and $75 per foot and make a profit. On the other hand, he was convinced that the Capex product was superior to the usual exhibit and, therefore, should command a higher price. The belief was reinforced when he visited a show and saw a display booth that he estimated weighed 800 pounds and that the exhibitor told him cost $1,000. A Capex prefab unit, superior in appearance and weighing only 80 pounds, could be sold for $450. Such a drastic saving in price, in Mr. Pease's opinion, would degrade the product.

1. *How should Mr. Pease market the prefab exhibits?*
2. *What price should he charge?*

42

HALOID XEROX, INC.

AFTER several years of experimenting and an investment of $1.5 million, Haloid Xerox developed a new machine for the office copying field. The new machine, called the "914," had many advantages over the copying machines already on the market; however, the 914 was also considerably more expensive to produce than were most competing products. These factors suggested a selling price considerably higher than the prices of competing products, but the exact price had not been determined. The management was considering not selling the 914 at all, but leasing it for a fixed fee per month or for a fee based on the amount of use made of the machine.

Prior to the development of the 914, Haloid Xerox had been selling copying processes primarily to the engineering field for the reproduction of engineering drawings and to the duplicating field for the making of offset masters. This equipment utilized xerography, an electrostatic process. Sales had more than tripled in the last ten years (Table 1). Until the development of the 914, this process had not been successfully adapted for the office copying field. Mimeographing, ditto, and offset processes had been used for many years for duplicating large quantities of typewritten or hand-drawn material. These methods were not satisfactory, however, for reproducing a few copies of a given page, as the cost of preparing the stencils or masters was too great. This led to the development, following World War II, of the office copying machine, a machine designed for making up to about fifteen copies of any given document.

In the late 1940's a number of manufacturers became conscious of the

TABLE 1

(Thousands of Dollars)

	Net Sales	Net Income
1949	$ 7,724	$182
1950	10,027	299
1951	12,897	302
1952	14,755	321
1953	15,751	370
1954	17,318	400
1955	21,391	450
1956	23,560	637
1957	25,808	645
1958	27,576	658

growing number of clerical employees in the United States and of the rapidly growing volume of paper work which businessmen, government employees, educators, and virtually every organization had to cope with. Beginning about 1950, several of these manufacturers entered the field with differing processes. Total sales in 1950 were estimated at around $60 million, and at approximately $225 million in 1959. Forecasts indicated that sales in 1965 would be between $400 million and $500 million. It was this rapidly growing market that attracted Haloid.

Prior to the entry of Haloid into the office copying field with its xerography process, there were four main processes and about thirty-five different companies competing for the market. Three different processes and three companies formed the main competition for Haloid: American Photocopy Equipment Company (APECO) led in the introduction of office copying machines in the United States with a machine using the diffusion process. With this process, light passed through a photographic-type negative to an original and was reflected back to the sensitized copy paper; this passed through a liquid developer and then ran through rollers that squeezed out the developer solution. The latter process pressed the two sheets together, and they had to be peeled apart by hand.

Eastman Kodak Company sold a machine using the verifax process, which was very similar to the diffusion process. Both the Eastman and APECO machines could be used to copy originals of almost any type—single sheets of paper, books, and paper on which the writing was on one side or on both sides. They were both wet processes. Minnesota Mining & Manufacturing Company sold the thermofax process. This was a dry process that used infrared rays, passing them through sensitized paper to the original. Carbon or metallic particles of the printing on the original were heated. The hot image, however, turned the copy paper dark. This process was limited to use with carbon copies or copies made with metallic inks. Writing by ball-point pens and many colors could not be reproduced by the thermofax process. The cheapest of the office copying processes was the diazo process, which was offered by a number of companies, such as Charles Bruning Company and the Ozalid Division of General Aniline & Film Corporation. This process passed light through the original to a paper coated with a special salt solution. As a result, the process was limited to use with originals that were translucent and were printed on only one side.

In the xerography process offered by Haloid, the original was projected to a charged surface of selenium plate by contact with exposure to light. Where the light struck the surface, an electrical charge was dissipated. Where the image on the original protected the plate from the light, the charge remained. Powdered ink with a negative charge was then dusted over the surface and was attracted to the charged areas. Paper was then placed over the surface and given a positive electrical charge to attract the ink, which was fused into the surface by heat. This process could be used with all types of originals in the same way that the diffusion and verifax processes could be used.

The Haloid 914 had one characteristic that distinguished it from its competitors—a characteristic that was both an advantage and a disadvantage: it made copies on ordinary office paper instead of on specially processed papers which the other methods required. Competitors relied on their sales of these specially treated papers for most of their income. In general, it was estimated that the competing processes obtained about 85 per cent of their income from the sale of the paper, as compared to only 15 per cent from the sale of the original equipment. In the case of the 914, however, sales of paper would be inconsequential, and the major income would have to come from the machine itself.

No competing machine could match the 914 in versatility. It could copy any document up to 9 × 14 inches in size, including colored material. The copies produced were dry and permanent and were sharp enough so that they could be used as originals or for further copying. Copies were produced at a rate of about six per minute; the operator simply placed the original document on the machine's scanning plate, set a dial for the number of copies desired, and pushed a button. When the number of copies had been produced, the machine shut itself off automatically. The operator did not need to feed the paper into the machine, as was the case with a number of other processes.

It was generally estimated that having a secretary retype a page cost somewhere between $0.68 and $2.85. The diazo process cost only about 1 cent per copy but was limited by the fact that it could reproduce only items on translucent originals. The other competing processes cost somewhere between 4 and 9 cents per copy for paper, ink, and other chemicals. The Haloid process would cost only about 1 cent per copy for paper and other supplies and would require no other chemicals.

The one big disadvantage of the Haloid 914 was its cost, which necessitated a price of several thousand dollars. Competing products sold for as little as $99.50. Table 2 shows the prices of the principal competitors. The Haloid management feared that its price might scare off many potential buyers. For this reason it was giving serious thought to the idea of leasing the machine. Competitive firms leased their products, but only in a small number of cases—perhaps 10 per cent. Typical leasing charges for these products are shown in Table 2.

APECO and Verifax provided permanent service guarantees for their machines as part of the sales price. This included the provision of all maintenance to keep the machine running properly. Actually, there was relatively little that could go wrong with the machines, although if, in time, they completely wore out, the customer would be expected to replace them. There had been no experience of this sort to date. Verifax

TABLE 2

PRICES AND RENTAL CHARGES FOR COMPETING REPRODUCTION EQUIPMENT

Product	Size of Material Handled	Price	Monthly Rental Charge
APECO*			
Smallest model.............8½″ × any†		$227.50	$ 7.50‡
Largest model.............. 16″ × any†		475.00	15.50§
Thermofax			
Smallest model.............8½″ × 11″		299.00	$20–$30‖
Largest model.............. 11″ × 16″		625.00	N.A.
Verifax			
Smallest model.............8½″ × 11″		99.50	No rental
Largest model.............. 10″ × 16″		425.00	$20#

  * American Photocopy Equipment Company.
  † This process was continuous, so that theoretically any length of material could be reproduced. In practice there were limits, as the reproduction paper was not generally available except in sheets.
  ‡ In addition, there was an initial deposit of $22.75.
  § In addition, there was an initial deposit of $47.50.
  ‖ If the machine was leased for one year, the rental was $30 per month; if leased for two or more years, the rental was $20 per month.
  # Three year lease minimum.

replaced all minor parts (less than $2.50) but charged the customer for major items. Bulbs and squeegees that were worn out with operation were replaced by the customer. Thermofax gave a six-month warranty with the sale of its product, but further service had to be paid for unless an annual service contract was purchased at a price of around $35, varying according to the machine. This entitled the purchaser to four quarterly inspections, emergency service on call, and all parts except bulbs and belts.

Actually, Haloid was going against the trend in the industry by introducing the 914. Competitors had been steadily turning out cheaper and cheaper copying units, although the cost of expendable supplies for each copy reproduced was relatively high. The market for the copying machines had been changing in a complementary manner. Virtually every organization, except for the very smallest, used office copiers. The largest users as a group were the government and manufacturing, insurance, and transportation companies. The larger the company, the more copiers there were relative to employees and the more extensively the copier was used. The large users, i.e., 100 or more copies per day, constituted about 10 per cent of the market.

The actual cost of producing the Haloid 914 would vary somewhat with the volume that was sold. However, the management estimated that it would cost about $2,500, on the average, to produce a single 914. Selling costs were expected to be about 30 per cent of sales. If it were decided to emphasize the leasing of the product, there were two alternatives at least. One would be to charge a fixed amount per week, per month, or per year for leasing the item. Management was concerned that this might scare off those who did not do a large amount of copy work. On the other hand, if the leasing charge were placed on a per copy basis, a customer might put the machine it its office and use it very little, so that there would be little or no income to Haloid. If the fixed per month charge for leasing were adopted, the company might use it very heavily and wear out the machine rapidly, whereas another company, using it a moderate amount, might preserve the machine over a much longer period of time.

All Haloid Xerox products were sold direct to consumers by salesmen located in seventeen branch offices throughout the United States. In Canada a wholly owned sales subsidiary distributed Haloid products. The company had three separate sales forces, which specialized according to product line: photographic equipment, manual xerographic equipment, and automatic xerographic equipment. In the three sales forces, there was a total of 160 salesmen. In addition, there were 185 field servicemen and about 80 other persons in the branch offices. Plans called for consolidation of the sales forces into one group handling all products, including the 914. While consolidating the sales operation, the management expected to double the number of salesmen and more than double the number of servicemen.

1. Should Haloid Xerox attempt to enter the copy machine market with the 914?

2. If the company were to enter this market, what pricing policies and what actual prices should it adopt?

43

CRYOVAC DIVISION, W. R. GRACE & COMPANY (A)

CRYOVAC introduced a new process for packaging and preserving such foods as fresh meats, poultry, cheese, and fish in 1947. Although there were some twenty other firms manufacturing fresh food packaging materials, none had the patented features of the Cryovac process, which management considered to be the only truly satisfactory method of packer packaging for self-service retail sale. From its inception, therefore, Cryovac sold its process at a considerably higher price, generally 50–100 per cent higher, than other packaging materials. The firm's sales climbed rapidly from $1.5 million in 1947 to about $39 million in 1957. The management planned sales of $48 million for 1958—an increase of $9 million over 1957. Actual sales in 1958, however, totaled only $42 million. Cryovac executives believed that this failure to achieve the planned sales volume was the result of prices higher than competitive prices during a period when economic and competitive factors were less favorable than they had been in the past.

Cryovac is the name of a vacuum-sealing process designed to protect products from damage and deterioration during handling, storing, and shipping. The process involves four steps:

1. The item to be packaged is placed in a loose-fitting bag made from a special plastic.
2. Air is withdrawn from the bag by a vacuum pump.
3. The neck of the bag is twisted tightly and sealed with a metal clip.
4. The package is then dipped in hot water at about 200° F., which causes the plastic to shrink and to cling tightly to the contours of the product like a second skin.

Cryovac bags are made from an airtight film that is a modified type of Saran, a plastic resin produced by Dow Chemical Corporation. When a food is sealed in a Cryovac bag and the air withdrawn, the food is protected against spoilage and shrinkage (loss of weight from loss of moisture) and the flavor does not deteriorate. The food can be seen clearly through the plastic. Many foods wrapped by Cryovac can be kept under refrigeration for many weeks without spoiling, whereas with other wrappers spoiling sets in within a week. Cryovac-wrapped meats can be frozen without the discoloration that usually occurs. A number of foods, such as ready-prepared corned beef, which had practically disappeared from meat counters, are now being sold again in Cryovac wrappings.

Cryovac's strongest selling points to food packers were that the Cryovac package would (1) stop shrinkage of the product completely, (2) control the color of the product, and (3) prevent spoilage and thus permit retail shelf life of from three to seven weeks versus a shelf life of only a few days to a week with other types of packages. Competitors in food-packaging materials had processes for packaging foods in plastic bags, but none had the airtight vacuum or the durability features of Cryovac.

Cryovac licensed their entire process to packers. This included sale of three items: the bags, the clips, and the equipment. Manual, semiautomatic or automatic equipment was available, depending on the needs and desires of the packer. The equipment included (1) a vacuumizing unit that drew out the air in the bags, (2) a clipping machine that fastened clips on the bags, and (3) a bath unit that shrank the bag tightly around the product. One person could operate one complete unit. Working with small-unit products, one man in an eight-hour day could package 1,000–1,200 units; with the automatic or semiautomatic equipment, he could do 2,000–3,000 units. On products packaged in larger units, one man could handle 800–1,000 units in a day with the manual equipment and 1,500–1,750 units with the automatic equipment.

Manual equipment generally cost $500–$700 for each set, and the automatic equipment $5,000–$7,000 a set. The equipment wore out very slowly, so that replacement sales were negligible. Small packers might buy one set; large national packers might buy seventy-five to one hundred sets. The bags were sold at prices that varied with the quantity bought, the size of the bag, the type, and the printing desired. About 60 per cent of all bags sold were printed. The price schedule for a typical bag size was as follows:

Nonprinted Bags		Printed Bags*	
Quantity Purchased	Price per Thousand	Quantity Purchased	Price per Thousand
1,000	$40.00	2,500 (Min. order)	$83.00
5,000	38.00	5,000	63.00
10,000	36.00	10,000	53.00
20,000	34.00	20,000	48.00
50,000	32.00	50,000	45.00
100,000	30.00	100,000	44.00
250,000	29.00	250,000	43.50
500,000	28.50	500,000	43.00

* The prices shown are for three-color printing.

It was possible for a packer to purchase bags on a split-shipment basis. He could place an order for a number of bags and have portions of the order shipped at different times within a six-month period; however, a minimum of 20,000 bags had to be shipped at any one time. The clips were sold in three sizes in cases of 10,000; medium size clips sold at about $25 per case.

A small meat packer who did about 25 per cent of his dollar volume in packaged meats would use the following Cryovac equipment: one semiautomatic vacuum and fastening machine set, one manual vacuum and fastening machine set, and one automatic shrink tunnel. This equipment would cost about $6,000 and would enable him to package up to 2,000 units a day. This packer would use $10,000 to $15,000 worth of bags and clips in a year.

Initially, the packers of poultry, especially turkeys, were the biggest customers for the Cryovac process. Locker plants were important customers, but after they reached a total number of about 15,000 in 1951, they began to decline in importance and by 1959 represented a negligible market. In 1951 Cryovac began an all-out campaign to convince meat and poultry packers of the desirability of prepackaged goods for consumers, a somewhat new concept at the time. To accomplish this task, Cryovac made an extensive appeal to retailers in the hope that retailers would encourage food packers to prepackage more products. Direct-mail pieces, articles in trade publications, demonstrations at trade shows and conventions, and calls by Cryovac salesmen were used. Cryovac salesmen also called on food packers with a presentation that included (1) a list of items to prepackage, (2) a description of how to prepackage them, (3) a statement of how to prepare the food for prepackaging, and (4) a blueprint of how to install a production line using the Cryovac process.

By 1953 many cheese packers, especially those in Wisconsin, were using the Cryovac process because they could age the cheese in the package. Fish and meat packers were also beginning to be important sales sources, but poultry packers were still the largest customers.

In 1956 the firm split into three regional divisions, each having its own plant and personnel. The western division included the territory west of Michigan to the Texas line, with headquarters in Cedar Rapids, Iowa; the eastern division was centered in Greenville, South Carolina; and the third division was in Canada. The general administrative office, where all research, promotion, and general policies were developed, was located in Cambridge, Massachusetts. In addition, a Chicago office was maintained to handle a group of large national accounts, which included Armour, Swift, Kraft, Wilson, A & P, and National Food Stores. These large accounts generally produced sales of between $100,000 and $1 million each per year. One salesman was required to handle two to four accounts. By 1956 national accounts represented approximately 25 per cent of Cryovac's volume.

Originally Cryovac had five salesmen, who called on some twenty-five to thirty distributors who sold the product to packers. The distributors were selected on the basis of experience in the food industry, ability to merchandise, and willingness to crusade for a new process that was costlier than competitive processes. The distributors realized an average 18 per cent discount from list price. In 1954 the company reappraised this policy in the light of the growing frozen-food market and the general consumer acceptance of prepackaged fresh foods. The executives believed that an all-out sales campaign was needed if Cryovac were to receive its share of the packaging market and that distributors could not do as effective a job as could Cryovac's own sales force. Prospects had to be sold aggressively because of the high cost of the Cryovac process, and accounts had to be serviced. Cryovac salesmen were more skilled in handling the service problems than were distributor salesmen. In addition, the Cryovac management believed that Cryovac salesmen were actually doing most of the selling for the distributors. Therefore, all distributors were dropped, and sixty salesmen were added to Cryovac's existing force, which had grown to twenty.

In 1956 the management decided on another major expansion of the sales force and about eighty salesmen were added, bringing the total to more than one hundred and sixty. Each salesman had an assigned territory and was expected to call on each account at least once every thirty days. A sizable and growing volume of business had been developed with smoked meats, and the company then campaigned to get the packers and wholesalers of red meats to use the Cryovac process. The advantages of aging such meats in the Cryovac package rather than unwrapped was emphasized. Normal practice was to age meats in a refrigerated warehouse and then to package them, using a process of one of Cryovac's competitors that would permit shelf life of only a few days. The Cryovac salesmen could cite the following problems in aging by this method: (1) weight loss due to shrinkage; (2) color loss from bacteria activity; and (3) the trimming required to take off the edges that had spoiled. Shrinkage ran to as much as 8 per cent of the weight of some meats but averaged about 4 per cent. Generally only the finest meats were aged—those sold to high-class restaurants and similar customers. Aging was believed to make meat more tender and to improve its flavor. Despite aggressive selling, Cryovac salesmen found considerable resistance to dropping the traditional method of aging red meat. This market segment, however, represented a large potential.

Cryovac faced competition from a few large firms and some twenty smaller firms. The larger ones were Visking, Tee-Pak, Milprint, Dobeckmun, Continental Can, and Goodyear. These firms had many other packaging lines that did not compete with Cryovac's line, but it was estimated that they had combined sales of $40 million in 1958 that could have been replaced by Cryovac. Total sales directly competitive to Cryovac probably were as high as $210 million annually.

All competitive firms sold packaging materials, but few sold a packaging process, and none had all the features of Cryovac's vacuum-sealing method. Cryovac, therefore, offered the best method for preventing shrinkage and assuring longer shelf life. It was generally accepted in the field that the Cryovac bag was of a quality superior to that of competitors. How much the added quality was worth was not clear. A typical comparison was a bag used for pork butts. Cryovac's bag sold for $44 per thousand and would preserve a butt for three weeks or more, compared to $30 per thousand for a competitor's bag that would be adequate protection for only ten to fourteen days.

Although the company sold flat film, pouches, and equipment, bags were the key item in the line. They represented the major part of the sales volume and produced the greatest margin. Therefore, it was the price competition in bags that was crucial; equipment sales and prices were relatively unimportant. Cryovac bags were priced from 50 to 80 per cent above competing bags. Cryovac tried to sell their complete process, including equipment, clips, and bags, at one time. Most firms that bought the process also bought bags from Cryovac. There was nothing, however, that prevented such customers from buying bags from other sources, although they could not get the same quality of bags elsewhere nor could they be used with the Cryovac packaging process.

In 1956–57 there was a rather pronounced effort by most food packers to reduce expenses because of a profit squeeze. Many firms reported to Cryovac that they were well satisfied with the line but that the advantages gained from Cryovac over other packaging lines in terms of what was needed did not justify the additional costs of the Cryovac line. Cryovac's competitors generally used the argument that meat packers should package to sell, not to keep, and that the most effective way to maximize profits was to package as cheaply as possible while maintaining minimum package requirements. Cryovac salesmen also ran into other objections, as follows:

1. The labor costs of operating the Cryovac process was generally 10–15 per cent higher than others because somewhat more skilled workers were needed. The manual and semiautomatic machines, especially, required a great deal of dexterity on the part of the operator.
2. The initial cost of the packaging line averaged 50 per cent more than competitive lines.
3. Cryovac offered no cash discount or free freight, as was the general practice in the field. All Cryovac prices were F.O.B. factory, and terms were net 30 days.
4. Cyrovac-wrapped fresh red meats changed color because of the absence of air. When the package was opened, however, the original color returned.

In considering the problem, the Cryovac general manager listed the things that Cryovac salesman had to offer:

1. A process that would stop shrinkage of the product completely, which would mean that a packer would incur virtually no weight loss during aging or handling.
2. A process that would retard color fade in smoked meat, making it more inviting to purchase, with resultant higher turnover.
3. A process that permitted the package to have a retail shelf life of three to seven weeks, depending on the product, which meant fewer returns and less dissatisfaction from consumers and retailers.
4. A bag that was stronger and clearer than any other plastic bag on the market.
5. The only process that permitted aging of product, when desirable, right in the package.

As an example of the savings possible through prevention of shrinkage loss, one Cryovac customer, a hotel and restaurant meat purveyor, reported the following savings from using the Cryovac process: A choice boneless sirloin strip steak might weigh 17 pounds and, at $1.50 per pound, be worth $25.50. The cost to package it with Cryovac, including the bag, clip, and labor, was 26.5 cents. Shrinkage during aging of such steaks usually ran 4 per cent or more. Such a shrinkage in this case cost the purveyor slightly over $1.00 in loss of weight, an amount far more than the cost of packaging. Meats aged outside of Cryovac developed mold, which had to be trimmed off, causing further loss of weight.

Figures from the various industries showed that average shrinkages were as follows: cheese, 3 per cent; smoked meats, 4 per cent; red meats, 6 per cent; and poultry, 3 per cent.

Meat wholesalers also found a saving in the use of Cryovac in that the longer shelf life it gave meat permitted them to build up inventory during slack periods. This resulted in labor savings and also permitted the wholesalers to buy larger quantities when they had opportunities to get lower prices.

Cryovac's management was disturbed by the apparent resistance in the market to its prices. This was particularly noticeable among smoked meat packers, whose preservation requirements were not as critical as in some other lines. Cryovac's margins were such that it could cut prices to some degree, but it could not meet the prices of lower-quality bags. If it cut prices, however, it would lose margin on all sales. There was a possibility that an intensified sales and promotion program could offset a price cut.

What pricing action, if any, should the Cryovac management take?

44

WITTEN CORPORATION

THE WITTEN CORPORATION, one of the largest manufacturers of stainless steel cooking utensils in the United States, was confronted with a pricing problem as the result of the growth of a new channel of distribution. Historically, the company's primary channel of distribution had been through hardware wholesalers to hardware retailers, but a proportion of sales had been made direct to large retailers, such as department stores, variety chains, and grocery chains. Prior to 1955, 75 per cent of sales had been to hardware wholesalers. After that date a shift developed in the relative importance of the two channels, and by 1959 only 55 per cent of sales were to hardware wholesalers and 45 per cent were direct to retailers. The increase in direct sales was almost entirely the result of increased sales to grocery chains.

Witten's price policy prior to 1955 had been based on a two-price system, one price for wholesalers and another for direct sales. Wholesalers received list price less 50 per cent and, in turn, sold to retailers for list less 33 ⅓ per cent. All direct sales were made at list price less 40 per cent. The larger discount to wholesalers was justified on the basis that they performed the functions of warehousing, distributing, billing, and offering of credit.

As sales to chains grew in importance, grocery chains in particular began demanding the wholesalers' price. The chains argued that they performed many functions of a wholesaler, such as warehousing and distribution. When Witten allowed the chains the same discount as wholesalers, the wholesalers raised strenuous objections. They argued that they were entitled to a larger discount than the chains and that the chains would use the larger discount to cut the consumer price. In some instances, chains had sold Witten items at prices below list even before they received the larger discount. The company did not wish to jeopardize its established position with the hardware wholesalers, but did wish to maintain its new position with the chains.

There was some division of Witten's business between wholesalers and chains according to price lines handled. The chains primarily carried the

TABLE 1

Typical Examples of Witten Prices

Item	List Price	Price to Wholesaler	Wholesaler Price to Retailer	Price Direct to Retailer
Low-priced items				
6-Inch frypan	$ 2.20	$1.10	$1.47	$1.10
10-Inch frypan	3.45	1.72	2.30	1.72
10-Inch de luxe frypan	3.98	1.99	2.65	1.99
High-priced items				
6-Quart saucepan	4.95	2.47	3.30	2.97
15-Inch deluxe frypan	10.95	5.48	7.31	6.57
8-Quart saucepan	7.95	3.98	5.30	4.76

lower-priced items in the line, while the hardware wholesalers concentrated on the higher-priced items. With this situation in mind, Witten developed another pricing policy in 1959 for the items in the lower end of its line. Under this policy, all buyers were given a 50 per cent discount from list. Table 1 shows prices of typical items in both the low-priced and the high-priced segments of Witten's line.

In the first four months of 1960, 25 per cent of the company's sales were in the lower-priced items and were sold at the same price to both chains and wholesalers. The trend toward sales of cooking utensils in chains was continuing, and it appeared to the Witten management that sales to chains would exceed sales to hardware wholesalers in the future. The chains were buying some items at list price less 40 per cent and some at list less 50 per cent, but they exerted continuing pressure for a straight list less 50 per cent on all items. Wholesalers, on the other hand, maintained their stand for a lower price than that given to chains.

While Witten was one of the largest producers of stainless steel utensils, it had considerable competition both from other stainless steel utensil firms and from manufacturers of other types of utensils, especially aluminum. The two largest competitors were firms that sold utensils on a door-to-door basis. There were a number of competitors, all smaller than Witten and less well known, that sold stainless steel utensils through channels similar to those used by Witten.

Witten's sales force consisted of thirty-five men, each responsible for all sales in his territory. The average salesman made from $7,000 to $8,000 a year from salary and commissions. In some territories the salesmen were supplemented by food brokers, who sold Witten products to the smaller grocery chains. The salesmen received credit for sales made in their territories by food brokers, but their commissions were reduced. Large chains were sold direct by management personnel. Salesmen performed all functions incident to completing sales but did not do missionary work with retailers, training of retail salesmen, or setting-up of displays.

Direct sales were made only to large retailers and chains. No quantity discounts were given. A minimum order requirement of a full case or one dozen items was established to deter small retailers from buying direct. Witten paid the freight on all orders from wholesalers of $250 or 250 pounds, and on orders from retailers of $150 or 150 pounds. All orders of less than these amounts were shipped F.O.B. Chicago. All bills carried 2 per cent/10 net 30 cash discount.

What pricing policy should Witten adopt?

45

OKLAHOMA OIL COMPANY

In July, 1956, the Standard Oil Company of New Jersey signed a purchase contract with Oklahoma Oil Company and Perfect Power Corporation, two independent oil marketers in the Chicago area, to acquire the marketing facilities of these companies, which consisted principally of 123 retail service stations. Of these, 76 were Oklahoma stations and 47 were Perfect Power. All the Perfect Power stations were company owned and operated, while 71 of the 76 Oklahoma stations were company owned and operated and 5 were operated by independent dealers who owned or leased the stations. Most major oil companies owned the majority of their service stations but leased them to independent operators on an annual basis. Both Oklahoma and Perfect Power characteristically had used price cutting and heavy promotion to build gasoline sales volume. They had not featured service or sales of related items, as did the more conventional nationally known marketers. In planning for the operation of these companies, the new management had to determine whether to continue the same over-all marketing policy or to shift the emphasis to the type of operation usually followed by Standard Oil of New Jersey in its other marketing affiliates.

The purchase of Oklahoma and Perfect Power by Standard of New Jersey was the result of considerable study of various areas, both foreign and domestic, where Standard of New Jersey might expand its markets. Projected population and industrial growth patterns indicated that the middle-western area of the United States was the third fastest growing section in the country. Although Standard Oil of New Jersey was the largest oil producer in the world, it had marketed at retail only along the eastern seaboard in thirteen states and the District of Columbia under the Esso brand name, in the Rocky Mountain states through the 100 per cent owned Carter Oil Company, and in Texas and New Mexico through the 78 per cent owned Humble Oil Company. It had had no marketing outlet in the Midwest. Standard of New Jersey accounted for about 12 per cent of the gasoline sold at retail in the United States. In Canada it held about a 23 per cent share of the retail gasoline market through the 70 per cent owned Imperial Oil Company.

After the directors had approved Jersey's entrance into the Midwest market, the question of how best to accomplish this mission was solved when it was found possible to purchase Oklahoma Oil and Perfect Power. It was felt essential to buy into the market, rather than attempt to establish new stations, because of the difficulty of acquiring desirable sites for service stations in properly zoned areas, securing permits, etc.

At the time of the purchase agreement with Oklahoma, the so-called "independents" marketed more than 30 per cent of the gasoline sold in the metropolitan Chicago area (Table 1).

TABLE 1

ESTIMATED NUMBER OF SERVICE STATIONS AND PER CENT OF
GASOLINE MARKET BY COMPANY IN THE CHICAGO
METROPOLITAN AREA: JULY, 1956

Company	No. of Stations	Per Cent of Market
Standard Oil Company (Indiana)...	940	29.5
Sinclair........................	900	13.0
Shell..........................	525	12.5
Texas.........................	435	7.5
Cities Service..................	360	3.0
Socony Mobile.................	300	3.0
Oklahoma and Perfect Power......	123	9.5
Other independents.............Unknown		22.0

The growth of the independent oil companies had started in the late 1930's after numerous antitrust actions. The larger oil companies had been content to concentrate on their producing and refining operations both because these functions were more profitable and because there would be a more healthy legal climate if more organizations were selling gasoline at retail.

Oklahoma Oil was founded in 1937 and, along with many other independents, had a phenoenal growth in the late 1940's and early 1950's. Generally speaking, the growth of the independent was accomplished by price cuts plus promotional schemes. The "gas-for-less" appeal was generally based upon a differential of approximately 2 cents per gallon below the posted price for the major oil companies' retail outlets. A differential of up to 4 cents per gallon sometimes existed, if the promotional costs were included. As long as the posted price of the independents did not exceed the 2-cent differential, however, the "majors" seemed content not to engage in a price war. This policy began to change in the 1950's as the independents became more successful.

In July, 1956, the 123 Oklahoma and Perfect Power stations pumped 8,837,000 gallons of gasoline at retail, or an average of almost 72,000 gallons per station. This volume was achieved with a price that was $\frac{1}{2}$–$1\frac{1}{2}$ cents per gallon below what was considered a normal price for comparable grades of gasoline sold by major brands. In earlier years of operation the price differential had been greater, but there was an apparent growing tendency for the large-volume independents in the Chicago metropolitan area to bring the price more nearly in line with the major brand marketers and to use some of what had been a wider differential on promotional gimmicks. Coupons or trading stamps had been extremely successful promotional devices for Oklahoma and Perfect Power. None of the major producers offered any type of trading stamp. Additional promotional schemes, such as free Sunday papers and merchandise give-aways, were also used successfully.

Typical Oklahoma and Perfect Power stations, as they existed in July of 1956, are shown in Exhibit 1. Essentially all the outlets were large-volume operations with eight or more pumps and were located on heavily traveled highways or traffic arteries. This contrasted with the neighborhood type station of two to six pumps, which were common among the major brand stations. In square footage occupied, the typical Oklahoma station covered 50–100 per cent more area than the average major brand outlet. In physical appearance the Oklahoma or Perfect Power station was generally more brilliantly lighted at night and had large billboards flanking the station proper. Often "Gas for Less" signs were prominently displayed, but actual prices were not prominently advertised but only posted at the pumps.

Oklahoma and Perfect Power stations usually sold oil but placed no emphasis on changing oil. One lift might be on the premises, but it was

EXHIBIT 1

TYPICAL OKLAHOMA AND PERFECT POWER SERVICE STATION: 1956

in the open instead of in an enclosed stall, as was common in the major-company stations. Antifreeze was featured and installed when necessary, but particular emphasis was placed on early season price appeals, with the aim of "selling" the customer on purchasing the antifreeze in cans and carrying it home, where he could install it later.

The large-volume independent stations usually catered more to the blue-collar trade and the price conscious transient trade. In order to capitalize on volume, these outlets usually remained open twenty-four hours a day. As a rule, the large-volume operations catered to men more than to women, who characteristically needed and were more impressed by the services offered by the major oil company outlets. Clean restrooms were promoted by the major company outlets more than by independents.

An industry study published in 1954 had the following comments on the large-volume independent stations:

Generally speaking, whenever one finds non-major company dealer operations, he finds some disparity in retail prices. Perhaps the strongest force operating toward retail price disparity in the market recently is the inauguration of the large-scale gasoline outlet. This type of unit is potentially a low-cost operation but must have large volume in order to realize its potentialities. (This probably should be a minimum of 75,000–100,000 gallons per month, as against 8,000–10,000 in conventional stations.) That is, the super-station (having 9–24 pumps and very large underground storage capacity) is a very efficient unit when utilized extensively. Under such conditions the whole cost of distributing gasoline (including that of carrying the wholesale function, which is substantially reduced) may be halved (i.e., the total cost may drop from 6¢–7¢ to 3¢–4¢).[1]

In its eastern states operation under the Esso brand name, Standard Oil of New Jersey operated its retail outlets in the conventional manner of the well-known major brand oil companies. Major oil companies tended to maintain uniform prices in the same market, and the Esso operation on the eastern seaboard had followed such a pattern. Superior service—which included oil changes; antifreeze installation; a full and extensive line of accessories, such as tires, batteries, fan belts, light bulbs, and replacement windshield-wiper blades; road service, including towing service; and even minor motor tuneups—was the characteristic competitive tool of the service stations of the major companies rather than price. Such nonprice appeals, supported by national or regional advertising stressing quality of product, had generally been the policy of Standard Oil of New Jersey.

A consideration in determining over-all marketing policies and strategy for the new Oklahoma and Perfect Power management was the problem of public, and also government, acceptance of the fact that the world's largest oil company had entered the Midwest market by purchasing a price-cutting independent. A continuation of the price-cutting, gas-for-less policies of the purchased companies might be seen differently when done under the management of Standard Oil of New Jersey than when carried on by minor firms in the industry.

---

[1] Ralph Cassady, Jr., *Price Making and Price Behavior in the Petroleum Industry*, (New Haven: Yale University Press, 1954), p. 257. In the early and middle 1950's the success of the large-volume independent had tended to shift the philosophy of some of the major oil companies as to their interest in controlling more of the marketing at retail of their products.

Pricing in the petroleum industry had for many years been complicated by government antitrust investigations concerning the legality of all major concerns following the price leadership of one firm acknowledged to be the major supplier in a particular area. "The Federal Trade Commission seems to have devised a term called 'conscious parallelism' which it uses to describe the unilateral adoption of substantially uniform business practices (especially with respect to prices) by competing business enterprises. The idea seems to be that if action is taken by one individual with the expectation that similar action will be taken by another, there is a conscious parallel action and hence a sort of collusion."[2] Thus, if the Oklahoma and Perfect Power prices were raised to the same level as those the major oil companies posted, there was danger that the companies might be accused of collusion. There was a question, however, as to what action Standard Oil (Indiana), the acknowledged price leader in the Midwest, would take if another major company maintained a price differential. A price war could result.

At the opposite end of the scale, it was felt that criticism might be received if the new management entered the Midwest market on a price-cutting basis. Competitors, especially the small ones, could conceivably charge "unfair trade" and "loss leader" tactics against the giant Standard of New Jersey.

A further problem facing the new management was whether to combine the two independents under a single name and, if such a combination were effected, whether to use either of the two previous company names or to establish a new name.

A court decision handed down in 1935 was pertinent to the thinking of company officials at this time. This decision involved a suit by Standard Oil Company (Indiana) against Esso Standard Oil Company, a subsidiary of Standard Oil Company of New Jersey. At that time, Standard Oil Company of New Jersey had entered the Midwest territory in the St. Louis area with stations labeled "Esso." The court held that Standard Oil Company (Indiana) had been marketing its product in this region for many years prior to the Esso invasion, hence the name Standard Oil and the letters "SO" meant "Standard Oil (Indiana)" to consumers in the Midwest. It further held that when Standard Oil Company of New Jersey first entered St. Louis with stations, selling under the name "Esso," confusion resulted in the minds of consumers, despite a notice on the stations reading "Not Connected with Standard Oil Company (Indiana)." Standard Oil of New Jersey, therefore, while welcome to do business in the Midwest, was enjoined from selling under its name in that region.

1. What pricing policy should the Oklahoma Oil Company adopt?

2. Should both Oklahoma and Perfect Power gasoline be sold under one brand name?

---

[2] *Ibid.,* p. 106.

46

SURE CUT CHAIN SAW COMPANY

IN FEBRUARY, 1958, the research and development department of Sure Cut Chain Saw Company reported that a new 3.5-horsepower chain saw, which had been under development for the past several years, would be ready for production in the fall of that year—much earlier than had been anticipated. This saw was lighter yet more rugged than the 3.5-horsepower model then being sold by Sure Cut and its competitors. Lower production costs would permit the new saw to sell for approximately 25 per cent less than existing comparable saws. The president of the company, upon the recommendation of the sales manager, ordered the new saw into production immediately, for announcement and sale to the trade commencing in the fall of 1958. This decision left the sales manager with the problem of how to dispose of a substantial inventory of the existing 3.5-horsepower saws before the new model reached the market.

The Sure Cut Chain Saw Company produced and marketed a line of chain saws powered by small horsepower motors. Sales in 1957 were $1,285,000. The industry had grown spectacularly from 1950 to 1957, and industry sales for 1958 were estimated at about 200,000 units. The chain saw industry was dominated by two companies: McCulloch and Homelite, which collectively accounted for approximately 60 per cent of all sales. About thirty other companies shared the remaining 40 per cent of the market. The industry was becoming increasingly competitive. This resulted partly from the entry of several large firms that had purchased chain saw companies; for example, Remington Arms had purchased Mall Tool, Outboard Marine had acquired Industrial Engineering Limited, and Draper had purchased Titan.

The traditional distribution channel used by a majority of chain saw companies was from manufacturer to distributor to dealer. The Sure Cut Company had twenty-eight distributors throughout the United States. Each was assigned an exclusive area. It was the responsibility of these distributors to establish their own dealer organizations; however, the Sure Cut Company's five-man sales force helped each distributor, wherever possible, to secure and maintain dealers.

In all cases the Sure Cut distributors handled other products; in fact, chain saw sales were secondary. Twelve of the company's distributors were hardware wholesalers, five were industrial distributors, four were boat and outboard motor distributors, and the remaining seven represented a variety of types, including power equipment, garden supplies, and sporting goods. Seventeen of these distributors had set up separate departments to handle chain saw units and parts sales. Sure Cut executives estimated that their products were sold through approximately twelve hundred dealers. Many of these dealers were small specialized operators who sold mainly saws and provided service and spare parts.

The Sure Cut Company followed industry practices in its discount structure. It sold its saws to distributors at 40 per cent off list price. Distributors, in turn, sold to dealers at 25 per cent off list. Parts were sold at 45 per cent off list to distributors, who sold to dealers at 30 per cent off list; comparable discounts on chains were 47 per cent and 32 per cent. The only time that the foregoing discount structure was departed from was when a distributor bid on a contract with a municipality or some other special group and needed some price concession to enable him to make the low bid.

The company estimated that the life expectancy of a chain saw varied between one and five years, depending on the type of use. An increasing

TABLE 1

RETAIL PRICES OF 3.5- AND 5-HORSEPOWER CHAIN SAWS

Horsepower	Sure Cut	McCulloch	Homelite
3.5..............$268		$258	$274
5.0.............. 320		. . .	313
7.0.............. . . .		399	. . .

number of commercial cutters were trading in their saws after one year. The farm market, however, kept saws for about five years. Trade-ins presented a special problem to the industry. It was standard practice for each dealer to make his own trade. Manufacturers sometimes helped the dealer by allowing from $20 to $40 on a trade, depending on the model sold, but in most cases dealers set their own terms on trade-ins on the basis of reconditioning costs and expected resale price. The Sure Cut Company annually ran a spring promotion, allowing special discounts to its distributors for trade-ins. The company was especially anxious to replace competitive saws with its own brand because of the opportunity to sell spare parts and chain replacements.

Sure Cut's line consisted of five saws, of which the 3.5- and 5-horsepower units were the most popular. The 3.5-horsepower saw accounted for 63 per cent of the company's sales, and the 5-horsepower for 28 per cent. Retail prices for McCulloch, Homelite, and Sure Cut 3.5- and 5-horsepower units are shown in Table 1. The new 3.5-horsepower unit to be introduced by Sure Cut in the fall was scheduled to retail for $199.

Sure Cut's inventory at the end of February showed 3,012 units of the 3.5-horsepower saw. The sales manager, Mr. Heston, estimated distributor and dealer stocks to be another 1,800–2,000 units. From past shipment data, Mr. Heston determined that he might expect to ship 1,600–1,750 of these units between March 1 and September 1. In January and February,

Sure Cut had shipped 440 units. On the basis of this, he would have to dispose of about 1,300 additional units from March through September and also help the dealers and distributors dispose of their stocks.

After much discussion with the president, Mr. Heston developed a plan for reducing the retail price on the current 3.5-horsepower model to $215 with a trade-in. Through this he hoped to gain additional sales and reduce the inventories in preparation for the introduction of the new model in the fall. Effective immediately, he would grant distributors an extra $25 discount on every saw they purchased. In addition, the company's salesmen would visit all twenty-eight distributors and inventory their present stock of 3.5-horsepower units. Each distributor would receive a $25 credit for each unit in stock, which could be applied only on the purchase of additional units of the same model. These credits would be given only on purchases made before July 15, 1956.

Distributors, in turn, were to reduce prices to dealers by $35, provided the dealers purchased three or more units and agreed to sell the 3.5-horsepower units for $215 with a trade-in. The distributors were to inventory dealers' stocks and to grant a $35 credit for each unit. As with distributors, this credit would apply only on future purchases of the existing 3.5-horsepower units. Each distributor would report the inventory of each of his dealers, and Sure Cut would then credit the distributor's account for $25 for each unit. Mr. Heston realized that not all retail sales would be made with trade-ins, but he thought that the dealers would use the $35 credits to "discount" off the list price in varying amounts, which he would leave up to them.

Mr. Heston recognized that this price cut would reduce, if not eliminate, company profits. The manufacturing cost, including all overhead except sales, of the old 3.5-horsepower unit was 63.76 per cent of the manufacturer's former selling price, or $102.53.

Should Mr. Heston's plan be accepted?

D. Selling, Advertising, and Promotion

47

CANDYGRAM, INC.

LATE IN 1958, CandyGram, Inc., in conjunction with Western Union and Stevens Candy Kitchens, Inc., was considering launching a new service —candy by telegram. This service would make it possible to send a box of chocolates, accompanied by a personal telegram, anywhere in the

United States with the speed of a telegram alone. The candy would be delivered by Western Union messenger. The telegram would be inserted into the top of the candy box (Exhibit 1), where it would be clearly visible behind a transparent cover. The unit of candy and attached telegram would be called a CandyGram. CandyGram, Inc., would be responsible for all marketing activities except the delivery of the CandyGram to the ultimate consumer. Stevens Candy Kitchens would furnish the candy.

Maurice Sher, a restaurateur in Columbus, Ohio, originated the Candy-Gram idea, which he took to Stevens Candy Kitchens. Together they

EXHIBIT 1

SAMPLE CANDYGRAM

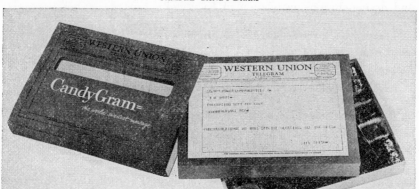

formed the CandyGram corporation to investigate the potential of the idea and to exploit it if feasible. Mr. Sher became chairman of the board of the new corporation and William H. Rentschler, president of Stevens Candy Kitchens, became president.

As the two executives conceived the plan, a CandyGram could be sent from anywhere in the United States to any other address in the country. CandyGrams could be ordered at any Western Union office or by telephone. Western Union would bill the customer for the cost of the candy plus the telegram. Upon receipt of a CandyGram order and message, the Western Union employee at the addressee station would remove the requested box of candy (one pound or two pounds) from a freezer located in the telegraph office, attach the telegram to the box top, slide the box with the "message top" into a decorative open-end sleeve (Exhibit 1), and deliver the CandyGram to the addressee. The sleeve was designed to be die-cut to show the recipient's name and address.

Stevens Candy Kitchens, Inc., of Chicago would produce all the candy. The hand-dipped chocolates, protected by special packaging, would be frozen shortly after they were made. They would thus remain in perfect condition indefinitely if kept frozen. It would take about two hours to thaw the candy; this was the estimated typical time required to deliver a CandyGram to the recipient's door. To send a CandyGram, a customer would pay $2.95 for the one-pound box and $5.00 for the two-pound box plus the cost of the message at regular Western Union telegraph rates.

Rentschler believed that rising personal incomes, increasing emphasis on special occasion giving, and the speed, convenience, and appeal of the CandyGram idea indicated that there would be a rich, "ready-to-act" market, both consumer and commercial, for CandyGrams. A consumer research study was undertaken to determine such factors as candy-giving habits of businessmen and housewives, importance of brand name in the candy industry, acceptance of frozen candy, and reactions to the CandyGram idea. The research organization's summary of its findings and its conclusions are shown in Exhibit 2.

EXHIBIT 2

Consumer Survey

Purpose

    A. To determine consumer habits in the purchase of flowers and candy as gifts.

    B. To determine consumer attitudes toward sending candy by wire, specifically via CandyGram.

Method

A total of 514 respondents, living in New York, San Francisco, Birmingham, and Des Moines, were personally interviewed in their homes. The interviews in New York were conducted during October, 1958, by Merrill Levitt and Associates; the interviews in the other three cities were carried out by National Field Service during the latter part of November, 1958. The respondents were selected from the A, B, and C socioeconomic strata (over $4,000 annual family income) because it was felt that low-income groups were not a potential market for CandyGram. The interviews were equally divided between men and women.

Because this survey is based on a quota-type sample, the results are not projectable to the total population, nor are the results to be taken strictly at their numerical face value; instead, the findings reflect general attitudes and habits in broad terms.

Summary of Findings

    1. Eight out of ten people are in the habit of giving candy as a gift, but only three out of ten would send candy to someone out of town if they had to choose between flowers and candy.

    2. The major reason for choosing flowers over candy as a gift to be sent to someone in another part of the country is the speed, ease, and convenience with which they can be sent. Conversely, the major reason for not sending candy is the fear that the product might spoil in the long transit.

    3. Candy is considered an especially appropriate gift for birthdays, Valentine's Day, and Mother's Day, while flowers are associated chiefly with illness, hospital, anniversaries, or as an expression of condolence.

    4. There seems to be no strong brand loyalty in candy purchasing; over half the people stated that they usually bought different brands of candy.

EXHIBIT 2—*Continued*

The results indicate, however, that brand loyalty is more of a factor in the large, cosmopolitan city than in the smaller, less sophisticated markets. Such brands as Schrafft, Loft, and Barton in New York and Whitman and See in San Francisco seem to have a loyal core of customers.

5. The three most important things people want to know about the candy before buying a new brand are: ingredients (assortment, type of chocolate), freshness, and taste.

6. "Good quality" in candy means good taste and good (pure) ingredients to the consumer. Freshness is not mentioned to any considerable extent, but this may well be due to the fact that people naturally assume good quality chocolates to be fresh without verbalizing this assumption.

7. Good chocolate and fresh nuts are important ingredients as far as the consumer is concerned. Revealing, however, is the fact that half the respondents could not express any opinion on which ingredient is important in the manufacture of candy. Many said that they never gave it any thought.

8. Two-thirds of the respondents had sent flowers by telegraph at one time or another, and they liked the convenience and speed of sending flowers in this fashion. The only major objection voiced by the respondents regarding flowers-by-wire was their uncertainty of what the recipient would actually receive. There is some feeling that the florist in the other city might substitute an inferior product.

9. Seven out of ten people thought that CandyGram was a good idea, and convenience, speed, and freshness were given as reasons for this belief. Those who thought candy-by-wire was a poor idea were primarily people who themselves did not like candy or who were not sure whether the donee liked to receive candy as a gift. Significant, however, is the expression of resistance to the CandyGram idea because of the unknown quality of the CandyGram chocolates. About one-quarter of the respondents who thought CandyGram to be a poor idea gave this as the reason for their opinion.

10. There is every reason to believe that people in the cosmopolitan cities will be more likely to send a CandyGram than will those living in less cosmopolitan areas—at least initially, until the new idea has sufficiently penetrated.

11. The preferred method of sending a CandyGram is via night letter, and birthdays, Easter, Valentine's Day and Mother's Day rank high as occasions for using the new service.

12. A two-pound Candy Gram was judged three times as popular as a one-pound by the respondents. It must be remembered, however, that a question on this subject tends to produce overstatement of actuality because of prestige reasons. When asked for the weight of the last box of candy they bought, most respondents indicated that it was a one-pound box.

13. There is no evidence of any serious objection to the fact that CandyGram is a frozen chocolate. Well over half of those who would be likely to use the service indicated that it made no difference or even that it was a good idea to freeze the candy. Nine out of ten thought that freezing candy had no effect on its flavor, and seven out of ten thought that freezing had no effect on the candy's appearance.

Conclusions

The study produced a strong consumer acceptance of the CandyGram idea and a very favorable picture of sales potential. This is evidenced by:

EXHIBIT 2—*Continued*

A. The general practice of giving candy as a gift.
B. The acceptance and use of the flower-by-wire service.
C. The fact that CandyGram would overcome most current objections to sending candy out of town.
D. The fact that people do not seem to reject the price of the service and that there seems to be no adverse opinion of frozen candy.

The study points to the distinct possibility that the CandyGram idea will be more readily accepted and used in the large cosmopolitan areas. Therefore, it may be well to concentrate initial advertising efforts in these markets.

In addition, there is evidence that, in order to realize the service's full potential, the consumer must be sold on the quality and taste of the product.

Western Union in 1958 transmitted more than 20 million social telegrams (Happy Birthday, Merry Christmas, etc.). The Florists Telegraph Delivery Association (FTDA) handled an additional 7.5 million orders valued at $56 million in 1957. Consumer candy sales in the United States totaled about $1.12 billion in 1958, according to the National Confectioners Association. This amounted to 16.4 pounds of candy per capita, an increase over the previous year.

From these facts Rentschler concluded that a big market already existed for gifts-by-wire, for telegraphed greetings, and for candy. He believed that the CandyGram idea combined the best features of a telegram and a gift in a unique manner. He thought the CandyGram idea was superior to the flowers-by-wire service for the following reasons:

1. The minimum order of flowers-by-wire was $5; the top price for a CandyGram was $5.
2. The uniformity possible with candy was not possible with flowers.
3. A telegram message could be sent with the candy but not with flowers.
4. The telegram and candy could be charged to Western Union; this was not possible with flowers unless the person had a charge account with the florist.

Rentschler thought that it would be inadvisable to feature the Stevens Candy Kitchens' name with the advertising program and package design primarily for two reasons: he believed that the two names, Western Union and CandyGram, were sufficient and that to feature a third name would confuse the customer; and he had some reservations about the advisability of associating the Stevens' name with CandyGram. The one-pound box of CandyGram candy would sell for $2.95 but would normally sell in stores for about $2.00; similarly the two-pound box that would be sold by CandyGram for $5.00 would normally sell for about $4.00. The extra dollar charged by CandyGram would go to pay the 75-cent delivery fee paid to Western Union and to cover the costs of freezing and handling the candy.

Shipping the candy was no unusual problem, as the same procedure would be used that had been developed by Stevens Candy Kitchens in shipping to its 1,500 retailers all over the United States. This procedure involved the purchase of special containers in which the frozen candy and dry ice were placed. The containers were then shipped by less-than-truck-load lots. Less-than-truck-load rates from Chicago were $4.50 per hundredweight to New York and $9.50 to Los Angeles. The minimum shipment was 100 pounds.

Rentschler expected to spend about $175,000 to $200,000 during the first year on all types of promotional efforts on behalf of CandyGram. However, he was not sure as to the best types of disposition of the fund.

Stevens Candy Kitchens would sell candy to CandyGram, Inc., at regular wholesale prices, which would include the special box made for CandyGram. CandyGram would ship the boxed candy via refrigerated trucking lines to as many Western Union offices throughout the nation as it thought desirable. Rentschler planned to stock the candy in six hundred key Western Union offices as a start. The boxed candy would be stored in freezers located in each of these Western Union offices. CandyGram would provide the freezers (17-cu.-ft. models), which it could lease from Admiral Corporation at a cost of $225 per year for three years, after which the freezers would be owned by CandyGram. The freezers held 72 one-pound and 72 two-pound boxes of candy. Western Union would maintain inventory control on the candy in the freezers, deliver the CandyGrams, and collect for them. It would retain the price of the telegram and a 75-cent flat fee for each CandyGram delivered. The rest of the CandyGram price would be remitted to CandyGram, Inc.

The price of a CandyGram would automatically include the charge for the standard fifteen-word telegraph message. If longer messages were sent, there would be an additional charge. Regular rates on telegrams up to fifteen words in length varied by distance; the charge for a message from Chicago to Denver was $1.60. A CandyGram would be sent to the Western Union office stocking the candy that was nearest to the addressee. This office would deliver the CandyGram if the address were in the immediate vicinity. Otherwise, it would mail the candy and the message. Delivery through the mail would require, at the most, two days. First class mail postage was 78 cents for the one-pound package and 96 cents for the two-pound package.

Stevens Candy Kitchens signed an exclusive twenty-five-year pact with CandyGram to furnish all the candy required. Western Union would sign a contract giving CandyGram exclusive rights to any business of this type for six years. An agreement with Admiral Corporation would call for payment of freezer rentals in equal monthly installments.

Stevens Candy Kitchens was a medium-sized candy manufacturer of medium-priced, hand-dipped chocolates, most of which retailed for $1.35–$2.00 per pound. It sold its line direct to department stores, drugstores, supermarkets, and confectionery shops all over the United States. The typical retail discount was 40 per cent off the suggested retail selling price. Trucking firms transported the line from the plant in Chicago to the customers. Stevens Candy Kitchens had four major direct competitors. Like most candy manufacturers of this type, 65 per cent of its sales were made at Christmas, Easter, Valentine's Day, and Mother's Day. Consequently, Rentschler, as president of Stevens, was greatly interested in the CandyGram idea, since it seemed likely to increase everyday business.

1. *Should CandyGram, Inc., proceed with the CandyGram plan?*

2. *What selling program should Mr. Rentschler establish if the CandyGram plan were put into operation?*

48

BAYLINE SCHOOL FOR GIRLS

THE BAYLINE SCHOOL FOR GIRLS had been located in one of the suburbs in the San Francisco–Oakland area for over thirty-five years. In the last ten years the school had experienced increasing difficulty in attracting new students. It did not have an endowment and depended solely on tuition for operating income. Tuition did not cover all expenses, and deficits were usually made up each year by gifts from trustees of the school. It had become increasingly difficult to balance the budget; therefore the Board of Trustees decided to consult a firm that specialized in solving fund-raising problems of educational institutions. The board asked the consultants to develop a program for recruiting new students and for raising endowment funds.

Bayline offered a complete curriculum for all grade levels from preschool through high school. It was a day school only and did not have boarding students. At the preschool and kindergarten levels, both boys and girls were accepted, but from the first grade on it was exclusively a girl's school. Tuition ranged from $430 a year for full-time preschool to $975 a year for high school. Bus service and lunches were provided by the school at additional charge.

Bayline had an excellent scholastic reputation and was highly selective in screening applicants. Because of its high scholastic standards, many applicants were turned down each year, even in those years when enrollment was not up to the school limit. Over 90 per cent of Bayline graduates went on to college.

The school drew students from the area approximately within a ten-mile radius. This area included most of Oakland, a number of smaller suburbs, and a part of San Francisco. Faculty and staff members of the universities in the area were allowed 30 per cent discount on tuition, and a significant portion of students were daughters of these people. Maximum enrollment was about 230 students but had ranged between 175 and 180 in the past few years.

The population of the area served by the school had grown rapidly in the past ten years. The ten-mile-radius area, which had included a population of about 500,000 twenty years before, now had over a million. The public school system had more than kept pace and was considered one of the best in the country. During this twenty-year period, Bayline's position in the community had declined. Poor management had been a factor early in the period, and changes made by the board of trustees in trying to correct this situation caused hard feelings with some alumni. The result of these actions was the loss of the support of over half the alumni in the area, many of whom were influential members of their communities. The competition from the public schools had also had its effect on Bayline. Coupled with these factors was an apparent change in public attitude toward private schools that tended to decrease their prestige. This had been tempered somewhat by the recent national emphasis on education and by the publicity given to the problems of public schools.

About 120 students usually continued from one year to the next. New students were not accepted for the eighth and twelfth grades, since these were considered final years for elementary and high school levels. There had never been a case of a girl's going all the way through Bayline, first through twelfth grades, but about 50 per cent of the students who started either the elementary or the high school sequences finished that level.

The director of enrollment had been responsible for recruiting new students. Recommendations by parents and alumni furnished the main leads to prospective students. Also, many inquiries came directly from parents interested in sending their daughters to a private school. The director of enrollment was responsible for following up these recommendations and inquiries. This was done mainly through telephone contact or by mail. A prospect list was also maintained, which averaged approximately 200–250 families, with additions and deletions being made regularly. The parents on the prospect list were mailed information about the school from time to time and received invitations to school functions, such as parent teas and graduation exercises. A limited amount of personal contact was made with prospects by the director of enrollment and other members of the staff. Main emphasis was placed on getting prospects to visit the school. Past experience showed that the school enrolled one student out of every thirty qualified prospects.

Bayline advertised in the newspapers of the nearby communities. Thirteen advertisements a year were run in each of four newspapers. These were one-column, editorial-type advertisements that discussed the advantages of Bayline as a private school. The total cost of this advertising program was around $2,000 per year. In addition, the school made annual mailings of a brochure to good prospects. No specific promotional activities had been directed toward fund raising.

The management consultants believed that the school must broaden its entire scope of promotion activities. They recommended that the school hire a director of development to manage the over-all promotion and fund-raising program. The development director's primary responsibility would be to work with the consultants, at first, in developing the promotion and fund-raising programs and then to put the programs into effect. At this time, the new student situation for the following September was critical. The school needed 125 new students for the fall term to get enrollment to the point at which tuition would cover most of the expenses. The trustees also believed that Bayline would have to raise $50,000 for operating expenses in the next year to put it in a safe financial position.

The consultants' recommendation was approved in April and a director of development was hired almost immediately at a salary of $9,500 a year. Working closely with the consultants, he immediately tackled the problem of recruiting students. Through directories of local churches, clubs, and other institutions and through information from alumni and friends in the area, he expanded the prospect list from 200 to over 1,000. This list was qualified as well as possible by geographic areas, social organizations, church groups, and family income. The best prospects, those personally recommended by alumni or friends and those who initiated their original contact with the school, were singled out for personal calls. A direct-mail campaign was planned to reach the rest of the prospects. Through a series of three mailings, which would cost about $600 in total, it was hoped to single out the best prospects of this group for personal calls.

The director of development planned to divide his time equally between student recruiting, fund-raising activities, and public relations. His activities were hampered by the fact that he did not have a secretary and handled much of the detail work personally. He and the consultants were further hampered by the head mistress of the school, who at first was not in complete accord with their ideas. She stressed the point of maintaining the dignity and prestige of the school and insisted that all plans and activities, down to the smallest detail, be cleared through her. She would not approve the use of prepared mailing lists or of any "crash"-type program that would hint that the school was in any trouble.

Plans for public relations activities included making contacts with the business community, social organizations, and church groups in the area to convince them of the need for a private school in the community. Personal calls on ministers, educators, and other influential people in the community were planned to obtain their help in recommending prospective students. The director also planned to renew the alumni organization, which had broken down as a result of changes made by the board of trustees during the earlier period of management difficulties.

Fund-raising activities involved two problems. First, the sources of funds had to be located, and, second, ways of giving money that would appeal to different groups and types of people had to be established. The primary groups that were considered good prospects were the business community, foundations, parents of students, alumni, trustees, and students. The director of development planned to establish a fund-raising organization, consisting of alumni and parents of students, to make individual appeals. He planned to appear personally before these groups.

Plans were made to set up categories of gifts so that people or groups could make their gifts for the purpose in which they were most interested. For example, different funds, such as a building fund, a science-laboratory fund, a library fund, or a scholarship fund, would be established. Subject areas were to be divided into units of cost per year so that contributors could "buy" one or more units and would know just how much their money contributed to the operation of the school.

By the end of June the programs planned by the director of development with the consultants were under way. Many contacts had been made with the business community, influential individuals, and important organizations. The direct-mail campaign to recruit new students had not brought any significant results. About twenty-five new students were enrolled for the fall term, and about $2,000 had been raised. A gift of $6,500 was promised if the school could match it.

Was the Bayline promotion program sound?

49

ABBOTT LABORATORIES (B)

IN 1950 Abbott Laboratories, one of the leading United States manufacturers of drug products, culminated ten years of research and testing of cyclamate, a new chemical compound, for use as a noncaloric sweetener. The product was given the trade name Sucaryl and was the first new noncaloric sweetener to be developed since the early 1900's, when saccharin was first introduced. Sucaryl was introduced to two markets simultaneously—in a packaged form for consumers and in bulk to dietetic food and drink processors. The packaged Sucaryl was marketed through Abbott's distribution organization to drugstores only. The chemical sales division was given responsibility for bulk sales direct to food and beverage processors.

During the period 1950–55, the chemical sales division did some advertising through trade journals, but in accordance with company policy there was no consumer advertising of Sucaryl except for point-of-sale and window displays for packaged Sucaryl sold through drugstores. Abbott manufactured and marketed Sucaryl under a license from Du Pont, which held the patent on cyclamate. It was not an exclusive license, and by 1955 other chemical companies had started to enter the market with bulk cyclamate. The company then faced the problem of establishing the brand name of Sucaryl firmly in the market to hold off competition.

Abbott Laboratories maintained plants in seventeen foreign countries and sales offices in almost every country in the world. Net sales in 1958 were in excess of $116 million. Abbott distributed its pharmaceutical products primarily through its own marketing organization. Warehouses were located in twenty-one strategic spots throughout the country to assure quick delivery. Historically, company policy had been not to advertise to consumers. Promotion was done primarily through detail men who contacted doctors and druggists to inform them of new products or further uses of other products. In addition, direct mail and trade journals were used to reach doctors, hospitals, and druggists, and point-of-sale displays were given to druggists for products that could be sold without prescription, such as vitamins or Sucaryl.

By 1955 Abbott had two competitors in the bulk market in addition to Du Pont. None of these competitors had put any emphasis on the consumer market for noncaloric sweeteners. At this time Abbott did 75 per cent of the bulk cyclamate business, Pfizer had about 15 per cent of the market, Du Pont about 8 per cent, and Merck about 2 per cent. The company realized that, as competition increased, the main factors in controlling market share would be the reputation of the company and the establishment of the trade name in the consumers' minds. There was no difference in the chemical compound cyclamate. The company directors therefore decided to make Sucaryl an exception to the advertising policy of the company and to begin a consumer promotion campaign to establish firmly the Sucaryl trademark.

Up to the introduction of Sucaryl, saccharin had been the only noncaloric sweetener approved by the federal Food and Drug Administration. Saccharin had not been used widely by dietetic food and beverage processors because it often left a metallic aftertaste in the consumer's mouth. But saccharin was the only noncaloric sweetener available for diabetics and other people who could not use sugar. Abbott's tests showed cyclamate to be stable in all food and beverage processing, and taste tests indicated its aftertaste incidence to be much lower than saccharin's. There were other dietetic foods on the market that utilized the natural sweetness of fruits or other foods or that contained no sweeteners at all.

Many problems arose in the first stages of marketing Sucaryl to food and drink processors. Although the product had been approved by the federal Food and Drug Administration, many states had laws against using such additives in processed foods. So, state by state, Abbott had to prove its case for Sucaryl. By 1952 all but nine states approved Sucaryl for use in processed foods and drinks, and by 1955 the toughest of these had been won over. The second problem was price. In 1950 saccharin was selling for $1.80 per pound and had a sweetening power 400 times that of sugar. Sucaryl, on the other hand, was sold at $3.50 per pound, and its sweetening power was only 30 times that of sugar. As a result, Sucaryl cost users about 26 times as much as saccharin per pound of sweetener. By 1955, volume production brought the price down to $2.95 per pound, which, as a sweetening agent, about equalled the cost of sugar. In 1958 the price was reduced to $1.95 per pound.

The chemical sales division undertook the responsibility for merchandising the Sucaryl trademark. It was primarily concerned with protecting its bulk market from competition. The promotion program for packaged Sucaryl for consumers was administered independently of the bulk program. The chemical sales division was only a three-man division in 1950, and it handled all sales of chemicals and drugs to industrial users. By 1955 the organization had expanded to include a general manager, a sales manager, an assistant sales manager, and five salesmen. Much of this expansion was due to the increasing sales of bulk Sucaryl, which had reached 379,000 pounds in 1955 and 575,000 pounds in 1958.

The program developed for merchandising the Sucaryl trademark was based on the fact that the people who used noncaloric sweeteners at home were also customers for processed foods and drinks that used a noncaloric sweetener. The market for noncaloric sweeteners included diabetics and overweight and other diet-conscious people. A market study done by Abbott in 1956 revealed that one out of every three Americans was either overweight or concerned about his weight. Sales of dietetic canned fruits had risen from 100,000 cases in 1950 to over 3 million cases in 1956, and sales of dietetic soft drinks had risen from 1 million cases a year in 1950 to over 15 million cases in 1956. A study of supermarket sales reported that dietetic foods represent 1.5 per cent of total store sales. These studies of the dietetic food market included low sodium and "natural" foods as well as sugar-free foods.

The proposed program was to advertise the Sucaryl trademark to consumers (Exhibit 1). The ads would be designed to get consumers to buy dietetic foods that were sweetened with Sucaryl and would emphasize that foods or beverages sweetened with Sucaryl would carry the Sucaryl trademark on their labels. The company offered the trademark to all customers to use on their labels. Some customers were already using the name Sucaryl or the trademark on their labels in 1955. The company thought that such action would help pre-sell customers' products. It was hoped that this program would develop strong consumer demand for products sweetened with Sucaryl and, thereby, make it difficult for a competitor to draw away Abbott's bulk customers, since none of the competitors' sweeteners were known in the consumer market. In conjunction with the consumer ads, Abbott would run ads in trade journals that reached food and soft drink processors, showing the current consumer ads and citing the benefits of these to Abbot customers.

EXHIBIT 1

Exhibits 1 and 2 are the front and back, respectively, of a proposed two-page gatefold ad to be run in trade journals in 1958.

The campaign for packaged Sucaryl started in 1955, but the trademark program did not get into full swing until 1958, although two consumer ads were run in 1957. The 1958 program called for five three-quarter page ads to run in the *Saturday Evening Post*. These would aim at selling dietetic foods and drinks sweetened with Sucaryl. In the same months, ads would be run in the trade magazines, as shown in Exhibits 1 and 2. The 1958 campaign for packaged Sucaryl called for ads in the *Saturday Evening Post, Time, Readers' Digest, Ladies' Home Journal,*

EXHIBIT 2

Here's Sucaryl's current "ad-of-the-month"

WILL
YOU
BE
OUR
GUEST?

56 calories
when you sweeten with sugar

8 calories
when you use Sucaryl

You can't taste the difference, but
Sucaryl makes it lots easier to cut down calories

Sucaryl•
Non-caloric Sweetener—No Bitter Aftertaste

and several other leading magazines. The advertising budgets were as
shown in the accompanying tabulation.

Year	Packaged	Bulk
1955	$ 804,000	$ 71,000
1956	1,194,000	58,000
1957	1,497,000	200,000
1958	1,350,000	259,000

Should Abbott's proposed promotion program be adopted?

50

CRYOVAC DIVISION, W. R. GRACE & COMPANY (B)

CRYOVAC sold a patented process for vacuum packing meats, poultry, fish,
and cheese products in transparent plastic bags. The process protected the
foods against shrinkage and deterioration while moving from producer
to consumer. The Cryovac process was introduced in 1947, and by 1958
sales had reached $42 million. During this decade the firm's promotional

program varied widely as the result of changes in the process, in users of the process, in the level of acceptance, and in the nature of competition. In 1959 Cryovac's sales promotion director was considering how to integrate the hodgepodge of various activities into a total promotional program.

Prior to Cryovac's entrance into the industry, some twenty-five firms sold various types of packaging supplies and processes to the fresh food industry. In 1958 sales of these firms in competition with Cryovac were estimated at $210 million, but none offered certain advantages that Cryovac believed that its process had. This process eliminated air from the

TABLE 1

CRYOVAC SALES AND PROMOTION BUDGET: 1948–58

| | | Promotion Budget | |
| | Sales | | Per Cent |
Year	(Millions)	Dollars	of Sales
1948	$ 1.5	$ 45,000	3.00
1950	7.5	75,000	1.00
1951	12	93,000	0.78
1952	15	172,500	1.15
1953	25.5	165,000	0.65
1954	30.	324,000	1.08
1955	34.5	349,500	1.01
1956	37.5	481,500	1.28
1957	39	1,185,000	3.04
1958	42	468,000	1.11

plastic bag, thus preventing the drying effect that air has on fresh foods; permitted these foods to keep their appearance and taste over a longer period; and prevented shrinkage (loss of weight as the result of loss of moisture). These factors permitted retail stores to keep foods packaged by Cryovac on the shelf from three to seven weeks, depending on the item, instead of the few days otherwise possible. After a few years' experience in the packaging field, Cryovac also developed a bag that permitted aging of the meats and cheese right in the package, something that food packers had never been able to accomplish before. Aging in Cryovac packages prevented mold formation and thus saved the expense of trimming and the loss of weight from trimming, as well as the saving from lack of shrinkage.

Machinery that would permit one man to package approximately two thousand units a day cost from $5,000 to $7,000. Bags cost from $25 to over $100 per thousand, depending on size, quality, and quantity purchased. The major share of Cryovac's sales were in the bags. Considering all factors, the cost of the Cryovac process was 50–80 per cent greater than other packaging processes.

The Cryovac process had four simple steps: (1) the item to be packaged was placed in a loose-fitting plastic bag; (2) air was withdrawn by a vacuum pump; (3) the neck of the bag was twisted tightly and fastened with a metal clip; and (4) the package was then dipped in hot water at about 200°F., which caused the plastic film to shrink and to cling tightly to the contours of the product like a second skin. The bags were made from a special Saran film, manufactured by Dow Chemical Company, which was tasteless, odorless, nontoxic, transparent, and tough and flexible at all normal market and home temperatures, including temperatures in freezers. The bag was generally considered to be of very high quality.

Cryovac's yearly sales and promotion budgets are shown in Table 1.

The average advertising and promotion budget in the fresh food packaging industry ran about 1.67 per cent of sales, while the Cryovac budget was about 1.2 per cent.

TABLE 2

NUMBER OF ESTABLISHMENTS IN SELECTED AREAS OF FOOD
PRODUCTION AND DISTRIBUTION*

Meat packing plants	2,367
Prepared meats	1,316
Poultry dressing plants	1,309
Meat wholesalers	4,357
Fish and seafood distributors	1,808
Cheese producers	1,419
Fresh fruit and vegetable wholesalers	6,520
Grocery stores	279,440
Retail meat markets	22,896
Retail fish and seafood markets	4,458

* Census of Business, 1954.

The firm's first promotion manager viewed the company's main problem as one of education. In the period prior to 1951 he set out to educate all levels of the trade—food packers, wholesalers, retailers, and consumers—as to what the Cryovac process was and what it meant to them. Table 2 shows the number of establishments in the different areas of the food trade. To do this he used the following methods:

Publicity. With an almost negligible budget, the company's public relations firm obtained a considerable amount of publicity mention and feature presentation of the process in consumer and industrial publications. Most of the consumer publicity was developed around the idea of placing a girl in a bathing suit in a Cryovac bag and shrinking the bag to fit her "like a second skin." Laboratory reports on applications research and case history testimonials were the basis for the trade publicity program.

Technical brochures. Manuals were developed showing how to use the process for various applications with products such as pork, fish, and poultry.

Movies. Originally black-and-white movies were prepared in plants where turkeys, fish, and meat were being packaged. Later, colored movies with sound were developed and became a basic sales tool.

Trade advertising. Cryovac went into this area very sparingly because it did not have the budget to do otherwise and because the management did not know in what media to advertise, since markets were still relatively undefined. The small amount of trade advertising that was run was largely technical and explanatory in nature, showing how the process worked.

By 1951 the company's executives believed that the basic general education job had been done, the important basic markets for the process had been determined, and the company was actively engaged in selling the product in those markets. Consequently, the promotional activity shifted from general education to selling Cryovac for specific markets and customers. Sales were over $10 million, and the company had established a very strong position in the turkey industry with nearly 85 per cent of the turkeys in the country being packed in Cryovac bags.

The sales organization included twenty full-time salesmen. In addition, thirty distributors sold the line throughout the country. Although there were still some quality control problems in the process, the sales outlook was considered bright. During the 1951–1954 period, advertising and promotion programs were used to sell the major packers and to sell the distributors' salesmen.

During 1951 Cryovac's process began to be used on smoked meats. By 1952 a great many of the independent meat packers were using Cryovac for smoked meat, but the firm was unable to secure the business of major national packers, such as Swift, Armour, and Wilson. The promotional manager thought product endorsements from customers rather than from competitors (small packers) might be effective. Consequently, the company gathered testimonials from leading retailers all over the country endorsing Cryovac's value as a package to protect smoked meats. The company used these in a program that was designed to establish the company as resourceful and aggressive. A dramatic presentation was developed. Each of the testimonials obtained from store operators was reproduced on an 8½ × 11-inch black-and-white page featuring a picture of the store manager, his store, and a statement about Cryovac. These were gathered into 8- and 12-page booklets and bound with four-color covers that showed a variety of products and labels using Cryovac.

These booklets were then inserted in their entirety in the *National Provisioner*, a meat industry publication, leading off with a 12-page insertion, followed by three 8-page inserts at weekly intervals, and then twelve more 8-page insertions at biweekly intervals, thus covering a total span of twenty-eight full weeks with a campaign of 132 pages.

Reprints of these ads were carried by the salesmen when they called on the packers. The total cost of the campaign was only a little more than $22,500, about one-third of the total advertising budget. The campaign served its purpose of opening the door at the major packing companies. Distributor salesmen had to be sold on the value of following up this and other trade promotion and advertising programs. A weekly "Sales Reporter" was used to stimulate interest and stir up morale among the distributor salesmen by providing them with sales information and success stories on Cryovac. This program was never entirely successful, and in 1954 distributors were dropped. Cryovac expanded its sales force to about eighty men to take over the work formerly done by the distributors.

As Cryovac applications and customers multiplied, it was decided to start using direct mail to reach specific individuals. The objective was to keep Cryovac continuously before them and actually to sell new applications. To accomplish this, Cryovac's monthly external house organ, "Marketing Q's," was launched. This featured case histories, technical information on new applications, and general sales and promotion information on Cryovac. It was sent to a list of over five thousand prospects and customers in the meat, poultry, and dairy industries, as well as to selected retail chain buyers throughout the country on a list supplied by the salesmen themselves.

The firm's executives believed that one of the problems, as well as one of the advantages, of the Cryovac process was that it was just as important to retailers and consumers as it was to Cryovac's customers. The executives believed that their future success would depend not only on how well they were able to sell their customers, but on how well Cryovac and Cryovac's customers were able to merchandise the process to retailers and consumers. From 1954 to 1957 this concept guided the advertising and promotion policies of the firm.

Cryovac executives believed that their packer customers were backward in their merchandising efforts to the point that they would be slow to merchandise Cryovac on their own. Therefore, Cryovac set out to merchandise the process to the retail trade and to consumers and to increase its merchandising aid to packers.

Cryovac ran a schedule of four-color ads every month for three years in the two leading trade magazines of the retail trade. Coinciding with this color-insert campaign was a stepped-up direct-mail program. This used the external house organ, "Marketing Q's," whose retail coverage reached over ten thousand stores, and individual series mailings telling retailers why they should buy meats packed in Cryovac. The objective of this advertising was to establish Cryovac in the minds of the retail store managers as the best packaging material on the market. From 1955 on, Cryovac gave packers direct-mail and give-away brochures to be used in the sales of Cryovac-packaged products to the retailers. In many cases, the company also created and designed special brochures for individual packers.

Cryovac also tried to help packers and retailers merchandise Cryovac-packed products to consumers. A series of merchandising kits were prepared that included point-of-purchase materials, suggested ad layouts, TV commercials, and various other consumer advertising suggestions. These were designed to help the packers sell consumers on Cryovac-packed items. A good many packers complained that Cryovac was wasting "their money" on this material, but many of them developed respect for the Cryovac salesman as the one packaging salesman who always seemed to have something new to offer. A good many packer advertisements featured the Cryovac trademark prominently, and the Cryovac trademark appeared on more than 50 per cent of the half-billion Cryovac bags that were sold.

This identification of Cryovac packaging led the management to decide that it was ready to sell consumers directly. By building a franchise at the consumer level for Cryovac-packaged products, the company could control the future of the business to a greater extent. Consumer advertising was thought of as an insurance policy against future competition and a way to stimulate faster sales growth at the retail and packer levels.

Consumer promotion got under way in 1955 with a series of food editor luncheons, which were conducted throughout the country to interest the consumer press in Cryovac. In the fall of 1956 sales were exceptionally good, profits were high, and the outlook seemed bright. The sales force was being doubled to more than 160 salesmen. Therefore, the management decided to try a national consumer advertising campaign.

The firm's advertising agency presented a program of national advertising, using four-color photos of various food products packaged in Cryovac. The ads ran in a series of full-page ads in such magazines as *Life, Good Housekeeping,* and *Better Homes and Gardens* from April through November, 1957, coinciding with the peak consumption periods of each of the six products to be featured. The total budget for this program came to $750,000. The specific objectives were as follows:

1. To build awareness among consumers of Cryovac as a packaging material that made foods more desirable.
2. To build consumer preference for foods packaged in Cryovac.
3. To insure that Cryovac's position in the market would be maintained.
4. To stimulate packers to use Cryovac on more new products.
5. To hasten acceptance of new Cryovac packaging materials in the packaging industry.
6. To get Cryovac customers to use Cryovac as a merchandising tool.
7. In the long run to increase investor interest in the company.

The complete consumer campaign was not considered a success for the following reasons:

1. The packers were not convinced that this was a good way to spend "their money" and complained that the firm was asking them to promote Cryovac, not their products.

TABLE 3

PROPORTION OF PROMOTION BUDGET SPENT ON BASIC AREAS

	Wholesalers	Packers	Retailers	Consumers	Institutions
1947–50	50%	50%	Negligible	..	..
1950–53	25	65	10	..	..
1953–56		55	45	..	..
1957–59		25	6	65%	15%

2. The retailers also rejected the idea of promoting a packaging material at the point-of-sale, consequently very few of the point-of-purchase materials were used. Little tie-in of national ads at store level took place.

3. The Cryovac sales force could not see that the program helped in any material way to improve their sales, particularly when related to the comparatively large amount of time they were forced to devote to it.

In the fall of 1957 the business picture was just opposite to that of the previous year. Sales and profits were not up to expectations, and the promotion budget for 1958 was cut drastically.

In planning the advertising and promotion program for 1959, the promotion director summarized past policies as shown in Tables 3 and 4.

TABLE 4

DISTRIBUTION OF PROMOTION BUDGET BY METHOD USED

Years	Promotion Method	Approximate Percentage
1950–52	Advertising in trade media	75
	Publicity	10
	Promotion, including movies	15
1953–54	Advertising	55
	Direct mail, promotion, publicity, and general sales tools	45
1955	Advertising	50
	Sales promotion, including direct mail	50
1956	Advertising	40
	Sales promotion	60
1957	Consumer advertising and promotion	65
	Trade advertising	12
	Sales promotion	23
1958	Trade advertising	40
	Sales promotion	60
1959	Trade advertising	37
	Sales promotion	63

What should be Cryovac's promotion program for 1959 ?

51

PLAYSKOOL MANUFACTURING COMPANY

LATE IN 1958 the advertising manager of the Playskool Manufacturing Company was reviewing past advertising expenditures in connection with the preparation of next year's budget. The company produced toys for children between the ages of two and ten, but concentrated on a complete line of preschool wood educational toys. The advertising budget in 1958 was approximately $200,000. Most of these funds were used to purchase space in toy catalogues distributed by wholesalers and department stores. About $35,000 was spent for package inserts that showed the entire line and that were included with each toy; $15,000 was used for trade advertising; $10,000 was used for direct mail to school officials and teachers; and $5,000 for booths at school conventions.

Playskool, with an average annual sales increase of about 10 per cent per year since 1939, had become the leader in sales of preschool wood educational toys. The company had about forty competitors, but only one of these made wood and educational toys exclusively. Educational toys for preschool children accounted for approximately 7 per cent of the toy industry's $1.5 billion annual sales volume. Out of this total, Playskool's share was somewhat better than 5 per cent. Pretax net profit margins were generally between 15 and 20 per cent of sales.

Playskool's line generally retailed from 79 cents to $9.00 per toy, with the typical sale in the $1.00–$3.00 category. Included in the line were push toys, pull toys, co-ordination toys, play materials (such as blocks), construction toys, puzzle plaques, and pounding toys. About 90 per cent of all sales were made in toys designed for preschool children. In general, the company's toys were priced slightly higher than other toys of a comparable nature.

Since the company's inception, the management had endeavored to secure consumer brand loyalty through the establishment of a favorable corporate image. To support this policy, the company had undertaken consumer advertising for many years prior to 1954. It was one of only four or five toy manufacturers who advertised to consumers. Playskool, however, typically promoted its entire line of toys, while competitors generally carried out one-item campaigns. Approximately 80 per cent of the Playskool budget had been spent for advertisements in such magazines as *Good Housekeeping*, *Woman's Day*, and *Parent's Magazine*. Management believed that such magazines had good consumer reputations, which would support the image they desired for their line. In addition, they found that these magazines obtained the best consumer inquiry and response.

In 1954 the toy industry became heavily involved in co-operative advertising. At that time, a catalogue printing firm sold a group of whole-salers on the idea that a catalogue, paid for principally by toy manu-facturers, would be a good promotional device. Wholesaler salesmen could use the catalogue to sell the retailer by offering large quantities, either free or for a nominal sum, for redistribution under the store's name to its customers. Wholesalers were generally enthusiastic about the idea and placed heavy pressure upon manufacturers to subscribe to catalogues in order to have their toys represented. Playskool executives thought that they had no other alternative but to follow this trend. By 1958 the company's products were represented in some forty catalogues, thirty of which were produced by department stores and the remainder by toy wholesalers. The large expenditures that this required forced the company to drop its consumer advertising entirely. During 1958 this co-operative advertising cost approximately 5 per cent of sales to depart-ment stores and 2.5 per cent of sales to jobbers. No co-operative ad-vertising funds had as yet been given to chain stores and mail-order accounts, which represented slightly more than one-third of the com-pany's total volume.

The educational toy market varied somewhat from that of the rest of the toy industry. First, its sales did not vary as much seasonally as did those of the industry. Some 70–75 per cent of the toy industry's sales were made during the Christmas season. Second, people tended to shop for specific types of educational toys, whereas the greater share of most other toys were bought on impulse.

With the move to catalogues, Playskool executives became disturbed lest the abandonment of consumer advertising would result in a reduction in consumer loyalty and a loss of corporate image. Toy catalogues, they believed, were not adequate for their purpose. As a consequence, the firm began a school advertising campaign on a limited basis. The purpose of this campaign was to acquaint school principals, administrators, teach-ers, nurses, counselors, and other people dealing with preschool children with Playskool toys. Executives believed that these individuals would be in a very good position to recommend toys, particularly when parents visited the classrooms to observe their children.

Playskool's management thought that teachers were generally responsi-ble for the purchase of new toys for the classroom each year. Funds were obtained from petty cash or from the principal, and purchases were made from one or more school supply wholesalers. When new schools were built, distributors were usually asked to make bids for the total initial requirements.

To reach the school market, Playskool developed a two-part program, each part of which cost about $5,000. The first was directed toward school supply wholesalers and consisted of the preparation of about 1.5 million inserts for placement in the catalogues distributed to schools by the wholesaler salesmen. In 1958 Playskool inserts appeared in about sixty toy catalogues of this type printed by major wholesalers. Playskool also sent representatives to the school supply wholesaler conventions.

The second part of the program was directed toward school officials and consisted of display booths at five of the major annual school conventions. These conventions, such as the one held by the National Education Association and its various subgroups, were attended primarily by school administrators and elementary school principals. Playskool representatives also attended the convention of the National Kindergarten Association. Various school supply distributors also took booths at these conventions.

The advertising manager was concerned about the effectiveness of these campaigns and whether they were achieving the goals the company sought. Sales to schools had increased from $25,000 in 1954 to approximately $150,000 in 1958. The 1958 volume would be only about $20,000 more than that in 1957. The advertising manager was not certain whether this growth represented a greater share of the market or simply growth of the entire market. He also was not sure whether the campaign had produced any awareness of the Playskool name with either teacher or child or whether any of the information about the educational value of the toys filtered back to parents or retail store owners.

One fault in the program, the advertising manager speculated, was that it might not be adequate. There were about forty school supply distributors who used no co-operative advertising. There were also hundreds of local school conventions that could be attended. Lists of kindergarten schoolteachers' names and addresses were probably available, and there was a trade school publication, *Our Schools*, which covered all elementary grades and which accepted advertising. On the other hand, it was possible that some or all of the funds used in this way were being wasted and could be spent elsewhere to better advantage. While the company was currently appearing in most group catalogues outside the school field, the advertising manager thought that a number of individual store and wholesaler catalogues were still not showing Playskool toys. The manager was somewhat restricted by a general management policy that advertising costs should not exceed 3 per cent of sales.

What changes, if any, should Playskool make in its advertising program?

52

INTERNATIONAL MINERALS AND CHEMICAL CORPORATION (A)

The three main divisions of the International Minerals and Chemical Corporation faced a common problem of how to differentiate their products from those of competitors. These divisions were:

1. The phosphate minerals division, which mined phosphate rock needed for fertilizers.
2. The phosphate chemicals division, which processed phosphate rock to produce refined phosphate products for fertilizers.
3. The potash division, which mined potash needed for fertilizers.

International Minerals was one of the largest suppliers of raw materials for fertilizers. In addition to these materials, the company supplied minerals to industry and consumers. The feldspar department of the industrial minerals division, a smaller division, was the world's largest producer of aluminous materials, feldspar, nepheline syenite, and aplite, essential to the manufacture of ceramic ware and glass; and of bonding clays and additives for foundry sands. The amino products division, a minor division, manufactured and marketed Ac'cent, a food seasoning. Another of this division's products was L-glutamine, an ingredient es-

TABLE 1

INTERNATIONAL MINERALS AND CHEMICAL CORPORATION—
NET SALES AND NET PROFITS: 1953–58
(000 Omitted)

Year	Net Sales	Net Profits
1953	$ 88,837	$7,030
1954	93,592	6,044
1955	96,485	6,322
1956	96,626	5,402
1957	106,189	6,961
1958	103,662	5,273

sential in the production of Salk polio vaccine. Net sales and profits for 1953 through 1958 are shown in Table 1.

Each of the fertilizer material divisions operated individually and maintained its own sales staff, but they had a common market—fertilizer processors and distributors. Their customers were not necessarily the same because of the different types of fertilizers required and manufactured. The phosphate minerals division had two salesmen calling on approximately 100 accounts and prospects. Their territories were the northern and southern halves of the country. International Minerals did not ship west of the Rockies because of freight costs. The phosphate chemicals division had four salesmen calling on 320 accounts, and the potash division had eight salesmen and four district managers, two of whom were also salesmen, serving about 800 accounts. The salesmen were paid a salary plus an incentive bonus on sales over their quota. This bonus could not exceed 25 per cent of the man's salary.

International's salesmen were mainly chemical engineers with previous experience in the fertilizer field. The company gave them extensive product training, which included a tour of duty at the mining operations and other on-the-job training. The company made a policy of continuing such training to keep the salesmen abreast of new developments and had recently intensified its training in sales methods and marketing.

Price competition was practically nonexistent among the three major suppliers in this industry because, as one executive put it, ". . . no one company can enjoy a price advantage very long. Someone else is sure to cut under him and the first thing you know nobody is making any money." Price lists were published annually by all companies in the late spring. Typically, there was little difference among them. Freight was not a factor because all major companies mined raw materials in approximately the same areas. Potash deposits were located near Carlsbad, New Mexico, and phosphate deposits were in Florida. Raw phosphate rock sold generally for $6–$7 a ton, the price varying with the grade and type of grind. Processed phosphate rock sold for $40 a ton and potash for $22–$36 a ton, depending on grade and form. Pretax profit from sales of phosphates and potash averaged about 13 per cent of sales. Because the sources of these products were limited and all suppliers mined in the same areas, customers were not convinced that any significant quality differences existed.

In addition to the divisions that were directly connected with the fertilizer market, International Minerals and Chemical Corporation (IMC) also maintained several fertilizer processing plants. Potential customers and customers of the three materials divisions in the regions where these plants were located often resented the competition from their supplier of raw materials. In addition to this problem, the demand for fertilizer in 1957 was beginning to level off and there was a threat of price competition from European exporters of potash and fertilizers. The discovery and development of new deposits of potash in Canada pointed toward further increases in supply. These problems led the company to seek some way to differentiate its products or itself, to strengthen its market position, and to increase its share of the market. This task was assigned to the marketing vice-president, a staff officer of the corporation, who began by engaging a marketing research firm to make a survey of what buyers of phosphate and potash wanted of a supplier.

The research firm interviewed 94 fertilizer companies, which accounted for 40 per cent of the total fertilizer production in the United States. They found that 78 per cent of the companies interviewed were receiving technical engineering assistance from their suppliers, 37 per cent advertising assistance, 20 per cent general information, and 12 per cent sales assistance. These companies were asked what type of services they would like to receive from a supplier, and the following were named, listed in order of most frequent response: (1) technical engineering, (2) sales services, (3) advertising services, and (4) general management, which included office procedure, accounting systems, and management ideas. When respondents were asked to rate the three major suppliers in the industry, the responses showed IMC to be below, or no better than even with, other suppliers in such factors as general reputation, speed of service, and shipping and traffic help. Questions on sales effectiveness and product attributes brought answers that showed that IMC was not receiving full credit for many of its attainments in those areas.

From the research data, the marketing vice-president concluded that fertilizer manufacturers automatically expected technical service from their suppliers and wanted more help in selling their products. Furthermore, since neither IMC nor most other suppliers were offering advertising and sales service, the company saw an opportunity to gain a competitive advantage in this area. The low rating on technical service and assistance given to IMC indicated that the firm was not receiving credit for the services that it did offer.

Analysis of the survey data was complicated by the fact that the three major companies in the industry did not compete directly in all products. The three basic ingredients of fertilizers were potash, phosphate, and nitrogen. One major competitor sold only nitrogen and phosphate, while the other sold only potash. International Minerals sold potash and phosphate. It was the only one of the three that also manufactured and sold fertilizer, and it was thought that the survey responses reflected some of the customers' resentment in having one of their suppliers as a competitor. One competitor maintained a pilot plant to work out customers' technical problems. The marketing staff believed that this contributed greatly to the consistently higher ratings given this competitor by customers.

In general, fertilizer companies were small local operations, the market areas of which were limited to a 50–250-mile radius around the plants. Management was usually concentrated in one man, often the owner, who managed the plant and sales. There were usually two to three salesmen, often part-time men, who worked on a straight commission basis. These companies sold to retail dealers and direct to farmers in their market areas. Through local advertising, these fertilizer companies often developed strong brand loyalty in their areas. There were also several large fertilizer manufacturers who operated on a national basis.

On the basis of the information obtained in the customer survey, the marketing division developed IMC's "Full Orbit Service" program, which was designed to help customers sell more fertilizer by helping them with problems in six major areas: market analysis, sales meetings, sales manpower, advertising and sales promotion, transportation, and technical service.

A series of "how-to-do" manuals on the first four subjects was developed for customer use. The manuals on transportation and technical service were based primarily on presenting facts about International

EXHIBIT 1

NOW.... FROM
a new concept of service
To help you
sell more
fertilizer
profitably

Minerals' transportation department and technical staff and their ability to solve problems in these areas for customers. All the manuals were keyed to specific problems in the fertilizer business.

The manuals alone were not considered to be sufficient, and a training program for the eighteen salesmen and managers of the three divisions involved was planned so that they would be able to help customers use the manuals as well as to present ideas on specific customer problems. In addition, it was planned to make the staff of the marketing division available to customers to work out problems. A team from the marketing division would organize conferences in different areas of the country that would deal with specific problems, such as how to conduct sales meetings or how to plan an advertising program. All the customers and prospective customers in the area would be invited to these conferences. In addition, this team would be available to give customers individual help on specific problems.

The "kick-off" for the "Full Orbit Service" program was scheduled for May, 1958, with a sales meeting in Chicago to introduce the plan to the salesmen and advertisements in three trade journals, *Commercial Fertilizer, Farm Chemicals*, and *Agricultural Chemicals*, to introduce the program to the trade (Exhibit 1). This was to be followed by another ad in the same journals in July. A copy of this ad with a Zippo-type lighter engraved with the slogan "Out of This World Service for Down to Earth Results" would be mailed to each customer. In August, a pre-release of the ad scheduled to run in September would be sent to all customers with a "Full Orbit" ball-point pen. In October a direct mailing would be made to customers and prospects of the Answer Graph, a device that enabled the customer to dial any one of 100 questions and get the specific page of one of the "how-to-do" books where the question was answered. November advertising would carry testimonials of customers who had used "Full Orbit Service." News stories on Full Orbit, carried by leading trade and business magazines, lent authoritative weight to the program.

It was thought by November that the salesmen would have made personal contacts with all the customers of the three divisions to explain "Full Orbit Services." Customers were re-assigned to avoid double calling by salesmen where a customer happened to buy from two or more divisions. In those cases in which it was thought that calls by both salesmen were necessary in the future, a joint call was to be arranged to present the "Full Orbit Service" program.

A special presentation booklet was developed for the salesmen's use. This booklet gave a short history of the company; described the products of the three divisions involved, pointing up quality and services offered by International Minerals; and presented the "Full Orbit Service" program. The salesmen were expected to go through the booklet with the customer then report back to the company the customer's reactions and requests for any of the handbooks.

The marketing division was given responsibility for supervising the program. Records would be kept of customer reactions and of requests for more information, whether made through salesmen or directly to the home office. Direct requests for handbooks or assistance would be forwarded for immediate action to the responsible division.

In order to get the testimonials needed for future advertising, a $50 prize was established for the first usable testimonial submitted by a salesman, $100 for the most usable testimonials by January 1, 1959, and new hats for all salesmen in the division that submitted the most testimonials by January 1, 1959. In addition, the division that showed the most usage of "Full Orbit Service" among its customers by January 1, 1959, would receive a golf jacket for each man.

The costs of the "Full Orbit" program were to be allocated to the advertising budgets of the three divisions involved. The initial costs of printing the manuals, of sales meetings, and of sales training in 1958 would result in a 50 per cent increase in advertising costs for the three divisions for that year. The increase in these costs in the following years as a result of the "Full Orbit" program were not expected to be significant. The total advertising budget for these three divisions was approximately $300,000 in 1957.

Was the "Full Orbit Service" program sound promotional strategy for International Minerals and Chemical Corporation?

53

LORD'S DEPARTMENT STORE

LORD'S DEPARTMENT STORE was the oldest department store in Evanston, Illinois, a suburb of Chicago. Evanston had a large retail shopping center that had particularly strong appeal in soft goods. Total retail sales in the city in 1956 were estimated at $132 million, of which $30 million were made by the three department stores. Despite the obvious appeal of the Evanston shopping center, Lord's management felt at a definite disadvantage in promoting the sale of its merchandise and was seeking to improve its promotional program.

Evanston's location, immediately adjacent to Chicago, meant that it was covered by the metropolitan newspapers. The only publication in Evanston itself was a weekly, magazine-style paper, the *Evanston Review*, which carried local items of personal interest. Since this paper came out Thursday mornings, it was not a good medium for promoting special events except on that day. Even then it had disadvantages because the editorial material was not as current as that in daily newspapers and so did not encourage immediate readership as did the daily newspapers. Moreover, the *Evanston Review* was restricted primarily to the city of Evanston, whereas the shopping center drew customers from a much wider area, including many other suburbs and major parts of Chicago itself.

Lord's specialized in medium to better quality and carried the wide assortment of merchandise usually found in department stores. It attempted to fit its selection between those of the other two department stores in town; however, it tended to be competitive with the one handling the higher-quality line. One of these department stores was part of a local chain, while the other was a branch of Marshall Field and Company, the largest store in Chicago. Lord's had typically maintained about a 10 per cent share of the department store business in Evanston and was thought to have strong loyalty from the old-time residents of the community. It was located in a large three-story building, well situated with respect to the traffic flow of the shopping center.

The Evanston trading area was a large one, extending twenty-five miles north and west and a considerable distance south into Chicago itself. Following World War II, there was a very rapid growth in the suburban parts of this trading area. Major specialty shops from Chicago opened branches in Evanston. Traffic congestion appeared in downtown Evanston, and parking became increasingly difficult. In 1956, Old Orchard, a very large shopping center with over one hundred stores, was built immediately west of Evanston. It was located between the Evanston shopping center and much of the trading area from which Evanston drew. Old Orchard had as much floor space as all the shopping goods stores in downtown Evanston and much more parking space, but it did not have the public transportation facilities that the city had. A second, smaller, but still significant shopping center—Edens Plaza—was built between Evanston and another segment of its retail trading area.

These developments had their effect on retail sales in Evanston, especially sales of shopping goods. A report issued by the Chamber of Commerce showed that the index of retail sales in Evanston stood at 94.6 in the second quarter of 1957, as compared to 100 in the same quarter of 1954. Using the same base, the index stood at 117.6 for the entire Chicago area. During the same period, 1954–57, shopping goods dropped from 40 per cent of total retail sales in Evanston to 30 per cent.

Newspaper advertising had traditionally been an important factor in the development of department store sales. Because of the special problems previously described, Lord's use of local advertising had always been limited. The changes taking place in Evanston's retail trade in 1958 caused the advertising manager of Lord's to review his program in search of more effective ways of promoting sales.

Lord's generally based its advertising expenditures on the advertising expenditure to sales relationship suggested by the National Retail Dry

Goods Association studies. Consequently, the company spent between 2.5 and 3 per cent of projected sales on advertising. In 1958, $92,000 was budgeted for advertising to be spent as follows: newspapers, $72,000; mail-order pieces, $4,000–$5,000; local radio, $2,500–$3,000; mechanical production costs, $8,000; and special promotions (fashion shows, display pieces), $5,000–$6,000.

The advertising department was organized as shown in the accompanying chart. The advertising manager reported directly to the company's president. Outside specialized agencies were frequently used for certain mechanical production needs and for other special purposes.

Lord's used two local weekly newspapers in its advertising. Both were more like a magazine in appearance and format than like a newspaper. They were printed by gravure; consequently, advertising reproduction

was of a superior type. One of the local weeklies, the *Evanston Review*, with a circulation of 24,000, came out each Thursday morning. Its full-page rates were as follows: 1 insertion, $210.00; 13-time contract, $175.00; 26-time contract, $147.50; and 52-time contract, $115.50. Lord's used an average of six full pages per week. The store had a yearly contract, a special discount for the number of pages bought, and a number of preferred positions without additional charge. The other local papers, the "Hollister Group," were really a series of papers that covered several nearby suburbs. About 1½ pages per week were inserted in these papers, which were used mostly for store-wide or major sales events. The store also had a yearly contract with the "Hollister Group." Table 1 shows the circulation and rates of these papers.

For major sales events, ads were placed in the leading Chicago paper, which had a special section on Thursdays and Sundays for the northern part of the city and the suburbs. Full pages in the special northern section cost $500 if purchased under an annual contract for twenty pages. The circulation of this section was about 285,000, but some of this probably was in areas from which Lord's drew relatively few customers. Twenty full pages a year were taken under a yearly contract in this section. The store used newspaper advertisements exclusively to promote goods, except for three institutional ads that appeared for Christmas, Easter, and Thanksgiving.

The advertising manager was not satisfied with the newspaper advertising. In his opinon the two local newspapers did not give sufficient impact for effective promotional advertising. Since the news content of the weeklies did not require immediate attention by the reader, they were often not read completely even by the end of the day of their publication (Thursday). The advertising manager thought responses to the ads in these weeklies sometimes were delayed several weeks. Thursday was Lord's second-best sales day of the week, but the timing of the local newspapers did not permit their use for special promotions on that day. These limitations caused the advertising manager to wonder whether the local papers should be used at all.

TABLE 1

THE "HOLLISTER GROUP" PAPERS

Paper	Circulation
Glencoe News	2,125
Glenview Announcements	5,100
Northbrook Star	3,050
Wilmette Life	6,125
Winnetka Talk	4,350
	Rate
Full-page rate in one paper	$ 98.00
Full-page rate in two papers	129.50
Full-page rate in three papers	157.50
Full-page rate in all papers	203.00

The department and specialty stores that had branches in Evanston used advertising in the metropolitan newspapers effectively because the same ads would draw customers to both their central and their suburban stores. While two of the city papers printed special editions designed for suburban sale, there was still a great deal of wasted readership as far as Lord's was concerned. The suburban issue of one paper reached a circulation of over 300,000, while Evanston's trading area included less than half of that figure. Therefore, the advertising manager believed that Lord's could not use the metropolitan papers effectively because (1) the larger retail organizations with heavy expenditures could dominate these papers, thereby limiting the effectiveness of Lord's advertising, and (2) the high rates charged by these newspapers were based, in part, on circulation that was outside Lord's trading area.

The advertising manager was experimenting with other types of media to serve as substitutes for newspapers. A well-developed mailing list of about 46,000 names from charge accounts and other regular customers was kept up to date and utilized on particular occasions. The advertising manager believed that this medium was very successful, but he did not wish to destroy its usefulness by too frequent mailings. He believed that this medium should be utilized a maximum of four times a year as follows: (1) the anniversary sale in September; (2) the January white goods sale; (3) the Easter sale; and (4) the special summer sale in July. In addition, advertising inserts furnished by manufacturers were enclosed each month with the charge customers' statements.

The 1958 anniversary sale, held in September, was typical of these direct mail events. The following data describe the promotional effort:

Total pieces mailed	46,000
Cost of mailing	$ 1,500
Paper stock	$280
Typesetting	150
Reproducing plates	50
Mailing	770
Personnel	250
Sales (2 days)	$32,700

In 1957 this event produced $28,000 in sales. The four-time-a-year mailing had been started in 1955. The advertising manager planned to continue it unchanged.

Six to eight times a year an Evanston radio station was used to promote special sales events, such as dollar days, the January white sale, and special "festivals." At these times, Lord's spent between $400 and $500 on radio advertising. Spot announcements were used exclusively. Such details as the time of announcements and the frequency were left to the radio station. The advertising manager believed that radio should not be used in any other way or with greater frequency. The station broadcasts were received over an area with a forty-mile radius, which included most of the Chicago metropolitan area. The station management estimated its audience at approximately one million. Costs for spot announcements within seven consecutive days were:

No. of Announcements	1-Minute Spots	½-Minute Spots
15	$135	$ 82.50
25	200	125.00
35	245	157.50
70	350	245.00

About four times a year a fashion show was presented, in addition to a number of manufacturers' special showings. In recent years a special Christmas toy display using nearly one complete floor of the store was designed and constructed by an outside agency. The cost of such special displays in 1958 was budgeted between $5,000 and $6,000. The advertising manager preferred to use an outside agency to prepare these special displays because his small staff was unable to take care of the work involved.

Lord's offered the usual department store services to its customers, including interior decorating, personalized shopping (during Christmas season only), all types of charge accounts, delivery of goods, and parking facilities. The latter were limited in space, with room for about fifty cars, but the store was seeking a nearby piece of property that could be used for additional parking facilities.

Lord's had been extremely successful in keeping customer loyalty. In a number of instances, the store had three generations of shoppers from a single family. In 1956 it was ascertained that about 60 per cent of the firm's total volume came from customers located in the town of Evanston itself, about 15 per cent from suburbs north of Evanston, and about 10 per cent from suburbs west of Evanston. The latter group, and to some extent those from north of Evanston, were subject to interception by the new shopping centers.

The advertising manager believed that the newspaper advertising, which accounted for almost 90 per cent of the promotion budget, was ineffective. To compete effectively with the growing competition in the area, he believed that special promotions were necessary.

What action should the advertising manager take?

54

HALLMARK GREETING CARDS

THE HALLMARK COMPANY had produced high-quality and distinctive greeting cards, party decorations, and gift wrapping materials for almost fifty years. The firm's slogan, "When you care enough to send the very best," typified the kind of merchandise and company image that Hallmark hoped to maintain. In 1958 the firm had approximately 30 per cent of the greeting card market. In recent years it had concentrated most of its advertising in television, and was concerned with the customary problems of what types of programs to sponsor, the best times to advertise, and the most effective frequency of advertising.

Greeting cards were by far the main item in the Hallmark line. The use of greeting cards increased rapidly after World War II; total consumer expenditures for such cards reached $550 million in 1958. This represented the sale of about five billion cards, valued at $275 million at manufacturers' prices and compared with sales of about three billion cards ten years earlier.

Hallmark was the largest firm in the industry. Its sales in 1958 were larger than the combined sales of its three largest competitors—Norcross, Gibson, and Rust Craft. Its 1958 volume was 10 per cent larger than in 1957 and 200 per cent larger than in 1948. Estimated net profits after taxes ran 6–7 per cent of sales—about the same as for the other leading firms in the field.

Hallmark's line included over 11,000 different items, including cards, gift wrappings, ribbons, party decorations, and similar items. The "everyday" line, which included items in steady demand throughout the year—birthday and anniversary items—was considered the "bread-and-butter" line and accounted for 25 per cent of the total volume. Four special days —Easter, Valentine's Day, Mother's Day, and Father's Day—accounted for another 25 per cent, and the remaining 50 per cent of sales was concentrated in the Christmas season. Hallmark salesmen sold the line direct to some 20,000 retailers throughout the United States. The firm sought to distribute only through retailers similar in character to the Hallmark line, i.e., retailers who emphasized quality and wide assortments rather than price. This policy limited the company to stationery stores, gift shops, and department stores, and excluded such outlets as variety chains and drugstores. The management believed that this limited distribution enabled its retailers to develop more volume and thus encourage them to do a more aggressive selling job.

Prior to 1951 Hallmark had used radio and magazine advertising. In that year it entered television for the first time with a fifteen-minute weekly program in which Sarah Churchill interviewed famous personalities. To coincide with the Christmas season in 1951, Hallmark sponsored a special Sunday afternoon two-hour presentation of Hamlet, starring Maurice Evans. Radio and magazine advertising were continued throughout the year.

From 1946 to 1955 the firm sponsored the *Hallmark Hall of Fame*, a half-hour, weekly, dramatic-type radio program over the NBC network. This became one of the leading radio shows of its time and was consistently rated in the top ten of all radio shows. Despite the fact that it maintained this high rating, the show was dropped in 1955 because television had reduced its audience to less than five million. In 1953 while the radio program was still being presented, a television *Hallmark Hall of Fame* was started as a half-hour network program on Sunday afternoons at 5:30. The nature of the television show was such that simulcasting of it on radio was impractical.

As television became more important as an advertising medium, Hallmark gave more attention to its use. Foote, Cone and Belding had been the Hallmark advertising agency for many years. The two together developed the following set of criteria for use in buying television advertising time:

1. Television programs will be of a distinctive quality so that the consumer association will be appropriate to the type of product Hallmark offers.
2. Hallmark will sponsor all programs exclusively in order to achieve maximum advertising penetration and program-to-product association. No co-sponsors will be accepted.

3. The advertising will reach the widest audience possible, especially those that are considered by sociologists as the social influencers. Individuals who influence social modes and activities and who purchase Hallmark products will become important word-of-mouth advertisers.
4. The cost of reaching each potential customer, as measured by (a) various ratings and (b) sales results, will be a major factor in determining how, when, and where the television advertising budget will be spent.
5. Television advertising must help dealers in selling the Hallmark line. The success or failure of any advertising campaign depends to a large extent on the retail dealers handling the line. The only way Hallmark can maintain its line in the better stores is to insure that the line produces sales for the retailer.

To gain the best terms for this new television *Hallmark Hall of Fame* show, Hallmark purchased a fifty-two-week series. At the end of the season the advertising agency analyzed the results and drew the following conclusions:

1. A weekly show tended to have a quality of sameness. Letters from viewers suggested that the same audience was obtained week after week and that a large segment of the market did not see the show at any time.
2. Retail dealers did not show continued enthusiasm. A weekly show did not suggest to them a special promotional effort by Hallmark. The weekly show was accepted as a routine type of promotion, since it occurred each and every week both on radio and on television.
3. Sales for both the everyday line and the holiday line failed to show the increases that had been generally expected.

Consequently, at the end of the 1953 television year, the advertising agency negotiated a new contract with the National Broadcasting Company with a stipulation that was a radical departure from customary sponsoring contracts. For the 1954–55 television season, the *Hallmark Hall of Fame* was presented every third week as a one-hour dramatic program and once in the spring and fall as a two-hour spectacular. The two-hour spectaculars were timed to coincide with the Easter and Christmas greeting card seasons and were so successful in terms of ratings and sales that a new format was developed for the following years. For the 1956–57 season, seven two-hour spectaculars were sponsored, and in 1957–58 and 1958–59 six spectaculars were presented—one each in October, November, December, February, March, and April. To economize and to concentrate all efforts on the spectaculars, all radio and other television programs were dropped, but some magazine advertising was continued. This concentration on spectaculars permitted the firm to save 25–30 per cent on its advertising budget. Sales in 1958 were almost 50 per cent higher than in 1956.

To reach as wide an audience as possible with the spectaculars, several further changes were made in the *Hall of Fame* shows as follows:

1. A wider variety of programs, to include comedies and musicals.
2. The use of movie stars or special stories to interest a larger audience. For example, to reach the teen-agers, Tab Hunter was featured in a

EXHIBIT 1

When you care enough to send the very best

musical based on Hans Christian Andersen's *Hans Brinker*, and an all-Negro drama was presented in the *Green Pastures*.
3. Obtaining different time and day spots to reach new viewers. It was believed that the same people tended to watch television at a particular hour each Sunday.

The following schedule shows the spectaculars for the 1958–59 season:

October: *Johnny Belinda*—drama—Monday, 9:30 P.M.[1]
November: *Kiss Me Kate*—musical comedy—Thursday, 9 P.M.

---

[1] All times are Eastern Standard or Daylight Time.

December: Hallmark Christmas Tree—original family-type show—Sunday, 7 P.M.

February: Original drama—Thursday, 9:30 P.M.

March: *Green Pastures* (repeat)—drama—Monday, 9:30 P.M.

April: *Ah! Wilderness*—comedy—Tuesday, 9:30 P.M.

Magazine advertising was continued but major emphasis was put on television. Magazine expenditures fluctuated according to TV expenditures—if TV costs went up, magazine advertising went down. Magazine advertising expenditures for the years 1952–58 were as follows:

1952	$125,000	1956	180,000
1953	160,000	1957	225,000
1954	240,000	1958	315,000
1955	130,000		

In 1958–59 Hallmark called its magazine campaign the "Leadership Campaign." This campaign featured a series of full-page ads in magazines, such as *Life, Look,* the *Saturday Evening Post,* and *Holiday.* The ads were very simple—a large picture showed a human interest scene in which a Hallmark card was appropriately displayed. The only copy was the statement, "When you care enough to send the very best—Hallmark cards." A copy of one of these ads is shown as Exhibit 1.

1. *Appraise the Hallmark advertising program.*
2. *Should the 1958–59 program be continued in 1959–60?*

55

SIMONIZ CORPORATION

THE SIMONIZ CORPORATION was one of the largest manufacturers of car and household waxing and polishing products. Over the past ten years the car wax industry had prospered as the number of cars in use increased substantially year after year. With the introduction of the new 1959 models, however, the automobile manufacturers featured new finishes that they claimed did not require waxing to the extent needed by automobiles in prior years. The claims varied by manufacturer and by type of paint used and ranged from statements that the finish would need no waxing for three years to claims that it would never need waxing. A typical claim appeared in a Chevrolet advertisement in *Life* magazine which ran as follows: "Magic-Mirror finish—a new type that keeps its shine without waxing or polishing for up to three years." Such claims naturally disturbed the Simoniz management, which immediately began to consider what action, if any, it should take.

The new finishes were of two general types—acrylic and melamine. When they were first available the Simoniz laboratory started testing them and, by the time they were featured by the car producers, had completed two and one-half years of research on them. The laboratory findings are summarized below:

1. The acrylic finish is a synthetic lacquer. Commercially, its two largest manufacturers are Du Pont (lucite) and Ditzler (duracril). The melamine finish is an enamel that combines a new melamine resin with aklyd to form a harder resin.
2. These finishes offer new high-luster retention and a slower rate of chalking.
3. Acrylic lacquers are used as standard finish on all 1959 General Motors cars. Melamine enamels are the standard finish on all 1959 Ford and Chrysler cars.
4. Although there is a slower rate of chalking, new finishes still require waxing or polishing soon after purchse date.
5. A great percentage of acrylic finishes are of the metallic type, which actually have less initial luster than do conventional lacquers. Laboratory findings show that waxing or polishing metallic lacquers improves their luster.
6. Acrylics are most susceptible to solvents in road tar and asphalts, which leave dark spots on light acrylic finishes.
7. Simoniz products are in no way harmful to the new finishes.

The laboratory was continuing tests through 1959, with the objective of determing what the long-term effects of weather would be on the new finishes when they were unwaxed, as compared to when they were waxed.

Simoniz executives believed that most of the claims were exaggerated. Nevertheless, they constituted a danger to the wax and polish industry and, in turn, to Simoniz. Some of the most apparent dangers were:

1. The "no need to wax" advertising by the car manufacturers would have some effect simply because of the greater weight of car advertising as compared to wax and polish advertising, despite the fact that the new finishes would not perform as advertised.
2. Since the new paints were not supposed to need waxing until after a longer period of service than conventional finishes, consumers could fall out of the habit of maintaining the finish through waxing.
3. Car waxing and polishing of old as well as new cars could diminish because of consumers' reaction to the claim that waxing was unnecessary.
4. The advice in new car manuals to wash cars frequently could also reduce the use of wax and polish.
5. Competition among manufacturers could expand promotion of the "no wax" idea even further.

There were some brighter sides to the situation. Simoniz executives believed that there was a possibility that the awareness of the importance of car finishes built up through this advertising might actually interest more people in keeping their cars looking better. Some other points that appeared favorable were the following:

1. Simoniz' Family Opinion Studies of 1952 and 1955 showed conclusively that the prime polish and wax market was with owners of cars two to

five years old. Since laboratory results showed that even the new finishes required attention after two years, there appeared to be no direct threat to this market.

2. Acrylic and melamine finishes had harder paint surfaces and therefore showed results from one-step waxing that were superior to prior finishes. This could induce people to wax their cars more frequently.

3. The introduction of Instant Simoniz, a new brand, simultaneously with the new finishes implied that it was an ideal product for use on the new

EXHIBIT 1

LETTER SENT TO KEY OUTLETS

SIMONIZ COMPANY

2100 Indiana Avenue Chicago 16, Illinois

EXECUTIVE OFFICES

November 14, 1958

Gentlemen:

Some of our friends in the trade have been asking us about the "New" finishes, the acrylics and melamines, that car manufacturers are promoting so heavily now.

Since both you and the Simoniz Company have a strong interest in car finishes, we thought that you might be interested in what the technical appraisal of these finishes has been here at Simoniz.

First of all, we have, of course, been studying, testing and comparing these "New" finishes for <u>nearly</u> <u>three</u> <u>years</u>. These tests have been carried out extensively in the Simoniz Laboratories to provide specific technical information. These Laboratory results have been proven by on-the-car tests with production-line cars in actual use.

WHAT ARE THE REAL FACTS? On the basis of these careful studies, we can state these conclusions:

1 The "New" finishes still require the same kind of care. For lasting beauty, for protection and for long life, the "New" finishes <u>need</u> to be cleaned, waxed and polished.

2 In certain respects, the acrylic finishes are more delicate than the old finishes since they will stain easier when exposed to the solvents in road tars and oils.

3 Simoniz waxes, polishes, and cleaners are not harmful in any way to the "New" finishes. Certainly, the "New" finishes need Simoniz care.

Let's remember that over 93% of the total car market in 1959 will still be in old finishes. Within a few months, 100% of all cars with the "New" finishes, as well as those with old finishes, will see the need for car finish care as they begin to lose their initial "showroom shine."

Let's remember that the "New" finishes look better, last longer, <u>need</u> SIMONIZE care.

Yours very truly,

D. E. Cluck
Director of Sales

finishes. Cursory tests showed a highly favorable result when Instant Simoniz was used on the new finishes.

4. The emphasis on beauty in new car sales built up a pride of ownership that caused buyers of new cars to want to keep them looking their best.

As the leading manufacturer of automotive waxes and polishes, the Simoniz management believed that it should lead in establishing a policy relative to this threat to the industry. Several alternatives were available, either singly or in combinations. The wax companies could continue in their usual manner, they could develop advertising programs saying that the new finishes needed wax, they could emphasize the need to wax new cars to keep them looking new, or they could emphasize new waxes for the new finishes. It was conceivable that the wax industry could go to the automobile industry and ask the latter to drop the claims for the new finishes. Undoubtedly there were other possibilities.

As immediate steps, the Simoniz management undertook the following:

1. A letter was sent to all key outlets explaining the Simoniz position relative to the new finishes (Exhibit 1).
2. A similar letter was sent to all Simoniz Company personnel.

EXHIBIT 2

1959 CAR OWNER MANUAL RECOMMENDATIONS
FOR WAXING AND POLISHING THE "NEW" ACRYLIC AND MELAMINE CAR FINISHES

1. FORD (Melamine Enamel)

"To help protect the new-car appearance of the painted surfaces of your '59 Ford, apply a good automobile wax or polish . . . to the finish regularly."

2. BUICK (Acrylic)

"The use of waxes or polishes is generally not recommended for 60 days* after application of paint."

3. PONTIAC (Acrylic)

"Properly applied polishes and waxes of known quality will help maintain the appearance of your car."

4. OLDSMOBILE (Acrylic)

"Frequent washing and an occasional thorough cleaning and polishing is recommended."

5. CHEVROLET (Acrylic)

"If the car is to be polished, any of the approved 8 cleaners on page 28 of this book may be used."†

---

* DuPont Company, one of the leading acrylic paint manufacturers recently advised their customers that the 60-day limit is now lowered to only 4 days.

† For obvious reasons, they list only their own products, plus porcelainize.

EXHIBIT 3

SAMPLE SIMONIZ ADVERTISEMENT

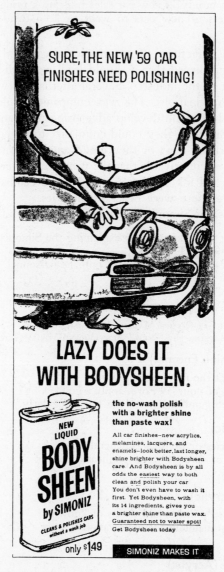

3. A study was made of the 1959 new car owner manuals to determine what they said in the wax and polish section. A summary of excerpts was mailed to all Simoniz representatives. (Exhibit 2).

4. A car manual excerpt was prepared for dealers to mail to their customers.

5. All Simoniz products' packages were changed so that "Ideal for use on all new finishes" would be included on all Simoniz automotive products. Two examples were:

VISTA: "Ideal for all car finishes, including acrylic."

INSTANT SIMONIZ: "Miracle formula—ideal for all car finishes. All car finishes—new acrylics, melamines, lacquers and enamels—look better, last longer, shine brighter with Instant Simoniz care."

6. All advertising of Simoniz waxes included a statement to the effect that the new acrylic and melamine finishes looked better and lasted longer if protected by the advertised wax. An example is shown as Exhibit 3.

7. All automotive product display material, selling brochures, cost sheets and trade flyers included the statement, "Ideal for use on all car finishes."

1. *Were the actions taken by Simoniz sound?*
2. *What other actions, if any, should the company take?*

56

INTERNATIONAL HARVESTER MOTOR TRUCK DIVISION (B)

LATE IN 1958 the advertising department of International Harvester faced the problem of what to do with its co-operative advertising program. The program was similar to that used prior to 1957 by all the major companies in the automobile industry. Dealers were required to pay a set amount into a company administered advertising fund on each truck they purchased. In 1956 General Motors suddenly dropped its co-operative program, and by 1958 all other major automobile and truck manufacturers had followed suit, except for International Harvester. It was in this climate that the management was reappraising its advertising policy.

A co-operative advertising fund was set up for each dealer at International Harvester headquarters. Upon delivery of a truck to a dealer and his payment of the invoice, a credit equaling the advertising charge billed plus the amount contributed by the company was posted to the individual dealer's account. The amount billed varied in accordance with the size of the truck. Ten dollars was billed for a small pick-up truck, and the amount increased to $15, $20, and $30 for larger trucks. The charge against the dealer was billed as a separate entry on each invoice over and above the basic truck cost, excise tax, and all extras. For each dollar so paid by a dealer, the company added 50 cents to the co-operative fund. The total credit built up in each dealer's account was used exclusively for advertising in his local territory. International Harvester controlled all local advertising charged against the co-operative account. Through its advertising agency it prepared and placed, at national rates, all co-operative advertising. Dealers, however, selected the actual media used from the following: newspaper, radio, television, outdoor posters, *Trail* magazine (a company-prepared publication), movie playlets, and direct mail.

Harvester required all dealers to estimate the probable amount of co-operative advertising funds available for each fiscal year and to prepare a tentative budget in triplicate. The original copy was submitted to the consumer relations department at company headquarters, the duplicate was forwarded to the district manager, and the third copy was held by the dealer. Company instructions outlining the preparation of tentative budgets suggested that the average dealer might budget 50 per cent of his co-operative funds for newspaper space, 25 per cent for direct mail, and the balance for radio, outdoor, *Trail* magazine, etc. Tentative budgets were used as a guide for planning by the consumer relations department. No advertising was placed, however, unless funds were actually available in the specific dealer's account at the time.

Dealers could not place advertisements and then bill the co-operative fund. No changes in the layout or copy prepared by the home office were authorized without the prior approval of the consumer relations department. Dealers were notified in advance of any co-op advertising to be done in their areas. No funds from any dealer's co-op account were ever used for national advertising. In the case of direct-mail advertising, the only costs charged to the co-op account of a dealer were the direct costs, such as addressing, postage, and handling. Harvester paid for all creative and mechanical preparation costs of co-op advertising.

International Harvester Motor Truck Division had been administering a co-op advertising program for its dealers since 1949. At first most dealers spent the bulk of their funds in newspapers, but Harvester had been urging them to spend more in other media. In cases in which it was uneconomical or impracticable for the company's advertising agency to buy at national rates the type of advertising that the dealer preferred, the dealer could, after obtaining permission from the consumer relations department, place advertising in strictly local media, such as small local radio stations, and charge it against the co-op account. During the average year about $1,000,000 was collected from International Harvester truck dealers through co-op billings, and $500,000 was added by the company. The half-million contributed by the company comprised about one-tenth of its annual advertising and promotion budget, which in an average year was about $5 million.

The automotive industry in general had used co-operative advertising programs similar to the one described above since the early days of automobile manufacturing. General Motors had maintained such a program since 1925. In a surprise move in early December, 1956, General Motors announced that it was scrapping the dealers' co-operative advertising program. Coincidentally, the Department of Justice announced that its Antitrust Division had been investigating the General Motors' dealer advertising fund. Attorney General Herbert Brownell, Jr., declined to say at that time whether the company's action would terminate the investigation, but he said: "The Department of Justice welcomes the announcement by G. M. of its abolition of the dealer advertising fund. This step should help to eliminate some of the sources of friction between dealer and manufacturer."[1] At the time, GM was requiring dealers to contribute to the co-op fund an amount from $20 per car for Chevrolets to $45 for certain Cadillac models. Earlier in 1956 some GM dealers had claimed at the Senate investigation of GM dealer relations that dealers had contributed $70 million to the fund, while GM had put in only $20 million. It was alleged that this $90 million total represented the largest portion of GM's advertising, which totaled $160 million in 1955, including the co-op funds. Early in 1957 Chrysler, Ford, and American Motors followed General Motors' action and discontinued their co-op advertising programs.

After discontinuing the program, GM announced that it would increase the price of its Chevrolets by $20 and use the increase for advertising purposes. Ford announced that it was preparing a new plan for local advertising that "would take greater cognizance of basic marketing factors such as sales potential, actual sales, and population distribution than was possible under the dealer cooperative advertising program."[2] A Mercury advertising official was quoted as follows: "We do not anticipate significant changes in the use of the newspaper medium, although it is inevitable that there may be some reduction in the newspapers used—particularly those secondary and supplementary newspapers that tended to fall in a marginal category under the cooperative plan."[3]

At the time the "Big Three" discontinued the dealer charge for co-op advertising, they added the charge as a part of the list or wholesale price to the dealer. Industry spokesmen pointed out that such action increased the price of the vehicle to the consumer. This increase was brought about because, when $20 was added to the factory price of a unit, 10 per cent, or $2, more was paid to the government in excise taxes, and, in addition, when the $20 was included in the dealer's list, he tended to figure his markup on a cost that was $20 higher. The normal dealer markup was about one-third of cost, thus resulting in an extra $6 markup when $20 was added to the cost price.

The consumer relations department of International Harvester believed that its co-op program for truck dealers always worked better than the programs of the larger companies because the Harvester dealer organization was smaller and easier to reach than that of any of the larger automotive companies. Harvester prided itself on the degree to which it handled its co-op fund in accordance with dealers' wishes. The large

[1] *Editor & Publisher*, December 8, 1956, p. 17.
[2] *Editor & Publisher*, April 27, 1957, p. 98.
[3] *Ibid.*

automobile manufacturers had been more arbitrary. In all cases the Harvester dealer co-op fund was used for the individual dealer in the local area from which the funds originated.

International Harvester distributed its motor trucks through two channels: (1) about 5,000 dealers, who sold from 55 per cent to 60 per cent of the company's average yearly production of about 100,000 trucks, and (2) about 165 company-owned branches located primarily in the larger metropolitan areas, which accounted for 40–45 per cent of the company's truck sales. The truck dealers generally were combination dealerships, either selling a line of Harvester farm equipment with the trucks or handling such other business franchises as automotive products, tires, and appliances. About 85 per cent of all dealers held one or more franchises in addition to the Harvester trucks, while about 15 per cent held no other franchise and sold only International trucks. In 1958 the Harvester motor truck division made sales of $515 million, or 47 per cent of International Harvester's total sales volume. This amounted to 13 per cent of the national motor truck market.

Only the 5,000 company dealers participated in the co-op advertising program. All truck advertising placed by company-owned branches was controlled by the consumer relations department at company headquarters and charged to the truck division's advertising budget, which had no relationship to co-operative funds. When company branches were located contiguous to or overlapped territories covered by dealers, some benefit from co-op advertising funds could accrue to the branches at no cost to them. On the other hand, advertising placed especially for the benefit of a specific branch could also benefit dealers located in the vicinity.

The consumer relations department decided in the fall of 1958 to reappraise the truck division's co-operative advertising plan. In addition to the questions raised by the General Motors action, some criticism of the co-op program was heard from dealers and also from various district managers. The criticism generally came from some of the more independent dealers, who believed that they were capable of handling and placing their own local advertising and resented the arbitrary contribution that was charged to them each time they bought a truck. Criticism was also leveled at the "red tape" involved in making tentative motor truck co-operative advertising budgets and getting permission to do unusual types of local advertising. Exhibit 1 shows an example of how the consumer relations department recommended that a local dealer should plan and budget his co-operative advertising funds for the ensuing year. It was believed that if such a plan were prepared each year by all dealers for credits accruing to them from the co-op plan, they would also consider more carefully their own advertising, which they paid for directly. The advantage accruing to International Harvester as a company from the headquarters control of a portion of the dealer's local advertising was primarily the uniformity and consistency of impact on a nation-wide basis that could thus be obtained.

EXHIBIT 1

SUGGESTED CO-OPERATIVE ADVERTISING BUDGET
(EXAMPLE FOR SMALL DEALER)

Truck Models	Sales Forecast	Co-operative Credit			Total Estimated Credit
		Dealer	Company	Total	
L-110,L-120,L-130.........12		$10.00	$ 5.00	$15.00	$180.00
LM-120, LM-150, etc....... 8		15.00	7.50	22.50	180.00
L-170,L-180,etc........... 5		20.00	10.00	30.00	150.00
L-210,L-220,etc........... 0		30.00	15.00	45.00	0.00
Total.............25					$510.00

TENTATIVE BUDGET (ESTIMATED FUND OF $510)

	Amount	Per Cent of Estimated Funds
Direct mail (based on total mailing list of 300 names at 50 cents per name)...................................	$150.00	30
Internation *Trail* (based on 40 names of owners of five or more trucks at 75 cents per name)......................	30.00	6
Newspaper space (based on 5,000 lines at 5 cents per line).....	250.00	49
Other local media—radio, billboard, etc......................	80.00	15
Total...	$510.00	100

At the request of the motor truck division, the consumer relations department surveyed dealers, district managers, assistant district managers, and branch managers to obtain their opinion of the company's present motor truck advertising, both national and co-operative. Approximately one-fifth of the company's truck dealers were selected to receive a questionnaire entitled "International Truck Advertising Survey" (Exhibit 2). The sample included all large dealers and a representative group of the medium and smaller dealers picked at random. In addition, all district managers, assistant district managers, and branch managers were asked to complete a separate questionnaire.

EXHIBIT 2

INTERNATIONAL TRUCK ADVERTISING SURVEY

Return to District Manager

Dealer_____
City_____ State_____
District_____

Please return by December 8, 1958

1. Please list below the business franchises in addition to International Trucks that you now have (automotive products, tires, appliances, etc.) State specific name of franchise.

_____   _____
_____   _____

EXHIBIT 2—*Continued*

2. How many new I.H. trucks do you sell in an average year in each of these groups?
    Models 100 through 140 _____
    Models 150 through 195 _____
    Models 200 and up _____
    Total no. of trucks _____

3. How do you rate the appearance and content of recent International Truck advertising in the following media:

	Excellent	Fair	Poor	Haven't Noticed
General magazines (*Saturday Evening Post*)	( )	( )	( )	( )
Business magazines (*Nation's Business, Business Week, U.S. News & World Report*)	( )	( )	( )	( )
Farm magazines (Regional and state, etc.)	( )	( )	( )	( )
Trade magazines (State Trucking Association, regional trucking magazines, etc.)	( )	( )	( )	( )
Sunday supplements (*This Week, Parade, American Weekly*, etc.)	( )	( )	( )	( )
Local newspapers (your paper)	( )	( )	( )	( )
Outdoor posters (24-sheet panels)	( )	( )	( )	( )

4. How, in your opinion, does the International truck advertising which you have seen compare with competitive truck advertising:

	I.H. Is Better	I.H. Is as Good	I.H. Is Not as Good	Haven't Noticed
Compared with Ford	( )	( )	( )	( )
Compared with Chevrolet	( )	( )	( )	( )
Compared with Dodge	( )	( )	( )	( )
Compared with GMC	( )	( )	( )	( )
Compared with Mack	( )	( )	( )	( )
Compared with White	( )	( )	( )	( )
Compared with Willys	( )	( )	( )	( )

5. What suggestions, if any, do you have for improving the appearance and content of International truck advertising?

_____

_____

_____

_____

6. In your opinion, which of the following forms of advertising media do the most good in your market?

General magazines ( )
Business magazines ( )
Farm magazines ( )
Trade magazines ( )
Sunday supplements ( )
Newspaper ( )
Radio ( )

Fill in number 1 opposite the most effective media, number 2 opposite the second ranking media, and number 3 opposite the third (RANK ONLY THREE). Place an "x" opposite the *least* effective.

EXHIBIT 2—*Continued*

Television.........................( )
Outdoor—24-sheet.................( )
Road signs.......................( )
International *Trail*.................( )
Direct mail......................( )
Comments: _____

_____

7. How do you rate International *Trail* magazine?

( ) Excellent ( ) Fair ( ) Poor

7*a*. How many of your prospects are on your International *Trail* mailing list?

(Fill in number) _____

7*b*. Have prospects who receive *Trail* expressed interest in the magazine? (Check one)

Interested_____ Not interested_____

7*c*. Has *Trail* magazine been effective in promoting truck sales in your area?

Yes_____ No_____

8. What kind of local advertising do you now use on new trucks?

8*a*. For each kind of new truck advertising you use, roughly what per cent is paid for out of International Harvester motor truck dealer co-operative advertising funds?

(Check Those You Use)

(Per Cent Paid for Out of Co-op Funds)

Newspaper..................( ) _____
Direct mail.................( ) _____
Trail magazine...............( ) _____
Outdoor....................( ) _____
Radio......................( ) _____
TV........................( ) _____
Movie playlets..............( ) _____
Other_____ _____
None.......................( )

8*b*. Approximately, how much money over and above your co-operative funds do you estimate you spend in a year for advertising and promotional activities on new motor trucks in your area?

$_____

8*c*. Approximately, how much money do you estimate you spend in a year for advertising and promotional activities on other phases of your motor truck business such as: used trucks, parts, and service?

$_____

9. How do you feel about the present I.H. co-operative advertising plan for motor truck dealers? (Check one.)

I like the present plan. ( )
I don't like the present plan. ( )

EXHIBIT 2—*Continued*

10. Do you feel that the present national advertising program and local advertising you are receiving under the present co-op plan *plus* the advertising you do locally is adequate to promote International truck sales in your area? (Check one.)

Yes_____ No_____

Comments: _____

_____

_____

11. Based on your experience with the present I.H. motor truck dealer co-operative advertising plan, which of the following would you recommend? (Check one.)

( ) Continue the plan in its present form.
( ) Change the present plan.
( ) Discontinue the present plan.

12. If you recommend the plan be changed, please give us your suggestions.

_____

_____

13. We would appreciate any additional comments, recommendations, or suggestions you may wish to offer regarding advertising and promotional activities on International trucks. (Attach additional pages, if necessary.)

_____

_____

_____

_____

Signature_____

Title_____

Tables 1–6 show the results of the survey as tabulated for selected questions that pertained most directly to the co-operative advertising program. The replies received to question 8a were not tabulated, since the answers indicated some confusion on the part of dealers. Confusion ap-

TABLE 1

QUESTION 8: WHAT KIND OF LOCAL ADVERTISING DO YOU NOW USE ON NEW TRUCKS?
(INCLUDES ADVERTISING PAID FOR OUT OF CO-OP FUNDS AND BY DEALER HIMSELF)

Media Used to Advertise New Trucks	Dealers by No. of Trucks Sold Last Year				
	0–9	10–24	25–49	50–Up	All Dealers
Newspaper	79%	89%	89%	85%	87%
Direct mail	53	60	61	72	61
Trail magazine	49	62	70	74	64
Outdoor	22	30	37	48	34
Radio	15	31	48	51	36
TV	7	6	9	22	10
Movie playlets	5	16	18	15	15
No reply	12	4	1	3	4
No. dealers	(148)	(408)	(259)	(175)	(990)

parently arose because many of the dealers held other franchises for which there were co-operative advertising funds. Some of these dealers considered all advertising for all products in answering question 8*a*. It was obvious that the results were not comparable.

TABLE 2

QUESTION 8*b*: APPROXIMATELY HOW MUCH MONEY OVER AND ABOVE YOUR CO-OPERATIVE FUNDS DO YOU ESTIMATE YOU SPEND IN A YEAR FOR ADVERTISING AND PROMOTIONAL ACTIVITIES ON NEW MOTOR TRUCKS IN YOUR AREA?

Amount Spent above Co-op Funds	Dealers by No. of Trucks Sold				
	0–9	10–24	25–49	50–Up	All Dealers
None	9%	6%	3%	4%	5%
$1–$100	33	19	7	1	15
$101–$500	38	58	51	27	48
$501–$1000	1	4	21	29	12
$1001–Up	3	2	12	33	10
No reply	16	11	6	6	10
No. dealers	(148)	(408)	(259)	(175)	(990)

TABLE 3

QUESTION 9: HOW DO YOU FEEL ABOUT THE PRESENT I.H. CO-OPERATIVE PLAN FOR MOTOR TRUCK DEALERS?

Opinion	Dealers by No. of Trucks Sold					District Mgrs.	Branch Mgrs.
	0–9	10–24	25–49	50–Up	All Dealers		
Like plan	58%	61%	57%	53%	58%	56%	52%
Don't like plan	32	32	39	43	36	42	29
No reply	10	7	4	4	6	2	19
No. of respondents	(148)	(408)	(259)	(175)	(990)	(96)	(160)

TABLE 4

QUESTION 10: DO YOU FEEL THAT THE PRESENT NATIONAL ADVERTISING PROGRAM AND LOCAL ADVERTISING YOU ARE RECEIVING UNDER THE PRESENT CO-OP PLAN PLUS THE ADVERTISING YOU DO LOCALLY IS ADEQUATE TO PROMOTE INTERNATIONAL TRUCK SALES IN YOUR AREA?

Opinion	Dealers by No. of Trucks Sold					District Mgrs.	Branch Mgrs.
	0–9	10–24	25–49	50–Up	All Dealers		
Yes	55%	45%	36%	39%	43%	20%	28%
No	37	52	63	59	54	79	55
No reply	8	3	1	2	3	1	17
No. of respondents	(148)	(408)	(259)	(175)	(990)	(96)	(160)

TABLE 5

QUESTION 11: BASED ON YOUR EXPERIENCE WITH THE PRESENT I.H. MOTOR TRUCK
DEALER CO-OPERATIVE ADVERTISING PLAN, WHICH OF THE FOLLOWING WOULD YOU
RECOMMEND?

Opinion	Dealers by No. of Trucks Sold				All Dealers	District Managers	Branch Managers
	0–9	10–24	25–49	50–Up			
Continue plan in present form....	49%	49%	41%	38%	45%	34%	48%
Change plan.......	30	39	49	49	42	57	31
Discontinue.......	9	9	8	13	10	7	3
No reply.........	12	3	2	..	3	2	18
No. of Respondents	(148)	(408)	(259)	(175)	(990)	(96)	(160)

TABLE 6

SUMMARY OF DEALER COMMENTS ON MOTOR TRUCK CO-OPERATIVE
ADVERTISING PLAN

Comments requiring major changes in basic plan
Decentralized control... 124
Change in charges.. 58
Advertising agency fee excessive................................ 41
Miscellaneous administrative changes............................ 3
Additional ways of spending funds (94 made comments)
General (no specific recommendations)......................... 22
Used trucks.. 13
Parts and service.. 17
Specialty items (giveaways) and calendars..................... 20
Dealer signs... 26
Miscellaneous local publications............................. 15
Activities... 24
Miscellaneous ways to spend funds............................ 3

Comments requiring modifications of present plan
Desire more advertising.. 160
Desire placement and/or creation of advertising................ 104
Greater dealer "voice" and/or control.......................... 86
Greater company and/or agency guidance......................... 31
Simplify procedures.. 46
Require additional and/or better material...................... 61

Alternative activities if present plan discontinued
Factor advertising cost in truck price......................... 17
Dealers do own advertising..................................... 17
Advertising allowance plan..................................... 16
Miscellaneous comments... 11
No. of dealers... (990)

*Should International Harvester continue its truck co-operative advertising
program? If not, what alternative should it adopt?*

57

SURF MOTOR COMPANY

Surf Motor Company manufactured outboard motors for all types of boats. The industry was made up of only nine firms of any significance; four accounted for a majority of both dollar and unit sales. Surf was one of the smaller firms, with sales of about 5 per cent of the industry. For four consecutive years, Surf had exhibited at the three big boat shows in New York, Chicago, and San Francisco and at from two to seven smaller shows in other cities, such as Detroit and Miami. There were many other boat shows at which the company did not exhibit. Several of these were regional in scope, but the majority, probably several hundred in all, were local. The number of such shows was increasing annually. Although it exhibited at only a few of the larger shows, Surf's expenditure on these shows was 10–15 per cent of its over-all advertising budget. Therefore, management decided to study the value of such shows to determine whether Surf should continue to exhibit in the same shows, should expand to other shows, or should curtail activities of this type.

Virtually all boat shows were essentially public shows and were promoted as such. The manufacturers of motors, boats, trailers, and accessories displayed their latest products and took the names of interested consumers to turn over to the appropriate dealers. No actual sales were made. At the big shows some special arrangement was usually made so that dealers would have an opportunity to visit with the manufacturers at times when the public was not admitted. At the New York show, for example, there were three days during which the show was open only to dealers and at Chicago there were special hours during which dealers only were admitted. At these times manufacturers tried to take orders for their products. The big shows, however, were held during January, February, and March, while new models were usually introduced in October. As a result, most dealers had placed their initial orders for the new season before the shows opened.

In most of the smaller shows, no distinction was made between dealers and the general public; in fact, at the local shows dealers were usually the exhibitors. The Outboard Boating Club, the trade association to which eight of the nine outboard motor manufacturers belonged, urged its members to exhibit at as many shows as possible because such shows increased the acceptance of boating with the public. The Outboard Boating Club planned a new "trade only" show for the entire marine industry to be held, for the first time, in Chicago during October, 1960. It was anticipated that this show would become an annual event.

In planning its use of trade shows for 1960, Surf management decided that the new "trade only" show might serve its purposes better than the public shows at which it had been exhibiting. Surf participated in the three major shows annually and also in two to seven other, usually local, shows. All the major manufacturers exhibited at the three major shows; some, but never all, participated in the better-established local shows.

Surf paid approximately $4,000 for display space alone at each of the three major shows and about $400 for display space at the typical local show at which it exhibited. In addition to these costs, there were the costs of the exhibits themselves and of the personnel who were taken off their regular jobs to man them. The average cost for an exhibit was about $100 per lineal foot for original construction. Thereafter, the exhibit could be reused about twenty times, with a refurbishing cost of about 10 per cent of the original cost after each use. About one man-day of labor was needed to set up the average exhibit, and another day to take it down. At the large shows Surf usually had two men on duty at all times, which meant that four men had to be detailed to the show for a period of about ten days. At the local shows two men were usually enough, and the length of the show was shorter—about five days on the average at the shows in which Surf participated.

Surf management decided to make a special study at the Chicago show in February, 1960, to help in determining whether the company should continue its participation in such shows in the future. Four objectives were set for the study:

1. To discover the public image of Surf and of its major competitors.
2. To determine the effect of the show in changing the knowledge of and attitude toward Surf on the part of the public.
3. To determine the effectiveness of the Surf exhibit for informing the public on specific points concerning Surf motors.
4. To determine whether or not Surf motor owners differed in any important respects from owners of other brands.

The Chicago Boat Show was open for ten days. Despite a serious snowstorm, which almost halted traffic for the first few days of the show, the total attendance was 362,550. Over seven hundred exhibitors, representing all phases of the boating and water sport industry, participated. Two groups of respondents were interviewed. One group, considered the control group, was interviewed as the individuals entered the show; it was assumed that they had not been exposed to the show at that time. The other group, considered the experimental group, was interviewed as the individuals left the show; it was assumed that they had been exposed to the exhibits. The same questionnaire was administered to each group by trained interviewers. Classification data covering seven different characteristics were obtained, and the two groups, control and experimental, were compared on all seven factors. No significant differences were found on any of the characteristics at the 5 per cent level of significance.

Comparison of the experimental and control groups showed no significant differences in either attitude toward or knowledge of Surf or of any of the specific points about Surf motors that were emphasized in the exhibit. Surf was mentioned as a brand of outboard motor known by fewer respondents than any of its four major competitors. The brand of motor that respondents picked as their first choice if they were to buy one was very highly correlated to the awareness of that brand; that is, the brand that had the highest awareness also was the brand preferred by most, and the brand with the lowest awareness was preferred least. Similarly, the public image tended to be more favorable for the brands that were better known. The strongest single factor related to Surf's image was "low initial cost."

A trade association study of the 1959 boat show established a number of characteristics of the people attending the show:

From families that owned a motor and/or a boat, 66 per cent.
Males, 88 per cent.
Had attended previous shows, 58 per cent.
Came to the show "to look around," "to see the boats," "out of curiosity," or "for amusement," 75 per cent.
Respondents arriving with plans to purchase something, 15 per cent.
Respondents departing who actually had purchased something, 2 per cent.
The average party was composed of 3 persons—2.6 adults and 0.4 children.

The outboard-motor industry had grown very rapidly from the early 1930's, as shown in Table 1. In 1958 the Outboard Boating Club estimated that 4 million out of the 51 million households in the country owned outboard motors. The association's forecast was that sales would continue to expand to an annual level of 1,256,000 by 1970. Surf's sales had been growing steadily at about the same rate as the industry total.

TABLE 1

SALES AND MARKET DATA FOR OUTBOARD MOTORS FOR
SELECTED YEARS: 1934–59

	Unit Motor Sales (000)*	Outboard Motors in Use (000)	Retail Expenditures on Boating (000,000)	Recreational Boats in Use (000)
1934	23	N.A.†	N.A.	1,720
1939	120	N.A.	N.A.	1,998
1944	..	N.A.	N.A.	...
1949	329	2,643	$ 660	3,197
1954	479	3,740	1,000	5,510
1959	540	5,845	2,475	7,800

* Sales measured by manufacturers' shipments.
† N.A. = Not available.
Source: Outboard Boating Club.

What action should Surf management take relative to participation in trade shows?

58

AUNT JEMIMA'S BUTTERMILK PANCAKE MIX

In the fall of 1956 Quaker Oats Company introduced a new buttermilk pancake mix named "Aunt Jemima's New Deluxe Buttermilk Pancake Mix." Quaker Oats had marketed a standard pancake mix under the Aunt Jemima name for many years. This brand had become a household word, well known throughout the United States, and was by far the leading brand in the industry. In order to take advantage of the public acceptance of the name, Quaker began a program of product line expansion under the Aunt Jemima brand. A buckwheat pancake mix was the first item added, followed by a cornbread and a coffee cake mix. The buttermilk pancake mix was initially distributed to grocers late in 1956, but it was not until 1957 that it was really introduced to the consumer market, with a special promotion that was based on a premium offer. In July, 1958, the management was reviewing the results of this promotion.

Just before the introduction of the New Deluxe Buttermilk Pancake Mix, a national advertising campaign had been undertaken promoting the regular mix and the buckwheat mix. The theme of this campaign was "Perfect Pancakes in 10 Shakes" (Exhibit 1). The ads explained a new way to make Aunt Jemima pancakes by shaking the mix, eggs, and milk in a shaker. The campaign was intended to stimulate demand for pancakes by emphasizing the idea that mixes were convenient and quick and took the drudgery out of making pancakes. The ad copy suggested, "Use any shaker . . . even a glass jar." The results of this promotion were unanticipated. Many inquiries were received from readers as to where and how the shaker, which was illustrated in the ad, could be obtained. The shaker had been a prop furnished by the advertising agency, and Quaker Oats was not prepared to furnish such a shaker or even to suggest where one could be bought.

This experience suggested the campaign that was used to introduce the New Deluxe Buttermilk Pancake Mix. Copy featured the new mix as the third pancake mix under the Aunt Jemima label—"The famous two, plus one that's new." This campaign again featured the blue shaker with the large caption "Buttermilk Pancakes in 10 Shakes." This time, however, the shaker was offered as a free premium upon the return of three box tops, one from each of the three mixes—regular, buckwheat, and buttermilk. The ad was run as a full-page, four-color spread in such magazines as the *Ladies' Home Journal, Better Homes and Gardens,* and the *American Home.* This ad appeared in some of the magazines in October, 1957, and in others in November, 1957. The national magazines used had a gross circulation of 36 million and the total cost of the campaign was $139,000. The campaign brought 29,841 requests for the free shaker.

From the results of this promotion, management concluded that premium returns, about 0.08 per cent of the estimated circulation, were not satisfactory. The manager of the grocery products advertising division believed that the most important reason for the poor return was the requirement that box tops from all three of the mixes be sent in exchange for the free shaker. He estimated that each box of pancake mix would make from fifty to sixty pancakes. On this basis, a family of four persons would probably get four meals per box or twelve meals from the three boxes. If the offer did prompt the housewife to buy all three mixes at one time, he doubted that she would immediately tear the tops off all the boxes, since this would make them unsightly and unsatisfactory as storage containers for the unused portion of the contents.

Regardless of the reasons for the number of requests for the premium, the management decided that another campaign should be run in January and February of 1958 to provide more introductory push behind the Buttermilk Pancake Mix. The advertising copy was essentially the same (Exhibit 2), but the only medium used was the Metro Sunday Comics Network. A four-color, half-page ad was adopted. This time the free shaker was offered in return for one box top from the New Deluxe Buttermilk Pancake Mix. The estimated gross circulation of the Metro Sunday Comics Network was 14,110,264, and the cost was $33,690.

Requests for the premium shaker came in strongly over a two-month period after the ad was run and totaled 122,237, about 0.9% of the gross circulation. This was four times as many returns as had been received from the first campaign and was considerably greater than the advertising manager had anticipated. In appraising the total effort to date, the supervisor of premium promotion tabulated the results as shown in Table 1.

In addition to the direct advertising costs of these promotions, there were premium and trade promotion costs. The free shaker cost about 43 cents per unit, including handling and mailing. Each shaker represented a retail value to the customer of about $1.00. To gain trade support during the first campaign to introduce the Buttermilk Pancake Mix, Quaker Oats had employed a special introductory trade deal that was designed to encourage dealers to build larger stocks of all three mixes in preparation for the demand that would be created by the national advertising program and the premium offer. This trade deal was a price concession for the purchase of all three mixes at one time. Television and radio advertising had been used during the October–November campaign, but this advertising did not mention the premium offer. Total expenditures for television and radio advertising were $105,000.

Advertising costs for both compaigns totaled $277,690, including the

EXHIBIT 1

television and radio costs. Premiums cost approximately $65,000. There were additional costs of the trade promotion, but these were not readily available.

Sales of the three pancake mixes are shown in Table 2.

First put 1 cup milk in shaker. Add 1 egg and 1 tbsp. liquid shortening. (WESSON OIL)

Next Add 1 cup Aunt Jemima pancake mix.

Now the fun! Shake vigorously ten times

And pour out perfect pancakes every time.

Quaker sold directly to retailers at prices that varied somewhat according to quantity but averaged approximately as shown in Table 3. The retail prices shown in the table are also averages, since such prices varied slightly.

EXHIBIT 2

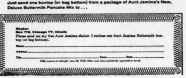

Buttermilk pancakes in 10 shakes !

Just the way you like them—these new Aunt Jemima Buttermilk pancakes! Dairy-fresh buttermilk right in the mix makes them twice as tender,... smooth as silk. And it's so easy to make 'em when you shake 'em. Pour the mixings in a shaker, shake 'em times, and pour out perfect buttermilk pancakes every time! Delicious Aunt Jemima Buttermilks. Shake up a batch tomorrow!

The famous TWO plus one that's NEW

Only Aunt Jemima gives you ALL THREE!

FREE SHAKER!

Just send one boxtop (or bag bottom) from a package of Aunt Jemima's New, Deluxe Buttermilk Pancake Mix to ...

Shaker
Box 712, Chicago 77, Illinois
Please send me my free Aunt Jemima shaker. I enclose one Aunt Jemima Buttermilk box-
top (or bag bottom).

Name
Address
City   Zone   State
Offer expires at midnight, June 30, 1958. Offer void where prohibited, regulated or taxed.

TABLE 1

RESULTS OF TWO PREMIUM CAMPAIGNS

	First Campaign	Second Campaign
Size of ad	Full-page	Half-page
Cost	$139,000	$33,690
Gross circulation	36,000,000	14,110,264
Cost per thousand circulation	$3.83	$2.39
Premium requests	29,841	122,237
Percentage requests to circulation	0.08%	0.9%

TABLE 2

QUAKER OATS SALES OF PANCAKE MIXES
FOR SELECTED PERIODS
(CASES OF TWELVE 1-POUND PACKAGES)*

Period	Regular Mix	Buckwheat Mix	Buttermilk Mix
1956			
August–September	246,978	49,940	.....
October–November	294,150	69,372	8,328
December–January	302,478	72,150	11,100
1957			
August–September	266,400	52,728	19,422
October–November	324,668	72,150	58,278
December–January	302,478	66,600	77,928
1958			
February–March	310,800	66,600	88,800
August–September	238,650	41,628	77,700

* All sales were not in cases of twelve 1-pound packages, but data have been reduced to this common denominator for comparative purposes.

TABLE 3

QUAKER OATS' AND RETAILERS' SELLING PRICES
(CASES OF TWELVE 1-POUND PACKAGES)

Item	Quaker Oats' Selling Price	Retailers' Selling Price
Regular mix	$1.89	$2.52
Buckwheat mix	2.01	2.52
Buttermilk mix	1.76	2.29

The supervisor of premium promotion completed his review of the promotion in July, 1958, and wrote a note to the marketing vice-president that concluded as follows: "We feel that this promotion has been an extremely successful program and points to the value of a new fresh approach, namely 'Pancakes in 10 Shakes' augmented by the free shaker offer. Our observations indicate that an integrated premium device used in conjunction with a new method of preparing our products or serving them has been instrumental in gaining greater trade acceptance of our programs than those ideas where the premium had no relation to the promotional idea."

In August the premium promotion and advertising supervisors wrote a letter to the Metro Sunday Comics Network relative to this promotion. The letter is reproduced as Exhibit 3.

Appraise the introductory promotion for Aunt Jemima's New Deluxe Buttermilk Pancake Mix.

EXHIBIT 3

LETTER FROM THE QUAKER OATS COMPANY TO THE METROPOLITAN
SUNDAY COMICS NETWORK

The Quaker Oats Company

MERCHANDISE MART PLAZA

CHICAGO 54, ILLINOIS

TELEPHONE WHITEHALL 4-0600

August 4, 1958

Mr. Harry Harlow
Metro Sunday Comics Network
Chicago 11, Illinois

Dear Harry:

While we can't go into detail, we, nevertheless, feel compelled to congratulate you and the Metro Comics Network for its share in an outstandingly successful premium promotion on our New Deluxe Aunt Jemima Buttermilk Pancake Mix.

Most impressive was a response two and one-half times as great as our calculated anticipation. Also impressive is the fact that the returns were strong during a 2-month period after the ad had run.

Doubtless, four very important factors, in determining the success of a premium promotion, are:

1. The ad itself,
2. The premium,
3. The related product,
4. The advertising medium.

We want to thank you for your contribution to our selection of a combination that materialized in spectacular success.

Sincerely yours,

J. P. Odell
Supervisor - Aunt Jemima Ready
Mixes Advertising

Ronald Bouras
Supervisor - Premium Promotion

JPO:NG

SECTION IV

Organizing to Carry Out the Plan

ONCE the major strategies are merged into a plan that specifies who will do what, an organizational structure must be set up. This organization must consider the needs of the marketing department and the relationship of the marketing department to the other departments within the enterprise. The firm's total organization must provide a communication system that permits and encourages the flow of information within individual departments and among the various departments. Inevitably, the marketing department comes into conflict with other departments, since it represents the needs of the market and thus takes the customer's point of view. Other departments, more often than not, will take the firm's point of view and hence will be more influenced by the firm's limited resources. Such a conflict situation is not necessarily bad so long as the organization provides a court of review where the differences are reconciled quickly.

Product planning is typically carried out by representatives from a number of departments, including marketing, research and development, and engineering. The marketing department has much to contribute here, since, through its salesmen and its marketing research unit, it has close contact with the needs of the market and with competitive activity. The marketing department must also co-ordinate closely with production. A few companies have gone so far as to give the marketing department the responsibility for production scheduling and inventory control.

Marketing embraces a great many functions, which are handled by a number of administrative units within the department. Over the past few years there has been a strong trend to place more and more activities under the command of the marketing manager. This trend represents a recognition of the fact that, if the firm is to be successful, its marketing operation must be integrated; that is, the marketing manager must be able to manipulate individual strategies in such a way as to achieve the optimum marketing mix.

A marketing department may include units responsible for such activities as the field sales force, advertising, service, marketing research, product planning, order or office management, shipping, sales personnel, and sales training. While each unit has a separate and distinct mission, all must work together closely to achieve the common objectives. The overlap between units is more important in some cases than in others. Sales and advertising, for example, must be very closely co-ordinated to prevent waste. While most companies still have a field sales unit and an advertising unit, more is being done at the marketing manager's level to insure co-ordination than ever before.

The sales unit and the service unit also have much in common. In many cases the salesman also functions as a service man. On the other hand, some firms have been reluctant to put service into the hands of the salesman for fear of dissipating his selling effort and killing the initiative for replacement selling where the existing machinery is still adequate if serviced properly.

The relationship between sales and order billing is obvious. Not only must orders be obtained in the field, but they must be processed efficiently within the office. The office staff ships the product and handles correspondence with the customer. Credit and collections are important parts of the office work. Since the drive to sell inevitably produces accounts with questionable credit, conflicts occur between the sales force and the credit department. If the credit manager follows a conservative credit policy, the field salesman, especially if he is working on a commission arrangement, will feel discriminated against. Sales can be lost if the credit manager does not handle customers diplomatically.

Several different types of organization are used in marketing departments. Most are based, in part, on a recognition of the importance of functional activities. The traditional functional organization calls for the work load of the marketing department to be handled by such functional units as advertising, personal or field selling, marketing research, export sales, service, product development, and office or clerical. These units typically report to the director of marketing. Such an organizational structure is "flat" in that a relatively large number of units report directly to the director of marketing.

Where the company sells more than one product, the organization described above might be modified to permit some product specialization. In its simplest form this change might take place within only the field sales force, with different salesmen reporting to different product sales managers. These product sales managers would report to the field sales manager. In extreme situations, completely separate functional organizations may be set up around different products; a marketing manager is established for each product or group of products, and he has a complete set of functional units reporting to him. There may be overlaps among product marketing managers; several may share the same staff functional unit, such as marketing research, or even the same sales force.

Many companies use a brand manager approach in their organization. This is especially true with those large consumer product companies that sell two or more brands within the same product class; for example, Procter and Gamble has several brands of detergent. Brand managers share the same field sales staff and compete for the time of the sales force. They have the responsibility for marketing the brand and make such decisions as those having to do with advertising, price, "deals," package design, and product improvements. They typically do not have their own marketing research unit or advertising staff but share these facilities with other brand managers.

Some marketing departments are organized around the type of customers to which the firm sells. Thus, a consumer food manufacturer may organize to accommodate sales to chains and to institutions as well as to wholesalers. In most such cases, the organization of the field sales force reflects this type of customer breakdown, while the remainder of the organization remains largely functional. Some firms go so far as to organize their sales force by industry.

The impact of geography on the organization is, of course, very important. Almost every company that sells over a wide area breaks down its sales force on at least a regional basis. Often the regions are further subdivided into districts. The home office may or may not make all major decisions.

As might be expected, the number of different types of marketing organizations is sizable. There is no single best type of organization. A firm must select that organizational structure that will achieve its plan most efficiently.

A. Marketing Organization

59

RHEEM MANUFACTURING COMPANY

ALMOST from its founding in 1930, Rheem Manufacturing Company had experienced growth and decentralization problems. By 1956 the firm consisted of eighteen domestic and seventeen foreign plants manufacturing a great variety of products. It was divided into six divisions, each of which operated as a distinct and separate entity. The management believed that this organization was unable to cope with the diversity and geographic distribution of the company's manufacturing and marketing operations. In 1955 the company had sales of $180 million, with earnings of $12 million before taxes, but in 1956 sales dropped to $174 million, with a loss of $16 million. Some executives were convinced that the way in which the company was organized was an important factor leading to the loss. Table 1 shows Rheem's sales and earnings for the years following World War II.

TABLE 1

RHEEM MANUFACTURING COMPANY SALES

AND EARNINGS: 1947–56

(MILLIONS)

Year	Sales	Earnings before Taxes
1947	$ 60	$ 5
1948	59	5
1949	50	4
1950	74	10
1951	94	13
1952	145	7
1953	188	13
1954	164	11
1955	180	13
1956	174	16 (loss)

Executives estimated that sales in 1956 were divided among product lines approximately as shown in the accompanying tabulation.

The company was divided into six major divisions—four geographical divisions and two product divisions, as shown in Exhibit 1. Each division was organized around one of six major plants in operation in 1956. Each

338

Product Lines	Per Cent
Steel and fiber shipping containers and automatic storage water heaters	40
Aviation and electronics equipment	25
Plumbing fixtures	10
Heating and air-conditioning equipment and gas ranges	10
Automotive parts	10
Foreign operations (Rheem International)	5

of these divisions was responsible for producing its own profit. Although there was some centralized direction, each division had a considerable amount of freedom in setting its own policies and essentially handled its own production, research, and distribution. The advantages believed inherent in this organization were that it would help cut costs by eliminating the necessity for a large central headquarters with a concentration of personnel and records and that it would let problems be solved at the lev-

EXHIBIT 1

RHEEM MANUFACTURING COMPANY ORGANIZATION CHART: 1956

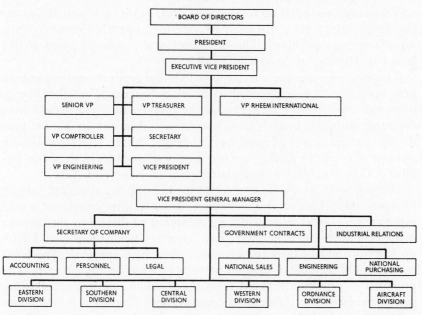

els where they occurred, thus eliminating red tape. One major difficulty of this centralized plan was that to some extent it did not allow full use of national marketing methods. For example, West Coast plants on occasion manufactured water heaters that in some details were different from those made by Midwest plants and had entirely separate sales staffs and separate advertising budgets. Each region produced containers that were sold by its own sales force. Production facilities were duplicated in several instances, although facilities were sometimes idle at some of the plants. Regional managers were not able to draw on production facilities of other regions even if they could not meet the demand in their region from their own production. On occasion, there was reluctance by some regional managers to develop new products with full vigor for fear that the necessary capital to launch them might not be available. The feeling was that, if funds were poured into new product development, current profits would be lower and the division would look bad in comparison with others.

Distribution gaps occurred in some territories and overlapping sales effort developed in others. For example, in New Orleans a plant made containers and water tanks and serviced an area with a radius of 150 miles, while in Houston, Texas, a plant made the same line and also serviced an area with a 150-mile radius. This left a gap that was not covered. On the other hand, in some territories two company salesmen, operating from different regional offices, would call on the same account. With stiffer competition developing in a number of lines, the management decided that a change in organization was mandatory.

Two criteria were set up for any new plan: (1) it must provide for national marketing, and (2) it must provide for centralized control of the manufacturing operations. The organization that was proposed to the Board of Directors is shown in Exhibit 2.

This new organization was developed around product lines rather than geographically. It was designed to provide "maximum autonomy with maximum control." This meant that the division managers would have operating authority in their divisions but would be responsible for producing specific results assigned by the central office. The eight-division product lines and headquarters and plant locations were as shown in Exhibit 3. The corporation headquarters was in New York City.

Division goals would be established by the division managers, subject to approval by the executive committee. The executive committee would maintain close supervision without attempting to dictate to the division managers how to run their day-to-day business. The divisions would draw up forecasts and budgets for executive committee approval. The committee would then check division performance against these targets. The proposed organization differed from the previous one in the following general ways: It (1) divided the company into product divisions rather than geographic divisions, (2) created an executive committee, and (3) placed the product divisions under the supervision and control of the executive committee rather than under a general manager.

To insure better co-ordination of the divisions, the executive committee would co-ordinate the sales policies, promotion policies, product standardization, research and development, and equipment purchases.

In the new organization, the Ordnance Division and the Aircraft Division remained essentially as they were but were combined and became

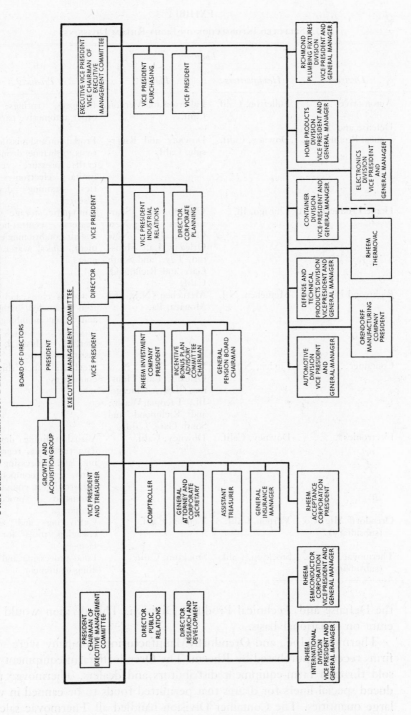

EXHIBIT 2

Proposed Organization Plan, Rheem Manufacturing Company

EXHIBIT 3

SELECTED INFORMATION ON EIGHT RHEEM DIVISIONS

	Location		
Division	Headquarters	Plants	Products
Automotive.........Fullerton, Calif.		Fullerton and Vernon, Calif.	Bumpers, springs, and other automotive parts
Defense and Technical Products.....Downey, Calif.		Downey and Riverside, Calif.	Propulsion and missile systems, ordnance, drone aircraft, pressure vessels, military electronics, optics, training devices, research
Home Products......Chicago, Ill.		Chicago, Ill.; Sparrows Pt., Md.; New Castle, Del.; New Orleans, La.; Houston, Tex.; and South Gate and Richmond, Calif.	Automatic storage water heaters, central-heating and air-conditioning equipment, tanks, water softeners
Richmond Plumbing..Metuchen, N.J.		Metuchen, N.J., and Monaca, Pa.	Vitreous china and cast-iron enameled bathroom and other plumbing fixtures for residential, commercial, industrial, and institutional use
Container...........Linden, N.J.		Linden, N.J.; New Orleans, La.; Houston, Tex.; Chicago, Ill.; Tacoma, Wash.; and Richmond and South Gate, Calif.	Steel and fiber shipping containers
Electronics.........Downey, Calif.		Downey, Calif.	Visual training devices; data recording, reproducing, and processing systems and components; industrial test equipment; automatic processing equipment
Orendorff Mfg. Co...Vernon, Calif. (subsidiary)		Vernon, Calif.	Cultivating and earth-engaging tools for the farm
Thermovac, Inc......Stockton, Calif. (subsidiary)		Stockton, Calif.	Food processing and handling equipment

the Defense and Technical Products Division. This division would operate on a national basis.

Thermovac, Inc., and Orendorff Manufacturing Company were small firms recently purchased by Rheem. The Orendorff farm equipment was sold through farm-equipment distributors and dealers. Thermovac produced special liners for drums that permitted foods to be canned in very large quantities. The Container Division handled all Thermovac sales.

The Electronics Division produced semiconductors, such as transistors, which were sold primarily to the military market.

The Home Products Division and Container Division were to be created from what had been the four regional divisions. The proposed Home Products Division organization is shown in Exhibit 4. Two separate segments were proposed in this division—one, under the national marketing manager, would handle sales of the branded items to distributors through the four regional organizations that existed under the old setup. The Rheem branded products were sold to distributors. The other segment, National Contract Sales, would handle all private-brand and component-parts business through six salesmen who covered the entire country. The Container Division would sell its drums on a national basis direct to firms in the petroleum, meat packing, and chemical industries. The five product managers were the contact men between sales and research and devel-

EXHIBIT 4

PROPOSED ORGANIZATION OF HOME PRODUCTS DIVISION,
RHEEM MANUFACTURING COMPANY

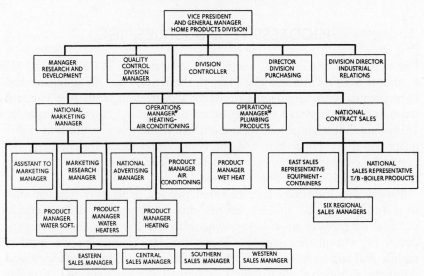

opment. They had no responsibility for sales or advertising, but they worked on product design and were consulted on the establishment of prices.

The Richmond Plumbing Fixtures Division, formerly the Richmond Radiator Company, which was acquired by Rheem Manufacturing Company in 1956, produced a line of items similar to those made by the Home Products Division. The Richmond Plumbing Fixtures Division operated as a separate division of the company, but close liaison permitted a teamed marketing approach by the Richmond Home Products Division.

Each of the divisions in the proposed plan would have its own sales and advertising organizations. The size of each sales force is shown in Table 2. No central sales or advertising department and no over-all institutional advertising were planned.

TABLE 2

DIVISION SALES FORCES UNDER PROPOSED ORGANIZATION

Division	Salesmen	Sales Supervisors
Home Products	40	5
Container	30–35	5
Richmond Plumbing	30	9
Automotive	8–10	1–2
Defense and Technical	8–10	1–2
Electronics	50	7
Orendorff	1	0

Should the proposed organization plan be adopted?

60

PROGRESSIVE INDUSTRIES, INC.

PROGRESSIVE Industries, Inc., had grown in sales from $25 million in 1940 to almost $260 million in 1958. Prior to the latter year, the company had been essentially an engineered products organization, with few standard items in its line, and had been organized on a highly centralized basis. By 1958 standardization of many products had made this organization inadequate for the volume done and the competition faced by the firm. An executive committee was appointed to prepare a plan for reorganizing the corporation's marketing operation.

Progressive Industries manufactured presses, generators, electric motors, hydraulic jacks, air compressors, dehumidifiers, and drilling equipment. Prior to 1948 most items were relatively complex and were produced for custom installations. Thereafter, standardization was pushed rapidly and within a decade 60 per cent of all units sold were standardized products, although these products accounted for less than half of dollar sales. Small air compressors, small generators, and small motors accounted for the major part of the sales of standardized items. These products were designed to fill a variety of general needs and most buyers were potential repeat purchasers. Nonstandardized items were sold on a one-time basis. Individual sales of the custom-built items varied from $5,000 to $500,000. Orders for the standardized products usually included several items and varied from $1,000 to $10,000.

The sales organization prior to 1958 was headed by a general marketing manager, who reported to a vice-president in charge of marketing. The United States was divided into five geographical regions, and each region, on the average, into five districts. The 275 salesmen, who worked under district managers, were mostly trained engineers and each sold the complete Progressive line. The custom-built items were sold direct to industrial and governmental customers, but the standardized products were sold through distributors to contractors, road builders, and other users of this type of equipment.

The executive committee studying the sales organization thought it was an inefficient use of manpower to have skilled engineers selling shelf items to distributors. Each salesman had a dollar quota in each product line, and thus they would sometimes concentrate on the standardized items at the expense of the custom items. Conversely, when a salesman worked on a large potential sale, he might be forced to ignore the standardized items, thereby antagonizing distributors. One salesman, for example, spent nearly all his time for over six months working on a government contract that finally resulted in a sale of $800,000. When calling on a distributor, a salesman might write an order for $1,000 in a matter of minutes. In selling custom items the salesman usually had to help design the equipment, work with as many as twenty different people, help install the product, and then service the installation as needed. When calling on distributors, he had to sell only one man. Salesmen were paid a salary plus a commission, which, on the average, amounted to only about 15 per cent of the salesman's total income. The average salesman earned about $700 a month.

To overcome the problems described above, the committee proposed that the sales force be divided into two parts, as shown in Exhibit 1. The new plan called for only four regions instead of five. Each regional sales manager would report to the general marketing manager and would supervise district office managers, who in turn would supervise the technical sales engineers. There would be twenty-two district office managers and two hundred technical sales engineers.

Also reporting to the general marketing manager would be a general manager of distributor sales. He would supervise four regional distributor sales managers who would supervise about seventy-five distributor sales representatives working out of twenty-three central cities.

The technical sales engineers would call on potential users of Progressive's custom-built equipment. If a salesman found a need for one of Progressive's standardized items, he would refer the prospect to the nearest distributor handling the line. A technical sales engineer would generally be considered 60 per cent engineer and 40 per cent salesman; in other words, emphasis would be placed on his ability to help companies solve problems through the purchase of Progressive products. These representatives would be paid a base salary of $600 per month plus one-fourth of 1 per cent commission on all sales. It was anticipated that about 85 per cent of the typical sales engineer's income would be salary and about 15 per cent commission.

The distributor sales representative's job would consist mainly of (1) selling distributors the standardized Progressive products, (2) educating and training distributors' salesmen, (3) helping distributors develop their assigned territories, and (4) helping distributors use the various advertising programs developed by the company. These representatives would be thought of first as salesmen and second as engineers. They would be paid $300 per month plus one-fourth of 1 per cent commission on all sales. It was expected that the typical representative's income would be about 65 per cent salary and 35 per cent commission.

EXHIBIT 1

Progressive Industries Marketing Division

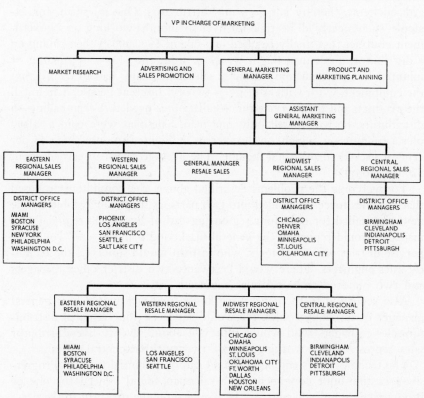

In most cases the distributor sales representatives would work out of the district technical sales offices, although there would be a few salesmen in cities with no district offices (e.g., Fort Worth) and a few district offices where there were no distributor sales representatives (e.g., Salt Lake City). These two groups would co-ordinate their activites in the sense that they would pass leads and other information to each other. Basically, however, they would operate as separate entities.

The committee also recommended the following changes in the organization of the marketing division at the main office: (1) the addition of a product and marketing planning section to help promote the use by the operating divisions of all needed marketing services from both inside and outside the company, (2) the addition of marketing research as a staff function, and (3) the enlargement of the centralized advertising and sales promotion department in order to bring its functions to bear on all marketing objectives.

The committee recommended that an account supervisor be appointed for each product division to work out over-all marketing plans. The central staff personnel would call regularly on these account supervisors to keep acquainted with the division problems so as to make central promotional and advertising plans more effective.

Should the committee's recommendations be accepted?

61

UNION CARBIDE PLASTICS COMPANY

UNION CARBIDE PLASTICS COMPANY was part of the Union Carbide Corporation, the second largest chemical corporation in the United States. Union Carbide Plastics Company had annual sales of $220 million, which made it one of the largest segments of the parent corporation, the total sales of which exceeded $1.25 billion. The company's marketing organization consisted of eight divisions divided on the basis of markets. In 1957 management was studying this organization and considering a complete reorganization of the company.

Exhibit 1 shows the organization as it existed. The sales vice-president supervised four general sales managers, each of whom had responsibility for two customer-process divisions. While these divisions had products designed for different uses, such as bonding, laminating, and molding, the plastics used were not mutually exclusive; that is, the bonding division used some of the same plastics that were used in the laminating and molding divisions. The management believed that each of these customer-process groups had peculiar marketing problems, and therefore a separate sales force was organized in each division.

The headquarters of all eight divisions were located in New York City. The sales forces varied considerably by size, from as few as six salesmen in the flexible packaging materials division to forty salesmen in the molding materials division. Those divisions that had a larger number of salesmen had several assistant sales managers, and in the molding, sheeting, and surface coatings divisions there were several zone managers who were responsible for specified geographical areas and among them, in each division, covered the entire market area of the United States. Generally speaking, all field sales management personnel, that is, general sales

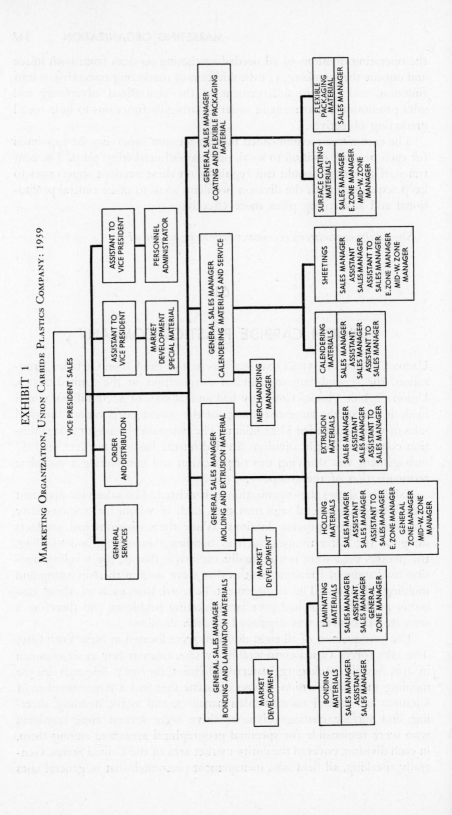

EXHIBIT 1

MARKETING ORGANIZATION, UNION CARBIDE PLASTICS COMPANY: 1959

managers, sales managers, assistant sales managers, and zone managers, spent about half their time on actual supervision and about half in market and product planning.

The salesmen were highly skilled sales engineers, who rendered a great deal of technical advice and service to their customers. On the average, each salesman had about fifty accounts, some of which were quite large; it was not unusual for accounts to purchase over $100,000 annually. The customers were all manufacturers who used plastics in their products. While continuing relationships with these customers were the usual thing, purchases were made on the basis of one or a few months' needs at a time, so that several purchases were made by each customer during the period of a year. Salesmen spent almost all their time working with established customers. Relatively little prospecting for new customers was done.

In studying its organization, the Plastics Company management became convinced that there were areas for improvement as follows: (1) It was becoming increasingly difficult for the various sales managers to do the two general types of work that they were expected to do—that is, supervise and plan. Management believed that there would be advantages in separating the activities—having one person concentrate entirely on planning and another on supervising. (2) Because of the time spent in planning, sales managers were not giving salesmen as close supervision as they should. Management believed that considerably closer supervision was necessary. (3) Marketing decisions were often made too far away from the actual point at which the problems arose. Since management was mostly concentrated in New York City, problems tended to gravitate there for solution. As a result, people making decisions often had little firsthand knowledge of the problems involved, and a good deal of time elapsed between the recognition of a problem and an actual decision. Such a simple thing as an adjustment of a customer's complaint often had to go to New York City for decision. (4) The existing organization also separated management from customers by too wide a gap. In some cases, customers had no contact with anyone in the Plastics Company except the salesman. As a result of such a situation, a great deal of authority and responsibility remained in New York City; very little was decentralized anywhere in the field.

The proposed new organization, shown in Exhibit 2, separated the direct selling from the planning activities. Under the vice-president of sales two divisions—a direct selling group (line sales) and a planning group (product marketing)—were established. Line sales included a number of the old staff positions that had reported to the vice-president of sales and included six regional offices that would report to the sales manager, who, in turn, would report to the director of sales. Each of the six proposed regional managers would have complete responsibility for the sale of all Plastics Company products in his region. All the salesmen in that geographical area would report to this regional manager. The salesmen would no longer be divided strictly along customer-process lines. Some would probably remain specialists in one customer-process line, while others would probably handle more than one customer-process line. It would be up to the regional manager to assign salesmen in the way that he thought best suited his region.

The product-marketing operation, a staff function and the second of the two major proposed groups reporting to the vice-president of sales,

EXHIBIT 2

PROPOSED MARKETING ORGANIZATION, UNION CARBIDE PLASTICS COMPANY

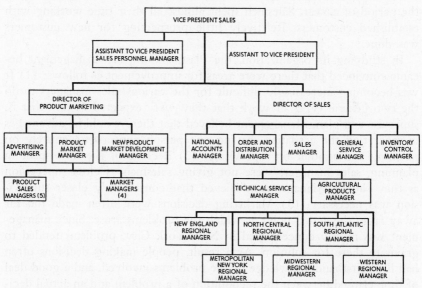

was divided into three parts: advertising, product market, and new product market development. The product market manager would have two types of managers reporting to him. One included a group of five product sales managers and the other a group of four market managers. The product sales managers were to be divided according to basic plastic products, such as phenolics and vinyls, and the market managers according to the major markets served by the company, such as flexible packaging, flooring, and sound records. By developing expertness in their assigned product or market areas and by working closely together, the product sales managers and market managers would support line sales in such a manner that the selling effort would be aimed at maximizing sales profits on all established products in all established markets. The product sales managers' primary responsibilities would be to represent sales to other departments, such as production and development, and to plan for the availability of the right products in sufficient quantities, properly priced, and of proper quality to meet customer needs and maintain company profits. The market managers' primary responsibilities would be to plan marketing programs to be implemented by line sales, to assist the management of advertising in planning and developing promotional and advertising programs, and to participate actively in the industry associations of customers.

The functions of the new-product market-development group would be the same as for the product market operation except that it would deal with new products in old and new markets rather than with the established or existing products and markets. Its objective would be to introduce and develop new products and new market opportunities to the point where they were commercially established and the planning functions on these products and markets could be turned over to the product market operation, thereby permitting new product market development to move on to other new products and markets.

Should the proposed organization plan be adopted?

62

THE OLNER COMPANY

THE OLNER COMPANY, with sales in excess of $61 million, was made up of six divisions that produced a variety of industrial and consumer goods. The company had initially been a producer of industrial air-conditioners but after the war had completed successfully a series of mergers with other companies, which had resulted in its present complex of six divisions. The company followed the policy of decentralization, and each division was relatively autonomous. The divisions sold under their own brand names and had their own sales forces, their own dealer organizations, and their own advertising programs. Exhibit 1 shows the six divisions and their sales organizations; Exhibit 2 shows their sales and advertising budgets.

In 1952, after the last merger had been completed, the company formally set up a headquarters staff. The purpose of this staff was financial —that is, to set up a consolidated budget, to plan the cash needs for the organization as a whole, and to handle tax returns. Heretofore most of this had been left to each division, which was headed by an executive vice-president. In 1954 a vice-president in charge of production for the corporation was appointed and assigned to the headquarter's staff. His responsibility was to consolidate the manufacturing activities of all divisions wherever possible. In 1956 a vice-president in charge of marketing was added to the central staff. His mission was to consolidate all marketing budgets; administer the institutional advertising program; set standards for the selection, training, control, and evaluation of salesmen by the individual divisions; and direct the firm's publicity work, which was handled by an outside consulting firm.

None of the divisions had an adequate organization for developing and evaluating marketing data or for conducting marketing surveys. All divi-

EXHIBIT 1

MARKETING DEPARTMENTS OF THE SIX OLNER DIVISIONS

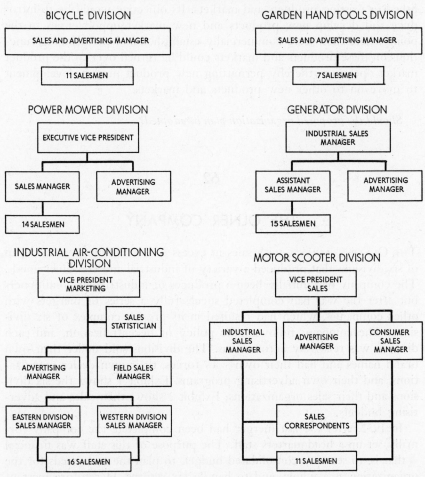

sions, with the exception of the industrial air-conditioning division and the generator division, relied on the secretarial staff to keep sales records. The industrial air-conditioning division had a sales statistician who kept records on sales and expenses and did some evaluation of these records. In the generator division, the industrial sales manager spent a large share of his time in the field, while the assistant sales manager handled most of the inside work.

In 1958 the staff of the vice-president of marketing consisted of a secretary and two assistants. He had no authority to deal directly with the divisions but instead reported to the president of the corporation, who, in turn, made recommendations to the executive vice-presidents in charge of the individual divisions. In commenting on the scope of his authority, the vice-president in charge of marketing said, "I'm strictly a staff officer of the parent company. I wish I could say that all my recommendations were accepted and put into effect—but that time is a long way off. This company is primarily production oriented and since we have been in a seller's market off and on for the past ten years or so, it is doubtful if my recommendations will carry much weight until we experience a tough

EXHIBIT 2

SALES AND ADVERTISING BUDGETS AND MAJOR MARKETS
FOR THE SIX OLNER DIVISIONS: 1958

Division	Sales	Advertising Budget	Major Markets
Bicycle	$ 3,000,000	$ 200,000	Private brands and consumer
Power mower	8,000,000	410,000	Consumer
Industrial air-conditioning	28,000,000	260,000	Industrial
Garden hand tools	4,500,000	70,000	Private brands
Generator	16,000,000	165,000	Electrical contractors
Motor scooter	2,500,000	185,000	Industrial
Total	$62,000,000	$1,290,000	

selling period. My relationships with each division's advertising and selling managers are quite ambiguous. Frankly, I accomplish more through persuasion than by going through the formal organization. We certainly aren't scientific in the way in which we go about things. We really know very little about our market and still less about our selling costs. Most of our divisional sales and advertising managers are old-timers. They have been around a long time and I don't think they're about to adopt any new methods overnight."

In 1958 the company experienced a sales setback, and as a consequence the president ordered his staff to make recommendations regarding what actions they thought should be taken to reduce costs in the years ahead. The vice-president in charge of marketing used this opportunity to include in his report a recommendation for the establishment of a marketing research unit in his department. In his report he commented on the addition of the necessary personnel and the staff for this activity as follows: "Much of our difficulty centers around the fact that we do not know whether we are producing the right products for the right markets. I suspect that in some cases we are actually producing too good a product for the price at which we sell it. Further, we really have no idea of our sales costs and whether or not we are doing the most efficient job possible. I propose that a marketing research unit be set up which will give us data which will help us allocate better our sales resources." The president's reaction to this recommendation was favorable. He indicated, however, that before setting up such a department he would like to have the views of an outside consultant as to how it should be organized. The vice-president in charge of marketing concurred with this recommendation and employed an outside consulting firm to do this job. Their report follows:

> This report was prepared at the request of Mr. James Erickson, Vice-President of Marketing, Olner Manufacturing Company.
> Our firm was directed to present views regarding the following:
>   1. The mission of a marketing research unit within the marketing department of the central headquarters staff of the Olner Company.
>   2. The organization and operation of such a unit with particular reference to the activities that such a unit should undertake and the kinds of people needed to perform these activities.

To accomplish the above objectives, it was necessary to study the marketing needs and organization of the company. Thus, it was important to know what personnel was doing what marketing research work, if any, and what difficulties the various divisions were experiencing owing to a lack of marketing information.

Objectives of a Marketing Research Unit

The main or central objectives of such a unit would be to provide management with information that would help them make "better decisions." It would operate solely on a staff basis and would, of course, have no line responsibilities. The unit should not just collect information but should organize it in such a way as to present management with recommendations for action. This is an important point since otherwise the unit will turn into merely a statistical unit. In other words, a plea is made for the development of a unit staffed with sufficiently high caliber persons to counsel management on marketing problems.

A quick study of the activities of the various Olner divisions reveals that marketing management in these activities does not have the information by which they can lay down how the firm's resources should be used. Lacking this information, they are unable to set up a detailed plan whereby such basic strategies as product and product line, personal selling, advertising, dealer organizations, and price are integrated on a total basis. Nowhere did our analyst find any evidence whereby the individual divisions were attempting to identify the various segments of the markets in which they sell. Nor did we find that the product and product line were being considered in light of the needs of the individuals comprising these various market segments. Channels of distribution have not received any real attention by anyone in the organization for quite some period of time. Thus, it is possible that a considerable overlap exists among the various divisions. Some integration work is probably needed in the foreseeable future. Personal selling activities are not spelled out clearly nor, for that matter, are sales territories. While individual salesmen in some divisions fill out a call report, no detailed analysis is made from these records. No sales analysis of any detailed type is even being attempted. While quotas are assigned individual salesmen, these figures have been determined largely on a historic basis.

None of the Olner divisions have any marketing research personnel assigned to the marketing departments. Obviously the sales managers do not have the time or the specialized talents to do either sales analysis or marketing survey work. It is therefore suggested that a marketing research unit be set up at corporation headquarters to prepare detailed marketing plans for all divisions. These would be submitted for approval by the Olner vice-president in charge of marketing. These plans would then be reviewed by this individual and modified where necessary. They would then be passed up the line to the president who would, in turn, take these matters up in the presence of the vice-president in charge of marketing with each of the divisions' vice-presidents and their marketing staffs.

Generally speaking, this new unit would activate all types of marketing research projects, although the following would be the most important: (1) product research, (2) market research, (3) sales organization research, (4) channels of distribution research, (5) advertising research. We recommend strongly that the unit have as its operating head a man with the title "Director of Marketing Research and Sales Planning." This individual would, of course, report to Olner's vice-president in charge of marketing.

In the long run, the unit would be organized so that a senior analyst would be in charge of the research work carried on for each division. For the most part, the sales analysis and planning work, using sales record data obtained largely from accounting, would tend to dominate the work load and activities of the unit. Thus, the research director will, of necessity, have to be skilled in such work. This will call for a knowledge of the marketing operations of the various divisions plus skills in accounting, forecasting, budgeting, and statistics.

Because of the heterogeneity of the company product line, individual industry experience will probably be an important factor in the selection of those individuals who will specialize in working on the activities of the individual divisions. In the long run, the unit should break down into two major divisions: (1) sales planning and (2) survey research—with a specialist in charge of each. In connection with the survey work, it is not anticipated that the corporation would or should undertake its own work. Rather, such work should be farmed out to local research firms. A specialist, however, in survey work should supervise and "ride herd" on such projects.

Initially, the company should employ a limited staff to "get off the ground." It is urged that a research director be hired plus an associate research director to head up the sales planning work. In addition, it is thought that at least four analysts should be employed plus three typists. It is not recommended that a survey specialist be hired at this time. The first thing to do is to "mine" the information which is currently available within the division and within the accounting department of the corporate headquarters. The annual out-of-pocket salary costs for the above personnel are estimated as follows:

Research director................	$25,000
Section chief....................	15,000
4 Analysts at $8,000 to $9,000 each................$32,000–	36,000
3 Secretaries and/or clerical workers at $4,000 each.................	12,000
Total...................$84,000–	88,000

Assuming that the general principles contained in this report are accepted, it is urged:

1. That departmental responsibilities or missions be detailed for this new unit.
2. That job descriptions be prepared for each position in the new unit.
3. That specifications or profiles be prepared for the individuals to fit these positions.
4. That a final departmental budget be prepared which would include allocation of overhead costs.

Once the above steps have been undertaken, then plans should be drawn up as to how to proceed to hire personnel, the physical facilities required to house this staff, the operating protocol needed to establish the department and make it operational, and the control procedures needed by the vice-president in charge of marketing to administer the unit. This report does not undertake to accomplish these things simply because it was not thought wise to go any further before some over-all acceptance of the ideas expressed throughout this report was forthcoming.

Should the vice-president in charge of marketing accept the recommendations made by the consulting firm relative to the formation and organization of a marketing research unit?

B. Co-ordinating Marketing and Other Activities

63

HENRY RESEARCH CORPORATION

THE HENRY RESEARCH CORPORATION produced an extensive line of non-destructive magnetic testing equipment for use in a wide variety of manu-facturing, maintenance, and repair functions in industry. The expressed policy of the company was not to sell a testing instrument as such but to sell a means whereby a customer could solve a problem. It had always been difficult to co-ordinate the company's marketing department and its research and engineering department because of the technical nature of the testing instruments and the necessity of constantly developing new instruments and modifying existing ones to suit individual customers' needs. The importance of proper co-ordination between these depart-ments was emphasized by a problem brought about by the introduction by Henry Research in 1954 of a completely new line of testing equip-ment generally described as "electronic." By 1958 it was obvious that this new line of equipment had not lived up to sales expectations. Research, engineering, and sales expenses devoted to the line in 1957 alone amounted to $420,000, while total sales of electronic equipment were only $358,000 in the same year. In 1957 sales of all electronic testing equipment were approximately 3 per cent of the company's total sales. Table 1 shows sales of electronic testing equipment by year. Despite the poor results to date, the management was convinced that electronic equipment had a large potential.

Henry Research Corporation was founded in 1929 by Mr. V. M. Danby, a physicist and consulting engineer who developed a magnetic dust inspection method that conclusively located cracks in oil well pipe. The company grew rapidly, and company officials pointed with pride to the fact that it furnished testing instruments to practically every manufacturing industry. Many products, ranging from aircraft to shotguns,

TABLE 1

SHIPMENTS OF ELECTRONIC EQUIPMENT BY YEAR

Year	Sales
1954	$228,000
1955	232,000
1956	262,000
1957	358,000
1st half of 1958	278,000

had to be tested during manufacture and overhaul to locate any breaks or weak points that might endanger the life or property of the purchaser. Henry Research furnished a nondestructive, economical test for this purpose. Other inspection processes were developed for use with newer metals, such as aluminum, magnesium, bronze, tungsten carbide, and even certain ceramics and glass.

Through the years, as the company had grown, the sales personnel or field engineers had had the responsibility for recognizing their customers' needs for inspection as their customers developed new products. It was the responsibility of the sales engineers to advise their respective branch and regional sales managers of new problems existing in customers' plants. These needs were discussed with the marketing vice-president and the technical co-ordinator, who appraised the needs and passed them on to the research and engineering department. When a problem was thus passed on from the field, it was often difficult for the marketing vice-president to appraise the importance of the new development on which a customer might be working. Many times a customer's enthusiasm for a new or modified type of testing instrument would have no relationship to possible future demands for such an instrument, even though the research and engineering department could develop a satisfactory answer for the particular customer's problem.

A typically difficult field was that of aircraft manufacturing. As air speeds became greater, the need for testing engines and airframe parts became more critical. Often the Henry Research field engineers were urged by their customers to develop testing methods and instruments for assemblies or parts that might be in only the developmental stage, and at such a stage even aircraft manufacturers could not tell whether contracts would be obtained in a volume sufficient to support development of new testing instruments.

As a result of the difficulty of estimating sales potential for possible new testing methods, the amount of emphasis given to new projects by the marketing department in passing them to research and engineering depended to a large degree on the judgment of the marketing vice-president or the technical co-ordinator. This in turn was influenced by the ability of the sales engineers to "sell" the idea to their superiors.

Another difficulty often encountered in co-ordination between the marketing and the research and engineering departments was that, after a problem had been passed to research and engineering, priority might be determined by that department's interest in the problem or by whether it thought that it would have a reasonable chance of coming up with a solution quickly and easily. In other situations it might approach a problem "on its own," without having received any specific indication from the marketing department as to the potential market for such a product or testing method.

In the early 1950's the company's research department was attracted to the new electronic testing equipment as a potentially profitable related field. This method of testing, known as "eddy current testing," had been developed by a German physicist, Dr. Foerster, and was relatively unknown in the United States. According to Dr. Foerster, the method had been researched for a period of some twenty years and by 1950 was in use commercially in numerous industrial plants in Germany. The principles of this electronic type of testing were based upon the measurement of the impedance and phase relationships of electric current passing through coils. The amount of impedance depended upon the physical properties of the material being tested. Such testing instruments, it was claimed, not only could easily locate defects, both surface and subsurface, but could detect variations in diameter, grade, tensile strength, and hardness. The obvious relationship of eddy current testing to the company's line and the description of its potential led the company to enter into a patent and licensing agreement with Dr. Foerster whereby his equipment could be distributed by Henry Research in the United States.

The company dominated the magnetic testing field; as a result, there was little competitive pressure on the development of new testing methods. The electronic testing field was different—there were more competitors and Henry Research was less well established. If the company delayed in developing an electronic testing method for a new product, there was a real risk that a competitor would beat them to it.

Initially, numerous types of Dr. Foerster's instruments were imported, and a research team was set up to determine what products could be tested by the new instruments and what modifications would have to be made so that they would be commercially applicable for use by industrial plants in the United States. It was not long before the conclusion was reached that, although basic theoretical work had progressed in Europe for over twenty years, most of the testing instruments as imported were

EXHIBIT 1

HENRY RESEARCH ORGANIZATION DURING INTRODUCTION AND DEVELOPMENT OF EDATEST
LINE OF ELECTRONIC TESTING INSTRUMENTS

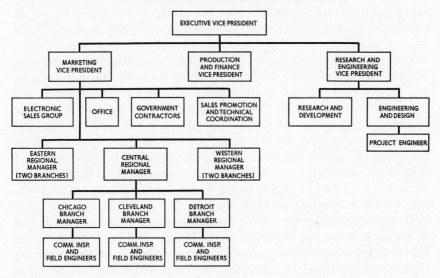

not suitable for commercial distribution to any of the company's customers.

Modifications were made, and much field work was done by the research and Edatest engineering department, which proceeded energetically with the problems of making the Edatest line, which included all eddy current types of instruments applicable to customers' needs. The problems involved were so complex that about three-fourths of all research and engineering personnel were devoting full time to the Edatest line, leaving only about one-fourth to work on other company problems. In addition, a special electronic sales group of three men was organized to work with customers in adapting Edatest testing methods to their problems.

Henry Research was organized in three principal departments, namely, marketing; production and finance; and research and engineering. An abbreviated organization chart as of the time of the introduction and development of the Edatest line is shown in Exhibit 1.

The marketing department was responsible for all sales and was divided into three regions: eastern, central, and western. Each region was in charge of a regional sales manager. Under each region were two or three branches out of which the salesmen, called "field engineers," worked. A total of twenty-seven field engineers worked out of the seven branches. Each branch manager was responsible for the field engineers in his branch and for at least one, and in some cases for as many as four, commercial laboratories that tested products brought in from the field.

A field engineer was typically a well-trained technical man, whose salary ranged from $8,000 to $15,000 per year. He necessarily had to have a great deal of technical knowledge to appraise a particular customer's problem and determine whether Henry Research had a type of testing equipment that would suitably solve the problem or whether he should call on the research and engineering department for help in developing a new or modified type of equipment to solve the customer's problem.

Officials of Henry Research believed that the problem confronting the company concerning the large expenditure for sales and for research and development and the relatively small sales of Edatest equipment not only was important in itself but was indicative of the fact that better co-ordination between marketing and research and development was needed. The company, by the very nature of its products, had always been heavily research oriented, and the history of its new products had been that a great deal of money had to be expended in developing a new or modified method of testing to suit a customer's need before sales volume of any magnitude could be developed.

It was felt that, in the case of the development of the electronic line of testing instruments, too much of the impetus had come from the research and development department and not enough from the marketing department. The special electronics sales group, which had been set up to survey customers' needs for electronic testing equipment, had worked in a slightly "ivory-tower" atmosphere and had not sought the opinions of the field engineers (general salesmen) or kept them advised of details of developments. This situation apparently had tended to make the field engineers less interested in the new line of electronic equipment. The salesmen concentrated on the older lines of equipment, for which a demand was established and with which they were acquainted.

It was decided that organizational changes were necessary to correct the situation that had been highlighted by the electronic equipment experience. Exhibit 2 shows an abbreviated organization chart incorporating the principal changes that management decided were needed to develop better co-ordination between the marketing and the research and engineering departments. Principal changes in the marketing department were the establishment of a market research department, the transferring of electronic technical co-ordination from sales promotion to a separate section under research and engineering, and the elimination of the special electronics sales group.

EXHIBIT 2

HENRY RESEARCH ORGANIZATION, REFLECTING PRINCIPAL CHANGES TO EFFECT BETTER
CO-ORDINATION BETWEEN MARKETING AND RESEARCH AND ENGINEERING

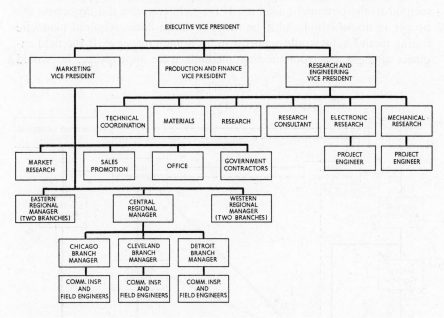

Special provision was made for better liaison between the marketing and the research and engineering departments concerning the new electronic lines by the creation of three new positions known as "regional electronic specialists." Their position in the organizational setup is indicated in Exhibit 3.

The duties of the technical co-ordinator did not change in the reorganization but were made into a full-time job and transferred to the research and engineering department. The technical co-ordinator was to maintain records of all applications, successful and unsuccessful, of the company's electronic testing methods; to furnish information on these applications and all other pertinent technical data to the field engineers, the regional electronic specialists, the sales promotion manager, and the regional and branch managers; to pass information from the field on customer problems and testing applications to the technical departments in the research and engineering department; and to pass requests for research from the field to the proper technical department, following research developments, and pass results back to the field.

Regional electronic specialists would set up testing laboratories in each sales region to work on customer problems. If they developed a successful testing method for a given problem, they were to report this to the technical co-ordinator, who would inform both the marketing and the research and the engineering departments.

It was expected that the new organization would function as follows: if a field engineer (salesman) found a testing problem that Henry Research had solved before, he would attempt to sell the company's testing method to the potential customer. If the field engineer did not know the proper testing method and if he thought the problem required magnetic testing methods, he would report it to his branch manager. If the field engineer thought electronic testing methods were appropriate, he would

EXHIBIT 3

SALES-ENGINEERING LIAISON—ELECTRONICS

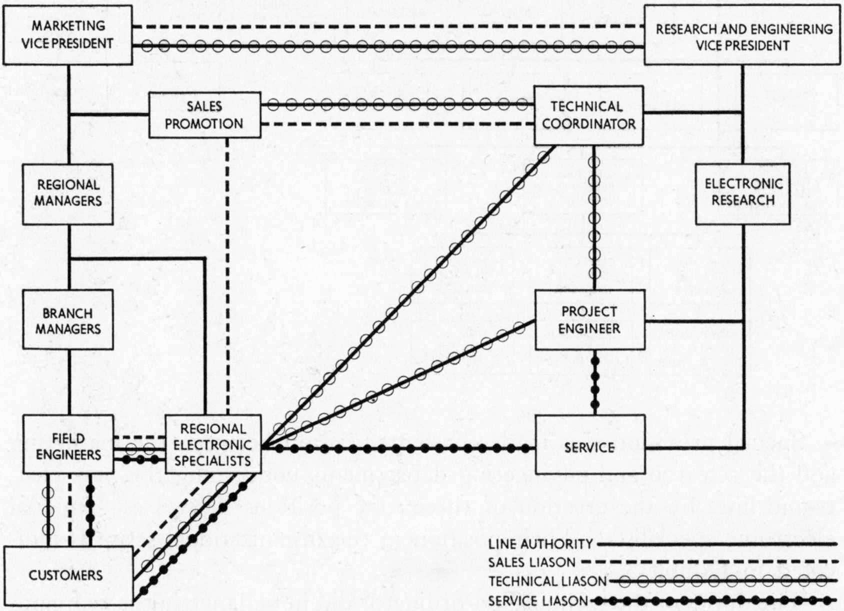

report the problem to the regional electronic specialist, who would attempt to solve it by work in his laboratory or at the customer's plant. If the field electronic specialist could not solve the problem, he and the field engineer would report the problem to the branch manager, from where it would be handled in the same manner as were magnetic testing problems.

Problems forwarded to branch managers were passed on to the regional managers, who would attempt to estimate the following:

1. Were Henry Research testing methods applicable to the problem?
2. How large was the potential sales volume for Henry Research?
3. What was the probability of technical success in solving the problem?
4. What was the probable cost of technical development?

If his estimates of the foregoing questions were favorable, the regional manager passed the problem to the marketing research department for a more formal estimate of the sales potential. This report was then submitted to the marketing vice-president, who sent it to the research and engineering department.

Would the new organization improve co-ordination between the marketing and the research and engineering departments?

64

BISSELL COMPANY

FOR EIGHTY years the Bissell Company produced and sold only one product—a carpet sweeper. During this time its sweeper dominated the market and was a household item in virtually every home in the country. The company was very stable, or even staid. The design of the carpet sweeper changed little over the years. It was a durable product, so that repeat sales were many years apart. In 1957 a change in management brought a new outlook to the firm, and a policy of expansion was adopted. A number of new products were added in rapid succession. As a result, it was necessary to consider the best type of organization to handle a rapid expansion of the product line.

In the past the firm had been a manufacturing organization, but with the new management it became a marketing organization. The president was the chief operating executive. Reporting to him were four vice-presidents—one each for research and development, manufacturing, and marketing, and one as controller. To guide the new product development of the company, a product committee was established. This was made up of the president of the company as chairman, each of the vice-presidents as named above, and the director of new products, who was secretary of the committee. The director of new products was made directly responsible for the co-ordination of all factors in new product development— from the original conception of new ideas to the final introduction of the product as a regular item in the Bissell line. This included responsibility for styling and packaging and the administration of the product budget, which was established at 2 per cent of gross sales.

As an initial step, the Product Committee established criteria that new products would have to meet before they would be added to the Bissell line. Criteria were as follows: (1) fulfill a need to the consumer; (2) fulfill a need to the trade; that is, it must be profitable to the dealer, it must be interesting enough to consumers to encourage interest and traffic, and it must be packaged in a way that would be easy for the dealers to handle and attractive to consumers; (3) fit into Bissell's existing channels of distribution; (4) incorporate a radical improvement to an existing product; and (5) be capable of manufacture at a reasonable cost.

An example of how the product development program worked within the limits of the organization described above and the standards established as guides can be seen following the development of one of Bissell's new products—a combination vacuum cleaner and floor scrubber. As the result of a marketing research project on consumer household cleaning habits, two ideas were developed. One was that the old Bissell carpet sweeper was likely to be replaced at some time in the future by an electric carpet sweeper, since more and more household chores were being done by electricity. A second, and at this point unrelated, idea was that scrubbing floors was still done in a primitive manner by most housewives; that is, they got down on their hands and knees with a bucket of water and a scrub brush. In September, 1958, the research and development department was given the job of developing products to fill these two needs. They were given a target date of February 1, 1959.

In its early work the research and development department concentrated on an electric vacuum cleaner. While working with an industrial design firm on this project, the department people began to see a possibility for a combination electric vacuum cleaner and floor scrubber. They had only crude ideas about how this could be done, but there seemed to be a definite indication that a combination was practicable. This idea was brought back to the Product Committee for evaluation. After consideration, the Product Committee made the decision to move ahead in the attempt to develop a combination electric vacuum cleaner and floor scrubber. By this time it was January 1, 1959. Since time was getting short, a stylist was added to the research development team and the target date for a fully stylized working model was moved up to February 15. This date was met.

The working models and drawings were then turned over to the engineering department for rough costing and tooling analysis. This work was completed by March 1. The marketing department was asked to develop a forecast of sales, which it found to be a very difficult task, since such a product had never been sold on the consumer market. The task was complicated by the fact that the unit as designed was capable of being sold either as a vacuum cleaner, as a floor scrubber separately, or as a combination unit. This made it necessary to estimate how many of each of the units would be sold separately and how many in the two-in-one combination. These rough estimates of sales and of production costs were returned to the Product Committee, which decided to go ahead. Research and development was directed to have a finished product from an engineering and styling standpoint by May 1, so that the manufacturing department could commence tooling by July 1. A new team, consisting of a member of the research and development department, an industrial design consulting firm, and a stylist, was formed to work toward these goals. It was decided to have the stylist work directly with the engineering people so that there would be no need for adjustment at the end, either to change the engineering aspects to meet the style needs, or to change the style to meet engineering problems. This new team was able to complete its work by the May 1 deadline, and twelve prototypes were made.

At this point, packaging design was started. A packaging committee was established consisting of the director of new products as chairman and representative of the Product Committee, a representative from the research and development department, and the advertising manager. This committee had responsibility for developing a package for the product. The final decision on the new package, however, was to be made by the Product Committee. The director of new products was expected to keep the Packaging Committee aware of any developments as far as the design of the product was concerned and to keep the Product Committee aware of the progress on development of the package.

The twelve prototypes that were available were divided between two uses: four were left with the research and development department for continued tests on such things as water lift, motor life, effectiveness in cleaning, and dust bag design. The other eight were sent to the company's advertising agency for test by a panel of fifty housewives. The research and development department found some serious problems in their further tests of the product. The life of the motor was not sufficiently long, the filter bag did not fit properly, and the scrubber foot was not correct. Similarly, the consumer tests brought in many consumer dissatisfactions that had not been anticipated: the unit was too heavy, the vacuum did not glide easily enough, and the scrubber left some residue on the floor after use. These problems were brought back to the Product Committee, which now had a difficult decision. If production was postponed any longer, the original target date for introducing the product could not be met. This difficulty was magnified when at this point the Hoover Company—the biggest name in standard vacuum cleaners—announced the introduction of a new product, a floor scrubber. If the product were taken to the board of directors for approval at this time, so that tooling could be commenced on June 1, the product could be introduced in the early spring of 1960. This meant, however, that a risk was being taken that the problems that had been discovered could be solved by the research and development department. The Product Committee decided to take this risk and presented the product to the board of directors for approval. The board granted this approval with one qualification—no product was to be shipped until another consumer panel had tested the revised products.

While the description of the development of the combination vacuum cleaner and floor scrubber indicates a great deal of work and concentration on this product, it should be noted that, at the same time, the director of new products had fifty projects in progress at some stage or another. It was planned that ultimately the department would have from 150 to 200 projects in the program at all times. Of course, many of these would never become fully developed products. Included in such products would be redesign and change in construction of existing products.

The responsibilities of the director of new products were established as follows: (1) to relate company objectives to new product ideas and recommend new product objectives and programs, (2) to direct and coordinate the product development program in all stages in all departments, (3) to develop classifications of new products, (4) to direct all marketing consumer research, (5) to direct all company styling, (6) to supervise company packaging, and (7) to distribute all information on newly developed products and new packages.

Should Bissell make any changes in its organization for new product development?

65

HYDRAULIC SYSTEMS COMPANY

HYDRAULIC SYSTEMS specialized in the development of control systems for airplanes. It was necessary for the company to maintain adequate testing facilities for the products it manufactured; however, differences in the character, extent, and timing of each test caused variations in the utilization of major testing equipment. This equipment represented an investment of approximately $1.5 million. Since the company had excess capacity for all the major types of test (Table 1), the management decided to investigate the possibility of doing contract testing for other industries and the government. Executives estimated that, if current excess testing capacity could be utilized fully for outside testing, the maximum revenue would be about $370,000 annually.

As a result of these preliminary investigations, the management of Hydraulic Systems engaged a management consulting firm to make a study of the market for contract testing, pricing practices, and other related problems that would be encountered in entering this market. The consultants submitted a final report that contained the following information:

I. *Evaluation of Testing Facilities*

The current mix of testing equipment is more extensive than that of almost any other testing laboratories in Philadelphia. The only other more complete testing laboratories are those of the Pennsylvania Testing Company. Several pieces of testing equipment are unique in this area. They are the air-flow equipment, the vibration facilities, and the leak tester. Sufficient space is available now for outside testing. In addition, through rearrangements of equipment, another 1,000 square feet of floor space could be made available.

II. *Personnel Requirements*

Additional personnel would be required at higher operating levels, just how many would be determined by type of outside testing done and the capacity for present individuals to absorb increased work load. The testing department at present is operating at 70 per cent of capacity with thirty-six people. It is estimated that an additional five people will be needed for each 10 per cent increase in operating level.

TABLE 1

HYDRAULIC SYSTEMS' TESTING CAPABILITIES AND
CURRENT UTILIZATION

Test	Per Cent Internal Utilization	Per Cent Available for Outside Testing
Functional:		
Air-flow and pneumatic-pressure cycle	36	64
Hydraulic tests	32.5–82*	18–67.5
Hydraulic impulse	63	37
Leak tests	100	..
Vibration tests	100	..
Cycle tests, applied motion	100	..
Environmental:		
Temperature effects:		
Low	23–65*	35–77
High	82	18
Vacuum tests	18	82
Salt-spray tests	27	73
Shock tests	9	91
Mechanical properties:		
Tensile tests	45–54*	46–55
Fatigue tests	67.5	32.5
Metallurgical tests	18–90*	10–82
Chemical tests:		
Alloy analysis	54	46
Chemical analysis	54	46

* Utilization varied for different pieces of equipment.

III. *Potential Dollar Volume Capacity for Outside Tests per Year*

Potential dollar volume from outside testing per year is estimated to be in excess of $370,000 (Table 2). Current prices charged for testing services range from $50 per hour for air-flow tests to $15 per hour for all other tests. The greatest dollar potential is from air-flow tests because of the higher price and the large excess capacity available. Table 2 shows the potential volume for each type of test based on a 40-hour workweek, 250 workdays a year, and an average down time of 2 per cent per machine. Table 2 also assumes optimum scheduling. Scheduling problems could reduce this potential by 20 per cent or more. Company officials estimate that the future testing needs of the company will not increase appreciably, so present usage levels will not change much in the long run.

TABLE 2

CURRENT MAXIMUM POTENTIAL DOLLAR VOLUME CAPACITY FOR OUTSIDE
TESTS PER YEAR

Test	Average Availability of Equipment (Hrs./Yr.)	Charge/Hr.	Dollar Potential
Functional:			
Air-flow and pneumatic-pressure cycle........3,060		$50	$153,000
Hydraulic tests...........................2,322		15	34,830
Hydraulic impulse........................ 504		15	7,560
Leak testing............................. ..		15	..
Vibration testing......................... ..		15	..
Cycle testing............................ ..		15	..
Environmental:			
Temperature effects......................2,358		15	35,370
Vacuum tests...........................1,494		15	22,410
Salt-spray tests..........................1,224		15	18,360
Shock tests.............................1,584		15	23,760
Mechanical properties:			
Tensile testing..........................1,548		15	23,220
Fatigue testing.......................... 414		15	6,210
Metallurgical testing.....................3,132		15	46,980
Chemical:			
Alloy analysis........................... ..*		15	..
Chemical inspection...................... ..		15	..
Total potential...$371,700			

* Additional equipment required for outside alloy analysis.

IV. Contract Testing Markets and Needs that Can Be Met by Hydraulics Systems' Present Facilities

Contract testing in the United States is performed by the government and its military agencies, universities, research and development firms, and commercial testing laboratories, which are either independent firms or divisions of manufacturing companies. Hydraulic Systems' testing operation would fall in the latter category, and the company's market would be that now served by commercial testing laboratories. Commercial testing laboratories currently perform about $200 million of contract testing per year, which includes all testing, much of which is outside the scope of Hydraulic Systems' present facilities. The market served by these commercial laboratories consists of two segments, testing sponsored by industrial concerns, either privately or under government subcontracts, and prime contract testing for the government.

In a survey conducted among users of contract testing, no important needs for additional outside testing facilities were uncovered. Industrial and government purchasers of outside testing reported that they had little difficulty in finding sources to meet their needs. Several firms reported some dissatisfaction with specific services of outside testing laboratories. Those services mentioned as unsatisfactory were: (1) the time required to obtain test results and (2) the failure of the laboratory to explain or interpret the test results.

There are twenty-five testing laboratories in the Philadelphia area that can be considered as potential competitors of Hydraulic Systems Company. The company, however, has a wider range of testing equipment than any of the other laboratories have, and the air-flow, vibration, and leak-testing equipment are unique in this area. The market is competitive, and testing will have to be sold aggressively, since most business will be obtained by capturing it from other testing laboratories.

The results of a survey conducted among metal-using firms indicate that the market area for Hydraulic Systems is limited to a 500-mile radius around Philadelphia. For reasons of either control or shipping costs, most companies consider 500 miles as the maximum distance they will go for testing. Further considerations of the market are therefore limited to this area.

Between 45 per cent and 50 per cent of the metal-using firms contacted reported using outside testing facilities in the past twelve months. The survey indicated that there was an element of irregularity in testing needs in the sense that these needs cannot be forecast, which might pose problems in scheduling. None of the firms indicated any seasonal patterns in their testing needs. The total volume of testing done in the area 500 miles around Philadelphia is estimated at just under $3 million. Hydraulic Systems' potential dollar volume capacity represents 14 per cent of this figure (Table 3).

TABLE 3

ESTIMATED INDUSTRIAL EXPENDITURES FOR TESTS THAT COULD BE DONE BY
HYDRAULICS SYSTEMS COMPANY

(Area within a 500-Mile Radius of Philadelphia)

| | | Hydraulic Systems' Capacity | |
Test	Outside Expenditures Per Year	Dollar Volume	As Per Cent of Total Expenditures
Functional	$ 783,000	$195,390	25
Environmental	706,500	99,900	14
Mechanical	1,098,000	76,410	7
Total	$2,587,500	$371,700	14

Government expenditures for testing on a contract basis were difficult to obtain because of security restrictions, lack of centralized information, and recent drastic revisions in military plans. Estimates by one government official and published information of the National Science Foundation place total government testing expenditures between $75 and $125 million annually. Geographical limitations are not a major factor in government testing. Expenditures for tests that fall within the limitations of Hydraulic Systems' laboratory are estimated at between $10 and $40 million per year. One army development center near Philadelphia estimates its expenditures last year for outside tests at $750,000.

Potential customers for Hydraulic Systems' testing laboratory lie primarily in the metalworking industries. Following is a list of industries rated as good prospects:

Aircraft
Aircraft engines and parts
Pumps and compressors
Refrigeration equipment
Machine tool accessories, precision tools
Blowers and fans
Collapsible tubes

Iron and steel foundries
Mechanical power transmission equipment
Valves and fittings
Materials handling equipment
Steel springs
Laundry equipment
Furnaces and ovens

V. *Pricing Contract Testing*

Other testing laboratories are currently using three pricing methods: standard prices, hourly rates, and negotiated prices. The negotiated prices are most common (Table 4).

TABLE 4

PRICING METHODS OF OTHER TESTING LABORATORIES

(Based on Information from 50 Reports)

	Per Cent Usage
Negotiated contract	63
Hourly rate	17
Standard price	11
Answer not definite	9

Specific prices are available from price lists issued by other testing laboratories. Standard prices have been established for many types of tests that occur rather frequently and are subject to established government specifications. Prices quoted on an hourly rate basis usually specify a rate for man-hours plus a rate for machine-hours (Table 5).

TABLE 5

PRICES QUOTED BY SPECIFIC TESTING FIRMS

Testing Firm Company	Test	Price
A	Tensile	$ 5.50/machine-hour
	Chemical	13.62/hour
B	Vibration	12.50/technician-hour
	Shock	15.00/engineering-hour
		10.00/machine-hour
C	Routine tests	8.50/engineering-hour
D	Hydraulics	10.00/engineering-hour
		5.00/machine-hour
E	Vibration, shock,	9.25/man-hour
	Tension, compression	6.50/machine-hour
F	Bending	6.10/per hour
G	Hydraulic	10.70/engineering-hour
		3.30/machine-hour
H	Hardness	1.50/test
	Tukon hardness	10.00/test
	Tensile (steel or brass)	3.50/machine-hour
	Tensile (aluminum or magnesium)	2.50/machine-hour
	Salt spray	15–30.00/test
	Bending	2.50/machine-hour
I	Salt spray	10.00/test
	Vibration	50.00/machine-hour
	Shock	50.00/machine-hour
J	Vibration	285–855.00/test
	Shock	54.00/machine-hour
	Sand and dust	60–72.00/test
Gov't. testing	Hardness	21.00/test

Profit markups are not generally available, but from the few laboratories that did reveal their markups, they varied from 4 per cent to 8 per cent of costs in government work and from 6 per cent to 12 per cent of costs for industrial work. These markups are subject to change, depending on a specific situation and the size of the bid.

The consultants recommended that Hydraulic Systems should enter contract testing on a conservative, well-planned, step-by-step basis. No expansion of testing facilities was recommended. Paper work administration, pricing and cost methods, sales training, call lists, and sales material had to be developed prior to entering contract testing. One salesman was considered sufficient to start the program and to carry it through the first year. It was recommended that direct mail solicitation be conducted on a periodic three-month basis. Long-range planning would include the development of a detailed brochure on testing services offered by Hydraulics Systems and the addition of one or more salesmen as business increased. Pricing would be based on insuring a profitable return over the direct costs of the testing. Indirect or overhead costs did not have to be fully covered in order to add to over-all profitability.

Should Hydraulic Systems adopt the consultant's recommendations? Consider the alternatives available to the company.

SECTION V

Putting the Plan into Action

AFTER the firm has determined its market niche, specified its major strategies, and organized to carry out its plan, it is ready to put the plan into action. This calls for doing a number of things, including selecting personnel; delegating responsibility; training, supervising, and paying personnel; working with outside firms, such as advertising agencies and marketing research firms; and storing and shipping the product. These types of activities are the fabric of everyday work and occupy the time of a great many individuals.

Managing the Sales Force

The operation of the sales force breaks down into recruiting, selecting, training, supervising, compensating, and controlling. These are not discrete and independent functions but are interdependent to varying degrees. The manager of the field force performs all these tasks continuously. Since some of these activities may be delegated to regional and even district offices, it is imperative that policies be established to provide for uniformity of action.

The recruiting and selection of salesmen must be related to the job to be accomplished by the sales force. Thus, a job analysis is the first step in the selection process and involves a description of the nature of the selling job and the duties to be performed.

The next step is to determine the characteristics a person should have in order to accomplish the specified duties. This is difficult because there are many different personal characteristics that can affect performance. Some characteristics, such as age, marital status, general health, and race, are easy to measure, but how does one measure a "pleasant personality" or "motivation to do a good job?" Since only rarely will a sales applicant have a near perfect set of the desired characteristics, it is necessary to balance strong against weak points.

Sales managers use a variety of indicators to assess the worth of a man applying for a job as salesman. Such indicators as the man's experience record, education, aptitude test scores, and behavior during one or more interviews are commonly used. The results are frequently compared against a profile of the firm's successful salesmen. No matter what "scientific" selection devices are used, the selection decision is still one of executive judgment and rests heavily on the diagnostic powers of the individuals who interview the candidate.

Most salesmen, when first hired, require some training. They need to know many things about the product and the company as well as how to do their assigned task. Many companies also operate training programs for their experienced salesmen. Obviously, the more complex and dynamic the selling job, the more important it is to have a well-conceived and well-implemented training program. Training programs have a variety of objectives, including imparting knowledge, developing selling skills, helping the individual develop self-confidence, and improving morale. Most companies employ a combination of classroom work and on-the-job training.

The amount and type of day-to-day supervision of the sales force depends upon the complexity of the selling process, the level of competency existing within the sales force, the concentration of accounts or the size of the sales territories, and the extent to which the sales organization is decentralized. Supervision frequently consists of a supervisor traveling with each salesman for a short period of time at intervals to observe how effectively he operates. During such a period the supervisor will do on-the-job training. Many salesmen, especially in concentrated markets, check with their immediate supervisors daily. Salesmen's reports and expense accounts provide management with information that is useful in determining the extent and frequency of supervision required by individual salesmen. Many firms have regular sales meetings at their branch offices, at which subjects of general interest are discussed.

There are many different kinds of sales compensation plans, but there are only three basic types. These are straight salary, straight commission, or a combination of the two. Each has advantages and disadvantages. In determining what compensation plan to use, the company must take into account such factors as the complexity of the plan and the ease with which it can be understood and administered, the incentive it provides, the stability of earnings it affords in both good and bad times, the degree to which it bases the salesman's income on things he controls, the degree to which it encourages economy in the total selling program, whether it discriminates against any group of salesmen, and the degree to which it is based on performance factors that can be measured objectively.

Relations with Advertising Agencies

Firms that use an advertising agency, as virtually all large advertisers do, must select an agency, set performance standards for it, and then determine the agency's performance relative to the standards. This is very difficult because the advertising job does not lend itself to objective measurement.

Relations between a client and its advertising agency represent an increasingly important problem because of the growing integration of advertising with the other marketing strategies and because of the increased size of the advertising appropriation. Many advertising agencies conceive of their jobs as more than creating ads and selecting the media in which they are to run. Some promote themselves as marketing agencies and point to their resources in product planning, merchandising, public relations, and marketing research. Some question whether advertising agencies should attempt to do more than serve as specialists in creating ads and selecting media, although it is clear that agencies cannot perform these tasks effectively in a vacuum; advertising can be accomplished successfully only if it is adapted to, and co-ordinated with, well-thought-out and well-implemented strategies in the other areas.

Many advertisers are not sure what they should receive in return for the 15 per cent commission that they pay, indirectly, to their agencies. Many do not understand why they are charged additional fees for some services. Since the effectiveness of the advertising program is usually difficult to ascertain, some advertisers demand that a certain number of people be assigned to work on their accounts. It is not uncommon for an advertiser to demand certain services "free," for example, marketing research that does not pertain to either copy or media selection. One way to minimize the problem of agency-client relations is for the agency to develop work plans in advance for the advertiser's approval.[1]

Physical Distribution

Physical distribution consists of moving actual goods from the point of production to the point of consumption. This involves decisions as to size and location of stocks, methods of transportation, and procedures for handling orders. These problems are closely related to, and greatly influenced by, channels of distribution problems. If wholesalers are used in the distribution channel, they may carry local stocks that the manufacturer otherwise may have to maintain. Many stock points located throughout the marketing area permit quick delivery to customers but increase costs. Rapid, and usually more expensive, transportation may be used to give quick delivery from central warehousing points. Electrical methods of transmitting and processing data permit more rapid handling of orders. Operations research has been used effectively in recent years to determine the optimum combinations of these factors. In all cases, the firm has the further decision of whether to maintain its own physical distribution facilities or to hire them from public contractors.

---

[1] See Ira W. Rubel, "Toward Better Advertiser-Agency Relations," *Harvard Business Review*, March–April, 1958, p. 111.

A. Managing the Sales Force

1. Field Sales Activities

66

AMERICAN HOSPITAL SUPPLY CORPORATION

THE AMERICAN HOSPITAL SUPPLY CORPORATION was the leading distributor in the United States of hospital supplies, equipment, furnishings, and scientific products. Over a period of years following World War II, the corporation acquired twenty different subsidiary companies and separated its own operation into four major divisions. Each of these divisions maintained a complete sales organization, and several of the subsidiaries had their own sales forces, so that it was possible in any one day for a hospital to be called on by as many as seven different salesmen representing American or one of its divisions or subsidiaries. While the management was convinced that intensive sales effort was important to maintain volume, some executives wondered whether they had gone too far and had too many salesmen calling on customers.

As its name implied, American attempted to handle all types of supplies used by hospitals. This included more than 20,000 different items, about 80 per cent of which were manufactured by nonaffiliated companies. Many of the items were manufactured according to American specifications, to be sold under its own private brand names of Tomac and Chieftain. There was a growing tendency, however, for the company to do more and more manufacturing in its subsidiaries. About 85 per cent of the company's business was in products that were used up or destroyed within a short period of time.

The corporation sold to more than 8,000 different customers throughout the United States, including almost all the hospitals, sanitariums, and related institutions, both public and private. Since some of the products used in hospitals were also used in other institutions and organizations, American had some sales outside the hospital field. Sales to industrial laboratories, for example, were growing.

Generally speaking, American's line could be classified into four categories: hospital supplies, hospital furnishings and equipment, intravenous products, and scientific products. The hospital supplies category included such things as dressings; sutures; various glass, wood, paper, plastic, steel,

376

and rubber goods; soaps, brushes, and other cleansing materials; operating and nursing supplies; surgical instruments; diagnostic instruments; surgeons' and nurses' gowns; operating room shoes; tableware for patients' food service; special fluids; hypodermic syringes and needles; thermometers; and a wide variety of miscellaneous items.

Hospital equipment included such items as operating tables, lighting equipment, sterilizers, stretchers, wheel chairs, oxygen equipment, regulators and control devices, receptacles of all types, and medical-surgical furniture for many uses. Hospital furnishings included all the items needed to equip wards, private rooms, offices, staff quarters, and various other functional departments. Beds, chairs, draperies, linens, pillows, blankets, bedspreads, tableware, and similar items were in this group. Intravenous products were items added directly to the blood stream, such as blood, plasma, and a wide variety of solutions that could carry food or drugs, that is, anesthetics and reladants. These products were packed, ready for use, in disposable sets. Scientific products included all the supplies and equipment needed to furnish laboratories.

The corporation was divided into four sales divisions: the hospital supply division, the scientific products division, the parenteral products division, and the international operations division. The hospital supply division sold the hospital supply and the hospital furnishings and equipment lines. The scientific products division sold the scientific products line, and the parenteral products division handled the intravenous products. The international division was responsible for all foreign operations. In addition to these divisions, there was a separate rehabilitation products department in the hospital supply division. This department specialized in such items as canes, crutches, revolving beds, exercise equipment, and hot packs. The hospital supply division sold these products, but the department had several technical specialists who handled such projects as the equipping of an entire new rehabilitation center.

American's growth had been dramatic. In 1940 sales were only $2.3 million; in 1945, $8.9 million; in 1950, $27.0 million; and by 1959, $77.8 million. The firm had twelve different geographical sales regions; these were located in Atlanta, Boston, Chicago, Columbus, Dallas, Kansas City, Los Angeles, Miami, Minneapolis, New York, Washington, D.C., and San Francisco. At each of these regional offices there were a supply warehouse and at least two sales forces, one representing the hospital supply division and one the scientific products division. The newest division, parenteral products, while not maintaining a staff in all the offices, covered the country through sales representatives. While the sales forces for the different divisions worked out of the same physical facilities, they were entirely separate, with a few minor exceptions.

The twenty wholly owned subsidiaries of the corporation, with their date of acquisition and main type of business, are shown in Exhibit 1. American handled all the leading brands of most products. It tried to get

EXHIBIT 1

WHOLLY OWNED SUBSIDIARIES OF AMERICAN HOSPITAL SUPPLY CORPORATION

Name	Date Acquired	Main Type of Business
Institutional Industries, Inc..	October 6, 1949	Manufactured steel hospital equipment, wheel chairs and furniture distributed by American.
Mealpack Corporation.....	December 1, 1949	Owned rights to and sold vacuum sealed food service equipment, which kept food hot or cold and flavorful for several hours.
Don Baxter, Inc..........	August 1, 1950	Manufactured intravenous solutions, blood bottles and administration sets, and distributed these in 13 western states.
E. & J. Mfg. Co..........	August 1, 1950	Manufactured anesthesia equipment and special apparatus for delivery room and nursery use.
Pharmaseal Laboratories, Inc.....................	August 1, 1950	Marketed plastic intravenous administration accessories and disposable enemas.
Campbell Laboratories, Inc.	July 1, 1953	Merchandised deodorants, body rubs, and other commercial chemical products.
V. Mueller & Co.........	December 31, 1954	Sold instruments, supplies, and equipment to the individual physician and in wholesale, retail, and surgical supply markets.
Star Surgical Instrument & Mfg. Co................	December 31, 1954	Manufactured precision surgical instruments and special surgical equipment.
American Hospital Supply Export Corp.............	January 1, 1955	Marketed hospital and laboratory supplies and equipment in Central and South America, especially on a contract basis.
Dade Reagents, Inc.......	July 1, 1956	Researched and manufactured blood typing serums, synthetic control materials, tubal nutrient solutions, laboratory glassware, and specialties.
American Hospital Supply Corp., Peru.............	October 23, 1957	Handled day-to-day demand for hospital and laboratory supplies and equipment in Venezuela.
Massillon Rubber Co......	January, 1959	Manufactured and marketed surgeons' gloves and rubber accessories.
Pharmaseal Mfg. Co.......	May 8, 1959	Manufactured plastic parts for disposable syringe and needle units.
Fisher & Burpe Division, Amer. Hosp. Supply Corp. (Canada) Ltd.............	October 31, 1959	Marketed hospital and laboratory supplies and equipment in Canada.
Amer. Hosp. Supply Corp., International, S.A.........	November 23, 1959	A Panamanian corporation for distributing hospital and laboratory supplies and equipment in the Caribbean area.
Amer. Hosp. Supply Corp. do Brasil Equipamento Hospitalar, Ltda.............	December 1, 1959	Marketed hospital and laboratory supplies and equipment in Brazil.
Hartman-Leddon Co., Inc..	January 8, 1960	Manufactured chemical and biological testing reagents for laboratory use.

Exhibit 1 *(Cont.)*

Name	Date Acquired	Main Type of Business
Arnar-Stone Laboratories, Inc.....................January 29, 1960		Along with its subsidiary, U.S. Standard Products Co. and U.S.S.P.'s division, the Charles C. Haskell Co., manufactured ethical (prescription) pharmaceuticals.
Hoffman-Pinther & Bosworth, S.A...............March 15, 1960		Marketed hospital and laboratory supplies and equipment in Mexico.

exclusive rights for the sale of all good products and was successful in a large number of cases. Some of these were exclusive with American but were sold in the same form, under a different brand name, by other companies. The relationship between American and its subsidiaries varied with each individual case. The Don Baxter subsidiary manufactured and distributed intravenous solutions, which it sold, through a sales force of more than thirty men, in thirteen western states. American sold the Baxter products exclusively in the thirty-seven other states under a special license agreement. The E. & J. Manufacturing Company products were sold by American as a wholesaler but were also sold by other wholesalers in competition with American. The same was true of Pharmaseal products, which were sold by American and by many competing wholesalers.

American had exclusive distribution rights for Institutional Industries products, but also handled competing lines. American did not handle products of the Mealpack Corporation at all, but its salesmen passed on leads to this subsidiary. When a sale was made on the basis of one of these leads, the salesman who first located the lead received a bonus of 2 per cent of the sale. Several of the fifteen Mealpack salesmen worked out of the American division offices, but they were entirely independent in their operation. Campbell Laboratories made products on order for American exclusively; no one else handled its products.

V. Mueller & Company had its own sales force of about fifty salesmen, who sold to doctors and hospitals. American sold no V. Mueller products but sold competing items to the same hospitals. V. Mueller also operated five retail stores, which sold to doctors and consumers. The Star Surgical Instrument Company manufactured products that were sold only by the V. Mueller Company. V. Mueller also handled other brands that were competitive with the Star products. Star also repaired instruments for surgeons and hospitals all over the United States, and American used it for this purpose. American salesmen sent items by mail to the Star Company for repair. Dade Reagents sold only to the scientific products division of the American Corporation, but the division also handled other items that competed with the Dade products. American had handled Massillon Rubber Company products prior to its acquisition of the company in 1959. This arrangement continued after American acquired control, but Massillon also continued to sell to other wholesalers with which it had done business previously.

Hartman-Leddon Company sold to the scientific products division but also continued to sell to competing wholesalers, as it had done prior to its acquisition. Arnar-Stone Laboratories sold a small part of its products through the hospital supply division but sold the bulk of its production to drug wholesalers, who sold to retail druggists. The most important part of the work of the thirty salesmen, however, was detailing Arnar-Stone products to physicians.

There were only three national hospital supply wholesalers in the United States—two besides American. American was easily the largest, being as large as the other two firms combined. In addition, there were about twenty-five regional wholesalers and perhaps five hundred local suppliers. American had between 6 and 9 per cent of the total market. Most hospitals tended to buy from three or four different wholesale suppliers. American attempted to handle everything needed by a hospital and developed a sizable volume in its contract division, where it undertook to equip entire new hospitals. More than seven hundred new hospitals or additions had been equipped on this basis.

Under the various arrangements with the subsidiary companies, it was possible that seven different salesmen might call on a hospital in one day —one salesman representing the hospital supply division of the corporation, a second representing the scientific products division, a third the Don Baxter subsidiary, a fourth the parenteral products division, a fifth Mealpack Corporation, a sixth V. Mueller and Company, and a seventh the rehabilitation products department of the hospital supply division. In addition, salesmen for other wholesalers might call, selling E. & J., Pharmaseal, Massillon, and Hartman-Leddon products, which were produced by American subsidiaries. In the opinion of American's management, most of the large hospitals who bought from them were aware of the corporation's ownership of these subsidiaries.

American's sales coverage of its customers and prospects had grown more intense over the years. Experiments had shown that by increasing the calls on a given hospital from once a month to once a week, the volume of business secured from that hospital increased almost 400 per cent. This had led the management to push for more frequent calls wherever it was feasible economically. As a result, hospital supply and scientific products salesmen called on every hospital in the United States at least once a month and on 80–90 per cent of all hospitals at least once every two weeks. The hospital supply division had about 150 salesmen in 1959, and the scientific products division about 125. The parenteral products division had 30 salesmen. They did not call so frequently as the salesmen in the other divisions because their products were usually purchased on the basis of annual contracts; however, they tried to call on all hospitals at least once every four weeks and on hospitals with more than 250 beds once every one to two weeks.

The hospital supply division's salesmen tended to call on the purchasing agents in the hospitals and to sell the widest variety of products. When new items were offered, purchasing agents normally sent them to the hospitals' department supervisors, such as the operating room supervisor, the director of nurses, the central supply superintendent, etc. These people would pass on the product and recommend to the purchasing agent that he buy or not buy it. Salesmen, of course, attempted to see these department heads; in some cases they were not able to do this, but in most instances, with some imagination and aggressiveness, they were able to accomplish the contact. In small hospitals, much of the purchasing was done directly by department supervisors. However, this situation was becoming less and less frequent. In large hospitals there tended to be a standards committee, made up of department heads, which reviewed purchasing practices and all new products.

The products sold by the scientific products division were sold primarily to hospital laboratories. These products tended to be purchased separately by the pathologist who headed the laboratory. All orders for these products were processed ultimately through the purchasing agent, but the laboratory products were specialized to the extent that the purchasing agents normally did not know much about them and did not feel competent to deal with them. Thus, scientific products salesmen called on the pathologist, who made the actual buying decisions. In recent years the scientific products division had begun to penetrate the laboratory market of industrial organizations. This represented a large new potential, as these laboratories were three or four times as large in total as laboratories in hospitals. This market was quite different in its methods of purchasing, however, so the scientific products division was experimenting by having three or four men concentrate on developing this new market, while the main sales force continued to sell only to hospital laboratories.

Parenteral salesmen called on hospital administrators, purchasing agents, pharmacists, central supply personnel, anesthesiologists, intravenous nurses, chief surgeons, pediatricians, and other key members of the medical staff. When seeking a contract, the salesmen called on all these people, unless his judgment of a particular situation indicated that some of them were not influential there. He had to be able to discuss the technical use of blood collecting and transfusing equipment as well as the therapeutic values of intravenous solutions. In general, the salesmen needed a premedical background and a strong interest in medicine. The company then gave them from two to three years of training before sending them out by themselves as salesmen.

Intravenous products were sold on the basis of a contract that was really a service agreement, with a strong moral obligation on the part of both the hospital and American to follow the terms of the agreement.

This did not require the hospital to buy all intravenous products from American, but from a price standpoint it was usually advantageous to concentrate purchases with one source. Under one of these contracts, products were shipped on order—usually in lots of 6–8 cases to make up a 100-pound-minimum freight shipment. After obtaining a contract, American instituted a training program at the hospital to acquaint all pertinent personnel with the use of their products. Frequently, these training programs required a team of men working shifts for forty-eight straight hours in order to cover all the hospital personnel on different shifts.

The average order by a hospital supply division salesman was $204 and averaged 2.56 lines on the invoice; the typical scientific products division order was 4.7 lines and $93; and parenteral division orders averaged $400 and 4 lines. Both the hospital supply division and the scientific products division maintained complete stocks of rapidly moving items at all the twelve geographical region offices throughout the country. Furniture and large equipment were shipped direct from the manufacturer. The hospital supply division salesmen were essentially salesmen, but they had to keep up to date on the technical aspects of hospitals and the products used by them. On the other hand, scientific products salesmen were more often technically trained. Many of them had worked in hospital laboratories before coming to work for American Hospital Supply Corporation. Salesmen from both these divisions typically spent about one hour on a call to a large hospital but somewhat longer on a call to a smaller hospital.

Sales of the hospital supply division tended to be larger in the smaller hospitals. Many manufacturers reserved the right to sell to some hospitals directly, and these were typically the large hospitals of 100 beds or more. Johnson & Johnson, for example, sold through American and other wholesalers, but reserved the right to sell directly to hospitals of 100 or more beds when it was necessary to meet price competition. The margin on dressings was likely to be quite low, and, as a result, this sort of product was sold largely on a direct basis. American obtained margins of 12–17 per cent on dressings; other products had wider margins, varying upward from 15 to 25 per cent on furniture. Since the management was convinced that more frequent calls and better coverage invariably resulted in better service to customers and increased sales, the company was constantly studying sales territories. An analysis of an individual salesman's business usually showed that he was getting about 80 per cent of his volume from 20 per cent of his accounts. It was common after making such an analysis to take the 80 per cent of accounts that were furnishing only 20 per cent of the business, and to combine them with part of the 80 per cent from an adjacent territory, and in this way to make a new territory in which a new salesman would be placed.

All the salesmen in the hospital supply division were paid on a straight commission basis. The percentage of commission varied considerably, depending upon the product. On sutures, for example, salesmen obtained 2 per cent on sales, whereas on surgical instruments they received 8 per cent. Generally, the salesman's commission varied according to the gross margin on the item, with the salesman getting about 20 per cent of the gross margin realized by the company. On the average, salesmen in the hospital supply division had annual gross incomes of about $13,000, but out of this they had to pay their own expenses. Some salesmen had gross incomes of as much as $25,000. The salesmen sold at prices established by American and could not vary these prices except with the regional manager's approval. In the case of a few old-time salesmen, this was varied, and they were given permission to adjust prices as they thought necessary to close sales. In the scientific products division, the salesmen were paid a salary plus an expense account with a bonus of from one-half of 1 per cent to 2 per cent for sales over quota.

American Hospital Supply Corporation made its appeal to customers on better service. It tried to maintain stocks on a more local basis and to give faster delivery than did competitors. Orders were shipped on the same day as received if the product was in stock, which about 80 per cent of the products were. No competitor had come close to this service. Items that were not stocked were immediately ordered from the manufacturer for drop shipment. Sales of the scientific products division required a more time-consuming and specialized type of selling than did sales of general hospital supplies and equipment. The initial sale, that is, getting the line established in the hospital, was the most important part of the job. Once the hospital had adopted the line, it usually continued to re-order on a somewhat automatic basis. Scientific product lines were distinctive and required enough specialized know-how that hospitals did not find it practical to switch frequently from one line to another. On some occasions, the scientific product division salesmen were assisted by staff specialists when highly technical knowledge was necessary on a particular sale.

From time to time salesmen reported that some hospital administrators thought that they were giving too much business to American and were inclined to buy from other hospital supply companies in order to distribute the business more evenly among suppliers.

Should American Hospital Supply Corporation combine the various sales forces into one, establish more sales divisions, or leave the organization as it was?

67

INTERNATIONAL MINERALS AND CHEMICAL CORPORATION (B)

THE TWO largest divisions of International Minerals and Chemical Corporation, the potash and the phosphate divisions, had a common market in fertilizer processors and distributors. These divisions accounted for over 50 per cent of the company's sales. They had operated independently, covering the same territory and maintaining separate sales forces. A plan to merge these divisions into one agricultural chemicals division was presented to the board of directors for a decision in 1959.

International Minerals was one of the largest suppliers of raw materials for fertilizers through its potash and phosphate divisions. The com-

TABLE 1

INTERNATIONAL MINERALS AND CHEMICALS CORPORATION
NET SALES AND NET PROFITS: 1953–58

(Millions)

Year	Net Sales	Net Profits
1953	$ 89	$7
1954	94	6
1955	96	6
1956	97	5
1957	106	7
1958	104	5

pany's plant food division sold processed fertilizers and plant foods and was actually in competition with some of the customers of the potash and phosphate divisions. The firm also sold minerals to industry through its industrial minerals division. The feldspar department of the industrial minerals division was the world's largest producer of aluminous materials, feldspar, nepheline, syenite, and aplite, which were essential to the manufacture of ceramics and glass; and of bonding clays and additives for foundry sands. The amino products division manufactured and marketed the company's only consumer product, Ac'cent, a food seasoning. Another of this division's products was L-glutamine, an ingredient essential in the production of Salk polio vaccine. Company net sales and profits for 1953 through 1958 are shown in Table 1.

The firm's organization in 1959 had resulted from its historical growth. International Minerals was a pioneer in the production and processing of phosphate, with fifty years of experience in phosphate mining. At one time the firm had had two phosphate divisions—a phosphate minerals division, which mined and sold raw phosphate, and a phosphate chemicals division, which produced and sold refined phosphate products. These were merged into the phosphate division in 1958. The company had no potash operation until 1940. By that time the phosphate divisions were well established, and a separate division was established for potash.

Fertilizers normally consisted of three basic ingredients—phosphate, potash, and nitrogen. International Minerals was the only firm that supplied both phosphate and potash. It had never produced nitrogen compounds, such as ammonium nitrate, used in fertilizers, because there had been an oversupply of such compounds. The proportion of the three ingredients in a fertilizer was dictated by soil conditions. Most fertilizer manufacturers established a formula based on the soil conditions in the area that they served. A few national fertilizer manufacturers had a formula for general use. In some cases phosphate, potash, or nitrogen compounds were applied directly to the soil as single chemicals rather than in compounds with the others.

The plan to combine International's potash and phosphate divisions was based on several considerations. The first and most important was the economy that could be achieved. Salesmen from the two divisions covered the same geographical territories and, in many cases, called on the same customers. In the phosphate division the minerals department had two salesmen under the domestic sales manager calling on 150 fertilizer accounts, and the chemicals department had four district sales managers (salesmen) under the sales manager of special products calling on 320 fertilizer accounts (Exhibit 1). The potash division had eight sales-

EXHIBIT 1

INTERNATIONAL MINERALS AND CHEMICAL CORPORATION, PHOSPHATE DIVISION
ORGANIZATION CHART

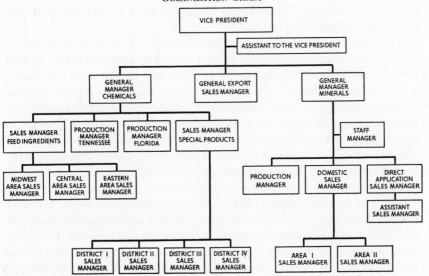

men and four district managers (two of whom were also salesmen) under the manager of agricultural sales, serving 500 fertilizer accounts (Exhibit 2).

Another factor favoring the combination of the two divisions was the fact that certain areas of the country used a large proportion of potash and little phosphate in fertilizers. Some of these areas were not served by International phosphate salesmen because the business available did not justify the cost of a salesman. With salesmen handling both potash and

EXHIBIT 2

INTERNATIONAL MINERALS AND CHEMICAL CORPORATION, POTASH DIVISION
ORGANIZATION CHART

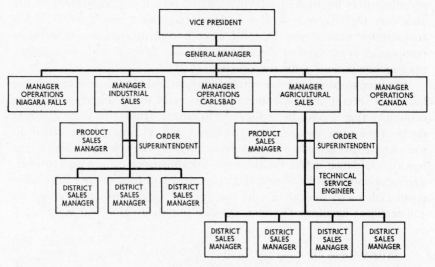

phosphate, however, International would be able to get some of this phosphate business.

The major share of fertilizer sales was made by small local manufacturers whose market areas were limited to a 50 to 250-mile radius around the plant. Management was usually concentrated in one man, the owner, who managed both the plant and sales. There were usually two or three salesmen, often part-time men, who worked on a straight commission basis. These companies sold to retail dealers and directly to farmers in their market areas. Through local advertising, these dealers often developed strong local brand loyalty. There were also several large fertilizer manufacturers who operated on a national basis.

International's salesmen were mainly chemical engineers, with previous experience in the fertilizer field. The company gave them extensive product training, which included a tour of duty at the mining operations and other on-the-job training at different stages of the business. This training was continued over the salesmen's careers to keep them abreast of new developments. In recent years the firm had intensified its training in sales methods and marketing. The salesmen were trained to help customers with general problems of soil testing and fertilizer-mix formulation, but International Minerals' technical service men were usually called in to handle the more technical details. The salesmen averaged from two to five calls per day, depending upon their territories. In most cases they called on the plant owners or, in the case of a larger firm, the purchasing agent or plant manager. Orders were usually for large quantities (e.g., $100,000), to be delivered over a period of from one to three months.

During informal discussions fertilizer customers reported that they would favor being served by a multiproduct firm that would serve them through one sales representative. To check further on this feeling among customers, International Minerals conducted an anonymous survey over a large segment of fertilizer manufacturers. In this survey a majority of companies reported that they favored one-man, multiproduct sales and service.

The introduction of a special promotion called the "Full Orbit" service program in 1958 resulted in a temporary reassignment of salesmen to avoid doubling up on calls in those cases in which a customer bought from two or more divisions. The "Full Orbit" program was designed to give customers help in all aspects of their businesses rather than merely in technical matters. Manuals were developed on market analysis, sales meetings, sales manpower, and advertising and sales promotion. These manuals were available to customers upon request. In addition, International Minerals offered direct help from its staff on transportation and technical matters. Later, this direct help was extended to all subjects. The salesmen and sales managers of International Minerals were given training in the areas covered by the "Full Orbit" program so that they would be able to help customers spot problems and make the best use of the program to solve these problems. As this program continued and became better established, International executives expected that salesmen would become more involved with their customers. This, the executives believed, would make it more important for a customer to deal with only one salesman.

The proposed merger of the phosphate and potash divisions called for the formation of an agricultural chemicals division, to be headed by two new vice-presidents of equal rank, one in charge of sales and one in charge of operations. Each would report directly to the president of the company (Exhibit 3). All mining and production operations would be combined under the vice-president of operations. The four sales departments of the phosphate division—feed ingredients, special products, domestic, and direct application—and the two sales departments of the potash division—industrial and agricultural—would be under the vice-president of sales. Three of these departments would continue as before, with no change in their sales organizations. They were the phosphate feed ingredients department, which consisted of a sales manager and three salesmen; the

EXHIBIT 3

INTERNATIONAL MINERALS AND CHEMICAL CORPORATION ORGANIZATION CHART, INCLUDING
PROPOSED AGRICULTURAL CHEMICALS DIVISION

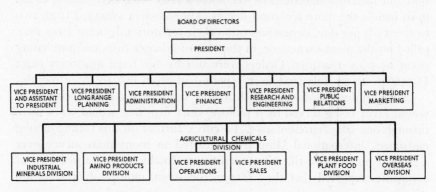

phosphate direct applications department, which consisted of a sales
manager, an assistant sales manager, and two salesmen; and the potash industrial chemicals sales department, which consisted of a sales manager,
three salesmen (district sales managers), and two staff members (Exhibit
4).

A major share of the sales of the phosphate and potash divisions was
made to fertilizer manufacturers through the special products and domes-

EXHIBIT 4

INTERNATIONAL MINERALS AND CHEMICAL CORPORATION, PROPOSED AGRICULTURAL
CHEMICALS DIVISION ORGANIZATION CHART

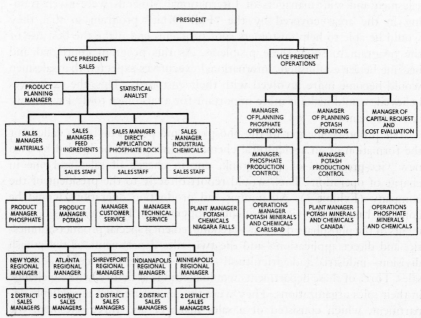

tic sales departments of the phosphate division, and the agricultural sales department of the potash division. It was proposed that these three departments be combined under the sales manager for materials. This department would be enlarged to include a staff of two product managers, one for phosphate and one for potash; a manager of customer service; and a manager of technical service. The district sales organization would include five regional managers and thirteen salesmen (district sales managers).

Management believed that the proposed reorganization would benefit customers in several ways. The customer would get more frequent, personalized sales service; one salesman would sell him all International Minerals' fertilizer ingredients. Orders could be co-ordinated better when the customer worked with one man. A single salesman would also give the customer a better idea of International Minerals as a supplier of a full line of potash and phosphate minerals.

Should the proposed reorganization be adopted?

2. Recruiting and Selecting Sales Force

68

THE EASTERLING COMPANY

LIKE most companies that sell direct to consumers in their homes, The Easterling Company experienced a very high turnover of sales personnel. Among the company's 1,600 salesmen, the annual turnover rate was almost 100 per cent. Since the records showed that salesmen who stayed with the company more than one year tended to make excellent incomes, the vice-president in charge of sales was convinced that a reduction in the turnover rate would be to the advantage of the salesmen as well as to the company. Consequently, he was constantly studying the recruiting, selecting, training, and supervising procedures used by Easterling to see whether they could be improved.

Easterling had five product lines—sterling silver flatware, stainless steel flatware, cutlery, china, and crystal. It did not manufacture any of these products but bought them from various manufacturers. Easterling sold these products on a house-to-house basis through its sales force. The salesmen, however, were not employees of Easterling but rather were independent business men who worked with the company on a yearly contract basis.

Salesmen worked on an "endless-chain" sales procedure. Whenever they made a sale, they asked the customer for names of friends who might be interested in seeing a demonstration of the product. The customer received a small gift, or a reduction in the price of any purchase made, for each name given, if the person(s) whose name she furnished agreed to receive an Easterling sales presentation. Since more than one prospect name was obtained on most sales, the salesmen always had a number of leads on which to work.

Once a prospect's name was obtained, the salesman called for an appointment, mentioning the friend from whom the name was obtained. At the time of the appointment, the salesman showed a basic pattern in each of the five lines and tried to close a sale. The largest single group of customers were young, single working girls of the lower- or middle-income class. The typical sale was about $100, and over a period of years the typical customer bought three different times. On the average, salesmen made a sale at one out of every three presentations. Most sales were made on the installment plan. The salesmen collected a down payment of 10 per cent, which he kept as part payment of his commission. The remainder of the commission was paid by Easterling within one month. The customer made all further payments direct to Easterling.

Salesmen received a straight 20 per cent commission on all sales. On the basis of one sale averaging $100 out of every three presentations, a salesman making eighteen presentations in a week could earn about $120. In addition, a salesman received $15 worth of Easterling merchandise for each new salesman he recruited, if the new person stayed long enough to make some sales. The firm also had contests in which salesmen could win prizes.

Easterling's sales organization was as shown in the accompanying chart.

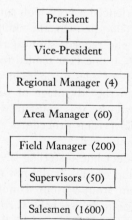

```
┌─────────────────────────┐
│        President        │
└─────────────────────────┘
             │
┌─────────────────────────┐
│     Vice-President       │
└─────────────────────────┘
             │
┌─────────────────────────┐
│   Regional Manager (4)   │
└─────────────────────────┘
             │
┌─────────────────────────┐
│   Area Manager (60)      │
└─────────────────────────┘
             │
┌─────────────────────────┐
│   Field Manager (200)    │
└─────────────────────────┘
             │
┌─────────────────────────┐
│    Supervisors (50)      │
└─────────────────────────┘
             │
┌─────────────────────────┐
│    Salesmen (1600)       │
└─────────────────────────┘
```

Regional managers were paid employees of Easterling and did no selling, but all other personnel were independent contractors. Area managers usually supervised about forty people in territories that included between 1½ and 2 million people. Most area managers worked directly with field managers and supervisors who handled the salesmen, but about 10 per cent of them had no field managers or supervisors below them. Some area managers spent part of their time selling. They received 20 per cent commission on all sales of their own plus 20 per cent on all other sales made in their areas. If a field manager worked under an area manager, the area manager received only 10 per cent on sales other than his own and the field manager got 10 per cent. Area managers were mostly men.

Most field managers did considerable selling as well as supervising. They were generally women. They received 20 per cent commission on all personal sales and 10 per cent on all sales made by salesmen whom they supervised. In some territories supervisors worked with five to seven salesmen under the supervision of field managers. In such instances the supervisors received 20 per cent commission on their personal sales and shared one-half of the 10 per cent given to the field managers. Both the field managers and the supervisors made about 60 per cent of their earnings by personal sales, and the other 40 per cent from the 10 or 5 per cent commission on the sales made by their subordinates.

Area managers not only decided how many field managers they wanted but also selected the actual ones that were hired. Similarly, the field managers determined the number of salesmen and supervisors they wanted, although the problem was usually one of finding enough. Since the supervisory personnel all shared in the total commission in their territories, they all made efforts to recruit new salesmen. The two principal methods used to find prospective salesmen were classified advertising and personal contacts.

Area managers and field managers were encouraged to advertise for recruits in their local papers. Easterling helped them with ideas, but the advertising was at the manager's expense. Exhibit 1 shows the general advice given to managers relative to newspaper advertising.

Exhibit 2 is an example of one of the suggested ads that the company furnished the managers.

Salesmen, field managers, and area managers were urged to ask their friends, acquaintances, and customers for the names of possible salesmen. Exhibit 3 is reproduced from Easterling's *Manager's Manual*. It suggests the procedure to be used for obtaining the names of potential salesmen from customers.

A field or area manager interviewed all prospective salesmen. Easterling furnished an interview guide (Exhibit 4), which it encouraged managers to use in interviewing to determine whether the prospect should be put under contract as a distributor. Easterling also furnished detailed instructions on how to handle such interviews.

The field manager, area manager, or supervisor usually conducted the

EXHIBIT 1

Newspaper Advertising

A steady supply of potential recruits will come through consistent newspaper advertising. Here are some tips on advertising:

Plan your advertising at least a month in advance. Give a month's schedule to the paper—then, if you wish, ask them to telephone you weekly for confirmation.

Save your own time by always inserting "Use of car necessary."

Instead of spending your own time waiting for telephone replies to an ad, pay a woman 25 cents per response handled. Coach her to say: "Mr. Leader is not here right now. I do not know all about the position advertised, but I'll have him call you later this afternoon. What number should he call? And your name, please?"

Keep your ads short. Long ads are considerably more expensive per response.

Consistency is very important. Keep an ad going always, and preferably with little change.

Trick wording doesn't usually pull as well as straightforward phrases.

Say just enough to get interest but don't attempt to tell the whole story. Remember that your ad objective is to get inquiries and interviews. You sell the opportunity during the interview.

Neighborhood papers cost less per line and are generally more satisfactory, though they must be run with more frequency.

Samples of ads are on another page. You will be kept advised of new ones that are getting good results.

EXHIBIT 2

Unusual Woman

For special position in uncrowded field. No cosmetics, books, or canvassing. Good education, outstanding personality essential. Age 25–40. Applicant preferred who needs to earn as much as $85 a week. Car necessary. Call ———.

training on an individual or small-group basis. The initial training involved a ten- to twelve-hour training program that was usually accomplished in sessions of two to three hours each. The training included such topics as: (1) building a prospect list; (2) arranging displays; (3) the sales display—presentation, closing the sale, completing the call; (4) company policies; and (5) answering objections. These training topics were outlined in detail in a coaching guide that Easterling had prepared for its managers.

After the formal training the new salesman went out with the supervisor on a few calls, usually three or four, or the supervisor accompanied the new salesman on her first few calls.

Each area manager had two monthly meetings, and each field manager or supervisor had two monthly meetings. Each meeting was usually a two-hour affair and was designed to stimulate the salesmen. All salesmen in the territory were expected to attend, although there was no particular

EXHIBIT 3

On the Sales Call

Easterling's top leaders ask for new salesmen on every sales call and condition their salesmen to do the same.

First ask your prospect for names of potential salesmen on page 9 of the Prospectus. Then at the close of the Sales Call, use the last (unnumbered) page in your Prospectus to probe. (Persistent probing is often necessary to get results.)

Another method: Just before leaving the home after a sales call, assume a casual attitude as you say:

You: Oh, by the way, Mrs. Customer, I wonder if you could do me a favor?

Customer: Surely, what is it?

You: Well, I have a problem. You see, everyone who looks at our tableware gives me six or more people to call on. I make twelve or more calls a week from which I get about 50 to 75 names. You can understand that I am steadily falling behind in my work.

Customer: I see your problem—but how can I help?

You: Well, my manager suggested that I find an assistant. He also suggested that I ask people like you for recommendations. The way he put it, "The people who have seen Easterling products are the best ones to recommend potential Easterling salesmen. They know the quality of our merchandise, they know how we work, and they can probably suggest a qualified person or two."

The type of person we like is someone who can work a minimum of twenty-five to thirty hours a week and who can use $50 to $75 more a week. Of course, many of our people make much more. The person we are looking for might be a lady between 25 and 50, or a young man. We find that women who need additional income to meet their family's needs, who are unattached, or whose families are grown, or women whose husbands travel all week, etc., are ideal for our work. [Show Horizon.]

I'm sure you have already thought of one or two. If you will give me the names, I shall be glad to contact them. And you will receive———(explain current recruiting offer) for every person you name who is accepted by Easterling.

Get names at this point, at least one or two.

Information to add as you probe for names:

You: There are many advantages to our program, Mrs. Customer. We call on only referred leads and have no trouble getting plenty. There are no deliveries; we sell on convenient budget terms as well as cash. Each customer usually buys two or three times. It is a dignified business and it's *fun!* Maybe you (if she looks o.k.) would qualify for the opportunity yourself, Mrs. Customer.

The same requirements prevail in recruiting as prevail in selling—you must build a large prospect list in order to get results.

penalty if they did not. All salesmen received the regular biweekly house organ, which carried new information and sales success stories.

Among the sixteen hundred salesmen, the annual turnover rate was nearly 100 per cent, but among the managers and supervisors 75 per cent had been with the firm three years, 50 per cent five years, and about 25 per cent over ten years.

EXHIBIT 4

SELECTION GUIDE—FEMALE: FOR TELEPHONE APPLICANTS AND/OR PERSONAL INTERVIEW

Name _____ Date _____

Address _____ City _____ Zone _____ State _____

Telephone _____ Car _____ Age _____

Family _____ Education _____

Sales Experience _____ Products Sold _____ How Long _____

Now Working _____ Where Employed _____

Appointment: Date _____ A.M. _____ P.M. _____

KEY DECISION QUESTIONS:

		Yes	No
1.	Do you have the independent use of a car?	☐	☐
2.	Can you work daytime and/or evenings minimum 25-30 hours per week?	☐	☐
3.	Does your family (husband) favor your working?	☐	☐
4.	Do you need to earn money?	☐	☐

QUALIFYING QUESTIONS	ABOVE AVERAGE		AVERAGE		BELOW AVERAGE	
Length of Residence	Over 5 Years	☐	1-5 Years	☐	Less than year	☐
Age	30-49	☐	24-29	☐	50-58	☐
Marital Status	Single Married	☐	Divorced	☐	Widow	☐
Last Worked	Employed Now	☐	Not employed. Worked within 2 yrs.	☐	Worked prior to past 2 yrs.	☐
Past Experience	Direct Sales Ran Own Business	☐	Teaching Civic Leader	☐	Store Clerk Office Work	☐
Hobbies	Extrovert	☐			Introvert	☐
Motivation	Educate Children Support sick family Wants to work Wants money	☐	Support self	☐	Add to income Improve home	☐
Conversation & Facial Reaction	Alert, sparkling	☐	Pleasant, friendly	☐	Sober, timid	☐
Dress & Personal Appearance	Very satisfactory	☐	Average	☐	Lacking in taste	☐
Social Ease	Quickly senses & gives courtesies to others	☐	Natural and Easy	☐	Stiff, clumsy	☐
Degree of Determination Shown or Judged	Very good	☐	Good	☐	Neutral	☐
Interviewer's Reaction	Excellent for our work	☐	Can succeed	☐	Not qualified	☐

Interviewer _____

Remarks after Interview--Reverse Side

The sales vice-president believed that the salesmen who stayed with the firm tended to have the following characteristics:

1. A belief in and appreciation of the line. They believed that they were doing a service by selling the line to the customers, especially to the young working girls.

2. Women between the ages of thirty and forty. Of the 50 per cent who were married, those with two or more children of school age worked out best.

3. Some college or business college exposure (a year or so).

4. A real necessity to earn money in rather large sums. Self-supporting women who had to support a number of people, such as children, parents, or family worked out well.

5. Had been or were socially active, such as a leader in a social club.

The vice-president of sales thought that too many women were being hired who did not have a real desire to earn considerable money continuously. He believed that many took the job to pay for some immediate need and left after such payment had been made. A sizable portion of those hired completed the training program and dropped out before going on the first call because their husbands would not permit them to do such work, because they changed their minds, or because they lost interest.

Easterling suffered no direct loss from the rapid turnover of salesmen. The recruiting and training costs were incurred by the area and field managers, who were independent contractors. Easterling furnished each salesman with a sample kit valued at $175, but this was returned or covered by the bond that each salesman had to buy at a cost of about $10 per year.

What should Easterling do to reduce the turnover of salesmen?

69

IMPERIAL BELTING COMPANY

FOR OVER fifty years Imperial Belting Company had been the sales leader of stitched canvas belting, which was used primarily with conveyors and elevators. Each of the nine men on the sales force was a highly trained industrial salesman with considerable knowledge of engineering problems, who earned between $8,000 and $10,000 annually. The general sales manager was concerned with salesman turnover; at least one salesman had left the company each year for the past several years. The sales that were lost while these men were being replaced plus the cost of training a new man, which was estimated at $10,000, made this turnover expensive.

The belting industry consisted of two major segments, manufacturers of rubber belts and manufacturers of canvas belts. There were approximately fifty companies making belts, of which some forty manufactured the rubber type and ten the canvas and cotton woven type. Imperial accounted for about 40 per cent of the total quality canvas belting business, or more than the next three largest canvas belting manufacturers combined. Canvas belts were considered to have a major advantage over the rubber variety—they resisted oils and acids and cost less to maintain. Imperial produced quality belts that sold for 5–15 per cent more than most competitive belts. The company executives believed that their belts lasted two to five times longer than most ordinary rubber or canvas belts.

Each Imperial salesman was expected to make about one hundred calls a month, of which about 20 per cent should produce sales; the typical order was for about $900. The sales manager expected that about 40 per cent of all calls would be made on new prospects and the remaining 60 per cent on established accounts. All established accounts were to be called on at least once a year. Larger-volume accounts were expected to receive from four to eight calls a year, depending on their size.

A new salesman normally needed nearly a year to acquire the technical information needed to be fully versed on the entire line. An ability to read blueprints was essential. Each salesman was on his own, once he was out in the field, except for monthly visits by the general sales manager. A

EXHIBIT 1

GEOGRAPHIC TERRITORY ASSIGNMENTS

Salesman 1: Connecticut, Massachusetts, Vermont, New Hampshire, Maine, 50 per cent of New York, and 50 per cent of New Jersey.

Salesman 2: Maryland, Delaware, Virginia, 50 per cent of West Virginia, 50 per cent of North Carolina, 50 per cent of Pennsylvania, and 50 per cent of New Jersey.

Salesman 3: Canada (basically Montreal and Toronto), 50 per cent of New York, 50 per cent of Pennsylvania, and 25 per cent of Ohio.

Salesman 4: Kentucky, 50 per cent of West Virginia, 75 per cent of Ohio, and 75 per cent of Indiana.

Salesman 5: Alabama, Georgia, S. Carolina, Tennessee, and 50 per cent of North Carolina.

Salesman 6: Michigan exclusively.

Salesman 7: Wisconsin, Minnesota, 50 per cent of Iowa, and 50 per cent of Illinois.

Salesman 8: 50 per cent of Illinois, 25 per cent of Indiana, and 50 per cent of Iowa.

Salesman 9: Arkansas, Colorado, Kansas, Mississippi, Nebraska, and Oklahoma.

two-day sales meeting was held once a year. All other contact with the home office was by mail or telephone. The nine sales territories are shown in Exhibit 1. Each salesman had to adapt his sales personality to a number of varied situations. On one occasion he might deal with the plant superintendent or with the maintenance foreman, who often had worked his way up from the ranks; at other times his contact would be with the chief engineer, who perhaps had one or more college degrees. The job description for an Imperial sales engineer is shown in Exhibit 2.

All salesmen received the same base salary—$6,000 a year—and expenses which averaged about the same amount. In addition, each salesman received a bonus of 10 per cent on all sales that exceeded the quota established for his territory.

The general sales manager recruited new salesmen primarily through newspaper advertising, employment agencies, and referral of noncompetitive salesmen by Imperial's customers. Management believed that the

EXHIBIT 2

JOB DESCRIPTION OF AN IMPERIAL SALES ENGINEER

A job description is a written record of the duties, responsibilities, skills, and requirements of a particular job. It is concerned with the job itself and not with the individual. The individual is selected and trained to perform the duties it outlines.

An Imperial representative is the sales manager of his territory and must perform the following essential functions for best performance. (1) sales, (2) service, (3) territory management, (4) sales promotion, (5) executive duties, and (6) good will.

1. Sales:
   Make regular, productive calls.
   Sell the line, demonstrate.
   Handle questions and objections.
   Estimate customer's potential needs.
   Emphasize quality.
   Explain company policies on price, delivery, credit.
   Explain benefits of product to customer.
   Get the order.
2. Service:
   Report product adaptability, complaints.
   Handle adjustments, returns, and allowances.
   Show customer how to get the most from the product.
   Advise and assist customer on his belt problems.
3. Territory Management:
   Arrange route for best coverage.
   Balance effort with customer against potential.
   Maintain sales portfolio, samples, kits.
4. Sales Promotion:
   Develop new prospects and new accounts.
   Call on conveyor manufacturers' headquarters.
   Present suggestions, layouts, and proposals.
5. Executive:
   Each night make a daily work plan for the next day.
   Prepare and submit daily reports to home office.
   Organize field activity for minimum travel and maximum calls.
   Prepare and submit special reports on trends and competition.
   Collect and submit data requested by home office.
   Investigate lost sales and the reasons for loss.
   Prepare reports on developments, trends, new objections met, and new
      ideas on meeting objections.
   Attend sales meetings.
   Build a prospect list.
6. Good Will:
   Counsel customers on their problems.
   Maintain loyalty and respect for firm represented.

sales force was not large enough to justify a sales training man; therefore, all training was done by the general sales manager. Since he had many other responsibilities, he was willing to pay a premium to obtain the services of an experienced industrial salesman.

Imperial executives had developed the following list of characteristics, which they believed a salesman would need to have in order to be successful with their firm:

1. Be married.
2. Have two or more children.
3. Be 28–35 years old.
4. Have had some engineering courses.
5. Be a college graduate.
6. Not be an only child in his family.
7. Enjoy traveling and being on his own.
8. Have a wife who would be a social asset.

A candidate for a selling position usually went through the following procedure:

1. Filled out an application blank.
2. Had preliminary interview with general sales manager (generally 15–20 minutes).
3. Awaited word relative to (1) checking on references given on application blank and (2) evaluation of interview.
4. If step 3 was favorable, he was asked to return with his wife for a final interview.

The general sales manager believed that the yearly turnover of at least one salesman was primarily the result of faulty selection, since he was not able to determine whether or not a candidate possessed the psychological attitudes that would fit him for the job. He could only guess at answers to such questions as: How well can he take being on his own? How well can he take company direction? Does he resist help? Should he be in selling at all?

To help him select salesmen, the sales manager decided to use the services of a psychological testing company, which would test prospective salesmen for $50 per candidate. The testing company suggested that each candidate be given a battery of six tests:

1. Mental ability (Otis Employment Test).
2. Personality portrait (Washburne S-A Inventory).
3. Social intelligence (George Washington University Series).
4. Personality adjustment (Bernreuter Personality Inventory).
5. Interests other than selling (Strong Vocational Interest Test for Men).
6. Sales aptitude (sales sense).

To verify the validity of these tests, the battery was given to each salesman in the company. From analysis of each salesman's test and the correlation of test scores, criteria were established to evaluate the test scores of potential salesmen, as shown in Exhibit 3. Upon seeing the results of these tests, the sales manager was convinced that they could be a useful tool to help separate the undesirable from the potentially good salesmen. Shortly after completion of this validity work, he was faced with the problem of hiring a salesman. After several months of recruiting, a number of candidates were obtained. Of the group, two men, Mr. Harold R. Overstreet and Mr. George Paddock, appeared to be the best

EXHIBIT 3

GRAPHIC TEST ANALYSIS

	Score to Be Not Less than	Score to Be Not More than
1. Mental ability		
Speed in arriving at conclusions on new problems	35	90
Accuracy in finding the right answers under time pressure	35	100
Capacity—mental adaptability and trainability	35	100
2. Personality portrait		
Stability—ability to take adversities or turndowns	65	90
Self-sufficiency—capacity to stand on one's own two feet	30	75
Objective-mindedness—treating situations unaffected by own feelings	75	95
Dominance—ability to control interviews and situations	60	90
Self-confidence—confidence in one's own ability to achieve	65	90
Social mixing qualities—need for group sociability	70	90
Aggressiveness and driving power	50	90
3. Social intelligence		
Tact and diplomacy—knowledge of diplomatic things to say and do	50	100
Sizing up—sizing up people in face-to-face social situations	75	100
Judging behavior—judging human behavior correctly	75	90
Sense of humor—ability to take kidding at one's own expense	75	95
4 Personal adjustment		
Sincerity in taking these tests	30	100
Happiness—tendency toward personal and domestic happiness	90	100
How others take to him—feeling of being accepted	50	95
How he takes to others—sympathetic interest in others	15	75
Purposiveness—goals and objectives in business	75	95
First things first—in business situations	90	100
Self-control—capacity for control in business situations	80	100
5. Sales aptitude		
Interest in selling as expressed by sales managers	A	...
Interest in selling tangibles	A	...
Interest in selling intangibles	A	...
Sales sense	85	100
6. Interests other than selling		
Engineer	C	...
Chemist	A	...
Production	B	...
Personnel	B	...
Accountant	No rating	...
Office worker	No rating	...
Purchasing agent	No rating	...
Advertising	No rating	...

prospects. The selection problem was a difficult one for the general sales manager because both candidates appeared to have equal abilities:

1. Both were married and had children.
2. Both had a wife who would be a social asset to their work.
3. Both had their own homes.
4. Both had about equal previous industrial selling experience.
5. Both were college graduates with over a year of study in engineering.
6. Both had been in the service as officers.
7. Both were in their early thirties.

EXHIBIT 4

GRAPHIC TEST ANALYSIS
George R. Paddock

	Danger	Desirable	Caution
1. Mental ability			
Speed in arriving at conclusions on new problems		40	
Accuracy in finding the right answers under time pressure		35	
Capacity—mental adaptability and trainability		35	
2. Personality portrait			
Stability—ability to take adversities or turndowns		84	
Self-sufficiency—capacity to stand on one's own two feet		35	
Objective-mindedness—treating situations unaffected by own feelings		93	
Dominance—ability to control interviews and situations		58	
Self-confidence—confidence in one's own ability to achieve		65	
Social mixing qualities—need for group sociability		88	
Aggressiveness and driving power		34	
3. Social intelligence			
Tact and diplomacy—knowledge of diplomatic things to say and do		34	
Sizing up—sizing up people in face-to-face social situations		99	
Judging behavior—judging human behavior correctly		29	
Sense of humor—ability to take kidding at one's own expense			99
4. Personal adjustment			
Sincerity in taking these tests		30	
Happiness—tendency toward personal and domestic happiness		99	
How others take to him—feeling of being accepted			20
How he takes to others—sympathetic interest in others		35	
Purposiveness—goals and objectives in business		75	
First things first—in business situations		99	
Self-control—capacity for control in business situations		74	
5. Sales aptitude			
Interest in selling as expressed by sales managers		A	
Interest in selling tangibles		A	
Interest in selling intangibles		B	
Sales sense			15
6. Interests other than selling			
Engineer			
Chemist			
Production		B-plus	
Personnel			
Accountant		A	
Office worker		A	
Purchasing agent		A	
Advertising			
7. Other factors			
Analytical tendency			X

Paddock and Overstreet took the aptitude tests, after which the testing firm submitted the reports shown as Exhibits 4 and 5. Each report consisted of a "graphic analysis" and a commentary by an analyst.

DETAILED ANALYSIS

Objective of this report: To evaluate Paddock for the position of industrial salesman.

1. *Mental ability:* The ratings are in line for the job. Paddock has the capacity for absorbing the essentials of new duties and responsibilities.

EXHIBIT 5

GRAPHIC TEST ANALYSIS
Harold R. Overstreet

	Danger	Desirable	Caution
1. Mental ability			
Speed in arriving at conclusions on new problems		55	
Accuracy in finding the right answers under time pressure		80	
Capacity—mental adaptability and trainability		45	
2. Personality portrait			
Stability—ability to take adversities or turndowns		65	
Self-sufficiency—capacity to stand on one's own two feet			21
Objective-mindedness—treating situations unaffected by own feelings		86	
Dominance—ability to control interviews and situations		78	
Self-confidence—confidence in one's own ability to achieve		75	
Social mixing qualities—need for group sociability		75	
Aggressiveness and driving power		84	
3. Social intelligence			
Tact and diplomacy—knowledge of diplomatic things to say and do		99	
Sizing up—sizing up people in face-to-face social situations		89	
Judging behavior—judging human behavior correctly		54	
Sense of humor—ability to take kidding at one's own expense		94	
4. Personal adjustment			
Sincerity in taking these tests		35	
Happiness—tendency toward personal and domestic happiness		99	
How others take to him—feeling of being accepted		94	
How he takes to others—sympathetic interest in others		15	
Purposiveness—goals and objectives in business		95	
First things first—in business situations		99	
Self-control—capacity for control in business situations		99	
5. Sales aptitude			
Interest in selling as expressed by sales managers		A	
Interest in selling tangibles		A	
Interest in selling intangibles		A	
Sales sense		90	
6. Interests other than selling			
Engineer			
Chemist			
Production			
Personnel		A	
Accountant			
Office worker			
Purchasing agent			
Advertising		B-Plus	
7. Other factors			

2. *Personality portrait:* Paddock has a strong personality portrait. He reveals capacities for taking it when it comes to the impact of disappointments, defeats, and obstacles and resistances. He has aggressiveness, inner energy, dominance, and driving power, as well as confidence in himself and his abilities and high objective-mindedness.

The following factors should be explored: Paddock was analytical in his approach to the test. Many technical men tend to be analytical, are accustomed to weighing carefully the pros and cons of situations before reaching decisions or making commitments. We have placed this tendency in the caution zone on the color chart because it is important to determine whether or not Paddock may still be in the state of "analysis" relative to the job opportunity being offered him with Imperial Belting. In other words, does Paddock have any uncertainties or doubts or mental reservations concerning the job or his ability to handle the job or the future. If so, these should be completely resolved before he is put on the payroll.

3. *Social intelligence:* Paddock has capacities for tact and for sizing up people in face-to-face social situations. He earned a fairly good rating for judging behavior.

Paddock earned a top rating for sense of humor. We have placed this is the caution zone on the color chart because it is important for him to recognize the fact that many of the people with whom he will be working out in the field cannot begin to match his own high sense of humor. He must be alerted against impressing such individuals as taking too lightly or airily situations that they would rather have him consider seriously.

4. *Personal adjustment:* Paddock seems to feel that others may not take to him too readily. Why? Is there any aspect of his appearance, speech, personal mannerisms, or background about which he is sensitive and which he believes others do not like in him?

Ratings for the other adjustment factors are in line for the job.

5. *Sales aptitude:* Paddock has live interest in selling, but his rating for sales sense is that of the individualist, and usually the individualist sells the hard way and only the rugged survives.

Paddock is not bringing what might be termed an inherent or intrinsic sales sense to the new job with Imperial Belting. Thus he is a risk for employment unless he has had very thorough and specific experience in exactly the same field of work in which he will be operating if employed as an Imperial Belting industrial salesman. If he has this experience, then he is a fair or calculated risk for employment by Imperial Belting; perhaps he will carry over in the new job some specific sales experiences he has had in the same or related field.

It is important in working with Paddock to make certain that at all times he follow through on specific Imperial Belting methods and techniques of selling rather than depend on his own individualist's approach to sales situations.

6. *Interests other than sales:* Paddock's other interests are in line for industrial selling, particularly his interests in manufacturing processes and in purchasing.

Conclusion and recommendation: Paddock is recommended for employment as an industrial salesman with Imperial Belting Company.

DETAILED ANALYSIS

Objective of this report: To evaluate Overstreet's potentials for a sales position with the Imperial Belting Company. In this capacity he would be covering New England and New York City, being away from home for several days to a week at a time, but never for week ends.

1. *Mental ability:* Overstreet's performance on the mental ability test is quite good. It indicates that he should be able to absorb training, new inforation, and new ideas without any particular difficulty.

2. *Personality portrait:* Overstreet appears to be a generally sociable individual who is quite amiable and amenable to guidance. He should be a good company man in terms of being willing to follow through on established policies and procedures without making sudden and unexpected changes on his own.

From that standpoint, he should be a good company man. He shows good over-all self-confidence, can take most emotional pressures without becoming easily discouraged, and is sufficiently objective-minded to be able to keep

most personal worries or troubles apart from his work. He shows good dominance, drive, and aggressiveness.

The marginal rating for self-sufficiency has positive as well as negative implications. From the positive standpoint, it reflects the type of individual who
fits well into a large, smoothly running organization, where he is expected to
operate as a member of a closely knit and well co-ordinated team.

By the same token, such a man typically needs to feel that he has the
support of his organization and of his manager behind him if he is to function
at his best. It is also important, from the standpoint of the traveling aspects of
of his job, that he have the full support of his family and those who are
nearest and dearest to him, since otherwise it may be difficult for him to "take"
traveling which keeps him away from home for days and nights at a time.
Not only his attitude but the attitude of his wife and family should be
checked carefully to be sure that all are in full accord with the desirability
of his entering into a position of this type.

It should also be noted that Overstreet apparently has high hopes and
great expectations for the future. He seems to expect big things to happen and
great events to occur. The question is: Are his "great expectations" realistic
and in accordance with the plans and expectations that management has for
him? If not, they could lead to ultimate disappointment and a letdown in his
efforts.

3. *Social intelligence:* Overstreet has a fine understanding of what it takes
to get along well with other people. He can be so highly tactful and diplo-
matic as to be almost suave, and he has fine capacity for sizing up other people face to face. He has a good understanding of human nature generally and
a fine sense of humor.

4. *Personal adjustment:* The indications are that Overstreet has made a
good adjustment to his home, personal, and business environments.

5. *Sales aptitude:* Overstreet has a strong interest in the selling field, or
the type commonly associated with men who regard that general field of work
as a career. Furthermore, he has an excellent understanding of and insight into
the "sales-wise" approach to situations.

6. *Interests other than sales:* Overstreet also has a strong interest in working with and handling personnel and a secondary interest along advertising,
merchandising and sales promotional lines.

Conclusion and recommendation: On the basis of the over-all test pattern,
Overstreet is recommended for employment as a salesman with the Imperial
Belting Company.

Which candidate, if any, should Imperial hire?

*Evaluate the use of this psychological testing program in recruiting sales-
men.*

70

DOVINSHER DRUG COMPANY

Dovinsher Drug Company hired David Lear as a salesman near the end
of 1957. All indications were that Lear was well qualified for the position,
and Bob Heller, the sales manager, anticipated that Lear would become
one of the firm's more productive salesmen. Less than a year later, Heller
was on the verge of firing Lear.

David Lear applied on November 28, 1957, for a position with Dovinsher Drug Company at the suggestion of a pharmacist friend who was employed at the Boynton Pharmacy, one of Dovinsher's customers. On his application, Lear gave the following as his reason for desiring to work for Dovinsher:

Having learned through Cliff Wilson of Boynton Pharmacy that Dovinsher Drug Company was seeking a representative for the Haywood area, I immediately began a personal investigation and found that Dovinsher Drug was a progressive organization and, by virtue of its marketing and research on hormone products, was a leader in its field.

With my experience in the service as a medical corpsman, coupled with the four-year pre-medical program in college and part-time as an industrial first-aid attendant, I feel convinced that I can succeed in medical sales.

By virtue of the aforementioned, and with the desire and temperament for meeting and conversing with people, I feel that I can be of use to myself and for the betterment of the organization.

Lear sent his application to the home office of Dovinsher; from there it was forwarded to Sam Foythner, who at the time was manager of the Haywood district. Foythner hired Lear after interviewing him once, pending a favorable retail credit report and a successful physical examination, both of which he (Foythner) instituted.

The following is a letter from Sam Foythner (district manager) to Bob Heller (sales manager), dated December 10, 1957:

Mr. David Lear is being employed by us on December 13. He is being hired as a replacement for Rudy Flemer after the first of the year.

We are not enclosing the file on Mr. Lear at this time, since it and his processing have not been completed. So far we have only his application and the investigational report from Retail Credit. Seemingly premature action is being taken to employ him because (*a*) of the action taken in Mr. Flemer's case, outlined in yesterday's correspondence, (*b*) Mr. Lear is unemployed, and (*c*) any other arrangements would have delayed our employing him until at least the second week in January, one month hence. Reference inquiries have been sent to previous employers, and his character references listed on his application. A physical has been scheduled for his first day of employment and training here. He has been given to understand that his permanency in Dovinsher employment is contingent upon our receiving favorable reports from these sources.

Mr. Lear will begin his employment on December 13 with training under Mr. Dunhill's supervision [new district manager to replace Foythner about January 1, 1958]. He should be on open expense until December 20, receiving fixed expense for the last one-third of the month. His starting salary is to be $550 per month. He has his own car, a 1955 Plymouth, which he intends to use on his territorial assignment with Dovinsher. Mr. Dunhill, I believe, can and will take care of all the supplies and equipment needed for Mr. Lear to start on territory. He has most of it here, and it will be supplemented by that taken over from Mr. Flemer.

Briefly, Mr. Lear is thirty-four years of age, married, and has one child less than two years of age. He is a nice-looking, neat-appearing, dark-complexioned individual (Slavic descent) with black hair, brown eyes, height 5 feet 9 inches, and weight 160 pounds. His wife, too, seen during my interview, is a dark, very attractive, sensible woman, age about twenty-five. Mr. Lear has completed pre-med at Haywood University and was a pharmacist mate in the Navy for three years. His background includes primarily four years as a chemist in customer service for Frampton Corporation. His only selling came from part-time work while attending school.

Mr. Lear's outside activities included:
Sports: basketball
Editor: high school newspaper
President: Slavic Youth Organization
Reading preferences: *Business Week, Chemical Week, Factory Management, Selling*

Mr. Lear's application and employment file should be completed within a few days. It will be sent to you at that time along with your file copy and the original, signed Letter of Employment.

The following are replies to letters sent by Foythner to references given by Lear:

Dear Mr. Foythner:

I have known Dave Lear since he was a child. He is honest, trustworthy, and very intelligent. I can recommend him without qualification whatsoever.

(*signed*) F. Gayton
Municipal Judge
City of Riverville

Dear Mr. Foythner:

It is a pleasure to recommend Mr. David Lear for a position on your staff.

I have known Mr. Lear and his family for several years and have always found them to be honest and stable members of the community. His appearance and way of presenting himself should make him a good addition to your group.

I have known many of the representatives of the Dovinsher Drug Company, and I feel confident he will be a successful member of the detail sales staff.

(*signed*) Sincerely yours,
Flavius P. Golus, M.D.

The following information was received from Lear's former employer, Frampton Corporation, on a form sent by Dovinsher:

Date of employment: 6/30/53—9/8/57
Reason for termination: Own volition
Position held: Chemist
Would you rehire: No
Quality of work: Good
Quantity of work: Good
Attitude: Fair
Attendance: Excellent

The following remark was added: "Lear left because he wanted to do sales work and we had no openings in that department."

The following Retail Credit Report was received December 11, 1957:

Sales ability and qualifications: Average

Scope of investigation: During the investigation of Mr. David Lear, the field investigator talked to a personal friend who has known him all during his lifetime, a present residential neighbor who has known him two years, a former employer who knew him four years, and also another employer with whom he worked for two months.

Summary of employment: David Lear was employed with the Frampton Corporation, a firm engaged in plating equipment manufacturing from 6/30/53 to 9/8/57. He was a chemist in their customers' service laboratory. He was on their training program and was doing very well until he became impatient, as he wanted to go into their sales field and they did not have an opening for him at this time. He had some customer contact work in which he would go out and help customers with their problems. He was a very competent worker and needed very little supervision. He left of his own accord for a position where he would be doing sales work. He is eligible for rehire.

Applicant was employed in the personnel department of the Valley Forge Iron Works, a large steel manufacturer from 11/18/46 to 1/15/47 when he returned from the service, prior to going to college. His record was clear with this firm.

The following report was received from Life Extension on Lear's physical examination: Class 1—Fit for any type of employment.

Memo from Foythner (district manager) to Thomas (division manager) concerning Dave Lear's personnel file, dated January 3, 1958:

> Attached is the file on our recently employed representative for the Haywood area, Mr. Dave Lear. Mr. Lear's file was held here in our pending file for completion; however, it appears that no more letters of reference are forthcoming. Should we receive additional references, we shall forward them to you immediately.

Memo from Thomas to Personnel Division:

> Mr. Foythner has employed Mr. Dave Lear for Territory 109, formerly covered by Mr. Flemer. His effective date of employment was December 13, 1957, with a starting salary of $6,600 per year. The file on Mr. Lear is attached.

Memo to Thomas from Lear concerning car depreciation fund (a fund built up monthly to cover depreciation of salesmen's cars; normally held by Dovinsher until a new car was purchased), dated January 15, 1958:

> It is respectfully requested that the car depreciation fund for January and February be sent directly to me. Thank you.

Memo to Dunhill (district manager) from Thomas (division manager), dated January 18, 1958:

> I believe you will recall from our telephone conversation that Mr. Lear is having a considerable amount of doctor bills due to the pernicious vomiting

of his four-month-old baby. He will use this money for medical payments. I suggest we give it to him for these two months only.

Memo from Thomas to Kraft (controller) concerning auto reserve—Mr. Lear, dated February 7, 1958:

This is an unusual request; however, it was approved in a conversation with Mr. Dunhill. Apparently Mr. Lear has incurred some bills through illness in his family and requests his entire auto reserve at this time. He would like to have his January deposit, and, in addition, send him the deduction for February. If an amount must be kept on deposit to keep the account current, please indicate this on the check stub.

Memo from Dunhill (district manager) to Burke (training director) concerning Dave Lear's attendance at training class, March 15, 1958; memo dated February 4, 1958:

Dave Lear and I worked together this past week for a couple of days. I believe he is ready for the training class despite the short time he has been on territory. But. . . .

Dave has a family problem which may not clear up before the training class and could seriously interfere with his doing as good a job as he might. He has a four-month-old daughter who has been vomiting perniciously since birth. They have spent a lot of medical time and money on the child and a definite diagnosis still has not been reached. I know he loses a lot of sleep at nights walking with the baby. Inasmuch as this is their firstborn, you could expect a number of telephone calls to Haywood while he is in training. There could be a possibility that he might be called home if surgery is indicated.

Dave has any number of times asked *when* he would be allowed to go in to our home office for training. If, on the basis of the above personal information, you would like to delay his training until the next class, the additional "field seasoning" would not hurt him a bit.

Memo from Frobisher (insurance manager) to Lear, dated March 4, 1958:

Request you complete and return the attached Automobile Insurance Agreement, which should have been submitted when you were first employed.

On March 15, Lear entered the training class, which met at the Dovinsher home office for one week out of each month.

Memo from Dunhill (district manager) to Lear concerning transfer of Sales Control Unit, dated April 8, 1958:

Dave, I just received final approval from Mr. Thomas for you to take over Territories 111–112, effective April 1, 1958, as you requested.

Needless to tell you these are key territories in our district, and it is not the usual thing to entrust two territories to a relatively new man. However, the showing you have made with Dovinsher in the relatively short time you've been with us, makes me believe that you will do a job in those territories and that two of them are not too much.

That's on the plus side of the ledger. Against making the switch was the change itself. By that I mean we've shifted men so frequently in the Haywood area in the past year that our accounts no doubt must wonder what we are doing. I'm sure you'll be able to satisfy any questions which may come up as the result of this switch in territories.

As you can appreciate, this change will no doubt make a lot of extra work for not a few people in our home office. The best way you and I can justify this change is to have your and my objective met with at least 100 per cent. Can you do it? I know you can or I wouldn't have passed along your request. Now it's up to you to prove I was right in requesting the change from Home Office.

I've asked Bud Gingold to have his territory records ready to pass on to you; would you make arrangements with him to pick up this material at the earliest possible date? You already know which Syndicated accounts you will be covering from my previous memo.

If there are any questions you'd like to go over, I'll be in Haywood during the week of April 25, staying at the Blakeston. How was the training class, Dave? I'll be interested to hear your impressions on that.

Memo from Thomas (division manager) to Lear, dated April 13, 1958:

To date we have not received your monthly summary for March. In order for you to be reimbursed for your expenses, it is necessary for us to have this report. Would you please forward it as soon as possible.

Memo from Lear to Thomas, dated May 9, 1958:

It was called to my attention that I had not submitted any copies of prescription blanks. I misplaced the bulletin pertaining to this matter and overlooked mailing them in.

This is wholly my fault and I am sorry this had to happen. I do not expect nor anticipate any credit for these Rx blanks. However, to show that I have obtained some, I am remitting these 21 blanks.

Memo from Dunhill to Thomas, dated May 12, 1958, concerning actual expenses and budget variances:

Thank you for the above report. I have gone over the report quite thoroughly and believe the biggest single headache as far as expenses go are samples. I'm about 40 per cent over my allotment.[1] The rest of the report doesn't look too bad for me. Attached are some figures which will be of interest to you and which I shall use at the District meeting (names hidden, of course).

It is quite evident from this breakdown that certain Haywood District representatives need education in the use of samples. Rest assured this will be taken care of in the immediate future. I have attempted to cut sample requests of the entire district to put myself more into line with my budget and naturally have had some objections from the men.

In the future may I be sent all sample requests from Mr. Lear and Mr. Gingold, whether they be the regular requests or requests for physicians on physician request forms.

Memo from Dunhill to Thomas, dated June 4, 1958:

I'll be looking for you on the 16th.

If you have no objections, I wish you would work with Lear on the 17th instead of Raymonds. Will you notify the man of your intention to work with him?

---

[1] Salesmen were allotted a certain number of samples per month. This limitation was necessary because of the high cost of drug samples.

Memo from Frobisher (insurance manager) to Lear, dated June 22, 1958:

Second Request

I have been advised that you are using your personally owned automobile for Dovinsher business. You are undoubtedly aware that it is our policy to cover all of our representatives under our Master Automobile Insurance Policy and we pay 50 per cent of the liability premium.

Please complete the attached insurance agreement and, if you desire the additional optional coverages, please check off the desired coverages. If you are currently carrying insurance, please cancel your policy and advise the date of cancellation so that I can make our effective date concurrent. If you have not been carrying insurance, you have been covered under our policy ever since you joined our company, beginning December 19, 1957.

Upon receipt of the completed attached form, I will be in communication with you concerning the premium payment, which is accomplished through monthly salary deductions. If you have any questions concerning this insurance, please do not hesitate to call upon me.

Memo from Frobisher to Dunhill (district manager), dated July 8, 1958:

Last December 15th we were formally advised through channels that Mr. Lear had been employed by us and was using his personally owned automobile for Dovinsher business. When I did not receive a completed Automobile Insurance Agreement we wrote to him on March 4th requesting that he complete the necessary form, which we enclosed. For some reason he did not answer my memo so I wrote again to him on June 22nd, a copy of which is attached.

I cannot understand why Mr. Lear will not complete the form or at least drop a note in connection with the matter.

Therefore, I will appreciate your discussing this matter with him the next time you see him and see what you can do about getting the form completed. As you know, it is our firm policy that all representatives must be insured under our Master Policy and that we pay 50 per cent of the premium. Furthermore, it would be mighty embarrassing if he became involved in a serious accident and we had not had an opportunity to register his automobile with the insurance company.

Your co-operation in handling this matter will be sincerely appreciated.

Memo from Dunhill to Lear, dated July 16, 1958:

As you have requested, you will be covering only Territory 111 sometime after the 15th of August. George O'Brien will be covering Territory 112 after we are able to train a man around that time for Territory 110 on the East Side. I would appreciate your arranging to transfer to Mr. O'Brien your records on Territory 112 at such time as the assignments are announced as firm.

The transfer of an up-to-date and neat route book to a new man is always an indication of the working habits of a representative. I know the material you transfer to Mr. O'Brien will be in the best possible arrangement you can make it, Dave.

Memo from Dunhill to Lear, dated July 30, 1958:

Dave, you remember when I called you a couple of weeks ago, I asked if you had submitted a route list for the month of July? I mentioned I had not received a photostat of it from the office so perhaps it had become misplaced, and asked if you would send me a copy of it. I have not as yet received it and of course the need has passed with the end of July. Now I find I have everyone's route list for August except yours. You remember these are due in the Home Office before the 15th of the month *preceding* the month for which they are made out. Would you please submit your route lists through the month of October to our Home Office as soon as possible?

Memo from Burke (training director) to Lear, dated August 5, 1958:

You did an excellent job in the final March Training Class Examination, Dave, with a score of 96 in sales and 94 in the medical section, ranking you fifth in both instances in your class.

We are attaching your papers, which I am sure you will like to look over and keep in your files as an excellent review.

We enjoyed having you here in the Home Office, and I am looking forward to seeing you in the Haywood area.

Memo from Lear to Professional Service Department, dated August 25, 1958:

I have been informed by our family doctor that he wishes to place my mother on Articol for bronchial asthma. She will be using (3) three tablets per day. As her need is decreased I will inform you. May I have the Articol tablets sent to my address.

Memo from Lear to Thomas (division manager), dated August 25, 1958:

I wonder if you can help me? I am desirous of purchasing a new home. Before I can do same, I must have certain information relayed for approval of a G.I. loan. I need an employment verification letter in triplicate, addressed to "Whom it may concern," including the following information:

a) Type of work—including qualifications, such as degree required, technical background, etc.
b) Base rate—this should include also bonuses, expenses, etc.
c) Earnings thus far.
d) Length of employment.

Any other information which would be conducive toward an approval of a loan will be appreciated. Thanking you, I remain,

The above memo was forwarded to the Personnel Division for preparation of "To whom it may concern" letter, which was sent to Lear on August 30.

Memo from Dunhill (district manager) to Lear, dated August 29, 1958:

Once again, Dave, I have everyone's route list for September except yours. Since I have not received the route lists requested exactly a month ago, I would like to ask you for the third time, will you please make these out and submit them to the Home Office for duplication.

Excerpt from Dunhill's monthly report for August, 1958:

Lear's operation has not been the best, and a personal interview with facts and figures was held. It is hoped this will increase his activities to what they can be.

Excerpt from Dunhill's monthly report for September:

Lear, who also appears to be delinquent in his activities, was interviewed for the third time, and suggestions were made as to how he could improve his operations.

Memo from Dunhill to Thomas (division manager), dated November 8, 1958:

As previously mentioned to you in our phone conversations, the above named man (Lear) has been leaving home late in the morning and coming home early in the afternoons. Lear's call activities have been discussed with him on previous occasions. They quickly increased and have been running consistently at about seven per day. One day, while in his neighborhood about 4:30 P.M., I drove by his house to find him home (October 21). The following Monday (October 24) he left for work at 10:50 A.M. and got home at 3:30 P.M. On October 25, he left home for work at 10:30 A.M. and made only two calls (Alpha Pharmacy and Hayes Drug Company) before noon—two places, incidentally, that are reputed to be purchasers of samples and whom Mr. Gingold (who was formerly with us) had reportedly sold samples to. I had lunch with Lear on this date, saying nothing about "accidentally" meeting him in the Hayes Drug Company.

In checking the daily report of activities with the physicians on whom he called, the following is presented. Using the excuse of a supposedly misplaced catalogue, I personally called on the physicians shown below on November 6:

Physician's Name	Date Reported Called on	Comments of M.D.
Dr. M. J. Hubinger	October 24	Did not see Lear. Someone left literature.
Dr. Henry Swift	October 24	Could have seen, doesn't remember him, though.
Dr. G. A. Read	October 24	Physician's day off.
Dr. George Lerch	October 24	Physician saw Lear.
Dr. E. S. Trueheart	October 24	Physician did not see, never in office in daytime.
Dr. L. E. Zeman	October 24	Saw Lear.
Dr. Laura L. Young	October 24	M.D. does not remember seeing him nor a detail on Articol.
Dr. Albert H. Campbell	October 21	M.D. said man left literature but hasn't seen Dovinsher man personally in long time.
Dr. J. M. Gillespie	October 21	M.D. did see him.
Dr. K. H. Packard	October 21	M.D. says he was too busy to see man who called; hasn't been detailed on Articol in months.
Dr. Ray A. Chandler	October 28	M.D. doesn't remember seeing Lear, but could have.
Dr. John R. Banach	October 28	M.D. saw Lear.
Dr. Fred La Mar	October 28	M.D. says he probably saw him, doesn't remember.
Dr. Thomas R. Koontz	October 28	M.D. saw him.

Lear admitted to me today that he has been faking reports because, as he put it: "A lot of others do it also." He also admitted leaving late in the mornings for work and coming home early. He gave as his reason "the amount of Saturday work" he has been doing. When asked why he did not submit reports for Saturday work, he had no answer.

Lear, almost from the first day he was hired (approximately one year ago), has been extremely difficult to supervise. He asked for and received a transfer from Territory 109, for which he was hired, to his present one, Territory 111 because it would be closer to home for him, and I thought this would improve his attitude and work activities. On three separate occasions Mr. Lear and I had discussions on how to improve his operation from planning a day's work on paper the evening before (three requests for this alone) to answering Home Office correspondence without repeated requests (see July 8, 1958, memo from Mr. Frobisher) to sending in route lists, Daily Report of Activities, etc. The last time I talked with Mr. Lear, he came to my home and we talked in the room I use for an office for nearly three hours. At that time he outlined those things on which he would begin to work and improve himself. Attached is my copy of this list (attachment A), along with notes made on items to talk to him about (attachment B). Of these, his sample requests have been less, due to my editing; nothing else has been accomplished.

Lear has been unable to adjust himself to writing orders in drug stores, depite demonstrations and personal counseling (he only sold three deals in two accounts).

Lear is bitter and may be vindictive about our conversations today. He was extremely difficult to talk with.

ATTACHMENT A

LIST PREPARED BY LEAR OF THINGS HE WOULD WORK ON
TO IMPROVE HIMSELF: SEPTEMBER 28, 1958

1. Supply information on activities to district manager and home office.
2. Maintain route book in good condition and up to date.
3. Report daily activities.
4. Read sales manual from cover to cover.
5. Call activities—increase M.D. calls.
6. Attention to correspondence—promptness.
7. Take sales course.
8. Watch gripes.
9. Sampling.

ATTACHMENT B

LIST PREPARED BY DUNHILL OF THINGS ABOUT WHICH TO TALK TO LEAR

Does he think company and I have been fair with him?
Been with company over six months.
Wants salary raise—conversation sometime back.
No real evidence of efforts.
Remind him of initial training—did little or no studying.
Attitude since then—surly to me and to home office; unco-operative.
Itinerary requests—three of them.
Doesn't appear that he is trying to co-operate with company and do things the way they outline them.
Belittles company in light of entertaining done by previous employer.
Conferences: hotel room, district sales meeting; at his home, August 3, 1958.
    Noted little change if any; typically is wanting to keep all of Hanford (large drug chain) purchases for self; suggest he try to be a little more co-operative.
Making out outline for next day's work—three requests.
Daily call average: first six months, 4 M.D.'s; first three months, 3.5 M.D.'s, second three months, 6.0 M.D.'s.
Samples: six physicians per day for twenty working days, 120 samples per month. Huge requests—more than anyone else in district.
Fatzler Drug letter: What did he do about it?

Route book: up to date—not on inspection.
Relations with accounts: i.e., direct account call with him where there were
two owners—irritating accounts.

1. *What action should be taken by Dovinsher with respect to Lear? By whom?*
2. *Could this situation have been prevented? How?*

3. Training the Sales Force

71

HEFFNER FOODS, INC.

HEFFNER FOODS, INC., was one of the largest food manufacturers in the United States. It maintained distribution of over one hundred food items through a sales force of 1,500–1,800 men who sold to retail food stores and buyers such as restaurants, schools, and hospitals. For many years the firm had had an extensive sales training program consisting of initial decentralized training, on-the-job training, and training at the company's central school. When the firm underwent a reorganization in which greater decentralization was effected, one of the changes was to close the central training school. The firm's training director believed that the training formerly given in the central school was essential and was not duplicated by the training given in the field. He urged the top management to provide the equivalent of this training in some manner.

The organization of the sales force prior to the decentralization was as shown in the accompanying chart.

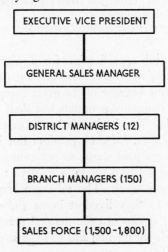

EXHIBIT I

POSITION SPECIFICATIONS

Position Title: General line salesman II
Location: branch office

General Duties and Responsibilities:

Sell and promote full line of the company's products to assigned distributive trade in a defined area within the local selling unit's territory. Plan and conduct product promotions and demonstrations and assist with merchandising procedures in other sales territories. Make collections, assist in establishing credit ratings for assigned accounts, and perform related duties as assigned.

Typical Duties:

1. Sell and promote full line of the company's products to distributive trade within an assigned territory of the local unit.
2. Solicit new accounts, and maintain good business relations with the established trade.
3. Make collections, assist in establishing credit ratings, and adjust claims and/or grievances of the trade whenever possible, such as: Contact those responsible for errors in pricing, product received but not ordered, faulty selection of product quality, delayed shipment, product ordered but not received, etc.
4. Merchandise the company's products through in-store advertising, displays, product promotions, etc., and check store stock to maintain and increase product distribution.
5. Contact the various sales departments at local chain units to check stock of product available for sale, for price changes, and to obtain additional product and market information.
6. Compile reports periodically, such as: tonnage, distribution, special product sales, and cash collections. Assist in conducting market and dealer surveys and reporting on them.
7. Perform related duties as assigned.

Qualifications:

Education: Equivalent to graduation from high school supplemented by the company's sales-training course.
Experience: Equivalent to three months' experience as student salesman.

Exhibit 1 shows the job specification for a salesman. These salesmen sold to individual stores, not to central buying offices of chains. The selling job was not routine because of the great competition. If a salesman was not effective, then company products lost shelf space, which was the equivalent of losing sales. To obtain a balanced sales effort among products, quotas were established for each product line in each territory. On the average, salesmen were paid about 80 per cent salary and 20 per cent incentive pay, which was based on sales relative to quota. The typical salary was $100–$125 per week. The salesmen required very little expense money because (1) they lived at home and worked in territories very near to home; (2) it was not the general practice in the food field to spend money entertaining clients; and (3) the salesmen were furnished

EXHIBIT II

Product Knowledge and Company Orientation Study Guide

I. The Sales Plan (Sales Information)
   A. A day on your sales territory
   B. Determining sales potential within territory
   C. Getting the facts on your sales territory
   D. Instructions for making a survey of the sales territory
   E. Determining sales potential for each prospect
II. Sales Opportunities (Sales Information)
   A. Background information on the company
   B. The know-how of selling
   C. Operating in the dealer's store
   D. Keeping records
   E. Bright prospects for the future
III. Know Your Territory (Sales Information)
   A. Population analysis
   B. People, occupation, income—store and product preferences
   C. Sales equipment
   D. Your territory and advertising
   E. Time on your territory
   F. Telephone selling
   G. Distribution problems
   H. The bakery market
   I. The restaurant market
   J. The sales manager's job
IV. Working with Dealers
   A series of technical booklets, each dealing with one product line.
V. Company Benefits

company cars that were maintained by the firm. Each salesman had 70–80 accounts in his territory; he called each week on the larger accounts and every two weeks on the smaller accounts. The approximately one hundred different company products included both perishables and non-perishables.

Prior to the reorganization, a salesman received the following training after he was hired by a local branch manager:

1. Individual study under the guidance of the branch manager for two to six weeks, depending on how fast the individual learned. Exhibit 2 shows the outline of the material covered. The salesman was given manuals covering company orientation and product information. After the salesman had studied the material, the branch manager gave him an oral examination.

2. Upon completion of step 1, the sales trainee then traveled with an experienced salesman for one week to observe. He discussed the successes and failures encountered by the experienced salesman with him.

3. The salesman was then given experience, on a relief selling basis, during vacations or sickness of other salesmen.

4. After a total of six months in steps 1, 2, and 3, the trainee went to company headquarters for a two-week class in merchandising and sales techniques at the company sales-training school. It was considered that this instruction was more effective at the time it was given than when the salesman was newly hired.

5. Upon completion of the sales training school program, the sales trainee became a company salesman and was assigned to a territory.

The company's sales school had two teachers who handled this training. Each two-week session included from twelve to fifteen trainees. Since turnover in the sales force was 10–15 per cent annually, sessions were held almost continually. The course involved twenty sessions, two a day for ten days, and included the following:

1. The sales trainee recorded a sales presentation—generally one which lasted from five to ten minutes.
2. By use of lectures and demonstrations, such as role-playing, the essentials of the sales process were studied and practiced during the next twelve sessions.
3. The trainee then recorded another sales presentation. Each trainee, with the help of the group, then analyzed and compared the second presentation with the first.
4. Each trainee was taught the mathematics of merchandising. Such items as margins, markups, and stock turnover were included.

When the company was reorganized, the general sales manager's position was abolished. Regional vice-presidents were established, each with complete authority over sales in his region. Consequently, the central training school was cancelled. This left the problem of how to continue the work done formerly by the central school, if at all. The following alternatives were viewed as possibilities:

1. Organize another central sales school.
2. Organize several schools—one for each region.
3. Drop the school completely.
4. Consolidate training within three or four regions.
5. Develop follow-up, on-the-job training material to be given by each branch manager.

In reviewing the situation with top management, the training director pointed out that the company school had the following merits:

1. Experience had shown that the central school training brought increased sales and earnings for the salesmen who received it.
2. It played an important role in such psychological ways as building greater interest in the salesman's job and in the company and its products and greater confidence in the salesman himself.
3. The central school afforded a good opportunity to control the content of the training in terms of uniformity and coverage.

The training director, however, pointed out what he felt to be two basic limitations of the central school:

1. The salesman did not receive instructions from his supervisor. The supervisor (branch manager) should be involved if maximum results from the training were to be realized.
2. The central school teachers were not in a position to keep track of the salesmen and correct later difficulties.

The training director was not sure of the comparative costs of the central school versus a decentralized school but believed that the costs would be approximately the same. The expenses that would be saved by elimination of the central school—two teachers, one clerical worker, and salesmen's traveling and living expenses while at the school—would tend to be offset by new costs if a decentralized system were established. The training director's position was not affected by the closing of the central school.

He also pointed out to top management that the changing nature of food retailing made training more important than ever. The individual retail units in the food field were steadily becoming larger. As a result, greater specialization was occurring in retail stores and higher-caliber men were being appointed to management positions in these stores. It was the training director's conviction that the success of the firm's salesmen would depend in the future less on personality and friendship and more on ability to merchandise and to help plan merchandise programs.

Finally, the training director pointed out that the company had traditionally promoted from within. The firm's president had come up through the sales ranks, and over 90 per cent of the branch managers were once company salesmen. He believed that good training contributed greatly to the retention of such men in the company during their early years as salesmen.

What type of sales training program should Heffner have?

72

THE TONI COMPANY

DURING the rapid growth of the Toni Company from 1950 to 1958, the personnel department had developed a training program to meet the needs of the expanding staff of marketing executives. By 1958 the personnel director thought that the company had reached a position where this training program should be supplemented by a broader program. He prepared a plan for a new training program and submitted it to the four department managers for review.

Under the proposed training program a college student who had completed at least his sophomore year would be brought into the company. A student with a C to A— average would be preferred. The program was to be a co-operative plan whereby the student would spend four quarters with Toni working full time at the mutual convenience of the company and himself. The ideal plan for a student finishing his sophomore year would be to spend three summers with Toni plus one quarter during one of his regular school years, to complete four quarters with the company prior to graduation. This particular program was not to be the only acceptable arrangement. Other quarters of the year could be used, and students who had completed their junior year of college would be considered. The personnel director hoped to help students integrate their school programs with job situations and planned that students would spend no more than two consecutive quarters at Toni at one time before returning to school. While working at Toni, the co-op students would be paid at a rate consistent with existing co-op systems operating in the area.

The personnel director believed that this program would, by giving the students job experience along with their study programs, produce men with a more realistic approach to their job future—men who would have a better idea of what they could do and wanted to do. The personnel director envisioned the program as part of the educational process for the students and did not propose that they should be required to commit themselves to working for Toni after graduation. Both the student and the company would have had a sufficient period to decide on the advisability of a long-term association, however, and, if both were interested, employment would be arranged. If the man who participated in the program returned to the company after graduation, they would have a greater appreciation of their position and value to the company. In any case, students with this training would be of more value to the business world in general.

The personnel director had certain reservations concerning the plan. He proposed to recruit students from the universities in the Chicago area but was not sure of the co-operation he would get from the schools. Since most of the candidates would come from the immediate area around Chicago, selection would have to be made from a relatively small pool of persons. He was not sure what interest students would have in the plan. Furthermore, although economic need was to be a factor in selecting students for the program, he did not want students to find the income so attractive that they would quit school.

The personnel director called a meeting of the four department directors who would be concerned with the proposed plan. The field sales organization was not included, since all employees started as salesmen and were moved up through the ranks. At this meeting, the following points were agreed upon:

1. Prospective candidates must be screened carefully to avoid unnecessary turnover.
2. It would be desirable to have a double team of students train in a department, whereby one student would train for two quarters while the other was in school, and vice versa. The department directors believed that most jobs required a minimum of six months to learn the essential skills, and a double team in a department would give continuity to the work.
3. The program should be as flexible as possible to permit the directors to use the co-op students where immediate needs existed and to permit students to show preference for positions in which they wished to gain experience.

The department directors thought that this type of program would help each student decide what program at school he wanted to follow. Furthermore, they thought that the students, being actively in school and getting new ideas, might offer some fresh approaches to their jobs. The public relations aspect of the program would probably be favorable for the company.

The department directors also expressed some concern about the mechanics of the plan. As they envisioned it, the directors would have to spend a considerable amount of time supervising the co-op students, and they doubted whether they could find this much time. The period that each student would spend with the company at one time would be six months or less, which would necessitate a constant refilling of these training positions and almost continuous training activities on the part of the directors. The department directors also noted that the company had a very low turnover of personnel and that new openings were not readily

TABLE 1

NUMBER OF EMPLOYEES PER DEPARTMENT

Department	Employees in Routine Work	Employees in Nonroutine Work	Total Employees
Market research	13	22	35
Advertising	5	5	10
Sales administration	15	12	27
Sales promotion	3	6	9

available. Because of this low turnover and because Toni could not be sure that the co-op student would want to return after graduation, the directors believed that the students would have to be given routine jobs during the training periods. Some directors were not sure that they had enough jobs in their departments to keep a co-op student busy.

To check this latter point more fully, the personnel director got a count on the number of employees in each of the four departments, as shown in Table 1. Each of the department directors was asked specifically whether he could use such a co-op student, and, if so, on what jobs he would use him. The market research director thought that he could use a student on such tasks as coding, tabulating, elementary analysis, and possibly for some media research that involved hunting data in various source books. The sales promotion director was doubtful that he could use a co-op student because his personnel were primarily highly trained technicians who did advertising production work or worked with retailers on co-operative advertising programs. The advertising director thought that he could not use a student because of the limited size of his staff and the lack of turnover. The sales administration director reported that he could use co-op students in a number of ways. He could use them to do statistical or analytical work on sales data, to make special studies, to carry through special projects, or as general "leg men."

Should the proposed training program be installed?

4. Supervising and Controlling the Sales Force

73

INTERNATIONAL HARVESTER MOTOR TRUCK DIVISION (C)

INTERNATIONAL HARVESTER'S share of the Los Angeles truck market had been declining for three years. The western regional manager believed that one of the major factors involved in this decline was the high rate of turnover among new salesmen. To overcome this problem, he proposed to have a special supervisor of recruiting and training who would take over these jobs for the three Los Angeles branches.

TABLE 1

NEW TRUCK REGISTRATIONS IN FOUR MAJOR MARKETS
FOR THREE MOST RECENT YEARS

Market	Current Year*			Last Year			Two Years Ago		
	Industry	Inter-national No.	Per Cent	Industry	Inter-national No.	Per Cent	Industry	Inter-national No.	Per Cent
Los Angeles	19,513	1,085	5.6	23,540	1,768	7.5	17,825	1,542	8.7
Chicago	11,618	1,690	14.5	15,801	2,145	13.6	13,343	1,528	11.5
Philadelphia	6,233	660	10.6	8,213	838	10.2	6,924	719	10.4
New York	14,587	1,897	13.0	20,549	3,037	14.8	17,236	2,179	12.6

* First ten months only.

A study of new truck registrations for the four most important metropolitan markets in the United States for the last two years and the first ten months of the current year (Table 1) showed clearly that International was not sharing in the Los Angeles market to the same degree that it did in the other major markets.

International's share of the new truck registrations in the Los Angeles metropolitan market, which included all Los Angeles County, had declined from 8.7 per cent of the industry total in 1952 to 5.6 per cent for the first ten months of 1954. International was concerned not only because of this drop but also because the company's industry participation in Los Angeles was extremely poor when compared with that in the other major markets. In Chicago, International had 14.5 per cent of the industry's sales, in Philadelphia it had 10.6 per cent, and in New York 13.0 per cent.

The motor truck division was of great importance to the International Harvester Company. More than 30 per cent of the firm's total sales volume came from the sale of motor trucks, service, and parts. The total yearly volume of this division exceeded one-quarter of a billion dollars. International ranked third in total truck registrations among all companies in the industry, and in the heavier class of vehicles it ranked first. The company had been well known for many years for its large motor equipment, particularly for vehicles weighing 16,000 pounds and over.

International sold its trucks through its own retail branches and through independent dealers. The Los Angeles area had more outlets than other metropolitan areas because of its geographic expanse. There were three branches and eighteen dealers in the Los Angeles metropolitan area and the western regional manager had proposed establishing five more branches. Branches accounted for 72 per cent of the 1,085 International trucks sold in the Los Angeles market, a fairly typical proportion for large cities.

The company had experienced difficulty in securing and holding good dealers in the area because of the strong competition from combination car and truck dealers with a sales volume advantage and because of the high capital investment required for land, facilities, tools, and inventories. The logical prospects for International franchises were the automobile dealers who did not sell any line of trucks. In discussing contracts with these firms, International cited the fact that the motor truck line could be merchandised without a significant increase in overhead costs; typically, little additional space or equipment was needed. Direct selling expense was the chief additional cost. Despite the validity of this argument, it did not seem to be a strong attraction for dealers.

There were thirty-eight International retail salesmen in the Los Angeles area. They worked out of the three branches. The three branches each had a manager who was responsible for directing all phases of branch activities, including sales and service. One of his responsibilities was recruiting and training new salesmen. Because of the many demands on the branch managers, it was thought that they were unable to give adequate time to accomplish the training and supervision necessary for the development and increased productivity of new salesmen. Annual salesman turnover was 50 per cent in Los Angeles, as compared with 8 per cent in Chicago, 5 per cent in New York, and 15 per cent in Philadelphia.

International Harvester's salesmen in the Los Angeles area were of three distinct types. About half the salesmen were "old-timers" who had built up a substantial clientele and handled most of the fleet accounts. Within this group there were two categories—the salesmen who had specific territories and possibly some additional fleet accounts outside their territories and the salesmen who were specialists in given industries and sold only to those industries. For example, one man sold only mixing trucks to the companies who supplied ready-mixed concrete for construction, road building, etc. The other half of the sales force consisted of new salesmen. These men were each assigned a territory and had full responsibility for the territory except for those accounts which were assigned to the more experienced men.

Compensation was different for each of the three types of salesman. The new salesmen were paid a straight salary during their training period. After a man had accumulated some experience and built up a clientele, his compensation was changed to a combination of a base salary and commissions. The salary portion was less than his training salary but was sufficient to cover basic living expenses. On each small truck sold to a nonfleet owner, the salesman received a 3 per cent commission computed on the sale price. If a trade-in were involved, the commission was computed on the net cash transaction, but a minimum commission of $25 was paid for each truck sold. A 5 per cent commission was paid on sales of used vehicles. Commission rates were scaled downward for sales to fleet owners and on sales of the larger vehicles. The salesmen who specialized in one particular industry were paid on a salary-plus-bonus arrangement. These men generally had a sales volume in excess of $300,000 annually, and their bonuses were calculated on the relationship of sales to expenses.

The turnover was heaviest among the newer, less experienced salesmen. The western regional manager attributed some of the turnover to the fact that the older salesmen were taking the "gravy" in the fleet accounts and leaving the single-truck market for the new salesmen. The lack of supervision and training, however, he believed to be a more important factor. Because of this lack of training the new salesmen did not reach the point at which they could increase their income through commissions rapidly enough and soon became dissatisfied and left. This turnover created a morale problem, which contributed to further turnover because, since new salesmen did not last long, the other members of the staff tended to belittle them.

To correct the declining truck sales in the Los Angeles area, the regional manager created a new position in the regional staff called the "supervisor of recruiting and sales training." It was believed that such an individual could contribute a great deal in training sales personnel in all ways. He would establish procedures for branch managers to follow in recruiting and supervising new salesmen. In addition, he would work directly with salesmen in on-the-job training, making calls with the salesmen and holding weekly training meetings to establish methods of allocating time, finding and evaluating new prospects, and conducting sales presentations. The supervisor of recruiting and training would work with all three of the branches in the area as part of the regional office staff. Branch managers would continue to have the responsibility for recruiting new salesmen and for their sales results.

Was the appointment of a supervisor of recruiting and training a sound step toward better performance in the Los Angeles area?

74

SPECTOR FREIGHT SYSTEM, INC.

THE SALESMEN for Spector Freight System, Inc., one of the largest trucking systems serving the midwestern and eastern sections of the United States, had been working with little or no guidance from line management. There were duplication of territories and wasted time in nonproductive calls and entertainment. The result was an inefficient use of salesmen. To correct this situation, Mr. Val Williams, vice-president of marketing, undertook to develop, test, and implement a program to increase the productivity of the salesmen.

Spector Freight System, Inc., served primarily the midwestern, middle Atlantic, and eastern sections of the United States. It had twenty-eight terminals located throughout these areas and more than 3,500 operating units—local delivery trucks, tractors, and trailers. The company handled approximately 1.8 million shipments in 1959, and total revenues exceeded $47 million—an increase of more than 100 per cent over 1950.

The sales organization had consisted of a vice-president of sales, a director of sales, and four district sales managers, all located at the main office in Chicago. The company's seventy salesmen reported to the district sales managers, but, because of their location, the district managers had little contact with the salesmen except through reports and correspondence.

One of the first changes made by Williams was to revamp the organization and put the salesmen under the terminal managers. About half the terminal managers had been promoted from the sales department; the others had come from the operations department. Where there were more than three salesmen operating out of a terminal, a sales supervisor was added to the staff to handle administrative sales details. The sales supervisors also had territories of their own and devoted about 60 per cent of their time to selling and 40 per cent to administrative work.

The terminal managers reported to the district managers, who were moved to the district offices located approximately in the center of each district. Each district had a sales manager who was responsible to the district manager. The sales managers had only staff responsibility and had no line authority over terminal managers except through the district managers. The districts were all under the vice-president of operations (Exhibit 1).

The salesman's duties were to call on any and all accounts in his territory that had need for trucking service and to sell them on using Spector service. He normally called on the traffic manager or the shipping clerk. Frequent contacts with accounts were necessary to set up shipping

EXHIBIT 1

Spector Organization Chart

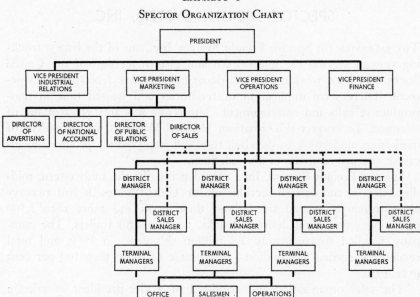

and routing schedules. Regular shippers usually planned these schedules from one week to a month in advance. Since rates were regulated by the government, the main sales points were speed, availability, and service. All salesmen were paid a straight salary.

The sales program was broken down into seven parts: (1) territory screening, (2) account classification, (3) sales call pattern, (4) production requirements, (5) production planning, (6) budgeting sales expense, and (7) time analysis. Each of these parts was taken under study to develop methods and standards for the salesmen's performance. The program was turned over to the salesmen in the form shown in Exhibits 2 and 3.

EXHIBIT 2

Spector Sales Production Plan

1. Territory Screening

The following screening steps are basic to the initial planning for a new sales territory. *Every* sales territory, however, should be rescreened at least once

EXHIBIT 2 (*Cont.*)

each year, and which of these steps will be required for this rescreening is dependent upon the local circumstances. You as a salesman and manager of your territory along with your terminal sales supervisor will determine the need and can use these steps as a guide.

a. Outbound Accounts

(1) Current Active Accounts

A clerk can arrange an alphabetical card listing of accounts from your account ledger. These cards should include the account name, address, phone number, name of the person to be contacted, commodity involved, and tonnage accomplishment for the past six periods. NOTE: This grouping should include all accounts in your ledger even though some may show no activity. In certain instances where your record cards are not complete, a summary should be made of the bills of lading covering the foregoing period of time in order to insure an accurate record of current active accounts.

(2) Prospective Accounts

Compile a card listing of the prospective accounts not included in your ledger listing. Your first approach should be from your knowledge of your territory. Your next approach should be to take major industry classifications, such as, chemical, electrical, parts manufacturers, paint manufacturers, drugs, etc., secure classified listings from chamber of commerce guides, industrial guides, classified phone directories, etc., and list those businesses that are not included in step (1).

(3) Composite List

A clerk should then arrange all cards in alphabetical order, and a review of the card listing should be made by you and the terminal manager or sales supervisor to insure as thorough an analysis as possible.

b. Inbound Accounts

(1) Current Active Accounts

A clerk can compile a card listing of inbound accounts from your ledger where you maintain separate records of inbound accounts. Add to these your cards on every active inbound account of which you have knowledge in your territory. Review the past three periods' inbound manifests to add any accounts not listed through a study of your ledger or by your knowledge.

(2) Prospective Accounts

Have a clerk compile an alphabetical card listing of inbound leads for the last six periods. Also compile a card listing of prospects based on your knowledge of the territory.

(3) Composite List

Have a clerk compile the composite list alphabetically to be reviewed by you and the terminal manager to insure as complete a listing as possible.

NOTE: At this stage both card lists should be reviewed and screened for duplications, local business only, etc.

Account Classification

a. Account Coding

When the cards are completed on *all* accounts in a territory, divide them into eight groups under two major headings, namely "ACTIVE" and "PROSPECTIVE."

EXHIBIT 2 *(Cont.)*

(1) "A" Accounts

(*a*) Active Accounts

An Active "A" Account is defined as one that produces $500 or more of LTL revenue during a majority of the thirteen four-week accounting periods during the year.

(*b*) Prospective Accounts

An account that cannot be classified as an Active "A" Account under the qualifications listed in (*a*) immediately above, but that has the potential of producing that volume of LTL revenue, will be classified as an "A" Prospective Account.

(2) "B" Accounts

(*a*) Active Accounts

An Active "B" Account is defined as one that produces $500 or more TL revenue during a majority of the thirteen four-week accounting periods of the year.

(*b*) Prospective Accounts

An account that cannot be classified as an Active "B" Account, but that has the potential of producing that volume of TL revenue described in (*a*) immediately above, will be classified as a "B" Prospective Account.

(3) Accounts with Both TL and LTL Volume

(*a*) In situations in which an account is presently supplying a volume of TL and LTL revenue to meet both "A" and "B" account requirements, the account will be classified as an Active "A" Account regardless of the TL revenue produced.

(*b*) A Prospective Account will be classified "A" or "B" according to the most immediate potential, whether LTL or TL.

(4) "C" Accounts

(*a*) Active Accounts

An Active "C" Account is defined as one that produces $200–$500 LTL or TL revenue during a majority of the thirteen four-week accounting periods and because of the size or nature of its business activity is unlikely to produce more revenue. Because of this limitation it would not be classified as an "A" or "B" Prospective.

(*b*) Prospective Accounts

An Account that cannot be classified as an Active "C" Account, but that has the potential of producing that volume of LTL or TL revenue described in (*a*) immediately above, will be classified as "C" Prospective.

(5) "D" Accounts

(*a*) Active Accounts

An Active "D" Account is defined as one that produces less than $200 revenue per period and because of the size or nature of its business activity is unlikely to produce any more revenue than that. Generally, the small shipper or occasional shipper will fall in this category.

(*b*) Prospective Accounts

A Prospective "D" Account is defined as one that cannot be classified in any category above but that does have the potential of producing some revenue.

(6) Short-Haul Operations

The definitions and classifications covered previously are designed for the long-haul operations; however, they will also apply to short-

EXHIBIT 2 (*Cont.*)

haul operations, except that the revenue requirements will be reduced. These situations will be handled on an individual basis and the general office sales department, working with the local sales department, will determine the respective revenue criteria.

3. Sales Call Pattern

Your salary plus your expenses divided by the number of calls you make will determine a cost-per-sales call. This cost can be economically invested only in ratio to a return, either immediate or potential. It is possible, therefore, to work out an average call pattern that you can afford to invest on the various categories of accounts. Following is the average pattern proved out through an analysis of Spector's sales activity over the past couple of years.

Active "A" accounts:	1 call every 4 weeks—12 per year	
Active "B" accounts:	1 " " 4 " —12 " "	
Prospective "A" accounts:	1 " " 5 " —10 " "	
Prospective "B" accounts:	1 " " 6 " — 8 " "	
All "C" accounts:	1 " " 7 " — 7 " "	
All "D" accounts:	1 " " 8 " — 6 " "	

NOTE: After you have made 3 calls on a prospective account with no production results, the account should be reviewed by the terminal manager or the district sales manager and yourself. It may be necessary to call on the district or home office for special sales assistance to "crack" the account. It is most important that all the factors relating to the nonproductivity of the account be identified. Such an account presents a sales problem that can be solved only with planning and campaigning. There is questionable economic justification for a continued investment of sales-call time with no signs of return. On the other hand, if the account has a potential we had best find a way to secure it for Spector.

4. Production Requirements

With this type of plan a Spector salesman should average 12 calls a day. His work should be planned on the basis of a 48-week year, which means 240 working days or 2,880 calls per year.

5. Production Planning

The next step in the sales plan is to divide the territory into sections on a geographical basis. The territory may best be divided into four, six, or eight sections, depending on the area to be covered. When the sections have been established, the cards should then be sorted into section groups. Each section will include the various account classifications, both active and prospective. The next step is to take each section and project the coverage time involved, using the formula in 3. You should now begin to lay out specific 4-week call plans by setting in your twelve customers a day on a production calendar or spread sheet.

NOTE: You should use a call division formula of 75 per cent active and 25 per cent prospective. Therefore, each day you would have nine active accounts and three prospects. This division, of course, is based on the fact that even active accounts are prospects in the sense that we must get more business from these active accounts than what we are currently enjoying.

6. Sales Expense

The sales call pattern, once established, will also serve as a businesslike budgeter of the entertainment expense that can be profitably directed to a specific account.

EXHIBIT 2 (*Cont.*)

All extra sales expense items, such as luncheons, dinners, ball games, traffic functions, and similar expenditures, can be allotted in terms of the type or classification of the account. An Active "A" Account may be entitled to 3 luncheons and 1 traffic club function per year; an Active "B" Account may likewise be a 3 luncheon and 1 traffic function account.

The number of luncheon, dinners, etc., per account is not nearly so important as that each one be according to a sales plan. These expenditures are justifiable in terms of the business they produce. To approach this expense problem otherwise is to suggest that they should not be allowed. To produce the desirable sales result, it is encumbent upon every one of us to spend every sales dollar and every sales minute where it will do the most good.

7. Time Analysis

Every salesman's life is the story of man versus time. The prime shortcoming of salesmen on this question of time is their lack of systematic attention to it. Here is a list of items to keep in mind as you devote your attention to helping yourself make even more productive use of your time:

a. A simplification of paperwork, with some thought to having clerical help assume part of the burden.

b. Increased sales per call.

c. Scheduling calls practically and intelligently.

d. Enlisting co-operation of customers.

e. Capitalizing on service calls for prospecting in the area.

f. Greater use of the telephone.

g. Use "unavailable" waiting time.

h. Concentrate on new customers in an area where we presently have few customers.

i. Have a "second possibility" in event appointments are cancelled.

Observe the "Time Expense Account" form. You may find it very helpful to fill in a form such as this for each of several weeks. It could help you focus your attention on the less productive time you use up during a day and indicate the places where you can make more selling time available to yourself.

In developing the program, management first turned to company records to classify accounts. The company had 300 national accounts that were handled by the director of national accounts. He had four national account executives, each with 75 accounts. These were accounts that shipped large volumes of merchandise and accounted for a major portion of Spector's revenue. The accounts handled by the salesmen were generally smaller. Accounts were classified by the type and amount of business they produced. LTL (less-than-truck-load) business was classified over TL (truck-load) because it was more profitable business. Standardized methods were developed for screening and classifying accounts in each territory.

The sales call pattern was developed from information received from customers and from past experience of salesmen. Spector learned that most customers scheduled shipping at the same time that production was scheduled and that the trucking service representative should be on

EXHIBIT 3

TIME EXPENSE ACCOUNT FORM

Kind of Activity	Monday	Tuesday	Wed-nesday	Thurs-day	Friday	Saturday	Minutes (Total)
Records and reports							
Travel							
Waiting							
Interview							
Work with cus-tomers							
Telephone							
Service calls							
Complaints							
Prospecting and pre-approach							
Planning and Study							
Entertainment							
Personal							
Miscellaneous							
Total							
No. of calls							

hand at that time. A survey was conducted among customers to get their ideas on how often a salesman should call.

Considerable testing was done on the number of calls a salesman could make in a day. Special salesmen and management personnel went out in different areas and tried making 8, 10, 12, 14, and up to 20 calls a day. It was found that, if the salesman made over 14 calls per day, he did not have enough time to spend with each customer. If the salesman made less than 12 calls per day, he was loafing. As a result of these tests and other information that showed sales calls averaged about 26 minutes, management settled on 12 calls per day as the standard.

To make 12 calls a day required planning. Each territory was divided into sections, the number depending upon the area to be covered. The salesman was to take the accounts in each section and work out the optimum grouping so that he could make 12 calls a day. Management determined that the salesman should spend 75 per cent of his time with customers and 25 per cent with prospects. This meant 9 calls a day on

EXHIBIT 4

SALES CALL REPORT FORM

103299

SPECTOR MID-STATES   SALES CALL RECORD

Date_____

Firm_____

Address_____ City_____

Talked to ._____ Title_____

Active ☐   Prospective ☐   New Prospect ☐

Outbound ☐   Inbound ☐   Out and In ☐

Call Accomplishments_____

_____

_____

_____

_____

_____

_____

_____

_____

_____

My last call on this account was on_____

Lead Number_____Routing Order ☐

Salesman_____Acct. Class_____

customers and 3 on prospects. The salesman was to plan his activities four weeks in advance.

Management felt that this sales call pattern would also help in budgeting expenses. Expenses were not considered important in themselves but had to be justifiable in terms of business produced.

Each salesman was given a ring binder that contained call report forms in triplicate. A call report was submitted for each call. Management encouraged salesmen to make out call reports during the interview with the customer, noting the important points discussed, any complaints, and schedules. It was thought that the customer would be more impressed if he knew that his ideas would come to the attention of Spector management. The salesman kept one copy of the report, one went to the terminal manager, and one to the district sales manager (Exhibit 4.)

Quotas were established for each territory on the basis of past performance and total business available. The quotas were broken down on a weekly basis. The salesmen were paid a weekly bonus, which was determined by three factors: sales over quota, number of calls, and sales expenses. The bonus was allocated on a point system, with ten points as the maximum. This maximum represented the total bonus that a salesman could earn in his territory; the dollar amount of bonus varied among territories. Of the ten points, eight were allocated to sales over quota, one to number of calls, and one to sales expenses. The degree to which a salesman exceeded his quota determined how many of the eight points would be credited to his bonus. If he did not make his quota, he lost all eight points. Similarly for the number of calls, he received one point. If the salesman made 60 calls (12 calls a day, 5 days a week), he received the full point for number of calls; if he made 59 calls, he received 0.8 point; if 58 calls, 0.6 point, etc. If sales expenses were held to 2 cents per hundred pounds of truck-load freight and 4 cents per hundred pounds of less than truck-load freight shipped from his territory, the salesman got the one point for sales expenses. If expenses were higher, the point credit was reduced proportionately.

1. *Would the new plan result in more efficient use of Spector salesmen?*
2. *What further improvements could be made?*

75

AMERICAN PHOTOCOPY EQUIPMENT COMPANY

THE SALES manager of APECO (American Photocopy Equipment Company), the leading manufacturer of photocopying machines in the United States, believed that, while no major sales problems existed at the moment, the company would, in the near future, have to develop a new program for handling the supply part of its business if it were going to maintain its industry leadership position.

The sale of supplies (sensitized paper and developing chemicals) accounted for 70 per cent of APECO's volume. The firm produced its own chemicals but bought the paper that it resold. The reason for the sales manager's concern was that two independent companies that did not manufacture machines had recently brought out lines of sensitized paper and developer for photocopying machines. These were marketed through office supply wholesalers and retailers. According to the 1954 Census of Business, there were over 1,500 office supply wholesalers, many of which sold direct to larger businesses, and 2,216 office supply dealers. Dealers often had sales forces calling regularly on stores and offices. They typically received discounts of about 40 per cent off list price.

About thirty-five different companies competed in the office copying field. APECO had led the industry in the introduction of office copying machines in the United States with a machine that used the "diffusion transfer" process. APECO had over 90 per cent of the market for this type of equipment. In the "diffusion transfer" process, light was passed through a photographic-type negative to an original and reflected back onto this negative. The exposed sheet was then placed with a "transfer" sheet and passed, by means of motor-drive rollers, through a liquid developer to a set of exit rollers that squeezed out the excess solution. This developing process pressed the two sheets together, and, when they were peeled apart, a finished positive copy resulted. Through the sale of this equipment and the compatible supplies APECO sales had grown from $2.5 million in 1952 to over $24.8 million in 1959.

Eastman Kodak Company sold a machine using a dye transfer process that gave results similar to the diffusion process. Haloid Xerox, Inc., marketed a process that used a projection process to produce an image on an electrically charged plate. The image was transferred to copy paper by use of negatively charged powdered inks. These two competing processes and APECO's could be used to copy almost any original. Minnesota Mining and Manufacturing Company sold the Thermofax process, which used heat to produce a copy. This process was limited to use with originals that had been printed with carbon or metallic based inks. The least expensive process on the market was the diazo process. This process could be used only to copy translucent originals with printing on only one side. Several firms marketed this process. Charles Bruning Company and Ozalid Division of General Aniline and Film Company were two of the major ones.

In addition to marketing a complete line of photocopy machines, APECO's line included the ComBind, which was a portable machine to punch and bind papers or booklets with a plastic binding element. APECO also marketed the Ply-On Laminator, which was a desk-top machine that permanently sealed any type of document or card in clear, flexible plastic. APECO, of course, marketed a complete line of supplies for all their machines. All these products were sold directly to the user by 353 company salesmen in the United States and Canada. In addition, APECO had sales offices throughout South America and Europe.

The APECO sales organization was headed by a national sales manager. Under him were two assistant national sales managers and five divisional sales managers. The national sales manager was also responsible for the functions performed by the sales promotion manager and the market research department (Exhibit 1).

EXHIBIT 1

APECO Sales Organization

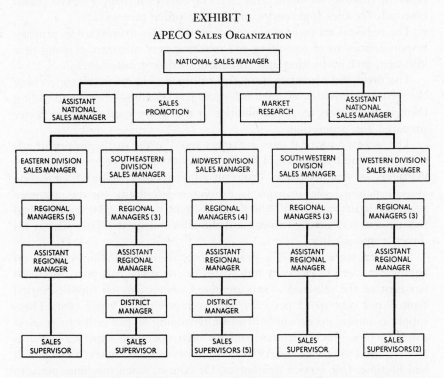

Each divisional sales manager was responsible for one of the five major market areas of the United States. A division consisted of from three to five regions, each with a regional manager in charge. The regional managers were responsible, through their own efforts and those of the district sales managers and sales supervisors under them, for the direct supervision of the field salesmen. The sales supervisors and district managers reported directly to the regional managers, and the regional managers, in turn, reported directly to the divisional managers. In each division one of the regional managers had an assistant regional manager, who divided his time between selling and working in the regional office. This was part of an advanced training program for grooming future management personnel.

The sales supervisor was a senior salesman who operated a territory and also aided in sales training. APECO maintained a continuous training program for all salesmen. A sales supervisor usually was assigned the responsibility of from three to six salesmen, in addition to any new salesmen who might be assigned to him for training. The initial training period for a news salesman varied from six weeks, for men who had had previous selling experience, to three to five months for men with no previous experience.

The district managers, likewise, operated sales territories. These men supervised from five to nine salesmen and, in addition, had the responsibility of running the branch offices. The district managers served simultaneously as sales supervisors and branch office managers.

The regional manager was a full-time field sales manager. His primary responsibilities were recruiting and selecting new salesmen, training new salesmen, and motivating and stimulating existing salesmen.

The divisional managers were also full-time field managers supervising the general activities of regional managers, training them, and aiding them in their areas of responsibilities so that these men might be better prepared for promotion.

The assistant national sales managers acted in the dual capacity of administrators and field men. They aided divisional managers and regional managers as was necessary. From an administrative point of view, one assistant national sales manager had direct responsibility for the customer relations department, while the other assistant national sales manager had the national service department and the sales statistical department as his direct responsibility.

Salesmen were paid on a straight commission basis. Commissions on equipment were 25 per cent and usually accounted for approximately 60 per cent of the salesman's total income. Commissions on supplies varied from 5 per cent to 15 per cent, but averaged about 9 per cent. These supply commissions accounted for the remaining 40 per cent of the salesman's income. Each salesman paid his own operating expenses and was also required to service the APECO machines in his territory, all of which had lifetime, free service guarantees. Of course, when machines actually wore out, they had to be replaced. The company had a trade-in policy on replacement sales. The effective life of the machines was estimated at five years or more. Many salesmen hired part-time servicemen to help service their customers. This service usually involved making minor repairs and adjustments and training new operators. The average APECO salesman grossed between $11,000 and $12,000 a year from commissions.

Each salesman was assigned a territory and received commissions on all business emanating from his territory. When a salesman was assigned to a new territory, he was normally given approximately one hundred accounts to start. This meant an immediate income of approximately $250 per month from the sale of supplies. The territories were established on a statistical basis, that is, such items as total population, number of business establishments, and number of manufacturing organizations were taken into consideration. Each man was assigned a sales quota, and these quotas were uniform throughout the country. In 1959 the quota for each man was six machine sales per month. In 1960 the quota was raised to seven machine sales per month. There was no quota on supplies.

The company had an extensive advertising program, which was divided between publication advertising and direct mail. The salesmen received an average of thirty inquiries per month as a result of this advertising program. In addition, salesmen continuously received referrals from existing customers. APECO also had a "chain reaction" program that provided all salesmen with the information pertaining to any sale to a nationally known organization.

Company statistics showed that the average salesman made from four to six calls per day and gave two or three demonstrations per day. These demonstrations were actual presentations of the machines to a prospective buyer. The salesmen averaged between one and two sales for every seven demonstrations made. The sale involved the basic machine plus the necessary operating supplies. The basic machine in the APECO line varied in price from $227.50 to $423.50. The ComBind machine was priced at $223.50 and the Ply-On Laminator at $335.00.

In addition to selling machines, the company expected the salesmen to call regularly on existing accounts. In almost all cases, a customer purchasing an APECO machine would continue to use APECO supplies. The average customer purchased approximately $30 worth of supplies a month, which was worth $2.50 in commissions for the salesman.

To help in defining the potential problem in holding the supply part of his business, the sales manager made a survey among inactive accounts that sought the reasons why APECO had not been getting business from them. All accounts that had not ordered within the past year were assigned to salesmen for investigation. This survey uncovered the fact that a small percentage of the accounts had been lost as a result of the lack of contact between the salesman and the customer. On the basis of the survey findings, the sales manager established a routine follow-up program, which he believed had regained the bulk of the accounts that had strayed to competition.

The average small account was to be called on every ninety days by either the APECO salesman or his serviceman. The machine was checked over thoroughly, supplies were inventoried, and, if any additional instructions were necessary, the operator was made familiar with them. When a salesman or serviceman made a service call, he asked the owner or operator of the machine to sign a "no charge service invoice." These were kept by the salesman as a record of the service extended to each customer.

Large national accounts were handled somewhat differently. One of the big insurance companies was typical. This firm was on a routine thirty-day follow-up. Every thirty days each of the one hundred salesmen who had one of the insurance company's offices in his territory called on the local office and inspected and adjusted the equipment. The branch managers of the insurance office were required to sign a "no charge service invoice" (which was the same one used for small accounts). These "no charge service invoices" were forwarded to the customer relations department at the home office and checked against the master list to make certain that all the branch offices of the insurance company had been called on. The invoices were then forwarded to the salesman covering the home office of this insurance company. This salesman, in turn, presented them to the proper individual in charge of branch office operation.

All new salesmen were required to turn in daily call reports to their regional managers. Most regional managers required these reports only until such time as a man was firmly established in his territory. Once there was no question of this man's operation, these reports were discontinued.

On the bases of past experience and the sales-to-demonstration ratio, a man could make a good income from merely selling machines. The supply business followed more or less automatically. The loss of the supply business from several small accounts did not seriously affect a salesman's income. The rapid growth that APECO had enjoyed had overshadowed any loss of accounts that might have occurred through lack of close contact between salesman and customer. It was extremely difficult to separate these losses into those that might be using another make of supplies and those that might have discontinued the use of the equipment through a change in their office requirements. With the entry of additional competitors into the supply field, the sales manager believed that APECO was going to have to become more customer conscious. Since the new competitors did not manufacture photocopy machines, they could stress the sales of supplies only to organizations that already had equipment.

Was any further action needed to prepare APECO to hold its supply business? If so, what?

76

WHEELER TRACTOR COMPANY

The Wheeler Tractor Company produced a specialized line of rototillers and two-wheel walking garden tractors. The latter could easily be converted into a snow plow by adding a special snow plow fixture. The rototillers sold at retail for $139.60–$168.75, and the garden tractors (complete with snow-plow attachments) for $269.95–$359.95. The company sold its entire output to a leading mail-order firm until 1956, when it launched its own brand with a force of three salesmen calling on dealers. In the first nine months of 1959 the company had sales of $224,241 of its own brand, and sales for the entire year were projected at $298,405. The president, while pleased with the progress in sales, was concerned about the continuing heavy sales cost. In 1958 the total sales cost for the company's own brand totaled $114,852[1] on sales of $274,241.

The sales manager pointed out that high sales expenses were necessary because salesmen had to locate, train, and service dealers. He hoped that sales costs as a per cent of sales had hit their peak. He did not expect sales costs to decrease, but he did anticipate an increase in sales. "Also, this is the kind of product," he said, "that has to be sold direct to the dealer. Almost without exception the industry follows this pattern. I'm sure we couldn't hold many of our better dealers if we went the distributor route. And don't forget that distributors don't carry much of an inventory either. We'd end up doing a lot of drop shipping."

Dealers received a 32 per cent discount from list price, and distributors received a 47 per cent discount. The company had distribution in only the middle-western states of Minnesota, Wisconsin, Michigan, Iowa, Ohio, Illinois, Indiana, Missouri, Kentucky, and Kansas. A variety of dealer types, including garden supply stores, power equipment dealers, hardware stores, appliance stores, general stores, farm equipment dealers, filling stations, garages, department stores, and auto and truck dealers were serviced by the three salesmen. In the first three years a substantial number of dealers had either terminated their franchises voluntarily or had them terminated by Wheeler. During the first nine months of 1959 sixty-five dealers were added and thirty-one dealers dropped their franchises.

The company's sales records consisted mainly of a sales ledger book divided into four parts—one for each salesman and one for the sales manager, who spent a majority of his time in the field soliciting new accounts. There was a separate page for each dealer, on which the date of each sales visit and the dollar amount of each order were recorded. Sales by product were not recorded, only total dollar sales.

In discussing the sales budget, the president urged the sales manager to try to get more production out of the existing sales force by having them limit the time they spent with smaller accounts. The sales manager did not think that it was possible to limit the time spent with "small accounts" because many dealers were just getting started and, therefore, needed a lot of attention. In any case, all dealers started as small accounts. Nevertheless, he decided to analyze his records before submitting his final budget to the president.

---

[1] Advertising, $29,200; salesmen's salaries and expenses, $52,895; sales manager's salary and expenses, $20,909; and office help, $11,848.

The sales manager's secretary was responsible for maintaining the sales ledger. He therefore discussed with her the need for a sales analysis and concluded by requesting her to draw up dummy tables showing the kinds of data that could be obtained from the ledger. Two days later he received the tables, which showed figures for the first nine months of 1959 (Tables 1 and 2).

TABLE 1

DOLLAR SALES AND NUMBER OF ACTIVE DEALERS BY MONTH: JANUARY–SEPTEMBER, 1959*

Month	Sales	No. of Dealers
January	$29,631	214
February	24,824	225
March	20,368	227
April	3,347	232
May	6,616	245
June	13,608	245
July	44,875	252
August	64,919	247
September	16,053	248

* Data were not yet available for the last three months of the year.

TABLE 2

NUMBER OF DEALERS, NUMBER OF DEALER CALLS, SALES VOLUME, AND DIRECT SALES COSTS BY ANNUAL SALES TO DEALER: 1959*

1959 Sales to Dealer	No. of Dealers	Per Cent of Dealers	No. of Calls	Per Cent of Dealer Calls	Sales Volume	Per Cent of Total Sales	Direct Sales Costs†	Sales Costs as Per Cent of Sales Volume	Sales Costs as Per Cent of Total Direct Sales Costs‡
$0–$499§	162	58.1	155	32.0	$ 20,757	9.3	$ 5,817	28.0	32.0
500–999	42	15.1	62	12.8	29,358	13.1	2,327	7.9	12.8
1,000–1,499	22	7.9	52	10.7	29,118	13.0	1,952	6.7	10.7
1,500–1,999	18	6.5	72	14.8	30,625	13.7	2,702	8.8	14.8
2,000–2,499	14	5.0	61	12.6	31,710	14.1	2,289	7.2	12.6
2,500–2,999	6	2.2	29	6.0	17,742	7.9	1,088	6.1	6.0
3,000–3,499	4	1.4	17	3.5	13,302	5.9	638	4.8	3.5
3,500–3,999	4	1.4	17	3.5	14,830	6.6	638	4.3	3.5
4,000–4,499	4	1.4	8	1.6	16,227	7.2	300	1.9	1.6
4,500–4,999	1	0.4	6	1.2	6,089	2.7	225	3.7	1.2
5,000 and over	2	0.7	6	1.2	14,483	6.5	225	1.6	1.2
Totals	279	100.1‖	485	99.9‖	$224,241	100.0	$18,202#	8.1	99.9‖
New business**			648				$24,319		
Grand Total	1133				$224,241	100.0	$42,521	18.5	

* First nine months only.

† Includes salesmen's salaries and expenses only. A per call cost of $37.53 was obtained by dividing total sales costs ($41,596) by the number of calls (1133).

‡ Excludes cost of new business calls.

§ Includes 17 dealers to whom no sales were made in this period.

‖ Does not add to 100.0 because of rounding.

Does not add to total because of rounding.

** "New business" calls were calls on prospective dealers that did not result in sales.

1. *What changes, if any, should be made in the allocation of salesmen's time?*

2. *Could more useful data be drawn from the sales records? What data?*

3. *Should different sales records be kept? What records?*

77

TALCOTT AND COMPANY

TALCOTT AND COMPANY manufactured and sold a wide variety of paper products for both industrial and household use. One of its product lines, multiwall bags, was used for packaging cement, fertilizer, chemicals, animal feeds, sugar, charcoal briquets, and other consumer and industrial products. Its sales of multiwall bags were concentrated in the eleven western states; however, company executives wished to expand into the Midwest market. With that thought in mind, a new multiwall bag factory was built in Milledgeville, Georgia. As the plant neared completion in 1957, the marketing manager began to plan how to enter this new market. One problem was to decide how many salesmen were needed, where they should be located, and what territories they should have.

Talcott and Company owned and operated timber lands, sawmills, wood pulp and paper mills, and manufacturing plants for making paper into a variety of products. The latter included newsprint and other printing papers, wrapping and packaging paper products (such as kraft paper, multiwall paper bags, waxed papers, and flexible packaging materials), paperboard products (such as corrugated and solid fiber shipping containers), and tissue and sanitary papers (such as facial and bathroom tissue and paper towels). The "Jay" and "Silfen" brand names were used on consumer items. The company also sold part of its timber in the form of lumber, plywood, and shingles. Sales were heavily concentrated on the West Coast and totaled $461 million in 1957, more than twice the figure of ten years earlier. Multiwall bag sales accounted for less than 10 per cent of the total in both years.

In November, 1955, the Northwoods Corporation merged with Talcott and Company. It had, among other plants, a pulp and kraft paper mill at Milledgeville, Georgia. The acquisition of this mill gave Talcott the raw material source it needed for making multiwall bags east of the Rocky Mountains. Accordingly, a bag manufacturing plant was built adjacent to the mill.

Since Talcott had no previous sales experience in the Midwest area, considerable information was needed before sales plans and sales territories could be established. Consequently, the company conducted a survey of bag users in eight midwestern states[1] to determine who used multiwall bags and the users' size, location, and other characteristics. Instead of hiring a commercial research firm to make the survey, the marketing manager used the five new salesmen who were to take over

[1] The states were Iowa, Missouri, Wisconsin, Illinois, Indiana, Kentucky, Michigan, and Ohio.

the eight-state area when sales efforts actually began. None of these men had had any previous experience selling multiwall bags, but all had attended the company's three-month sales training school. The purpose of the school was to familiarize new salesmen with the company, the paper industry in general, and specific Talcott products, such as multiwall bags. Preparations for the survey started in November, 1956; the field work was completed by July 1957; and the Milledgeville bag plant opened two months later. The survey cost less than $50,000, the principal part of which was salaries and expenses of the five men for the eight-month period.

The salesmen spent a month familiarizing themselves with the techniques and problems of interviewing. They "acted out" interviews among themselves and tape recorded these practice interviews so that each man could hear himself and others and thereby recognize the weak points of each presentation. At the end of the month, the manager assigned each salesman to a section of a state; as soon as the man completed the section, he moved on to the next area. Each salesman called on all the possible users of multiwall bags in his area, as shown on a list supplied by the company's market research department. To prepare the list, the market research department had assembled names and addresses of firms listed in trade magazines and trade association directories of the cement, fertilizer, and other industries making products that could be packaged in multiwall bags. However, the salesmen discovered that not all the firms listed were actual bag users. For example, a fertilizer manufacturer might make either or both solid or liquid fertilizer, yet Talcott could consider him a potential customer only if he made solid fertilizer and only if he sold some of his output in bags as contrasted with selling it in bulk. In addition, it was necessary to determine whether the manufacturer used paper or textile (burlap) bags. As a result, some of the survey calls were unproductive from the standpoint of reaching potential customers. It was discovered, however, that there were potential customers who had not been listed; the salesmen believed that they learned about most of these firms from bag users whom they visited.

The salesman's responsibility was to meet each potential customer personally and to learn what he could about the types and approximate quantities of bags used annually; the number and types of packaging machines used (the latter affected the types and sizes of bags needed); the number of bag suppliers from whom the customer bought; his delivery requirements (i.e., whether he ordered frequently and in small quantities or ordered in large lots and carried a considerable inventory); whether he received shipments by truck or by rail; and the relative importance to him of price, service, and reciprocity as buying motives. The salesman also attempted to judge the customer's receptiveness to Talcott as a new supplier. Following the salesman's visit, Talcott mailed a letter to each firm on which the salesman had called, thanking the firm's officials for their co-operation.

The salesmen's estimates of bag purchases by each firm, and the resulting statewide totals, were compared with available industry data on bag shipments to each state, and the estimates were adjusted proportionately, so that the total estimate for each state agreed with the industry figure. The data on shipments were tabulated by an industry trade association, the Paper Shipping Sack Manufacturers' Association, from its members' reports of monthly bag shipments. Though individual buyers or sellers were not identified in the reports, an association member could determine his own market share by comparing his shipments with the industry total. Discrepancies between the company estimates by states and the industry shipment figures could occur because of inaccurate estimates by the salesmen, because of inaccurate industry figures resulting from incorrect reports by member firms, or because of the purchasing policies of the bag users. For example, a manufacturing plant located in Missouri might have a headquarters office in Chicago or New York, where purchasing was done, yet shipments would be made to the Missouri plant.

From the estimates of bag consumption thus obtained,[2] the marketing manager divided the eight-state area among the five available salesmen as shown in Exhibit 1.

The marketing manager realized that the territories were too large for the salesmen, both in geographical size and in relation to the time the salesmen should spend with each potential customer. The latter was directly related to the volume of the firm's bag purchases, i.e., the greater the bag consumption, the more frequent should be the salesmen's calls. Talcott had found that a salesman could make an average of four calls a day, or a thousand calls a year, based on a five-day week, fifty-week year. The marketing manager estimated that the number of calls needed ranged from a minimum of twelve calls per year to a maximum of fifty-two. On the average, salesmen were expected to call at least twelve times a year on firms buying between 100,000 and 1 million bags annually, twenty-four times a year on those buying between 1 million and 2 million bags, and thirty-six or more times a year on buyers using more than 2 million bags. Some of the largest bag users were manufacturers of cement, flour, chemicals, and animal feeds; the largest of these firms used as many as 25 million bags annually.

The marketing manager knew that he would need more salesmen to cover the eight states adequately, but he could not justify to Talcott management the hiring of additional salesmen until the existing men were making enough sales to cover their cost to the company. The company

---

[2] Of all the information the salesmen obtained, only the bag consumption figures were used in establishing sales territories. The salesmen used the rest of the information in subsequent sales calls.

EXHIBIT 1

SALES TERRITORIES FOR MULTIWALL BAGS IN EIGHT MIDWESTERN STATES, WITH
ESTIMATED BAG CONSUMPTION, NUMBER OF FIRMS BUYING BAGS, AND
NUMBER OF SALES CALLS NEEDED

Office	Salesman*	Territory Covered	No. Firms Buying Bags	Estimated Annual Bag Purchases	No. of Sales Calls Needed per Year
Columbus, Ohio......Howard		Ohio	135	111,507,000	1,888
		Eastern Mich.	32	37,818,000	502
		Total	167	149,325,000	2,390
Chicago, Ill..........Albright		Part of			
		Northern Ill.	43	40,012,000	752
		Wisconsin	50	31,663,000	728
		Northern Ind.	24	12,958,000	264
		Western Mich.	21	4,928,000	224
		Total	138	89,561,000	1,968
Chicago, Ill..........Orland		Part of			
		Northern Ill.	68	81,928,000	976
		Eastern Iowa	35	18,051,000	436
		Total	103	99,979,000	1,412
St. Louis, Mo........Roberts		Southern Ill.	41	31,204,000	502
		Southern Ind.	30	27,544,000	356
		Kentucky	32	16,296,000	383
		Eastern Mo.	31	35,904,000	541
		Total	131	110,948,000	1,782
Kansas City, Mo.....Tinsley		Western Iowa	40	18,612,000	646
		Western Mo.	41	59,686,000	697
		Kansas†	31	27,500,000	462
		Nebraska‡	14	17,534,000	241
		Total	126	123,332,000	2,046
Grand Total...			665	573,145,000	9,598

* Fictitious names.
† Though these states were not included in the survey, their bag consumption by firm was estimated from a previous survey, and they were made a part of the Kansas City sales territory on that basis.

had found that this point was reached when a man sold approximately 1,500,000 bags a year, which represented about $200,000 in annual sales. The marketing manager also realized that, if it later became necessary to divide the present territories, the salesmen might be upset at losing part of the territories they had worked to develop. To overcome this problem, the marketing manager planned to offer the present salesmen their choice of any new territories that might be carved from the existing areas.

The decision to locate an office in Columbus, Ohio, illustrates the factors considered by the marketing manager in establishing the territories. The Columbus territory included Ohio and eastern Michigan; the principal cities in this area, from the standpoint of bag consumption, were Cleveland, Toledo, Detroit, Columbus, and Cincinnati. Annual bag consumption in Cleveland of 34 million bags was approximately 1.7 times as great as that of Detroit, approximately 2.5 as great as Columbus, and approximately 4.6 times as great as either Cincinnati or Toledo. The marketing manager established the office in Columbus because of its central location among these cities. He reasoned that a salesman would be more likely to call on Cincinnati, Detroit, and Cleveland bag users if he were based somewhat centrally rather than at any one of them. The salesman also would be less likely to have to be away from home on week ends, because of the shorter travel distances involved (i.e.. the shorter distance from Columbus to any of the other cities—than from Cincinnati, for example, to Cleveland or Detroit). The company believed it was important to the salesman's family life, and consequently his job satisfaction, for him to be at home on week ends. The marketing manager anticipated, however, that the Cleveland-Toledo area eventually would warrant a sales office because of the large bag consumption in Cleveland.

Company executives did not establish sales quotas from the data on estimated purchases. The executives realized that many of the firms that were buying bags probably were well satisfied with their present suppliers and would be unlikely to switch suddenly to Talcott. As a result, the estimated bag consumption data for a territory were considered only very rough guides to the actual sales that the company could expect to make. This was especially true of bag users whose purchasing offices were located in other parts of the country.

Evaluate the company's approach to the establishment of sales territories.

78

WHITING CORPORATION

FOR MANY years, Whiting Corporation's management thought that it could control sales operations without requiring its salesmen to fill out call reports. In the years following World War II, however, total company sales grew to the point where the vice-president in charge of marketing believed that it was necessary to establish a number of additional controls. One of the controls he proposed was to have each salesman make out a weekly call report.

Whiting was engaged primarily in the manufacture of material handling equipment of the capital good type. Its main lines and the typical length of life of each were as follows:

1. Cranes, 10–15 years.
2. Transportation equipment (maintenance equipment for railway shops), 20 years.
3. Cupolas and accessories for the foundry industry, 20 years.
4. Furnaces, ovens, and pulverizers for the foundry industry, 20 years.
5. Electric arc furnaces for steel scrap melting, 20 years.
6. Industrial evaporators, spray dryers, and crystalizers, 20 years.

7. Trambeam (overhead monorail system), 10 years.
8. Trackmobile (a small vehicle that runs on railway track or off; used to move railway cars), 4 years.

Nearly all items were tailor-made to suit customers' needs except the Trambeam and Trackmobile, which were standardized and sold through distributors. Individual sales ran as high as $1 million, but the typical sale was about $25,000. Trackmobiles were produced in three different models that varied in price from $9,000 to $20,000.

The company employed forty-six sales engineers, who were super-

EXHIBIT 1

ORGANIZATION OF THE MARKETING DIVISION, WHITING CORPORATION

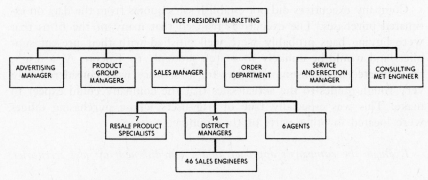

vised by fourteen district managers. The latter also did selling (Exhibit 1). The district sales offices were located as follows:

1. Charlotte, N. C.
2. Chicago, Ill.
3. Cincinnati, Ohio
4. Cleveland, Ohio
5. Detroit, Mich.
6. Houston, Tex.
7. Minneapolis, Minn.
8. New York, N. Y.
9. Norwalk, Calif.
10. Philadelphia, Pa.
11. Pittsburgh, Pa.
12. St. Louis, Mo.
13. Seattle, Wash.
14. Whiting International (Export) New York, N. Y.

Sales agents were used to sell the lines in a few areas where it was believed that sales did not justify coverage by Whiting's own sales force. The sales agents did essentially the same job as the company's own sales force and received a commission of 10 per cent; however, they handled other noncompetitive lines. They were supervised by the general sales manager. The agents were located in the following cities:

1. Buffalo, N. Y.
2. Binghamton, N. Y.
3. Ohaha, Neb.
4. Salt Lake City, Utah
5. Denver, Colo.
6. El Paso, Tex.

The Trambeam and Trackmobiles and some foundry items were sold through 180 distributors and direct by the Whiting sales force. The district managers were responsible for the distributors in their territories, and the sales engineers called on them. The resale product specialists, each of which had about one-seventh of the country to serve, handled all special problems on these items for both the distributors and the company salesmen. These specialists were called in for technical problems and also for such marketing problems as conducting sales meetings for distributors.

The product group managers were key men. Salesmen sent descriptions of material handling jobs to these men, who devised the appropriate method of doing the job and turned this information over to the engineering department for the design of the specific equipment needed. The product managers determined the actual prices quoted to customers and planned the promotion programs for their products, subject only to the limitations of the firm's total promotion budget and the competition of other product managers for promotion funds. Each product group manager was required to go into the field on at least one job per month.

Whiting was a significant factor in each of the industries in which it competed, as shown in Table 1.

TABLE 1

COMPETITIVE SITUATION IN MAJOR INDUSTRIES SERVED BY WHITING

Line	No. of Competitors	Total Industry Sales	Whiting's Market Share
Cranes	30	$80,000,000	7%
Transportation equipment	6	2,000,000	40
Foundry equipment	11	14,000,000	30
Electric-arc furnaces	17	35,000,000	15
Industrial evaporators, etc.	7	2,000,000	20
Trambeam	17	35,000,000	12
Trackmobile	13	4,500,000	40

Whiting's sales engineers were college graduates who had majored in some form of engineering. It generally took two years of training in the factory before a salesman was prepared to go into the field to sell the complete Whiting line. The salesmen were paid on a salary-plus-bonus system. Each district was given a quota for each product line and had to make the quota in each to be eligible for a bonus. Bonuses were paid to a district on the basis of the extent to which it exceeded its quota. If a district earned a bonus, the district manager decided, with the approval of the general sales manager, the distribution of the bonus among the men in his district. Bonuses were paid semiannually. On the average, about 80 per cent of each salesman's income was his salary, and rest was bonus, but this varied considerably. Each salesman was reimbursed for all expenses incurred in connection with his duties. Exact data were not available, but it was generally believed that the typical salesman made about thirty calls per month, which resulted in sales of about $34,000.

A salesman generally called on a prospective customer as a follow-up to an inquiry made as a result of the company's promotional efforts by direct mail, by trade publication advertising, or at a trade show. The typical sequence of events to obtaining an order was as follows:

1. The salesman followed up an inquiry by calling on the purchasing agent, who directed the salesman to confer with the appropriate engineer, who gave job requirements to the salesman.
2. The salesman sent the job requirements to the appropriate product manager, who worked up a preliminary proposal and specifications.
3. The sales engineer took the preliminary proposal back to the prospect.
4. The prospect called the salesman to discuss specification changes and to request that a definite bid for the job be made.
5. The salesman sent specification changes to the product manager for a final bid.
6. The product manager made a definite bid which the salesman delivered to the prospect.

It generally was from two to six months between the time of the inquiry and the final sale. The ratio of inquiries to sales was about 4.5 to 1. Salesmen communicated with the product group managers primarily by mail. They could suggest product design and prices to the product managers, but the latter made the decisions. The salesman's job was to interpret the customer's problem to the product manager and the product

EXHIBIT 2

WEEKLY REPORT

WHITING CORPORATION				WEEKLY CALL REPORT	CLOCK NUMBER	WEEK ENDING	SALESMAN
DATE	TOWN	STATE	COMPANY CALLED ON	MEN INTERVIEWED AND TITLE			PRODUCT

INSTRUCTIONS	USE THESE ABBREVIATIONS		BREAKDOWN IN HOURS				PRODUCT BREAKDOWN IN HOURS									
			OFFICE	TRAVEL	SELLING	TOTAL	C	L	CU	EF	SW	T	TB	TM	SP	TOTAL
1. RECORD ALL PERSONAL CALLS DURING EACH WEEK.	CRANE	C	SUN.													
2. MAIL TO HARVEY NOT LATER THAN MONDAY.	LADLES, FURN. ETC.	L	MON.													
3. USE EXTRA SHEETS IF NECESSARY.	CUPOLAS AND ACCES.	CU	TUES.													
4. ALLOCATE TOTAL TIME OF WORKING DAY REGARDLESS OF HOURS IN BEHALF OF EACH PRODUCT.	ELECTRIC FURNACE	EF	WED.													
	INDL. EVAPORATORS ETC.	SW	THUR.													
5. YOUR TIME ESTIMATES ARE USED TO ALLOCATE YOUR SALARY AND EXPENSES TO PRODUCT.	TRANSPORTATION	T														
	TRAMBEAM	TB	FRI.													
	TRACKMOBILE	TM	SAT.													
PRINT NAMES · GIVE INITIALS AND TITLES	SPECIAL PRODUCTS	SP														
			TOTALS													

manager's ideas to the customer. This required considerable engineering knowledge.

The vice-president in charge of marketing was able to tell the number of new accounts obtained, the size of each sale, and the items sold from the records prepared by each product manager when bid prices were determined. In addition, expense records were submitted monthly by each salesman. The vice-president thought that he should have additional information and designed the Weekly Call Report shown as Exhibit 2. This report was to be sent directly to the vice-president, but in practice most salesmen sent it with their weekly expense account statements. Since the expense accounts had to be approved by the district managers, the call reports also went to the district managers, who forwarded them to the home office. The salesmen were to report the total hours worked each day. In determining the breakdown of time among products, the salesmen were to use their own judgment. In practice, if a salesman talked to a customer about three products, he usually charged one-third of his time to each of the products.

1. *Was the new call report necessary?*
2. *Should the vice-president of marketing have additional information?*

5. Compensating the Sales Force

79

ALISON PUMP AND EQUIPMENT COMPANY

THE RESIGNATION of a sales division manager of the Alison Pump and Equipment Company led to a search for a replacement. Company executives, however, found no one in any of the three sales divisions who they felt had sufficient managerial capacity to warrant the promotion. As a result, an executive committee was appointed to investigate the reasons for the lack of management potential among the firm's sales personnel.

The Alison Company manufactured pumping and regulating equipment for use in regulating the flow of gaseous and liquid materials. Some specific applications of this equipment were the automatic control of fluid storage tanks and automatic fire sprinkler systems. The company's total sales in 1958 were $22 million. This volume was the result of a steady growth from sales of $14 million in 1955 to $16 million in 1956 and $19 million in 1957.

The sales department was organized into three divisions employing 190 men. The northern division, the largest of the three, had 101 men; the

EXHIBIT 1

ORGANIZATION CHART OF THE SALES OPERATION, AT THE DIVISION LEVEL, OF
THE ALISON PUMP AND EQUIPMENT COMPANY: 1957

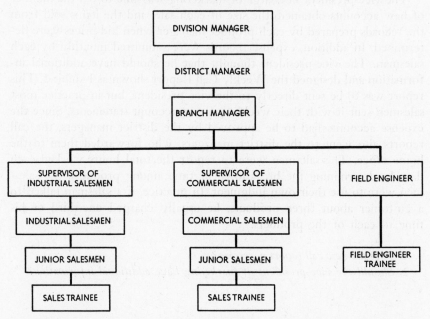

central division had 69 men; and the southern division had 20 men. Exhibit 1 shows the organization of a sales division. Both industrial and commercial salesmen were employed; the former sold direct to original equipment manufacturers, and the latter to plumbing wholesalers, general industrial distributors, and specialized distributors of pumping equipment.

Company executives investigating the lack of managerial potential in the sales divisions reviewed, among other things, the sales compensation program. All sales personnel were paid a straight salary. District and branch managers received annual sales bonuses in addition to their salaries. The amount of each man's bonus depended on the sales vice-president's general impression of the relative performance of the branches. No detailed analysis of the sales and expenses of each branch was made. Until April 1956 industrial and commercial salesmen had also participated in the bonus. At that time all but a few of the outstanding men were dropped from the bonus plan; their salaries, however, were increased accordingly. Whether or not a salesman continued to receive a bonus depended on the opinion of the branch manager about the salesman's sales record.

The income ranges of Alison personnel are shown in Table 1 and are compared with data from the *Salesmen's Compensation Survey, 1956,* of the American Management Association, and a study entitled *Annual Sal-*

TABLE 1

COMPARISON OF MONTHLY INCOME RANGE OF ALISON SALES PERSONNEL
WITH COMPARABLE DATA FROM AMA AND TRADE ASSOCIATION SURVEY

Job Title	Alison		AMA*		Trade Association	
	Lowest Income	Highest Income	Lowest Income	Highest Income	Lowest Income	Highest Income
District manager........	$820	$1,883	$700	$1,320	$660	$1,400
Branch manager........	480	1,180	400§	1,130	460	1,360
Salesman†	310	890	620	1,100	340	1,100
Sales trainee‡	330	500	280§	560	340	560

* The AMA information was obtained through a national survey and was reported by industry groups and by types of products manufactured by each group. The industry group "accessory materials and equipment" is shown here. Products included in this group were electrical and mechanical control equipment, tools, dies, and packaging and printing materials, etc. Within this industry group the data are limited to firms that have approximately $20 million annual sales and that pay their employees on a salary and bonus basis.

† Alison data include the positions of sales supervisors, industrial salesmen, commercial salesmen, and field engineers. These job classifications were grouped to permit more significant comparison with the AMA and trade association data.

‡ Alison data include the positions of junior salesmen, sales trainees, and field engineer trainees. These job classifications were grouped to permit more useful comparison with the AMA and trade association data.

§ These AMA data are not directly comparable because the AMA survey included such a small number of individuals in the classification "accessory materials and equipment" that data from other industries were combined with them to provide a larger base. Since the AMA figures thereby included personnel from lower-paying industries, such as food and nondurable goods, the result was to lower the minimum figure of the rate range.

ary Rates of Sales Personnel, 1956, prepared by an industry trade association.

The National Industrial Conference Board reported in the January, 1957, issue of Management Record the results of a survey of college recruiting practices for two hundred companies. The average monthly starting salary for engineering graduates for 1956 was $415, and for 1957, $433. The Alison Company was unable to hire college graduates as either field engineer trainees or sales trainees at its starting salary of $330 per month. Consequently, the firm was forced to hire as engineers men with certificates from engineering trade schools.

Company executives concluded, after studying the current compensation program, that a considerable degree of salary inequity had been created throughout the sales force. They also decided that the salary program had been inadequate to attract and hold the quantity and quality of salesmen needed to build the organization for the future. Consequently, they proposed, as a means of improving the present system, the following measures: (1) a job content study, (2) a new salary structure, and (3) a procedure for installing and administering the new salary program.

The job content study was to begin with the preparation of job descriptions by the district and branch managers. Each job description was to classify each sales function by job activity (e.g., direct selling, administration, training of new salesmen, etc.) and to explain the specific procedures and techniques of each function. Exhibit 4, appended to this case, summarizes the completed job descriptions that were developed.

The relative importance of each of the jobs was then established by arranging them in order from the most important to the least important. The two considerations on which the rankings were based were: (1) the jobs must be distinctly separated according to the difference in job requirements, and (2) promotional opportunities must be clearly and logically substantiated and must be consistent with the company's organization policy. The result of the job ranking is shown in Exhibit 2. The

EXHIBIT 2

Job Grading Chart Showing Relative Rank of Each Job

Grade	Administrative	Sales	Engineering
12	District manager		
11			
10	Branch manager (A)		
9	Branch manager (B)		
8		Supervisor of industrial salesmen (A)	
7	Branch manager (C)	Supervisor of industrial salesmen (B) Supervisor of commercial salesmen (A)	
6		Industrial salesmen (A)	
5		Industrial salesmen (B) Commercial salesmen (A)	Field engineer (A)
4		Commercial salesmen (B)	
3		Junior salesmen	Field engineer (B)
2			
1		Sales trainee	Field engineer trainee

grade relationship that one job held to another was determined solely by the relative value of each job to the company. Within each grade there was a salary range. An individual employee's level of job performance was to be recognized by his position in the salary range for his job grade.

To allow for the fact that all branches were not the same size, either in sales volume or in number of sales personnel, three branch levels, A, B, and C, were established. Level A represented those branches with sales in excess of $1 million; level B included branches with sales volumes between $200,000 and $1 million; and level C included branches with sales of less than $200,000. Company officials believe that they should not pay a branch manager or industrial salesman in an A-level branch (Chicago, for example) the same salary as a counterpart in a B-level branch (Peoria,

Ill., for example). The duties of the branch manager or industrial sales-man of all three levels, however, were covered by the same job description.

A specific salary structure was proposed, with the following objectives in mind:

1. The level of compensation should be in relation to salaries paid for similar jobs in other industries.
2. There should be a continuous and integrated salary structure for all sales personnel.
3. Each job grade should have a salary range for all jobs included within the grade. The range should consist of a minimum, mid-point, and maximum salary figure, so that an individual's salary could be adjusted in relation to his development and level of contribution.
4. The current level of salaries should be reviewed in relation to any proposed structure, so that the cost to the company of adopting the new salaries could be determined.
5. The base salary structure itself should provide a reasonable standard of living.

The recommended salary structure is shown in Table 2.

TABLE 2

RECOMMENDED SALARY STRUCTURE

| | Annual Salary Range | | |
Grade	Minimum	Mid-Point	Maximum
12...............	$12,370	$14,550	$16,735
11...............	11,245	13,230	15,215
10...............	10,220	12,025	13,830
9...............	9,295	10,935	12,575
8...............	8,450	9,940	11,430
7...............	7,770	9,035	10,300
6...............	7,145	8,215	9,280
5...............	6,570	7,465	8,365
4...............	6,040	6,790	7,535
3...............	5,610	6,170	6,790
2...............	5,100	5,610	6,170
1...............	4,590	5,100	5,610

The salary structure was developed by establishing the mid-point for Grade 1 at $5,100 and moving each succeeding mid-point 10 per cent higher (rounding these figures to the nearest $5). The minimum and maximum levels of the ranges for grades 1–3 were established at approximately 10 per cent below and above each mid-point; for grades 4–7 the minimum and maximum spreads from the mid-point were 11, 12, 13, and 14 per cent, respectively. Grades 8–12 had a 15 per cent range below and above the mid-point. A greater salary range for the higher jobs was proposed in order to allow for the increased responsibility of some of the jobs and because individuals were very likely to remain in a higher job for a longer period of time.

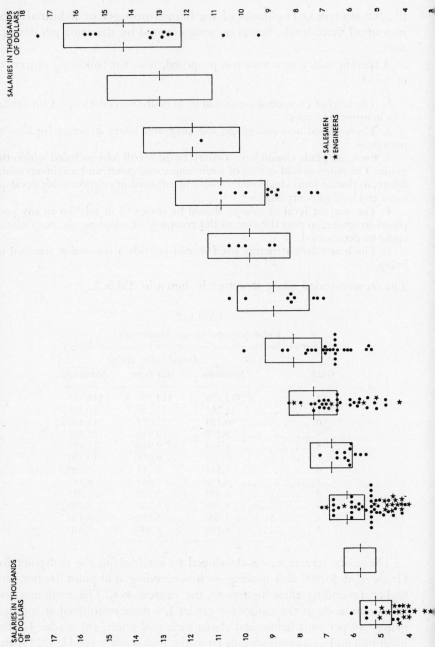

EXHIBIT 3

INDIVIDUAL ANNUAL SALARIES COMPARED WITH PROPOSED SALARY STRUCTURE

• SALESMEN
★ ENGINEERS

Exhibit 3 shows the distribution of the existing individual annual salaries compared with the proposed salary structure (the latter is shown by the vertical bars). Table 3 shows both the detail from which Exhibit 3 was developed and the cost of the proposed salary structure.

TABLE 3

INDIVIDUAL ANNUAL SALARIES COMPARED WITH PROPOSED SALARY STRUCTURE

Grade	No. of Employees	Present Total Salaries	Present Average Salaries	Proposed Mid-Point Salaries	Proposed Total Salaries	Present Average Salaries as Per Cent of Proposed Mid-point
1......	25	$ 113,230	$ 4,529	$ 5,100	$ 127,500	88.8
2......	..	..	..	5,610	..	..
3......	54	285,990	5,296	6,170	333,180	85.8
4......	12	74,588	6,216	6,790	81,480	91.5
5......	35	223,474	6,385	7,465	261,275	85.5
6......	26	179,573	6,907	8,215	213,590	84.1
7......	9	75,332	8,370	9,035	81,315	92.6
8......	5	49,094	9,819	9,940	49,700	98.8
9......	11	99,571	9,052	10,935	120,285	82.8
10......	1	11,700	11,700	12,025	12,025	97.3
11......	..	..	..	13,230	..	..
12......	12	164,165	13,680	14,550	174,600	94.0
Totals.	190	$1,276,717	$ 6,720	$ 7,658	$1,454,950	87.8

Data from the American Management Association's *Salesmen's Compensation Survey: Second Report, 1957–58* were used to determine the similarity of the proposed salary structure to existing industry salaries. Table 4 is a comparison of the two sets of salaries for selected positions. The AMA figures could not be used as an absolute measure because the sampling was rather small for the sales category used. In addition, the data were not classified by the educational background required for the specified job, and Alison officials believed that the AMA rates were, as a result, somewhat depressed by firms that typically hired less than college graduates for the majority of their sales positions.

The Alison executive committee believed that the proposed salary plan should be put into effect gradually. They believed that it would be neither practical nor prudent to move all existing employees who were below the minimum salary level to the new minimum rates. For that matter, no employee should be considered for a salary increase until some process of performance evaluation was established. By the same token, there should be no attempt at a wholesale "housecleaning," for fear that the sales structure of the company would collapse. The executives believed that a period of from one to three years should be taken to weed out gradually personnel whose performance did not merit the proposed salaries. Normal attrition would accomplish much of the weeding process during this time, but some direct discharges would be necessary.

TABLE 4

COMPARISON OF PORTION OF PROPOSED SALARY SCALE WITH AMA "SALESMEN'S
COMPENSATION SURVEY: SECOND REPORT, 1957–58"*

		Proposed	Ranges		
Source	Job Title	Grade	Minimum	Mid-Point	Maximum
Alison......Sales trainee................ 1			$ 4,590	$ 5,100	$ 5,610
AMA.......Trainee..........................			4,500	5,000	5,500
Alison......Junior salesman............ 3			5,610	6,170	6,790
AMA.......Salesman, grade 1...................			5,400	6,400	6,700
Alison......Industrial salesman (B)...... 5			6,570	7,465	8,365
AMA.......Salesman, grade 2..................			6,200	7,300	7,900
Alison......Industrial salesman (A)...... 6			7,145	8,215	9,280
AMA.......Salesman, grade 3..................			8,400	8,900	9,700
Alison......Branch manager (A).........10			10,220	12,025	13,830
AMA.......District manager...................			7,200	10,700	13,500†
Alison......District manager...........12			12,370	14,550	16,735
AMA.......Regional manager..................			9,100	12,000	19,000†

* The category "Industrial Products—Accessory Equipment" was used. Note the data from this AMA report do not agree entirely with the data in the 1956 report that are shown in Exhibit 2. In addition to the change in date, the industry category is defined somewhat differently and different job classifications are shown.
† These ranges include bonus payment.

The following provisions were suggested as a guide to the reviewing and adjusting of the salaries of all employees:

1. Salaries of sales personnel below the minimum for their grade should be increased to or toward the minimum only where warranted. If the amount below the minimum is excessive, or the individual is not yet qualified, the adjustment to the minimum should not be made in a single step.

2. The salaries of employees in the lower portion of the ranges who are performing their jobs in a satisfactory manner should be increased in order to move them into a more equitable salary relationship with other employees and into a more appropriate relationship to the proposed salary ranges.

3. Employees who now exceed the mid-point but are below maximum, and whose work performance is outstanding, should also be raised so that they will maintain their relative salary position with other employees.

4. The salaries for employees who are currently above the maximum for their grade should not be cut, but efforts should be made to promote these individuals if at all possible. If promotion is not feasible, then the employee's salary status, and the company's intention to let the salary stand as is, should be discussed with the employee immediately.

The executive committee recommended that the new salary program be adopted as soon as district and branch managers were trained in their responsibilities for salary administration. Salary administration, they thought, should be initiated at the branch level. It should be the branch manager's responsibility to recommend merit increases for his personnel, subject to the approval of his district manager; to evaluate employee performance and to counsel with employees about their growth and development in their jobs; and to prepare an annual salary budget. The primary objective of the review of an employee's performance by his superior should be to encourage the individual's development and improvement. The secondary purpose of the review should be to determine whether a salary increase was merited. By conducting these reviews on the anniversary date of the individual's employment, the supervisor would be relieved of making all the reviews in a short space of time. It was hoped that this would also help the supervisor avoid the tendency to rate employees relative to each other rather than relative to the requirements of their job. A form suggested for the employee review is shown as Exhibit 5 appended to this case. Since performance review or rating would be a matter of subjective judgment, the executive committee recommended that all ratings be reviewed by both branch and district managers. All ratings would be discussed with the employees involved.

The executives believed special effort would be necessary to prevent this performance rating from deteriorating into a justification for salary adjustment. After reviewing an employee's performance, however, it would be natural to consider whether his salary should be increased. The following factors were proposed for consideration in determining the frequency and amount of increases: (1) the performance of the individual on his job, (2) his position in his salary range, (3) the grade of his job and his length of service in the particular job, and (4) the date and amount of the last salary increase. The normal salary increase should be from 10 to 15 per cent. Exceptional or unusual considerations might result in larger increases. When salary adjustments were considered, the minimum salary for a grade should be thought of as the starting salary for a qualified but inexperienced person. The mid-point should represent a "going" salary for satisfactory job performance, and the maximum should be reserved for those few individuals whose performance was exceptional and outstanding in every respect.

According to the committee's plan, qualified personnel in any sales area of the company should be considered when promotional opportunities occurred. A promotion would permit the company to utilize more fully the abilities of an individual and, by so doing, increase the chances of keeping the person with the company.

It was emphasized that the proposed program was not meant to be inflexible—salary scales and job descriptions would be reviewed periodically to see whether they were still pertinent and adequate, and the suggested procedures for administering the program would likewise be reviewed to determine their usefulness and effectiveness. In this way the program would be changed to accommodate changing conditions both within and without the company.

Evaluate the company's existing compensation program and the executive committee's proposals for revising it.

EXHIBIT 4

JOB DESCRIPTIONS

District manager. Directs, co-ordinates, and controls activities of branch managers and agents to achieve established company goals with respect to the promotion, sale, and service of company products and customer relations in the territory under his jurisdiction. This is primarily an administrative function. Most of the district manager's time will be taken by branch problems and general administrative activities. It is advisable that he program and schedule some branch visits each month.

Branch manager. Is responsible for the successful and profitable operation of his branch through the promotion, sale, and service of company products and the maintenance of good customer relations within his assigned territory. Directs, co-ordinates, and controls activities of sales personnel under his jurisdiction. Spends major portion of his time in direct sales activities. This is the highest level of selling responsibility in the company wherein both indentity as a salesman and direct responsibility for sales activities are maintained. In addition to direct sales activities, he must maintain contact with major accounts in his territory as well as with architects, consulting engineers, and contractors.

Supervisor, industrial salesmen; supervisor, commercial salesmen. Each supervisor oversees and co-ordinates, under the direction of the branch manager, the activities and sales functions of all personnel in the sales department; he also engages in direct sales activities. This function subdivides into two primary activities. In the first place, the supervisor will call on and sell primary accounts and develop new sources of business. As a second phase of his activities, he will assist the salesmen under his supervision in the performance of their assignments. This may range in scope from a sales contact call to quoting a job. In some respects, the supervisor is comparable to some branch managers. His problems, duties and responsibilities are not too far removed from the operational procedures in a small branch office.

Industrial salesman. Maintains customer contact and is responsible for customer relations within his territory. Keeps potential buyers informed of Alison products and services. Called upon to adapt existing products to new or varied circumstances. Sales efforts may necessitate detailed layouts and specifications prior to installation and may result in new product design. Successful sales activity here is largely dependent upon the general engineering ability of the salesman. He is required to know and understand a multiplicity of industrial operations and manufacturing procedures in order to sell in the industrial field. He must be able to adapt his engineering knowledge and his understanding of the capabilities of Alison equipment to meet a varied and sometimes highly technical market. This function requires diversity in sales activities in that he calls on design engineers, contractors, industrial concerns, and original equipment manufacturers.

Commercial salesman. Maintains customer contact and is responsible for customer relations within his territory. Keeps potential buyers informed on products and prices. Activities consist primarily of contacting plumbers and plumbing suppliers or jobbers and selling them stock or catalogue items. Must maintain contact with architects and consulting engineers to get suitable specifications for, and to promote, equipment. Must use building reports and correctly interpret and evaluate them. Sales ability rather than engineering training is the most important prerequisite for this job. Must be able to read construction drawings and have mechanical aptitude. Some activity in this field may call for new uses of standard products, and for this reason the salesman must have thorough knowledge of all standard products. While the plumbing layouts are most often uniform from building to building, the salesman must have a basic

EXHIBIT 4 *(Cont.)*

understanding of the plumbing contractors' problems if he is to meet the design needs satisfactorily. A basic knowledge of drafting and mechanical drawing is advisable.

Field engineer. Obtains specifications for a job and estimates cost preparatory to the company's bidding a project. Lays out the control system for a successfully bid job and orders material and equipment for installation. The field engineer will save the industrial salesman a great deal of time if he can accurately take off the specifications for a project. The sales force should be able to rely on his estimates of installation and equipment costs and the installation superintendent should be able to rely on his layout of the proposed control system.

Junior salesman. Works with and assists experienced sales personnel initially, but will, at the discretion of his manager, ultimately be permitted to engage in independent sales activities. May estimate and price jobs under direction. The position of junior salesman is, initially, an extension of the sales training program. In its later stages, however, the function approaches the status of a fully qualified salesman. The length of time an individual will remain as a junior salesman depends upon his ability to expand his knowledge of the company's product line, and his ability to carry his share of the sales responsibilities.

Sales trainee. Follows a program for learning the company's products, services, policies, and sales techniques. There is no specific time limit for the training period, though experience would seem to indicate that it may last from one to two years, depending upon the individual. Mechanical engineers with a B.S. degree, or its equivalent, are preferred. Careful appraisal must be made of the individual during this period.

Field-engineer trainee. Follows a program for learning the company's products, services, policies, and field engineering and installation techniques. There is no specific time limit for the training period. The trainee completes his training period when judged sufficiently skilled to assume engineering responsibility for major projects. An engineering education, or its equivalent, is preferred.

EXHIBIT 5

EMPLOYEE PERFORMANCE REVIEW

Name_____ Date_____

Job assignment_____ Date of birth_____

On job since_____ Employment date_____

Reviewed by_____

Recorded by_____

1. How good is this employee on the job?_____

2. How well does he get along with others in the department?_____

3. What are his strongest points?_____

4. What are his weakest points?_____

5. Looking back over the last six months, would you say that he has:
   ( ) Improved
   ( ) Remained the same
   ( ) Become less satisfactory

6. What would you say were his goals for the future?_____

EXHIBIT 5 (*Cont.*)

7. As his supervisor, what specific plan do you have for him in the next six months?

_____

_____

8. General comments not covered above:_____

_____

_____

9. Do you plan to go over this review with him?_____

10. If so, what specific points should be made?_____

_____

80

LIQUID CHEMICAL COMPANY, INC.

Liquid Chemical Company had developed rapidly in the field of industrial chemicals during the thirties and by 1945 had assumed a position of industry leadership in certain fields. In the process of growth, the company had followed an aggressive policy of product research and product line diversification. Executives soon became aware that new products could sustain wider margins than could well established products. As products grew in popularity and age, they tended to become very competitive in both price and service. As a result of this situation, the executives decided to concentrate sales effort on the newer and more profitable items.

Competition was especially strong in the chemical industry because most industrial chemicals were homogeneous and provided the individual manufacturer with no differentiated selling points. Liquid Chemical sold its line in every major marketing area in the United States through a sales force of ninety-three men, who were organized into fourteen districts. In 1956 its sales exceeded $10 million.

In the years following World War II, Mr. Howarth, the sales manager, became convinced that the salesmen tended to push the established items in which large poundage could be sold easily rather than the more profitable new items. In 1956, therefore, he instituted a new compensation system for the sales force that was designed to stimulate sales of the more profitable lines.

When the new compensation plan was presented to the salesmen at the annual meeting in October, it was received with enthusiasm. Each man was given a written statement of the plan (Exhibit 1). All products were classified into one of four categories, A, B, C, or D, and sales volume

EXHIBIT 1

COMMISSION SCHEDULE FOR INDUSTRIAL CHEMICAL SALESMEN, FISCAL YEAR 1957

I. Period Covered by the Schedule

Schedule will become effective October 28, 1956, for the fiscal year ending October 26, 1957.

II. Definitions

A. "Salary" shall be defined as actual salary earned for the computed period, excluding suggestion awards, contest awards, and commission payments.

B. "Volume" shall be defined as actual shipments of products into each territory as shown by invoices, but excluding shipments made to Liquid Chemical Company and subsidiaries, product that is returned, and "no charge" and sample shipments.

III. Employees Covered by the Schedule

Commission payments are limited to full-time sales personnel, who are assigned and responsible for specific sales territories. Sales managers are not eligible to participate.

IV. Sales Volume Standards

The home office will assign total yearly standards to each district. The local sales managers will assign standards to each sales territory for:
(*a*) The first quarter.
(*b*) The first and second quarters, combined.
(*c*) The first, second, and third quarters, combined.
(*d*) The first, second, third, and fourth quarters, combined.

V. Qualifications for Commission

To qualify for quarterly commission payments participants must:
A. Equal or exceed the total assigned volume standard.
B. Equal or exceed 75 per cent of the total assigned volume standard in product categories A and B as shown below.
C. Equal or exceed 50 per cent of the total assigned volume standard in product categories C and D as shown below.

At the end of the first quarter, sales results will be compared to the first-quarter standard; at the end of the second quarter, to the first- and second-quarter standard; at the end of the third quarter to the first-, second-, and third-quarter standard; and at the end of the fourth quarter to the first-, second-, third-, and fourth-quarter standard.

VI. Payments of Extra Compensation

A. Commission payments will be made quarterly on the basis of the schedule of commission rates given in Section VIII below, payments to be on the basis of accumulated volume at the end of each quarter, less commission previously paid. Such payments are subject to all federal, state and local income tax and payroll tax laws.

B. In no case will participants be required to refund commissions received in previous periods.

C. In the event that a salesman transfers, retires, resigns, is discharged, or dies during the life of this schedule, and provided that his territory

EXHIBIT 1 (*Cont.*)

qualifies at the close of the period under the provisions of Paragraph V above, he shall be entitled to commission calculated on the basis of his performance to the date of his transfer, separation, or death. To determine the amount of commission earned by the salesman during the quarter in which he transfers, retires, resigns, is discharged, or dies, divide the total number of pounds actually shipped into the territory during the quarter by the salesman up to the time of his transfer, separation, or death, by the total number of pounds shipped into the territory during the quarter. Apply the resulting percentage to the total territory commission earned during the quarter. Total commissions paid out cannot exceed the total commission earned by a territory for any quarter.

    D. Maximum payments for each computation shall not exceed 35 per cent of salesman's salary.

VII. Reservation of Management

    A. The company reserves the absolute right to select the individuals eligible to participate in the schedule.

    B. Any action taken hereunder shall not be held or construed to create a contract that any employee shall be retained in the service of the company, and Liquid Chemical Company expressly reserves, unaffected hereby, its right to discharge, without liability other than for salary or for wages due and unpaid commission earned hereunder, any employee, whenever its interest, in its judgment, so requires.

    C. The company reserves the right to deduct from any payment hereunder amounts due it from the participant.

    D. All sales territory standards are subject to approval by the home office. After standards are set for each sales territory, neither the standards nor the territory can be changed during the fiscal year without approval of the home office, provided that any change in standards shall not be effective until the next quarter, and in no event shall such change be retroactive.

    E. The foregoing is subject to all federal or state laws and regulations now in effect or which may hereafter be enacted or promulgated.

VIII. Commission Rates for Salesmen

	Per Cent Improvement over Standard	Commission Rate on Improvement over Standard
Category A	0 and under 10	$0.25 Cwt.
	10 and under 20	0.35 "
	20 and under 30	0.45 "
	30 and under 40	0.55 "
	40 and under 50	0.65 "
	50 and up	0.75 "
Category B	0 and under 10	0.15 "
	10 and under 20	0.18 "
	20 and under 30	0.21 "
	30 and under 40	0.25 "
	40 and under 50	0.30 "
	50 and up	0.35 "

EXHIBIT 1 (*Cont.*)

	0 and under 10	0.06 Cwt.
	10 and under 20	0.08 "
Category C......	20 and under 30	0.09 "
	30 and under 40	0.11 "
	40 and under 50	0.13 "
	50 and up	0.15 "
	0 and under 10	0.005 "
	10 and under 20	0.02 "
Category D......	20 and under 30	0.03 "
	30 and under 40	0.04 "
	40 and under 50	0.05 "
	50 and up	0.06 "

Category A...... { Diphenylamine
Ethyl cellulose
Chloroform

Category B...... { Pyridine compounds
Acetone
Cellulose derivatives
Refined napthalene
Ether
Glycerine

Category C...... { Carbon tetrachloride
Sodium carbonate

Category D......Lime

standards were set for each salesman for each category. The highest profit items were in category A, the next highest in B, the next in C, and the least profitable in D. Salesmen were to receive commissions on all sales over the standards set for them. The rate of commission was higher on the A and B categories to encourage the salesmen to put more effort on these products.

To insure that the salesmen did not neglect the large-volume items entirely, it was provided that no commission would be paid unless certain minimums were met in each product category. This encouraged efforts to sell the complete line to each customer, thus tending to increase sales relative to expenses.

The yearly sales volume standards were set in the Detroit home office by computing the average sales for the three preceding years. These standards were set for each district separately, and the figures were sent to the district sales managers, who broke them down for individual salesmen, each of whom was provided with a standard for each of the four product categories. Adjustments sometimes were made for the geographical transfer of large accounts and similar situations over which the salesman had no control.

EXHIBIT 2

COMMISSION PLAN
Territory Standards
19__ Fiscal Year

Territory No._____
Salesman _____
District _____

Approvals

Sales Manager _____

Detroit office _____

Category		First 3 Months		First 6 Months		First 9 Months		Fiscal Year	
		Pounds	Amount $	Pounds	Amount $	Pounds	Amount $	Pounds	Amount $
A	Sales								
	Standard								
B	Sales								
	Standard								
C	Sales								
	Standard								
D	Sales								
	Standard								
Total	Sales								
	Standard								

In order to gain the maximum impact on the salesmen and to keep them trying to enlarge their commissions, each salesman was sent a monthly report of shipments into his territory and given a form on which to record these and his standards and to compute his commissions (Exhibit 2). This made deficiencies and commission possibilities readily apparent to each salesman. The home office kept the form shown as Exhibit 3 as the

EXHIBIT 3

SALES COMMISSION CONTROL FORM

Salesman_____   District_____
Territory No._____   Periods Ending————

-1-	-2-	-3-	-4-	-5-	-6-	-7-
			Improvement over Standard			
Product	Shipments Pounds	Standard Pounds	Pounds	%	Com. Per Cwt.	Commission Amount
Category A:						
AA Diphenylamine						
AB Ethyl cellulose						
AR Chloroform						
Total A						
Category B:						
BC Pyridine compounds						
BR Acetone						
BE Cellulose derivatives						
BF Refined naphthalene						
BG Ether						
BH Glycerine						
Total B						
Category C:						
CJ Carbon tetrachloride						
CK Sodium carbonate						
Total C						
Category D:						
DL Lime						
Grand total						

Less commission paid previous quarters this fiscal year

Amount of commission payable for this quarter

Approvals:

              Auditor   Sales Manager

basis for running the plan. The commission earned by each salesman was computed on the form at the end of each quarter. The sales department continued to assemble and evaluate the information that made up the Salesman's Period Report shown as Exhibit 4. Mr. Howarth always made a particular point of noting the "cost to sell ratio" which was the ratio of the salesman's expenses, including salary, to his dollar sales.

EXHIBIT 4

SALESMAN'S PERIOD REPORT

District _____ Period Ending _____ Salesman _____ Territory No. _____

Code	Product	Current Period		Same Period Last Year		Accumulated Pounds This Year	Accumulated $ Volume This Year	Accumulated Pounds Last Year	Accumulated $ Volume Last Year	New Customers
		Pounds	$ Value	Pounds	$ Value					
AA	Diphenylamine									
AB	Ethyl cellulose									
AR	Chloroform									
	Total A category									
BC	Pyridine compounds									
BD	Acetone									
BE	Cellulose derivatives									
BF	Refined naphthalene									
BG	Ether									
BH	Glycerine									
	Total B category									
CJ	Carbon tetrachloride									
CK	Sodium carbonate									
	Total C category									
DL	Lime									
	Grand Total (Categories A + B + C + D)									

Expenses this Period _____   Cost to sell this period _____
Accumulated _____   Accumulated _____

To determine the gross margin by which products were classified into the various categories, it was assumed that the manufacturing costs, excluding the cost of raw materials, were the same for all products. This was approximately correct, since the production method was a process system. Raw material costs and selling prices did differ considerably between products. The gross margin was computed by subtracting the raw material cost per pound from the revenue per pound. Margins and prices varied within each category; the data in Table 1 show the average in each

TABLE 1

AVERAGE PRICES AND MARGINS WITHIN PRODUCT CATEGORIES

Category	Average Price per Cwt.	Price Range per Cwt.	Average Per Cent Gross Margin*
A	$68	$35–$200	73
B	24	19– 50	65
C	18	10– 22	65
D	8	7– 15	40

* Gross margin is defined here as the difference between raw material cost and selling price. Total costs, other than raw material costs, are approximately 40 per cent of sales for each product category. It was estimated that category D products paid their full costs, including their full share of overhead, but did not contribute directly to net profit.

group. Management normally assumed that selling costs were the same for each category; however, selling costs actually were somewhat less on the larger-volume items.

Sales of each product category for the three years preceding the establishment of the plan and for 1957, the first year in which the plan was in effect, are shown in Table 2.

TABLE 2

SALES BY PRODUCT CATEGORY: 1954–57
(THOUSANDS OF POUNDS)

Year	Category A Pounds	Per Cent	Category B Pounds	Per Cent	Category C Pounds	Per Cent	Category D Pounds	Per Cent	Total Pounds	Per Cent
1954	3,250	7.4	17,149	39.0	5,121	11.6	18,423	42.0	43,951	100
1955	3,375	7.2	17,927	38.4	5,949	12.7	19,631	42.0	46,882	100
1956	3,327	6.8	19,926	40.1	6,682	13.8	19,664	39.6	49,599	100
1957	3,475	6.8	20,982	40.8	6,705	13.2	20,211	39.5	51,373	100

An index of total industry shipments was computed each year by the industry trade association from reports of its members and estimates of the part of the industry not represented in the association. These indexes are given in Table 3.

Of the 93 salesmen eligible for commission in 1957, 68 earned a commission. Commission earnings ranged from 0 to $1,688.61, and the total commissions paid amounted to $14,500. To evaluate the program further, Howarth selected five salesmen at random and studied their results during 1957. To get a comprehensive look at the data, he assembled all the varia-

TABLE 3

INDEX OF SHIPMENTS OF INDUSTRIAL CHEMICALS: 1954–57
(1954 = 100)

Year	Index	Year	Index
1954................100		1956................112	
1955................106		1957................115	

tions from the standards, as reported on the bonus computation forms, into one table. To make the data comparable, he used the variations expressed as percentages. Exhibit 5 shows the data in tabular form.

In a report to the marketing vice-president, Mr. Howarth stated: "It is evident that a salesman cannot make a substantial commission unless he concentrates on higher-priced products. The plan has accomplished what we wanted, that is, to get the salesman quality conscious. It has resulted in the sale of the more profitable products and boosted both our volume and our profits."

EXHIBIT 5

PERCENTAGE VARIATIONS OF ACTUAL SALES FROM STANDARDS BY CUMULATIVE QUARTERS,
BY CATEGORY FOR FIVE SELECTED SALESMEN: 1957

Category	Salesman	Q_1	Q_1 and Q_2	Q_1–Q_3	Q_1–Q_4
A	1	+105.9	+137.4	+89.0	+66.0
	2	+ 10.1	+ 14.6	+14.7	+15.0
	3	− 33.0	+ 74.4	+67.2	+52.0
	4	+ 77.9	+ 57.0	+80.9	+63.3
	5	+ 0.4	− 24.0	−20.9	−25.1
B	1	+ 28.7	+ 14.5	− 8.0	+ 3.3
	2	+ 95.5	+ 99.2	+93.2	+67.2
	3	+ 14.1	+ 5.8	+ 5.0	+18.0
	4	+ 88.6	+ 91.6	+92.8	+89.3
	5	+ 18.3	+ 23.6	+ 0.5	+14.9
C	1	+103.4	+ 9.0	− 3.0	− 9.0
	2	+ 37.3	− 37.0	−25.7	+11.3
	3	− 65.0	− 31.0	−67.0	+70.0
	4	+ 39.4	+ 40.8	+46.8	+40.7
	5	+100.2	+ 94.4	+44.2	+18.8
D	1	+ 1.2	+ 8.3	− 2.0	+ 1.2
	2	− 36.0	− 1.0	−32.0	+21.2
	3	− 42.0	− 30.0	−28.0	−25.0
	4	− 3.5	+ 6.1	− 0.7	+ 5.2
	5	+ 76.0	+ 65.9	+45.9	+51.8
Total all products	1	+ 22.1	+ 32.1	+12.0	+10.6
	2	+ 28.4	+ 51.6	+37.4	+33.5
	3	− 16.6	− 23.0	−25.6	−20.0
	4	+ 47.6	+ 47.7	+52.4	+52.1
	5	+ 52.7	+ 46.7	+22.8	+29.8

Was the new compensation plan sound?

81

NESBIT WIRE PRODUCTS COMPANY

NESBIT WIRE PRODUCTS COMPANY made two types of wire products: consumer gift items and industrial items. Following its formation in 1951, Nesbit had annual sales that fluctuated closely around $200,000. Losses were incurred each year from 1951–57. Late in 1958 it appeared that the firm would have a sizable increase in annual sales and would make a considerable profit. In view of this, Harold Bowen, the president, was undecided as to what bonus he should give his salesman.

Bowen was the original organizer of the firm and had served as chief designer, engineer, production manager, and sales manager. Late in 1957 he decided to hire a sales manager who could spend full time in selling. He found Maynard Hanson, who was out of work at the time but who had many contacts in the giftware field and had had experience with several companies selling to this industry. Hanson agreed to join Nesbit as sales manager at the small salary of $125 a week, with the understanding that if he was successful in increasing sales he would be rewarded properly. He joined the company on January 1, 1958.

During the next six months sales and losses continued essentially as in previous years. During this period Hanson exhibited the Nesbit gift products at several trade shows and established manufacturers' agents to handle the Nesbit gift line in major cities throughout the country. The gift items were sold to gift wholesalers and direct to large department and variety chain stores. Bowen continued to sell to industrial accounts that were handled on a contract basis. Bowen also continued with his designing, engineering, production, and general supervisory work.

In May, Barclay Company, which had seen one of the Nesbit gift items at a trade show, asked to handle the item as one of the gifts that they would give to women who had Barclay parties in their homes. Barclay sold direct to consumers, primarily through the party system. A woman was given a gift for having a Barclay party in her home. At these parties the Barclay line was demonstrated, and those who wished to buy products could do so. The Nesbit item that Barclay selected for a gift item was a Lazy Susan made of wire with glass trays, which Bowen had designed several years earlier. The Lazy Suzan immediately became a very popular item with Barclay, and orders totaling 100,000 units, approximately $148,000, were received during the next four months. Orders also began to come in for the same item from department stores all over the country. Many of the best-known stores in the United States, including Marshall Field, Macy, Hudson, and Neiman Marcus ordered the Lazy Suzan. Other products in the line sold better than in any previous year but in nowhere near the volume of the Lazy Suzan, which made up 50 per cent of Nesbit's sales for the year and almost 75 per cent of the giftware sales. Industrial sales continued at about the same level as in previous years, and it appeared that they would total about $175,000 in 1958.

Late in November the company's board of directors met to consider necessary actions to complete the year and to plan for 1959. From the record to date and the orders on hand, it was reasonably certain that Nesbit would have sales of about $500,000 for the year, with a net profit of approximately $90,000 before taxes. The question was raised as to what should be done for Hanson. All members of the board agreed that he should be given a bonus. Opinions varied, however, as to the amount of the bonus, with one member favoring a figure as low as $500 and another a figure as high as $10,000. In the discussion that ensued, Bowen, the president, pointed out that he believed Hanson was responsible for much of the success of the company during the year.

Hanson had talked with Bowen repeatedly in recent weeks, asking how much he would be given as a bonus. Bowen had refused to say and in turn had asked how much Hanson thought that he should have. Hanson refused to commit himself but did mention that on a previous occasion he had worked with a firm that had promised to take care of him if he "produced," but had not done so, and he had left them. One of the members of the board reported that he had heard through a mutual contact that Hanson would leave if he did not get a very substantial bonus, which this member thought would be in the neighborhood of $8,000 or $10,000. Others reported that men of similar ability made salaries in the neighborhood of $20,000. Another board member reported that he understood that Hanson had lost some previous jobs because of drunkenness. There had been no trouble with him in this regard since he had been at Nesbit. This board member felt, however, that, if given a large bonus, Hanson might celebrate and not be seen for some time. Another member said that if a bonus as small as $5,000 were given Hanson, he would undoubtedly leave the company.

All members of the board agreed that Hanson had done a good job and that he should be retained if at all possible. Hanson had told Bowen that the $500,000 sales in 1958 were "only the beginning, and next year I can raise sales to $1 million."

After considerable discussion, the board directed Bowen to approach Hanson with the offer of a bonus of $4,000 and to see what his reaction was. If he objected that this was not sufficient, further thought would be given to the matter.

Was the board of directors' decision sound?

B. Advertising Activities

1. Selecting the Advertising Agency

82

HOLMES COMPANY

THE HOLMES COMPANY produced a line of prestige men's toiletries, including such items as shaving cream, after-shave lotion, stick deodorant, and talcum powder. Yardley and Shulton were its main competitors. Holmes sold its product line nationally through such outlets as drugstores and department stores. Early in 1958 the agency that had been handling the Holmes account for ten years resigned because its West Coast office had succeeded in obtaining the advertising of a large cosmetics firm that was about to enter the men's toiletry field. The Holmes Company was thus faced with the necessity of selecting a new advertising agency.

The president appointed a three-man committee, comprised of the vice-president in charge of sales, the vice-president in charge of advertising, and himself, to screen and make the final decision as to a new agency. The president indicated at the first meeting of this committee that it need not be hurried in making this decision, since the present agency's resignation was not effective for about four months. He asked the vice-president in charge of advertising and the vice-president in charge of sales each to prepare a procedure or plan for screening and selecting an agency. The president pointed out that he had already received telegrams, phone calls, and letters from a total of twelve agencies that were interested in soliciting the Holmes $650,000 advertising account.

At the next meeting of the committee the advertising vice-president presented his plan, the first step of which consisted in setting down in writing the criteria to use in selecting the new agency. These criteria were that the agency (1) must be located in the same city as the Holmes Company; (2) should have a good reputation for keeping accounts; (3) should have only a few accounts of over $1 million, since, otherwise, the Holmes Company would be "lost in bigness"; (4) must have had experience with accounts whose products were sold through drugstores and department stores; and (5) must have experience with products advertised on a prestige basis.

The advertising vice-president had made a list of all agencies that had indicated an interest in the Holmes account. To this list he had added those agencies recommended by the former agency and others that he believed would do a good job if they had the account. He had reviewed this list with the vice-president in charge of sales and the president and, at their suggestion, had added three more names to the list, making a total of twenty agencies. The vice-president for advertising proposed that this list of agencies be screened on the basis of the criteria he recommended to the committee. This would result in the elimination of some of the agencies. A questionnaire would be sent to the remaining agencies. On the basis of the replies received, the committee would make further eliminations. The proposed questionnaire appears as Exhibit 1.

EXHIBIT 1

ADVERTISING AGENCY QUESTIONNAIRE
(Please give your answers in a separate report)

1. What are your 1958 anticipated billings?
   A. If your agency has multiple offices, please tell us what office would handle our account *and* what you expect the 1958 billings to be for this office.
2. What has been your growth pattern for the past five years (since 1952)?
3. Please give us a brief history of your agency.
4. Who are your corporate officers? What are their ages? How long have they been associated with your agency?
   A. If your agency has multiple offices, please provide us with an organizational chart for the office that would handle our account.
5. What accounts are currently served by your agency? How long have you had each account?
   A. If your agency has multiple offices, please tell us what accounts are currently served by the office which would handle our account. Also, how long have you had each account?
6. How does the billing of your agency break down by type of media (percentagewise), that is, what percentage of your media expenditures were for newspapers, radio, TV, magazines, etc.?
   A. If your agency has multiple offices, please tell us how the billings break down by media for the office that would handle our account.
7. Please indicate what experience your agency has had with accounts similar to ours. Be sure to tell us the background and experience of the individuals associated with these similar accounts. We are interested in account, merchandising, media, copy and art, and research personnel. If your agency has multiple offices, please answer this question only for the office that would handle our account.
8. What account, merchandising, media, copy and art, and research personnel would be assigned to our account? What per cent of each individual's time would be available to us? What will each individual do with the remainder of his time?
9. Please describe completely how your agency would be compensated for its services to our account.
10. If your agency is invited to make a formal solicitation of our account, what information from us will you need?

The committee would then visit each of the remaining agencies to get to know the personnel generally and particularly the individuals the agency indicated would service the Holmes account. The plan called for the committee to meet and talk for five or ten minutes each with representatives from the media, research, copy, art, and merchandising departments in each agency and then to spend one to one and one-half hours with the potential account executives and account supervisor.

As a result of these visits, the number of agencies for consideration would be further limited. Those still in the running would be investigated more thoroughly, and inquiries would be made of several of their accounts to get ideas on their merits. Each of the agencies still under consideration following this screening would be asked to prepare a two-hour presentation for the committee and to recommend an advertising program for the Holmes Company for the coming year.

This two-hour presentation would be a complete one and would include copy, media, dealer promotional aids, and research recommendations. So that the agencies would be able to prepare a realistic presentation, each would receive the Holmes advertising budget for the year, the total sales of the Holmes Company for the past five years, the media schedule for the present year, ad proofs, TV commercials, and four marketing-research studies that had been completed within the past year. One of these research studies was a small scale motivational research project, done by the previous agency; two were concerned with dealer attitudes toward the Holmes Company; and the fourth was an estimate of the sales of all men's toiletries, broken down by major products and by major marketing areas. Agency representatives would also be permitted to interview committee members for no more than two hours to gain other needed information. The committee would make its final selection on the basis of these presentations.

The vice-president for sales suggested a procedure different from the foregoing. He proposed that the company engage an experienced marketing consulting firm to screen the interested agencies and to present to the committee four or five agencies for final consideration. This, he thought, would save a large measure of executive time that would otherwise be spent in committee work. He had talked with several marketing consultants and had found that the job would cost approximately $5,000. The procedure followed by the consultants would probably be similar to that outlined by the advertising vice-president. The sales manager believed, however, that consultants would do a more thorough and objective job than the Holmes committee. The consultants would investigate all aspects of the agency, primarily through direct contacts and through agency clients.

Which method for selecting a new agency should be adopted?

2. Working with the Advertising

83

ALLGOOD DAIRY COMPANY

THE ALLGOOD DAIRY COMPANY, with sales of over $17 million in 1957, was located in one of the largest metropolitan areas in the United States. The company's line consisted of such items as milk, butter, cream, ice cream, and cottage cheese. These products were sold through home-delivery routes and in stores. In 1957 the company spent $653,000 on advertising—$525,000 through its advertising agency, which had served the company for the past twelve years. In August, 1958, the advertising manager of the Allgood Dairy Company was killed in an automobile accident, and his assistant was promoted to this job. The new advertising manager, John McCarthy, 33 years of age, was a man who had been a former salesman with the company. He had been in the advertising department for about two years.

John McCarthy had been at his new job for about a month when he was surprised to learn that the agency account executive handling the company's account, George Roberts, also serviced another account—a frozen-food packer. He was even more surprised to learn that Mr. Roberts devoted only about half his time to servicing the Allgood account. In talking to the Allgood sales manager about this, McCarthy said, "I think, frankly, that our account is big enough to warrant the services of a full-time account executive. There is plenty for him to do because each product has a separate promotion schedule. He should be spending some time with your department and with our merchandising crews." After some discussion the sales manager advised him to find out from the account executive just who in the agency did what on the account.[1]

In response to the request for a detailed statement Mr. McCarthy re-

---

[1] The primary function of an advertising agency is to place advertising for a company in appropriate media. In carrying out this function, the agency works with the company in planning and creating the type of advertising program that the company will use. Many agencies maintain marketing research facilities to provide data on which advertising budget and program decisions can be made. After a client company has determined its advertising budget and a general idea of what the advertising is to achieve, the agency's creative department develops preliminary ideas for the program. From these ideas a detailed program is worked out with the company including the actual ads and the media schedules to be used. Work on the program within the agency is under the supervision of an account supervisor, who may handle several accounts, depending upon their size. The account executive is under the account supervisor and is the agency's contact man with the client company. He co-ordinates agency and client ideas and works with the client in co-ordinating other phases of sales promotion with advertising. He may handle one or

ceived the following information regarding what personnel worked on the Allgood Dairy account, with their total time in man-equivalents as follows: (1) account supervisor, 25 per cent; (2) account executive, 50 per cent; (3) print copy, art, and production, one man; (4) radio, TV, copy, and production, 50 per cent; and (5) media man, 25 per cent. Actually seven persons worked on the Allgood account in categories 3, 4 and 5.

He was also told that the servicing of his account required help from the agency's marketing research and merchandising department. George Roberts further pointed out that it was necessary for the agency to spend funds on secretarial, accounting, and plans board personnel directly related to the account. There was also the question of overhead, including rent, light, taxes, supplies, management, and legal fees. Roberts also indicated that in 1957 the agency spent about $3,000 on the account for outside copy and media research.

The advertising manager, with the help of a friend of his who sold art supplies to studios and agencies, priced out the personnel services that he received from the agency. According to his best estimates, the agency was making a direct expenditure of $35,750 per year on his account. He arrived at his estimates as shown in Table 1.

TABLE 1

Account supervisor @ $25,000, 25%.....................	$ 6,500
Account executive @ $16,000, 50%......................	8,000
Copy, art, production @ $10,000, 100%..................	10,000
Radio, TV copy and production @ $12,000, 50%...........	6,000
Media man @ $9,000, 25%.............................	2,250
Copy and media research, $3,000........................	3,000
Grand total......................................	$35,750

In 1957 the agency billed $525,000 on this account. At a 15 per cent commission rate, this meant that the agency received $78,750. McCarthy then subtracted from this amount the estimated direct expenses, arriving at a residual amount of $43,000, out of which the agency would have to pay indirect personnel and overhead costs and make its profit. He was convinced that this amount was far in excess of its indirect expenses incurred on Allgood and believed that the agency was making too great a profit from his account. He thought that even if he got the full time of the account executive, George Roberts, the amount would still be too great.

In discussing his findings with the account executive, he was surprised to find that the latter was not taken aback by the amount estimated as

more accounts, depending on their size and the time required to service properly these accounts.

Advertising agencies receive 15 per cent of the advertising expenditures billed through it.

being retained for overhead and profits. Roberts said, "You are about 20 to 25 per cent too low on your direct personnel cost estimates. When you throw in direct secretarial and accounting costs, you will probably find that our out-of-pocket expenses on your account total around $45,-000. This leaves only around $33,000 to cover overhead and profit. This is about the same ratio we try to work off on all our accounts."

What action, if any, should John McCarthy take with regard to the amount of service received from the agency?

84

FREEMAN COMPANY

THE FREEMAN COMPANY, with headquarters in a large city on the West Coast, produced and sold nationally under its own label a line of canned fruits, vegetables, and juices, as well as a line of canned specialty items, including olives, orange segments, syrup, and avocados. The company sold its products through a sales force of eighty-six men direct to chain stores and wholesalers for resale to food outlets. A separate force of twenty-eight men sold the line to wholesalers who specialized in selling to the restaurant, hotel, and institutional markets. In 1957 the company spent $3.4 million in advertising its products. A new advertising director was appointed in 1958, and one of his first projects was to investigate the way his departmental organization fitted that of Freeman's advertising agency.

The company's marketing department was organized into three major departments: the sales department, the advertising department, and the marketing research and planning department. All departments reported to the vice-president in charge of marketing. The two personal selling organizations—consumer and institutional—reported to the director of sales. The advertising department was divided into three major units as follows: (1) publicity, (2) media advertising, and (3) production. The activities of the production-unit centered on the production of point-of-sale materials, including streamers, window displays, shelf displays, and island displays. These three units reported directly to the advertising director. Exhibit 1 shows the organization.

The co-ordination of the various departments within the marketing division was effected largely through the use of a planning committee. The membership of this committee consisted of the director of sales, the advertising director, the director of marketing research and sales planning, and the vice-president in charge of marketing, who served as the

EXHIBIT 1

MARKETING ORGANIZATION, FREEMAN COMPANY

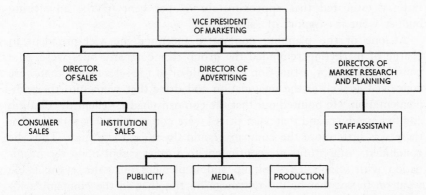

chairman. This group concentrated much of its activity around the budget for the marketing division. It did, however, exercise a control function and had to approve all major changes within the individual departments and also passed on all final advertising plans that were presented by the company's agency.

The Freeman Company's advertising was handled by the Newel Becker Agency. This agency had served the company for over twenty years and had originally been hired by the former advertising director. The new advertising director, Mr. Dabney, had previously served as an account executive with a large New York agency and in this capacity had serviced a large ready-to-eat cereal account.

An area that required a great deal of Mr. Dabney's time concerned working with the sales department to co-ordinate his department's activities with the sales events that the sales department maintained throughout the year. In 1957 the company conducted a total of sixty-seven sales events. These all required co-operation from the advertising department, since it was not only necessary to feature these events in the firm's print, radio, and TV advertising, but it was also necessary for the production unit of the advertising department to develop, with the help of the agency, special point-of-purchase materials. These special events sometimes centered on price, but their aim was typically to relate a company product to a special menu that was applicable to the given season of the year. For example, one special event involved tie-in advertising of certain vegetables with cheese during National Cheese Week. While most of these sales events were national, some were local or regional, thereby placing a considerable strain on the development of special copy and media to meet these requirements. A typical local event was a tie-in of syrup with Boy Scout or Girl Scout Pancake Day parties in individual communities. Twenty-two of the sixty-seven sales events were run in co-operation with other national advertisers of food products or with associations representing groups of food processors. For example, the company co-operated annually with a large ice cream seller by featuring the use of certain of its products as a topping for ice cream desserts. Mr. Dabney estimated that approximately 65 per cent of the advertising budget went in support of sales events.

At one of the planning committee meetings the vice-president in charge of marketing reminded the group that company sales were, to a considerable extent, a function of the caliber of the sales events that were conceived as well as the imagination and drive that went into their implementation. He pointed out that the company had excellent distribution and fine products and that their prices were competitive. He thought that there was little more the company could do along these lines. Thus, he concluded, "our profits are contingent to a great extent upon the imagination with which we think up and implement our sales events." He went on to say that he did not mean by this that all the company's advertising resources should be spent on the development and execution of sales events, since, in his opinion, there yet remained the problem of reminder and image-building advertising. He did think, however, that the sales event constituted the means by which the company could best accomplish its profit mission. He added that he was not satisfied completely with the sales events that were scheduled for the remainder of 1958. He specifically pointed out to Mr. Dabney that he thought the agency was not contributing as much as it should to the development of new sales events ideas. He asked Mr. Dabney to think about this particular problem and to present at the next planning committee meeting a plan whereby this problem might be overcome.

At the next planning committee meeting, Mr. Dabney presented to the group his ideas about how the company's agency might better serve the needs of the company. He pointed out that he had not discussed them yet with the agency account supervisor because he did not wish to present him with the plan until he had the complete support of the company's marketing division. He stated that in his opinion the agency would be quick to support the idea. Mr. Dabney's thesis was that the development of possible ideas for a sales event should be the result of interaction between the company's marketing division and the agency's personnel. He believed that the first step of the development of possible ideas should be to obtain a census of ideas from both the agency and the marketing division. Following this, the relative importance of each sales idea should be evaluated.

In order to accomplish both these steps, Dabney argued that a maximum amount of creative thinking must be brought to bear on the problem. He suggested that the company set up product committees and that similar committees be activated within the agency. He thought that the company should set up four major product sales events committees, which would be organized on a permanent basis. These four committees would be: canned fruits, canned vegetables, canned juices, and canned specialties. He believed that each committee should consist of a chairman plus at least two other members and that the personnel resources of the marketing division permitted the utilization of twelve persons in such capacities. He stressed the fact that each committee should always have one representative from the sales department and another from the advertising department.

In discussing the composition of the comparable committees that would be set up within the agency, he said, "Here we don't have too much of a problem because at the present time they have four account executives working on our account. Each of these account executives could serve as chairman of one of their committees. I think their committees should probably have more people on them than ours. I would like to see representatives from the merchandising, creative, and research departments serving on each of these agency committees."

It was Mr. Dabney's idea that these committees, within both the company and the agency, would convene separately to discuss all possible sales events ideas conceived individually and by the group. Committees would be charged with spelling out the exact nature of the idea as well as indicating what resources would be required to implement it. Representatives from the various departments, within both the agency and the company, would report back to their respective department heads, who would then review the plans, ideas, etc., discussed by the committee and through this same representative make any suggestions to the committee that he thought pertinent. This review by the individual department would require a scheduling of frequent departmental meetings. At a specific point in time, which would be indicated to all concerned, the agency and company committees would terminate their activities in preparation for presenting their ideas to a review board. Dabney pointed out that there would be no discussion of ideas between the company and agency committees at any time during this formulative period. Both the company and the agency would set up separate review boards. In the case of the company, each of the four product committees would report to a review board made up of the vice-president in charge of marketing, the sales director, the advertising director, and the marketing research and planning director.

In the case of the agency, the review committee would consist of the account supervisor, the merchandising director, the marketing research director, the creative director, and the media director.

At these review meetings the appropriate committee chairman would present, in as much detail as possible, all the sales events ideas his committee believed to be pertinent. The review board would discuss each one and in this way develop new ideas, delete others, and change still others. The objective of the review board activity would be to reduce the number of worthwhile ideas to some workable number. In some cases, Mr. Dabney pointed out, it might be necessary for the individual committee to go back and get additional information or evidence to support or deny the feasibility of a particular idea or question.

Following the action taken by the agency and the company review board, the remaining ideas would be submitted to a joint company-agency committee, which would be comprised of the personnel serving on the two separate review boards. The goal of this joint meeting would be to inform all concerned of the various ideas and to receive suggestions for accepting or rejecting any and all events ideas. It would be up to this joint committee to determine which ideas would be considered sufficiently worthwhile for further detail. Thus, the committee would cut down the total number of entries to a reasonable number and also indicate which ideas needed further exploration before final action could be taken.

Following the decisions of the review board, the job of detailing the ideas would be assigned to joint company-agency groups. There would be four such groups, corresponding to the four original product committees. In other words, the agency and its related company product committee would be merged, thereby consisting of seven members. Each of these groups would be forced to specify in detail the central theme, the resources needed, the media to be used, and the total budget for each sales event. When it was necessary, two or more product committees might meet together to co-ordinate activities—as when more than one product type was involved in a single sales event. It was Mr. Dabney's belief that the product groups should be working on about twice as many sales events as the company could use for any one year. He felt that if this were not the case the company might have a shortage of events.

After the individual sales events were planned out in writing, the joint committee would present them to the joint review board, who would be responsible for deciding exactly what sales events would be undertaken for the following year. Mr. Dabney made it clear that, while the review board consisted of several members from the agency, it would still be up to the company to make the final decision. He pointed out that the review board would then delegate the responsibility of dovetailing all the sales events into an over-all written marketing plan to a subcommittee comprised of the advertising director, the sales director, and the agency account supervisor. Upon completion of the over-all marketing plan for a given year, it would be submitted to the company's planning committee for final approval. At this time a detailed budget would accompany the final plan.

In closing, Mr. Dabney pointed out that he expected to be criticized regarding his new plan because of the total number of meetings involved. He stated: "Granted that they are numerous and granted further that much time will be spent by many persons in such meetings, still it is necessary to remember that these meetings serve as informational devices as well as planning. It is doubtful that the intelligent spending of many millions of dollars can take place without an elaborate planning procedure —especially when creative ideas are so very important and when it is necessary to co-ordinate the activities of so many different people, many of whom are from both the company and the agency."

Should the planning committee approve Mr. Dabney's plan for developing and implementing sales events?

85

HOWARD RIETER AND ASSOCIATES

HOWARD RIETER AND ASSOCIATES, an advertising agency billing over $15 million, was approached by one of its accounts, Thompson Industries, Inc., for advice on a proposed research study to determine the corporate image of the Thompson Company. Thompson had no marketing research director and frequently asked the advertising agency to help design surveys. Usually, the agency did not charge for this type of consultation. In the current case, discussions between the agency's marketing research director and the advertising director of Thompson Industries continued over a period of two months. At the conclusion, Thompson asked the agency to draw up a research proposal for doing the entire project on a fee basis. After a proposal was submitted, the agency was authorized to proceed with the job, which was completed several months later. The results were presented to Thompson in a standard report form. The agency then submitted a bill of $6,400. The Thompson advertising director protested the amount of the bill, stating that he believed it to be exorbitant, since data were obtained from only eighty-nine respondents in sixty-three companies.

Thompson Industries, Inc., was one of the large manufacturers of electrical motors in the United States. It produced a variety of motors, of both a standard and a special order nature, which it sold direct to a large number of different industries through its own sales force. Sales exceeded $42 million. Most of its products were component parts that were incorporated in other products that, in turn, were sold for both consumer and industrial use. Thompson invested heavily in product development research and in research to discover new applications of its products.

The request for the image study grew out of the advertising director's opinion that Thompson should spend a larger share of its advertising appropriation on institutional advertising depicting the company as a leader in research on electrical motors. Most of the annual advertising budget of $600,000 was spent in promoting specific product features and pointing out how these features could solve certain problems.

When the agency had submitted the research proposal, the account executive who had presented it to the Thompson advertising director had told the latter that the work would be done on a cost-plus basis. At that time the advertising director did not question the way in which the final bill would be totaled. Later, however, he stated that he was of the opinion that the cost would include only salaries of personnel working on the project and out-of-pocket expenses that the agency incurred on the job.

The Rieter research department had formulated the objectives of the study, prepared and tested the questionnaire, drawn the sample, contracted with an outside agency for the field work, supervised and helped train the interviewers, validated 15 per cent of the interviews, edited and tabulated the returns, prepared the final report, and presented the results to the management of Thompson Industries. To help in designing an effective questionnaire, two analysts had spent time in the field; one of them spent a week discussing the project with fifteen known Thompson customers. The research director had estimated that he spent a total of ten working days himself on the project.

In deciding upon the amount to charge Thompson Industries, the Rieter marketing research director had reviewed the costs connected with the job. He classified these costs as shown below:

1. Direct personnel costs for planning, analysis, and preparation
   of report..$1,488.10
2. Field interviewing cost—invoice received from survey firm........ 1,733.70
3. Direct expenses including travel to client, field travel for pilot
   interviewing, phone calls, meals, etc........................... 501.40
4. Typing of final report....................................... 149.50
5. Questionnaire printing....................................... 78.80

   Total..$3,951.50

A six-month study by the Rieter research department had shown that 72 per cent of all department personnel salaries could be allocated to specific jobs. The remaining 28 per cent was accounted for by vacations, illnesses, departmental meetings, committee meetings, and discussions with members of the agency that could not be related directly to any specific job. The total annual salaries for the marketing research department amounted to $68,942.45. In addition to this 28 per cent of salaries, which was considered "overhead" cost, the research department incurred expenses of approximately $20,000 a year, which included a share of top management salaries, rent, heat, insurance, telephone, postage, depreciation of furniture and fixtures, supplies, association memberships, and library costs.

In pricing the job to Thompson Industries, the research director had followed a standard agency procedure for research billing. Direct personnel costs were doubled, and all other direct costs were added, giving a total of $5,439.60. To this the director added 17.65 per cent for agency overhead. This brought the total of $6,399.68, which he rounded to $6,400.

When Thompson Industries objected to the bill, the Rieter research director reviewed the billing procedure with the account supervisor. The latter asked how independent research firms would have priced the job. The research director replied: "As near as I know, they would charge a higher rate, since they have to receive markup of from 50 to 100 per cent to cover their overhead, instead of our 17.65 per cent. If Thompson had gone to an independent research company, they would have had to have a great deal more preliminary work done, since the independent firm would not have been familiar with the business. The job would have cost $8,000 to $10,000 on this basis."

The account supervisor pointed out that each interview cost $70, which he thought was extremely high. He said, "The cost per interview is the thing that's killing us on this job; it's the thing the Thompson people point to every time they talk to me about it."

The research director thought that the cost per interview was misleading and should not be used as a base by which to judge the total job. He discussed the various steps that had to be undertaken prior to finding and interviewing respondents. He pointed out that much time had been spent in trying to "educate" the Thompson advertising director on the kind of questionnaire that was needed. He noted that, of the $1,488.10 direct personnel charges, about $600 was for his own time in planning the job. The account supervisor agreed that the cost records were undoubtedly right, but he did not think the client could be made to understand the mechanics of a research projet. He did not know how much the final bill should be, but it was his opinion that the agency would have to reduce it substantially.

1. *Evaluate the pricing policy followed by the marketing research director.*
2. *What should be the final amount of the bill to Thompson Industries?*

C. Physical Distribution

86

THE MAYTAG COMPANY

THE MAYTAG COMPANY of Newton, Iowa, was one of the large, well-known manufacturers of major appliances for the home, with sales in excess of $100 million. Over its sixty-year history, it evolved a system of physical distribution that included the maintenance of stocks at 114 points throughout the United States. In 1959 it was studying this distribution system to see whether a more efficient location of stocks could be developed and still give satisfactory service to retail dealers.

Maytag specialized in manufacturing washing machines, both the wringer type and the automatic; however, by 1959 it was also producing automatic electric clothes dryers. The company marketed ironers and home freezers produced by another manufacturer. Sales had grown rapidly following the end of World War II, as shown in Table 1. All the

TABLE 1

Maytag Sales: 1949–58

Year	Sales (Millions)
1958	$105.8
1957	98.6
1956	113.0
1955	93.1
1954	81.1
1953	89.0
1952	86.9
1951	82.7
1950	83.8
1949	60.0

products were sold under the Maytag name; no products were produced for other brands.

Maytag products were sold in every community in the United States through a network of approximately 15,000 retailers. Most of these retailers were served directly by the Maytag organization through ten branch sales offices and 118 salesmen, who were called regional sales managers. In addition, there were eight independent distributors who had specific territories assigned to them and five distributors, which were subsidiaries of the Maytag Company but which operated as if they were independent wholesalers. The independent distributors were located in Cambridge, Mass.; Philadelphia, Pa.; Chicago, Ill.; Dayton, Ohio; Cleveland, Ohio; Atlanta, Ga.; Jacksonville, Fla.; and Colorado Springs, Colo. The distributors who were subsidiaries of the Maytag Company were located in New York City; Detroit, Mich.; Dallas, Tex.; Los Angeles, Calif.; and Portland, Ore. Each of the distributors, both the independent ones and the ones owned by Maytag, had sales forces of their own that covered their territories.

Physical distribution of the Maytag appliances was handled through a system separate from the sales organization. Maytag salesmen (regional sales managers) called on the retail dealers in their territories. When orders were obtained, they were sent to the home plant in Newton, Iowa, if they were large enough to warrant direct shipment; otherwise, they were sent to the closest point at which a stock was maintained. Exhibit 1 shows the location of the stocks at the 114 points throughout the United States.

These stocking points were of four distinct types. Seventy-six of them were known as primary dealers. In fact, these were not dealers in the usual sense of the term but were more like warehouses. They did, however, take title to the products; that is, they actually bought appliances from the Maytag Company in Newton, Iowa, took title to them, and

EXHIBIT 1

MAYTAG POINTS OF DISTRIBUTION

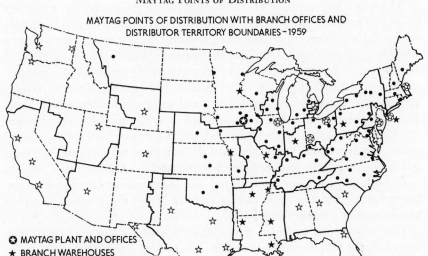

MAYTAG POINTS OF DISTRIBUTION WITH BRANCH OFFICES AND
DISTRIBUTOR TERRITORY BOUNDARIES - 1959

✪ MAYTAG PLANT AND OFFICES
★ BRANCH WAREHOUSES
☆ DISTRIBUTOR WAREHOUSES
✹ CITY DISTRIBUTOR WAREHOUSES
• PRIMARY DEALER WAREHOUSES

maintained stocks at their own risks. These primary dealers did not sell at retail. They shipped only on orders from Maytag salesmen and only to retail dealers from whom these salesmen solicited orders. In general, these primary dealers were independent operations established as side-lines to warehousing companies, trucking companies, or financing companies. Originally, they had been established on the basis of one in each sales territory, and, in general, this situation still existed in areas where primary dealers were used.

The second type of physical distribution was that made through branch warehouses, of which there were ten. Five were concentrated in the Louisiana-Mississippi-Arkansas area and the others in the Great Lakes area. These branch warehouses were similar to primary dealers except that Maytag maintained ownership of the stored merchandise. Thus the branches tended to be stocks of appliances maintained in public warehouses. As in the case of primary dealers, the warehouse operators shipped from these stocks to local retailers on the receipt of orders from Maytag salesmen. The branch warehouses differed in one other respect from the primary dealers. Maytag Company had a fixed policy of no credit; all shipments were made on a C.O.D. basis. Primary dealers, however, being independent operators, could give credit to retailers if they wished, and many of them did. Retailers who received shipments from Maytag branch warehouses were billed by Maytag directly. Retailers who received shipments from primary dealers' stocks were billed by the primary dealers for these shipments, although in those cases in which they received direct shipments from the factory, they were billed by Maytag.

The other two types of distribution points were essentially variations of one type—the independent distributor warehouse. City distributors varied slightly from other distributors in that they worked more closely with Maytag personnel. One Maytag salesman normally worked directly with city distributors—almost as a sales manager for them. There were five of these city distributors. The other distributors were similar, even though some of them were owned by Maytag and some were independent. Each was a regular wholesaler, who handled Maytag products, maintained stocks, sold to dealers, gave credit, serviced the retailer, and settled adjustments. Among them they maintained twenty-three warehouses. Maytag's sales force had little responsibility for the sales of distributors. Contacts with both the company owned and the independent distributors were maintained at the executive level. Exhibit 2 shows the physical distribution system in graphic form.

Distributors had exclusive sales rights in their territories. In all other areas Maytag sold directly to retailers. If an order was large enough to be shipped economically direct from the Newton plant, such shipment was made. The primary dealer serving that area received no credit for the sale. If, however, the order obtained from the retailer by the salesman was small, it was usually more advantageous to obtain the shipment from the primary dealer. On a national basis, about 40 per cent of all sales were made direct to retailers and shipped from the Newton plant. This varied widely, however. In some areas up to 70 per cent of all sales were shipped direct to the retailers from the main plant, while in other areas this was as low as 10 per cent.

Primary dealers bought at carload prices. They received a carload shipment, stored it in their warehousing space, and sold smaller lots to retailers at prices established by Maytag. Primary dealers' margins varied by product and according to the size of the orders received from retailers. The price the retailer paid was exactly the same whether he received the shipment from the primary dealer's stock or from the manufacturer's stock in Newton, Iowa. The difference was only in the transportation costs that were paid by the retailer. Some primary delers operated more than one stock warehouse for Maytag. In cases of this type they could

EXHIBIT 2

PHYSICAL FLOW OF MAYTAG APPLIANCES

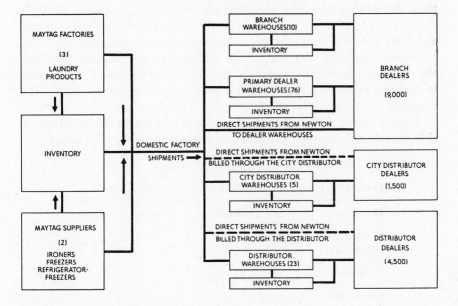

obtain split-car shipments from the Newton plant. Such a shipment was a carload that was delivered to two different locations. Occasionally Maytag could arrange split-car shipments to two different primary dealers, when they were not separated by great distance and when orders from the two, put together, would make a carload.

Primary dealers could order only in carload lots, which were 50 or more units, or in split-car lots, which were 25–29 units. If the price per unit was set at X for a carload of automatic washers, then the price per unit in split-car lots was X plus $2. Primary dealers and Maytag branch warehouses sold to retailers—usually in lots of less than 25, although sometimes in lots above that figure. Very seldom were carload shipments made to retailers from these warehousing points. Normally, all carload shipments were made from the Newton plant. When shipments of automatic washers were made to retailers in lots of 25–49, the retailer was billed at a price of X (the unit price in carload lots) plus $2. In lots of 10–24, the retailer was billed at X plus $8, and in lots of 1–9 the retailer was billed at X plus $10. The price differential varied in amount by type of product. In all cases the transportation charges in less-than-carload lots from the local stocking point were added, in addition to shipment costs from Newton to the stocking point at carload rates. Of course, where a retailer obtained a carload shipment direct from the Newton plant, the transportation costs were simply the carload costs from Newton to the dealer.

Distributors owned by Maytag and the independent distributors had exclusive territories, in which all sales were credited to them. In each of these distributing firms, the president had the authority to make all decisions. As such, he might give credit to retailers, even though Maytag had a definite policy against this. Distributor discounts varied from 12 to 17 per cent, depending somewhat upon the services that Maytag provided the distributor and the services that the distributor furnished the retailers in the area. In all cases the distributor paid freight charges out of his discount.

Table 2 shows the freight rate for carload and less-than-carload quantities to selected locations in the United States from the Newton, Iowa,

TABLE 2

FREIGHT RATES PER CWT. FROM NEWTON, IOWA, TO SELECTED CITIES

Destination	Carload Rates*	Less-than-Carload Rates
Los Angeles	$3.70	$8.99
Denver	1.97	4.04
Dallas	2.00	4.10
Minneapolis	.80	2.35
Kansas City	1.10	2.35
Indianapolis	1.47	2.95
Newark	2.65	5.29
Pittsburgh	2.02	4.04

* In almost all cases, carload quantities were 22,000 lbs. at a minimum, although there were a few variations from this figure.

plant. All factory stocks were maintained at Newton, where all production was located.

All long shipments, such as to California and to the East Coast, were usually made by rail freight; shipments for shorter distances, such as to Kansas City and Chicago, were usually made by truck. Minneapolis was the exception to this, however, as an unusually attractive carload rate had been negotiated with the railroad for shipments to that city. Automatic washers, when packed for shipment, weighed approximately 260 pounds each. Wringer-type washers weighed 150 pounds. Except for those receiving firms that had railway sidings, there was a trucking charge at the end of the rail haul. Delivery of single units from the railway freight yards to any location in a major city tended to run around $5, although this varied slightly. Local delivery from a stocking point, such as a primary dealer, to a retailer cost a similar amount. When more than one unit was shipped at one time, the local hauling rates usually declined slightly on a "per unit" basis.

Trucking charges for hauls beyond local areas varied, but Table 3 shows approximate rates.

Warehousing charges, which Maytag had to pay where it operated branch warehouses, varied considerably from one location to another.

TABLE 3

ApproximatE Trucking Rates for Washing Machines per Cwt.
for Selected Distances

Size of Shipment	Distance			
	50 miles	100 miles	500 miles	1,000 miles
Minimum charge..............$3.91	$3.91	$4.70	$6.65	
Under 200 lbs................... 1.49	..	..	..	
200–2,000 lbs.................. 1.29	..	..	..	
Over 2,000 lbs................. .97	..	..	..	
16,000 lbs. (truck load).......... .60	..	..	..	
Under 1,000 lbs................ ..	1.80	..	..	
1,000–2,000 lbs................ ..	1.60	..	..	
Under 2,000 lbs................ ..	..	3.31	..	
Over 2,000 lbs................. ..	1.54	2.92	..	
Over 5,000 lbs................. ..	1.18	2.48	..	
16,000 lbs. (truck load).......... ..	.79	1.62	..	
Under 5,000 lbs................ ..	..	..	4.80	
Over 5,000 lbs................. ..	..	..	4.55	
18,000 lbs. (truck load).......... ..	..	..	2.55	

On the average, however, there were certain charges that were fairly standard. Warehouses generally separated their charges according to the services provided, but in every instance there was a handling charge that varied from 90 cents to $1.00 per unit and a storage charge which varied from 60 to 75 cents per unit per month. If the warehouse billed the retailers, there was an additional charge.

Most of Maytag's competitors had a considerably smaller number of distribution points. Norge probably had the next largest number—around ninety in the judgment of the Maytag management. They were not certain of this figure, however, as many of Norge's distributors could have operated more than one branch stock. Frigidaire probably had the smallest number of distribution points—about forty-five throughout the country.

Most competitors maintained a few manufacturers' warehouses in different regions of the country, where they maintained stocks. This was particularly true of manufacturers who produced a wide variety of appliances at different locations in the country and needed points at which they could concentrate stocks of the various appliances. From these regional warehouses they could then ship mixed lots of the various appliances to their dealers. These regional warehouses usually worked with the railroads on a special rate. The railroads permitted them to have what was called "storage in transit." For example, a manufacturer located in Cincinnati could ship a carload to his warehouse in Denver, store the products there for a period of time, and later, when a sale was made to a distributor in, say, Seattle, ship a carload of these same products or a mixture of various products on to Seattle. The manufacturer was charged the carload rate from Cincinnati to Seattle plus a special fee of $16 or $17 per car for the "storage-in-transit" charge.

Maytag maintained only the one manufacturer's storage point, at Newton, and so was unable to use this type of service. Maytag's distributors, however, often used the split-car rail service. The distributor in California, for example, operated three branch stocks. He might order a carload shipment from Newton, Iowa, and have part of it delivered to his branch in San Diego and part to his Los Angeles warehouse. He could get the carload rate plus a small additional charge for the two stops. Such a distributor might also obtain a sizable order that was not as large as a carload lot. In this case, the distributor could arrange for a split-car shipment, one half of the shipment going directly to the retailer and the other half going to one of his warehouse stocks.

From almost any point in the United States, Maytag could deliver to a retailer within two days after receipt of his order. Quick delivery, however, was not considered a major point in the appliance business. It was much more important in the case of repair parts than in the case of new appliances. Maytag maintained parts depots at its Kansas City, Indianapolis, and Minneapolis branches. From these locations parts were sold to independent jobbers throughout the United States. These jobbers, who handled parts for many different brands of appliances, normally served local dealers on a quick delivery basis.

All distribution points maintained complete stocks; that is, they had stocks of all major models and products that Maytag produced. The only exception to this policy was in the case of colored appliances. The demand for these appliances varied widely among sections of the country. In California, for example, a significant portion of sales were made in the colored units, whereas in Minneapolis very few colored units were sold. Because of this, most distribution points did not carry complete stocks of the colored units but ordered them on a special basis from the home plant or a branch warehouse designated as a "color distribution point." In these cases Maytag "equalized" freight; that is, shipped the single or small number of units but charged the addressee only the carload rate.

Should the Maytag distribution system be changed? In what way?

87

GROCERY SPECIALTIES, INC.

GROCERY SPECIALTIES, INC., produced colored, flavored cones for ice cream, which it sold to the consumer trade. The firm was located in

Kansas City, Missouri; its only major competitor was in New York City. The competitor's sales were concentrated along the East Coast and totaled approximately $2 million annually. Grocery Specialties executives planned a major effort to break into the eastern market. One of the principal problems that had to be solved was that of physical distribution of the product.

The company's cones were sold under the brand name "Tastee Cones" and were available in five flavors—chocolate, strawberry, orange, cherry, and lime. They were sold in boxes of one dozen at a retail price that varied between 20 and 25 cents. Grocery Specialties sold through food brokers, but the product was shipped directly to the brokers' customers —primarily grocery wholesalers, chain stores, and buying groups. Two different physical distribution plans were considered as part of the program for invading the eastern market. Grocery Specialties could ship directly to eastern customers from its warehouse in Kansas City; the time in transit would vary between five and fifteen days. The other alternative was to establish a warehouse on the East Coast, probably in New York, ship by truck to the warehouse, and deliver by truck from the warehouse. Executives estimated that delivery time from a New York address would vary from two to five days, depending on the customer's location.

Before a decision had been made on this question, an American Airlines representative suggested that air freight from Kansas City might be a better solution. Grocery Specialties had never used air freight, but the management was sufficiently interested to permit the airline to study its problems and to submit a proposal. The following information is taken from the airline's report.

As a basis for comparing air freight with other means of distribution, the alternative of a warehouse in New York City was assumed. The motor freight rate to New York from Kansas City is $6.05 per hundred pounds, and warehouse charges in New York are as shown in Table 1.

There are additional warehouse costs that would be incurred to varying degrees. Some of these are: reconditioning packages—50 cents per carton, cost of new cartons and containers, cost of replacing damaged merchandise, New York state franchise tax, insurance on stock in warehouse, and cost of capital tied up in warehouse stock.

If only the specific warehouse costs listed previously are included, the total cost of handling 100 pounds by motor freight and warehousing in New York would be as shown in Table 2.

If a similar 100-pound shipment were made by air freight direct to the customer, the charge would be as shown in Table 3.

Pickup and delivery charges are considerably less for larger shipments. For example, such charges would be only $4.00 for a 300-pound shipment, making the total cost per hundred pounds only $9.68.

There are a number of added advantages that accrue from using air freight. Some of them are:

1. It will eliminate all warehouse costs as mentioned above in New York City as well as in other key distribution cities that may be used.

TABLE 1

WAREHOUSE CHARGES IN NEW YORK

Charges for:	Per Cwt.
Storage*	$0.30 per month
Handling†	0.40
Receiving‡	0.50
Shipping§	0.50
Marking‖	0.75
Delivery#	1.00
Total	$3.45

* The storage charge for one month, or portion thereof, has been used, even though some stock may remain in the warehouse for a longer period. A higher charge would, therefore, sometimes be incurred.

† The handling charge is the charge for labor involved in moving goods into and out of the warehouse.

‡ This receiving charge may be a little high, since many shipments may be over 100 pounds. The rate per pound decreases as the size of shipment increases.

§ Shipping charges are computed at the rate of 25 cents per order. The charge shown is based on the assumption that the average shipment will be 50 pounds.

‖ The marking charge is a charge for marking cartons shipped with the name and address of the customer and the order number. The charge shown is based on 100 pounds, made up of 25 cartons, each containing 6 boxes of one dozen cones.

Delivery charges from the warehouse for any shipment up to 2,000 pounds are as follows: Manhattan, $0.85; Bronx, $0.95; Brooklyn, $1.10; and Long Island, $1.35. As a general average, $1.00 has been used for delivery charges. Additional and much higher charges will be incurred when delivering from the New York warehouse to such cities as Boston, Philadelphia, Pittsburgh, Washington, and others.

TABLE 2

COST PER CWT. FOR MOTOR FREIGHT AND WAREHOUSING IN NEW YORK

Motor freight charge	$6.05
U.S. transportation tax	0.18
Warehouse charges	3.45
Total	$9.68

TABLE 3

COST PER CWT. FOR AIR FREIGHT AND DELIVERY IN NEW YORK

Air freight charge	$ 8.00
U.S. transportation tax	0.33
Pickup in Kansas City and delivery in New York	3.00
Total	$11.33

2. It permits flexibility of inventory, which may be needed because of unexpected seasonal changes in the tastes of customers.

3. It permits operation with less over-all inventory by supplying all outlets through one central distribution point, namely Kansas City. This will reduce the cost of capital that would be tied up in the larger inventory.

4. Through the use of air freight direct from Kansas City to the customers, Grocery Specialties, Inc., would be able to effect faster delivery to the points in the area discussed than could be obtained out of a warehouse in New York. This speed would greatly enhance the competitive advantage that Grocery Specialties has over the competitive firm in New York.

For the purpose of comparing how this same distribution pattern can work in other cities within the eastern area, the motor freight charges and air freight charges to other major cities are shown below:

TABLE 4

Motor Freight and Air Freight Costs to Selected Destinations

| | | Air Freight Rates per:* | |
Kansas City to:	Motor Freight Rates per 100 lbs.	100 lbs.	100 lbs., with min. of 300 lbs.
Baltimore.........................$5.67		$ 9.80	$ 8.30
Boston.......................... 6.38		11.45	10.15
Cleveland....................... 4.85		9.30	7.65
New York....................... 6.05		11.00	9.40
Philadelphia.................... 5.86		10.45	8.90
Pittsburg....................... 4.90		9.10	7.60
Washington.................... 5.42		9.50	8.15

* Rates include pick up and delivery.

What method(s) of physical distribution should Grocery Specialties adopt?

88

JUNE MALLORY, INC.

June Mallory, Inc., was a nationally known mail-order retailer of women's high-fashion apparel. Originally the mail-order business was a sideline to a fashion designing business, but after World War II the mail-order volume expanded rapidly to an annual total of $15,000,000. The firm was located in Los Angeles, and the bulk of its mail-order business came from the West Coast. In 1950 the management moved the mail-order operation to Des Moines, Iowa, believing that a larger national business could be developed from a central location. All orders were shipped from Des Moines by parcel post, but in 1958 the management was considering a proposal by American Airlines to use air freight.

Various airlines, including American, had made efforts over the years to sell June Mallory on air freight, but analysis by company executives showed that the use of air transportation would increase shipment costs approximately 50 per cent. Several articles in trade journals describing the use of air freight by other firms, some of which were fashion merchandising firms, caused the management to ask American Airlines to study

June Mallory's situation again and to submit a report on possible uses of air freight.

Upon examining June Mallory's records, the airline analysts found that sales in California had declined approximately 50 per cent since the mail-order business had been moved to Des Moines. The airline decided to base its sales argument on the ability of air freight to enable Mallory to regain this lost volume. When the mail-order business had been in Los Angeles, the average delivery in California took from two to three days. After the move to Des Moines, the average delivery time for orders from California had increased to five or six days. The Mallory executives agreed with the airline suggestion that this delay in delivery might have something to do with the decline in sales. Air freight to Los Angeles and San Francisco and parcel post from those locations would reduce delivery time on 90 per cent of the California orders to one or two days. The following basic factors were developed:

> Current annual mail-order net sales in California, $1,200,000
> Unit sales in California, $120,000
> Average unit invoice value, $10
> Average unit weight, 2 lbs.
> Parcel post time in transit, 5–6 days
> Parcel post charges per unit, $0.33
> Air freight parcel post time in transit, 1–2 days
> Air freight parcel post charges per unit, $0.50

Mallory records showed that 20–30 per cent of gross sales in California were returned because the customer refused to accept the package when it arrived or returned it after receiving it. When the office had been in Los Angeles, such returns represented only 10–15 per cent of gross sales. From this information the airline salesman theorized that each day of delay in delivery of an order resulted in a 5 per cent increase in returns. On the basis of this, the airline prepared the following analysis of Mallory's California sales:

> Annual gross sales in California, $1,500,000
> Average days delayed in transit, compared with air-freight service from Des Moines to San Francisco/Los Angeles, 4 days
> Annual percentage of orders returned as a result of delay in transit (4 days @ 5 per cent), 20 per cent
> Annual net dollar sales lost due to resultant returns, $300,000
> Profit lost on above lost sales (at least 10 per cent), $30,000
>
> Total annual unit sales in California, $120,000
> Unit cost of delivery, $0.33
> Total annual cost of parcel post to California, $39,600
> Total annual cost of air freight service to California (150,000 units @ $0.50), $75,000
> Total annual added cost of air freight, $35,400

Should June Mallory, Inc., use air freight to serve the California market?

89

THE WATERBYRD BOAT COMPANY

IN AUGUST, 1957, the management of the Waterbyrd Boat Company of Minneapolis, Minnesota, was considering the establishment of additional branch plants to assemble its line of nationally advertised aluminum outboard motor boats. Currently all parts were being fabricated by the company in its main plant in Minneapolis. Assembly of boats was carried out at the main plant and at a branch plant in Memphis, Tennessee. The company officers believed that the only way the company could achieve effective national distribution was through a system of branch assembly plants.

Waterbyrd sold some boats in each of the forty-eight states, but 75 per cent of its sales were direct to dealers located within approximately five hundred miles of its main plant or its assembly plant. Beyond this radius, transportation costs of assembled boats, in less than carload lots, generally totaled 10 per cent or more of the retail price. Crating costs, necessary for shipment on common carriers, added another 5 per cent. Because of these additional costs it was difficult for the company to secure many dealers beyond its major marketing area. Exhibit 1 shows the distribution of company sales by state.

The Waterbyrd Company had grown steadily since it was founded shortly after World War II. Increased leisure time and higher incomes for wage earners had created a strong and growing demand for water sport equipment of all types, and the outboard boating industry had tripled its sales between 1947 and 1956. The trade estimated that Americans were spending more money on boating than on any other sport. Sales for the boating industry amounted to 400,000 units in the twelve months ending July 30, 1957, and a 15 per cent increase was predicted for the next year. Sales and profits for Waterbyrd had quadrupled since 1952, and unit volume had reached a record 20,000 in 1956.

Outboard motor boats were produced by a large number of small manufacturers. Wood, aluminum, and fiberglass were common construction materials. Wood, including marine plywood, had been the traditional popular choice, but was currently losing part of its market to both aluminum and fiberglass. In 1957 about one-third of all boats produced were made of aluminum, and 22 per cent of fiberglass. One of the major aluminum producers estimated that by 1961 the annual market for aluminum boats would reach 210,500 units, more than a 60 per cent increase over 1957.

The growing popularity of aluminum and fiberglass was explained by their reduced need for maintenance as compared to wood and by their

EXHIBIT 1

DISTRIBUTION OF INDUSTRY AND WATERBYRD UNIT SALES BY STATES:
1956–57 SEASON

State	Industry	Waterbyrd	Waterbyrd Percentage of Industry Sales
Alabama	1.65%	1.41%	4.3%
Arizona	0.51	0.29	2.6
Arkansas	0.84	1.57	9.3
California	8.55	0.40	0.2
Colorado	0.47	1.37	14.6
Connecticut	1.43	4.56	16.0
Delaware	0.39	0.02	0.2
District of Columbia	0.37	0.00	0.0
Florida	6.43	0.48	0.3
Georgia	1.92	1.73	4.5
Idaho	0.36	0.11	1.4
Illinois	5.16	6.18	6.0
Indiana	2.65	2.77	5.3
Iowa	1.60	3.67	11.5
Kansas	1.21	1.49	6.2
Kentucky	0.86	1.58	9.2
Louisiana	2.48	4.44	8.9
Maine	0.91	0.14	0.7
Maryland	1.40	0.75	2.7
Massachusetts	2.93	0.46	0.7
Michigan	6.80	3.06	2.3
Minnesota	3.75	16.24	21.6
Mississippi	0.55	1.65	15.0
Missouri	2.44	7.15	14.7
Montana	0.42	0.19	2.2
Nebraska	0.53	0.80	7.2
Nevada	0.12	0.02	1.0
New Hampshire	0.56	0.20	0.2
New Jersey	3.02	1.36	2.3
New Mexico	0.28	0.22	3.7
New York	7.87	4.83	3.2
North Carolina	1.08	0.38	1.7
North Dakota	0.34	0.66	3.7
Ohio	5.34	1.72	1.6
Oklahoma	1.79	2.54	7.1
Oregon	1.42	0.11	0.4
Pennsylvania	2.95	1.08	2.7
Rhode Island	0.48	0.05	0.4
South Carolina	1.09	0.84	3.8
South Dakota	0.29	0.73	11.7
Tennessee	1.90	4.21	11.1
Texas	5.77	5.75	5.0
Utah	0.37	0.19	2.6
Vermont	0.29	0.01	0.1
Virginia	1.26	0.65	2.5
Washington	2.93	0.54	0.9
West Virginia	0.37	0.73	9.8
Wisconsin	3.75	10.57	14.0
Wyoming	0.12	0.11	4.7
Total U.S.	100.00%	100.00%	5%

Source: Company records and Outboard Boating Club of America.

lighter weight, which made it possible to haul them more easily on top of cars or trailers. Fiberglass had the additional advantages of being readily moldable into highly styled lines, retaining permanently impregnated colors, and being easy to repair. Aluminum was generally regarded as a sturdier material and somewhat lighter than fiberglass. It suffered, however, from a belief that exposure to salt air and salt water would corrode the metal. While this had been true at one time, improved alloys, developed following World War II, had eliminated much of this problem. Some unsightly superficial oxidation still appeared, however, if the boat was not painted. As a result of these factors demand for boats made of the three materials varied among different regions of the country (Exhibit 2). Most

EXHIBIT 2

GEOGRAPHIC DISTRIBUTION OF UNIT SALES BY HULL MATERIALS: 1956

Region	Wood	Plastic	Aluminum	Total Boat Sales
Great Lakes	12.4%	11.9%	20.6%	44.9%
Atlantic Coast (fresh)	4.8	1.5	1.8	8.1
" " (salt)	16.6	0.7	0.6	17.9
Gulf Coast (fresh)	1.0	0.8	1.0	2.8
" " (salt)	3.2	0.5	0.2	3.9
West Coast (fresh)	0.8	0.4	0.2	1.4
" " (salt)	2.0	1.0	0.4	3.4
Other	5.0	5.1	7.5	17.6
Totals	45.8%	21.9%	32.3%	100.0%

Source: Outboard Boating Club of America.

retail dealers of any size, however, carried boats made from each of the three materials.

In addition to the three types of material, the industry provided the consumer with a broad array of different boat designs to fit particular purposes. Models ranged from small prams and plain fishing boats to streamlined runabouts and day cruisers. The current trend was to larger and "flashier" models to match the increasing horsepower available from new outboard motors. Some cruisers with sleeping and eating facilities were beginning to appear. Style was becoming an increasingly important factor, and sporty models boasted sleek lines, automobile-type headlights, and tail fins. Colorful and rugged upholstery materials made it possible to have interiors that matched the luxury look of an expensive automobile convertible.

Prices varied with the type of boat and ranged from two hundred dollars to more than a thousand. Accessories, such as plexiglass windshields, steering wheels and control equipment, fancy marine hardware, fitted cushions, speedometers, and battery boxes could boost the price several hundred dollars more. Policies of manufacturers differed as to what accessory equipment was offered on the standard hulls. Price comparisons between models of different manufacturers were, consequently, not too easy to make. In addition to the boat, the boating enthusiast usually bought a motor and a trailer, which on the average cost an additional thousand dollars.

The Waterbyrd line of boats included twelve basic hull designs, which were modified into thirty-five models for fishing, water skiing, and day cruising. (Exhibit 3 shows list prices F.O.B. Minneapolis and shipping

EXHIBIT 3

PRICES AND WEIGHTS OF SELECTED BOAT MODELS FROM THE WATERBYRD LINE

Style	Length (Feet)	Price Retail F.O.B. Minn.	Weight Net*	Weight Shipping†
The Pelican (fishing)	12	$ 175	90	125
The Gull (utility)	14	$ 355	200	260
The Ouzel (sports runabout)	15	$ 740	370	652
The Flamingo (day cruiser)	16	$1,100	650	800

* For carlot shipments.
† For less-than-carlot shipments; includes crate.
Source: Company records.

weights for a representative portion of the line.) Dealers were allowed a trade discount of 30 per cent from the list price and a 5 per cent quantity discount if they bought in carload lots. Purchase in carload lots also saved the dealer the cost of crating because the boats could be secured on racks when the whole car was utilized. In less-than-carload lots the boats had to be individually crated. Besides its expense, crating also added to the shipping weight.

A large proportion of Waterbyrd's sales outside the areas immediately surrounding its plants were made through seven distributors. These distributors were actually large retailers who had started supplying smaller dealers near them. They had increased this business, purchased large trucks with which to haul the boats, and sold over areas that, in two or three cases, covered several states. They received a trade discount of 30 and 10 per cent on all carload purchases, although the sales manager of Waterbyrd believed that they probably sold at least 50 per cent of their volume through their own retail facilities. Distributors maintained all necessary contacts with their dealers and were quite jealous of any company interference. As a result, Waterbyrd management's relationship with such dealers seldom extended beyond the mailing of general sales literature.

Carload freight rates were considerably lower than less-than-carlot (l.c.l.) rates, often more than 50 per cent lower (Exhibit 4). It was difficult, however, to fit the variety of boats on a given order into a single standard freight car. As a result, the company frequently could not take full advantage of the lower carlot rate. Shippers were charged for a minimum of 10,000 pounds on carlot shipments. This meant that the minimum rate between Minneapolis and Albany, for example, would be $449,

EXHIBIT 4

FREIGHT RATES PER CWT. FOR ALUMINUM BOATS IN CARLOTS AND LESS-
THAN-CARLOTS AND FOR CARLOTS OF BOAT PARTS BETWEEN
MINNEAPOLIS AND SELECTED CITIES

| | Boats | | Boat Parts |
	Carlot*	L.C.L.	Carlot†
Los Angeles................	$7.10	$17.05	$5.43
Portland....................	7.24	17.05	5.43
Pittsburgh..................	3.68	8.70	2.80
Albany.....................	4.49	10.58	3.20
Memphis....................	3.68	10.78	2.82
Jacksonville................	3.25‡	9.56‡	3.90

* 10,000-lb. minimum per car.
† 24,000-lb. minimum per car.
‡ From Memphis.

regardless of the number of boats that could be fitted into the car. The sales manager estimated that the saving on carlot shipments was, consequently, likely to be only about 30 per cent of the difference between the carlot and the l.c.l. rates. He thought that if the company could plan its shipments, instead of shipping to the order of the distributor, perhaps 40 per cent of the difference between the two rates could be saved.

Despite the handicap of the freight charges, a few of the company's distributors and more distant dealers were doing an excellent job of selling Waterbyrd boats in their territories. The company had about one thousand dealers, most of which were located within the major marketing areas immediately adjacent to the two plants. The sales manager preferred to sell direct to dealers rather than through distributors because of the added margin for the company. Wherever branch plants were established, it would be feasible to sell direct to the dealers within a 500-mile radius.

Competition in the aluminum boat field consisted of forty manufacturers that sold 97.5 per cent of the volume. These manufacturers were located over the entire country, as indicated in Exhibit 5. The sales manager pointed out that some of the more aggressive companies were already establishing branch plants and that some were beginning to handle both fiberglass and plywood boats in addition to aluminum boats.

In considering the problems associated with the expansion of the company's sales, the sales manager pointed out that storage facilities at the Minneapolis location were almost fully utilized under current production schedules. Manufacturing and assembly facilities, however, could be operated on a third shift. Current assembly costs were regarded as about $5 per boat cheaper in Minneapolis than at Memphis because of the more efficient painting equipment and the better materials handling system that were used with the larger volume of boats at the main plant. Freight rates for shipping unassembled boat parts were less than carlot rates for assem-

EXHIBIT 5

LOCATIONS OF MANUFACTURERS OF ALUMINUM BOATS

East (4)	*Midwest (16)*	*Southwest (7)*
Elmira, N.Y.	Cadillac, Mich.	Dallas, Tex. (2)
Marathon, N.Y.	St. Charles, Mich.	Grand Prairie, Tex.
Pleasantville, N.Y.	Sturgis, Mich.	Little Rock, Ark.
Portland, Me.	Tecumseh, Mich.	Marathon, Ark.
	White Pigeon, Mich.	Monticello, Ark.
South (6)	Dixon, Mo.	Miami, Okla.
	Richland, Mo.	
Atlanta, Ga.	Goshen, Ind.	*Far West (7)*
Memphis, Tenn. (3)	Middlebury, Ind. (2)	
McKensie, Tenn.	Syracuse, Ind.	Salt Lake City, Utah
Orlando, Fla.	Little Falls, Minn.	Colville, Wash.
	Minneapolis, Minn.	Spokane, Wash. (2)
	Perham, Minn.	Fresno, Calif. (2)
	Webster City, Iowa	San Raphael, Calif.
	Topeka, Kan.	

Source: Company records.

bled boats, and freight cars could be fully utilized (Exhibit 4). Costs for a minimum-sized assembly plant were estimated at about $250,000. This would include 15,000 square feet of assembly space and 15,000 square feet for storage plus all necessary mechanical equipment. Management believed that a volume of 5,000 units would be necessary to support such a plant profitably. Storage facilities in public warehouses to which the company could ship in carlots were also available on a monthly basis. The annual rental for such space was $1.00–$1.50 per square foot, plus handling charges. The average boat required about 12 square feet for storage.

Should the Waterbyrd Company establish new branch plants? If so, how many and at what locations?

SECTION VI

Controlling the Operation

Good control is a function of how well the other steps in the administrative process have been conceived and implemented. Control is dependent upon the proper definition of the firm's marketing niche, the formulation of an adequate plan, and the development of a suitable organization. For example, the specification of quantitative goals is an essential part of setting objectives; these same goals become standards for control. Control is also a part of the organizational structure because one cannot develop such a structure without building authority provisions into it. To define responsibility is a form of control.

The marketing executive must try to control many different things, including a number of diverse types of individuals, sales results, a variety of costs, and project completion dates. He must make certain that the firm's position in the market is not in jeopardy for any reason and that its market niche, major strategies, and organization are in harmony.

Setting Standards

Standards must be set before effective control can take place. These must be identified and tied to individual responsibility. Unfortunately, standards for some of the units comprising the marketing department are difficult to set in any precise way. For example, what kind of standards can be set for the advertising unit? How can the performance of this unit be ascertained, since to do so requires measurement of the effectiveness of the advertising? Yet someone has to control this operation, which means that some sort of standards are involved even though they may not be stated precisely and may change over time.

How does one set standards for measuring the performance of the marketing research unit? Quantitative standards of value are impossible, but control is necessary. As a result, some qualitative standard is used, perhaps the opinion of the marketing manager, based on general impressions.

Control over the sales force is precise compared to that exercised over the advertising and marketing research units. In the process of assigning responsibility among the various geographical administrative units for achieving forecast sales, quotas are developed for the various subunits down to the individual salesman. These quotas become control standards. Not all firms use quotas; for example, it is quite difficult to set meaningful quotas for missionary salesmen.

Sales quotas can be expressed in dollars or units, although the latter is preferable, since prices change over time. Quotas are typically assigned on an annual basis but are broken down by months. Quarterly reviews are common so that quotas may be adjusted in light of changing conditions. Some firms use more than one quota; one is given to the salesmen for incentive purposes, and another is used for the budget.

Quotas, as standards, are often used for promotion and pay purposes. Many firms use a compensation system that calls for the individual salesman to receive a certain stipulated commission on all sales over quota. In this situation, quotas must be set with particular care, else expense or morale problems will develop.

Failure to reach quota does not necessarily mean that the salesman is at fault. Changes may occur in the market place which make the quota invalid. Other controls may then be used to appraise the salesman's work. The number of calls made, the expenses incurred, the number of new accounts opened, and the loss of key accounts are all factors for which control standards may be set.

Selection of Strategic Control Areas and Taking Corrective Action

Assuming that standards have been set wherever possible, the next step is to select the areas where control is most important. A top marketing executive cannot possibly control everything and everybody directly, nor should he, since to do so would destroy his organizational system. It is the mark of a competent executive to know *what* to check, *where* to check, and *when* to check. There are some strategic control areas that need to be checked continuously, such as total sales, market shares by products, sales expenses, and sales to key accounts. Situations may arise that require the executive to set up a temporary control system, for example, the introduction of a new product.

Much control work is delegated and the assumption made that only abnormal situations will filter to the top. This delegation implies that there is a hierarchy of control with certain levels of management making certain checks at frequent intervals, while other levels of management make other checks less frequently. Branch managers may check sales by individual salesmen daily, whereas the marketing manager may review results by salesmen only annually, if at all.

Control is essentially a negative activity unless corrective action is taken where indicated. First, the executive makes certain that performance did not meet the standards. This may mean a review of both "performance" and "standard" criteria. If either has become invalid, he must still take corrective action, but the type of such action will depend upon his findings relative to the validity of the two measures. If the standards are not valid owing to "unforeseen competition," he may take corrective action by attempting to make the standard valid by, for example, authorizing a price cut to match competition, or he may choose to change the standard. The executive may, on the other hand, take corrective action by discharging the individual, transferring him, or retraining him. No matter what corrective action he takes, the executive will end up with another control problem, since he will have set in motion a new and different set of forces, which, in turn, must be controlled.

90

MARMAN, INCORPORATED

WHEN the accounting department of the Marman Company, a large manufacturer of power lawn mowers, installed a machine accounting system, all company executives were given a briefing on its operation. The sales manager was impressed by the ease with which large quantities of data could be processed and later discussed with the company's treasurer the possibility of using the new installation for processing and summarizing sales data for control purposes. The treasurer assured him that this was possible and suggested that he prepare a written statement specifying the kinds of sales data needed and the sources from which such data could be obtained.

The Marman Company distributed its line of power lawn mowers through 137 distributors to over 4,500 dealers located throughout the United States. Sales exceeded $8 million. The company's seventeen salesmen were supervised by two field sales managers. The home office staff consisted of a sales manager, an assistant sales manager, a service manager, and three sales correspondents. Marman had no marketing research department.

Salesmen called primarily on distributors but also made calls with distributor salesmen on dealers who needed special attention. Marman salesmen were expected to keep distributor inventories of power mowers at optimum levels and to assist distributors in co-operative advertising plans. They also handled distributor complaints and credit problems when they arose.

Unit and dollar sales records by salesmen were kept manually in the sales department for each of the seven models. The accounting department provided the sales department with similar sales information by distributors. These data were summarized monthly from invoice records. A record of salaries and expenses on each salesman was kept by the assistant sales manager in a confidential ledger available only to the sales manager. Salesmen sent in weekly reports listing the calls made each day and the expenses incurred. This report was used to determine the total travel expenses of each salesman as well as yearly reports on mileage, entertainment, food, lodging, telephone and telegram, mailing, laundry and dry cleaning, and miscellaneous.

The company received warranty cards on about 70 per cent of sales. These cards showed the customer's name and address, the model purchased, the date purchased, the dealer who sold it, and the dealer's address. These cards were not used by the sales department but were referred to occasionally by the service department. They were filed by date of sale.

The sales manager turned over to the assistant sales manager the job of drawing up a report specifying the kind and source of sales data needed by the department to control and evaluate the sales force and the sources of such data. The assistant sales manager spent the next several days working on this assignment. His report is reproduced below:

To: Mr. Ralph Beard, Sales Manager
From: John Jorgenson
Subject: Machine system for sales department

At your request I have prepared a report indicating the kinds of information needed for continuous control of our sales activities. Since I do not know the nature of the new or intended accounting forms or procedures, I did not attempt to lay out a step-by-step procedure indicating the flow of such data from our records to the machines.

Kinds of Information Needed

1. Sales quotas and actual sales, in units and dollars for each model by territory, monthly and cumulatively for the year to date for the current year and last year.
2. Sales to each distributor grouped by sales territory for each model, quarterly and for year to date for the current year and last year. The same data should be shown monthly and cumulatively for key distributors.
3. Number of calls, sales per call, and cost per call made on each distributor and for each sales territory, semiannually and annually for the current year and last year.
4. Sales by distributor size (dollar volume of purchases from Marman) grouped by sales territory, semiannually and annually for current year and last year.
5. Financial rating of distributors.

Sources of Basic Data

The data required can be obtained from six sources:
1. Call reports made by salesmen.
2. Shipment papers or invoices which show dollar sales and unit sales by product.
3. Salary and expenses by salesmen.
4. Returns and credits from accounting records.
5. Distributor classification data from distributor control records.
6. A special study will be necessary to set up a method of allocating sales costs by distributor.

The treasurer estimated that to handle the additional load these reports would entail, he would have to hire another key punch operator. During peak periods, overtime work by others would be required. He estimated that the sales reports would add about $10,000 annually to his department operating costs.

Should the assistant sales manager's recommended sales analyses be established?

91

IDEAL INDUSTRIES

IN FORTY years Ideal Industries grew from a small business operating out of the owner's home to a $5-million business in 1959. The firm's product line consisted of over one hundred different products of varying importance. In attempting to develop a method for assessing the profitability of the various products, the new general sales manager found that he needed a practical method of allocating sales costs.

Ideal Industries' growth had been accomplished by the continual addition of new products. The products were mostly industrial tools and electrical supplies and equipment used in the building and contracting industries or as attachments to machine tools used in production or in plant maintenance functions. The complexity of the product line and the relative unimportance of any one product to the company's distributors made the selling and distribution of the company's products a difficult task. A great deal of selling effort had to be aimed directly at the ultimate customers in order to create demand for Ideal's products so that distributors would be interested in handling them.

Ideal's products could be divided into three broad classes. One group of products was used extensively by electrical contractors. Gradual addition of these products had come about because of the company's original connection with the electrical industry. Some of the principal items of this line were all types of wire connectors and wire nuts; plastic crimp connectors; fish tape reels, pullers, and winders, which were all items used by electricians when "fishing" wire through long conduit runs; "wire lube," a special lubricant applied by hand or brush to make the pulling of wire easier and to relieve strains on wire insulation during the pulling; and all types of electricians' tools, such as wire cutters, wire strippers, and pliers. All these items were distributed through more than 1,500 electrical distributors, and most of them sold for less than $50.

The second largest group of products manufactured by Ideal Industries was used principally by electrical and machinery manufacturers and was generally distributed through mill supply distributors. This line included driving centers—a patented device that, when attached to lathes, saved machining time by the elimination of chucks and clamps to hold the work in the lathe; live centers of various types for lathe work; etchers; electric markers; demagnetizers; tachometers; and large industrial tank and hand-type cleaners.

The third group of products was sold for plant maintenance and general industry use and was distributed primarily through a small group of specialty distributors. One of these products was a resurfacer for eliminating ridges, grooves, pits, and burns from commutators and slip rings in electric motors. Another type of specialty distributor handled rotary impact drills, attachments, and bits.

Some items, such as industrial cleaners and blowers, soldering sets, and wire strippers, were handled by all three types of distributors—electrical distributors, mill supply houses, and specialty distributors—but such "across-the-board" distribution was not usual because of the unrelated items from one product line to the next.

Approximately one half of Ideal's total sales was accomplished through manufacturers' agents, while the company's sales force of twenty-five salesmen was responsible for the other half. The sales manager estimated that approximately half the average company salesman's time was spent working with final customers, and half was spent in selling to distributors. If a sale was made to a final customer, it was placed with the area distributor of the customer's choice. Three regional managers supervised the agents and the company salesmen. Agents received an average commission of slightly less than 10 per cent. Salesmen's incomes averaged $6,000 to $10,000, including salary and bonus; expenses were paid by the company.

Over the years it had not been unusual for Ideal to add as many as five new products in a single year. Some new products were not closely related to the rest of the line. For instance, a rotary impact drill attachment had been introduced that required the sales department to find a complete new group of distributors in addition to those presently distributing the company's lines. Although the management realized that the profitability of the various products varied widely, it did not know exactly how profitable or unprofitable individual products were.

In an effort to determine which products should be given more emphasis and which, if any, should be dropped, the sales manager and the comptroller set up a special procedure. Exhibit 1 illustrates the procedure for three products.

Material and labor costs of producing a product were readily available from cost accounting records. Overhead production expenses were allocated to each product on the basis of total labor costs. These three items (material, labor, and production overhead) were added together to get the figures shown as "Direct Cost" in the example in Exhibit 1. Direct costs were deducted from sales to get gross margin.

Expenses were allocated to specific products in two steps. Such items as administration, shipping, and cash discounts were allocated against each product on the basis of sales. For example, if Product A accounted for 5 per cent of the company's sales, it would be charged with 5 per cent of the expenses mentioned above. Advertising and engineering expenses were charged to individual products directly. To arrive at an

EXHIBIT 1

Example of Evaluation of Profit Contribution by Product Line

Product	Net Sales	Direct Cost	Gross Profit	Per Cent	Total Allocated Expense	Contribution to Net Profit	Per Cent	Inventory	Annual Turnover Rate
A...........	$ 500,000	$300,000	$200,000	40.0	$162,000	$ 38,000	7.6	$ 60,000	5.0
B...........	180,000	90,000	90,000	50.0	91,000	(1,000)	(0.5)	45,000	2.0
C...........	340,000	140,000	200,000	58.8	120,000	80,000	23.5	35,000	4.0
Total A, B, C......	1,020,000	530,000	490,000	48.8	373,000	117,000	11.4	140,000	3.78
Total A, C......	840,000	440,000	400,000	47.6	282,000	118,000	14.0	95,000	4.63

adjusted gross profit that could be used as a profitability guide, it was also necessary to charge sales expenses directly to products. To do this, the company needed information from which to determine the proper allocation of sales expenses.

Ideal Industries' sales expense, including agents' commissions, was 17.8 per cent of sales. The sales manager estimated that the salesmen spent about half their time in actual customer calls. On the average, they made five calls a day—about half on distributors and half on distributors' customers. Some of the distributors handled a large percentage of the Ideal line, while others handled only a few specialized items. Most customers of distributors were interested in a narrower part of the Ideal line than were the distributors. To determine how sales expenses should be allocated, the sales manager devised a new salesman's report called "Salesman's Daily Record." Copies of the front and back of this report are shown as Exhibits 2 and 3. It was to be prepared in triplicate. If the form worked out in practice, it was proposed to convert it into a card that would be marked with special pencil so that it could be analyzed by machine.

EXHIBIT 2

SALESMAN'S DAILY RECORD—FRONT

Salesman

Date Office

Ideal Industries Inc.

Salesman's Daily Record

1. MAKE A RECORD OF EACH DAY USING AS MANY SHEETS AS NECESSARY
2. CHECK TYPE OF CALL PURPOSE AND PRODUCTS COVERED CHECK RESULTS IF LISTED: WRITE IN UNDER 'COMMENTS' IF NOT LISTED

CUSTOMER	TYPE OF CALL		PURPOSE OF CALL		PRODUCTS COVERED						RESULTS	COMMENTS
INDIVIDUAL:	☐ D1	☐ U1	☐ P1	☐ P 7	☐ 111	☐ 134	☐ 215	☐ 310	☐ 10	☐ 80	☐ R1	
FIRM:	☐ D2	☐ U2	☐ P2	☐ P 8	☐ 112	☐ 135	☐ 216	☐ 320	☐ 20	☐ 90	☐ R2	
	☐ D3	☐ U3	☐ P3	☐ P 9	☐ 113	☐ 136	☐ 221	☐ 415	☐ 21	☐ —	☐ R3	
ADDRESS:	☐ D4	☐ U4	☐ P4	☐ P10	☐ 114	☐ 137	☐ 222	☐ 416	☐ 22	☐ —	☐ R4	
	☐ D5	☐ U5	☐ P5	☐ P11	☐ 117	☐ 211	☐ 223	☐ 417	☐ 30	☐ —	☐ R5	
	☐ D6	☐ U6	☐ P6	☐ P12	☐ 118	☐ 212	☐ 231	☐ 418	☐ 40	☐ —	☐ R6	
CITY: STATE:	☐ D7	☐ U7	TIME SPENT		☐ 120	☐ 213	☐ 232	☐ —	☐ 50	☐ —	☐ R7	
	☐ D8	☐ U8	I	S	☐ 131	☐ 214	☐ 250	☐ —	☐ 70	☐ —	☐ R8	
INDIVIDUAL:	☐ D1	☐ U1	☐ P1	☐ P 7	☐ 111	☐ 134	☐ 215	☐ 310	☐ 10	☐ 80	☐ R1	
FIRM:	☐ D2	☐ U2	☐ P2	☐ P 8	☐ 112	☐ 135	☐ 216	☐ 320	☐ 20	☐ 90	☐ R2	
	☐ D3	☐ U3	☐ P3	☐ P 9	☐ 113	☐ 136	☐ 221	☐ 415	☐ 21	☐ —	☐ R3	
ADDRESS:	☐ D4	☐ U4	☐ P4	☐ P10	☐ 114	☐ 137	☐ 222	☐ 416	☐ 22	☐ —	☐ R4	
	☐ D5	☐ U5	☐ P5	☐ P11	☐ 117	☐ 211	☐ 223	☐ 417	☐ 30	☐ —	☐ R5	
	☐ D6	☐ U6	☐ P6	☐ P12	☐ 118	☐ 212	☐ 231	☐ 418	☐ 40	☐ —	☐ R6	
CITY: STATE:	☐ D7	☐ U7	TIME SPENT		☐ 120	☐ 213	☐ 232	☐ —	☐ 50	☐ —	☐ R7	
	☐ D8	☐ U8	I	S	☐ 131	☐ 214	☐ 250	☐ —	☐ 70	☐ —	☐ R8	
INDIVIDUAL:	☐ D1	☐ U1	☐ P1	☐ P 7	☐ 111	☐ 134	☐ 215	☐ 310	☐ 10	☐ 80	☐ R1	
FIRM:	☐ D2	☐ U2	☐ P2	☐ P 8	☐ 112	☐ 135	☐ 216	☐ 320	☐ 20	☐ 90	☐ R2	
	☐ D3	☐ U3	☐ P3	☐ P 9	☐ 113	☐ 136	☐ 221	☐ 415	☐ 21	☐ —	☐ R3	
ADDRESS:	☐ D4	☐ U4	☐ P4	☐ P10	☐ 114	☐ 137	☐ 222	☐ 416	☐ 22	☐ —	☐ R4	
	☐ D5	☐ U5	☐ P5	☐ P11	☐ 117	☐ 211	☐ 223	☐ 417	☐ 30	☐ —	☐ R5	
	☐ D6	☐ U6	☐ P6	☐ P12	☐ 118	☐ 212	☐ 231	☐ 418	☐ 40	☐ —	☐ R6	
CITY: STATE:	☐ D7	☐ U7	TIME SPENT		☐ 120	☐ 213	☐ 232	☐ —	☐ 50	☐ —	☐ R7	
	☐ D8	☐ U8	I	S	☐ 131	☐ 214	☐ 250	☐ —	☐ 70	☐ —	☐ R8	
INDIVIDUAL:	☐ D1	☐ U1	☐ P1	☐ P 7	☐ 111	☐ 134	☐ 215	☐ 310	☐ 10	☐ 80	☐ R1	
FIRM:	☐ D2	☐ U2	☐ P2	☐ P 8	☐ 112	☐ 135	☐ 216	☐ 320	☐ 20	☐ 90	☐ R2	
	☐ D3	☐ U3	☐ P3	☐ P 9	☐ 113	☐ 136	☐ 221	☐ 415	☐ 21	☐ —	☐ R3	
ADDRESS:	☐ D4	☐ U4	☐ P4	☐ P10	☐ 114	☐ 137	☐ 222	☐ 416	☐ 22	☐ —	☐ R4	
	☐ D5	☐ U5	☐ P5	☐ P11	☐ 117	☐ 211	☐ 223	☐ 417	☐ 30	☐ —	☐ R5	
	☐ D6	☐ U6	☐ P6	☐ P12	☐ 118	☐ 212	☐ 231	☐ 418	☐ 40	☐ —	☐ R6	
CITY: STATE:	☐ D7	☐ U7	TIME SPENT		☐ 120	☐ 213	☐ 232	☐ —	☐ 50	☐ —	☐ R7	
	☐ D8	☐ U8	I	S	☐ 131	☐ 214	☐ 250	☐ —	☐ 70	☐ —	☐ R8	
INDIVIDUAL:	☐ D1	☐ U1	☐ P1	☐ P 7	☐ 111	☐ 134	☐ 215	☐ 310	☐ 10	☐ 80	☐ R1	
FIRM:	☐ D2	☐ U2	☐ P2	☐ P 8	☐ 112	☐ 135	☐ 216	☐ 320	☐ 20	☐ 90	☐ R2	
	☐ D3	☐ U3	☐ P3	☐ P 9	☐ 113	☐ 136	☐ 221	☐ 415	☐ 21	☐ —	☐ R3	
ADDRESS:	☐ D4	☐ U4	☐ P4	☐ P10	☐ 114	☐ 137	☐ 222	☐ 416	☐ 22	☐ —	☐ R4	
	☐ D5	☐ U5	☐ P5	☐ P11	☐ 117	☐ 211	☐ 223	☐ 417	☐ 30	☐ —	☐ R5	
	☐ D6	☐ U6	☐ P6	☐ P12	☐ 118	☐ 212	☐ 231	☐ 418	☐ 40	☐ —	☐ R6	
CITY: STATE:	☐ D7	☐ U7	TIME SPENT		☐ 120	☐ 213	☐ 232	☐ —	☐ 50	☐ —	☐ R7	
	☐ D8	☐ U8	I	S	☐ 131	☐ 214	☐ 250	☐ —	☐ 70	☐ —	☐ R8	

EXHIBIT 3

Salesman's Daily Record—Back

Type of Call	Purpose of Call	Products Covered	Results!
Distributor:	P1.....Inventory	111..Wirenut conn.	231..Thermo Grip	R1....Obtained order
D1.........Electrical	P2.....Counter work	112..Plastic conn.	232..Thermo Tip	R2.....Added new distributor
D2.........Industrial	P3.....Sales meeting	113..Porcelain conn.	250..RIDA	
D3.........Specialty	P4.....Calls with dist.	114..Set-screw conn.	310..Live centers	R3....Placed promotional material
D4.........Non-stocking	salesman	117..Crimp conn.	320..Driving centers	
D5.........Simplet only	P5.....Line Expansion	120..Prod. strippers	415..Etchers	R4....Demonstrated products checked
D6.........Other	P6.....Inquiry follow-up	131..Fish tape	416..Markers	
	P7.....Demonstration	134..Wire lube	417..Demagnetizers	R5....Other (specify)
	P8.....Complaint	135..Hand strippers	418..Tachometers	
	P9.....New account	136..Voltage testers	10..Hub lugs	
User:	P10.....Product approval	137..Misc. elec. tools	20..Conduit fittings	
U1.........OEM	(written into specs.)	211..Abrasive stones	21..Pulling elbow	
U2.........Contractor	P11.....Other	212..Grinders	22..Universal box	
U3.........Utility		213..Undercutters	30..Vap-Oil-Tite	
U4.........Industrial		214..Saws	40..Fluor. hangers	
maintenance		215..Small tools	50..Ferrules	
U5.........Production		216..Insulation test.	70..Vapor-tight	
U6.........Architect		221..Hand blowers	80..Fixture hang.	
U7.........Other		222..Tank cleaners	90..Misc. spec.	
		223..Accessories		

Instructions for preparation of the reports were sent to salesmen in the following form:

You will note that there are three different colored sheets—white, yellow, and pink. All listings are to be completed in triplicate; the white sheet is the original, carbon paper will be found at the back of the pad. Only outside calls to a customer's place of business or location of work are to be recorded—telephone calls to or from a customer while in your office are not to be recorded.

On some calls, primarily industrial users, you may talk to several men within the same company. If you discuss different products with each man, list each as a separate call, even though all are at the same company. If you talk with several men at a distributor call, however, list only one call, since you will be discussing the same product groups with all the men.

As far as actually filling in the form is concerned, it is practically self-explanatory. The explanation of the code letters and numbers is printed on the back of every pink sheet. This is your copy of the report, and we suggest you leave them in the pad for handy reference.

Under "Type of Call," only one category is to be checked for each call. If the type of customer you call on is not specifically listed, check "Other" and list the type under "Comments." Purpose of your call can be one or several—please check all those applicable, again listing under "Comments" any not specifically printed.

Time spent will be a very important part of our statistical analysis. Here we are concerned with only the time you actually spend working with or talking to a customer. This *does not* include travel time, waiting time, or time spent in your office. Please show this time spent on each call to the nearest tenth (0.1) of an hour for ease in calculation.

Under "Products Covered" check only those product groups that you have discussed with the customer. This may be just one product or a half-dozen product groups—put a check in a square for each product or product group covered.

If you think that the "Results" printed are not adequate, check "Other," and list the result, as you see it, in the "Comments" column. This latter column is also to be used for any notes you think appropriate. Use the back of the white and yellow sheets for additional comments.

1. *Was the proposed procedure for allocating costs to products sound?*

2. *What other information of value, if any, could the sales manager obtain from the new salesman reports?*

92

O'CONNOR AND O'CONNOR, INC.

O'CONNOR AND O'CONNOR, INC., was a large manufacturer of control devices, which it sold through eighty-six company-owned branches. Total sales approached $90 million. The company had a recurring problem of how to evaluate the sales performance of each of these branches. To aid with this problem, the management set up a program for determining the relative sales potential for each branch territory. These potentials were then used as standards against which to compare actual sales results.

Almost all products were sold through the branches to industrial users, although a minor portion of sales went through the branches to plumbing and heating wholesalers and mill supply houses. Sales to industrial firms were primarily for use in (1) new industrial construction, (2) maintenance and repair of existing facilities, and (3) as parts in original equipment produced.

The F. W. Dodge reports and data on industrial construction awards permitted an excellent estimate of the new construction to be erected during a year in each county of the United States. The sales potential for control devices in new construction in each county was estimated to be in the same percentage to the United States total as was the average of the new construction in the county in the last two years, as shown in the Dodge reports, to the average of the national total in the same years. The average of the past two years was used to reduce the effect of unusually large or small amounts of new construction in a county in any one year. New construction, however, accounted for only a portion of O'Connor and O'Connor's total volume; a large portion of the controls were sold to industrial users for maintenance and repair and for use as component parts in original equipment. To measure this portion of the market, the "O'Connor Index of Production" was developed. The name was selected by the marketing research department to dignify the standard and to make it easier to "sell" to the sales executives who were to use it.

The O'Connor Index of Production, or O.I.P., was a market factor that was based on the amount of total industry in each county of the United States, expressed as a percentage of the total for the nation. For example, the Chicago Branch covered eleven counties in Indiana and nine counties in Illinois. The O.I.P. for this branch was the total of the O.I.P.'s for each of these twenty counties, and was expressed as 1.17. This was interpreted to mean that 1.17 per cent of the total United States potential for controls (excluding the new construction market) was in the Chicago Branch's territory.

To compute the O.I.P., all industries were classified into twenty major groups. The number of employees in each group in each county was determined from the *Census of Manufacturers* and kept up to date by data on social security tax payments reported in *County Business Patterns* and data from *Sales Management*'s "Survey of Industrial Buying Power." In this way, the number of employees in each of the twenty major industry groups in each of the 3,072 counties in the United States was computed each year. The employees in each industry group were then summed for the entire country, and the number in each county was expressed as a percentage of the total. Thus, a given county might have 1 per cent of the country's food and kindred products industry employees, 0.2 per cent of the tobacco industry employees, 0.07 per cent of the chemical industry, etc. The relative number of employees of an industry in a county was taken as a measure of the relative amount of that industry in the county.

The next step was to compute the importance of each county for all industry combined. The number of employees in each industry group was weighted according to that industry's relative value to O'Connor and O'Connor in sales possibilities. These weights were based on the percentage of the firm's sales in past years to each industry group. For example, the food and kindred products industry might have a weight of 8, the tobacco industry a weight of 1, and the chemical and allied products industry a weight of 15. The total of the 20 weights was 100. The weighted number of employees in all 20 industry groups was then totaled for each county and the total expressed as a percentage of the weighted number of employees for the entire United States.

As a result of the preceding computations, the company had:

1. The percentage of each individual industry that was in each county.
2. The percentage of all industry, weighted according to each industry's relative sales value to O'Connor, that was in each county.
3. The percentage of O'Connor sales potential for maintenance and original equipment in each sales territory, trading area, branch territory, or district. This was computed by adding the potentials of the counties in each such territory.

Sales performance standards were developed for each branch early each year. These standards involved a combination of the potential sales for new construction, as shown by the index developed from the Dodge data, and the potential for maintenance and original equipment, as determined by the O.I.P. O'Connor did not know what percentage of its sales was for new construction but estimated that the figure was about 50 per cent, although this probably varied from year to year. Therefore, the average of the Dodge index and the O.I.P. was taken as the market index for each county. The sum of these county market indices for the counties in a territory was the territory market index. The ratio of sales in each branch the previous year to the branch market index was determined. At first the average of sales per market index of the 60 per cent of the branches in each district having the highest ratios was used as the guide in determining the sales performance standard for each branch in that district for the coming year. Exhibit 1 illustrates the process for thirteen branches in one district.

Experience over several years indicated that using an average of the sales per market index for the top 60 per cent of the branches was not entirely satisfactory. The smaller branches tended to have higher ratios of sales to market index than did the larger branches, apparently because competition was less severe in the more sparse territories. As a result, in the small branches the sales consistently exceeded the sales performance

EXHIBIT 1

COMPUTATION OF BRANCH SALES PERFORMANCE STANDARDS BY TOP 60 PER CENT METHOD*

Branch	Dodge Index	O.I.P. Index	Market Index†	Actual Sales Last Year (Thousands)	Sales per Market Index‡ (Thousands)	Sales Performance Standard Based on Sales per Market Index of Top 60 Per Cent of Branches§ (Thousands)
A..........	0.30	0.24	0.27	$ 380	$1,407‖	$ 343
B..........	0.43	0.41	0.42	450	1,071‖	533
C..........	0.19	0.24	0.22	230	1,045‖	279
D..........	1.38	1.16	1.27	985	776	1,612
E..........	1.95	2.12	2.04	1,535	752	2,589
F..........	2.15	2.43	2.29	1,640	716	2,906
G..........	3.03	3.13	3.08	2,060	669	3,908
H..........	0.35	0.49	0.42	680	1,619‖	533
I..........	0.32	0.25	0.29	375	1,293‖	368
J..........	0.57	0.63	0.60	755	1,258‖	761
K..........	0.29	0.29	0.29	350	1,207‖	368
L..........	0.78	0.70	0.74	905	1,223‖	939
M..........	0.37	0.35	0.35	365	1,043	444
District total......	12.11	12.44	12.28	$10,710		$15,583

* All sales figures rounded to nearest thousand.
† Average of Dodge index and O.I.P. index.
‡ Actual sales divided by the branch market index.
§ Total actual sales of the top 60 per cent of branches ($4,125,000) divided by total market index of the top 60 per cent of branches (3.25); this quotient ($1,269,000) multiplied by each individual branch market index to get sales performance standard for each branch.
‖ One of the 60 per cent of branches with highest sales per market index.

standards, while the large branches seldom were up to their standards. To help correct this situation, an average of sales per market index for all branches in a district was used to calculate the sales performance standards. There were eight districts in the United States, so each district tended to be homogeneous. To be sure that the standards offered incentive to all branches, 20 per cent was added to each standard computed in this way. Exhibit 2 illustrates the effect of using this method to compute quotas for the same district as shown in Exhibit 1.

The sales performance standard was not a quota. Quotas were used by O'Connor, but greater weight was given to past sales in their construction. Sales performance standards were designed to indicate how a branch or salesman was performing relative to the size of the market in his territory. A quota was a measure of what the management thought could actually be sold in a territory "with extra effort."

Several other uses were made of the O'Connor market index. The company had found that branches often did not put on additional salesmen because they did not want to take accounts away from their present salesmen. This resulted, in some cases, in situations in which the existing salesmen were merely skimming the market because they did not have time to cover it thoroughly. If the market index per salesman was un-

EXHIBIT 2

COMPUTATION OF BRANCH SALES PERFORMANCE STANDARDS BY AVERAGE
OF ALL BRANCHES METHOD*

Branch	Market Index	Actual Sales Last Year (Thousands)	Sales per Market Index† (Thousands)	Sales Goal Based on Average Sales per Market Index‡ (Thousands)	Sales Performance Standard Based on Average Sales per Market Index Plus 20 Per Cent Incentive§ (Thousands)
A............	0.27	$ 380	$1,407	$ 235	$ 304
B............	0.42	450	1,071	366	439
C............	0.22	230	1,045	192	230
D............	1.27	985	776	1,107	1,328
E............	2.04	1,535	752	1,779	2,135
F............	2.29	1,640	716	1,997	2,396
G............	3.08	2,060	669	2,686	3,223
H............	0.42	680	1,619	366	439
I............	0.29	375	1,293	253	304
J............	0.60	755	1,258	523	628
K	0.29	350	1,207	253	304
L............	0.74	905	1,223	645	774
M............	0.35	365	1,043	305	336
District total...	12.28	$10,710	......	$10,707	$12,870

* All sales figures rounded to nearest thousand.
† Actual sales divided by branch market index.
‡ Total actual sales divided by total market index; this quotient ($872,000) then multiplied by individual branch market index.
§ Sales goal multiplied by 1.20 (20 per cent incentive).

usually large in a branch, management reasoned that it was an indication that more salesmen were needed. This measure of potential was an aid to the sales manager in convincing branch managers of their need for more salesmen. Since the market index could be broken down by counties, it was useful in placing salesmen and in defining sales territories. As a result of the studies of branches, the company found that there was a greater relationship between sales and the number of salesmen in a branch than there was between sales and the market potential for those branches. This led to further emphasis on building larger sales forces in the understaffed areas.

A further use of the market index was to determine locations for new branches or to determine whether certain branch operations should be discontinued. Since the market index was broken down by counties, it was an easy job to calculate the potential in a given trading area by totaling up the market indices for the counties within the area.

In addition to its use in computing the market index, the O.I.P. was also used to determine whether a specific branch was getting its share of business from each of the industry groups in its territory. In the development of the O.I.P., the relative importance of each county was calculated for each of the twenty industry groups. It was thereby possible to tell whether a branch was making sales to each industry relative to its potential by comparing the branch's share of potential to share of sales for each industry. Moreover, the branch managers could be told exactly which counties in their territories had certain industries, and in some cases actual lists of specific firms in an industry were prepared for the branch managers by the home office.

Some problems still cropped up in the various uses of the market index and the sales performance standards developed from it. There was considerable variation in the performance of the branches when measured against the standards. A branch that was well above its standard one year might fall below the next, or vice versa. On several occasions, extensive study of individual branches was begun when they fell below their standards. Before the studies were finished, another year's results were in, and the branches had exceeded their standards. In other instances difficulties were encountered with multiplant firms. A salesman in one branch might sell valves and fittings to the main office of a firm, which then had the items shipped to plants in other territories.

These difficulties caused some doubts in the minds of the executives as to the degree of confidence that they should put in the market index as a measure of potential.

1. *Was the market index a satisfactory measure of sales potential?*
2. *Were the sales potential figures used to the best advantage?*

93

THE DUPORT COMPANY

THE DUPORT COMPANY manufactured the concentrate for Genii, a bottled carbonated grapefruit drink. The company had franchised bottlers in forty-four states but had varying coverage of the population of these states. In planning future expansion and franchising of new bottlers, Mr. Herbert Walker, president of Duport, thought that the company should have some idea of the potential of each state. By concentrating on those areas where the potential was the greatest, Mr. Walker believed that Duport could make the greatest gains at the least cost.

The Duport Company was not a bottling company. It manufactured concentrated flavors that were used in making carbonated soft drinks. Bottlers purchased the concentrate and mixed it with carbonated water to produce a soft drink. This was then bottled for distribution. Besides the Genii concentrate, Duport also sold assorted flavors, ginger ale, root beer, orange, etc., for bottling in 24-ounce bottles under the Walker label. The Walker brand was not nationally advertised but had a strong following in several of the major metropolitan markets.

Duport had 150 bottlers franchised to bottle Genii in the United

States. The company also had bottlers in South America, Canada, and western Europe. Duport had established a distinctive bottle design and labels, which all bottlers used. An 8-ounce bottle was used for Genii. The terms of the franchise required bottlers to use only concentrate purchased from Duport for bottling Genii,[1] to use the bottle and label specified for Genii by Duport, and to maintain certain standards of quality. The bottlers were required to send periodic samples of bottled Genii to Duport for quality checks. The franchise granted the bottlers an exclusive territory.

The bottlers were also expected to promote Genii in their area through sales effort and advertising. Duport participated in co-operative advertising with the bottlers. Most of the franchised bottlers had an advertising account with Duport. The bottler paid an extra charge of one dollar for each gallon of concentrate. This was matched by Duport and set aside in the advertising account. The bottler would then forward any bills for advertising Genii to Duport for payment out of his advertising account. Also, the cost of displays and other promotional materials provided the bottler by Duport were deducted from this account. Duport allowed the bottlers, particularly newly franchised bottlers, some latitude in drawing against future accruals in their advertising accounts.

Duport conducted a national advertising campaign for Genii. It advertised regularly in the *Saturday Evening Post* and had occasional television spots. Also, regional campaigns were conducted from time to time primarily through newspapers. Duport provided bottlers with mats and ideas for local advertising.

The first step in determining potentials was to attempt to isolate those factors that affected soft drink sales. Mr. Walker had learned of studies by other soft drink companies that had found that temperature and income were factors that affected soft drink sales. He asked his statistical department to do a correlation analysis involving per capita consumption in bottles of all soft drinks, mean annual temperature, and per capita income, by states (Table 1). They found that there was a significant correlation among these factors but that temperature was by far the most important factor. Appendix A is a summary of their results.

From the estimating equation developed in the calculations, the statistical department calculated the expected demand, by states, based on the mean annual temperature and per capita income. This was then compared with actual sales to determine what states were above or below the expected demand (Table 1).

Having these data in hand, Mr. Walker asked that Genii sales in bottles per capita be analyzed with temperature and income to see what correlation existed. Since Duport in no case had 100 per cent coverage of a state, per capita consumption in bottles was estimated for that portion of the population that was reached by franchised bottlers. The results of this

---

[1] Imitations were available from competitive companies.

TABLE 1

CORRELATION OF PER CAPITA SOFT DRINK CONSUMPTION AND SELECTED FACTORS

State	Bottles of All Soft Drinks Consumed Annually per Capita* X_1	Mean Annual Temperature† X_2	Annual Income per Capita‡ X_3 (100's)	"Expected" Sales Y_{123}	Actual Sales Less Expected Sales X_1-Y_{123}	Bottles of Genii Consumed Annually per Capita§ X_4	Expected Sales Y_{423}	Per Cent of State Population under Franchise by Duport
Alabama	200	66°	$13	253	−53	1.8	4.1	63.9
Arizona	150	62	17	216	−66	9.4	3.9	18.8
Arkansas	237	63	11	236	+1	3.3	4.2	55.9
California	135	56	25	158	−23	8.2	3.5	8.4
Colorado	121	52	19	146	−25	3.3	3.7	83.4
Connecticut	118	50	27	114	+4	2.1	3.3	4.9
Delaware	217	54	28	138	+79	..	..	..
Florida	242	72	18	277	−35	3.7	4.0	23.4
Georgia	295	64	14	277	+18	1.3	4.1	18.0
Idaho	85	46	16	114	−29	5.5	3.7	70.8
Illinois	141	52	24	134	+7	3.0	3.5	75.8
Indiana	184	52	20	144	+42	2.2	3.6	28.9
Iowa	104	50	16	140	−36	3.0	3.8	30.3
Kansas	143	56	17	177	−34	3.7	3.8	18.6
Kentucky	230	56	13	186	+44	5.1	4.0	66.4
Louisiana	269	69	15	265	+4	3.1	4.1	33.9
Maine	111	41	16	82	+29	2.4	3.7	88.3
Maryland	217	54	21	154	+63	14.4	3.6	5.4
Massachusetts	114	47	22	107	+7	2.8	3.5	38.6
Michigan	108	47	21	109	−1	1.0	3.5	75.6
Minnesota	108	41	18	77	+31	4.2	3.6	85.6
Mississippi	248	65	10	251	−3	4.8	4.2	57.2
Missouri	203	57	19	178	+25	3.6	3.7	35.2
Montana	77	44	19	94	−17	4.0	3.6	89.0
Nebraska	97	49	16	133	−36	2.7	3.8	39.0
Nevada	166	48	24	108	+58	2.8	3.4	16.3
New Hampshire	177	35	18	38	+139	3.7	3.5	67.9
New Jersey	143	54	24	147	−4	0.9	3.5	66.2
New Mexico	157	56	15	181	−24	..	..	..
New York	111	48	25	106	+5	4.0	3.4	30.2
North Carolina	330	59	13	205	+125	6.4	4.0	42.3
North Dakota	63	39	14	74	−11	2.5	3.7	68.7
Ohio	165	51	22	133	+32	1.9	3.6	24.3
Oklahoma	184	62	16	218	−34	1.0	4.0	66.1
Oregon	68	51	19	140	−72	2.4	3.7	74.3
Pennsylvania	121	50	20	131	−10	1.8	3.6	28.1
Rhode Island	138	50	20	131	+7	..	..	..
South Carolina	237	65	12	247	−10	3.3	4.2	73.0
South Dakota	95	45	13	115	−20	7.8	3.8	44.5
Tennessee	236	60	13	212	+24	4.0	4.0	96.6
Texas	222	69	17	261	−39	3.7	4.0	36.6
Utah	100	50	16	140	−40	5.7	3.8	81.3
Vermont	64	44	16	101	−37	..	..	..
Virginia	270	58	16	191	+79	5.8	3.9	26.7
Washington	77	49	20	124	−47	3.4	3.6	38.6
West Virginia	144	55	15	174	−30	1.2	3.9	65.2
Wisconsin	97	46	19	107	−10	2.2	3.6	55.2
Wyoming	102	46	19	107	−5	2.5	3.6	18.6

* Source: *National Bottler's Gazette*, "The Soft Drink Industry—A Market Study."
† Source: U.S. Weather Bureau, *Climatological Data—National Summary, 1956*, Vol. 7, No. 13.
‡ Source: U.S. Dept. of Commerce, *Office of Business Economics, U.S. Income and Output*, a supplement to the *Survey of Current Business*, November, 1958.
§ Based on percentage of population under franchise in each state.

analysis were somewhat disappointing. There seemed to be little significant relationship between Duport sales and temperature and income, either individually or together. A summary of the results is shown in Appendix B.

APPENDIX A

CORRELATION ANALYSIS OF BOTTLES OF ALL SOFT DRINKS CONSUMED ANNUALLY PER CAPITA (X_1), MEAN ANNUAL TEMPERATURE (X_2), AND ANNUAL PER CAPITA INCOME (X_3), BY STATES*

Simple correlation. Bottles of all soft drinks consumed per capita (X_1) and mean annual temperature (X_2) by states:

Estimating equation:	$Y_{12} = 6.81\ X_2 - 206.7$
Standard error of estimate:	$S_{12} = 40.5$
Coefficient of correlation:	$r_{12} = .804$

Simple correlation. Bottles of all soft drinks consumed per capita (X_1) and per capita income (X_3) by states:

Estimating equation:	$Y_{13} = 257 - 5.51\ X_3$
Standard error of estimate:	$S_{13} = 78.4$
Coefficient of correlation:	$r_{13} = -.29$

Multiple correlation. Bottles of all soft drinks consumed per capita (X_1), mean annual temperature (X_2), and per capita income (X_3) by states:

Estimating equation:	$Y_{123} = 6.46X_2 - 2.37X_3 - 145.5$
Standard error of estimate:	$S_{123} = 39$
Coefficient of correlation:	$r_{123} = .814$
Coefficients of partial correlation:	$r_{12.3} = .784,\ r_{13.2} = -.258$

* Forty-seven states only. New Hampshire eliminated from calculation because of extreme variation.

APPENDIX B

CORRELATION ANALYSIS OF BOTTLES OF GENII CONSUMED ANNUALLY PER CAPITA (X_4), MEAN ANNUAL TEMPERATURE (X_2) AND ANNUAL PER CAPITA INCOME (X_3) BY STATES

Simple correlation. Bottles of Genii consumed per capita (X_4) and mean annual temperature (X_2) by states:

Estimating equation:	$Y_{42} = .019\ X_2 + 2.74$
Standard error of estimate:	$S_{42} = 2.48$
Coefficient of correlation:	$r_{42} = .065$

Simple correlation. Bottles of Genii consumed per capita (X_4) and per capita income (X_2) by states:

Estimating equation:	$Y_{43} = 4.33 - .032\ X_3$
Standard error of estimate:	$S_{43} = 2.48$
Coefficient of correlation:	$r_{43} = -.053$

Multiple correlation. Bottles of Genii consumed per capita (X_4), mean annual temperature (X_2), and per capita income (X_3) by states:

Estimating equation:	$Y_{423} = 3.764 + .0136\ X_2 - .0409\ X_3$
Standard error of estimate:	$S_{423} = 2.46$
Coefficient of correlation:	$r_{423} = .081$

1. *Is this analysis useful in selecting areas for new franchises?*
2. *Where should Duport plan to locate new franchises?*

94

SURENESS COMPANY

THE SURENESS COMPANY produced and distributed nationally a complete line of large and small appliances, such as dishwashers, laundry units, dryers, refrigerators, home freezers, electric stoves, air-conditioners, irons, toasters, blenders, beaters, and squeezers. The company was one of the largest in the industry, and sales had doubled since 1946. As a result of this expansion the company had made a number of important organizational changes. In 1955 it employed the services of an outside consulting firm to study the productivity of its executives.

As part of its study approach, the consulting firm assigned one of its senior account executives, Phillip Harms, to interview all company executives to determine their views on how their productivity could be improved. Prior to interviewing each executive the consultant studied the man's personnel record, the general nature of his work, his position in the organizational structure, and the number and type of persons reporting to him. Following is an interview with the sales manager.

STALEY: I'm glad that top management has decided to study the productivity of its executives. This company can certainly use some help on this subject. We're all working too many hours, and I, for one, don't see any relief in sight. In my own case I know I work a lot longer than forty hours each week and so does my boss, the vice-president of marketing.

HARMS: How much time would you guess you put in each week? Could you break this down by type of work activity?

STALEY: Both of your questions are tough to answer, since some weeks I spend a majority of my time in the field. There's one stretch around the first of the year when I'm in the field for better than a solid month. That's the time when we introduce our new models.

HARMS: Well, I can see why your problem is a little different from some of the other executives I've talked to—but why not tell me what you did last week. You were here all last week, weren't you?

STALEY: Yes, I was here last week, but I'm not sure that it was a typical week. Well, O.K., let's try it on for size and see what happens. You'll want to make some notes, won't you? Should I have my secretary record our discussion?

HARMS: No, I'll just do a little scribbling from time to time. Go ahead.

STALEY: I usually get to the office about 8 o'clock, which is a half-hour before the bell rings. By the time my secretary gets in, I have her work pretty well lined up for the day. From about 8:30 or 8:45 to nearly 10:00 I'm dictating and handling papers. I feel that paper work is important in a big company like this, and if I don't keep on top of it I'm really in trouble. Of course, I do a lot of my work over the telephone, especially with my district sales managers.

After 10 o'clock I don't have any prescribed routine. It all depends on where the fire is and what's going on in the vice-president's office. I'd guess I average an hour a day with him. He wants to know everything that goes on in this department, so I find that I spend a lot of time briefing him on our activities.

When I was new on this job I was glad that he was there with a net to bail me out, but I've had this job for almost two years and he still seems to worry about everything I do. Say, I assume that whatever I tell you is confidential. I have a note here from the president that says that I'm not to hold anything back.

HARMS: That's right. Nothing you tell me will ever be revealed. That's why I didn't want your secretary to take any minutes of this meeting.

STALEY: Well, don't misunderstand me—I've got a swell boss—but the company would be a lot better off if he spent more of his time working on over-all company problems instead of worrying about my operations. He does the same thing with the advertising manager and the sales engineering manager. I can't speak for them, but in my case it's like he was still running the department and I was the assistant manager.

HARMS: What kinds of matters do you discuss with him?

STALEY: Everything. About once a day he asks me to come up for a meeting. He then asks how things are going, and the first thing you know he's got me telling him about all my problems. Also, he remembers them and asks me later what I did about them. Of course, sometimes he tells me what to do— and how to do it. He's got a sharp memory and wants me to report back on the action I took. But heck, I'm a big boy now and can make most of my own decisions. Also, he gets a copy of all my sales-analysis reports.

HARMS: What kinds of reports are these?

STALEY: These are reports that come out weekly from our sales analysis unit showing sales by product item, by distributor, by sales district, and so on. They show sales for the week, sales cumulated for the year, sales for the same period last year, and the quota. Boy, when I'm off quota he's really on my back. I suppose in some cases he's got a right to be. I'll say one thing, though; he's a guy you can talk to. He'll listen to me, and for the most part he'll let me do what I want. Of course, we've been working together for over ten years now.

One problem with trying to keep him fully informed is that I have to be on top of everything. This means that I do many of the things that probably should be left to some of my staff. I think one of the problems that this company has is delegation. My boss should delegate more, and if he would then I could do more delegating.

HARMS: Could you be a little more specific about this matter of delegation?

STALEY: Well, delegation is an abstract subject, but take the matter of signatures. When I was assistant sales manager, no one could sign a letter except the boss. When I took over, I studied the situation and found that four members of my staff wrote 80 per cent of the letters in this office. Therefore, I told these people that they could sign for me but that before the letters were mailed I would check them. I was told by the V.P. that it wouldn't work, but it's worked fine so far.

HARMS: If you check all the letters, then how does this save you any time?

STALEY: I don't really read them—I just glance at them. From this I can tell what's important, and these I read more carefully. It only takes me about fifteen or twenty minutes a day to check these letters, but, before I delegated responsibility, it took me almost an hour. Also, I've noticed that I find fewer errors. People know they've got the responsibility, whereas before they could rely— or thought they could—on me to catch their mistakes. Now they have the responsibility.

HARMS: Do you have any other thoughts on delegation?

STALEY: Well, we have a tough situation here that prevents me from doing all the delegation I'd like. My assistant is an old-timer—been with the company for over twenty years. He's a nice guy and a real salesman. Trouble is, he can't administer. He used to be a district manager, but his health went bad and the doctor said he'd have to get an office job with regular hours and no traveling. He knows all the salesmen and many of our big accounts. If I want any information about the history of a salesman or a big account, I just ask him, and the chances are he'll give me a quick and accurate fill-in.

But he's no administrator. I find that I have to do part of his job. He's terrible about answering correspondence or even routing things. About twice a week I sit down with him at his desk and go over the stuff in his "in" basket. He doesn't seem to mind. I don't know what he'd do if he had a really tough boss.

HARMS: Do you have any other people on your staff to whom you feel you can't delegate?

STALEY: Yes, I do. I have a research director who at times drives me nuts. He's a smart technician who knows his statistics, but he can't see the forest for the trees. Research isn't any good unless it's problem oriented. It's got to help solve a marketing problem. Well, I have to practically tell this research specialist what the study objectives should be. What's more, I have to suggest the kinds of information he should get in order to solve the problem. But after that he's a good man. He does have difficulty writing a final report. Several times I've had to take his reports home and rewrite them so that my boss will be able to understand them.

HARMS: Can you tell me more about how you spend your day?

STALEY: Let's see—we were up to about 10 in the morning, just after I'd finished dictating to my secretary. Well, as I said, I don't have a regular schedule after that. I spend about an hour a day with my boss and probably average about another hour a day working with our advertising manager and the head of our sales engineering department. Then there are always several long distance phone calls from the field from salesmen or customers. Some of these I can turn over to my assistant, but usually I figure that if it's important enough to warrant a long distance call, it's important enough for me to answer. I always have some personal visitors—salesmen, product men, and so on. I like to talk with them if only for a few minutes, since it gives me a feeling of knowing what's going on in the market. There are also plenty of committee meetings—production co-ordination, styling, incentives, and so on. The higher one gets in an organization, the more committees he's on. But I don't mind too much—I learn a lot. By the time 5 o'clock comes my "in" basket is filled up again and so I load a lot of things in my brief case and head for home. I do all my magazine reading at home—they'd think I was loafing if they caught me reading on the job. I know I'd feel that way if I found any of my men doing it. I never get a chance to do any really good reading. At times I worry about this, because if I ever get promoted I probably ought to know about such things as the tariff, the national debt, the important trends in business, and so on. I even come down here on Saturdays and work trying to get caught up. When we're planning our activities for the next year, I find I'm head over heels in work—days, nights, and week-ends. My wife hardly knows me, and soon I'll need an introduction to my kids. Speaking of the time, I'm afraid I'll have to beg off for today. I've got to make a meeting date. I'm late now.

HARMS: You've been very co-operative. Would you object to my talking to any of your staff?

STALEY: No; just as long as you arrange a time that is convenient for them.

After Staley had left, Harms paid a visit to the company's research director, Don Hartwig. He explained who he was and what he wanted and asked when he could get together with Hartwig. The latter replied that "now" was as good a time as any.

HARMS: Delegation is always a big problem in a company as large as this. Still there are always ways in which it can be improved. Do you have any suggestions as to what can be done about it within this office? You probably got a note from the president saying I'd be around. Everything will be kept absolutely confidential.

HARTWIG: Gee, this is something I haven't thought about for quite some time. All in all, I think things run pretty smoothly around here. I have some problems with my boss, Mr. Staley, but they're not too serious. His biggest trouble is that he works too hard and expects everybody who works for him to do the same. Generally speaking, he's a real good guy, but he insists at times on spelling things out too much. Sometimes he spells things out so much that I'm boxed in. Also, he tries to tell me how to make surveys. He's way out of touch with the latest research techniques. He hasn't been in research for ten years, and a lot has happened since then. But I guess it's natural for a guy to be interested in a field he used to be pretty good in.

I have a relatively small section here—only about a half-dozen people. We farm out any big stuff, and our advertising agency helps a lot. They have a research man full time on this account. I don't really have many delegation problems. I'll tell you a guy you really ought to talk with who has this problem. He's Matt Keerney, Staley's assistant. He's a wonderful guy and in his day was probably the best salesman in the company. His health got bad, and they gave him a desk job. He really knows his stuff and advises Staley on just about everything. In fact, I'm not sure he doesn't make most of his decisions. Staley treats him O.K., except he's always after him for not following company procedures. Matt isn't a paper hound, but he can get more done with a phone call than any of the rest of us could with a dozen letters. You ought to talk with him. Trouble is, he's on vacation right now and won't be back for a couple of weeks.

HARMS: It's just about lunch time and I've a luncheon date with somebody from the advertising department. Can I come back sometime and talk again?

HARTWIG: You sure can. Any time.

Sometime later Harms talked at length with the vice-president of marketing, Fred Kroll. Part of the interview dealt with the problem of delegation. On this subject Kroll said:

In my job I don't have much of a problem of delegation. I have only about five people who report to me. Take my sales manager, for example. He's one of my boys. We've been together for a long time, but, despite all this, there are times, I'm sure, when he feels that I won't get off his back. But this is a "dog eat dog" business. You have to keep the pressure on day and night. I'm responsible for the total marketing operation, which runs well over one hundred million dollars a year. If I'm not on top of the latest price cut, the latest merchandising gimmick, the latest "deal," I don't feel that I'm doing my job. You have to push your men—drive them—because, if you don't, you'll wake up some morning and find that some competitor has stolen part of your market. I'm considered by some people to be old-fashioned—I won't delegate my life away—but I get results and that's what counts.

Harms then asked what he thought about the delegation in the sales department. Kroll replied:

I don't pay much attention to whether Staley delegates or not. I figure that's his business. I don't tell him how to run his people. I never hear any complaints, so I guess he's probably doing O.K. Staley has one problem though —he brings me too damn many problems. For example, yesterday he wanted my advice on what to do with a San Francisco department store that had refused delivery of their last order. How should I know what he should do? I know what I'd do because Bob Scope, the buyer in the Frisco store, is an old friend of mine. Another thing about Staley is that he's not out in the field enough. You don't sell appliances by sitting in the home office. He ought to be out there on the firing line. But Staley's a good man—we all have some faults. He's one of the best in the business. Sometimes I wish he knew just how good he really is.

What changes, if any, should be made in supervisory procedures of the Sureness Company?

95

SERIES PRINTING COMPANY, INC.

FOLLOWING World War II, competition in the printing industry increased steadily and profits of most firms declined accordingly. Series Printing Company was no exception. As they studied the problem, however, Series executives became convinced that poor salesmanship was part of the difficulty. It was easy for salesmen to exaggerate the danger of lower competitive prices and to seek orders by cutting prices instead of selling more aggressively. Dick Kreutzer, the marketing vice-president, believed that management was also at fault. Heavy pressure was exerted to keep sales expanding, with the result that both sales managers and salesmen were too quick to yield to pressure for lower prices for fear of losing volume. Kreutzer thought that profits could be increased by shifting the emphasis from volume to profit. In 1959 he proposed a new plan for compensating salesmen, which was designed to encourage sales managers and salesmen to increase profit instead of volume.

Series Printing Company was incorporated in 1925 after the merger of two printing plants in Philadelphia. By 1940 it was the largest printer of tickets, cards, and advertising specialties on the East Coast. Series expanded into a national operation after the war by acquiring plants in Chicago and St. Louis. Late in 1956 it merged with a large West Coast company to become the largest printer of its type in the country. The Series line included tickets of all kinds; business cards; serially numbered cards, such as those used for direct mailings; and advertising specialties, such as display cards, promotional pieces, and package inserts. Sales rose from just over $6 million in 1948 to over $18 million in 1958. Table 1 shows sales and earnings for the period 1948–58.

TABLE 1

SERIES PRINTING COMPANY, INC., SALES AND NET EARNINGS: 1948–58

Year	Sales (Thousands)	Net Earnings (Thousands)	Net Earnings— Per Cent of Sales
1948	$ 6,072	$ 517	8.5
1949	8,556	684	8.0
1950	8,737	695	8.0
1951	7,650	584	7.6
1952	10,320	803	7.8
1953	14,170	805	5.7
1954	11,890	684	5.8
1955	12,500	676	5.4
1956	12,400	906	7.3
1957	17,230	1,091	6.3
1958	18,400	1,215	6.6

Sales managers and salesmen were paid a straight salary plus expenses, which included the use of a company car. Most salesmen were assigned to territories for which they had full responsibility. Exceptions to this policy were senior salesmen who handled one or a few very large accounts and the salesmen who sold advertising specialties for which no specific territories were assigned. The Philadelphia plant, for example, had twenty salesmen. Twelve were assigned territories; four senior salesmen handled only their established accounts or specific accounts assigned to them by the sales manager; two men were each assigned to a large account, which demanded the full-time service of one salesman; and two salesmen sold advertising specialties. This plant had a general sales manager and four assistant sales managers. One of these four was responsible for advertising specialty sales only and had the two specialty salesmen under him. Each of the other three assistant sales managers supervised six salesmen.

The selling process normally required a minimum of two calls. On the first call the salesman would obtain the job specifications. He would take these to the estimating department, which would compute the cost and add a profit margin to obtain the "full" price. The sales manager than established the actual price for the job on the basis of the return on investment expected by management, the general price level in the market, and the competitive situation in that particular account. He had to rely heavily on the salesman's evaluation of competitors' prices to the account. The salesman took the sales manager's price to the customer, but he was usually authorized to bargain if he met considerable resistance to the price. It was in this area, management believed, that more incentive to fight for the higher price was needed to bolster profits.

In 1957 the firm installed a new cost estimating procedure, which provided a better base for establishing prices and gave a better picture of where profits were actually earned. Previously, prices had been determined by adding a profit percentage to the full cost, which included material cost, manufacturing cost, and sales and administrative cost. Sales and administrative costs were determined by applying an average percentage to the total factory cost, which included material and converting costs. Management believed that, since the company was in the business of converting material into a finished product, profits should be based on the amount of converting done rather than on total costs. In this way customers would be charged essentially on the basis of their use of Series Printing facilities. The new cost estimating concept called for the application of sales and administrative costs to factory converting costs rather than to total factory cost, which included material. This, of

EXHIBIT 1

COMPARISON OF PROFIT-ON-FULL-COST AND PROFIT-ON-CONVERTING-COST
METHODS OF PRICING HYPOTHETICAL JOBS

	Hypothetical Jobs			
	1	*2*	*3*	*4*
Profit-on-Full-Cost Method*				
Material............................	$ 70.00	$ 60.00	$ 40.00	$ 30.00
Factory converting costs..................	30.00	40.00	60.00	70.00
Total factory cost................	100.00	100.00	100.00	100.00
Sales and administration expense — 10 per cent of full factory cost................	10.00	10.00	10.00	10.00
Full cost.............................	110.00	110.00	110.00	110.00
Profit — 10.9 per cent of full cost..........	12.00	12.00	12.00	12.00
Price to customer.....................	$122.00	$122.00	$122.00	$122.00
Profit-on-Converting-Cost Method†				
Factory converting cost..................	$ 30.00	$ 40.00	$ 60.00	$ 70.00
Sales and administration expense — 25 per cent of factory converting cost..........	7.50	10.00	15.00	17.50
Total converting cost...............	37.50	50.00	75.00	87.50
Profit — 24 per cent of total converting cost..	9.00	12.00	18.00	21.00
Material.............................	70.00	60.00	40.00	30.00
Price to customer.....................	$116.50	$122.00	$133.00	$138.50

* Sales and administrative expenses computed on total factory cost and profit computed on full cost.
† Sales and administrative expenses computed on factory converting cost and profit computed on total converting cost.

course, resulted in a higher percentage figure than under the old method. A profit goal of a 20 per cent return on invested capital after taxes was established. On the basis of past experience, this was equivalent to 10.9 per cent of full cost. It was determined that under the new system this could be achieved by adding 24 per cent to total converting costs. Exhibit 1 illustrates the two estimating systems on four hypothetical jobs requiring different ratios of converting cost to material. The old method tended to overprice the easy-to-make items and underprice the more complex.

The sales compensation plan proposed by Kreutzer was based on the new profit-on-converting-cost method of pricing. The basic theory behind the plan was to set a profit requirement and a volume allowance for each salesman and to pay a bonus based on the volume sold and the profit obtained by the salesman. Kreutzer believed that this compensation plan would make the salesman realize the effect of price cuts on profits and cause them to try to sell at full price to earn bonuses.

The profit requirement for each salesman was established as a percentage of total converting cost. This percentage was set after an analysis of each salesman's accounts to determine the percentage obtained on them in the past and after further appraising likely competition in his area in the future. The company's goal of a 20 per cent return on invested capital after taxes required that a profit of 24 per cent of converting costs be added to total costs at the 1958 volume. This was not feasible in all cases because competitive conditions were the final determinant of prices, and in some areas competition did not permit margins of this size; in fact, for some very large accounts, it was necessary to price below total cost to get the business. At the end of each month the estimated profit percentage obtained by each salesman was computed. If it exceeded his profit requirement, he earned a bonus.

The volume allowance for each salesman was set at a level that, in most cases, would cover salary and selling expenses, including the company car. Since the profit requirement was in terms of a percentage, it was necessary to have some incentive to encourage salesmen to strive for volume as well as a high profit ratio. For most salesmen, past experience indicated that selling costs were between 10 and 15 per cent of total converting costs. Therefore, the volume allowance was usually such as to keep the selling costs in this range. If a salesman's volume did not cover these costs, a proportional deduction would be made from any profit bonus earned. For any sales above the requirement, the salesman would receive a credit.

Each salesman would be assigned an "incentive base salary" which the company considered to be the minimum amount that a Series Printing salesman should earn. The amount for most salesmen would be $500 per month, but in cases of new salesmen it would be lower, and in cases of some of the senior salesman, whose salaries were much higher, the "incentive base salary" would be higher. It was proposed that actual salaries not be changed at the time the new plan was adopted. Thus, the "incentive base salary" would, in many cases, differ from the actual salary received by the salesmen. Each salesman would also be assigned a "participation factor," which would determine the degree to which he would particpate in the total credits that he earned. This "participation factor" would be set after consideration of the salesman's present sales volume, his salary, and the degree of responsibility given him in handling his territory. It was also contemplated that this factor might be adjusted to prevent individual salesmen from earning unusually large incomes because of unusual circumstances. It was planned that almost all "participation factors" would be set at 10 per cent at the start.

To encourage efforts to get new business, special consideration was given to new accounts during the first six months after they were obtained. If the profit percentage level of the new account was less than the salesman's profit requirement, which would result in a reduction in the salesman's profit bonus, the account would be handled separately and 2.5 per cent of the volume of converting cost would be added to his bonus. At the end of the six months, the account would be reviewed by the sales manager and a decision made as to whether it was profitable enough to retain or whether it should be dropped. If the account were retained, it would be handled as a regular account from then on, but the salesman's over-all profit requirement would be adjusted to reflect the influence of the profit percentage on the new account, as determined from the first six months' experience.

An individual formula was developed for each man on the basis of the foregoing factors. A profit requirement was established as a percentage of the total converting cost of the volume sold by the salesman. A volume allowance was established such that this percentage of the converting costs of the salesman's volume would approximate his salary and expenses. In most cases this was 10 per cent, but there were exceptions where certain salesmen with high-volume, low-profit territories were assigned higher-volume allowances to enable them to earn more incentive on the basis of volume, since they would get little or no profit bonus. "Participation factors" varied from 5 to 15 per cent but generally were 10 per cent. Thus a salesman's "formula" was a series of three percentages; for example, 35–10–10 per cent. This meant that his profit requirement was 35 per cent, his volume allowance was 10 per cent, and his "participation factor" was 10 per cent.

By the middle of each month the salesmen would receive a detailed analysis of their previous month's business, which would show their total converting costs and profit, broken down by customer and by each order shipped. Each salesman would also receive a statement of his salary and total expenses for the month. From these data each salesman could calculate his bonus for that month. The bonus for any month would be paid at the end of the succeeding month. Each month was to be computed separately. In no month would a salesman be paid less than his regular salary. The detailed analysis gave an accurate picture of where profits were coming from in a territory and hence showed where the salesman would have to work to raise the profit level. Each salesman's "formula" would be reviewed periodically.

Exhibit 2 shows the calculation of the bonus for four hypothetical salesmen. The formula for each salesman is shown in the first three percentages at the top of each column—the profit requirement, the

EXHIBIT 2

Calculation of Sales Bonus for Four Hypothetical Salesmen

	Hypothetical Salesmen			
	1	2	3	4
Profit requirement (see A below)......	25%	35%	10%	15%
Volume allowance (see B below)......	15%	10%	20%	15%
Participation factor (see C below).....	10%	10%	10%	5%
Incentive base salary.................$	500	$ 500	$ 600	$ 500
Total converting costs...............$	12,000	$ 5,000	$20,000	$25,000
"Actual" profit......................$	4,000	$ 2,500	$ 2,000	$ 5,000
Actual salary.......................$	600	$ 400	$ 900	$ 750
Actual expenses.....................$	300	$ 200	$ 300	$ 400
New account converting costs.........		$ 1,800	.....	$ 4,000
A. Profit credit computation				
"Actual" profit................$	4,000	$ 2,500	$ 2,000	$ 5,000
Less profit requirement × total				
converting costs.............	3,000	1,750	2,000	3,750
Gross profit credit.........$	1,000	$ 750	$ ...	$ 1,250
B. Volume credit computation				
Volume allowance × total con-				
verting costs.................$	1,800	$ 500	$ 4,000	$ 3,750
Less incentive base salary plus				
expenses.................	800	700	900	900
Gross volume credit........$	1,000	$ − 200	$ 3,100	$ 2,850
C. Participation by salesman				
A plus B.....................$	2,000	$ 550	$ 3,200	$ 4,100
Participation factor applied to A				
plus B......................$	200	$ 55	$ 310	$ 205
Plus incentive base salary........	500	500	600	500
2½ per cent of new account total				
converting costs..............	...	45	...	100
Salesman's formula income.......$	700	$ 600	$ 910	$ 805
Less actual salary.............	600	400	900	750
Net bonus....................$	100	$ 200	$ 10	$ 55

volume allowance, and the participation factor. The "actual" profit on a salesman's sales for the month was determined by the estimating department and was really a revised estimate of profit. The estimating department analyzed each order after it had been run. If, as sometimes happened, the method of running an order through the plant differed from that assumed at the time that costs were originally estimated, a new cost was estimated. This sometimes changed the profitability of an order considerably. The profit requirement, which was determined by applying the profit requirement to the total converting cost, was then deducted from this "actual" profit. The remainder was the gross profit credit. To compute the gross credit for volume, the volume allowance was applied to the total converting cost, and the total of the incentive base salary and expenses was deducted from the result. The net bonus was then computed by applying the participation factor to the sum of the gross profit credit and the gross volume credit, adding any new account bonus, adding the incentive base salary, and deducting the actual salary drawn.

There were certain territories and salesmen to whom a formula would not be assigned because it was considered impossible to develop a workable formula for them. This group included older salesmen drawing a very high salary, new salesmen just starting, and salesmen in underdeveloped territories. Monthly sales volume of about $20,000, which would entail about $5,000 in converting costs, was considered to be the minimum volume needed before a workable formula could be developed. No salaries would be cut as a result of the new plan, but $500 plus cost-of-living increases in the future, would be the maximum salary that any new salesman would draw in the future.

A sales incentive plan was also developed for the sales managers of each plant. The formulas were similar to those for the salesmen, except that the profit requirement was based on the actual profit made by the manager's plant rather than on estimated profit. The top executives of Series Printing believed that this was a fair basis for the sales managers because they had more control over actual profits. The volume allowance and the participation factor were established on the same bases as those of the salesmen except at lower levels, since the sales managers' incentives were calculated on the total performance of their plants.

Flexibility was considered to be an important part of the plan, and sales managers were expected to review formulas periodically and to adjust for changes in territories. In some cases a salesman might have one large account in his territory in which he had little or no control over the price level for competitive reasons. Any changes he could make in other accounts would be insignificant in relation to this account. In such a case, management might decide to handle that account separately to allow the man's performance with the other accounts to determine his incentive. In the case of a general price change, all formulas would be reviewed. The sales manager of each plant would have authority to make changes in formulas, but these changes would be subject to review and approval by top management.

Should Series Printing Company adopt the proposed sales compensation plan?

SECTION VII

Reappraising the Marketing Program

THE control process leads naturally to a reappraisal of specific parts of the marketing program. At regular intervals, however, there should be a comprehensive reappraisal of the entire marketing program. This does not follow automatically from day-to-day operations, but must be consciously scheduled. This reappraisal should include a reasoned evaluation of all the steps in the administrative process, including the control system itself.

The control procedure will provide much of the information by which the executive reappraises the firm's marketing niche, the broad plans, the organizational system, and the control mechanism itself. Control information, however, tends to be obtained piecemeal and does not necessarily reveal subtle shifts or trends in the market. When viewed over a longer period, such as a year, the normal control data may indicate some less obvious developments. Nevertheless, the marketing manager may need data collected solely for the reappraisal function. For example, if channels of distribution were changing rapidly, a special analysis of the future of channels used by the firm might be very appropriate. Or changes in leisure habits of the population might have long-term implications for the firm which required special study.

The marketing manager should set up a regular time for reappraisal —probably once a year. Prior to this time, he should request all routine data that will be needed to put in the most usable form and that desired special information be collected.

96

THE EVERSHARP PEN COMPANY

THE EVERSHARP PEN COMPANY introduced a new "Fountain Ball" pen in the late summer of 1958. The pen, which was new both in appearance and in some functional features, was designed for the large but competitive "one-dollar" ball-point pen market. The marketing program was planned carefully, and specific sales goals were established. At the end of the firm's fiscal year on March 1, 1959, sales were approximately 20 per cent short of the goal, and the management decided to reappraise the entire marketing procedure.

Effective January 1, 1958, the Parker Pen Company had acquired 100 per cent ownership of the writing instrument division of Eversharp, Inc., for $1,600,000, and established a Parker subsidiary called the Eversharp Pen Company. Eversharp had been a major factor in the writing instrument market for many years, but sales had suffered after World War II, and by 1957 the company had lost much of its prestige with the trade. Surveys indicated, however, that the Eversharp name still had considerable value among consumers. Eversharp's profits had dropped badly in the ten years from 1947 to 1957. Its difficulties coincided with the introduction and growth of the ball-point pen. It spite of several false starts, the ball-point pen had taken over a major share of the market by 1957. Sales of ball-point pens in that year totaled almost 300,000,000 units, with a dollar value of $68,000,000. Total unit sales of fountain pens in the same year were only 40,000,000, but the dollar volume was about $55 million.

Eversharp had entered the ball-point pen market in 1945, after purchasing the American rights to the Biro (Argentina) ball-point pen patents. Although Eversharp was successful in generating an all time high company sales volume in the next several years, it never became a major factor in the ball-point market. The primary cause for this failure was attributed to the poor quality of the product during this period. Eversharp's reticence to push ball-point pens over the traditional fountain pens was also a contributing factor.

In the late 1940's the market for ball-point pens fell off because of unsatisfactory performance resulting from inferior inks and lack of proper mechanical means for controlling the flow of the inks. These problems were soon solved, and by the early 1950's ball-point pens again were a significant part of the pen industry. Parker successfully marketed its "Jotter" in 1954 in the medium price range. Its typical retail price was $2.95. Two years later, Parker reduced the price on its new "T Ball

Jotter" to $1.95. During this period, Paper Mate, Scripto, and others introduced pens to sell in the $1.00 class and ball-point pens became entrenched as the established mass writing instrument. By this time, Eversharp had lost much of its position in the writing instrument field.

By 1957 Parker was an important factor in the medium- and higher-priced pen field. Its products, however, covered only about the top half of the price range in the writing instrument field, and it was interested in entering the lower-priced market. The decision was made to buy a "name" with which to enter the lower-priced field rather than to produce lower-priced pens under the name of Parker or to attempt to introduce a new brand name. When it was discovered that Eversharp was for sale, the purchase was made.

Parker's marketing research department surveyed the low-priced pen market and selected $1.00 as the retail price at which the new Eversharp pen should sell. The survey indicated that about one-quarter of the ball-point pen market was centered around this price. Competition was extremely keen at this price and was dominated in 1958 by Paper Mate and Scripto. There were numerous private brands and unadvertised brands selling at or near $1.00. Parker set out to capture a substantial share of the $1.00 market as quickly as possible through its new Eversharp division; a 15 per cent share of this market was believed possible during the first year of production.

The ball-point pen market had two major segments of almost equal potential—the consumer market and the premium market. The consumer market consisted of all individuals who used writing instruments. Popular-priced ball-point pens were available to consumers in almost every type of retail outlet, including cafes and service stations. Vending machines that sold ball-point pens for 25–50 cents were common.

The premium market consisted primarily of merchants, manufacturers, and other businesses that used ball-point pens as gifts to attract new customers. Some manufacturers attached ball-point pens to their products as premiums. They often ordered in quantities of millions directly from the pen manufacturer. Merchants and others using the pens as gifts normally bought from wholesalers in quantities of 100–1,000 units.

Parker's management established several basic product policies for the new Eversharp pen. The new pen was to be equal to or better in quality than any other pen being retailed for $1.00. It had to have style, be unique in performance, and sell for 98 cents. Product development was started immediately. In a period of eight months the development staff completed its assignment, and production started in September, 1958.

The new pen was a triangle shaped instrument designed to fit more comfortably and naturally in the triangle formed between the thumb and the two writing fingers. The triangle shape was stylish as well as functional, giving what management termed a "continental modern" look to the instrument. A secret formula produced a high density ink, which was transferred to the writer's paper by a textured metal ball point that enabled the pen to write darker and with the characteristics of a fountain pen. This was the feature that led to the pen's name, "The Fountain Ball." Company executives believed that this feature made the pen superior to any $1.00 pen on the market.

Ball-point pens could be divided into two categories. The first was the cheap pen, usually selling for under 49 cents at retail and often as low as 10 cents each. This product was sold on the basis of price alone; no advertising or promotion was expended. This "price" class also included ball-point pens sold for give-away purposes, on which the giver usually had his name printed. Although no accurate data were available, these cheap pens probably accounted for well over 50 per cent of the ball-point pens produced in 1957. Unadvertised brands tended to dominate this market because of the "longer" discounts they offered.

The second class of ball-point pens included pens that were sold by brand, for which the manufacturers endeavored by promotion, advertising, and product quality to create a specialized demand. The dollar retail price tended to be the lower end of this class. It was this area in which Eversharp decided to make its big push.

Surveys showed the most important retail outlets for $1.00 ball-point pens to be those shown in Table 1. Distribution to these outlets normally

TABLE 1

MOST IMPORTANT RETAIL OUTLETS DISTRIBUTING
BRAND-NAME BALL-POINT PENS

Outlet	Approximate No. in U.S.
Drugstores	44,000
Stationery stores	27,000
Department stores	10,000
Variety stores	5,000
Magazine stands, cigar stores, etc.	14,000

was accomplished through wholesalers, the most important of which were drug, tobacco, and stationery wholesalers. Table 2 shows the number of wholesalers selling selected lines to those retailers who sold ball-point pens.

Eversharp's management anticipated difficulty in making wholesalers enthusiastic about handling and pushing still another ball-point pen in the one dollar category. Retail outlets in many cases considered that they were adequately supplied with a number of satisfactory writing instruments selling for one dollar. Although the name Eversharp was apparently in good repute with the average consumer, retailers and wholesalers did not think so highly of it.

The marketing plan called for a region-by-region approach. This was

TABLE 2

WHOLESALERS SELLING TO RETAILERS WHO HANDLED
BALL-POINT PENS

Type	Approximate No. in U.S.
General line drug	400
Specialty drug and toiletries	2,000
Stationery and office supplies	1,600
Books, magazines, and newspapers	1,900
General merchandise	600
Tobacco	2,900

thought necessary because of the limited manpower and advertising funds available. The introductory effort was concentrated on eleven major metropolitan markets, which represented 40 per cent of the total national potential market. Eleven salesmen were located in these markets, which were: Los Angeles, San Francisco, Chicago, St. Louis, Indianapolis, Dallas, Atlanta, Detroit, Boston, New York, and Philadelphia. Their primary duty was to sell the pen and its supporting promotional material to the important wholesalers in their areas. In addition to their sales work with wholesalers, the Eversharp salesmen called on pen shops, department stores, stationery stores, and chain drugstores to promote sales of the "Fountain Ball."

An attempt was made to have stocks in the hands of all important department stores and drug chains in a region and then to start advertising. The difficulties of this method were impressively illustrated in the New York market, where the editor of *Sales Management* magazine attempted to purchase a "Fountain Ball" after seeing an advertisement in his local paper. According to the article that he printed thereafter in his magazine, he visited twelve stores in the New York Grand Central area and could not find the new pen in any of them. Several dealers reported that they had never even heard of the item.

On the basis of the 98-cent price, Eversharp established the discount structure shown in Exhibit 1.

In order to introduce the new pen quickly, Eversharp appropriated approximately $1,000,000 for advertising during the first year (September, 1958–September, 1959). This was one of the largest advertising appropriations that had ever been put behind a new pen, to the best of the management's knowledge. It was anticipated that losses would be experienced during the first full year of operation of the Eversharp division but that by the end of the third year the new division should reach a breakeven point.

The Eversharp sales organization consisted of four salesmen in the trade division and five in the premium division when the company was taken over by Parker. At the time of acquisition, Eversharp was market-

EXHIBIT 1

DISCOUNT STRUCTURE FOR "FOUNTAIN BALL" PEN

Sales price......................................	$0.98
Dealer discount 50 per cent........................	0.49
Dealer cost.......................................	0.49
Wholesaler discount 10 per cent....................	0.05
Wholesaler cost...................................	0.44
Returns and allowances............................	0.02
Net to Eversharp.................................	0.42
Less production costs..............................	0.22
Balance for advertising, administration, sales expense, and profit......................................	0.20

ing and selling a line of six ball-point pens, a ball-point desk set, and three mechanical pencils. The premium division continued to sell the Eversharp merchandise, but the trade division concentrated on one product, the new "Fountain Ball." Seven salesmen were added to this division.

Although the "Fountain Ball" was introduced region by region, the management hoped to have the product available in every major United States market within one year. Initial promotion was directed at wholesalers, chain stores, large department stores, and stationers via trade advertising that announced the new "Fountain Ball" pen. Consumer advertising was then started on a regional basis. Major emphasis was placed on consumer advertising.

Heavy newspaper advertising and spot television commercials were scheduled for each key market to coincide with the time at which important retailers were expected to have stocks. There was some risk in this plan, since advertising commitments had to be made in advance and dealer ill will would be incurred if consumers, following the advertising, asked for the "Fountain Ball," only to discover the retailer had not stocked it, or if supplies were not sufficient to cover reorders that might develop.

Eversharp created a special merchandise dispenser for the new pen. A three-dimensional viewer was built into the display so that the consumer could see the difference between an ordinary stainless steel ball-point pen and the textured-tip featured in the "Fountain Ball."

By the end of Eversharp's fiscal year, March 1, 1959, the "Fountain Ball" had been introduced in thirty-four major markets in the United States. Management estimated that these thirty-four markets accounted for about 70 per cent of all retail sales of one-dollar ball-point pens. From September, 1958, to March, 1959, approximately $550,000 was spent on advertising. The initial effort in the eleven major markets was very successful, and during the introductory period Eversharp attained a larger share of the $1.00 pen market than did any other brand. But the impact of the introductory campaign could not be maintained, and the firm's share of market leveled off. Sales were almost 20 per cent short of the original sales target. Company officials were firmly convinced that Eversharp was offering the best value for $1.00 in the ball-point pen market. Therefore, they undertook a reappraisal of the marketing program.

What changes, if any, should be made in Eversharp's marketing program?

97

THE DOW CHEMICAL COMPANY

THE DOW CHEMICAL COMPANY was one of the nine firms producing ethylene glycol or "permanent" automotive antifreeze in 1958. Four of the producers sold antifreeze under their own brands (three also sold private label and bulk), while the others sold to marketers under private brands or sold in bulk to packagers and to automotive and farm equipment companies who used it in their new products during the winter months. Dow sold primarily to the private brand market but also sold some antifreeze in bulk. A number of developments took place during the 1958–59 season, however, that caused the management to reappraise this policy.

Glycol antifreeze was first introduced in 1927, when the Prestone brand was put on the market. Until that time, automotive vehicles had used alcohol in their cooling systems during cold weather. Since alcohol has a low boiling point, it often boiled away when engines became hot. The glycol antifreeze had a higher boiling point and did not evaporate, so it became known as "permanent" antifreeze, meaning it would last all winter. From its inception, the glycol antifreeze was successful, and its use grew rapidly, as indicated in Exhibit 1, which shows ethylene glycol production and the quantity consumed as antifreeze.[1]

By the 1957–58 market season, glycol antifreeze accounted for about 80 per cent of all antifreeze sales and totaled $275 million at retail prices. The number of producers had grown to nine—Dow, National Carbon (division of Union Carbide), Du Pont, Olin Mathieson, Allied, Wyandotte, Jefferson, General Aniline and Film, and Calcasieu. Three of these

---

[1] The close relationship of glycol-base antifreeze consumption and ethylene glycol production in 1953 and 1954 is to some extent misleading. There was a large inventory of antifreeze carried over from 1952. This led to a reduction in glycol production in the following years even though antifreeze consumption continued to rise.

EXHIBIT 1

U.S. PRODUCTION OF ETHYLENE GLYCOL AND CONSUMPTION OF GLYCOL-BASE ANTIFREEZE
(Millions of Pounds)

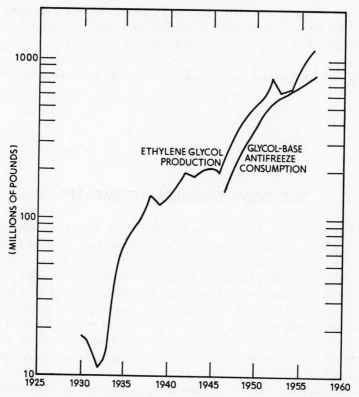

marketed their own national brands: National Carbon Company (Prestone), Du Pont (Zerex), and Olin Mathieson (Permanent Pyro). Commercial Solvents also marketed a national brand of glycol-base antifreeze (Peak), however, this firm only formulated the antifreeze; it did not produce glycol. These four national brands accounted for over half the market in 1957–58, with Prestone claiming about one third of the market by itself.

Dow, Commercial Solvents, Olin Mathieson, and Union Carbide (National Carbon's parent company) were the top suppliers of antifreeze for private brands, with Dow probably the largest. Most, if not all, of these firms also sold glycol to packagers who produced their own brand of antifreeze and also to some private label companies. The general makeup of the industry is shown in Exhibit 2.

The glycol used in all the "permanent" antifreeze was essentially the same. The only differences that existed among the major brands were in the additives and water content. "Permanent" antifreezes had three main problems in normal use: foaming, seepage, and rust. Antifreeze manufac-

EXHIBIT 2

GLYCOL ANTIFREEZE INDUSTRY ORGANIZATION AND CHANNELS OF DISTRIBUTION

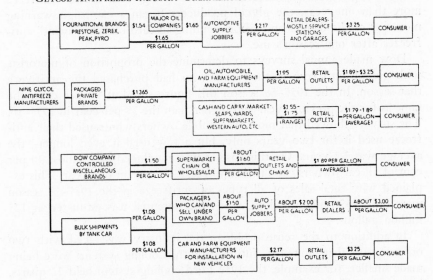

turers added chemicals to the basic glycol to inhibit these actions. Each firm guarded its inhibitor additive formulas carefully, although the same general principles were apparently used in all. Dow ran extensive tests on all leading formulations and was convinced that its product was equal or superior to any other.

Government specifications required that all glycol antifreezes contain not more than 5 per cent water. Presumably all brands met this standard, although Dow tests showed that some competitive brands varied occasionally as much as 22 per cent. The Dow brand composition by weight was as shown in the accompanying tabulation.

```
Total glycol.............................95% (min.)
    Ethylene glycol 95% (min.)
    Other glycols     5% (max.)
Inhibitors and dye........................ 2% (min.)
Water.................................... 3% (max.)
```

Over the years the "permanent" theme had been stressed by the glycol antifreeze industry. By the mid-1950's this idea had boomeranged. Glycol antifreezes had taken over more than two-thirds of the market, but many customers were using their glycol antifreeze more than one year. Some of these customers left antifreeze in their cars the year round, while others would drain their radiators in the spring and save the antifreeze for the next fall. The antifreeze qualities of glycol were perfectly good from one year to the next, but the inhibitors tended to break down with use. The maximum length of time that a "permanent-type" antifreeze could be used with safety varied widely even among cars of the same make and used under similar circumstances. This meant that reuse of antifreeze created a danger of damage to the engine and radiator. Because of this danger and the loss of business resulting from use of antifreeze more than one year, the glycol producers began a campaign warning motorists of the danger and recommending discard of "permanent" antifreezes after one season's use.

Dow made annual surveys to determine the proportion of motorists with glycol antifreeze in their cars who had purchased the antifreeze that season. In the 1957–58 season this figure stood at 80 per cent, the same as for the previous year and higher than the 78 per cent in 1955–56. The surveys showed that most automobile owners who reused their antifreeze used it for two years only, but a few used it even longer—the average was 2.2 years. On this basis it was concluded that almost 40 per cent of all car owners used their antifreeze more than one year. This explained why total sales of all types of antifreeze in the 1957–58 season were only 105 million gallons, when the potential was estimated at 125 million gallons.

In addition to the reuse problem, the industry was faced with two other factors that limited its future growth. Cooling systems were being made smaller; for example, the 1952 Ford cooling system held 22 quarts, but the 1958 Ford held only 19 quarts. There was some indication, however, that this trend had stopped. The second factor was that glycol had captured most of the antifreeze market, so there was little room left for expansion.

The Dow Chemical Company first entered the glycol antifreeze business in 1938, when it built a plant to produce ethylene glycol, which it sold to other firms for the formulation of antifreeze. In 1952 the management decided to formulate antifreeze itself. Rather than compete with the big, well-established national brands, Dow decided to produce under private brands only. About 75 per cent of all antifreeze was sold through automobile and oil companies, with a high-quality antifreeze to be sold under their own private label. The plan worked successfully, and soon Dow was one of the largest private brand manufacturers of antifreeze in the country. This made the antifreeze division a significant one even in a firm like Dow, which had sales of $675 million in 1958.

Contracts with private brand buyers usually specified that the buyer would take a minimum of 50,000 gallons during an antifreeze market year, which ran from April 1 to March 31. The antifreeze would be packaged in cans, designed according to the customer's preference. About 80 per cent of all sales were in gallon cans, quarts accounted for another 15 per cent, and the rest was in 55-gallon drums. The price quoted by Dow included delivery in truck loads or carloads to any one destination on a schedule set by the customer. In 1957 and 1958 this delivery became something of a problem, since customers gave shorter and shorter notice on delivery and asked for smaller and more frequent shipments.

If a given private brand buyer decided to drop Dow as his supplier, he was required to take any antifreeze that had been packaged for him; otherwise Dow did not force customers to take any leftover quantities even if their purchases were less than their contracts called for. Dow carried undelivered, packaged antifreeze from one season to the next at no charge. Some national brands were reported to let customers hold leftover inventories on a consignment basis without paying for them until the next season. All private brands were sold rather than shipped on consignment. If there was a price decline during the market year, however, customers were rebated the difference for any inventory in their hands up to 25 per cent of their purchases.

Dow's price to private brand buyers was guaranteed to be not more than 88 per cent of the national brand price to major marketers. For example, if the national brand price to an oil company was $1.65 per gallon, Dow's price would be $1.45 or less. If during the contract year the national brand cut its price, Dow would reduce its price, if necessary, to maintain the 88 per cent ratio. In practice, price cuts during the season have not occurred.

From the beginning, Dow made no effort to associate the Dow name with the private brands of antifreeze that it packaged. It was desirous, however, of building some consumer franchise and so devised an identifying label that could be used on the antifreeze it packaged. This label featured the name "Tri-Pro" and explained that the product contained triple protection against foaming, seepage, and rust. Some of the private brand customers did not like this label, since it associated the brand sold in their outlets with other brands sold in other outlets, possibly at different prices. When, in addition to these objections, a survey showed that only 7 per cent of antifreeze consumers specified a particular brand, Dow dropped the Tri-Pro label. After that, private brand cans had no Dow identification whatsoever. This created another problem; one farm supply firm wanted the antifreeze to have the Dow identification so that it would be associated with Dow agricultural chemicals, which the supply firm also handled.

Following Dow's successful entry into the antifreeze market, antifreeze sales executives continued to look aggressively for other opportunities to expand sales volume. One factor that interested them was the growing cash-and-carry segment of the market. Dow's research indicated that this segment accounted for about 25–30 per cent of all antifreeze sales and Du Pont published estimates of 39 per cent. This market was served by such retailers as Sears, Roebuck; Montgomery Ward; Western Auto Supply; and many miscellaneous retail outlets, including some supermarkets. Another sales department of the Dow Chemical Company, the plastic sales department, sold Saran Wrap to supermarkets through brokers. This seemed to offer a natural avenue for capturing some of this business. Accordingly, the antifreeze sales department established several brands for sale only to supermarkets through the plastic sales department.

The price to chains and wholesalers was about $1.50 per gallon—between the private brand and the national brand prices. These brands gave enough variety so that competing stores in a given market would not have to sell a brand carried by another store. It was also contemplated that chains might be given exclusive rights to brands if they so desired. No advertising of these brands was done, and there was no Dow identification on or with the brands.

The cash-and-carry brands brought quick complaints from Dow's established customers. Some private brand marketers objected strenuously when they learned that brands packaged by Dow were selling in supermarkets for $1.89 per gallon or even less. Dow's competitors were also selling to the cash-and-carry market, but they did not lose the opportunity to point out to the company's private brand customers that Dow was now competing with them in other channels.

Since all the leading antifreezes seemed essentially the same, product differentiation was difficult. Prestone spent about 30 cents per gallon, or about $9 million, advertising its brand in 1958, and Du Pont spent about $3 million promoting Zerex. Dow had no name to push in this manner and so decided that the way to differentiate its product was on the basis of sales and service. To do this, it devised programs with the following objectives: (1) decrease use of methanol-base (wood alcohol) antifreeze, (2) decrease reuse of antifreeze, (3) increase retail dealers' emphasis on selling private brands, and (4) show dealers how to sell antifreeze effectively.

The Dow advertising program had several facets. Trade magazine advertising was aimed at the oil companies to get them to push with their dealers the importance of draining old antifreeze in the spring. Other trade magazine advertising was aimed at service-station operators. A typical headline was: "It Pays To Sell *Your Company's* Antifreeze." Four "reasons why" were then given:

1. It is backed by your company's name and reputation.
2. Good service profits.
3. One family of fine products.
4. Extra assistance is given by Dow in promoting public awareness of good cooling-system maintenance.

Consumer advertising was more limited in 1958 than in previous years, but advertisements were placed in *Sports Illustrated* and the *Saturday Evening Post*. In the spring these ads tried to get people to drain their antifreeze. One headline was: "Save Your Engine—Not Your Antifreeze." In the fall consumers were urged to put in new antifreeze, but no brands were mentioned. A typical theme was: "Go to your favorite serviceman and buy his brand of antifreeze." Consideration was given to listing in these ads the private brands packaged by Dow, but a check with customers indicated that some of them would not want their brand listed with some of the other brands.

Dow furnished mailing pieces for oil companies to put in the monthly statements to credit card holders and for dealers to send to their customers. It also provided dealer window displays and instructions on how to use them.

Dow's main promotion effort, however, was through its sales force. The objective was to use this force to train the training staffs of the private brand buyers so that these staffs, in turn, could train their dealers. Dow set up a complete plan for a meeting of service station operators. These plans showed how to organize the meeting, provided a sound filmstrip, and listed the questions (with answers) that were likely to come up after the dealers had seen the film. Since the oil companies wanted their dealers to sell service, not antifreeze, this point was emphasized. The cooling system protection guarantee plan was an example. In this the oil companies through their dealers guaranteed to keep the customer's car full of antifreeze all winter if the customer had the dealer service the car at the time that the antifreeze was installed and at any time that antifreeze was lost during the winter. This gave the dealer a chance to sell other accessories also. One oil company increased its sale of antifreeze 15 per cent with this plan in the first year, but expanded sale of tires, batteries, and accessories 27 per cent.

Filmstrips of this type were available to private brand buyers and even to dealers on such subjects as cooling system maintenance, the importance of cooling systems in modern cars, and how to make service profitable. Dow also furnished technical manuals on cooling systems.

Although Dow intended to train the district managers only, the oil companies put considerable pressure to have the Dow salesmen, along with the district managers, put on the training sessions at dealer meetings. One oil company asked for a salesman for thirteen weeks during the 1958–59 season. The expense of this service was more than Dow wished to absorb.

In planning, Dow forecast the demand for glycol antifreeze for several years in the future. This forecast was based on a series of steps and several assumptions. First motor-vehicle registrations were projected as shown in Table 1.

TABLE 1

PROJECTED MOTOR VEHICLE POPULATION
(Thousands of Units)

Year	Passenger Cars	Trucks and Buses	Total	Tractors*
1959	59,230	11,378	70,608	5,060
1960	61,007	11,719	72,726	5,210
1961	62,837	12,071	74,908	5,370
1962	64,722	12,433	77,155	5,530
1963	66,664	12,806	79,470	5,700
1964	68,664	13,190	81,854	5,870
1965	70,724	13,586	84,310	6,050

* Estimated from 1955 data.

From past experience it was determined that the average requirement of antifreeze per vehicle was 1.65 gallons for passenger cars, 1.95 gallons for trucks, and 2.54 gallons for tractors. On this basis annual antifreeze requirements were projected as shown in Table 2.

TABLE 2

Projected Potential Antifreeze Requirements
(Millions of Gallons)

Year	Passenger Cars	Trucks and Buses	Tractors	Total
1959	97.73	22.53	12.85	133.11
1960	100.66	23.21	13.23	137.10
1961	103.67	23.90	13.64	141.21
1962	106.79	24.62	14.05	145.46
1963	109.99	25.35	14.48	149.82
1964	113.29	26.12	14.91	154.32
1965	116.68	26.90	15.37	158.95

With this market potential, the volume of glycol antifreeze actually sold in any year would depend on: (1) the percentage of the total market gained by glycol and (2) the amount of antifreeze reuse. Table 3 shows

TABLE 3

Potential Glycol Antifreeze Market
(Alcohol Usage Assumed to Be 15 Per Cent)
(Millions of Gallons)

Year	Reuse			
	0 Per Cent	15 Per Cent	25 Per Cent	35 Per Cent
1959	113.1	104.6	99.0	93.3
1960	116.5	107.8	101.9	96.1
1961	120.0	111.0	105.0	99.0
1962	123.6	114.3	108.1	102.0
1963	127.3	117.7	111.4	105.0
1964	131.6	121.7	115.1	108.6
1965	135.1	125.0	118.2	111.5

the glycol market forecast on the basis of glycol's obtaining 85 per cent of the total antifreeze market and reuse at various selected levels.

Several other uncertainties existed in these forecasts. The increasing use of air-conditioning in cars increased the potential market, since a 20–25 per cent antifreeze solution had to be used in cooling systems of some cars with air-conditioning during the summer months. The antifreeze companies recommended putting new antifreeze in such vehicles in both spring and fall. On the other hand, automobile manufacturers were experimenting with gas turbine engines with no cooling systems, and there was the idea of sealed engines, in which the cooling system would be sealed at the factory and no further coolant would be added during the life of the engine. Such engines would have to be cast in one piece so that there would be no gaskets through which exhaust gases could leak into the cooling system.

In addition to these general industry factors, Dow faced a number of competitive risks in the future. Pricing was becoming more competitive. Even the national brands, which suggested a fixed price of $3.25 per gallon, were finding increasing instances of price cutting. More producers were entering the glycol antifreeze market. In 1958 Continental Oil Company; Cities Service; Sears, Roebuck; and Mineral Industries combined to build a glycol plant for the production of antifreeze. The first three had been Dow customers. Dow anticipated that the new plant would not only produce the needs of the owning firms, but would also have excess production to sell in the general market.

What action should Dow take?

98

LUB-SEAL MANUFACTURING COMPANY

THE LUB-SEAL MANUFACTURING COMPANY, one of the largest producers of shaft seals and lubricating devices in the United States, had experienced erratic sales in shaft seals, and in recent years its share of this market had declined. In 1957 the company engaged the services of a market planning and research firm to analyze the seal market and to recommend a course of action to be taken by the company to better its position.

Lub-Seal was a recognized leader in the field of lubricating devices. A survey made by a leading trade publication showed that Lub-Seal led its nearest competitor by 573 per cent as the first choice of companies to be considered when buying oilers. Company executives believed that the firm had the world's largest inventory of lubricating devices. The technical skill and long experience of the Lub-Seal engineering staff was recognized in the industry. Many companies brought lubricating problems to Lub-Seal, and a number of innovations had resulted from collaboration with customers. In general, however, lubricating devices were standardized and were sold through distributors. The company did not hold a comparable position in the shaft seal segment of its business, which accounted for a relatively small percentage of its total volume. The possibilities for growth, however, were considered much better in the shaft seal field than in lubricating devices.

The seal division of the company specialized in the development and manufacture of mechanical shaft seals for rotating shafts. Shaft seals were designed to retain a liquid or a gas within a cavity along a rotating shaft;

for example, shaft seals prevented the oil in automobile transmissions from leaking along the drive shafts. The seal was accomplished by a leak-proof contact between a stationary ring seal, against which the flat, smooth surface of a shaft shoulder washer pressed. In the case of a unit seal, the entire seal was made as a unit that could be attached to a shaft and housing. Some seals for high-speed and high-temperature situations became complex and expensive (Exhibits 1 and 2). Most of the better

EXHIBIT 1

UNIT SEAL

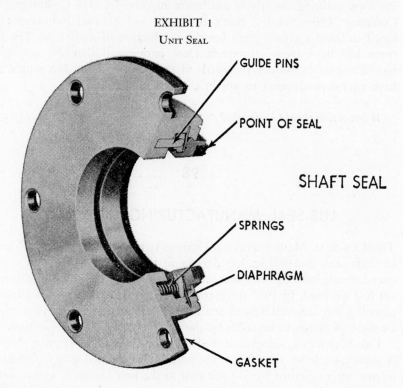

GUIDE PINS

POINT OF SEAL

SHAFT SEAL

SPRINGS

DIAPHRAGM

GASKET

PUMP SEAL

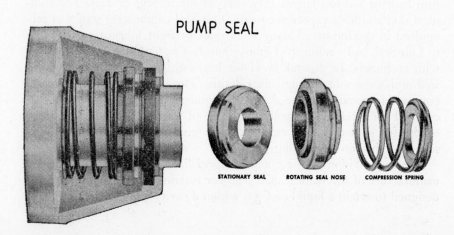

STATIONARY SEAL   ROTATING SEAL NOSE   COMPRESSION SPRING

EXHIBIT 2

SHAFT AND PUMP SEALS

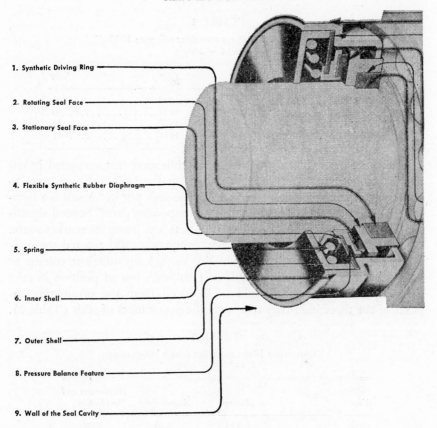

1. Synthetic Driving Ring
2. Rotating Seal Face
3. Stationary Seal Face
4. Flexible Synthetic Rubber Diaphragm
5. Spring
6. Inner Shell
7. Outer Shell
8. Pressure Balance Feature
9. Wall of the Seal Cavity

shaft seals were designed for specific situations, but many of the lower-priced ones were standardized.

Lub-Seal was one of the leading, although not the largest, shaft seal manufacturers. The company's strategy was to work with its customers on shaft seal problems and to attempt to have customers' design engineers specify Lub-Seal mechanical shaft seals. The company had only one full-time sales representative in the seal division. Two manufacturers' representatives also handled the Lub-Seal line of seals, but their sales were so small (less than 5 per cent) that they were considered unimportant.

Sales of shaft seals were concentrated among thirteen customers, which accounted for 95 per cent of Lub-Seal's volume in this division. Three customers accounted for 61 per cent of the total volume; their individual percentages were: Customer S, 24 per cent; Customer T, 19 per cent; and Customer U, 18 per cent. This left Lub-Seal in a vulnerable position. The loss of one of these accounts would be a major setback to the company.

Lub-Seal's sales of shaft seals varied greatly from one year to the next. Table 1 shows an index of sales volume from 1950 to 1957.

TABLE 1

INDEX OF LUB-SEAL SALES OF SHAFT SEALS: 1950–57
(1954 = 100)

Year	Sales	Year	Sales
1950	14	1954	100
1951	23	1955	50
1952	108	1956	51
1953	138	1957	97

There was no trade organization or publication that compiled industry sales figures. As a result, it was difficult for Lub-Seal executives to estimate the industry volume because, as one man put it, "A seal is a component part of a component part of a component part." Several significant facts, however, indicated that Lub-Seal was losing its market share. One of these facts was that seven new competitors had entered the market in the last three years and were able to pick up sufficient volume to stay in business. Another indicator of Lub-Seal's loss of position in sales of mechanical shaft seals could be deduced from the production indexes of the three industries that were the major users of seals (Table 2).

TABLE 2

PRODUCTION INDEXES OF SELECTED INDUSTRIES
(1947–49 = 100)

Year	Aircraft	Automobiles	Appliances and Heaters
1950	124	159	132
1951	211	127	112
1952	368	103	99
1953	465	146	118
1954	474	131	111
1955	481	190	138
1956	548	138	143
1957	574	151	121

Source: *Survey of Current Business.*

Competitors of Lub-Seal manufactured a broader line of seals than did Lub-Seal. Many of them produced static and lip seals that were not as effective but were less expensive than the mechanical shaft seals. As a result, they had a broader market, which covered the industries that demanded low-quality, low-cost seals. Lub-Seal concentrated on the market that wanted highly effective shaft seals and was willing to pay for them. The aircraft industry was the major market of this type. The company's largest competitor in this market was Company A, whose sales to the aircraft industry were estimated by Lub-Seal executives to exceed $3 million. Two of the new competitors in the shaft seal business. Company E and Company G, were aggressively competing for aircraft business. Using data from Dun & Bradstreet reports and from their own market contacts, Lub-Seal executives estimated that these two firms together sold over $1 million of mechanical shaft seals to the aircraft industry in 1957. There were several other major competitors whose sales volumes ran 50–60 per cent of Lub-Seal's. Table 3 lists all these firms in order of sales volume to the aircraft industry.

TABLE 3

mall caps>Mechanical Shaft Seal Sales to the Aircraft Industry: 1957*</small>

Company A..........$3,000,000	Company G...........$500,000
Lub-Seal.............. 1,140,000	Company H............ 500,000
Company B.......... 700,000	Company I............ 200,000
Company C.......... 700,000	Company J............ 200,000
Company D.......... 600,000	Company K........... 75,000
Company E.......... 550,000	Company L............ 50,000
Company F.......... 500,000	Company M........... ......

* As estimated by Lub-Seal executives from Dun & Bradstreet reports and company information.

In April, 1957, the market planning and research firm engaged by Lub-Seal Manufacturing Company submitted a preliminary report on its analysis of the firm's marketing problems. In the report the consultants proposed a marketing plan that they called a "co-ordinated shaft seal sales program." This report consisted of a rough estimate of the market for seals manufactured by Lub-Seal and recommendations for setting up a sales program. According to this report, the market for shaft seals was made up of five main segments as shown in the accompanying tabulation.

Market Segment	Application of Seal
Aircraft..............	Piston and jet engines
Appliance............	Automatic washers, dishwashers, and garbage disposal units
Automobile..........	Water pumps, automatic transmissions, and generators
Farm implement.......	Water pumps, transmissions, generators
Machine tools........	Transmissions, oil retainers

The total dollar volume of the market was estimated for 1957 and projected for 1960. Table 4 presents these figures broken down by type of seal and its application.

Although the automobile market represented one of the two largest segments of the market, the consultants thought that it was not a profitable market for Lub-Seal. It was highly competitive, and the potential profit margins did not appear to justify the risks. The appliance market demanded low-priced, low-quality seals capable of reasonable performance. On the other hand, the aircraft segment demanded high-quality seals that could meet high performance standards. This was the type of

TABLE 4

SALES POTENTIAL ESTIMATES FOR FACE-TYPE SHAFT SEALS

Type of Seal	Market Segment	1957	1960
Unit seal	Original equipment	$ 8,500,000	$11,000,000
	Automobile	$ 6,000,000*	
	Automatic washing machines	1,920,000†	
	Garbage disposal units	240,000‡	
	Dishwashers	168,000§	
	Farm implement and all other	172,000	
	Replacement	500,000	2,000,000
	Total unit seal	$ 9,000,000	$13,000,000
Pump seal	Original equipment		
	Water pumps of all types	3,700,000	4,000,000
	Replacement	300,000	500,000
	Total pump seal	$ 4,000,000	$ 4,500,000
High-speed shaft-type	Original equipment	6,800,000	12,500,000
and unit seals	Aircraft and accessories‖	$ 6,000,000	$11,300,000
	Machine tools and all other	800,000	1,000,000
	Replacement	200,000	200,000
	Total aircraft and high speed	$ 7,000,000	$12,500,000
	Total all types	$20,000,000	$30,000,000

* 6,000,000 at average of $1.00 each.
† 3,200,000 at $0.60.
‡ 400,000 at $0.60.
§ 280,000 at $0.60.
‖ Includes replacement seals bought at same time seals are purchased for installation in new equipment. These seals varied in price between $5.00 and $15.00.

product in which Lub-Seal specialized. Since price was of less importance in the aircraft industry, it appeared attractive for further development by Lub-Seal.

To determine the location of the market, the consultants made estimates of the sales potential for all types of mechanical face-type shaft seals for each of the forty-eight states. The estimates were broken down by three major industries—aircraft, automobile, and other users. This was done because of the peculiar problems each group involved, as well as because of their relative importance to the total. These estimates are shown in Table 5 for all states in which there was any significant potential.

These sales potential data for the aircraft and "other" industries were plotted on a map of the United States, and twelve sales territories were laid out, primarily on the basis of the potentials (Exhibit 3). The automobile figures were excluded because the consultants believed that it would be unwise to direct any considerable amount of effort toward that

TABLE 5

ESTIMATES OF SALES POTENTIALS FOR SHAFT SEALS
FOR SELECTED STATES BY INDUSTRY: 1957
(In Thousands)

| State | Total | Industry | | |
		Auto	Aircraft	Other
Alabama	$ 10	....	....	$ 10
California	903	$ 60	$ 468	375
Connecticut	1,716	12	1,618	86
Georgia	20	....	....	20
Illinois	1,565	338	702	525
Indiana	2,410	780	606	1,024
Iowa	231	....	96	135
Kansas	15	....	....	15
Kentucky	101	6	....	95
Maryland	81	36	....	45
Massachusetts	380	12	78	290
Michigan	3,260	2,189	156	915
Minnesota	358	18	....	340
Missouri	578	163	210	205
New Jersey	1,316	66	840	410
New York	1,420	630	180	610
North Carolina	27	12	....	15
Ohio	3,472	1,278	714	1,480
Oklahoma	26	6	....	20
Pennsylvania	1,467	85	332	1,050
Tennessee	91	6	....	85
Texas	70	....	....	70
West Virginia	12	12	....	....
Wisconsin	471	291	....	180
Total	$20,000	$6,000	$6,000	$8,000

EXHIBIT 3

STATE ESTIMATES OF FACE-TYPE SHAFT SEAL SALES POTENTIALS BY AIRCRAFT AND ALL
OTHER INDUSTRIES EXCLUDING AUTOMOBILE

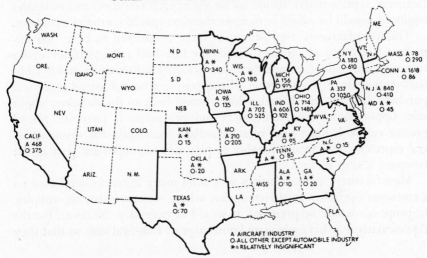

A AIRCRAFT INDUSTRY
O ALL OTHER EXCEPT AUTOMOBILE INDUSTRY
* = RELATIVELY INSIGNIFICANT

market. The sales territories followed state boundaries and were made up as shown below. Some rather large areas in the Northeast, South, and West were not included in any territory.

Territory	Area
1	Massachusetts and Connecticut
2	New Jersey and Delaware
3	New York
4	Pennsylvania and Maryland
5	Michigan
6	Ohio
7	Indiana
8	Kentucky, Tennessee, North Carolina, Alabama, and Georgia
9	Illinois
10	Minnesota, Wisconsin, and Iowa
11	Missouri, Kansas, Oklahoma, and Texas
12	California

Three basic alternatives were considered by the consultants in planning the type of sales representation needed in these territories: (1) full-time salesmen, (2) manufacturers' representatives who would handle the Lub-Seal line along with the products of other manufacturers, and (3) a combination of the first two alternatives.

The first alternative was considered impractical because some areas were believed to lack sufficient potential to support full-time sales representatives. There was enough potential, however, to support a part-time man, such as a manufacturers' representative. The second alternative was also considered to be out of the question because manufacturers' representatives could not provide the technical assistance to customers that was required in the sale of some shaft seals. Therefore, the third alternative, a combination of manufacturers' representatives and full-time sales engineers, was recommended as the best approach to the problem. A manufacturers' representative would be set up in each territory, and two sales engineers would be available to assist them on special customer problems.

The manufacturers' representatives were considered to have two important functions: (1) to win friends for Lub-Seal and (2) to serve as a two-way channel of communication, bringing information about Lub-Seal shaft seals to the attention of the people who influenced shaft seal purchase decisions and bringing information back to the company about sales opportunities from customers and prospects. If Lub-Seal placed greater emphasis upon sales of standardized shaft seals, the manufacturers' representatives would be able to play a more important part in the company's sales picture.

Manufacturers' representatives would, in many instances, send data on a customer's problem to the company, where recommendations, samples, or proposals would be prepared. It would be necessary, however, for the representatives to have adequate knowledge of Lub-Seal seals so that they could recognize potential applications and could report the necessary information. For these reasons, it was recommended that the company conduct a training program for the representatives, which would consist primarily of on-the-job training with one of Lub-Seal's engineers. An engineer would spend several weeks with each representative calling with him and instructing him about seal applications.

The commission scale for manufacturers' representatives in this field varied from 5 to 10 per cent, with 10 per cent apparently the most common. The consultant's report recommended setting an upper limit on what a representative could earn on any one order. This would eliminate the possibility of windfall earnings. A proposed commission scale set commissions for a single order shipped during any twelve-month period at 10 per cent on the first $25,000, 5 per cent on the next $25,000, and 2 per cent on everything above $50,000.

The sales engineers would be full-time, salaried employees of Lub-Seal. It was recommended that one of these men be specifically trained to work with the aircraft industry. Both men would be highly skilled in the application and development of seals. The sales engineers would be based at the home office and would travel where needed to assist the manufacturers' representatives with special problems or to work directly with customers considered as "house accounts."[1]

Salary considerations were important for the sales engineers. It was expected that these men would be technically competent, have sales personalities, and be willing to travel a great deal. They would need considerable drive and ambition to continue effectively over a period of time. The normal starting salary for personnel of this type in other industries was around $12,000. It was thought possible to hire men at a starting salary of $8,000–$10,000 and to adopt a profit-sharing plan.

The consultants recommended that all sales activities in the seal division be co-ordinated under one man with the title of "director of administrative sales." The sales engineers and manufacturers' representatives would report directly to him. He, in turn, would report to the vice-president of the seal division. In addition to responsibility for direct sales effort, he would also be responsible for all related activities such as the preparation of samples and proposals, quotations, sales promotion, and other customer services.

In June, 1957, the recommendations of the market research and planning concern were put into effect for approximately six months. Twelve manufacturers' representatives were selected and given a one-week training course at the home office before going into the field. Only two orders, each of less than $20,000, were received in the six-month period. At

---

[1] A house account was an account that was handled by one of the Lub-Seal executives despite the fact it might lie in a manufacturers' representative's area. The three large customers were house accounts. Company "S" was located in Territory 1, Company "T" in Territory 5, and Company "U" in Territory 6.

this point the management considered the operation unsuccessful and discontinued it. Shortly after the plan was implemented, some new shaft seals for jet engines and jet engine accessories, which had been developed in the company's laboratory and had been submitted for government contracts, were accepted for use on several types of jet engines. As a result, the company suddenly had the problem of a demand growing more rapidly than the firm's ability to supply it. Ninety-two per cent of Lub-Seal's 1957 sales were made to the aircraft industry.

1. *Should Lub-Seal have adopted the recommendations of the consultants?*

2. *Was the company correct in discontinuing the program at the end of six months?*

3. *What action, if any, should the company take at this time in establishing a sales program for the future?*

Index of Cases

INDEX OF CASES

This book has been set on the Linotype in 10 point Janson, leaded 2 points, and 9 point Janson, leaded 1 point. Section numbers are in 18 point Lydian Bold; section titles are in 24 point Lydian Cursive. Case titles are in 14 point Spartan Medium. The page size is 27 by 47 picas.